P9-DMC-957

WITHDRAWN

WITHDRAWN

Historical
Encyclopedia of
School Psychology

Historical Encyclopedia of School Psychology

Edited by
Thomas K. Fagan
and
Paul G. Warden

GREENWOOD PRESS
Westport, Connecticut • London

Library of Congress Cataloging-in-Publication Data

Historical encyclopedia of school psychology / edited by Thomas K.
  Fagan and Paul G. Warden.
    p. cm.
   Includes bibliographical references and index.
   ISBN 0–313–29015–6 (alk. paper)
   1. School psychology—History—Encyclopedias. 2. Educational
psychology—History—Encyclopedias. I. Fagan, Thomas. II. Warden,
Paul G.
LB1027.55.H57   1996
370.15'03—dc20   95–23614

British Library Cataloguing in Publication Data is available.

Library of Congress Catalog Card Number: 95–23614
ISBN: 0–313–29015–6

First published in 1996

Greenwood Press, 88 Post Road West, Westport, CT 06881
An imprint of Greenwood Publishing Group, Inc.

Printed in the United States of America

The paper used in this book complies with the
Permanent Paper Standard issued by the National
Information Standards Organization (Z39.48–1984).

10 9 8 7 6 5 4 3 2

Contents

Preface

Our affinity for a historical perspective became known to each of us almost thirty years ago. We were required to take Professor Harris Dante's History of Education class while in graduate education at Kent State University. For our required papers, we decided to do historical research on the emergence and early application of psychology in education, using original publications in psychology and education. Paul completed the course and traced the emergence of psychology until 1900. Tom completed the course the following term and covered the period 1900–1920. Tom has remained an avid historical buff and has written a great deal about the historical aspects of school psychology and of former leaders in, or related to, our profession.

Over the last three decades, we have worked together for the National Association of School Psychologists (NASP), shared other professional interests, and remained friends. Our families have visited often, and we watched the children grow up. We have often reminisced about our early years in Ohio, then the first decade of NASP. Whenever we would wander back to those times, our enthusiasm would show. Those were the good old days.

When thinking about a preface, we naturally wanted to proclaim our early years as the golden age of school psychology, to declare that that was a time when the field was growing rapidly, and there were a sense of urgency and excitement and an urgency of commitment that others have not experienced. We personally knew the many who were committed throughout the birth of NASP and its early struggles, the awakening of the giant in Washington, the Congress, and finally full educational rights for all children. It was a heady experience. However, upon reflection, we realized that earlier eras in school psychology must have been exciting for Witmer, for Gesell, for Woolley, and for Hollingworth and for many who followed in their footsteps. All of those identified with our field, or any field for that matter, had their good old days. This does not come out in the *Historical Encyclopedia,* but each who has preceded us had much to reminisce about. Each could say, "That's what I did for my profession."

Of the 105 contributing authors for this work, only a handful go back to our time. But all the contributors, young or old, will remember the Golden Age of school psychology as their time. All school psychologists will remember their time as the golden age of our field, but only if it were more than a job, if they felt they made a difference, if they could believe they left their mark. We say to those who will follow: Know who has preceded you, stand on their shoulders, then make your mark.

Thomas K. Fagan
Paul G. Warden

Introduction

Compared to several fields of psychology, school psychology has few published texts and reference works. The first book specifically about school psychology was written in 1930 (Hildreth, 1930). Few other books related to the field were written until the 1960s, a decade of considerable literary activity in school psychology. As the field matured since the 1960s, additional books and journals were published. Despite a sizable increase in literature in the past thirty years, the only recent general reference works are *The Handbook of School Psychology* (Reynolds and Gutkin, 1982; Gutkin and Reynolds, 1990) and *A Bibliographic Guide to the Literature of Professional School Psychology 1890–1985* (Fagan et al., 1985). In addition, until recently, little published information on the history of the field was available. Considerable historical research has been conducted and published in the past decade, and the history of school psychological services is now better understood and available in published form. The field has continued to be without a dictionary or encyclopedia of terms, events, persons, and concepts, though closely related fields such as psychology and special education have such works. This *Historical Encyclopedia* fills a void in the school psychology literature by providing a reference work of modest length to which school psychologists and others may quickly turn for historical and contemporary information.

The *Historical Encyclopedia* is suited for use in training programs for school psychologists and the academic libraries at these and other colleges and universities. The *Historical Encyclopedia* would also be of interest to graduate programs in educational, clinical, and counseling psychology and departments of special education. Undergraduate students planning graduate careers would find this reference work helpful. It is also useful to editors of journals in these fields and to individual practitioners as a quick reference to terms.

Because the encyclopedia had to be limited to about 500 entries, and the field of school psychology overlapped with other fields in psychology and education, a systematic, multistep process was employed to generate entries. This process was guided by seeking a level of specificity that represented the breadth of the field. The entry selection process was facilitated by an important distinction made between school psychology and educational psychology. While the former term refers to a professional practice specialty within psychology, educational psychology is considered a research-oriented field dealing with the problems of education and learning. A useful distinction is that educational psychology studies the general processes of learning and instruction, while school psychology studies the individual learner's adjustment to those processes. While some terms relevant to educational psychology are included, the *Historical Encyclopedia* is decidedly oriented to the field of school psychology and its historical traditions and development.

Following the editors' review of the literature in the field of school psychology, the following information domains relevant to the field of school psychology were identified:

Assessment

Interventions

Consultation

Research, Evaluation, and Accountability

In-service Education

Administration and Supervision

Major Events

Significant Persons

Training and Practice Settings

Organizations and Regulatory Agencies

Professional Issues

Using the domains, the editors generated about 400 entries. As a second step in the development of this reference work, a survey was sent to a panel of reviewers, who were asked to identify historically significant and potentially historically significant terms in the field of school psychology. The survey included a list of the domains and a few example entries in each domain previously generated by the editors. A total of 200 reviewers were surveyed, including state association historians, trainers, and practitioners of school psychology. Each reviewer was asked to consider the domains and example entries and to provide additional entries (and additional domains) for consideration in the *Encyclopedia*. Reviewers were also asked to indicate their interest in serving as a contributor to the work. The final selection of entries was made by the editors based on the survey and the previous list and a decision to limit the number of entries to no more than 500. At this point the domain structure was retired.

After a final list of entries was selected, the editors formally invited persons to contribute to the work as authors. Many of the contributors are established authors in the field who were invited by the editors regardless of whether they were part of the survey for selecting entries. Most contributors were asked to prepare at least three manuscripts (and preferably more) in an effort to keep the number of primary contributors below 100. The editors prepared many of the entries themselves. Entries were reviewed at least once by the editors and returned to authors for final revisions. The entire process of generating and writing entries was conducted during the period September 1993 through February 1995.

The entries provide a snapshot of areas that have influenced the development of school psychology over the century. The influences of assessment and intervention are observed in their contributing about 10 percent and 19 percent of the entries, respectively. The importance of persons and organizations and conferences is observed in their contributions of 10 percent and 12 percent, respectively. Approximately 8 percent of entries pertain to legal-ethical issues in the field, a strong showing based almost entirely on the past twenty-five years of the field's history. While assessment activities have dominated the practice of school psychology for decades, it is worth noting that the types of intervention (including consultation) substantially outnumber the types of assessment entries.

HOW TO USE THE ENCYCLOPEDIA

All entries appear in alphabetical order. Entries include the names of key deceased persons of national renown, events, places, concepts, and practices in the field of school psychology. Each entry includes a definition or description of the entry, followed by a discussion of the entry's historical context, if applicable, and concludes with a limited number of key bibliographic references for further information. While some entries may appear in reference works for other fields, the content of all entries is original. Within each entry, words marked with an asterisk indicate terms that appear elsewhere in the book as entries. At the end of most entries is a list of one or more other encyclopedia entries to which the reader may turn for related information. Thus, each entry leads to related entries either as marked with an asterisk or as identified at the end of the entry.

The overall index includes each entry with the page number of its appearance in bold. Numerous other index items are included to assist the reader in finding information related to entries. The index is designed to be user-friendly. In alphabetical order, it includes all 462 encyclopedia entries as well as important names, events, concepts, and terms that appear in the text. Because of their major significance to the field, the assessment, consultation, and therapy areas have been clustered as well as listed individually. For example, each type of assessment is indexed under the general term "assessment" as well as listed separately in the alphabetical index. The reader can thus quickly identify the location of assessment, consultation, or therapy items that will lead to additional sources within each entry. In order to limit the overall length of the index, clustering was done only for these three areas. While several index entries have been given subentries, we chose not to do this for "school psychology" and "school psychologist" since almost all entries refer to them in some manner.

In addition to the body of entries, the *Historical Encyclopedia* includes a list of contributors and an appendix entitled "Sources for Further Study," comprising major organizations in the field, major archival sources of information, journals in the field of school psychology, major books on school psychology, presidents of the Division of School Psychology—American Psychological Association and of the National Association of School Psychologists, and a list of historical overviews of school psychology.

The editors wish to express their appreciation to the 103 other persons who contributed to the writing of entries for the book. In addition, the book could not have been accomplished without the overall guidance of the publisher, especially the editorial assistance of Mildred Vasan. Special appreciation is extended to the members of our families, Alison Warden and Susan, Shannon, Lance, and Colleen Fagan.

REFERENCES

Fagan, T. K., F. J. Delugach, M. Mellon, and P. Schlitt. (1985). *A bibliographic guide to the literature of professional school psychology 1890–1985.* Washington, DC: National Association of School Psychologists.

Gutkin, T. B., and C. R. Reynolds. (Eds.). (1990). *The handbook of school psychology.* New York: Wiley.

Hildreth, G. H. (1930). *Psychological service for school problems.* Yonkers-on-Hudson, NY: World Book.

Reynolds, C. R., and T. B. Gutkin. (Eds.). (1982). *The handbook of school psychology.* New York: Wiley.

Historical
Encyclopedia of
School Psychology

A

ABAB DESIGNS. The ABAB design is a member of the broader category of interrupted time-series designs. More commonly, its applications are as a single-case design. The design evaluates the effects of an intervention through the alternation of a baseline phase (A), during which there is no intervention, and an intervention phase (B); these two phases are then repeated. During the second baseline phase, intervention is withdrawn. The design ends on an intervention phase, a desirable feature in many applied settings and an advantage over an ABA design (Barlow and Hersen, 1984). The design demonstrates the effects of an intervention and controls a variety of threats to internal validity to the extent that phase changes are accompanied quickly by changes in the target behavior(s) in expected directions.

Variations of the design include a variety of alternatives to the withdrawal of intervention during the second baseline phase since it may be undesirable or even unethical to withdraw intervention and revert behavior to baseline levels, differences in the order (e.g., BABA) and number of phases, as well as the number of different interventions implemented (Kazdin, 1982).

See also EXPERIMENTAL DESIGN; MULTIPLE BASELINE.

REFERENCES

Barlow, D. H., and M. Hersen. (1984). *Single case experimental designs: Strategies for studying behavior change* (2d ed.). New York: Pergamon Press.
Kazdin, A. E. (1982). *Single-case research designs: Methods for clinical and applied settings.* New York: Oxford University Press.

Daniel H. Tingstrom

ABILITY GROUPING. Ability grouping is defined as any organizational plan designed to reduce the heterogeneity of the groups created in terms of aptitude, affective, psychomotor, or style variables. Ability or homogeneous grouping takes place when students are classified according to one or more factors that purport to affect learning. Students are then grouped according to their similarities on the factor(s). Two kinds of grouping, within-class and between-class grouping, are reported in the literature. Between-class grouping can be tracking according to general, business, vocational, and college preparatory tracks, or it may involve block scheduling where most students of the same "type" attend common classes together. Tracking based on academic aptitude may lead to classes labeled gifted, accelerated, honors, or advanced placement for high achievers and remedial, special education,* Chapter One, and the like for low achievers. There are arguments pro and con as to the effectiveness of this kind of tracking (Corno and Snow, 1986; Slavin, 1990). Within-class grouping is typically used in reading and mathematics at the early elementary level. Separation may be based on developmental readiness, aptitude, and/or knowledge of prerequisite skills. Different textbooks may be used, and students progress at different learning rates. Here, according to Slavin (1987), ability grouping has been successful. Generally, the arguments against ability grouping focus on either the lack of effect on achievement or the effects of labeling. The labeling argument asserts that labels are bad for low-performing students. This, however, does not hold for academically strong students in gifted or honors classes.

See also COOPERATIVE LEARNING.

REFERENCES

Corno, L., and R. E. Snow. (1986). Adapting teaching to individual differences among learners. In M. C. Wittrock (Ed.), *Handbook of research on teaching* (3d ed., pp. 605–629). New York: Macmillan.

Dawson, M. M. (1995). Best practices in promoting alternatives to ability grouping. In A. Thomas and J. Grimes (Eds.), *Best practices in school psychology—III* (pp. 347–357). Washington, DC: National Association of School Psychologists.

Slavin, R. E. (1987). Ability grouping and student achievement in elementary schools: A best-evidence synthesis. *Review of Educational Research* 57, 347–350.

———. (1990). Achievement effects of ability grouping in secondary schools: A best-evidence synthesis. *Review of Educational Research* 60, 471–499.

Kay Sather Bull

ACADEMIC ASSESSMENT: NONTRADITIONAL. Nontraditional academic assessment is characterized as more sensitive to progress and improvements in the development of academic skills because such assessment is applied only in the particular classroom curriculum to which the child has been exposed. This approach was created in response to limitations of traditional academic assessment, including the fact that standardization samples were often not locally representative, and such tests possessed weak psychometric properties for purposes of instructional planning and decision making. Nontraditional assessment focuses on tracking gains in particular academic skills based on a student's performance related to the individual instructional objectives of the classroom.

Strengths and weaknesses can be identified that assist in instructional planning related particularly to developing and evaluating effective interventions.

Informal assessment and related approaches such as curriculum-based assessment* (CBA) and curriculum-based measurement* (CBM) are gaining in popularity with school psychologists,* special educators, and those working exclusively within general education. These approaches are considered nontraditional and have a shorter history and less frequent use than more traditional, norm-referenced procedures.

Informal assessment, which represents a nontraditional approach, refers to an approach that is nonstandardized and ongoing and includes analysis by teachers of multiple classroom products (e.g., written essay assignment). More recently, educators have begun to refer to informal assessment as authentic or performance assessment.

CBA and CBM, examples of nontraditional approaches that focus on the direct measurement of academic skills, refer to using direct and frequent measures of academic behavior that rely on a student's curriculum as the basis for constructing testing materials and decision making. Measures include developing probes such as short reading passages from basal readers or story starters for written expression. CBM refers to a specific approach to CBA and is designed for uses such as in special education* eligibility determination, evaluating intervention* effectiveness, and screening for program eligibility. CBM procedures include a set of short duration (one to three minutes) fluency tests in the basic skill areas of reading, spelling, written expression, and mathematics computation collected in a standardized format. Typically, local district norms are collected as part of the process to aid in interpretation of performance, suggesting that they are the most appropriate reference group to determine adequacy of progress.

See also ACADEMIC ASSESSMENT: TRADITIONAL; ASSESSMENT; CLASSIFICATION: EDUCATIONAL; SCREENING ASSESSMENT.

REFERENCES

Deno, S. L. (1985). Curriculum-based measurement: The emerging alternative. *Exceptional Children* 52, 219–232.
Shapiro, E. S. (1989). *Academic skills problems: Direct assessment and intervention.* New York: Guilford Press.
Shinn, M. R. (Ed.). (1989). *Curriculum-based measurement: Assessing special children.* New York: Guilford Press.

Yvette J. Cornett
Mark E. Swerdlik

ACADEMIC ASSESSMENT: TRADITIONAL. Academic assessment refers to an evaluation of students that describes their current level of academic functioning and assists prediction of future academic functioning, instructional decision making, and evaluating pupil progress. An early example occurred in

1856, when the Chicago public schools used written exams for promoting elementary school students and for admission to high school.

For school psychologists,* traditional (i.e., that which has the longest history and the most frequent use) academic assessment has included norm-referenced* and criterion-referenced* tests. Traditional academic assessment focuses on the relationship between reported skills on a test and classroom performance based on a measure of a representative sample of skills pertaining to a particular academic content area. For norm-referenced assessment, conclusions are based on comparing the results of a child's performance on an academic achievement test to a well-defined group of other children's performances, referred to as norms. Unlike norm-referenced tests, criterion-referenced tests focus on whether or not a student can perform the criterion behavior, that is, demonstrate a particular skill or demonstrate particular knowledge. A large number of norm- and criterion-referenced tests are commercially available and can be administered either individually or in a group testing format.

The strength of traditional, norm-referenced academic assessment is that the measures have a long history and typically have strong psychometric properties, including reliability,* validity,* and large and representative standardization samples. The results can be used primarily for decision making concerning categorizing children as "disabled," as is often required by law. Although the accuracy and efficacy of their use to differentially diagnose among disability categories have been questioned, the results of norm-referenced tests assist in identifying which students are in the greatest need for special education* services or which students require further evaluation (i.e., screening function). A main advantage of criterion-referenced testing is its value in instructional planning related to identifying a student's specific skills and the next logical step to teach.

A major weakness of norm-referenced tests is their content validity with the curriculum taught in the classroom, which limits their usefulness in planning and evaluating specific academic interventions. Criterion-referenced tests have been criticized for their inability to be applied at the upper end of the knowledge/skill continuum.

See also ACADEMIC ASSESSMENT: NONTRADITIONAL; ASSESSMENT; CLASSIFICATION: EDUCATIONAL; DIFFERENTIAL DIAGNOSIS; SCREENING ASSESSMENT.

REFERENCES

Salvia, J., and J. Ysseldyke. (1995). *Assessment.* Boston: Houghton Mifflin.
Sattler, J. (1988). *Assessment of children* (3d ed.). San Diego: Author.
Shapiro, E. S. (1989). *Academic skills problems: Direct assessment and intervention.* New York: Guilford Press.

Yvette J. Cornett
Mark E. Swerdlik

ACCOUNTABILITY: ENUMERATIVE DATA. Three types of data can be collected when evaluating the effectiveness of school psychological services—enumerative, process, and product (Fairchild, 1980). Enumerative data include records of the number of times various services are provided, such as the number of assessments completed, students counseled, parent conferences held, and team meetings attended. Enumerative data also include records of the amount of time spent providing school psychological services. A record of the time required to complete a comprehensive assessment and a yearly time analysis depicting the amounts and percentages of time devoted to the various services provided to consumers (Fairchild, 1974) are examples of such data. In a survey of the accountability efforts of school psychologists, the results revealed that 56 percent collect such data (Fairchild and Zins, 1993). Tabulation and time analysis are popular methods for data collection because they consume little time yet communicate valuable information regarding the range of services offered. The limitation of these data is that they do not provide information regarding the quality or effectiveness of services.

See also ACCOUNTABILITY: PROCESS DATA; ACCOUNTABILITY: PRODUCT DATA; PROGRAM EVALUATION.

REFERENCES

Fairchild, T. N. (1974). An analysis of the services performed by a school psychologist in an urban area: Implications for training programs. *Psychology in the Schools* 11, 275–281.

———. (1980). STEPPS: A model for the evaluation of school psychological services. *School Psychology Review* 9, 252–258.

Fairchild, T. N., and J. E. Zins. (1993). Accountability practices of school psychologists: 1991 national survey. *School Psychology Review* 21, 616–626.

Thomas N. Fairchild

ACCOUNTABILITY: PROCESS DATA. Since school psychologists were first challenged in the early 1970s to become more responsive to consumer needs and more accountable for their services, increased attention has been given to methods for collecting accountability data. One type of data to collect when evaluating school psychological services is process data, which focus on the process employed in achieving goals and objectives and provide information about the efficiency and effectiveness of procedures. Because school psychologists work with varied consumer groups using consultative and collaborative processes, much of their effectiveness is contingent upon how well they relate to, and communicate with, others. Process data provide information regarding school psychologists' work habits, initiative, accessibility, interpersonal skills, abilities to communicate information, abilities to create a climate conducive to counseling, and so on. Process data are typically collected using rating scales/questionnaires, interviews, or observation methods (Fairchild, 1975, 1985). Twenty-one percent of practicing school psychologists collect process data when evaluating their effectiveness. While process data require more time to collect, they are important because psychologists need to know how they are viewed by others. This information enables them to identify areas for self-improvement and make changes before unidentified areas of weakness sabotage their effectiveness. Practitioners may be providing a broad range of services and be potential resources for creating helpful intervention strategies, but if they are unorganized, manage time poorly, and lack interpersonal skills, their effectiveness is diminished.

See also ACCOUNTABILITY: ENUMERATIVE DATA; ACCOUNTABILITY: PRODUCT DATA; PROGRAM EVALUATION.

REFERENCES

Fairchild, T. N. (1975). Accountability: Practical suggestions for school psychologists. *Journal of School Psychology* 13, 149–159.
————. (1985). Obtaining consumer feedback as a means of evaluating school psychology intern performance. *Psychology in the Schools,* 22, 419–428.
Zins, J. E. (1985). Best practices for improving school psychology through accountability. In A. Thomas and J. Grimes (Eds.), *Best practices in school psychology* (pp. 493–503). Silver Spring, MD: National Association of School Psychologists.

Thomas N. Fairchild

ACCOUNTABILITY: PRODUCT DATA. Product data, also known as outcome data, provide information regarding the extent to which goals and objectives have been achieved and are a third type of data that can be collected when evaluating personnel effectiveness. Presently, the emphasis in the evaluation of school psychological services is on outcome measures. While enumerative and process data each provide important information, product data enable practitioners* to determine if their services are making a difference. For example, knowing that a psychologist counseled twenty-one students, spent ninety-four hours in counseling activities, established rapport, and was punctual for appointments does not reveal whether or not counseling goals were achieved. Knowing that consultation services were provided for forty-seven students experiencing academic and/or behavioral difficulties gives important enumerative data but does not communicate the degree to which desired behavior changes have been made. Product data communicate the extent to which school psychological services have resulted in successful outcomes. Product data are collected by 26 percent of practicing school psychologists, using a variety of methods, such as observation, case study, interview, rating scales/questionnaires, and pre/posttest measures. Consultation* and counseling services provide product data readily because such services require identification of goals and strategies for their accomplishment at the outset; product data are records of the degree to which goals have been achieved.

See also ACCOUNTABILITY: ENUMERATIVE DATA; ACCOUNTABIL-
ITY: PROCESS DATA; PROGRAM EVALUATION.

REFERENCES

Fairchild, T. N. (1976). School psychological services: An empirical comparison of
    two models. *Psychology in the Schools* 13, 156–162.
———. (1986). Self-evaluation methods for school psychologists. *School Psychology
    International* 7, 173–184.
Zins, J. E. (1990). Best practices in developing accountability procedures. In A.
    Thomas and J. Grimes (Eds.), *Best practices in school psychology—II* (pp.
    323–337). Silver Spring, MD: National Association of School Psychologists.

Thomas N. Fairchild

ACCREDITATION. Accreditation is a system through which educational institutions and educational programs associated with those institutions are recognized as having demonstrated performance that provides an acceptable level
of quality assurance to the public relative to the mission of the institution or
program (*Accreditation,* 1986). In most countries, central governmental agencies
are responsible for the oversight of educational institutions and programs. However, in the United States, because the Constitution reserves authority over education at all levels to the states, the jurisdiction of the federal government is
very limited (Blauch, 1959).

Accordingly, the accreditation of educational institutions and programs in the
United States is provided largely through nongovernmental organizations, and
participation is voluntary. However, accreditation is at least a consideration, if
not a major factor, in many differing types of decisions that significantly impact
institutions and programs (e.g., those of foundations and external funding agencies, prospective students, employers, and credentialing agencies). Because of
its interest in a reasonable level of quality assurance regarding institutions and
programs seeking financial support, the U.S. Department of Education bases
eligibility for federal funds, in part, on accreditation by nongovernmental organizations. Consequently, while technically voluntary, accreditation becomes
almost essential for many institutions and programs.

There are basically two types of accreditation: institutional and specialized.
Institutional accreditation addresses the institution as a whole and is based
largely on the mission of the institution and is granted by national or regional
organizations (e.g., Southern Association of Colleges and Schools). Standards
or criteria used to evaluate institutions tend to be generic in nature and to address
areas beyond just the academic program (e.g., financial resources). Institutional
accreditation is used to recognize high schools, as well as colleges and universities.

Specialized accreditation recognizes programs or institutions that tend to be
more narrowly defined and prepare professionals for specific disciplines or occupations (e.g., education, psychology). In this sense, accreditation represents a

symbol of respectability and the "professionalization" of a discipline. The fact that less than one-half of the institutions in the United States preparing teachers are nationally accredited is sometimes noted as one of the reasons that teaching may not yet have attained the same level of identity as a profession as that held by many other disciplines. Specialty accreditation also applies to areas in which there is attention to the issue of public welfare as it relates to professional competence. Criteria and standards that serve as the basis for accreditation are more specific in nature than those used in institutional accreditation and relate to reasonable expectations regarding the preparation of persons to enter a particular professional field of practice. Accreditation provides one means of quality control in the preparation of persons who are expected to serve the public.

Three different organizations are involved in the review of school psychology programs: the American Psychological Association* (APA), the National Council for Accreditation of Teacher Education* (NCATE), and the National Association of School Psychologists* (NASP). APA is the only agency recognized by the U.S. Department of Education to accredit psychology programs. NCATE is the only agency recognized for the accreditation of institutions preparing personnel to work in schools, and NASP is a constituent member within NCATE. School psychology programs prepare psychologists, many of whom work in schools. Consequently, the recognition of school psychology programs continues to be somewhat awkward with regard to jurisdiction. At the present time, APA accredits only doctoral-level programs. NCATE accredits education units (typically, colleges of education or other administrative units that house programs preparing professional education personnel), but not programs. NASP promotes standards for specialist, as well as doctoral-level, programs. However, NASP, as a member of another accrediting agency (NCATE), technically approves and "nationally recognizes," but does not accredit, programs. At the present time, accreditation by APA is probably more important for doctoral programs because of the relationship to psychological licensure for independent practice within individual states. Approval of specialist programs by NASP is important because of the relationship to national certification* in school psychology and the expanding access that credential provides to state credentialing for practice in the schools. NASP currently accepts APA accreditation of doctoral programs, contingent on documentation of appropriate internship policy and practice, in nationally recognizing programs.

See also PROGRAM APPROVAL; REGIONAL ACCREDITORS.

REFERENCES

Accreditation. (1986). Washington, DC: Council on Postsecondary Accreditation.

Blauch, L. E. (Ed.). (1959). *Accreditation in higher education.* Washington, DC: U.S. Department of Health, Education, and Welfare.

Michael J. Curtis

ACTUARIAL ASSESSMENT VERSUS CLINICAL JUDGMENT. Actuarial assessment and clinical judgment represent two very different approaches to interpreting psychological data for use in decision making about clinical diagnoses, treatment, and predicting future performance. Both approaches represent ways to integrate data obtained from a variety of different sources, such as tests, interviews, observations, and background data.

Actuarial assessment relies on normative data and statistical formulas. Decisions are based on the statistical relationship between current behaviors, including test performance, and future behaviors. Well-defined rules are created for classification/identification decisions. Advantages of this approach include efficiency in terms of making predictions in a variety of situations, high reliability,* and use for research. However, some argue that, at best, it demonstrates only low-level relationships, limiting its ability to accurately predict more important outcomes other than diagnoses.

Actuarial assessment with children has a briefer history, and fewer evaluative data are available than with adults. The best-known test utilizing an actuarial approach for adults is the Minnesota Multiphasic Personality Inventory (MMPI), first published in 1967. Recently, the MMPI—II has published adolescent norms. The MMPI has been used for such applications as predictions of potential dropouts and potentially abusive parents.

Assessment packages have also been developed for the diagnosis of learning and behavior problems. One comprehensive actuarial system, the McDermott Multidimensional Actuarial Classification System (M-MAC), received little application in the field. More recent examples of this approach include computer interpretation systems available for a number of different, commonly used tests.

Clinical judgment is characterized as having fewer formal rules for the interpretation of the data and relies more on intuitions, judgment, and experience of a highly skilled professional. An advantage of this approach is its flexibility in deriving interpretations, hypotheses, decisions, and predictions.

Research comparing the utility of both approaches have produced no clear conclusions. Studies have supported the supremacy of the actuarial model (Meehl, 1954), while others (Sawyer, 1966) support the clinical model. It is likely that the most useful approach to diagnosis and intervention* development includes a combination of both methods.

See also ASSESSMENT; CLASSIFICATION: EDUCATIONAL; CLASSIFICATION: PSYCHIATRIC; COMPUTER-ASSISTED TESTING.

REFERENCES

Achenbach, T. M., and C. S. Edelbrock. (1978). The classification of child psychopathology: A review and analysis of empirical efforts. *Psychological Bulletin* 85, 1275–1301.
Dawes, R. M., D. Faust, and P. E. Meehl. (1989). Clinical versus actuarial judgment. *Science* 243, 1668–1674.
Meehl, P. E. (1954). *Clinical versus statistical prediction: A theoretical analysis and a review of the evidence.* Minneapolis: University of Minnesota Press.

Sawyer, J. (1966). Measurement and prediction, clinical and statistical. *Psychological Bulletin* 66, 178–200.

Yvette J. Cornett
Mark E. Swerdlik

ADAPTIVE BEHAVIOR. Adaptive behavior definitions usually emphasize the concepts of personal independence and social responsibility expected of persons of a particular age in a specific setting. Adaptive behavior is a new name for the social competence construct that has been prominent in the mental retardation literature throughout most of the twentieth century (Reschly, 1990). Recent formulations of adaptive behavior have emphasized the individual's competencies in meeting expectations that vary by age and social context and the broadening use of the construct to applications with at-risk populations and other categories of disability (e.g., specific learning disability and behavior disorder).

Formal assessment of adaptive behavior typically uses the method of interviewing* or checklist completion by third-party respondents. The respondent typically is a parent or teacher who is asked to report on the individual's competencies in performing various tasks. Adaptive behavior measures typically do not involve structured testing or systematic observation of the individual. The interview or checklist methodology has the advantages of surveying a broad range of competencies in a relatively short period of time. The major disadvantages are the susceptibility to biasing response sets that may be unintentional on the part of the respondent (e.g., the tendency of parents to overestimate competencies) and the degree to which the respondent has opportunities to observe the actual performance of the skills on the inventory. Some adaptive behavior inventories involve estimations on a large number of items because the respondent has not had sufficient opportunities to observe the actual skills (Harrison and Kamphaus, 1987). Adaptive behavior conceptions and inventories typically include, depending on the age and functioning levels of clients, the domains of independent functioning, social functioning, functional academics or practical cognitive skills, motor/mobility skills, and occupational/vocational skills (McGrew and Bruininks, 1989).

Adaptive behavior is used most often in the context of mental retardation diagnoses and programming. Deficits in adaptive behavior typically are required in order for the individual to be accurately diagnosed as mentally retarded. Adaptive behavior programming, however, is important to all persons with disabilities and with at-risk populations because adaptive behavior competencies, independent of overall level of intellectual functioning, contribute to the adult adjustment of individuals in jobs, community participation, and personal relationships (Reschly, 1990). Although programming in adaptive behavior domains is important at all educational levels from preschool through high school, it is especially important at the secondary level as part of the transition of students with disabilities from school to adult roles.

See also ASSESSMENT; ASSISTIVE TECHNOLOGY; COMPREHENSIVE ASSESSMENT; VOCATIONAL ASSESSMENT.

REFERENCES

Harrison, P. L., and R. W. Kamphaus (Eds.). (1987). Adaptive behavior. *Journal of Special Education* 21(1).

Harrison, P. L., and B. Robinson. (1995). Best practices in the assessment of adaptive behavior. In A. Thomas and J. Grimes (Eds.), *Best practices in school psychology—III* (pp. 753–762). Washington, DC: National Association of School Psychologists.

McGrew, K., and R. Bruininks. (1989). The factor structure of adaptive behavior. *School Psychology Review* 18, 64–81.

Reschly, D. J. (1990). Adaptive behavior. In A. Thomas and J. Grimes (Eds.), *Best practices in school psychology (2d ed., pp. 29–42).* Washington, DC: National Association of School Psychologists.

Daniel J. Reschly

ADLERIAN THERAPY. Alfred Adler (1870–1937) was born in Vienna, where he met Sigmund Freud. By 1902, Adler and Freud had a close personal relationship that lasted for ten years. By 1912, Adler had developed an approach called individual psychology, which stressed the self as a subjective observer and focused on goal-directed causation of behaviors. Adler was the first to break away from Freud's psychoanalysis. Adler viewed personal distress and inadequate or maladaptive functioning as consequences of a person's maladaptive lifestyle. A lifestyle develops early in the family context. Birth order and family interactions contribute to notions of an ideal self and self-concerned goals, which, if achieved, represent a movement from inferiority to significance and security.

Adlerian therapy focuses on lifestyle assessment followed by interpretation of the purposes of the behavior. The therapist actively advises and encourages the client. Additional techniques are used to encourage the client to become aware of, and monitor, behavior and to try more adaptive behaviors.* These techniques are applicable to working with individuals, groups, and family constellations.

Adlerians have conceived of four dominant goals that operate with school-age children: attention, power, revenge, and inadequacy. The most widely recognized application of Adlerian conceptualizations and derived techniques has been incorporated into the training programs of Systematic Training for Effective Parenting (STEP) and Systematic Training for Effective Teaching (STET), published by American Guidance Services (AGS). These programs stress open communication (active listening, "I" messages), natural consequences, and encouragement. Both programs are widely used by mental health personnel and educators in consultation with parents and teachers.

See also PARENT-CHILD INTERACTION TRAINING; PARENT TRAINING.

REFERENCES

Ford, D. H., & H. B. Urban. (1967). *Systems of psychotherapy: A comparative study.* New York: Wiley.

Mosak, H. H., and R. Dreikurs. (1973). Adlerian psychotherapy. In R. Corsini (Ed.), *Current psychotherapies* (pp. 35–83). Itasca, IL: Peacock.

Rule, W. R. (1984). Adlerian methods. In J. G. Cull and L. B. Golden (Eds.), *Psychotherapeutic techniques in school psychology* (pp. 3–13). Springfield, IL: Charles C. Thomas.

Paul G. Warden

ADMINISTRATIVE SUPERVISION. Administrative supervision refers to either (1) oversight of the school psychologist's* work by a designated, hierarchically superior "supervisor" or (2) administrative functions that support the delivery of school psychological services by a person (often called "coordinator") who does not necessarily hold an organizationally superior position to the school psychologists in the service unit. These administrative functions may be contrasted with professional supervision,* in which the focus is on the school psychologist's professional development. In practice, the same person often provides both forms of supervision.

Historically, administrative supervision has been emphasized more in school settings than in hospitals and clinics, where professional psychologists have been more frequently treated as independent practitioners. In school systems, supervision of professional employees arose as an inspection function and was typically autocratic in nature. Beginning in the 1950s and 1960s, more collaborative and skill-sharing models of supervision gained prominence and continue to the present (Murphy, 1981).

Virtually all school-based psychologists report to an administrative superior. However, active, individual supervision of certificated school psychologists is not common, despite National Association of School Psychologists* (NASP) and American Psychological Association* (APA) professional standards* that encourage such supervision. Surprisingly, most school psychologists are supervised by someone who does not have "school psychologist" as a job title, and up to 30 percent of all supervisors may not have had any training as a school psychologist (Zins, Murphy, and Wess, 1989).

The school psychology* literature includes lengthy lists of administrative supervision functions, including recruitment, hiring and evaluation of staff, modeling best practices, developing a coherent philosophy of service for the unit, budget management and provision of supplies, scheduling, interpreting and communicating system policies, providing in-service staff training, and skill at negotiating the politics of the school system.

See also INTERNSHIP SUPERVISOR; PROFESSIONAL STANDARDS; UNIVERSITY TRAINER.

REFERENCES

Bowser, P. B. (1981). On school psychology supervision. *School Psychology Review* 10, 452–454.

Murphy, J. P. (1981). Roles, functions and competencies of supervisors of school psychologists. *School Psychology Review* 10, 417–424.

Zins, J. E., J. J. Murphy, and B. P. Wess. (1989). Supervision in school psychology: Current practices and congruence with professional standards. *School Psychology Review* 18, 56–63.

William Strein

ADVOCACY CONSULTATION. Advocacy consultation refers to an approach to consultation* where the consultant acts as a social interventionist, a change agent who pursues changes in policies and/or institutions for the perceived benefit of all who are purportedly served. This is seen as an effective change because of the opportunity to reach large numbers of people rather than maintaining a focus that is limited to individuals (Meyers, Gaughan, and Pitt, 1990). Advocacy consultants are more likely to promote their own set of values than is typical in other approaches to consultation (Lippitt and Lippitt, 1986). This approach is controversial due to its highly political, often confrontational nature. "Advocacy believes in power, influence, and politics as motivating forces behind human behavior" (Conoley and Conoley, 1982, p. 9). Because of its systemic orientation and far-reaching goals, advocacy consultation requires a wide range of skills and activities on the part of consultants. These include organizational, political, legal, negotiations, and public relations expertise, along with considerable tolerance for frustration, ambiguity, and conflict (Conoley and Conoley, 1982).

See also CASE CONSULTATION; CHILD ADVOCACY; CONSULTATION.

REFERENCES

Conoley, J. C., and C. W. Conoley. (1982). *School consultation: A guide to practice and training.* New York: Pergamon Press.

Lippitt, G., and R. Lippitt. (1986). *The consulting process in action.* San Diego: University Associates.

Meyers, J., E. Gaughan, and N. Pitt. (1990). Contributions of community psychology to school psychology. In T. B. Gutkin and C. R. Reynolds (Eds.), *The handbook of school psychology* (pp. 198–216). New York: Wiley.

Edward Gaughan
Joel Meyers

ALTERNATING TREATMENTS DESIGN. An alternating treatments design (also called multielement baseline design, multielement manipulation design, multiple schedule design, randomization design, and simultaneous treatment design) is a single-subject experimental design used to assess the relative effectiveness of two (or more) treatments. The treatment schedule is created by randomly assigning the order of the treatments for the subject, typically at fixed, closely scheduled intervals. For example, the subject might receive treatment 1 during weeks 2, 3, 5, 7, and 8 whereas treatment 2 is received during weeks 1,

4, 6, 9, and 10. Note the treatments are not actually alternating, to avoid potential validity threats such as ordering effects. Data are collected at each interval (a week, in this example). Data are analyzed by graphical technique—a clinically significant difference being indicated if consistently the criterion measure is higher on weeks corresponding to the assignment of a particular treatment. Among the advantages of this design, (1) the ethical dilemma of treatment withdrawal is avoided, (2) the time and effort needed to establish a baseline observation period are eliminated, and (3) multiple treatments can be efficiently examined. The major threat to the external validity of this design is potential carryover effects from one treatment to the other.

See also ABAB DESIGNS; EXPERIMENTAL DESIGN.

REFERENCES

Gay, L. R. (1992). *Educational research: Competencies for analysis and application* (4th ed.). New York: Merrill.
Kazdin, A. E. (1984). Statistical analyses for single-case experimental designs. In D. H. Barlow and M. Hersen, *Single-case experimental designs: Strategies for studying behavior change* (2d ed., pp. 285–324). New York: Pergamon Press.

William T. Coombs

ALTERNATIVE SCHOOLS. Alternative schools were established to meet the educational needs of students for whom the traditional school setting has not been successful. Alternative schools may operate as schools within a school or as separate programs away from a school. Common characteristics of successful alternative schools include flexible scheduling, small teacher/student ratio, nontraditional teaching strategies, applied academics or vocationally related experiences, acceleration of basic skills, and comprehensive student services (Donmoyer and Kos, 1993). Frequently mentioned is the importance of utilizing the appropriate staff for alternative programs. Recommended are those who have experience with disaffected youth, exhibit sensitivity and respect for their students, and have volunteered for the alternative setting assignment. Studies of successful alternative schools indicate that a personalized relationship between students and staff is common and desired, and students feel a sense of community that translates to a commitment to learning (Duckenfield, Hamby, and Smink, 1990).

See also SCHOOL SETTINGS; VOCATIONAL SCHOOL PSYCHOLOGY.

REFERENCES

Donmoyer, R., and R. Kos, (Eds.). (1993). *At-risk students: Portraits, policies, programs, and practices.* Albany: State University of New York Press.
Duckenfield, M., J. Hamby, and J. Smink. (1990). *Effective strategies for dropout prevention.* Clemson, SC: National Dropout Prevention Center.
Parffrey, V. (1990). An alternative to exclusion from school: The Tor Hill project. *Educational Psychology in Practice* 5, 216–221.

Leslie Hale

ALTERNATIVE SERVICE DELIVERY. The concept of "alternative service delivery" can be applied broadly to education and more specifically to the practice of school psychology.* In education, the 1980s marked an era of school reform movements, most notably, the regular education initiative* (REI) and similar calls for the full inclusion* of students with disabilities into general education. In this context, alternative service delivery refers to efforts to provide and support instruction for all students in the general education classroom, rather than pulling out and segregating students with disabilities, as in traditional special education models. The alternatives proposed include noncategorical assessments and interventions based on instructional need rather than diagnosis, with emphasis on prevention and early intervention. Poor instructional outcomes for disabled and at-risk students, minority overrepresentation in special education, practical problems in categorical labeling* of students and programs, and the creation of a dual system of special and general education are cited as justifications for an alternative model.

For alternative educational systems to be accepted and implemented, it is necessary that (1) general education assume responsibility for *all* children; (2) support staff are available to work with classroom teachers in modifying curriculum and instruction *within* the classroom, rather than pulling students out for assessment and intervention; (3) personnel preparation programs integrate traditionally "regular" and "special" education training; (4) school systems adopt more flexible structures for grouping and integrating students and programs; (5) regular education curricula incorporate community living and functional skills in order to meet the needs of all students; (6) instructional practices incorporate individualized instruction, cooperative learning, and adaptive learning environments approaches; and (7) assessment practices address instructional needs and student progress rather than diagnosis and classification.

The conceptualization of alternative service delivery in school psychology reflects the underlying philosophy of general school reform initiatives. Serving the needs of "special" children is regarded as part of a transformation of the larger system of schooling that will lead to more effective education of *all* children.

For many years, school psychologists have been challenged to expand their roles, to move away from "traditional" practices rooted in the medical model and instead embrace "alternative roles" emphasizing ecological, behavioral, and developmental approaches to consultation, intervention, and staff training. These roles are consistent with school psychologists' training in general psychology, child development, school organization, and instructional design. Consultation is regarded as the linchpin of alternative services, supporting collaboration among professionals and parents through a problem-solving process.

In delivering psychological services through "alternative" roles, school psychologists practice with far less emphasis on diagnostic activities geared toward identifying etiology and determining classifications and placements. Rather, there is much greater emphasis on ecological assessment,* application of principles of effective instruction and classroom management,* analysis of classroom systems and school organizations, parent involvement, training others in effective educational strategies, and the analysis and evaluation of instruction. In an alternative service delivery system, school psychologists function as collaborators, not experts.

Barriers to the implementation of alternative service delivery models in school psychology are both external and internal. These include difficulties upgrading credentialing standards and training practices, state and federal regulations that reinforce gatekeeping roles, funding procedures that maintain dual systems of special and general education, and the public's and professionals' resistance to change.

As school-based research demonstrates the positive impact of alternative school organizations and expanded roles for support personnel such as school psychologists, these "new" models will likely become more commonplace and may no longer be regarded as "alternative" practices.

See also ROLE CHANGE AND DIVERSITY; ROLE RESTRICTION; ROLES AND FUNCTIONS.

REFERENCES

Conoley, J., and T. Gutkin. (1986). School psychology: A reconceptualization of service delivery realities. In S. Elliott and J. Witt (Eds.), *The delivery of psychological services in schools: Concepts, processes, and issues* (pp. 393–424). Hillsdale, NJ: Erlbaum.

Graden, J., J. Zins, and M. Curtis (Eds.). (1988). *Alternative educational delivery systems: Enhancing instructional options for all students.* Washington, DC: National Association of School Psychologists.

Ysseldyke, J., M. Reynolds, and R. Weinberg. (1984). *School psychology: A blueprint for training and practice.* Minneapolis: National School Psychology Inservice Training Network.

Andrea Canter

AMERICAN ASSOCIATION OF APPLIED AND PREVENTIVE PSYCHOLOGY. The American Association of Applied and Preventive Psychology (AAAPP), an affiliate of the American Psychological Society (APS),* evolved from the failure of an effort within the American Psychological Association (APA)* to reorganize into separate assemblies, one of which would have been the Assembly for Scientific and Applied Psychology. With the reorganization defeated, the assembly membership voted to become the APS in 1988–1989. In 1990, the AAAPP was founded after changing its proposed name from the Society for Clinical and Preventive Psychology. Separate assemblies within the AAAPP include an Assembly of School Psychology Scientist-Practitioners. AAAPP's purpose is to promote, protect, and advance the interest of research-oriented applied and preventive psychology in science, professional application, and other means of improving human welfare. Its journal, *Applied and Preventive Psychology: Current Scientific Perspectives,* was first published in January

1992; its newsletter, *The Scientist Practitioner,* was first published in January 1991, and its annual convention, in conjunction with that of APS, was first held in June 1991. Its first president was George Albee. Contact: AAAPP, Department of Psychology/298, University of Nevada, Reno, NV 89557.

See also AMERICAN ASSOCIATION OF APPLIED PSYCHOLOGISTS.

Thomas K. Fagan

AMERICAN ASSOCIATION OF APPLIED PSYCHOLOGISTS. Founded in 1937, the American Association of Applied Psychologists (AAAP) evolved from a merger of the Association of Consulting Psychologists* (ACP) founded in 1930, and the American Psychological Association* (APA) section on clinical psychology, founded in 1919. The AAAP was a federation of four sections: clinical, educational, consulting, and industrial and business; a military section was added in the early 1940s. Like its ACP predecessor, the AAAP also had state affiliate organizations.

The AAAP was one of several groups that merged to form the reorganized American Psychological Association in 1944–1945. In that merger, each of the AAAP sections was granted division status in the reorganized APA. School psychologists* most commonly belonged to the AAAP clinical and educational sections. The founding of the APA Division of School Psychologists* was an outgrowth of the lack of specific identity for school psychologists in the AAAP.

See also AMERICAN ASSOCIATION OF APPLIED AND PREVENTIVE PSYCHOLOGY.

REFERENCES

English, H. B. (1938). Organization of the American Association of Applied
    Psychologists. *Journal of Consulting Psychology* 2, 7–16.
Fagan, T. K. (1993). Separate but equal: School psychology's search for organizational
    identity. *Journal of School Psychology* 31, 3–90.

Thomas K. Fagan

AMERICAN ASSOCIATION OF CLINICAL PSYCHOLOGISTS. The first group of applied psychologists established separate from the American Psychological Association* (APA), the American Association of Clinical Psychologists (AACP) was formed on December 28, 1917. The purposes of the group were to provide greater morale among professional psychologists and better media communication of ideas, to establish standards for professional work in clinical psychology, to encourage research, and to standardize and improve mental examination methods. After negotiations to resolve conflicts between the APA and the clinical psychologists, the AACP was disbanded on December 31, 1919, when the APA formed its first division, the section on clinical psychology.

REFERENCES

Fagan, T. K. (1993). Separate but equal: School psychology's search for organizational
    identity. *Journal of School Psychology* 31, 3–90.

Wallin, J.E.W. (1960). History of the struggles within the American Psychological
    Association to attain membership requirements, test standardization, certification
    of psychological practitioners, and professionalization. *Journal of General
    Psychology* 63, 287–308.

                                                                    Thomas K. Fagan

AMERICAN COUNSELING ASSOCIATION. With its headquarters in Alexandria, Virginia, the American Counseling Association (ACA), with approximately 60,000 members, represents counselors through sixteen subsidiary
organizations (e.g., American School Counselor Association, American Mental
Health Counselors Association). The current ACA evolved from the American
Personnel and Guidance Association (APGA), founded in 1952. In 1983, it
changed its name to the American Association for Counseling and Development
(AACD) and then changed to ACA in 1992.

The ACA publishes the *Journal of Counseling and Development,* several journals related to its subsidiary associations, and *Guidepost* (newsletter). The organization has fifty-six state branches and is involved in state licensure, national
certification, and program accreditation through its Council for Accreditation of
Counseling and Related Education Programs (CACREP). Contact: ACA, 5999
Stevenson Avenue, Alexandria, VA 22304.

See also COUNSELING PSYCHOLOGY.

REFERENCE

American Association for Counseling and Development, Professional Information
    Service. (1991). *AACD history.* Alexandria, VA: American Association for
    Counseling and Development. (mimeo, 4 pp.)

                                                                    Thomas K. Fagan

AMERICAN EDUCATIONAL RESEARCH ASSOCIATION. The aim of
the American Educational Research Association (AERA) is to "encourage and
improve educational research and its application, thereby increasing the contribution of education to human welfare" (Grinder, 1982). AERA began in 1915
with researchers drawn from school administration, but by 1930 its membership
shifted to academicians and numbered 222. The number of members rose to
1,262 by 1958 and to 8,350 by 1968 (Grinder, 1982). Currently, AERA's membership stands at 21,300. An annual meeting is held in the spring.

AERA's divisional structure, begun in the 1960s, includes administration;
curriculum studies, learning and instruction, measurement and research methodology, counseling and human development, history and historiography, social
context of education, school evaluation and program development, education in
the professions, and postsecondary education. There are over seventy special
interest groups, and the association publishes *Educational Researcher* (a
monthly magazine), as well as a number of journals and research reviews, including *Review of Educational Research, Review of Research in Education,*

American Educational Research Journal, Journal of Education Statistics, and *Educational Evaluation and Policy Analysis.* Contact: AERA, 1230 17th Street, NW, Washington, DC 20036-3078.

See also EDUCATIONAL PSYCHOLOGY; LITERATURE IN SCHOOL PSYCHOLOGY.

REFERENCE

Grinder, R. E. (1982). The AERA annual meeting as reflected in the recent history of the association. *Educational Researcher* 11, 7–11.

Judith S. Kaufman

AMERICAN PSYCHOLOGICAL ASSOCIATION. The American Psychological Association (APA) is one of the oldest scientific and professional organizations in the United States and the oldest representing the discipline of psychology. It was founded by G. Stanley Hall* at Clark University in Worcester, Massachusetts, on July 8, 1892. A centennial convention was held in Washington, D.C., in August 1992.

The twenty-six founding members were academic psychologist- philosophers who wished to create a scientific society to promote the advancement of psychology as a science (Cattell, 1895). APA modeled itself after the American Physiological Society (Evans, Sexton, and Cadwallader, 1992). At the start, APA was governed by a council consisting of the president, secretary-treasurer, and five additional directors. This system continued until the 1945 reorganization. Business meetings were held at the annual meeting, and mail votes were taken on various issues.

APA began publishing its proceedings in the *Psychological Review* in 1894 and in the *Psychological Bulletin* beginning in 1905. These journals were privately owned but were eventually sold to the association in the 1920s. The first journal initiated and published by the association was *Psychological Abstracts* in 1920. New journals have been added since the *American Psychologist* beginning in 1946. In 1994, APA published twenty-seven primary journals and a catalog of books.

In 1896, APA formed its first committee, known as the Committee on Physical and Mental Tests. A second committee was formed in 1898, called the Standing Committee on Psychological and Philosophical Terminology. Committees and task forces have been added continually.

In 1900, the association encouraged the formation of "local sections," which emerged in Cambridge, Massachusetts; Chicago; and New York. The latter became the Eastern Psychological Association in the 1930s. The Midwestern Psychological Association was formed in 1926, and the Western Psychological Association was formed at about the same time. Presently, there are seven affiliated regional associations.

Groups have periodically broken off and merged with APA. The philosophers formed the American Philosophical Association in 1901. Titchener led a group of experimental psychologists to establish their own group in 1904, and applied psychologists formed the Association for Consulting Psychologists* in 1930. The clinical section of APA was organized in 1919 after a group of practitioners organized the American Association of Clinical Psychologists* in 1917. The clinical section merged with the new American Association of Applied Psychologists* (AAAP) in 1937 (Fagan, 1993). Psychologists concerned with social problems created in 1937 the APA-affiliated Society for the Psychological Study of Social Issues. Groups of scientist-academicians formed the Psychonomic Society in 1960.

APA was reorganized in 1945 as a result of urging from the National Research Council, which wished to see consolidation of psychology organizations in anticipation of World War II. The reorganization was intended to give more recognition to interest groups among association members and to give greater attention to professional issues. Features of the reorganization included a divisional structure with nineteen charter divisions (there are currently fifty divisions), a Council of Representatives as a legislative body, a central office with an executive officer, boards overseeing several organization functions, and an increasing number of committees, beginning with ethics,* finance, and elections. The purpose of the association expanded to encompass the promotion of psychology as a science, as a profession, and as a means of promoting human welfare (Evans, Sexton, and Cadwallader, 1992). A further change to the organization was implemented in 1958 whereby state organizations received direct representation, and members used an apportionment system to determine which groups were represented on the council.

An attempt at APA reorganization failed in 1988. The movement to restructure was led by a group of academics identified with scientific and applied psychology but opposed by clinical practitioners, who had become the association's largest political force by the 1980s. After reorganization failed, many academic psychologists left to create the American Psychological Society.* Subsequently, the APA central office reorganized into four directorates: science, practice, public interest, and education, the first to give attention to science issues. In January 1992, APA moved into a new $85 million headquarters building. In 1994, there were over 124,000 members and affiliates of APA. Contact: American Psychological Association. 750 First Street, NE, Washington, DC 20002-4242.

See also AMERICAN PSYCHOLOGICAL ASSOCIATION ANNUAL CONVENTION; DIVISION OF SCHOOL PSYCHOLOGY.

REFERENCES

Cattell, J. Mc K. (1895). Report of the secretary and treasurer for 1894. *Psychological Review* 2, 149–152.
Evans, R. B., V. S. Sexton, and T. C. Cadwallader (Eds). (1992). *The American Psychological Association: A historical perspective.* Washington, DC: American Psychological Association.

Fagan, T. K. (1993). Separate but equal: School psychology's search for organizational identity. *Journal of School Psychology* 31, 3–90.

Jonathan Sandoval

AMERICAN PSYCHOLOGICAL ASSOCIATION ANNUAL CONVENTION. One of the principal activities of the American Psychological Association* (APA) is to bring its members together in an annual meeting. These meetings have always consisted of distinguished addresses, the delivery of scientific papers, and governance meetings. More recently, conventions have included symposia, poster sessions, workshops in which to learn new skills, job placement services, and exhibits of psychological books, products, and services.

The first regular meeting was held December 27, 1892, at the University of Pennsylvania. Until 1930, meetings were held generally between Christmas and New Year's Day, a time when other societies, particularly the American Association for the Advancement of Science (AAAS), also held their meetings. Many early APA meetings were held jointly with other associations such as AAAS and the American Philosophical Association (Hilgard, 1978). From 1930 through the 1980s, the meetings were held in late summer, typically over the Labor Day weekend. In the past decade, they have been held in mid-August.

Until 1951, APA conventions were held at universities offering studies in psychology, such as the University of Pennsylvania, Harvard, Columbia, Princeton, Johns Hopkins, Yale, and Cornell; the 1951 meeting was held in a Chicago hotel. By the 1980s, only a few large cities with several available hotels could host the convention (New York, Toronto, Los Angeles, Chicago, San Francisco, Atlanta).

In 1957, a convention slated for Miami Beach was shifted to New York because of concerns that African-American members would not be treated well in the South (Smith, 1992). Since that time, social issues, such as states not ratifying the equal rights amendment, and other local stances on issues have been used in the selection of convention locations.

With the 1946 reorganization of APA, the name "annual meeting" was changed to "annual convention," and a Central Office was established to manage APA affairs, including its convention. By the late 1960s, APA had an office of convention affairs to plan the convention (Crawford, 1992). This office has been headed for over two decades by Candy Won.

Each division of the APA, such as the Division of School Psychology,* is allocated program time for symposia, paper sessions, invited addresses, and poster sessions based on a formula taking into account the number of division members and the number of division members who attended the previous three meetings. In addition, the division receives time for a business meeting, a presidential address, committee meetings, and a social hour. Divisions may offer preconvention workshops.

REFERENCES

Crawford, M. P. (1992). Rapid growth and change at the American Psychological

Association: 1945 to 1970. In R. B. Evans, V. S. Sexton, and T. C. Cadwallader (Eds.), *The American Psychological Association: A historical perspective* (pp. 177–232). Washington, DC: American Psychological Association.

Hilgard, E. R. (Ed.). (1978). *American psychology in historical perspective.* Washington, DC: American Psychological Association.

Smith, M. B. (1992). The American Psychological Association and social responsibility. In R. B. Evans, V. S. Sexton, and T. C. Cadwallader (Eds.), *The American Psychological Association: A historical perspective* (pp. 327–346). Washington, DC: American Psychological Association.

Jonathan Sandoval

AMERICAN PSYCHOLOGICAL SOCIETY. The American Psychological Society (APS) evolved from the failure of an effort within the American Psychological Association* (APA) to reorganize into separate assemblies, one of which would have been the Assembly for Scientific and Applied Psychology. With the reorganization defeated, the assembly membership voted to become the APS in 1988. Dues were first collected in 1989, and the new association gained quickly in membership. The APS is strongly committed to maintaining the scientific base of psychology and, to a considerable extent, emerged from dissatisfactions with APA's growing professional orientation. The organization's journal, *Psychological Science,* was first published in January 1990; its newsletter, *The Observer,* was first published in October 1988; and its first annual convention was held in June 1989. A second journal, *Current Directions in Psychological Science,* was first published in 1992. Charles A. Kiesler, a former executive director of the APA, served as APS's first president. Contact: APS, P.O. Box 90457, Washington, DC 20090-0457.

See also AMERICAN ASSOCIATION OF APPLIED AND PREVENTIVE PSYCHOLOGY.

Thomas K. Fagan

AMERICANS WITH DISABILITIES ACT. The Americans with Disabilities Act (ADA) of 1990 (Public Law 101-336) is civil rights legislation for persons with disabilities. The Civil Rights Act of 1964 addressed racial and religious discrimination, and the Rehabilitation Act of 1973 protected the civil rights of persons with disabilities.

The authors of ADA recognized a continuing existence of discrimination and prejudice in spite of previous legislation and wanted to provide a clear mandate for the elimination of discrimination against individuals with disabilities. ADA was designed to provide clear, consistent, and enforceable standards for addressing discrimination. ADA specifically covers employment, public accommodations, transportation, state and local government operations, and telecommunications.

ADA is applicable to employers with fifteen or more employees. The qualified applicant, as well as the employee, is protected. Hiring, advancement, and discharge practices are included, as well as guidelines for medical examinations. Current use of illegal drugs or alcohol disqualifies a person as a qualified individual with disabilities. All public accommodations except private clubs and religious organizations are covered by ADA. Changes in policies and procedures, provisions for auxiliary aids and services, removal of physical barriers, and new construction design are prescribed. Regarding transportation, public bus systems, privately operated bus and van companies, public rail systems, and the public facilities must be accessible to persons with disabilities. Some rail facilities are not required to be modified until the year 2010. Congress provided no funds to implement ADA, but tax laws were enacted to allow the Internal Revenue Service to provide relief to private business and industry.

State and local government's employment practices are covered by ADA. Their facilities are covered by the Rehabilitation Act of 1973. Lastly, telephone companies must offer telecommunications devices for the deaf (TDD).

See also OFFICE OF CIVIL RIGHTS; SECTION 504 OF THE REHABILITATION ACT.

REFERENCES

Americans with Disabilities Act of 1990, 42 U.S.C.A.; 12101 *et seq.* (West 1993).

U.S. Department of Justice. (1990). *The Americans with Disabilities Act.* (CRD Publication No. 10). Washington, DC: U.S. Government Printing Office.

Paul G. Warden

ANGER CONTROL TRAINING. Problems with anger have traditionally been dealt with either through changing the consequences of the behavior or through finding a cause and removing it (a feeling or a cognition). Recent focus has been directed to teaching skills that (hypothetically) mediate adjustment. New understanding is combined with behavioral rehearsal to get new behavior.

One example is the *Dealing with Anger* series of videos (available from Research Press), which employs a social learning model. Teaching the adolescent self-control strategies is the goal of *Adolescent Anger Control* (Feindler and Ecton, 1986). Students are taught to identify anger triggers and to learn coping self-statements and relaxation. Spivack, Shure, and Platt (1976) assume that a core of social problem-solving skills mediates social adjustment. The learning and use of these skills can result in nonviolent problem solving. A basic skill is thinking of alternatives. An advanced skill is perspective taking.

An alternative to aggressive behavior to settle disputes is peer mediation (Schmidt, Friedman, and Marvel, 1992). Students are chosen who express an interest in solving disputes and who are judged as "fair," with an ability to appreciate various points of view and some skill in problem solving.

See also CONFLICT RESOLUTION/PEER MEDIATION; SELF-MANAGEMENT; SOCIAL SKILLS TRAINING.

REFERENCES

Feindler, E. L., and R. B. Ecton. (1986). *Adolescent anger control.* New York: Pergamon Press.

Schmidt, F., A. Friedman, and J. Marvel. (1992). *Mediation for kids*. Miami Beach: Grace Contrino Abrams Peace Education Foundation.
Spivack, G., M. B. Shure, and J. J. Platt. (1976). *The problem solving approach to adjustment*. San Francisco: Jossey-Bass.

William B. Jennings

APA/NASP JOINT AWARD FOR DISTRICT PROGRAM EXCEL-LENCE. In April 1978, Beeman N. Phillips, editor of the *Journal of School Psychology,* suggested that the journal provide an award to a school psychological services unit. Since the journal's Board of Directors declined the offer, Phillips presented the idea to Cal Dyer of the Executive Council for Division 16* (school psychology) of the American Psychological Association* (APA). Division 16 liked the concept and invited the National Association of School Psychologists* (NASP) to cosponsor the award.

At the time of its creation, the biennial award was the only practice-oriented national recognition for a service unit. William C. Hoffman chaired the first APA—Division 16/NASP Joint Selection Committee, consisting of John H. Jackson, Mark E. Swerdlik, and Deborah Vensel. James C. Paavola, of the Memphis City School Mental Health Center (MCSMHC), received the first award at an American Psychological Association assembly in Washington, D.C.; subsequently, staff from the MCSMHC presented a program description at the 1983 NASP convention in Detroit. Issues of the NASP *Communiqué* and the Division 16 *School Psychologist* contain articles describing the award recipients, with details about the winning programs.

REFERENCES

Fagan, T. K. (1993). Separate but equal: School psychology's search for organizational identity. *Journal of School Psychology* 31, 3–90.
Memphis receives award for excellence. (1982). *Communique* 11 (1), 6. Additional information appears in *Communique* 11 (4) and 11 (5).

Philip B. Bowser

APTITUDES. An aptitude refers to a potential to learn a specific skill such as art or music. Aptitudes can also be conceived very broadly, such as intelligence* or achievement and also as readiness* for learning in preschool through graduate or professional school. Aptitudes are conceived to reflect physical and mental abilities as well as motivation and interest.* Aptitudes develop from contributions of both heredity and the nature of the environment in which the aptitudes are nurtured.

There exist important distinctions between such concepts as aptitude and achievement; although both refer to learning to some degree, aptitudes are broader and represent abilities developed under uncontrolled and undefined conditions. Achievement refers to an ability developed with specific training and is usually limited to one particular subject area.

Aptitude tests for young children are referred to as readiness tests and assess a child's readiness for learning. For older persons, the term "aptitude" is substituted for readiness. Common examples of aptitude tests include the Metropolitan Readiness Test, used at the kindergarten level; the Differential Aptitude Test (DAT), commonly administered at the high school level; the Scholastic Aptitude Test (SAT), used for college admission; and the Graduate Record Exam (GRE), used by many graduate schools.

See also ASSESSMENT; VOCATIONAL ASSESSMENT.

REFERENCES

Anastasi, A. (1986). *Psychological testing* (6th ed.). New York: Macmillan.
Cohen, R. J., M. E. Swerdlik, and D. K. Smith. (1992). *Psychological testing and assessment. An introduction to tests and measurement* (2d ed.). Mountain View, CA: Mayfield.
Cronbach, L. J. (1990). *Essentials of psychological testing* (5th ed.). New York: HarperCollins.

Yvette J. Cornett
Mark E. Swerdlik

APTITUDE-TREATMENT INTERACTION MODEL. Suppose (hypothetically) a researcher is interested in whether average reading comprehension scores are higher for children taught by the traditional instruction method (treatment 1) or by a new instruction method utilizing mnemonic reminders (treatment 2). Further suppose that the reading literature has documented that IQ (aptitude) has a strong impact on reading comprehension scores. If differences in average reading comprehension scores between the two methods of instruction are not constant for every level (low, moderate, high) of IQ, then an aptitude-treatment model best fits the data. This model would be applicable, for example, if average reading comprehension scores were higher for high-IQ children using the traditional method of instruction whereas low-IQ children benefited most from the mnemonic reminder method.

While the aptitude-treatment interaction model is valid from a theoretical perspective, efforts to demonstrate the interaction have generally met with failure due to major methodological problems in trying to actually measure aptitude.

See also APTITUDES; TREATMENT INTEGRITY; VALIDITY.

REFERENCES

McClave, J. T., and F. H. Dietrich. (1988). *Statistics.* San Francisco: Dellen.
Marjoribanks, K. M. (1988). Interaction effects. In J. P. Keeves (Ed.), *Educational research, methodology, and measurement: An international handbook* (pp. 664–672). New York: Pergamon Press.
Ysseldyke, J. E., and P. K. Mirkin. (1990). The use of assessment information to plan instructional interventions: A review of the research. In T. B. Gutkin and C. R.

Reynolds (Eds.), *The handbook of school psychology* (pp. 663–682). New York: Wiley.

William T. Coombs

ART THERAPY. Art therapy often draws from psychoanalytic theory. Artistic production is viewed as a bridge between the inner world of a person and the outer world around him or her. Art expression can be free from external guidelines, as contrasted to crafts, which require the construction of end products patterned after a model (crafts can produce satisfaction and pride). But art can be chaotic or malevolent, and art often expresses the inner world, the unconscious world to many art therapists. By the expression of this inner world through art, the relationship of the client to the inner world can be understood. Forbidden wishes can be expressed symbolically. By helping the client produce emotionally charged art, the client can become more accepting of repressed feelings and ideas. The ego can now deal with the expression through sublimation—or, in the case of adults, transference—and its subsequent resolution.

Art therapy is seen as a vehicle for psychological assessment. The selection of a medium such as drawing, painting, or clay modeling; the quality of artwork; the formal character; the subject matter; and the client's attitude all provide information to the art therapist. Though children are more inclined to freely enter into artistic activity, certain limitations are recognized when working with children with disabilities, for example, neurological impairment.

The expression of the inner world through art or music or dance can be conceptualized within other theoretical orientations, for example, humanistic psychology.

For more information, contact the American Art Therapy Association, 1202 Allanson Road, Mundelein, IL 60060.

REFERENCES

Dalley, T., G. Rifkind, and K. Terry. (1993). *Three voices of art therapy: Image, client, therapist.* New York: Routledge.
Kramer, E., and E. Ulman. (1982). Art therapy. In C. R. Reynolds and T. B. Gutkin (Eds.), *The handbook of school psychology* (pp. 656–666). New York: Wiley.
Robbins, A. (Ed.). (1980). *Expressive therapy: A creative arts approach to depth-oriented treatment.* New York: Human Sciences.

Paul G. Warden

ASSERTIVENESS TRAINING. Assertiveness is identifying and claiming one's rights and expressing one's competence. To take such a stand has been interpreted by Western culture as a positive behavior (Feschbach and Feschbach, 1986). At the same time, men and boys who assert themselves have been reinforced and supported far more consistently than have women and girls (Kelley et al., 1980), and people of European ancestry have been more accepted in their assertiveness than have people of culturally and linguistically diverse groups

(Henry and Piercy, 1984). In this social context, assertiveness training has the potential for supporting people typically disenfranchised and unsupported, while at the same time altering aggressive interpersonal behaviors that sustain such variations in social acceptance.

Assertiveness training is among the most popular techniques in contemporary clinical practice. These approaches stem primarily from the work of Joseph Wolpe. Although Wolpe was not the first to identify the importance of supporting assertive behaviors, his ideas became public when the psychological community began to be interested in behavioral theory and, therefore, more open to Wolpe's ideas of systematic desensitization* and their application in assertiveness training.

Wolpe's techniques are evident in the use of behavioral rehearsal, in which individuals use role play or visualization to practice more assertive interpersonal responses. Other techniques for assertiveness training are the cognitive strategies, such as rational-emotive therapy,* rational restructuring, and self-instructional training through which individuals are brought to question dysfunctional cognition underlying habitual nonassertive responses. Group assertiveness training has been found to be as effective as individual assertiveness training, with the natural opportunity in groups for overt practice with a variety of interpersonal partners and for discussion and social reinforcement of assertiveness skills.

See also ANGER CONTROL TRAINING; GENDER ISSUES.

REFERENCES

Feshbach, S., and N. D. Feshbach. (1986). Aggression and altruism: A personality perspective. In C. Zahn-Waxler, E. M. Cummings, and R. Iannotti (Eds.), *Altruism and aggression: Biological and social origins* (pp. 189–217). New York: Cambridge University Press.

Henry, W. J., and F. P. Piercy (1984). Assertive/aggressive ratings of women as a function of raters' race and sex. *Journal of Non-White Concerns in Personnel and Guidance* 12, 85–98.

Kelley, J. A., J. M. Kearn, B. G. Kirkley, J. N. Patterson, and T. M. Keane. (1980). Reactions to assertive versus unassertive behavior: Differential effects for males and females and implications for assertiveness training. *Behavior Therapy* 11, 670–682.

Mary Henning-Stout

ASSESSMENT (DIRECT AND INDIRECT). The role of the school psychologist* traditionally has revolved around the assessment of students. Assessment is a process of identifying problems and making decisions to remediate those problems. In the past, assessment has been equated with testing. However, the two terms are not synonymous; testing is one tool of assessment. Others include behavioral observations, interviews, rating scales, and case histories. Assessment is used by school psychologists to assist them in making referrals, screening, classification, instructional planning, and/or pupil progress decisions for students' academic, behavioral, or physical difficulties (Salvia and Ysseldyke, 1995). In order to make such decisions, a multifactored approach to assessment should be utilized. A multifactored assessment implies that multiple sources of information collected through multiple methods are gathered prior to making decisions related to an individual child's educational placement or progress. Multiple methods include both direct and indirect forms of assessment.

Direct assessment refers to the gathering of quantifiable information about a student in a one-to-one situation involving a school psychologist and a student (Fagan and Wise, 1994). Through direct assessment, school psychologists can observe a student in a structured situation as well as obtain data with which to compare a student to his or her peers.

Indirect assessment involves consultation* with teachers, parents, administrators, and others to clarify problems and develop solutions; direct classroom and home observations; record reviews; and interviews with significant persons in a student's life. Often, problems can be solved by engaging in indirect assessment, and, thus, direct assessment may not be required.

See also COMPREHENSIVE ASSESSMENT; INTERVIEWING; MULTI-TRAIT–MULTIMETHOD MATRIX; NATURALISTIC OBSERVATION.

REFERENCES

Fagan, T. K., and P. S. Wise (1994). *School psychology: Past, present, and future.* White Plains, NY: Longman.
Salvia, J., and J. E. Ysseldyke (1995). *Assessment* (6th ed.). Boston: Houghton Mifflin.
Karen T. Carey

ASSISTIVE TECHNOLOGY. Assistive technology includes computerized devices to assist the handicapped in completing such basic life skills as communication, motor control, visual and auditory reception and perception, transportation, and reading and writing. Visually impaired individuals use computerized braille readers and writers, audiotapes of a wide variety of materials, and large-sized type presented a letter or a word at a time at a self-controlled pace and read aloud by the computer if desired. Hearing-impaired individuals use computerized hearing aids that adjust to block out background sounds and emphasize human speech or cochlea implants to help propel sound into the inner ear. Motor-impaired or physically impaired individuals use computerized wheelchairs that demand little or no muscle movement, computerized lifts to enter automobiles or buses, and electronic sensors attached to muscles to stimulate muscle movements and allow the person to "ride" a stationary bicycle. If physical impairments prevent communication, the individual may point to words or phrases on a language board or use eye switches attached to a computer that scans words or phrases until a blink selects the desired object. Regular or adapted word processors provide a means to circumvent fine-motor control problems or problems with below-average writing fluency. Self-paced reading instructional programs teach basic skills in a highly motivating and infinitely patient environment for those who require more repetition and a slower pace of learning. Computer-assisted instruction (CAI) monitors progress and presents information in units that may be repeated or branched to other units to focus on skills not yet mastered. Assistive technology also monitors life functions in individuals who would need immediate assistance in an emergency.

See also COMPUTER-ASSISTED TESTING.

REFERENCES

Chandler, S. K., T. Czerlinsky, and P. Wehman. (1993). Provisions of assistive technology: Bridging the gap to accessibility. In P. Wehman (Ed.), *The ADA mandate for social change* (pp. 117–133). Baltimore: Brookes.
Parette, H. P., and A. VanBiervliet (1991). School-age children with disabilities: Technology implications for counselors. *Elementary School Guidance and Counseling* 25(3), 182–193.

C. Sue McCullough

ASSOCIATION FOR ADVANCEMENT OF BEHAVIOR THERAPY. The Association for Advancement of Behavior Therapy (AABT) is an international organization of mental health professionals and students interested in behavior therapy,* cognitive behavior therapy, behavioral assessment,* applied behavior analysis, and their application in understanding and improving the human condition. The organization has been in existence since 1967. There are now over 4,300 mental health professional and student members.

AABT publishes journals (*Cognitive and Behavioral Practice* and *Behavior Therapy*), newsletters, directories, pamphlets, and fact sheets. An annual convention provides continuing education and research-reporting opportunities. AABT's Referral Service and Media and Community Connection operate as public services. Fact sheets have been developed by AABT members on such topics as adolescent suicide, acquired immunodeficiency syndrome (AIDS) prevention, alcohol abuse, attention-deficit hyperactivity disorder (ADHD), autism, bed-wetting, eating disorders, helping children cope with divorce, obsessive-compulsive disorder (OCD), parent training, shyness and social phobia and are available for purchase by mental health professionals and free to the public. More information is available from AABT, 305 Seventh Avenue, New York, NY 10001; phone 800-685-AABT.

See also ASSOCIATION FOR BEHAVIOR ANALYSIS; CLASSIFICATION: PSYCHIATRIC; COGNITIVE BEHAVIOR MODIFICATION.

REFERENCE

Association for Advancement of Behavior Therapy 27th Annual Conference Media Information Package, Atlanta, GA, 1993.

Robbie N. Sharp

ASSOCIATION FOR BEHAVIOR ANALYSIS. An international organization, the Association for Behavior Analysis (ABA) has been dedicated to advancing the science of behavior and its application since its beginnings in 1974. Its purview encompasses contemporary scientific and social issues, theoretical advances, and the dissemination of professional and public information. ABA, an organization of 2,366 members, is affiliated with numerous state and regional chapters and actively promotes the international development of behavior analysis.

ABA's activities include membership services (e.g., special interest groups), journal support (*Behavior Analyst*), directories (e.g., graduate training, membership), a newsletter, and an annual convention. ABA is supported by the American Psychological Association* to offer continuing education workshops. The organization also certifies graduate training programs in behavior analysis.

More information is available by contacting the ABA, 258 Wood Hall, Western Michigan University, Kalamazoo, MI 49008-5052; phone 616-387-4494.

See also ASSOCIATION FOR ADVANCEMENT OF BEHAVIOR THERAPY; BEHAVIOR THERAPY.

Robbie N. Sharp

ASSOCIATION OF CONSULTING PSYCHOLOGISTS. Founded in 1930, the Association of Consulting Psychologists (ACP) evolved from an expansion of the New York State Association of Consulting Psychologists, founded in 1921. Its membership included doctoral consulting psychologists in the fields of business, education, industry, law, medicine, mental hygiene, social service, and vocational guidance. It may have been the first applied psychology association to have state affiliate organizations. In 1935, the ACP started a newsletter, *The Consulting Psychologist,* published at least seven times per year, and in 1937 it started the *Journal of Consulting Psychology.* The ACP disbanded in 1938, after the American Association of Applied Psychologists* was founded.

REFERENCES

Fagan, T. K. (1993). Separate but equal: School psychology's search for organizational identity. *Journal of School Psychology* 31, 3–90.
Symonds, J. P. (1937). Toward unity. *Journal of Consulting Psychology* 1, 23–24.

Thomas K. Fagan

ASSOCIATION OF PSYCHOLOGY POSTDOCTORAL AND INTERNSHIP CENTERS. The Association of Psychology Postdoctoral and Internship Centers (APPIC) was organized in 1968 to encourage high-quality psychology training and to serve as an exchange agency for information among postdoctoral and internship centers and a source of providing information to students seeking internships. In this latter aspect, APPIC has managed a clearinghouse for internship* placement since 1976. The association is involved in policy making and activities of organizations related to APPIC goals, including the directorates, boards, and committees of the American Psychological Association* (APA), the Association of State and Provincial Psychology Boards,* and the National Register of Health Service Providers in Psychology.* With criteria closely related to those of the APA, APPIC maintains a directory of qualified postdoctoral and internship centers. APA-approved internships are automatically included in the directory. Contact: APPIC, 733 15th Street NW, Suite 717, Washington, DC 20005.

See also ACCREDITATION.

Thomas K. Fagan

ASSOCIATION OF STATE AND PROVINCIAL PSYCHOLOGY BOARDS. The Association of State and Provincial Psychology Boards (ASPPB) (formerly, American Association of State Psychology Boards) is an association of American and Canadian regulatory boards of psychology whose purpose is to promote sound administration and facilitate communication among member boards. The ASPPB also recommends policy and legal perspectives regarding licensure, disciplinary actions, and other administrative decisions made by each board.

One of the primary tasks has been the development, validation, and organization of the semiannual forms of the Examination for Professional Practice in Psychology* (EPPP), which is now required for licensure in all states and provinces, and to provide information to candidates. The association also publishes the most comprehensive description of licensing* information in the United States and Canada. Information can be obtained relative to each jurisdiction about the types of statutes that exist, levels of licensure, rules and regulations, requirements for licensure (e.g., academic degree, exams, cutoff scores), and a description of the board. Contact: Association of State and Provincial Psychology Boards, P.O. Box 4386, Montgomery, AL 36103.

REFERENCE

Carlson, H. S. (1978). The AASPB story: The beginnings and first 16 years of the American Association of State Psychology Boards, 1961–1977. *American Psychologist* 33, 486–495.

Robert N. Wendt

AUTHORITY. The concept of authority as it relates to the public school refers to the responsibility of administrators, such as superintendents and principals, for preparing and implementing educational programs. Such authority is vested by school boards, operating under mandates of state and federal laws. School psychologists have no administrative authority except when it is sanctioned by those in administrative positions. They can, however, demonstrate an "authority of expertise," or expert power* that represents the possession of relevant knowledge, and of referent power* because of their ability to identify with the interest of their clients (Fagan and Wise, 1994). As a member of an evaluation team, the psychologist provides data that identify the academic, social, and/or emotional development of both "normal" and "special" children (Shinn, 1989).

Although the psychologist functions as a consultant in such situations, there is often a misperception that the position involves a degree of authority, which creates potential professional rancor. When a school psychologist assumes an authoritative role (e.g., pupil personnel director), an opportunity exists for seeing problems from a broader perspective. However, care must be taken to avoid generating problems, as efforts are made to meet the conflicting demands of disparate roles.

See also CENTRALIZED VERSUS DECENTRALIZED SERVICES.

REFERENCES

Fagan, T. K., and P. S. Wise. (1994). *School psychology: Past, present and future.* White Plains, NY: Longman.
Shinn, M. (Ed.). (1989). *Curriculum based measurement: Assessing special children.* New York: Guilford Press.

Donald M. Wonderly

B

BAKER, HARRY J. Harry Jay Baker (1889–1981), director of the Psychological Clinic in the Detroit public schools (1920–1960), was a frequent author, active participant in many professional organizations, and visiting lecturer at many universities across North America. He received three degrees from the University of Michigan, earning an A.B. in 1913, M.A. in 1918, and Ph.D. in 1920. He was a superintendent of schools in two Ohio towns (1913–1917).

Baker is best known as the author of the *Detroit Learning Aptitude Test* (with Bernice Leland) and three editions of *Introduction to Exceptional Children* (1944, 1953, and 1959), as president of the (National) Council for Exceptional Children from 1935 to 1937, and as president of the American Psychological Association's Division of School Psychologists in 1946–1947.

A member of nine national professional organizations, he was also quite active in local groups, serving as president of the Detroit Psychological Association, Social Workers of Metropolitan Detroit, Detroit chapter of Phi Delta Kappa, Boys Work Council of Metropolitan Detroit, Guidance Association of Metropolitan Detroit, and Kiwanis Club No. 1 of Detroit.

Following publication of *Characteristic Differences in Bright and Dull Pupils* (1927) and another book on remedial teaching (1929), he was chair of the Committee on Behavior Problems at the White House Conference of Child Health and Protection (1930). His final major publication was *Biographical Sagas of Will Power* (1970). He died in San Diego on September 30, 1981.

REFERENCE

Lord, F. E. (1982). In memoriam, Harry J. Baker. *Exceptional Children* 48, 293.

Joseph L. French

BARDON, JACK I. Jack Irving Bardon was born on October 24, 1925, in Cleveland, Ohio, and died on November 9, 1993, in Greensboro, North Carolina.

After serving in the military in World War II, he received his B.A. degree in 1949 from Cleveland College of Western Reserve University with a major in psychology and a minor in education. In 1951, he received his M.A. in psychology and in 1956 the Ph.D. in clinical psychology* at the University of Pennsylvania. Influenced by several significant school psychologists in the 1950s and 1960s, Bardon was among those who helped to bridge the educational and clinical psychology traditions of the field and promulgated the concept of a psychology of schooling* in preference to the traditional concept of school psychology.* He worked with others to forge the first doctor of psychology (Psy.D.) program in school psychology at Rutgers University during his tenure there from 1960 to 1976. Prior to Rutgers, he worked as a school psychologist in the Princeton Borough Schools (New Jersey) from 1952 to 1958 and as its coordinator of special services, 1958–1960. His last academic position was as Excellence Professor at the University of North Carolina–Greensboro from 1976 until the time of his death.

REFERENCES

Bardon, J. I. (1981). A personalized account of the development and status of school psychology. *Journal of School Psychology* 19, 199–210.
———. (1992). Perspectives on school psychology. *The School Psychologist* (Division 16-APA newsletter) 46(1), 4–5.
Fagan, T. K. (1994). Tribute to Jack I. Bardon. *The School Psychologist* (Division 16, APA Newsletter) 48(2), 3–6, 20.

Thomas K. Fagan

BEHAVIORAL ASSESSMENT. Behavioral assessment is an approach to evaluation distinguished by a set of assumptions that dictate the interpretation of data obtained by various methods. The primary goal of behavioral assessment is to identify those aspects of the environment that maintain the behaviors of concern, rather than to determine potential underlying psychological causes. Expected outcomes of behavioral assessment are identifying potential targets for intervention,* determining possible strategies for intervention, and providing an ongoing assessment of behavior over time.

One of the most important and influential articles defining behavioral assessment was provided by Hartmann, Roper, and Bradford (1978) in the premier issue of the *Journal of Behavioral Assessment* (which became the *Journal of Psychopathology and Behavioral Assessment* in 1985). In their article, Hartmann et al. described a series of assumptions, implications, uses of data, and other characteristics that distinguished behavioral and traditional assessment methodologies. A cornerstone assumption of behavioral assessment is that observable behavior is assumed to be situationally specific rather than cross-situational (as with more traditional approaches to assessment). This assumption requires that the degree to which behavior occurs across settings and time be assessed. As such, behavior is viewed as a sample of a behavioral repertoire rather than as a sign of other underlying pathology. The presence of trait personality character-istics is de-emphasized. Additionally, the causes of behavior are assumed to be found in the environmental conditions maintaining current behavior. Emphasis tends to be on intraindividual, rather than interindividual, change. Given this emphasis on environmental events, more direct methods of assessment, such as systematic observation, are used.

Historically, the process of behavioral assessment was embedded within the development of behavioral interventions commonly associated with operant con-ditioning.* These interventions often focused on observable behaviors and ex-cluded consideration of cognitive and emotional aspects of the behavior change process. As such, behavioral assessment was devoted primarily to the identifi-cation of antecedent and consequent conditions surrounding the occurrence of observable behavior. Early writers in behavioral assessment tended to emphasize the importance of an assessment of the environmental events surrounding be-havior.

With the emergence of cognitive behavior therapy and a recognition of the influence that thought and emotion play in the prediction of behavior, behavioral assessment incorporated cognitive and emotional components into its conceptual framework. In one of the first models for behavioral assessment, Cone (1978) identified a three-dimensional model that contained a modality of assessment (motoric, cognitive, and physiological), the content of assessment* (direct to indirect), and the universes of generalization (scorer, item, time, setting, method, dimension). A key element in Cone's model was the recognition that all behavior contains components that are observable (motoric), covert (cognitive), and in-ternal (physiological).

Cone's methods of behavioral assessment have been elaborated by describing in more detail the direct-to-indirect approaches to evaluation. A method was defined by Cone (1978) on this dimension, depending on the degree to which a procedure assessed behavior at a time that the behavior actually occurred. If behavior was assessed when it actually happened, it was considered a direct method of assessment. If behavior was assessed at a time or means removed from the actual occurrence of the behavior, it was considered an indirect method. Specifically, direct methods consisted of direct observation in the natural setting, direct observation in an analogue setting, and self-monitoring. In all of these methods, behavior was assessed as it actually occurred. Indirect methods were self-reports and informant reports, primarily through the use of rating scales and/or interviews.

The recognition of the presence of a continuum of behavioral assessment methods resulted in a revision of Cone's conceptualization of the generalization dimensions of his model. In his revision, Cone emphasized the importance of accuracy as a key component in the evaluation of behavioral assessment methods as well as providing a description of behavioral assessment that included nom-othetic and idiographic approaches.

Behavioral assessment emerged primarily from behavioral child clinical psychology. In particular, Mash and Terdal (1981) provided one of the first comprehensive volumes devoted to the behavioral assessment of children. However, the emphasis was clearly placed on the assessment of children in clinical, rather than school, settings. Extension of behavioral assessment to school psychology* was offered initially by Kratochwill (1982), Shapiro (1987), and Shapiro and Kratochwill (1988). Drawing on the clinical methodologies developed for nonschool settings,* school-based assessment procedures were incorporated into the evaluation process, such as teachers as informants, problem identification interviews, direct classroom observation, and the assessment of academic skills problems.

See also ASSESSMENT (DIRECT AND INDIRECT); BEHAVIOR MODIFICATION; COGNITIVE BEHAVIOR MODIFICATION; ECOLOGICAL ASSESSMENT; INTERVIEWING.

REFERENCES

Cone, J. D. (1978) The Behavioral Assessment Grid (BAG): A conceptual framework and a taxonomy. *Behavior Therapy* 8, 411–426.
Hartmann, D. P., B. L. Roper, and D. C. Bradford. (1978). Some relationships between behavioral and traditional assessment. *Journal of Behavioral Assessment* 1, 3–21.
Mash, E. J., and L. G. Terdal. (1981). *Behavioral assessment of childhood disorders* (2d ed.). New York: Guilford Press.
Shapiro, E. S. (1987). *Behavioral assessment in school psychology.* Hillsdale, NJ: Erlbaum.
Shapiro, E. S., and T. R. Kratochwill (Eds.). (1988). *Behavioral assessment in schools: Conceptual foundations and practical applications.* New York: Guilford Press.

                                                                        Edward S. Shapiro

BEHAVIORAL CONSULTATION. Behavioral consultation refers to one of the three most frequently identified models of school psychological consultation,* the others being mental health consultation* and systems and organizational consultation.* Behavioral consultation is distinguished by its ties to the principles of behavioral psychology.

Common to other models of consultation, behavioral consultation uses a problem-solving procedure. With some variation among authors, the problem-solving approach usually involves a version of the following steps: (1) problem identification, (2) problem clarification, (3) intervention design, (4) implementation, and (5) treatment evaluation. The consultant (e.g., school psychologist) guides the consultee (e.g., teacher, parent) through the problem-solving steps.

In the classic version of behavioral consultation most identified with Bergan (Bergan and Kratochwill, 1990), adherence to behavioral principles underlies movement through the problem-solving steps. During problem identification (step 1), consultees are helped to be very specific in identifying problems and in ranking problems in terms of priorities. The objective is to help the consultee answer questions such as "Which of the various *specific* problems that Johnny

is presenting is the most important to address now?'' In step 2, problem clarification, the consultant works with the consultee to arrive at a behaviorally
specific (operationally defined) description of the problem. The problem is described in language that allows its frequency, intensity, and/or duration to be
objectively measured. Baseline data are gathered to provide a benchmark with
which the results of interventions will be compared.

Intervention design (step 3) proceeds with the designation of a goal statement
for the problem behavior, as well as intermediate objectives that are realistic
and measurable. Interventions are usually based on operant conditioning* techniques, where the problem behavior is reduced or eliminated through some combination of extinction and aversive consequences, along with positive
reinforcement of desired behavior. In cases where the problem is a behavioral
deficit rather than an excess, the procedures will be largely ones of reinforcing
successive approximations of the desired behavior until the goal state is reached.
The final part of step 3 is the specification of the respective responsibilities of
the consultant and consultee in carrying out the intervention and measuring
outcomes. It is a general principle of consultation that interventions are implemented as much as possible by the consultee, thus serving to generalize the
effects of intervention and to expand the consultee's professional competence.

Step 4 is the implementation of the intervention, with step 5, evaluation,
occurring during intervention. Attainment of objectives and goals leads to termination of the program or its modification (e.g., fading) to facilitate maintenance of gains. If objectives are not met, the consultant and consultee recycle
through the steps of the problem-solving model to improve the treatment program.

A variation of the behavioral consultation model called the social learning
theory model (SLM) has been developed and relies more heavily on cognitive-
behavioral, than operant, psychology (Brown and Schulte, 1987). The two models share a foundation in the scientific bases of behavioral psychology and the
use of the problem-solving steps. However, the social learning model has as its
conceptual base the notion of reciprocal determinism,* which considers interaction of behavior, environment, and cognitions (covert behavior), rather than
focusing primarily on the environment. Although operant techniques may be
part of the social learning model, this model also employs such techniques as
modeling,* desensitization, cognitive restructuring, and self-monitoring.

Although evidence exists for the effectiveness of behavioral consultation (Bergan and Kratochwill, 1990; Medway and Updyke, 1985), there are criticisms.
Behavioral consultation may be a poor fit with most definitions of consultation.
Consultation is often described as a collaborative problem-solving process involving two or more persons of equal status. The consultee is seen as free to
accept or reject consultant input. It can be argued that behavioral consultation
involves a more directive and instructional role on the part of the consultant
than is true in other consultation models (e.g., mental health consultation). Although the consultant and consultee still must agree on such things as problem

definition and intervention plans, the consultant tends to play a leadership role in influencing the consultee to use a step-by-step behavioral analysis approach leading almost exclusively to behavioral interventions. One of the reasons evidence exists for its effectiveness may relate to the relative ease of studying a model that is so rigidly, behaviorally bound with its insistence on objectively measurable outcomes. Despite these limited criticisms, behavioral consultation has made significant contributions to school psychology research and practice and is likely to remain one of the most important practice options available to school psychologists in the future.

See also COLLABORATIVE CONSULTATION; CONSULTATION; METACOGNITIVE SKILLS; SELF-MANAGEMENT.

REFERENCES

Bergan, J. R., and T. R. Kratochwill. (1990). *Behavioral consultation and therapy.* New York: Plenum Press.
Brown, D., and A. C. Schulte. (1987). A social learning model of consultation. *Professional Psychology: Research and Practice* 18, 283–287.
Kratochwill, T. R., S. N. Elliott, and P. C. Rotto. (1995). Best practices in school-based behavioral consultation. In A. Thomas and J. Grimes (Eds.), *Best practices in school* psychology—III (pp. 519–537). Washington, DC: National Association of School Psychologists.
Medway, F. J., and J. F. Updyke. (1985). Meta-analysis of consultation outcome studies. *American Journal of Community Psychology* 13, 489–504.

Edward Gaughan
Joel Meyers

BEHAVIOR MODIFICATION. Behavior modification was originally conceptualized as the systematic application of the principles of operant conditioning* originally developed by B. F. Skinner (1953). Although some early writers in the area distinguished behavior modification from behavior therapy,* the term has evolved and become synonymous with behavior therapy.

See also BEHAVIORAL ASSESSMENT; COGNITIVE BEHAVIOR MODIFICATION; INTERVENTION (DIRECT AND INDIRECT); SELF-MANAGEMENT.

REFERENCES

O'Leary, K. D., and S. G. O'Leary (Eds.). (1972). *Classroom management: The successful use of behavior modification.* New York: Pergamon Press.
Skinner, B. F. (1953). *Science and human behavior.* New York: Macmillan.
Sulzer, B., and G. R. Mayer. (1972). *Behavior modification procedures for school personnel.* Hinsdale, IL: Dryden Press.

Edward S. Shapiro

BEHAVIOR THERAPY. Behavior therapy refers to an approach to behavior change that focuses on the teaching of new patterns of behavioral responses. In contrast to other forms of therapy that emphasize underlying psychological or biological causes to explain and alter behavior patterns, behavior therapy emphasizes understanding and changing the environmental events that maintain behaviors. The primary focus of behavior therapy is educational.

Originally based on the principles of operant conditioning,* behavior therapy is the systematic application of these techniques. Many behavior therapy interventions focus extensively on principles of positive reinforcement. As described by Skinner in 1953, any event that increases the probability that the response will be repeated is, by definition, a positive reinforcer. Using this principle, behavior therapy interventions attempt to identify such events and then use these events contingently to alter the probability of occurrence of identified, desirable behaviors.

One such procedure is called differential reinforcement of low rates (DRL). In this procedure, a desirable behavior that currently occurs at a low rate is targeted. Individuals are assessed to determine potential events and consequences that currently maintain other high-rate behaviors. These events are considered positive reinforcers. In a DRL procedure, these positive reinforcers are then provided contingently on the occurrence of the low-rate behavior. At the same time, undesirable high-rate behaviors are no longer reinforced. The procedure results in the gradual increase of the low-rate behavior with reduction in occurrence of the undesirable high-rate behavior.

For example, a student currently calls out in class and rarely raises his hand. The teacher identifies that special use of the computer is a highly desirable event, thus considered a positive reinforcer. A DRL procedure would require the teacher to ignore all call-out behavior and to provide two minutes of free computer use for each time the student raises his hand. The result of this procedure should be a gradual increase in hand raising (the desirable behavior) with a concomitant decrease in calling out.

Another principle of operant conditioning used in the development of some behavior therapy interventions is negative reinforcement. Specifically, negative reinforcement is defined as the increase of a behavior contingent on the removal of an aversive stimulus. This principle is often confused with punishment. Because the outcome of negative reinforcement is to increase a desired behavior (rather than decrease an undesirable behavior), negative reinforcement is not punishment.

For example, a student who begins to become disruptive after receiving an assignment from his teacher is sent out of the classroom for misbehavior. If his behavior worsens, he has been negatively reinforced for his disruption and, thus, may tend to act out more often in class in order to escape the work that was assigned.

Another procedure that is commonly associated with behavior therapy is time-out from positive reinforcement. Often called simply ''time-out,'' the procedure involves removing the opportunity for individuals to receive positive reinforcement for a period of time contingent on their behavior. The procedure can include both exclusionary time-out, where the individual is physically removed from the positively reinforcing environment, and nonexclusionary time-out, where the opportunity is removed, but the individual is not physically removed. The effectiveness of time-out requires that the environment from which the individual is removed be considered positively reinforcing.

Over the last twenty years, behavior therapy interventions have incorporated significant aspects of cognitive psychology. These interventions, known as cognitive behavior therapy, emphasize the thought and emotional processes that are covert antecedents to observable behavioral events. Distinguished by the works of Kanfer (1977), Beck et al. (1979), and Ellis (1973), this approach to behavior therapy attempts to determine the particular self-statements and emotional responses that individuals may be using that result in undesirable behavior. Interventions are designed to challenge and alter these self-statements.

A good example of this approach to behavior therapy is the work of Beck et al. (1979), who developed a model for the treatment of depression. Their model identifies a triad of negative self-statements that results in the maintenance of depression. Treatment involves requiring individuals to challenge and alter these negative self-perceptions.

Cognitive behavior therapy interventions have also been developed for numerous other problems common to settings in which school psychologists work. These include social skills training,* problem-solving training, and self-instruction training.

See also BEHAVIORAL ASSESSMENT; BEHAVIOR MODIFICATION; COGNITIVE BEHAVIOR MODIFICATION; INTERVENTION (DIRECT AND INDIRECT); SELF-MANAGEMENT.

REFERENCES

Beck, A. T., A. J. Rush, B. F. Shaw, and G. Emery. (1979). *Cognitive therapy of depression.* New York: Guilford Press.
Ellis, A. (1973). *Humanistic psychotherapy: The rational-emotive approach.* New York: McGraw-Hill.
Kanfer, F. H. (1977). The many faces of self-control, or behavior modification changes its focus. In R. B. Stuart (Ed.), *Behavioral self-management: Strategies, techniques, and outcome* (pp. 1–48). New York: Brunner/Mazel.

                                                                      Edward S. Shapiro

BIBLIOTHERAPY. Bibliotherapy, in its simplest terms, is helping through books. Specifically, bibliotherapy is the guided use of literature to influence development, an interactive process between the reader and books that is used to facilitate specific clinical outcomes and minor adjustment problems and to meet the growth and adjustment needs of children and adolescents (Pardeck, 1993). The bibliotherapeutic process has its roots in Freudian psychotherapy incorporating the principles of learning theory: people learn by imitation. The traditional approach to bibliotherapy involves an interactive process between the reader and literature under the guidance of a counselor. The less traditional model is self-help bibliotherapy with no therapist feedback.

See also MODELING.

REFERENCES

Cohen, L. J. (1994). Phenomenology of therapeutic reading with implications for research and practice of bibliotherapy. *Arts in psychotherapy* 21, 37–44.

Pardeck, J. T. (1993). *Using bibliotherapy in clinical practice: A guide to self-help books.* Westport, CT: Greenwood Press.

Pardeck, J. T., and J. A. Pardeck. (1993). *Bibliotherapy: A clinical approach for helping children.* Langhorne, PA: Gordon and Breach Science.

Kathleen R. Ryter

BILINGUAL ASSESSMENT. Bilingual assessment refers to a comprehensive model for evaluating the cognitive abilities, academic skills, and social-emotional characteristics of students who are culturally diverse and/or limited in English proficiency (LEP) or have varying degrees of bilingual proficiency, yet are dominant in a language other than English.

Historically, the concept of bilingual assessment emerged during the 1960s as a result of a concern with the lower performance on standardized intelligence tests and the overrepresentation* in special education* classes of students from ethnic minority backgrounds. This concern resulted in a number of legal action suits (e.g., *Diana v. California State Board of Education,* 1968; *Lau v. Nichols,* 1974) and led to greater scrutiny regarding the validity of commonly used instruments and assessment practices with these students. Research on test bias with children of diverse racial, ethnic, and socioeconomic background supported the validity of commonly used instruments (e.g., Wechsler Scales) in predicting achievement. However, the student's acculturation level, language proficiency, and background experience and the language of test administration were some of the factors found to affect test performance. Public Law 94-142,* the Education of All Handicapped Act, provided the legal mandate for the evaluation of these children in their dominant language and for the provision of appropriate instruction. The relevant literature discusses best practices in the assessment of LEP and bilingual children (e.g., Figueroa, 1990), educational issues, and appropriate pedagogical practices (e.g., Cummins, 1984; Varona and Garcia, 1990).

See also *LARRY P. v. RILES;* NONBIASED ASSESSMENT; NONVERBAL ASSESSMENT.

REFERENCES

Cummins, J. (1984). *Bilingualism and special education: Issues in assessment and pedagogy.* Clevedon, Avon, England: Multilingual Matters.

Figueroa, R. A. (1990). Best practices in the assessment of bilingual children. In A. Thomas and J. Grimes (Eds.), *Best practices in school psychology—II* (pp. 93–106). Washington, DC: National Association of School Psychologists.

Lopez, E. C. (1995). Best practices in working with bilingual children. In A. Thomas and J. Grimes (Eds.), *Best practices in school psychology—III* (pp. 1111–1121). Washington, DC: National Association of School Psychologists.

Varona, A., and E. E. Garcia (Eds.). (1990). *Children at risk: Poverty, minority status and other issues in educational equity.* Washington, DC: National Association of School Psychologists.

Giselle B. Esquivel

BINET, ALFRED. Among the most prominent persons in mental testing is Alfred Binet, who was born July 11, 1857, at Nice, France, and died in Paris on October 18, 1911. Binet completed a *licence* in law in 1878 and then pursued, but did not complete, a medical degree. Binet's early interest in psychology was influenced by Charcot's work in hypnosis. Binet then pursued other experimental topics, eventually arriving at his interest in mental testing. For much of his career, Binet served as director of the Laboratory of Physiological Psychology at the Sorbonne. Following a period of experimental research with Victor Henri, he accepted a collaborative research arrangement with Theodore Simon. Simon's proximity to mentally retarded subjects and Binet's membership with the Society for the Psychological Study of the Child formed the basis for significant research. Binet's active involvement with the society led to his appointment to a study commission of the Ministry of Public Instruction "from the vantage point of which he saw the compelling need to find a way to differentiate those children who could learn normally from those who could not" (Wolf, 1973, pp. 21–22). After failing to obtain academic positions at three French universities, Binet produced with Theodore Simon, in 1905, the first intelligence scale "oriented to 'tasks or behavior' rather than to so-called faculties" (Wolf, 1973, p. 29). The scale was part of a more comprehensive process for differentiating normal and retarded children, and it was revised in 1908 and 1911. His test was introduced in America by Henry Goddard,* who developed his own revision. The most popular American revision was that of Louis Terman* in 1916. Binet's scales ingrained the concept of mental age in testing for decades.

Among Binet's achievements was the founding (with Dr. Henri Beaunis) of the first French psychology journal, *L'Annee psychologique,* in 1895. He was a significant figure in early French psychology, and the studies of his two daughters likely influenced the subsequent research of Jean Piaget. Though Binet was neither trained nor served as a school psychologist,* he has had an enormous impact on the practice of school psychology.*

See also COGNITIVE ASSESSMENT: TRADITIONAL.

REFERENCES

DuBois, P. H. (1970). *A history of psychological testing.* Boston: Allyn and Bacon.

Thorndike, R. M., and D. F. Lohman. (1990). *A century of ability testing.* Chicago: Riverside.

Wolf, T. H. (1973). *Alfred Binet.* Chicago: University of Chicago Press.

Thomas K. Fagan

BIOFEEDBACK. Biofeedback refers to a procedure in which psychophysiological equipment is used to measure the physiological functioning of a person to attempt to achieve enhanced voluntary control over that function by the use of behavior modification.* The physiological measurements are given as feedback to the person to provide a concrete measure of how to associate behavior modification interventions with a specific physiological outcome state. The five most common physiological measures used are electromyography (EMG) as an index of muscle tension, temperature feedback to indicate blood flow volume in the extremities, electrodermal feedback (GSR) to measure level of arousal and stress, electroencephalography (EEG) to measure arousal level in various areas of the brain, and electrocardiography (EKG) to assess heart rate. The procedure is used to treat persons with various types of sleep disturbances, chronic headaches, panic disorders, muscle spasms, chronic pain, phobias, high blood pressure, and certain types of gastrointestinal disorders. Two or more techniques may be paired to treat disorders such as epilepsy, Parkinson's disease, peptic ulcers, and Tourette syndrome. A treatment series usually runs from ten to twenty individual sessions, with occasional follow-up meetings sometimes given. Cost is about the same as individual psychotherapy and is often covered by health insurance.

See also COGNITIVE BEHAVIOR MODIFICATION; COGNITIVE THERAPY; RELAXATION TRAINING; STRESS REDUCTION THERAPY; SYSTEMATIC DESENSITIZATION.

REFERENCES

Fischer-Williams, M., A. Nigel, and D. Sovine. (1981). *A textbook of biological feedback.* New York: Human Sciences Press.
Lee, S. (1991). Biofeedback as a treatment for childhood hyperactivity: A critical review of the literature. *Psychological Reports* 68, 163–192.
Yates, A. (1980). *Biofeedback and the modification of behavior.* New York: Plenum Press.

Raymond E. Webster

BOULDER CONFERENCE. Prior to 1949, most psychology programs trained psychologists in general and experimental psychology. Psychologists who wished to practice psychology in applied settings often had to gain clinical experience on the job following attainment of their Ph.D. The Boulder conference was convened in Boulder, Colorado, in 1949 to develop guidelines for graduate-level psychology programs to follow for the training of clinical psychologists. The philosophy of clinical psychology training that emerged during the Boulder conference is referred to as the Boulder model. The model philosophy is that a clinical psychologist's training should be grounded in basic research and that clinical application follows from basic research. In recent times, this model has been referred to as the scientist-practitioner model.* As of 1992, the majority of graduate-level professional psychology programs reported using the Boulder model to guide their training process.

See also PROFESSIONAL TRAINING MODEL.

REFERENCES

Frank, G. (1986). The Boulder model revisited: The training of the clinical
    psychologist for research. *Psychological Reports* 58, 579–585.
O'Sullivan, J. J., and R. P. Quevillon. (1992). 40 years later. Is the Boulder model still
    alive? *American Psychologist* 47, 67–70.
Raimy, V. C. (1950). *Training in clinical psychology.* New York: Prentice-Hall.

                                                                              Mark D. Shriver
                                                                              Jack J. Kramer

BOWER, ELI M. Eli "Mike" Bower was born on October 5, 1917, in New York. He received his B.S. degree in biology at New York University, his M.A. degree in guidance at Columbia University, and his Ed.D. degree in psychology and guidance at Stanford University. In 1950, Bower joined the California State Department of Education as a consultant and worked there to formulate prevention programs designed to enhance the social and emotional development of children. Bower's writings on children with emotionally based educational handicaps influenced the Public Law 94-142* definition of emotional disturbance. He believed that public schools must address the needs of children with emotional handicaps and must develop programs that would facilitate the mental health of all children and prevent the manifestation of emotional disturbance in individuals. His research and writings have influenced the practice of school psychology,* particularly in emphasizing the importance of prevention* and in developing models for implementing primary and secondary prevention programs in schools. His research resulted in numerous publications, including his most renowned book, *The Early Identification of Emotionally Disturbed Children in Schools* (Bower, 1981).

From 1962 to 1968, Bower served as a consultant in mental health and education at the National Institute of Mental Health in Bethesda, Maryland. In 1968, he joined the faculty at the University of California–Berkeley as a professor of educational psychology and became professor emeritus in 1986. Bower served as the president of the American Orthopsychiatric Association from 1971 to 1972 and was awarded fellow status by the American Psychological Association.* He died in 1991.

REFERENCES

Beth-Halachmy, S. (1993). Eli M. Bower: Understanding primary prevention and
    promoting emotional development in young children. *The School Psychologist*
    47(3), 2–3.
Bower, E. M. (1981). *Early identification of emotionally handicapped children in
    school* (3d ed.) Springfield, IL: Charles C. Thomas.

                                                                         Shani Beth-Halachmy

BRIEF PSYCHOTHERAPY. The literature on brief psychotherapy is consistent in defining this form of psychotherapy as any psychotherapy that does not exceed twenty-five sessions (Koss and Butcher, 1986). In fact, Koss and Butcher point out that brief psychotherapies include psychodynamically* oriented therapies, cognitive behavioral therapies,* behavioral therapies,* crisis-oriented therapies, and brief verbal therapies.

Although most individuals think of Freudian psychoanalysis as a long-term, in-depth treatment that usually lasts many years, this was not always the case. In fact, Freud, in his early work, emphasized a briefer, more solution-focused approach, which sometimes lasted only four to six sessions (Bauer and Kobos, 1987).

O'Hanlon and Weiner-Davis (1989) trace the evolution of psychotherapy from the more traditional therapies that looked to the past to the present-centered approaches of the 1960s and, most recently, toward a more short-term, solution-focus, which is much more future-oriented. Although all brief psychotherapies do not share either the solution-focus or the future orientation, there are several characteristics common to most brief psychotherapies. Koss and Butcher (1986) point out that all brief therapies have limited time and limited goals, stress a quick development of the therapeutic alliance, stay focused, have high therapist activity, encourage therapeutic flexibility, and initiate treatment for the client as soon as possible.

Several factors can account for the recent move toward briefer psychotherapies (Koss and Butcher, 1986). Clients generally enter treatment expecting therapy to be short. Brief therapy has been shown to be effective even with chronic problems. There appears to be no difference in effectiveness studies between brief therapy and longer therapies. Perhaps the strongest factor is the reluctance of insurance companies to reimburse for longer-term treatments.

See also CRISIS INTERVENTION.

REFERENCES

Bauer, G. P., and J. C. Kobos. (1987). *Brief therapy.* Norvale, NJ: Jason Aronson.
Koss, M. P., and J. N. Butcher. (1986). Research on brief psychotherapy. In A. Bergin and S. Garfield (Eds.), *Handbook of psychotherapy and behavior change* (pp. 627–670). New York: Wiley.
O'Hanlon, W. H., and M. Weiner-Davis. (1989). *In search of solutions.* New York: Norton.

Donald L. Boswell

BROWN v. BOARD OF EDUCATION. In *Brown v. Board of Education* (1954), under the Fourteenth Amendment to the U.S. Constitution, the Supreme Court ruled that school segregation by race denied the right of equal protection to African-American students. The ruling stated that separate but equal was not equal. Subsequently, the civil rights movement to integrate schools in the South and public facilities led to national strife. Though implemented over several decades and a prime factor in court-ordered busing for school desegregation, the *Brown v. Board of Education* ruling effectively ended the separate but equal doctrine of segregated schooling. The continued presence of discrimination in society had to be addressed by the Congress of the United States with the passage of the Civil Rights Act of 1964.

Even though segregation by schools was outlawed, tracking students by aptitude test scores segregated students along racial lines within individual schools. Within-school segregation was confronted in federal court. In *Hobson v. Hansen* (1967, 1969), the Court ruled tracking of students a violation of equal protection under the Fourteenth Amendment.

See also *MARSHALL v. GEORGIA*.

REFERENCE

Jacob-Timm, and T. Hartshorne. (1994). *Ethics and law for school psychologists* (2d ed.). Brandon, VT: Clinical Psychology.

Paul G. Warden

BUREAUS OF CHILD STUDY. When applied psychology first emerged in educational settings, the titles of those settings were varied but were often called bureaus of child study or of educational research and measurement. Among the more historically significant was the Chicago public schools' Department of Scientific Pedagogy and Child Study, founded in 1899 and later called the Bureau of Child Study. The Chicago bureau is considered the first organized psychological service in a public school setting. According to Wallin* (1914), there were nineteen such clinics in school settings, and their order of establishment was Chicago (1898); Rochester (1907); New York City (1908); Providence, Oakland, Hibbing, and Cincinnati (1911); Grand Rapids, Seattle, Philadelphia, Springfield, Massachusetts, New Orleans, and Milwaukee (1912); Buffalo, Washington, D.C., Albany, Los Angeles, and Trenton (1913), and Detroit (1914).

The early mission of these agencies was usually a mixture of child study research and individual clinical practice, reflecting the orientations of G. Stanley Hall* and Lightner Witmer.* After the first few decades of the twentieth century, these agencies were typically doing individual clinical child study associated with the growing offering of special educational services in the schools. The research functions faded by comparison but were supplemented by bureaus of educational research affiliated with the colleges of education at major state universities. The pattern has continued to the present, with few school systems conducting their own research programs and instead emphasizing individual child study and services. Whereas the title "bureau of child study" was relatively common in the early part of the century, the title is rare today as a designation for a school-based agency for the provision of psychological services. The Chicago Public Schools Bureau has retained its title and is among the most famous.

See also FIRST PSYCHOLOGICAL CLINIC.

REFERENCES

Hollingworth, L. S. (1933). Psychological service for public schools. *Teachers College Record* 34, 368–379.

Martens, E. H. (1939). *Clinical organization for child guidance within the schools.* (Office of Education Bulletin No. 15). Washington, DC: U.S. Government Printing Office.

Wallin, J.E.W. (1914). *The mental health of the school child* (Chapter 18). New Haven, CT: Yale University Press.

Thomas K. Fagan

C

CAREER ASSESSMENT. Career assessment is a consumer-friendly, ongoing, developmental, and interactive process that integrates data collection and decision making with effective planning and implementation of activities (e.g., training, placement, counseling, support services). The long-term goal of this process is the selection of an appropriate vocational choice. This interdisciplinary process begins in elementary school and continues through adulthood. The client's cognitive and psychological functioning is addressed through psychological testing. Assessment* of mastery of academic and functional living skills contributes to the decision-making process. In addition, assessments of vocational interests,* values, temperament,* work-related behaviors, aptitudes,* physical capacities, learning styles, and training needs help to determine the most appropriate course of action for effective career planning. Results from a variety of methods, tools, and assessment procedures are cross-validated using alternative approaches such as behavioral observations, self-reports, manual dexterity tests, commercially developed assessment systems, surveys and inventories, structured interviews, and work samples (Harrington, 1982). Accuracy of the decision-making process can be increased by reviewing job analyses that provide specifics such as physical, perceptual, and motor dexterity requirements of the job, essential academic skills needed, and tools and equipment used (Sitlington and Wimmer, 1978). Job information is essential for a good person–job match, such as knowledge of needed affective and social skills, worker trait requirements (e.g., speed and accuracy), training and educational requirements, characteristics of supervision, environmental factors (e.g., noise, dust, heat), salary and fringe benefits, entry requirements, and dress codes.

See also VOCATIONAL ASSESSMENT.

REFERENCES

Harrington, T. F. (1982). *Handbook of career planning for special needs students.* Rockville, MD: Aspen Systems Corporation.

Levinson, E. M. (1995). Best practices in vocational assessment in the schools. In A. Thomas and J. Grimes (Eds.), *Best practices in school psychology—III* (pp. 741–751). Washington, DC: National Association of School Psychologists.

Sitlington, P. L., and D. Wimmer. (1978). Vocational assessment techniques for the handicapped adolescent. *Career Development for Exceptional Individuals 1,* 74–87.

Peggy A. Hicks

CAREER DEVELOPMENT. Career development definitions range from one extreme of equating it to one's occupation to the other extreme of encompassing all the activities of a person's life. Current definitions encompass the major life roles of a person across the life span, including occupation, family, community, and leisure, as aspects of career development (McDaniels and Gysbers, 1992).

The origins of the field are generally attributed to Frank Parsons, who started the Boston Vocation Bureau in 1908 in response to the economic changes of the times. His philosophy was that if one knew oneself and knew the major aspects of occupations and synthesized this information, one would be able to make career decisions that were beneficial to the individual and to the employer.

In 1955, Donald Super published his classic article illuminating his theory that career development encompasses both personal growth and development as well as vocational growth and development. His theory, the life-span, life-space approach, encompasses the life roles of individuals, the stages of vocational development, exploration, establishment, maintenance, and decline, and the interactions of them over a lifetime.

John Holland's theories evolved from his thinking that personalities can be grouped into six general types. He also theorized that occupations can be classified into the same six types. Choosing an occupation is an extension of one's personality, so when one finds congruence between the two, it optimizes a person's satisfaction with life (Brown, Brooks, and Associates, 1990).

See also CAREER ASSESSMENT; COUNSELING PSYCHOLOGY.

REFERENCES

Brown, D., L. Brooks, and Associates. (1990). *Career choice and development* (rev. ed.). San Francisco: Jossey-Bass.

McDaniels, C., and N. Gysbers. (1992). *Counseling for career development.* San Francisco: Jossey-Bass.

Super, D. E. (1955). Personality integration through vocational counseling. *Journal of Counseling Psychology 2,* 217–226.

Terrie Anne Varga
Donald L. Boswell

CASE CONSULTATION. The term "case consultation" refers to one of the four categories of mental health consultation* described by Gerald Caplan in both his seminal book *Theory and Practice of Mental Health Consultation* (Caplan, 1970) and his more recent revision (Caplan and Caplan, 1993). The four categories include (1) client-centered case consultation, (2) consultee-centered case consultation, (3) program-centered administrative consultation, and (4) consultee-centered administrative consultation. Case consultation refers to the first two types of consultation in Caplan's model.

In case consultation, the consultant (e.g., school psychologist*) works with a consultee (e.g., teacher, administrator) to remediate the difficulties of a particular client. In both client-centered and consultee-centered consultation, the consultant uses his or her specialized skills and knowledge to help the consultee deal with a work problem about a particular client (case) as opposed to an entire group of cases, such as a classroom, school, or district. The goal is to alleviate the problems of the present case and to help the consultee respond more effectively to similar cases in the future.

In client-centered case consultation, the consultant focuses both assessment* and intervention* activity on the client, supplementing the consultee's own professional skills with his or her own in designing a program to effectively influence the client's presenting problems. In consultee-centered case consultation, the consultant's orientation is toward understanding and modifying what about the consultee prevents him or her from responding to the case with maximum effectiveness. The reasons for consultee-centered case consultation include lack of knowledge, lack of skill, lack of self-confidence, and/or lack of professional objectivity on the part of the consultee (Caplan, 1970, Caplan and Caplan, 1993).

The effectiveness of both types of case consultation is evaluated based on changes in a particular client. However, either type of case consultation can have potential benefit for other clients with whom the consultee interacts now and in the future.

See also BEHAVIORAL CONSULTATION; COLLABORATIVE CONSULTATION; CONSULTATION.

REFERENCES

Caplan, G. (1970). *Theory and practice of mental health consultation.* New York: Basic Books.
Caplan, G., and R. B. Caplan. (1993). *Mental health consultation and collaboration.* San Francisco: Jossey-Bass.

Edward Gaughan
Joel Meyers

CASELOAD. Caseload refers to the number of cases or clients managed during a particular period of time. Cases will be in varying stages, from initial contact through termination of services, including follow-up services,* if appropriate. The ratio of school psychologists* to children served varies widely from a favorable ratio of 1 school psychologist to 500 schoolchildren to an unfavorable ratio of 1:9,000 (Fagan and Wise, 1994). The National Association of School Psychologists (NASP), in its 1992 *Standards for the Provision of School Psychological Services,* recommends a ratio of 1 school psychologist per 1,000 children, with a maximum of four schools served. Recent surveys suggest 100 child studies per year is typical for practitioners. The diversity of role and function of the practicing school psychologist and the specific goals and objectives of the setting will determine the appropriate caseload.

See also ROLES AND FUNCTIONS; SERVICE RATIOS.

REFERENCES

Fagan, T. K., and P. S. Wise. (1994). *School psychology: Past, present, future.* White Plains, NY: Longman.

National Association of School Psychologists. (1992). *Standards for the provision of school psychological services.* Washington, DC: Author.

Reschly, D. J., and L. M. Connolly. (1990). Comparison of school psychologists in the city and country: Is there a "rural" school psychology? *School Psychology Review* 19, 534–549.

Kathleen R. Ryter

CATTERALL, CALVIN D. Calvin D. Catterall was born in Mount Shasta, California, on April 30, 1925, and died when accidentally hit by a train in Orleans, France, on July 3, 1984. He completed his undergraduate work at the University of the Pacific and master's and Ph.D. (1964) at the University of Southern California. As a school psychologist, he was active in the California Association of School Psychologists and Psychometrists, serving twice as its president. He served on the faculty of Ohio State University and later entered private practice. Active in national and international affairs, he was elected president of the National Association of School Psychologists* (NASP) (1971–1972) and contributed significantly to the formation of international colloquia* on school psychology that evolved into the International School Psychology Association*. His most notable career accomplishments were in international school psychology, including his three-volume series *Psychology in the Schools in International Perspective* (1976, 1977, 1979).

REFERENCE

Fagan, T. K., and H. Bischoff. (1984). In memoriam: Calvin D. Catterall 1925–1984. *The School Psychologist* (Division 16, APA Newsletter) 38(6), 5. (Item also appears in NASP *Communique,* 1984, 13(1), 1, 4.)

Thomas K. Fagan

CENTRALIZED VERSUS DECENTRALIZED SERVICES. School psychological services can be organized, structured, and managed on a centralized, decentralized, or combined centralized/decentralized basis. In essence, these terms refer to the manner in which psychological services are established, managed, and delivered to consumers. Each variation has implications for the roles of the individual psychological services provider, as well as for the potential effectiveness and efficiency of the overall psychological services unit.

With centralized services, school psychologists* are usually assigned to, or housed at, the location of the school district central administration. Such an arrangement is intended to enable supervisory personnel to provide greater direction and control over day-to-day operations, thereby making individual psychologists more directly responsible and accountable. In addition, at least some members of the psychological services unit may have the opportunity to develop competence or expertise in a small number of areas. Further, the activities of the overall psychological services unit can be more closely managed and coordinated. Thus, as service needs vary from one school to the next and at different times of the year, this arrangement makes it possible to adjust the quantity and types of services provided in response to these changing needs. Further, this style promotes regular and early interactions and problem solving among school psychology peers due to their frequent contact with one another during staff meetings, in-service training, and other visits to the central administration location (Curtis and Zins, 1986; Elkin, 1963). Although services might be more flexible in meeting changing needs, at the same time they usually are more distant from the clients* served, which may result in less understanding and responsiveness to their specific needs, and there tends to be more bureaucracy. Traditionally, centralized services have been the norm and continue to be more common in large, urban districts than they are in rural settings and small districts. Many rural districts, however, locate their psychological services unit in the district administration building because of its central location, rather than for management purposes.

A decentralized management approach allows school psychological services providers to operate more autonomously on a day-to-day basis, which suggests a greater amount of trust by the central administration. This type of organizational arrangement also enables each practitioner to become more knowledgeable about, and familiar with, the specific needs and organizational climate of an individual school. Because the emphasis of services delivery is determined at the individual practitioner level, changes in services can be made rapidly, based on emerging needs, but there may be less coordination of efforts among the overall psychological services unit. Further, there tends to be less interaction among psychology colleagues due to fewer natural opportunities to interact (Curtis and Zins, 1986). Additionally, the monitoring of professional performance (or accountability*) is more difficult and relies heavily on the efforts of the individual practitioner, who must design recording systems, generate outcome measures, and take a systems-level perspective so that decisions can be made regarding appropriate patterns of psychological service delivery. It also requires the psychologist to conduct needs assessments* and to generate strategic plans to address specific school needs. Thus, decentralized services usually are closer to the clients but also less coordinated (Elliott and Witt, 1986). In practice, most psychological services units are probably organized along a centralized-decentralized continuum rather than at either extreme.

See also RURAL SCHOOL PSYCHOLOGY; SCHOOL SETTINGS; SUBURBAN SCHOOL PSYCHOLOGY.

REFERENCES

Curtis, M. J., and J. E. Zins. (1986). The organization and structuring of psychological services within educational settings. In S. N. Elliott and J. C. Witt (Eds.), *The delivery of psychological services in schools: Concepts, processes, and issues* (pp. 109–138). Hillsdale, NJ: Erlbaum.

Elkin, V. B. (1963). Structuring school psychological services: Internal and interdisciplinary considerations. In M. G. Gottsegen and G. B. Gottsegen (Eds.), *Professional school psychology,* Vol. 2 (pp. 200–226). New York: Grune and Stratton.

Elliott, S. N., and J. C. Witt. (1986). Fundamental questions and dimensions of psychological service delivery in schools. In S. N. Elliott and J. C. Witt (Eds.), *The delivery of psychological services in schools: Concepts, processes, and issues* (pp. 1–26). Hillsdale, NJ: Erlbaum.

Joseph E. Zins

CERTIFICATE OF ADVANCED STUDY. A certificate of advanced study is awarded by some graduate programs in school psychology* in lieu of the specialist degree.* As training requirements in school psychology have expanded to the current entry-level standard of sixty semester credits recommended by the National Association of School Psychologists,* there was a need to recognize the additional study beyond the master's degree.* Some training programs have used the specialist degree to accomplish this purpose, while others award a certificate of advanced study (Prus, White, and Pendleton, 1988). Credit requirements range from fifty-four to ninety-nine semester credits, with most programs requiring sixty-five to seventy semester credits. Although most state departments of education* require specialist-level training (a minimum of sixty semester credits), only seventeen states require the specialist degree (Batsche, Knoff, and Peterson, 1989). The exact title of the advanced certificate varies among programs, with certificate of advanced graduate study (CAGS) and certificate of advanced study in school psychology most commonly used. Other titles include professional diploma program in school psychology, certificate of advanced study, school psychology specialist certificate, and sixth-year professional certificate (Smith and Henning, in press).

See also NATIONAL CERTIFICATION IN SCHOOL PSYCHOLOGY; TRAINING MODELS.

REFERENCES

Batsche, G. M., H. M. Knoff, and D. W. Peterson. (1989). Trends in credentialing and practice standards. *School Psychology Review* 18, 193–202.

Prus, J., G. White, and A. Pendleton. (1988). *Handbook of certification/licensure requirements for school psychologists* (4th ed). Washington, DC: National Association of School Psychologists.

Smith, D. K., and A. Henning. (in press). *Directory of school psychology graduate programs* (4th ed.). Washington, DC: National Association of School Psychologists.

Douglas K. Smith

CERTIFICATION. Much of the professional regulation of school psychology* occurs through credentialing—a procedure for granting titles and functions to persons following their training. In school psychology, credentialing occurs through certification and licensing*. Though the terms are often used interchangeably, certification has referred to practice credentials granted by a state education agency for practice in settings under the authority of that agency (usually referred to as the school sector), and licensing has referred to practice credentials granted by a state board of examiners in psychology for private, independent, and agency practice (usually referred to as the nonschool sector). Certification may also refer to a nonpractice, recognition credential given by a national organization such as the American Psychological Association* (APA) or the National Association of School Psychologists* (NASP).

The earliest state-level credentials for school psychologists originated in the 1930s with state department of education certification standards in New York and Pennsylvania. Following World War II, psychologists began to be licensed for private practice by a separate state-level board of examiners in psychology whose jurisdiction was statewide, with broad practice exemptions for government agencies, including the public schools. The separate state agency credentialing models for certification and licensing were available in almost every state by the 1970s. The requirements for state education agency certification vary, with titles and practice responsibilities often aligned with degree and field experiences. Many states certify with one title and degree level, while some have multiple levels and titles. A directory of certification requirements is published by NASP.

See also CERTIFICATION TESTS.

REFERENCES

Fagan, T. K., and P. S. Wise. (1994). *School psychology: Past, present, and future* (Chapter 7). White Plains, NY: Longman.

Prus, J. S., G. W. White, and A. Pendleton. (1987). *Handbook of certification and licensure requirements for school psychologists.* Washington, DC: National Association of School Psychologists.

Pryzwansky, W. B. (1993). The regulation of school psychology: A historical perspective on certification, licensure, and accreditation. *Journal of School Psychology* 31, 219–235.

Thomas K. Fagan

CERTIFICATION TESTS. Acquiring a certificate to practice often requires the successful completion of a certification test. The earliest such test appears to be that used by the New York City schools in the mid-1920s, a time when that school system used its own certification requirements in the absence of state-level certification* for school psychologists. In the credentialing process by state boards of education, certification tests have been infrequent because the certificate has been aligned with graduate-level training requirements and degrees with their own quality controls. Since the establishment of the national certification system by the National Association of School Psychologists* (NASP), the completion of the advanced school psychology test of the National Teacher Examination* (NTE) has been implemented in several states and required by the NASP certification process.

The Examination for Practice of Professional Psychology* (EPPP) was developed by the Educational Testing Service for use by all state boards of examiners in licensing professional psychologists for practice in the nonschool sector. The structures of certification tests are typically pencil-and-paper and multiple-choice.

See also NATIONAL CERTIFICATION IN SCHOOL PSYCHOLOGY.

Thomas K. Fagan

CHANGING CRITERION DESIGNS. Changing criterion designs are used to assess gradually shaped behavioral change, after establishing a baseline period of performance, by repeatedly showing that the degree of behavioral change corresponds to the degree of change in the researcher-defined criterion. Suppose a researcher is interested in evaluating a physical education aerobics component for ninth grade students. The aerobics level is monitored by having pupils exercise on a stationary rowing machine. During the baseline period, each student is allowed to self-determine the exercise intensity and duration (no intervention). After the baseline period, students are notified that they may receive extra credit points based on the amount of their aerobic exercise (intervention), as determined by the amount of distance traversed on the rowing machine. A light goes on when the aerobic intensity is sufficiently high to earn extra credit points, and a visible electronic counter documents the cumulative point total. The purpose of the changing criterion is, in this case, to increase aerobic intensity. The criterion is initially set so that extra credit points are earned if students row 10 percent faster than their established baseline rate. When this performance criterion is met, the criterion is set so that points are earned if students row 20 percent faster than the baseline rate. Next, the criterion is changed to 30 percent faster than the baseline rate, and so forth. Data collected using this design are analyzed graphically. Behavioral change should increase (or decrease) corresponding to increases (or decreases) in the criterion. Withdrawal of the criterion should result in behavior similar to that observed during the baseline period.

See also ABAB DESIGNS; EXPERIMENTAL DESIGN; MULTIPLE BASELINE.

REFERENCES

Deluca, R. V., and S. W. Holborn. (1992). Effects of a variable-ratio reinforcement schedule with changing criteria on exercise in obese and nonobese boys. *Journal of Applied Behavior Analysis* 25, 671–679.

Kazdin, A. E. (1994). *Behavior modification in applied settings* (5th ed.). Pacific Grove, CA: Brooks/Cole.

William T. Coombs

CHILD ADVOCACY. Child advocacy means taking positions and actions to assure respect for the needs and rights of persons under eighteen years of age. While advocacy is usually justified for any class of people on the basis of recognized and asserted human needs and principles of justice, advocacy for children is further supported by recognition of their relative powerlessness to effectively advocate for themselves. Child advocacy has been identified as occurring in a recognizable form since the late nineteenth century in efforts to improve infant mortality and child health, provide education, reduce child labor exploitation, and protect children from abuse and neglect. Advocacy efforts have often focused on the establishment of organizations, agencies, or forums (e.g., National Congress of Parents and Teachers,* Children's Bureau, White House Conferences, the International Year of the Child) intended to work toward social change. The child advocacy movement has progressed beyond single-issue imperatives and construction of well-intended declarations to produce the United Nations (UN) Convention on the Rights of the Child (adopted in 1989). This international treaty appears to provide the broad, comprehensive base and the positive ideology necessary for rallying and coordinating child advocacy. The "best interests of the child" principle, with which legal and psychological specialties have struggled for decades, is a central theme of the UN convention. It continues to hold promise for providing a conceptual model and practical criteria for advocacy, but fulfillment of that promise awaits adequate definition and support for the construct. Though much emphasis has been given to advocacy that deals with institutional responsibilities and failures to assure rights and avoid problems, it can focus on individual cases as well as class conditions. The ombudsman for children programs, which began in Sweden and Norway and are now being recommended for the United States, provides opportunities for mediation between the children as individuals or a class and societal institutions. Recently, the need to balance or resolve conflicts between respecting the child's needs for protection and nurturance versus participation and self-determination has come to the forefront to challenge advocates to recognize both the special vulnerabilities and "person" status of children. For example, serious debate has focused on the appropriateness of self-advocacy for children, including provision of "standing in court." Mental health and child development specialists have been actively involved in child advocacy since its early stages, for example, defining "child advocacy" first, proposing the "best interests of the child" concept, recommending that developmental competencies guide rights and responsibilities determinations, identifying advocacy as a critical element in helping emotionally disordered children. The profession of school psychology* has established a high-priority commitment to advocacy both for children as a class and for the individual child whom its professionals serve, as stated in the purposes and professional practices statements of its national and international associations.

See also ADVOCACY CONSULTATION; CHILDREN'S RIGHTS; PRESIDENTIAL COMMISSIONS AND WHITE HOUSE CONFERENCES.

REFERENCES

Jensen, M. A., and S. G. Goffin (Eds.). (1993). *Visions of entitlement: The care and education of America's children.* Albany, NY: SUNY.

Melton, G. (1983). *Child advocacy: Psychological issues and interventions.* New York: Plenum Press.

Takanishi, R. (1978). Childhood as a social issue: Historical roots of contemporary child advocacy movements. *Journal of Social Issues* 34, 2, 8–28.

Stuart N. Hart

CHILDREN'S RIGHTS. The term "children's rights" refers to entitlements and assurances for persons under eighteen years of age, supported by legal, institutional, public, and individual opinion and action. Human rights are generally considered to express recognition of, and support for, the natural and inalienable rights of persons, which emanate from an understanding of human needs and potential. Children have been the last among the major classes of human beings to have their rights seriously considered. Over the last 500 years, in the Western world, the treatment of children has advanced as conceptions of children have progressed from their being considered nonentities, miniature adults, valuable economic property, resources for a better future, valuable for emotional support, and, to a limited degree, persons. Beginning in the nineteenth century and continuing during the twentieth century, children's rights trends have emphasized protection and nurturance particularly, as indicated by movements to end exploitation in labor, to provide and compel education, to establish a paternal juvenile court system, and to reduce child abuse and neglect. During the last half of the twentieth century, some progress has been made in assuring children due process and considering them persons under the law, with the provision of limited choice rights. The recent progression of views on children's rights is partially represented in the formal positions of the *Universal Declaration of Human Rights* (1948), *United Nations Declaration of the Rights of the Child* (1959), *Declaration of the Psychological Rights of the Child* (1979), and the *United Nations (UN) Convention on the Rights of the Child* (1989). The last two documents have special significance. The Declaration of the Psychological Rights of the Child was produced by school, child, and educational psychologists throughout the world as their contribution to the International Year of the Child (1979). Its formulation was directed by Calvin Catterall, a prominent U.S. school psychologist who was the primary founder of the International School Psychology Association. While most constructions of children's rights are essentially psychological in nature, this declaration was the first to give specific attention to psychological rights, including three major themes: love and freedom from fear; personal, spiritual, and social development; education and play. The National Association of School Psychologists* (NASP) committed itself to this declaration in 1980 and established, jointly with Indiana University's School of Education, the Office for the Study of the Psychological Rights of the Child to work to clarify and advance children's rights. The UN Convention on the Rights of the Child was adopted unanimously by the United Nations General Assembly in 1989. It represents a major qualitative advance in children's rights in that it is an international treaty that (1) deals comprehensively with protection, nurturance, participation, and self-determination rights and includes two articles specific to education and (2) has been ratified by more nations than any previous international human rights treaty. The convention requires that the best interests of the child prevail in all legal and administrative decisions and that the child's evolving capacities be considered in providing direction for the exercise of rights by the child. Children, recognized as both being and becoming and as dependent on, and vulnerable to, those with greater power, represent a special class for whom developmental considerations must be substantial. Psychology and education are recognized to have quite important roles to play in helping society understand, rear, and respect children, particularly, as they combine to serve in schools and to provide expertise regarding children's best interests and evolving capacities. Organized school psychology (NASP and the American Psychological Association* [APA] Division 16) has endorsed the UN convention and has been actively working with other nongovernmental organizations, through the National Committee for the Rights of the Child, to advance children's rights.

See also CHILD ADVOCACY; CLIENT; CORPORAL PUNISHMENT; PROFESSIONAL STANDARDS.

REFERENCES

Hart, S. N. (Ed.). (1982). The psychological rights of the child. *Viewpoints in Teaching and Learning* 58, 1.
Hart, S. N., and D. P. Prasse, (Eds.). (1991). Children's rights and education. *School Psychology Review* 20(3), 339–416.
Horowitz, R. M., and H. A. Davidson (Eds.). (1984). *Legal rights of children.* New York: McGraw-Hill.

Stuart N. Hart

CHILD TESTIMONY. The last few decades have witnessed dramatic increases in reporting all types of child abuse. Concomitantly, growing numbers of children have been clinically interviewed, tested, and interrogated by police, lawyers, and functionaries of the courts. In addition, there has been an increase in accusations of child abuse by litigants in custody battles. As part of the legal proceedings, mental health experts are asked to assess young children to determine if they were abused. Some experts believe that young children are incapable of lying and that their memories of abuse are never wrong. Others maintain that large numbers of child witnesses are given false memories of abuse through suggestion and repeated questioning. Despite the eventual outcomes of full evaluations, school psychologists and other school personnel must report all cases of suspected abuse.

Research indicates that children do not develop accurate memories until about three or four years of age. Also, with time, memories fade, and gaps are filled in or fabricated. These may depend on other events and suggestions by therapists or may be caused by the child's belief system. It is clear that skilled interviewers, understanding children's desire to please, can place memories in children's minds. Accurate evaluation of memories of abuse should include developmentally appropriate assessment,* which usually includes projective techniques and play therapy* with young children. If appropriate and not devastating to the child, there should be observations of the child interacting with suspects. The suspects and important caregivers should be interviewed and requested to fill out appropriate parent/teacher/caregiver diagnostic rating scales designed to assess symptoms of abuse. Abused children often develop posttraumatic stress disorder, and, therefore, the expert should be familiar with this syndrome.

School psychologists are frequently aware of educator abuse of students, especially in the form of emotional maltreatment. This places the psychologist, an employee of the district in which the abuse is alleged, in an ethical and legal dilemma. If psychologists report the abuse, as required by law, they may jeopardize their jobs and relations with school staff and administrators. However, psychologists are responsible for reporting all types of abuse and may have to help parents and the victim deal with the issue. This may involve helping parents to develop appropriate methods of documenting the abuse. It may also involve gathering data and testifying against the abusive educator.

See also CHILD ADVOCACY; CHILDREN'S RIGHTS; CORPORAL PUNISHMENT; LEGAL-ETHICAL DILEMMA.

REFERENCES

Doris, J. (1991). *The suggestibility of children's recollections.* Washington, DC: American Psychological Association.
Goodman, G. S., and B. L. Bottoms, (Eds.). (1993). *Child victims, child witnesses.* New York: Guilford Press.
Hyman, I. (1990). *Reading, writing, and the hickory stick.* Lexington, MA: Lexington Books.

Irwin A. Hyman

CLASSICAL CONDITIONING. Ivan Pavlov is credited with what is often called classical conditioning, Pavlovian conditioning, or respondent conditioning. During his famous experiments, he was able to demonstrate that dogs that normally salivated when presented with meat could be conditioned to salivate to the sound of a metronome if the sound (conditioned stimulus) was presented before the meat (unconditioned stimulus). Classical conditioning elicits a response from a subject, and the response is thought to be involuntary (i.e., salivation, fear). This is in contrast to operant conditioning,* in which a response is initiated to obtain a reinforcer and is thought to be voluntary.

Work has continued to broaden understanding of classical conditioning beyond automatic formations of associations to include attentional, memory, and expectancy components. From those subsequent experiments, psychological practitioners have gained insight into learned helplessness as well as effective ways for dealing with a client's debilitating behavior. Habits such as smoking and behavior disorders have been treated by extinction, counterconditioning, and flooding, all relying on characteristics of the classical conditioning model. Joseph Wolpe's systematic desensitization is an effective technique for dealing with phobias, utilizing reciprocal inhibition to confront and reverse the phobia.

See also BEHAVIOR MODIFICATION; BEHAVIOR THERAPY.

REFERENCES

Hergenhahn, B. R., and M. H. Olson. (1993). *An introduction to theories of learning* (4th ed.). Englewood Cliffs, NJ: Prentice-Hall.
Nietzel, M. T., D. A. Bernstein, and R. Milich. (1991). *Introduction to clinical psychology* (3d ed.). Englewood Cliffs, NJ: Prentice-Hall.

Paul G. Warden

CLASSIFICATION: EDUCATIONAL. The Individuals with Disabilities Education Act (IDEA), Public Law 101-476,* (1990) guarantees all children with disabilities between the ages of three and twenty-one the right to a free, appropriate public education* (FAPE) designed to meet their individual needs. In 1986, the Education of the Handicapped Amendment (Public Law 99-457*) extended evaluative services (but not mandatory FAPE) to include children below the age of three. Each state has developed guidelines to comply with federal laws that identify minimum standards. However, where state standards are higher, they prevail.

In order to be eligible for special education* and related services,* a child must have one or more of the following conditions: mental retardation, hearing impairment, speech or language impairment, visual impairment, serious emotional disturbance, orthopedic impairment, autism, traumatic brain injury, other health impairment (e.g., nephritis), or a specific learning disability. Should the existence of any of these conditions be suspected, it must be shown that the condition interferes with the child's ability to learn in the regular classroom without assistance ranging from an adapted regular education program to special class placement. (The *Diagnostic and Statistical Manual of Mental Disorders* [DSM IV] provides specific categorization of all phases of disability but does not provide for remedial programs as required by IDEA.)

A condition known as attention-deficit disorder (ADD) has been a source of controversy during the drafting of the amendments to IDEA. The issue is still under study. At present, no separate program exists for children with ADD. If problems associated with ADD are deemed by the placement team to be interfering with a child's ability to learn in a regular education environment, the child may be served under the categories of other health impairment, specific learning disability, or serious emotional disturbance.

In order to confirm eligibility for one of the special education programs, a multifactored evaluation (MFE) must be conducted. Either a parent or the school may request such an evaluation. A signed parental consent form is required. Should a parent refuse, the school has the recourse of initiating an impartial hearing to conduct an evaluation if it feels that a special program is the only way to provide for the child's needs.

The purpose of the evaluation is to determine the child's strengths and disabilities. Areas generally tested are intellectual and academic abilities, language proficiency, physical condition, social and emotional factors, and adaptive behaviors.* Health, vision, and hearing are also checked. When a signed parent permission to evaluate is provided, and parents receive the necessary ''procedural safeguards''* information, the evaluation may be conducted.

Generally, the school psychologist coordinates and conducts the major parts of the evaluation. Only certificated psychologists may conduct an intellectual and personality assessment.* Information is also gathered from speech pathologists, physical education instructors, nurses, physicians (where appropriate), and classroom teachers as well as parents and any other professionals involved with the child. If the evaluation shows that the child needs special education services, an individual education program* (IEP) is written, based on the information gathered from the MFE. Parents have the right to accept or reject either test results or special education placement. If accepted, an IEP is written, and both parents and school personnel give input as to the needs and related services to be provided for the child.

The IEP must contain present levels of educational performance; annual goals, including short-term learning objectives, specific educational services, and amount of time spent in regular education programs; how the IEP will be evaluated; and a recommendation for placement in settings to provide for the maximum interaction with students without disabilities. Provisions are also made for a reevaluation to be conducted at least once every three years.

When issues arise that cannot be resolved through conference discussions, impartial hearing* officers are at the disposal of both the parents and the school. Each district has a detailed description of due process procedures.* With the knowledge, expertise, and caution exhibited by the school psychologist, due process should usually be unnecessary.

Although not part of the classification system of federal law 94–142, many states have developed criteria and are serving children identified as gifted, with programs beginning at the primary level.

See also CLASSIFICATION: PSYCHIATRIC.

REFERENCES

Public Law (P.L.) 101-476. Individuals with Disabilities Education Act, 1990. (104
    Stat. 1103.)
Shinn, M. R. (Ed.). (1989). Curriculum-based measurement: Assessing special children.
    New York: Guilford Press.

                                                                            Barbara W. Wonderly

CLASSIFICATION: PSYCHIATRIC. The *Diagnostic and Statistical Manual of Mental Disorders* (DSM) is considered the official taxonomy of psychiatric disorders in the United States and is used widely in hospitals, psychiatric clinics, and mental health facilities.

The American Psychiatric Association (APA) presented the first edition in 1952 with an official glossary of diagnostic categories. It reflected Adolf Meyer's psychobiological view that disorders are reactions of the personality to psychological, social, and biological factors. The second edition coincided with the development of the international classification of diseases (ICD-8) in 1968 and implied no specific theoretical framework for understanding disorders. The DSM III was published in 1979, reflecting the current state of psychiatric knowledge and maintaining compatibility with the new ICD-9, which included all its revised categories for mental disorders.

DSM III-R was published in 1987, and DSM IV in 1994, each reflecting the most updated view of mental disorders and epidemiology. It remains atheoretical in etiology, except when cause is well established, and it is descriptive in its definitions of conditions, listing characteristic features in identifiable behavioral signs or symptoms.

The goal of the task groups working on DSM IV was to provide a practical guide to clinical practice that would be usable across settings. Diagnostic categories are based on empirical research from published literature, reanalysis of collected data, and new field trials. A balance was struck in revision with respect to traditional terminology, research data, and consensus of the field. It is compatible with ICD-10, published by the World Health Organization in 1992, so that medical codes on Axis III can be consistent.

The multiaxial evaluation system ensures that relevant information about physical conditions, severity of psychosocial stressors, and global assessment of functioning are presented with the diagnosis of the disorder. A mental disorder is considered a "clinically significant behavioral or psychological syndrome or pattern that occurs in a person and that is associated with present distress or disability or with a significantly increased risk of suffering" (APA, 1987, p. 12). The concept defines a boundary between normalcy and pathology.

The syndrome or pattern of behavior must be outside an expected response to events in terms of severity, duration, and/or frequency of symptoms and considered a psychological or biological dysfunction of the person. Deviant or nonconforming behaviors are not considered mental disorders unless there are also symptoms of dysfunction. A new section covers culturally related features.

Major categories include the following:

- Disorders first diagnosed in infancy, childhood, or adolescence
- Delirium, dementia, and amnestic and other cognitive disorders
- Mental disorders due to a general medical condition not elsewhere classified
- Substance-related disorders
- Schizophrenia and other psychotic disorders
- Mood disorders
- Anxiety disorders
- Somatoform disorders
- Dissociative disorders
- Factitious disorders
- Sexual and gender identity disorders
- Sleep disorders
- Eating disorders
- Impulse control disorders not elsewhere classified
- Adjustment disorders
- Personality disorders
- Other conditions that may be a focus of clinical attention

The manual lists specific criteria to be used in making each diagnosis. These criteria are based on clinical judgment, with the descriptive nature of the criteria enhancing diagnostic reliability. For each disorder, essential features, associated features, age of onset, course of the disorder, degree of impairment, complications, predisposing factors, prevalence, gender ratio, familial pattern, and differential diagnoses are described, as well as the diagnostic criteria, making the manual a full encyclopedic reference for psychiatric conditions.

Most psychiatric classification systems focus on adults, with few categories for children's disorders. The DSM I listed two such categories, adjustment reaction and childhood schizophrenia. The Group for the Advancement of Psychiatry recommended a more complete system for classifying children's disorders, using three basic criteria: psychosomatic, developmental, and psychosocial. From these, ten major categories were proposed in 1966. In 1968, the new DSM II did not incorporate these concepts; instead, a limited number of specific childhood categories were used. The DSM III-R broadened the number of diagnostic categories, and the new DSM IV further refined the taxonomy to include mental retardation, specific learning, pervasive developmental, attention deficit and disruptive, anxiety, feeding and eating, gender identity, motor skills, tic, elimination, and communication disorders.

New categories for childhood disorders in DSM IV include learning disorders, problems related to abuse and neglect, relational problems, and additional conditions that may be a focus of clinical attention, such as acculturation, academic, identity, and antisocial problems. The pervasive developmental disorder category has expanded to include Rett's, Aspergers, and childhood disintegrative disorders.

Respectively, these categories are consistent with the ICD-10 classification system used in hospitals throughout the world, but not with the educational taxonomy outlined in Public Law 94-142* and subsequent amendments and used in the public school systems nationwide. ICD-10 is a valuable tool, however, for elucidating and understanding behavioral and emotional disorders of childhood and adolescence for purposes of intervention and treatment planning.

See also CLASSIFICATION: EDUCATIONAL.

REFERENCES

American Psychiatric Association. (1987). *Diagnostic and statistical manual of mental disorders* (3rd ed.) Washington, DC: Author.
———. (1994). *Diagnostic and statistical manual of mental disorders* (4th ed.). Washington, DC: Author.

Susan Kupisch

CLASSROOM MANAGEMENT. Classroom management can be defined as procedures required to establish and maintain a classroom environment in which instruction and learning can occur. Classroom management is typically regarded from two perspectives: (1) *proactive* and (2) *reactive*. Gettinger (1988) suggests that classroom management historically has focused on discipline and control of misbehavior, implying that behavior must be controlled and/or reduced before effective instruction can occur. This describes reactive classroom management. More recently, there has been an emphasis on structuring the classroom environment and using teaching strategies that prevent misbehavior and promote academic performance. This is known as proactive classroom management.

Gettinger (1988) described proactive classroom management as having three characteristics. First, it emphasizes planning, prevention, and anticipation of potential behavior problems rather than responding to them after they have occurred. Second, it integrates methods that promote appropriate student behavior as well as student achievement. Based on Kounin's (1970) research, these methods include ''withitness'' (the teacher's being aware of what is going on at all times in the classroom), ''overlapping'' (being able to do more than one thing at a time, such as teaching a lesson and intervening on a problem behavior), ''group alerting'' (prompting noninvolved students in lessons by using challenge-arousal techniques), and ''smoothness and momentum in lessons'' (briskly paced instruction with a minimum of slowdowns). Third, proactive classroom management emphasizes group, rather than individual, behavior. Proactive classroom management incorporates effective instruction with preventive techniques that greatly reduce the frequency of behavior problems in classrooms. It emphasizes the antecedents rather than the consequences of behavior.

Reactive classroom management focuses on the consequences of behavior. Reactive strategies involve intervention procedures based on principles of applied behavior analysis, which include variations of reinforcement (positive and negative) and punishment (positive and negative) (Kazdin, 1984). Examples of positive reinforcement include verbal praise, access to preferred activities, differential reinforcement, tokens/stars, or positive written comments on schoolwork. Negative reinforcement involves setting up contingencies whereby students can avoid aversive consequences by performing desired behavior (e.g., completing class work to avoid staying in for recess). Positive punishment is the presentation of aversive consequences that reduce behavior (e.g., verbal reprimands, overcorrection). Negative punishment is the removal of a specified amount of a positive reinforcer and includes procedures such as response cost (fines) and time-out (removal of all positive reinforcement for a set time period).

See also BEHAVIORAL ASSESSMENT; BEHAVIORAL CONSULTATION; BEHAVIOR MODIFICATION; OPERANT CONDITIONING.

REFERENCES

Gettinger, M. (1988). Methods of proactive classroom management. *School Psychology Review* 17, 227–242.
Kazdin, A. (1984). *Behavior modification in applied settings.* Homewood, IL: Dorsey Press.
Kounin, J. (1970). *Discipline and group management in classrooms.* New York: Holt, Rinehart, and Winston.

Frank M. Gresham

CLIENT. While school psychologists* clearly have clients, the identity of the client changes with situations, thereby creating significant challenges. One's model of practice, including medical,* child advocacy,* consultation,* and systems,* is influential, with the first two generally pointing to the child as client, the third to whoever is the consultee, along with that entity's clients, and the fourth to interactions among individuals, groups, and organizations. While one could resolve this issue by making all of these clients, both the National Association of School Psychologists* (NASP) and the American Psychological Association* (APA) ethical standards caution about divided loyalties. Conflicts of interest between and among school personnel, parents, and child pose a serious ethical dilemma for school psychologists. Whose best interests do they represent? The problem of resolving such dilemmas was recognized at the Thayer conference* (Cutts, 1955, p. 87) and at the Spring Hill conference* (Trachtman, 1981) and is discussed in most recent school psychology texts. While these latter discussions have helped to elucidate the issues (e.g., Stewart, 1986), no definitive answer to the question of clientage exists, and school psychologists are generally advised to tread carefully and attempt to resolve conflicts in a way that is beneficial to all parties involved.

See also CHILD ADVOCACY; CODES OF ETHICS; PROFESSIONAL STANDARDS.

REFERENCES

Cutts, N. E. (Ed.). (1955). *School psychologists at mid-century.* Washington, DC: American Psychological Association.
Stewart, K. J. (1986). Disentangling the complexities of clientage. In S. N. Elliott and J. C. Witt (Eds.), *The delivery of psychological services in schools: Concepts, processes, and issues* (pp. 81–107). Hillsdale, NJ: Erlbaum.
Trachtman, G. M. (1981). On such a full sea. *School Psychology Review* 10, 138–181.

Timothy S. Hartshorne

CLINIC. The mental health clinic provides psychiatric, psychological, and social work services on an outpatient basis, as opposed to a residential or inpatient basis. Mental health clinics first began to appear in the United States in the late 1800s but remained relatively uncommon until the 1940s, when demand for psychiatric treatment for returning veterans led to a major expansion of both inpatient and outpatient services. Additional impetus was provided by the success of psychotropic medications in the 1950s, which allowed many inpatients to return to community care, and by the Community Mental Health Centers Act of 1963, which provided federal funds to assist in the establishment of public community mental health centers.

Early influences on children's mental health services include Lightner Witmer's* laboratory clinic at the University of Pennsylvania (established 1896), which focused on applying psychological principles to help educators solve children's learning problems, and William Healy's Psychopathic Institute (established 1909), which advised the Chicago public schools and the Chicago juvenile court on the prevention and treatment of child and adolescent behavior problems. Child outpatient mental health services are currently provided in a variety of clinic-based settings, including community mental health centers, child guidance clinics, private counseling or psychiatric clinics, university counseling or psychiatric clinics, and school-based clinics.

See also HOSPITAL SETTINGS; UNIVERSITY-BASED CLINICS.

REFERENCES

Kupers, T. A. (1981). *Public therapy: The practice of psychotherapy in the public mental health clinic.* New York: Free Press.
Martens, E. H. (1939). *Clinical organization for child guidance within the schools.* Washington, DC: U.S. Government Printing Office (Bulletin 1939, No. 15).
Tulipan, A. B., and S. Feldman. (1969). *Psychiatric clinics in transition.* New York: Brunner/Mazel.
White, M. A., and M. W. Harris. (1961). *The school psychologist.* New York: Harper.

W. Val McClanahan

CLINICAL PSYCHOLOGY. Clinical psychology is a specialty of professional psychology in which the providers are licensed by a state board of examiners of psychologists* to deliver assessment, consultation, and intervention services directed to "correcting the emotional conflicts, personality disturbances, and skill deficits underlying a person's distress and/or dysfunction" (American Psychological Association, 1981, p. 5).

Authors in the field date the beginning of the profession to Lightner Witmer's* establishing the psychological clinic at the University of Pennsylvania in 1896. During that same year, he presented his vision of clinical psychology to his colleagues at the meeting of the American Psychological Association.* His vision was poorly received for a number of reasons, not the least being that those psychologists who were fashioning themselves as scientists were not accepting of the application of psychology to individual clients. The rift that appeared early in the profession between the scientist and the practitioner has been a source of contention ever since and related to the scientist-practitioner model* presented at the national conference on clinical training at Boulder, Colorado, in 1949. Yet, tension continues to exist and is demonstrated by a scientist faction's breaking away from the American Psychological Association in 1988 to form the American Psychological Society.*

The idiographic nature of the delivery of clinical psychological services has been the focus of critics who suspect the validity of such clinical methods, though substantial research has been done with assessment and intervention practices. The efforts over the last twenty years of clinicians, through the American Psychological Association, to gain privileges reserved for psychiatrists, such as third-party payments and hospital and prescription privileges,* have been sources of concern to academic psychologists and even some clinical psychologists.

The dramatic growth and role expansion of clinical psychology have been attributed to the need for clinical psychologists during and following World War II. The Veterans Administration (VA) hospitals had thousands of emotionally and physically impaired returning soldiers needing services. The VA and, later, the U.S. Public Health Service provided training grants to universities to prepare psychologists for hospital positions. Subsequently, clinical psychologists moved into other mental health settings and into private practice.

The ubiquitous application of clinical psychological services across ages, settings, and various presenting symptomatology has brought prestige to, envy of, and criticism of, the specialty.

See also COUNSELING PSYCHOLOGY; SCHOOL PSYCHOLOGY.

REFERENCES

American Psychological Association. (1981). *Specialty guidelines for the delivery of services by clinical psychologists.* Washington, DC: Author.
Reisman, J. M. (1976). *A history of clinical psychology.* New York: Irvington.
Witmer, L. (1907). Clinical psychology. *The Psychological Clinic* 1, 1–9.

Paul G. Warden

COALITIONS. A coalition is a union of organizations seeking similar ends. Coalitions unify groups when communicating with policymakers and stakeholders. They are a strong source of both information and power. Speaking with one voice, a coalition's endorsement of a position enables the policymakers to measure the breadth of the support across a variety of constituents. It avoids the guild-driven, narrowly focused image that a single profession or organization presents. Coalitions provide member organizations the opportunity to problem-solve and to refine a proposal so that it meets agreed-upon needs. School psychologists organize and participate in coalitions of organizations that include consumers in education, mental health, and related human services. The National Association of School Psychologists* belongs to several national coalitions, including the National Alliance of Pupil Services Organizations, Committee for Education Funding, National Mental Health/Special Education Coalition, National Coalition for Parent Involvement in Education, Coalition to Abolish Corporal Punishment, Comprehensive School Health Planning Group, National Consortium for Child and Adolescent Mental Health, Federation of Families for Children's Mental Health, and the Consortium for Citizens with Disabilities.

See also HOME-SCHOOL-COMMUNITY COLLABORATION; NATIONAL MENTAL HEALTH ASSOCIATION; SUPPORT GROUPS.

REFERENCES

Dwyer, K. P. (1994). *Best practices in government relations.* Silver Spring, MD: National Association of School Psychologists.
National Association of School Psychologists. (1994). *Annual Report 1993–1994.* Silver Spring, MD: Author.

Kevin P. Dwyer

CODES OF ETHICS. A professional code of ethics is a set of standards developed to guide the conduct of the practitioner in his or her professional interactions with others. Both the National Association of School Psychologists* (NASP) and the American Psychological Association* (APA) have adopted ethical codes. These codes are based on the consensus of association members about what constitutes appropriate professional conduct. In joining either NASP or APA, members agree to abide by the association's ethical code. Sanctions for ethics violations include expulsion from the association, probation, censure, or reprimand.

Ethical codes are periodically revised to address new and emerging ethical issues. Principles for professional ethics were first adopted by NASP in 1974 and revised in 1984 and 1992. First published in 1953, APA's code of ethics was revised and republished eight times between 1958 and 1990. The current version, "Ethical Principles of Psychologists and Code of Conduct," was adopted in 1992.

The ethical codes of NASP and APA are composed of broad ethical principles, along with more specific rule statements. Broad principles or themes common to both codes include respect for the dignity of persons (engaging in actions that respect client self-determination, autonomy, and privacy), beneficence or responsible caring (choosing actions that are likely to benefit the client or at least do no harm), integrity in professional relationships (being honest and trustworthy in professional relationships), and responsibility to community and society (using the science of psychology in ways that promote human welfare).

Ethical codes serve to protect the public by sensitizing professionals to the ethical aspects of service delivery, educating practitioners about the parameters of appropriate professional conduct, and helping professionals to monitor their own behavior. By encouraging appropriate professional conduct, associations such as NASP and APA strive to ensure that each person served receives the highest quality of service and, therefore, build and maintain public trust in psychologists and psychology.

See also PROFESSIONAL STANDARDS.

REFERENCES

American Psychological Association. (1992). Ethical principles of psychologists and code of conduct. *American Psychologist* 47, 1597–1611.
Jacob-Timm, S., and T. S. Hartshorne. (1994) *Ethics and law for school psychologists* (2d ed.). Brandon, VT: Clinical Psychology.
National Association of School Psychologists. (1992). Principles for professional ethics. *Professional conduct manual* (pp. 1–23). Silver Spring, MD: Author.

Susan Jacob-Timm

COGNITIVE ASSESSMENT: NONTRADITIONAL. Nontraditional cognitive assessment falls into two categories—methods operationalized into tests and those that exist only as experimental tasks. Formalized nontraditional tests include the Kaufman Assessment Battery for Children (K-ABC) (Kaufman and Kaufman, 1983), Woodcock-Johnson Psychoeducational Battery-Revised (WJ-R) (Woodcock and Johnson, 1989), Differential Ability Scales (DAS) (Elliott, 1990), and Das-Naglieri Cognitive Assessment System (DNCAS) (Das and Naglieri, forthcoming). Experimental nontraditional systems include dynamic assessment* (Carlson and Widel, Haywood, Lidz), information processing (Hunt, 1990), and multiple intelligence (Gardner, Sternberg). What distinguishes nontraditional from traditional is that these methods go beyond the general intelligence* view to measure specific dimensions of cognition.

Nontraditional cognitive assessment was developed out of a concern that traditional tests (Binet and Wechsler) have significant limitations. How authors attempted to improve traditional cognitive assessment methods directly influenced the construction of their instruments and, ultimately, their degree of success. The K-ABC and DAS differ from traditional approaches in how they measure ability—the former does so from a cognitive perspective (sequential/simultaneous processes), and the latter stresses the need for subtest specificity. The WJ-R and DNCAS differ from traditional tests in that they both provide a broader definition of intelligence and a theory of cognitive processing. The WJ-R measures eight broad intellectual abilities, and the DNCAS defines human functioning according to the planning, attention, simultaneous, and successive (PASS) cognitive processing theory. The K-ABC, WJ-R, and DNCAS all have an emphasis on measuring cognitive processes. Although advantages vary, what the authors all share is a background in traditional testing coupled with an intention to improve traditional IQ tests.

Experimental nontraditional researchers who came from cognitive psychology labs (Carlson, Das, Hunt, Jensen) or general psychology settings (Gardner, Haywood, Sternberg) also recognized the need for alternative models of intelligence. Typically, they proposed theories that define the mental processes associated with simple and complex levels of human performance. Some of these approaches (Gardner, Sternberg) have been widely recognized, although Sternberg says that Gardner's theory appears to be impossible to quantify and that convergent and discriminant validity remains to be shown for his own theory. Similarly, conversion of experimental methods into workable systems of assessment remains to be achieved for many of these experimentally based approaches.

Nontraditional cognitive assessment holds the potential to improve the state of the art in significant ways. At this point in the development of the field, many believe that scientific findings will reveal the most valid approaches. It seems clear that research in cognition and information processing may eventually yield new forms of individually administered intelligence tests of a type never before available. This important evolutionary step away from traditional theoretical models of intelligence toward cognitive processing-based reconceptualizations of intelligence has been made because of the view that traditional technology, now nearly 100 years old, should not be maintained into the twenty-first century. This sentiment is gaining acceptance in contemporary psychology and education.

See also ASSESSMENT (DIRECT AND INDIRECT); COGNITIVE ASSESSMENT: TRADITIONAL.

REFERENCES

Das, J. P., and J. A. Naglieri. (forthcoming). Das-Naglieri Cognitive Assessment
    System. Chicago: Riverside.
Elliott, C. D. (1990). Differential Ability Scales (DAS) administration and scoring
    manual. San Antonio, TX: Psychological Corporation.
Kaufman, A. S., and N. L. Kaufman. (1983). Kaufman Assessment Battery for
    Children. Circle Pines, MN: American Guidance.
Woodcock, R. W., and M. B. Johnson. (1989). Woodcock-Johnson Tests of Cognitive
    Ability: Standard and supplemental batteries. Chicago: Riverside.

Jack A. Naglieri

COGNITIVE ASSESSMENT: TRADITIONAL. The Random House dictionary defines an intelligence test as "any of various tests, as the Binet-Simon scale, designed to measure the native mental ability or capacity of an individual'' (1973, p. 739). The appearance of this entry in the dictionary speaks to the importance and influence of this technology. In psychology generally, intelligence tests have been an integral part of professional practice. Typically, school psychologists* have used the Stanford-Binet and the Wechsler scales to evaluate general intelligence.* These traditional measures have also been used throughout the world to evaluate general intelligence, using items of verbal and nonverbal content. Both tests represent a theoretical view of general intelligence organized according to the content of the subtests, which distinguishes them from more recently proposed nontraditional ones. The Wechsler and Binet scales represent one of the most significant accomplishments of applied psychology in the twentieth century.

Although intelligence tests are the product of modern society, the concept of intelligence was not recently discovered. Intelligence was discussed by Hindu scholars in the Bhagavadgita (500 B.C.) and by the Greeks (Aristotle's writings around 400 B.C.) and was even used by the Chinese (2000 B.C.) for selection purposes. Intelligence tests in use today are rooted in studies of individual differences that began during the 1800s. For example, Sir Francis Galton studied individual differences in sensory perceptions and physical characteristics (which led him to discover the unique aspects of fingerprints). The availability of a more complete test of intelligence had, and continues to have, a significant impact on the field of school psychology.

The availability of the first practical intelligence test developed by Binet and Simon in 1905 marked a significant moment in the history of psychology. This important contribution was made for the purpose of identifying the mentally retarded only about twenty-five years after the first psychological laboratory was founded. The Binet-Simon scale was distinctive because it measured more than simple sensory functions and provided a measure of higher mental activities, using items that were ranked by difficulty and used to establish a child's mental age. The scale was adapted by scholars in the United States and was modified, extended, and standardized by Lewis Terman.* His 1916 version, the Stanford-Binet, became the standard in the field and was revised in 1937, 1960, 1972, and 1986. Thus, for nearly ninety years, the field of psychology has had the Binet scale, and it has been an integral part of the practice of school psychology since the profession began.

In 1930, a clinical psychologist at Bellevue Hospital in New York provided an alternative to the Binet that provided an overall score like the Binet and separate scale (verbal and performance) and subtest scores. The Wechsler-Bellevue and its offspring—the Wechsler Preschool and Primary Scale, Wechsler Intelligence Scale for Children, and the Wechsler Adult Intelligence Scale—have had a sustained and substantial impact on the measurement of individual differences throughout the world. The Wechsler scales provide standard score-based IQs, verbal and performance scales, interpretable subtests, and excellent reliability and standardization samples, which have made them the most widely used tests of their kind. The Wechsler, like the Binet, continues to provide school psychologists with the most psychometrically advanced methods of evaluating general intelligence.

See also ASSESSMENT: DIRECT AND INDIRECT; COGNITIVE ASSESSMENT: NONTRADITIONAL.

REFERENCES

Kaufman, A. S. (1994). *Intelligent testing with the WISC-III.* New York: Wiley.
Matarazzo, J. D. (1972). *Wechsler's measurement and appraisal of adult intelligence.* Baltimore: Williams and Wilkins.
Sattler, J. M. (1990). *Assessment of children.* San Diego: Author.
Thorndike, R. M., and D. F. Lohman. (1990). *A century of ability testing.* Chicago: Riverside.

Jack A. Naglieri

COGNITIVE BEHAVIOR MODIFICATION. Cognitive behavior modification, typically referred to as CBM, is an individualized psychotherapeutic procedure in which cognitively based strategies are used to control, focus, and direct underlying cognitive processes associated with specific behaviors in acceptable and appropriately effective ways. CBM has several practical characteristics that distinguish it from other types of behavior management procedures. The first major distinction is that the individual is the primary mechanism by which change is generated and occurs. During the initial phases of CBM training, the therapist is typically involved in instruction. But, as treatment progresses, this relationship gradually changes to focus increasing personal responsibility on the individual receiving the treatment. Physiological and/or neurological causes of maladaptive behaviors are not considered relevant.

The main mechanisms used to initiate these cognitive and behavioral changes during treatment are verbalization and modeling* as teaching procedures. The purpose of therapeutic verbalization is to facilitate the development of covert, cognitive self-mediation and mental rehearsal strategies during stress-inducing times. Persons are also taught how to identify variables that lead to emotional distress and to develop a specific set of internal cognitive and accompanying behavioral response patterns to deal with these stressors, with the goal to assist in attaining maximum self-control.

The usual sequence of training during treatment involves identifying and defining the problem, attention focusing, developing a resolution to the problem, modeling, practicing using self-instruction, and verbal cuing to remind the person to inhibit targeted negative behavior and to reinforce a positive behavior in its place.

CBM has been used successfully with a number of different problem behaviors, including noncompliant behaviors in school for both regular and special education students, control of hyperactive behavior in children, social skills difficulties, assertiveness training,* stress management, and anxiety-based disorders.

See also COGNITIVE THERAPY; RELAXATION TRAINING; SOCIAL SKILLS TRAINING; STRESS REDUCTION THERAPY; SYSTEMATIC DESENSITIZATION.

REFERENCES

Cohen, J. J., and M. C. Fish. (1993). *Handbook of school-based intervention.* San Francisco: Jossey-Bass.
Manning, B. (1988). Application of cognitive behavior modification: First and third graders' self-management of classroom behaviors. *American Educational Research Journal* 25(2), 193–212.
Meichenbaum, D. (1977). *Cognitive-behavior modification: An integrative approach.* New York: Plenum Press.

Raymond E. Webster

COGNITIVE THERAPY. Cognitive therapy is a psychotherapeutic approach based on the presumption that people's feelings and behaviors reflect unique perception, interpretation, and cognitive organization of their social environment and interactions with others. Assumptions that form the basis for these perceptual and interpretive sets are called schemata. Maladaptive schemata, which are generated in response to specific social transactions experienced as stressful by the person, produce psychological and behavioral disturbances. Cognitive processing is viewed as the result of both behavior and underlying biological and neurochemical factors.

Specific therapeutic strategies typically include behavior modification,* verbal processing to enhance personal insight and knowledge, examination of how maladaptive schemata were originally developed from earlier experiences, and what the original purpose was for these beliefs. Cognitive mediation is seen as a critical element that modulates a person's emotional and behavioral reactions. Therapeutic techniques used include thought-stopping, role modeling, rehearsal, hypothesis testing, and visual imagery.

Treatment focuses on symptom identification and relief, with an active collaborative relationship formed between the patient and therapist. The primary focus is on solution of present problems and how the person cognitively experiences these problems internally in terms of attitudes, thoughts, feelings, and beliefs. There is little emphasis placed on past issues from childhood, nor is interpretation of unconscious material often involved. A goal of treatment is to identify the person's logic associated with the schemata developed and how these two impact behavior and interactions with others.

No single integrated and unified model characterizes cognitive therapy. In fact, there are several related subsystems, including cognitive behavioral therapy, structural cognitive therapy, cognitive behavior modification,* rational-emotive therapy,* and multimodal therapy.

Historically, cognitive therapy reflects the synthesis of several different perspectives about the development of psychopathology. Basic assumptions about how people conceptualize and organize the world of personal experiences are derived from several perspectives, including Kelly's (1955) hypotheses about personal constructs that impact behavior and behavior change; Ellis's (1962) views about the relationship between irrational beliefs and feelings that produce dysfunctional behaviors; Beck's (1972) work on how cognitive distortions often underlie depression; Rogers's (1951) position that people's personalized meanings about events affect how they react to these events; and the general social learning model. Behavior therapy* in general has also made a significant contribution to cognitive therapy.

Research has shown that cognitive therapy can be an effective approach to use to treat depression, anxiety disorders, phobias, psychosomatic disorders, chronic pain, and social or interpersonal skills deficits. It has also been shown to be effective in teaching people to manage and control stress, as well as in resolving marital conflict.

See also CLASSIFICATION: PSYCHIATRIC; FAMILY THERAPY; MARRIAGE AND FAMILY THERAPY; RECIPROCAL DETERMINISM.

REFERENCES

Beck, A. (1972). *Depression: Causes and treatment.* Philadelphia: University of
        Pennsylvania Press.
Beck, A. T., A. Freeman, J. Pretzer, D. Davis, B. Fleming, R. Ottaviani, J. Beck, K.
        M. Simon, C. Padesky, J. Meyer, and L. Trexler. (1990). *Cognitive therapy of
        personality disorders.* New York: Guilford.
Ellis, A. (1962). *Reason and emotion in psychotherapy.* Secaucus, NJ: Lyle Stuart.
Kelly, G. (1955). *The psychology of personal constructs.* New York: Norton.
Rogers, C. (1951). *Client-centered therapy.* Boston: Houghton Mifflin.

Raymond E. Webster

COLLABORATION. Collaboration is a problem-solving model based on parity and shared responsibility among coequal adults with differing knowledge and skills. Collaboration grew out of the educational reform movements of the 1980s, particularly those stressing teacher empowerment and local decision making. The mandate for placing children with disabilities in the least restrictive environment, as embodied in PL 94-142* and its subsequent amendments, coupled with the regular education initiative* (REI), has caused school psychologists,* special education* teachers, and classroom teachers to work together to better serve children with disabilities and at-risk children in general education classrooms.

Collaboration is seen by its proponents as supplanting consultation* as the primary form of problem-solving interaction among professionals. Research during the 1980s indicates that teachers, administrators, and parents prefer the collaborative interaction to the consultative relationship, which is perceived as hierarchical and expert-driven in practice.

Some proponents of collaboration see it as an interactive style that can be utilized with different consultation models (Friend and Cook, 1992). Other proponents see it as a vehicle to establish a schoolwide climate of caring that involves all interactions, not only those focused on problem solving (Pugach and Johnson, 1995). Critical to collaboration are mastery of the skills for effective communication, problem solving, conflict resolution, and planning. Caplan and Caplan (1993) have proposed a model for mental health collaboration that they believe best represents the school psychologist's interactions with teachers.

See also COLLABORATIVE CONSULTATION; PROBLEM-SOLVING ASSESSMENT; PROBLEM-SOLVING CONSULTATION.

REFERENCES

Caplan, G., and R. B. Caplan. (1993). *Mental health consultation and collaboration.* San Francisco: Jossey-Bass.
Friend, M., and L. Cook. (1992). *Interactions: Collaboration skills for school professionals.* New York: Longman.
Pugach, M. C., and L. J. Johnson. (1995). *Collaborative practitioners, collaborative schools.* Denver: Love.

Paul G. Warden

COLLABORATIVE CONSULTATION. Collaborative consultation is a process for problem-solving interaction designed to diminish the perceived hierarchical relationships of more traditional, expert-driven models of consultation.* Collaborative consultation is similar to collaboration, a problem-solving model based on parity and shared responsibility among coequal professionals with differing knowledge and skills.

The need for professionals working together to serve the needs of students with disabilities and at-risk students is rooted in the educational reform movements of the 1980s, particularly, the importance of teachers' working together for empowerment and local decision making. The legacy of Public Law 94-142,* mandating the least restrictive environment (LRE), became a core concept of the regular education initiative* (REI). Special education* and regular (general) education were conceived of as needing to merge but retain their specialized components of education, and the need to reconceptualize special educators and school psychologists as partners with regular classroom teachers became apparent. Continuing to perceive school psychologists* as take-charge experts by classroom teachers defeats the achievement of meaningful partnerships needed to restructure the schools.

Collaborative consultation is a problem-solving process where the consultant and consultee mutually define the problem of the client, share expertise in defining the goal, and assume mutual responsibility for the efficacy of the solution. Research has indicated that teachers, administrators, and parents prefer the collaborative interaction to the consultative relationship. This body of research has primarily focused on school settings; a variant to mental health consultation* called "mental health collaboration" has been proposed for school psychologists and other agency-based professionals (Caplan and Caplan, 1993).

Friend and Cook (1992) suggest that collaborative consultation is a misinterpretation of collaboration,* which is not a model of consultation but an interactive style that can be utilized, when appropriate, with existing models of consultation. They contend that circumstances might require the expert model inherent in the traditional forms of consultation. Collaborative consultation has less appeal than collaboration to contemporary proponents of collaboration who conceive of consultation as connoting an inherently hierarchical form of interaction. Authors writing about consultation appear to focus on the collaborative aspects of collaborative consultation, but some perceive the consultant as having less interaction with the client than one would in a collaborative relationship.

Since traditional models of consultation have stressed that the decision to implement any intervention rests with the consultee, arguably the responsibility of outcomes with the client is retained by the consultee. The consultant functions in an advisory position. With collaboration, there is shared responsibility between the two professionals. Combining the concepts of collaboration and consultation tends to cloud the issue of responsibility and could lead to legal ambiguities.

See also BEHAVIORAL CONSULTATION; CASE CONSULTATION; CONSULTATION; MENTAL HEALTH CONSULTATION; PROCESS CONSULTATION.

REFERENCES

Brown, D., W. B. Pryzwansky, and A. C. Schulte. (1991). *Psychological consultation: Introduction to theory and practice* (2d ed.). Boston: Allyn and Bacon.
Caplan, G., and R. B. Caplan. (1993). *Mental health consultation and collaboration.* San Francisco: Jossey-Bass.
Friend, M., and L. Cook. (1992). *Interactions: Collaboration skills for school professionals.* New York: Longman.
Idol, L., P. Paolucci-Whitcomb, and A. Nevin. (1986). *Collaborative consultation.* Rockville, MD: Aspen.

Paul G. Warden

COLLECTIVE BARGAINING. Collective bargaining is the process by which organized groups of employees negotiate salary and working conditions with their employers. Collective bargaining is a formal process that occurs within a framework of rules governed by fair labor laws and regulations. Collective bargaining attempts to provide for an atmosphere of discussion, concessions, and compromises to avoid "job actions" (e.g., strikes) by labor and unfair practices by management. Procedures such as arbitration and fact-finding are available when the two parties cannot reach agreement. Strikes, once illegal, are available to workers as a final protest. Until the 1970s, many educators and school psychologists considered themselves professional, rather than nonprofessional, employees and shunned both collective bargaining and strikes. However, as state collective bargaining laws for all public employees became the norm in the major industrialized states, large numbers of educators were forced to form collective bargaining units. These are now affiliated with the two major teacher associations, the National Education Association (NEA) and the American Federation of Teachers (AFT). By definition, both may be considered professional unions.

As reflected in the sparse literature, few academicians and leaders in school psychology have been very interested in the theories, research, and practice of collective bargaining. A series of state and national surveys, mostly by Hyman and colleagues, that dealt with this issue, especially within the context of collective bargaining, started in the 1960s and ended in the 1970s. Those studies and a seminal article by Agin (1979) constitute the bulk of the extant, in-depth literature on school psychology and collective bargaining.

School psychologists who work in collective bargaining states must be represented by a union, most often the teachers' union. As a distinct minority in a district's teachers' union, school psychologists often do not share a community of interest with teachers. That is, (1) they are not instructional personnel, (2) they work independently of classrooms, (3) they often work different hours than teachers, (4) they have different entry levels of training, (5) they tend to have training and orientations toward problem solving that may be at variance with the attitudes and approaches of many teachers, (6) they may travel between schools or work in a central office away from classrooms, (7) they more often work with individual children rather than groups, (8) they often recommend what teachers should do with children, and (9) they have the power to block a teacher's request to classify and/or remove a student from a classroom. Because of these distinctions, negotiations for salaries, working conditions, roles, and functions often focus on teacher demands related to classroom concerns.

School psychologists who take an active part in union affairs, especially those who become officers, are more likely to benefit from collective bargaining than those who are not involved in teachers' unions. This may not be true in settings where psychologists belong to a separate union for school psychologists or for pupil personnel services* generally.

See also SALARY DETERMINATION; TEACHER ORGANIZATIONS.

REFERENCES

Agin, T. (1979). The school psychologist and collective bargaining. *School Psychology Digest* 8, 187–192.

Hyman, I., M. Javian, P. McGreevy, P. Roessner, and K. Straub. (1972). The school psychologist and negotiations. *School Psychologist* 27(2), 10–18.

Hyman, I., and K. Kaplinski. (1994). Will the real school psychologist please stand up: Does the past offer a prologue for the future of school psychology?—Role and function. *School Psychology Review* 24, 564–583.

Irwin A. Hyman

COMPETENCY-BASED CERTIFICATION. Competency-based certification refers to the practice of basing credentialing on demonstrated levels of proficiency in specific skills rather than on a transcript review of specific course work completed. Competency-based certification at one time was predicted to be the wave of the future (Miller and Engin, 1974). The process was envisioned as having candidates complete simulated assessment,* consultation,* and intervention* activities for a panel of expert judges. While this kind of examination process has not been implemented, the National Association of School Psychologists* (NASP) takes a competency-based approach in its training standards, and a number of states (e.g., North Carolina, Tennessee, West Virginia) specify competency areas rather than courses as the basis for school psychology certification.* Each competency area is described in detail, with standards and criteria for evaluating the presence of that competency. For example, the North Carolina standards describe "direct intervention" as one of seven major functions of school psychologists,* list a number of specific functions related to direct intervention (e.g., "teaches students how to develop effective learning strategies and personal and social skills"), and provide "sample evidences" that can be used to determine that an individual has mastered the skills (e.g., "assists students in developing self-monitoring strategies").

Due to the logistical and technical complexity of verifying each competency for every applicant, states that employ competency-based requirements usually tie their standards to approved, in-state training programs. That is, programs are approved on the basis of providing training in the required competencies; graduates present an institutional recommendation to the certification agency as evidence of competence. Because competencies are ultimately tied to program courses, critics contend this method is simply another form of transcript-based certification. Other major issues in implementing competency-based certification include the limited empirical basis for selecting competencies, determining who should evaluate applicants, developing valid measurement techniques, and determining whether the process ultimately results in better-qualified personnel.

The term sometimes is used to refer to passing competency exams, such as the exam developed by the Educational Testing Service (ETS) for the NASP national certification program. The National School Psychology Certification System* (NSPCS) uses NASP credentialing standards to define entry criteria, continuing professional development standards, and a passing score on the ETS exam. States are beginning to utilize the test and/or the full NSPCS to credential school psychologists (see Pryzwansky, 1993).

See also PROGRAM APPROVAL; SPECIALTY TRAINING AND CREDENTIALING.

REFERENCES

Miller, J. N., and A. Engin. (1974). Performance-based school psychology certification: Situational response testing. *Psychology in the Schools* 11, 422–424.
Prus, J. S., and G. W. White, (1990). A summary of certification and licensure

requirements for school psychologists. In A. Thomas and J. Grimes (Eds.), *Best practices in school psychology—II* (pp. 899–912). Washington, DC: National Association of School Psychologists.

Prus, J., M. J. Curtis, A. Draper, and S. Hunley. (1995). A summary of credentialing requirements for school psychologists in public school settings. In A. Thomas and J. Grimes (Eds.), *Best practices in school psychology—III* (pp. 1237–1247). Washington, DC: National Association of School Psychologists.

Pryzwansky, W. B. (1993). The regulation of school psychology: A historical perspective on certification, licensure, and accreditation. *Journal of School Psychology* 31, 219–235.

Kathleen M. Minke

COMPREHENSIVE ASSESSMENT. Comprehensive assessment involves the consideration of intellectual and nonintellectual factors believed to be relevant to a child's academic and social functioning. It includes, in addition to indices of intellectual and academic achievement, an examination of cumulative records, home visits, and consideration of the child's developmental, medical, and social histories. Historically, any comprehensive assessment conducted by a school psychologist* that involves intellectual functioning must be traced to psychologist Henry Goddard.* Goddard translated the Binet scales in 1908. The early support and acceptance of the use of the Binet intelligence scales assisted in defining an important function for the profession of psychology.

Historically, the use of some form of comprehensive assessment has undoubtedly been occurring since the translation of the Binet scales. What indices or procedures are included is determined by what information is needed to address the referral question. Assessment most always involves a measure of intellectual functioning, in that, in most cases, it explains, relatively, the greatest amount of variance in the child's school functioning. However, combining intellectual data with indices of academic achievement, information gleaned from cumulative records, home visits, and inspection of developmental, medical, and social histories affords a more definitive assessment of the individual child. Comprehensive assessments function as an archive of historical, psychometric, interview, and observational data gathered and integrated to help describe and explain the child's current functioning and to ultimately assist in the design and implementation of effective interventions.

Indices of academic achievement included in the comprehensive assessment most likely incorporate a norm-referenced test, teacher evaluations, and perhaps a curriculum-based measure such as that described by Shapiro and Lentz (1986). Inspection of cumulative records is conducted to collect information included in past psychoeducational evaluations, such as the child's academic achievement history, diagnostic impressions, history of intervention attempts, and any past involvement in special education. In addition, the cumulative record probably includes past results of speech and hearing examinations, behavioral assessments, and intelligence test data. Of particular importance with regard to the utility of inspecting the child's cumulative record are the history of any attempts at intervention and the consistency and persistence of the referral problem. Unfortunately, this area of the cumulative record is often incomplete, particularly with respect to the accurate description of the intervention, the fidelity of its implementation, monitoring, and follow-up data.

A home visit is a form of environmental assessment that incorporates direct observation of supposedly relevant variables. They are included in most comprehensive assessments in order to obtain information regarding the child's socioeconomic status, parental characteristics, physical characteristics of the home setting, and availability of educationally relevant materials. Variables such as the child's expected work habits, parental disciplinary approaches, supports and reinforcements for academic accomplishments, and opportunities for language development are also usually observed. Although there are published indices available for the assessment of the home environment, the majority of home visits are conducted without consideration or completion of a formal evaluation.

Consideration of the child's developmental history usually focuses on significant and relevant events that have a bearing on the child's academic and social functioning. These may include such events as divorce, death of a significant person, loss of pets, changes in the family's socioeconomic status, relocation of the family, changes in schools, births, and other significant events that are assumed to be related to the child's current functioning. In addition to the child's cumulative record, developmental histories are most often obtained through interviews with the child, teachers, and parents.

Medical histories and current medical status are often included in comprehensive assessments if aspects of the child's history or current status are relevant to his or her academic and social functioning. Typically, medical diagnostic impressions are included, along with descriptions and durations of medical interventions such as hospitalizations, psychiatric treatments, and medications. Data regarding vision and hearing test results, history of brain injury, neuropsychological findings, and analysis of language impairments are also commonly included and considered pertinent to the medical component of the comprehensive assessment.

Social histories that are included in comprehensive assessments are aligned with the child's family background, educational, and developmental histories. Again, as with other components of the comprehensive assessment, aspects of the child's social history are detailed on the assumption that they are relevant to current academic and social functioning. Of particular significance in this domain is the assessment of the child's acceptance by his or her classmates. Data are typically obtained through inspection of cumulative records, child and teacher interviews, and sociometric indices. The latter are becoming less common, due primarily to the difficulty in obtaining the classmates' parent's permissions for testing.

In summary, a comprehensive assessment, through inspection of cumulative records, home visits, and consideration of the child's developmental, medical, and social histories, attempts to describe and explain the reasons for the child's current academic and social functioning. Thorough descriptions of many of the different assessment procedures employed for the various components that make up the comprehensive assessment are presented in Thomas and Grimes (1995). It is assumed that the comprehensive assessment is a prerequisite for the design and implementation of effective interventions.

See also ACADEMIC ASSESSMENT; ASSESSMENT (DIRECT AND IN-DIRECT); COGNITIVE ASSESSMENT; ECOLOGICAL ASSESSMENT; PERSONALITY ASSESSMENT.

REFERENCES

Anastasi, A. (1976). *Psychological testing* (4th ed.). New York: Macmillan.
Shapiro, E. S., and F. E. Lentz. (1986). Behavioral assessment of academic behavior. In T. R. Kratochwill (Ed.), *Advances in school psychology,* Vol. 5 (pp. 87–139). Hillsdale, NJ: Erlbaum.
Thomas, A., and J. Grimes (Eds.). (1995). *Best practices in school psychology—III.* Washington, DC: National Association of School Psychologists.

Thomas J. Kehle

COMPULSORY ATTENDANCE LAWS. Compulsory attendance laws require parents, legal guardians, or those who have legal control over children to see that these minors are "educated" by requiring their school attendance a minimum number of days per year over several ages (e.g., seven through fourteen or sixteen). Legal authority for the state to provide for compulsory public instruction is found in the common-law doctrine of *parens patriae,* which maintains that, as father to all persons, the state has inherent prerogative to provide for the common wealth and individual welfare. The motivation for passage of compulsory attendance laws grew out of two major drives in the late nineteenth and early twentieth centuries. The drive to abolish child labor was aimed at protecting the poor and the immigrant from exploitation, while giving them the tools to improve themselves. From the drive for Americanization came the view that a common schooling amid the diversity of religions, languages, ethnic and national backgrounds, and socioeconomic classes was necessary to achieve a sound and durable political community.

States acted on these two drives by passing compulsory attendance laws in two major phases; 1850–1890 was the symbolic stage, and 1890–1920s and 1930s was the bureaucratic stage (Tyack, 1976). The first stage was "symbolic" because school attendance in many states was already very high before the laws were passed and because the laws were seldom enforced. However, the passage of state compulsory attendance laws following the Civil War and Reconstruction reflected very strong political feelings that national cohesion should be strengthened by increasing the common bonds of America through education. The laws varied considerably in their details, and up to 1890 or 1900, the enforcement was lax to nonexistent. During the "bureaucratic" stage, compulsory attendance

laws were transformed into reasonably effective statutes requiring school attendance, hiring truant officers, defining responsibilities, establishing and supporting truant schools, delegating jurisdictive power, and dealing with a variety of
child labor regulations. This stage also saw a massive effort to get youth into
high school, thus shifting young people from a career of work to a career of
schooling.

The authority of states to enact such laws was affirmed by the 1901 decision
of the Indiana Supreme Court, which mandated compulsory education and gave
the state a monopoly over the responsibility (McGee, 1987). Specific ages of
children affected and other requirements of compulsory attendance are set by
the statutes of each state and carried out by the policies and procedures of local
school boards. The courts have consistently found that the enactment of compulsory attendance laws is a valid expression of the public power of the state
(Reutter, 1985).

See also BROWN v. BOARD OF EDUCATION; PUBLIC LAW 94-142.

REFERENCES

Alexander, K. (1980). School law. St. Paul, MN: West.
McGee. J. C. (1987). Compulsory education: An overview of the law. (ERIC
    Reproduction Services No. ED 285 249, EA 019 586).
Reutter, E. E. (1985). The law of public education (3d ed.). Mineola, NY: Foundation
    Press.
Tyack, D. B. (1976). Ways of seeing: An essay on the history of compulsory
    schooling. Harvard Educational Review 46, 355–389.

                                                                            George W. Etheridge

COMPUTER-ASSISTED TESTING. Computer-assisted testing includes using a computer to (1) administer tests, (2) score tests, or (3) interpret tests. Some
programs do all three functions, such as programs that administer, score, and
interpret (1) personality tests, such as the Minnesota Multiphasic Personality
Inventory (MMPI), (2) vocational interest or career guidance tests, or (3)
achievement tests, such as the Scholastic Aptitude Test (SAT) or the Graduate
Record Examination (GRE). Others do only one or a combination of these three
functions, such as test scoring and interpretation programs that are widely available for both group and individually administered cognitive, achievement, and
personality tests.

In 1965, there were 4 test scoring programs, but by 1990, there were over
400. Early programs were often created to meet practice needs: producing standard scores from raw scores or determining a significant aptitude-achievement
discrepancy from a regression table. They were available through a network of
early computer-using professionals loosely affiliated through special interest
groups within professional organizations such as the National Association of
School Psychologists'* Computer and Technological Applications in School
Psychology (CTASP) group. CTASP produced a newsletter from 1982 to 1987

that featured software reviews and information about new programs across several computer platforms.

Computer-administered tests include intake interviews and tests of personality, perceptual and motor speed, impulse control, attention, vision tracking, audition, and memory. These are widely used in research as well as in clinical settings, particularly in the identification of cognitive deficits associated with neurological or neuropsychological problems. They require specialized hardware, software, and professional training.

Research is inconsistent on the comparability of computer-administered tests to traditional paper-and-pencil tests. Some show no significant differences in outcomes, while others show significant differences in particular scales within a test. Ethical considerations require that computerized test interpretations be reviewed by a clinician in order to integrate information other than the test results into the clinical interpretation.

Computer-adapted testing is a feasible and rapidly growing type of computerized assessment. Qualitatively different measuring tasks are possible with computer item displays that are not possible with traditional paper-and-pencil tests. Adaptive tests do not have fixed item content; rather, items are selected from a bank of items to provide estimates of ability scores employing item response theory (IRT) selection criteria.

Computer scoring and interpretation programs vary in quality and output. Some provide extensive statistical information, such as standard scores, percentiles, grade or age equivalents, intracognitive discrepancies, aptitude-achievement discrepancies, and cross-test comparisons. Others add a report-writing function to the data reported and include expert-based or statistically based interpretations of the data. Some are meant for use by the examiner only, to provide possible hypotheses to consider in interpreting the data. Others are configured for direct inclusion in a psychological report.

Computer-based test interpretation (CBTI) programs can give the appearance of credibility because of the complexity of the reports produced, and professionals and laypeople may attribute undeserved authority to such documents. However, the credibility and validity* of many CBTI programs remain largely unexamined. Judging the validity of a CBTI program is difficult due to restrictions imposed by proprietary programming security, copyright protection, and the enormous complexity of the programs themselves. Debate exists among program reviewers on the choice of raters (self or neutral), the evaluation criteria to use, and the nature of the output (clinical or actuarial).

See also NATIONAL ASSOCIATION OF SCHOOL PSYCHOLOGISTS INTEREST GROUPS; NATIONAL ASSOCIATION OF SCHOOL PSYCHOLOGISTS; PROFESSIONAL STANDARDS.

REFERENCES

American Psychological Association. (1986). *Guidelines for computer-based tests and interpretations.* Washington, DC: Author.

McCullough, C. S. (1990). Computerized assessment. In C. Reynolds and R. Kamphaus (Eds.), *Psychological assessment* (Vol. 1, pp. 723–747). New York: Guilford.

———. (1991). Evaluating the validity of multidimensional computer-based test interpretation programs. *Journal of School Psychology* 29, 279–292.

Mead, A. D., and F. Drasgow. (1993). Equivalence of computerized and paper-and-pencil cognitive ability tests: A meta-analysis. *Psychological Bulletin* 114, 449–458.

C. Sue McCullough

COMPUTERIZED REPORT WRITING. Computerized report writing can increase the length and completeness of a psychological report while significantly reducing the production time by as much as 75 percent. Automated report writing has been around in one form or another since psychologists began writing reports, utilizing such helps as (1) abbreviations for frequently used words or phrases, (2) collections of descriptive sentences or paragraphs for frequently repeated parts of the report, and (3) report-writing forms with fill-in-the-blank or check-off boxes.

Computerized report writing utilizes automated means to produce psychological reports while allowing for individualization of text. Various types are available, including (1) stand-alone programs that require answering a series of questions, then generate text that incorporates the information given; (2) stand-alone or integrated word-processing programs that can be customized into report-writing templates using glossaries, style sheets, coded search and replace functions, form text, starter text, clip art, drawing tools, imported and integrated database information, or graphs from spreadsheets or other graphing programs; (3) unidimensional or multidimensional programs developed for a specific test or tests that may or may not be transportable to a word-processing program for further integration with other text, graphics, or data.

Word processors are the most flexible means to automatize the report-writing process, by setting up templates containing information that is repeated across reports, then customizing the text to fit the client. Word-processing templates may be prepared for different types of reports; letters to clients, parents, or teachers; or quarterly or annual reports to administrators. Templates are saved as ''stationary'' files so that when they are opened, the template cannot be written over when the document is saved. Templates include (1) form text, such as headers, demographic information labels, test names and subtest names, test descriptions, tables for reporting data, or section headers; (2) starter text, such as incomplete sentences or paragraphs for frequently used phrases, topics, or questions, which may be modified as needed; (3) coded search and replace functions, such as inserting the client's name, pronouns, or other frequently repeated information in the report. Glossaries may be utilized for frequently used phrases or words, such as test names. Some word-processing programs allow programming of the glossary function, which can be used to set up a series of questions, the answers to which are inserted in the program where designated. Style sheets assure that formats are uniform and easily set up.

Data may be entered into a database integrated with the word-processing program and then linked to specified places in the report. Anytime the database is updated, the report would be updated too. Most stand-alone word-processing programs have a means to set up a simple database within the word-processing program itself, though these are limited to demographic information, such as names and addresses of clients, and are not practical for entering test data into the report.

Stand-alone report-writing programs have been criticized for using "canned" dialogue and for language that may not sound like the language the examiner might use. However, some programs allow entry of sentences and phrases in the examiner's own words, and some also allow modification of standard text within the program. It takes time to set up the computerized report-writing system, whichever type is chosen, but the time saved later more than repays the investment.

See also CODES OF ETHICS; PROFESSIONAL STANDARDS; REPORT WRITING.

REFERENCES

McCullough, C. S. (1990). Best practices for utilizing technology. In A. Thomas and J. Grimes (Eds.), *Best practices in school psychology—II* (pp. 773–786). Washington, DC: National Association of School Psychologists.

Parker, R. C. (1988). *Looking good in print: A guide to basic design in desktop publishing.* Chapel Hill, NC: Ventana Press.

Tallent, N. (1993). *Psychological report writing.* Englewood Cliffs, NJ: Prentice-Hall.

C. Sue McCullough

CONFIDENTIALITY. The term "confidentiality" refers to the practice not to reveal what is learned in a professional relationship except under conditions agreed to by the person sharing confidences. Although confidentiality is primarily a matter of professional ethics, in some states psychologists can be held liable under state law for impermissible breach of client* confidentiality.

Prior to the mid-1970s, many psychologists accepted the view that the promise of confidentiality is absolute and can be broken under no circumstances. However, in a landmark court case, *Tarasoff v. Regents of California** (1974), the court held that the confidential character of the psychologist–client relationship must yield in instances in which disclosure is essential to protect others from danger.

The ethical codes of psychologists now recognize that there are limits to the promise of confidentiality, and practitioners have an ethical obligation to identify the parameters of confidentiality at the onset of providing services. Limits of the promise of confidentiality are likely to vary, depending on the nature of the services offered, the age and maturity of the client, and the reason for referral. For example, in working with minors, the psychologist will most likely need to share information with others in order to assist the children. Consequently, in discussing confidentiality with student-clients, the psychologist should identify those who will be provided information, what types of information will be disclosed, and how such disclosure will benefit the student.

Three situations generally require a school psychologist* to reveal confidential client disclosures to others. First, confidential information is revealed when the client requests it and has given his or her informed consent* for the disclosure. Second, confidential information may be disclosed to others when there is a situation involving danger to the client or others (e.g., child abuse). This is referred to as the "duty to warn"* or "duty to protect." Third, it may be necessary for a psychologist to disclose confidential information when there is a legal obligation to testify in a court of law.

See also PARENT/GUARDIAN PERMISSION; PRIVILEGED COMMUNICATION.

REFERENCES

Jacob-Timm, S., and T. S. Hartshorne. (1994). *Ethics and law for school psychologists* (2d ed.). Brandon, VT: Clinical Psychology.
National Association of School Psychologists. (1992). *Professional conduct manual.* Silver Spring, MD: Author.
Tarasoff v. Regents of California, 529 P.2d 553 (1974).
Taylor, L., and H. S. Adelman. (1989). Reframing the confidentiality dilemma to work in children's best interests. *Professional Psychology: Research and Practice* 16, 226–235.

Susan Jacob-Timm

CONFLICT RESOLUTION/PEER MEDIATION. As a nonviolent method for settling disputes, conflict resolution in education evolved during the peace movement and collective bargaining upsurge in the 1960s. Training usually includes a formal set of procedures to improve one's ability to communicate, problem-solve, diffuse anger, and reach agreements. A school conflict resolution program may include any of the following approaches: training students in negotiation skills via a classroom curriculum, training teachers in negotiation and mediation skills, and training students as peer mediators.

In a peer mediation, program student mediators learn specific procedures to assist disputants with generating their own solutions. Mediators keep the disputants on the topic, help them evaluate their options, and guide them in reaching a balanced solution that both disputants can support. Peer mediation has been successfully implemented at all public school levels. Program evaluations indicate positive results, such as improved self-concept* of disputants and mediators, a decrease in the number of suspensions for fighting, and improved school climate.

See also ANGER CONTROL TRAINING.

REFERENCES

Benson, J., and J. Benson. (1993). *Peer mediation: Conflict resolution in schools. Journal of School Psychology* 31, 427–430.

Van-Slyck, M., and M. Stern. (1991). *Conflict resolution in educational settings: Assessing the impact of peer mediation programs.* New York: Guilford Press.

Leslie Hale

CONJOINT THERAPY. Broderick and Schrader (1981) report that the term ''conjoint therapy'' was coined by Don Jackson in 1959 in order to describe a psychotherapist's meeting together (or conjointly) with both husband and wife. Jackson believed that meeting with both the husband and wife was a more effective intervention for family problems than working with the various family members individually. In 1959, Jackson started the Mental Research Institute, which was devoted to working with families. Later that year he brought in Virginia Satir to work with him at the institute.

Satir, in 1964, published her seminal work on families, *Conjoint Family Therapy.* As a result, Satir was most influential in popularizing the use of conjoint therapy to treat families, as well as to popularize the term ''conjoint therapy.'' Satir, however, changed the focus of her work to the human growth movement in the 1960s and became the first director of the Esalen Institute (Broderick and Schrader, 1981).

Conjoint therapy is not entirely reserved for the treatment of marital problems. Many therapists believe that it is the most effective mode of treatment for individual problems as well. Individuals are seen as parts of larger family systems; the treatment of the system, according to this belief, will necessarily effect change in the individual in need of therapy.

Although conjoint therapy is widely practiced today, the term is somewhat antiquated. Typically, when couples are seen together for relationship problems, this is simply referred to as family therapy,* marital therapy, or couples therapy. When couples or families are seen together for the treatment of an individual in the family, this is most often referred to as systemic therapy.

See also GROUP THERAPY; MARRIAGE AND FAMILY THERAPY.

REFERENCES

Broderick, C. B., and S. S. Schrader. (1981). The history of professional marriage and family therapy. In A. Gurman and D. Kniskern (Eds.), *Handbook of family therapy* (pp. 5–35). New York: Brunner/Mazel.

Satir, V. (1964). *Conjoint family therapy.* Palo Alto: Science and Behavior Books.

Donald L. Boswell

CONSULTATION. Consultation was present in early professional relationships between members of the medical profession during the nineteenth century. One physician would consult with another, assumed to have specialized expertise, about a client the former was treating. This triadic relationship emerged in the 1900s in mental health and education.

Consultation, as we know it today, began in the post–World War II era with the work of Gerald Caplan's mental health consultation.* Behaviorism, community psychology, school psychology,* and organizational development have added perspectives to the growing body of literature on the theory and practice of consultation.

Issues about the presence or lack of theory, locus of consultation, and amount of direct intervention* are only a few areas dealt with from the multiple perspectives of academics and practitioners of consultation.

Many variations of consultation are of particular interest to school psychologists*:

Advocacy consultation*

Behavioral consultation*

Case consultation*

Collaboration*

Collaborative consultation*

Ecological consultation*

Mental health consultation*

Parent consultation*

Problem-solving consultation*

Systems and organizational consultation*

REFERENCES

Brown, D., W. B. Pryzwansky, and A. C. Schulte. (1995). *Psychological consultation: Introduction to theory and practice* (3d ed.). Boston: Allyn and Bacon.
Zins, J. E., and W. P. Erchul. (1995). Best practices in school consultation. In A. Thomas and J. Grimes (Eds.), *Best practices in school psychology—III* (pp. 609–623). Washington, DC: National Association of School Psychologists.

Paul G. Warden

CONTINUING PROFESSIONAL DEVELOPMENT. Continuing professional development (CPD) is participation in activities designed to enhance and upgrade professional skills. The National Association of School Psychologists'* *Continuing Professional Development Program* (1992) lists a number of CPD activities in which school psychologists* may engage. Typical CPD activities include participation in courses, workshops, and independent study programs. Other CPD activities include preparation of publications and presentations, participation in research studies, supervision of interns, and participation in professional organizations.

Commitment to a profession requires a lifetime of learning, particularly for professions in which the knowledge base rapidly changes or grows (Houle, 1980). CPD is necessary for all professionals, including school psychologists, to ensure provision of quality, state-of-the-art services throughout their careers. CPD may also be necessary to expand current job responsibilities or for a career change.

Tucker and Huerta (1984) noted that, although CPD activities grew following World War II, the activities were disorganized until professional accountability* movements in the 1960s. Professionals began to recognize the need for structured CPD activities when public dissatisfaction with professional services increased. In 1970, the continuing education unit (CEU) was created by the National Advisory Commission on Health Manpower and was subsequently adopted for use by many professional agencies.

School psychology* has experienced rapid growth in knowledge, research, ideas, technology, and standards. Thus, graduate training for school psychologists is sufficient to meet professional demands for only a few years following training, and CPD activities are a necessary responsibility of all school psychologists. The ethical standards of the National Association of School Psychologists and the American Psychological Association* require that school psychologists engage in CPD and ongoing education throughout their careers. Many local and state education agencies and credentialing agencies require CPD activities for school psychologists. In addition, nationally certified school psychologists are required to participate in, and document, CPD activities for renewal of certification (NASP, 1992).

See also ACCOUNTABILITY.

REFERENCES

Houle, C. O. (1980). *Continuing learning in the professions.* San Francisco: Jossey-Bass.
National Association of School Psychologists. (1992). *Continuing professional development program.* Silver Spring, MD: Author.
Tucker, B. A., and C. G. Huerta. (1984). *Continuing professional education* (Report No. CE 040 445). Washington, DC: National Institute of Education. (ERIC Document Reproduction Service No. ED 252 674)

Patti L. Harrison

CONTRACTUAL SERVICES. Independent contracting of school psychological services includes a variety of arrangements, including privatization and subcontracting through other public agencies. Local educational agencies (LEAs) may implement privatization through contracts that shift the delivery of services from the public to the private sector.

Examples of privatization in school psychological services include contracts between a school district and one or more individuals or between a district and a private agency, such as a private consulting firm or private mental health clinic. In most states, such individuals or employees of the private agency would be required to hold a license for the independent practice* of psychology but would not necessarily be required to hold a credential as a "school psychologist," depending on the rules of the state board of education.

Private contractors are frequently hired on a per diem or per case basis to provide assessments as required by special education regulations. In some states, particularly where personnel shortages are significant, private contractors may provide full-time or part-time services to small districts where there is no employee available or where district size does not justify hiring a full-time employee. A private agency might contract with several districts to provide only assessment services or a wide range of services as might typically be delivered by a school-based psychologist. Another independent contracting arrangement might exist when community mental health services are "colocated" in the public school setting.

In some parts of the country, particularly in rural areas, LEAs might contract with a public cooperative services agency or special education district to obtain services that may not be practically or economically delivered by small, individual LEAs. The cooperative unit might employ school psychologists who, in turn, provide services to one or more contracting districts. There is evidence that this model can be cost-effective and, in many situations, the only practical means of obtaining fully credentialed service providers (Benson, 1985).

When provided in accordance with recognized professional standards, contractual services can be as comprehensive and effective as school-based services. The National Association of School Psychologists'* (NASP) *Standards for the Provision of School Psychological Services* (NASP, 1992) and *Position Statement: Employing School Psychologists for Comprehensive Service Delivery* (NASP, 1993) address appropriate situations and conditions of contractual services. NASP generally advocates for full-time, school-based services wherever feasible and for the use of contracted services that *supplement,* not supplant, existing employee services.

See also INTERMEDIATE AGENCY; PRIVATE PRACTICE.

REFERENCES

Benson, A. J. (1985). School psychology service configurations: A regional approach. *School Psychology Review* 14, 421–428.
NASP. (1992). *Standards for the provision of school psychological services.* Washington, DC: Author.
———. (1993). *Position statement: Employing school psychologists for comprehensive service delivery.* Washington, DC: Author.

Andrea Canter

COOPERATIVE LEARNING. Cooperative learning models utilize small groups of students who interact in an atmosphere of cooperation to discuss, investigate, and resolve problems. Heterogeneous grouping focuses on individual responsibility and accountability to achieve a group goal. Most models evaluate students' performance based on individual improvement, which is then translated into group achievement. Positive interdependence is fostered, in contrast to negative interdependence, which can be a consequence of competitive learning.

Models vary as to the structuring of task specialization of each student's contribution to task accomplishment. Models also vary as to the amount of attention paid to group processing as a critical function of cooperative learning. The use of intergroup competition varies from model to model. Some models are designed for specific curricular areas (i.e., math, reading), while others have broad application across content areas.

The historical foundations of cooperative learning can be traced to the work of Johann Comenius (1592–1679), to the work of Joseph Lancaster in England during the 1700s, to the common schools movement in the United States in the early 1800s, to John Dewey in this century. More recently, the work of Kurt Lewin with group dynamics and Morton Deutch's work with cooperation versus competition have provided foundational conceptualizations for the current cooperative learning movement, which began in the mid-1970s.

Cooperative learning is a viable method for addressing individual differences* in the regular classroom. More attention should be directed to these models, along with more traditional teaching methods such as peer tutoring.* The emphasis on inclusive education requires school psychologists to encourage teachers to utilize a variety of techniques to meet the learning and social needs of students with disabilities and other students who are at risk.

See also ABILITY GROUPING.

REFERENCES

Brandt, R. S. (Ed.). (1991). *Cooperative learning and the collaborative school.* Alexandria, VA: Association for Supervision and Curriculum Development.
Peterson, D. W., and J. A. Miller. (1990). Best practices in peer-influenced learning. In A. Thomas and J. Grimes (Eds.), *Best practices in school psychology—II* (pp. 531–546). Washington, DC: National Association of School Psychologists.

Paul G. Warden

CORNELL, ETHEL L. Ethel Letitia Cornell (1892–1963; Ph.D. Columbia, 1919) is best remembered for carrying the banner for school psychology* in several settings, including the New York State Department of Education. She coauthored (with Warren W. Coxe)* a widely used performance scale for measuring intelligence* in 1934, initiated certification* requirements for psychologists in the state of New York in 1935, addressed school principals on the role of, and need for, psychologists, and represented school psychologists in the American Psychological Association* (APA).

Her Cornell-Coxe Performance Ability Scale included subtests based on the Army Performance Scale, adapted for primary school children. The subtests were Manikin and Profile (Object Assembly), (Kohs) Block Design, Picture Arrangement (derived from Decroly and Vermeylen), Digit Symbol, Memory for Designs, Cube Construction, and (Healy's) Picture Completion. Similar items later appeared in scales developed by David Wechsler.*

Cornell was a psychologist with the U.S. Army and Boston Psychopathic Hospital before becoming a research associate and psychologist in the New York

State Department of Education in 1920, a position she filled until 1954. New York and Pennsylvania's mid-1930s regulation of school psychologists became a model for other states and, later, for boards licensing psychologists for the nonschool sector.

In addresses and publications, Cornell (1936) emphasized the need for psychologists in schools because of their different points of view, special techniques of diagnosis and analysis, and ability as consultants. After divisions were officially recognized by the American Psychological Association, Cornell served as first secretary and third president of the Division of School Psychologists.

REFERENCES

Cornell, E. L. (1936). The school psychologist's contribution. *National Elementary Principal* 15, 561–566.
————. (1943). *The work of the school psychologist.* (Bulletin #1238). Albany: New York State Education Department.
Cornell, E. L., and W. W. Coxe. (1934) *A performance ability scale examination manual.* Yonkers-on-Hudson, NY: World Book.

Joseph L. French

CORPORAL PUNISHMENT. Corporal punishment (CP) is the infliction of pain to change behavior. The most common types of CP in America are spanking with the hand by parents and paddling with a wooden instrument in school. However, CP includes practices such as pinching, ear twisting, hair pulling, choking, kicking, knuckle rapping, punching, shoving, forcing children to assume physically painful positions, confining them for unreasonably long periods of time (e.g., in time-out), and forcing them to mouth or swallow noxious substances or to exercise to exhaustion. Contrary to the claims of its proponents that it is used only as a "last resort," studies of corporal punishment in schools indicate that it is often the first punishment for nonviolent and minor misbehaviors.

Studies of teachers, parents, and psychologists indicate that the best predictor of support for the use of CP is the amount received as a child. Modeling* is so powerful that childhood experiences of some psychologists cause them to distort theories of learning and development to support their advocacy for the use of CP. Conservative religious and political beliefs, low socioeconomic status (SES), and low educational level are associated with higher support of CP, as is living in rural or conservative areas. Boys, minority and poor children, and those who live in the South and Southwest are the most frequent recipients of CP in home and schools.

The infliction of pain can be very effective in temporarily extinguishing behavior. It is not effective in promoting new learning. When it is excessive, it arouses aggression, which may then be turned against the punisher, peers, or property. Corporal punishment at various frequencies, durations, and intensities can result in posttraumatic stress disorder (PTSD). Excessive use of CP in the home is frequently associated with conduct disorders and may be comorbid with PTSD. Studies indicate a relationship between the amount of CP experienced and, in some cases, witnessed and greater feelings of alienation, depression, delinquent behavior, and lower economic and occupational achievement in adults. Corporal punishment is the least effective method of discipline in almost all situations. Studies in schools demonstrate that eliminating corporal punishment does not increase misbehavior. Anthropological, historical, and contemporary studies indicate that societies can function without using CP.

In 1974, the American Psychological Association* (APA) Council of Representatives passed a resolution opposing corporal punishment in the schools. At that time, New Jersey and Massachusetts were the only states that forbade paddling schoolchildren. Recognizing the lack of an adequate database regarding school corporal punishment, APA and the American Civil Liberties Union (ACLU) helped establish the National Center for the Study of Corporal Punishment and Alternatives in the Schools in the school psychology department at Temple University in 1976. The research conducted by school psychology students has formed the social science database that has been used by advocates, jurists, legislatures, and the media to conduct the long, slow, state-by-state and school-by-school struggle to join almost all Western democracies in banning corporal punishment of schoolchildren.

See also CHILD ADVOCACY; CHILDREN'S RIGHTS; SOCIETY FOR PREVENTION OF CRUELTY TO CHILDREN.

REFERENCES

Hyman, I. (1990). *Reading, writing, and the hickory stick.* Lexington, MA: Lexington Books.

Hyman, I., J. Clarke and R. Erdlen. (1987). An analysis of physical abuse in American schools. *Aggressive Behavior* 13, 1–7.

Hyman, I. A., and J. Wise. (1979). *Corporal punishment in American education.* Philadelphia: Temple University Press.

Irwin A. Hyman

CORRECTIONAL SCHOOL PSYCHOLOGY. Applications of psychology in correctional facilities date to the early part of the twentieth century, especially applications for juvenile offenders. With increased provision of services to exceptional children and the provision of educational programs in correctional settings, opportunities for school psychologist employment in such settings grew. While much has been written about the practice of school psychology* in settings other than the traditional public school district, little has been written about the practice of school psychology in correctional settings. Correctional school psychology is one of several subspecializations of the psychological specialty of school psychology. The services provided by the correctional school psychologist include assessment,* program planning, consultation,* direct interventions,* and evaluation. The correctional subspecialization is linked to that of vocational school psychology,* and training is recommended in that area as well as in adolescent and adult psychology and the juvenile justice system. There are not yet training programs specifically for the correctional school psychology subspecialization.

See also SPECIALTY TRAINING AND CREDENTIALING.

REFERENCES

Morris, R. J., and Y. P. Morris. (1989). School psychology in residential treatment facilities. In R. C. D'Amato and R. S. Dean (Eds.), *The school psychologist in nontraditional settings: Integrating clients, services, and settings* (pp. 159–183). Hillsdale, NJ: Erlbaum.
Timm, F. H., J. Myrick, and J. Rosenberg. (1982). School psychologists in corrections: A new frontier. *Journal for Vocational Special Needs Education* 4(3), 25–28.

Thomas K. Fagan

COUNCIL OF DIRECTORS OF SCHOOL PSYCHOLOGY PROGRAMS.

The Council of Directors of School Psychology Programs (CDSPP) was formed in 1977 under the leadership of Beeman Phillips to promote doctoral-level preparation of school psychologists (Phillips, 1993). CDSPP goals include collecting, exchanging, and disseminating information relevant to doctoral preparation; creating an organization through which members could communicate with the American Psychological Association* (APA) and other organizations concerning issues relevant to doctoral education in school psychology; and assisting doctoral-level school psychology program directors in meeting other common missions.

The birth of CDSPP followed the emergence of doctoral-level school psychology. The American Board of Professional Psychology (ABPP) began awarding diplomates* in school psychology in 1968, and the first doctoral school psychology program was accredited by APA in 1971. As the numbers of doctoral-level programs increased steadily during the late 1970s and 1980s, CDSPP membership did too, growing from thirty-five member institutions in 1978 to seventy-five by 1990.

CDSPP meets yearly during the APA convention.* Over the years, it has devoted considerable attention to the following issues: encouraging more programs to be APA-accredited, developing suitable criteria for accrediting school psychology programs, promoting suitable internship* placements, increasing the accessibility of experienced nondoctoral school psychologists to doctoral education, promoting suitable levels for the credentialing of entry-level practitioners, and increasing the number of school psychologists on APA central office staff.

See also ACCREDITATION; TRAINERS OF SCHOOL PSYCHOLOGISTS; UNIVERSITY TRAINER.

REFERENCE

Phillips, B. N. (1993). Trainers of School Psychologists and Council of Directors of School Psychology Programs: A new chapter in the history of school psychology. *Journal of School Psychology* 31, 91–108.

Thomas Oakland

COUNCIL ON POSTSECONDARY ACCREDITATION. The Council on Postsecondary Accreditation (COPA) was a nongovernmental organization created for the purpose of facilitating and promoting the efforts of accrediting organizations. COPA itself was not an accreditation-granting organization. Until the mid-twentieth century, there were little communication and no coordination among the numerous accrediting bodies that existed across the United States, and specialized accrediting organizations were proliferating. The National Commission on Accrediting (NCA), created largely for the purpose of addressing concerns regarding the growing numbers of specialized accrediting agencies, and the National Committee of Regional Accrediting Agencies emerged. The latter became the Federation of Regional Accrediting Commissions of Higher Education (FRACHE) in 1969. The emergence of accreditation* as a condition for eligibility for federal funding stimulated interest in coordination among the many accrediting organizations. One result was the merger of the NCA and the FRACHE in 1975 to form the COPA.

The purposes of COPA were threefold: (1) to review and recognize accrediting organizations; (2) to facilitate the improvement of the accreditation process; and (3) to promote accreditation at the national level. COPA was organized into three ''assemblies'' to reflect the three primary constituencies among its voluntary membership. The Assembly of Institutional Accrediting Bodies comprised representatives of the nine regional commissions and six national associations that accredit institutions. The Assembly of Specialized Accrediting Bodies included approximately forty specialty organizations (e.g., American Psychological Association* (APA), National Council for Accreditation of Teacher Education* (NCATE)) that accredited professional preparation programs or single-purpose institutions. The Presidents Policy Assembly on Accreditation comprised representatives of seven major national postsecondary institutional organizations that were interested in accreditation but that did not themselves award accreditation (e.g., American Association of State Colleges and Universities).

COPA was governed by a nineteen-member Board of Directors. Disagreement among the different member constituencies, largely over the conflicts that existed prior to the creation of COPA regarding specialty versus institutional accreditation, eventually resulted in a vote by the Board of Directors to dissolve COPA, effective December 31, 1993. Efforts to establish successor organizations (e.g., Association of Specialized and Professional Accreditors, Commission on Recognition of Postsecondary Accreditation, and National Policy Board on

Higher Education Institutional Accreditation) were initiated immediately following the vote of dissolution. Although the eventual status of the emerging agencies remains unclear, the accrediting organizations relevant to school psychology (APA and NCATE) currently have joined one or more of these new associations (e.g., the Commission on Recognition of Postsecondary Accreditors).

See also REGIONAL ACCREDITORS.

REFERENCES

Chernay, Gloria. (undated). *Accreditation and the role of the Council on Postsecondary Accreditation.* Washington, DC: Council on Postsecondary Accreditation.

Council on Postsecondary Accreditation. (1989). *The COPA handbook.* Washington, DC: Author.

Michael J. Curtis

COUNSELING PSYCHOLOGY. Counseling psychology is a doctoral-level specialty of psychology in which the providers are licensed by a state board of examiners of psychologists* to deliver assessment, consultation, and intervention services "intended to help persons acquire or alter personal-social skills, improve adaptability to changing life demands, enhance environmental coping skills, and develop a variety of problem solving and decision-making capabilities" (American Psychological Association, 1981, p. 654). The orientation of services is developmental, with an emphasis on positive aspects of growth.

The taproot of counseling psychology is the vocational guidance movement, which began with Frank Parsons's Vocation Bureau in Boston in 1908. The movement grew after World War I and during the Great Depression of the 1930s. After World War II, university counseling centers were established to meet the vocational and personal needs of returning veterans.

The specialty traces its official inception to the founding of the Division of Counseling and Guidance of the American Psychological Association in 1946. When the profession shifted from its earlier roots of guidance and counseling and vocational counseling, counseling psychology followed the example of clinical psychology* by espousing doctoral-level training, accreditation,* and credentialing requirements through the American Psychological Association (Super, 1955). The growth of the specialty has been less clear than its 1946 inception implies, since subsequent university departments were derived from other counseling areas—school counseling and guidance, marriage and family counseling, student personnel, and vocational rehabilitation counseling. Strife among counseling psychologists and other counselors occasionally has occurred, particularly after a number of states enacted legislation for licensed professional counselors (LPC).

See also CLINICAL PSYCHOLOGY; SCHOOL PSYCHOLOGY.

REFERENCES

American Psychological Association. (1981). Specialty guidelines for the delivery of services by counseling psychologists. *American Psychologist* 36(6), 652–663.

Gelso, C. J., and B. R. Fretz. (1992). *Counseling psychology.* New York: Harcourt Brace Jovanovich.

Super, D. E. (1955). Transition: From vocational guidance to counseling psychology. *Journal of Counseling Psychology* 2, 3–9.

Paul G. Warden

COXE, WARREN W. Warren Winfred Coxe was born in Belvidere, Illinois, on July 19, 1886. He completed his B.S. at Dakota Wesleyan in 1911 and his Ph.D. at Ohio State University in 1923. He was a teacher and an elementary school principal in Minnesota and an assistant director of the Vocational Bureau of the Cincinnati Board of Education from 1916 to 1921 (also during this period he was employed as a psychologist at the Cincinnati General Hospital and a psychological examiner for the army) and then held administrative positions in educational research for the New York State Department of Education from 1923 to retirement. He was president (in 1937) of the New York State Association of Applied Psychologists (NYSAAP, an affiliate of the American Association of Applied Psychologists* [AAAP]) and of the American Statistical Association (1935–1937), a member of the American Educational Research Association* (AERA), and president (in 1930) of the New York State Educational Research Association. He became an associate member of the American Psychological Association* (APA) in 1934 and a fellow in 1937. With reference to the history of school psychology,* it is most notable that he was appointed temporary chairman of the Division of School Psychologists* (Division 16) of the American Psychological Association during its reorganization year, 1944–1945. Thus, Warren W. Coxe was the first executive officer of the division. For unknown reasons, Coxe appears not to have continued in any leadership roles with Division 16 beyond his year of chairmanship. According to the first APA Membership Directory (1948), Coxe was a member of Division 13 (consulting psychology) and apparently did not become a permanent member of Division 16. Coxe helped to develop the Cornell-Coxe Performance Ability Scale and the New York Rating Scale for School Habits.

Thomas K. Fagan

CRISIS INTERVENTION. Crisis intervention refers to helping others respond to critical events in their lives. Young people encounter a variety of crises, from parental divorce and separation to serious illnesses or violent deaths of family members and friends. While individuals react in unique ways to such events, for most people there is a sense of imbalance in their lives, accompanied by feelings of disorientation or confusion, sadness, fear, and/or denial. Such reactions may affect every aspect of a person's life, including physical and mental health, relationships with family and friends, and school or work performance.

School psychologists,* along with school counselors, school social workers, and others, are frequently called upon in times of crisis to help students, school personnel, and others cope with crises. Many school systems in recent years have developed plans for delivering crisis intervention services within schools. Such plans generally specify the personnel who will make up the crisis team, the chain of command, and the procedures to be followed (i.e., Will school be canceled? What services will be available to individual students?).

REFERENCES

Poland, S., G. Pitcher, and P. J. Lazarus. (1995). Best practices in crisis intervention. In A. Thomas and J. Grimes (Eds.), *Best practices in school psychology—III* (pp. 445–458). Washington, DC: National Association of School Psychologists.
———. (1992). *Crisis intervention in the schools.* New York: Guilford Press.
Sandoval, J. (Ed.). (1988). *Crisis counseling, intervention, and prevention in the schools.* Hillsdale, NJ: Erlbaum.

Paula Sachs Wise

CRITERION-REFERENCED ASSESSMENT. Criterion-referenced assessment is a process of collecting data to determine whether students have mastered specific skills when compared to explicit standards or objectives. Traditional criterion-referenced assessment data come from criterion-referenced tests consisting of hierarchically arranged skills. The test results often contribute to instructional planning and student progress decisions. Opponents of criterion-referenced assessments argue that their use encourages educators to teach the test items instead of the skill domains from which the items were sampled. These assessments also have been criticized because the behaviors sampled and mastery standards typically vary among tests, districts, and states.

Minimum competency testing* is a specific form of criterion-referenced assessment that involves evaluation of whether students have mastered basic/routine skills necessary for successful school and life functioning. According to Mizell (1979), state minimum competency testing programs have at least four general features: (1) performance standards/mastery objectives; (2) specific tests; (3) requirements that students must master performance standards before they can advance in grade, graduate, or receive their diploma; and (4) the requirement that remedial courses be provided to students who do not master the performance standards. Minimum competency testing is rooted in the basic skills movement of the 1970s and the educational objectives movement of the 1930s and 1960s. Public concern over student failure to acquire basic skills necessary for successful adult functioning was the impetus for the basic skills movement. Identification of behaviors that students are expected to have acquired by the conclusion of their formal education was the aim of the educational objectives movement. Minimum competency tests provide a resource for persons interested in clarifying essential learning objectives.

Performance, authentic, and portfolio assessments are specific forms of criterion-referenced assessment that are currently popular in the field of education. These assessment approaches differ from minimum competency, traditional criterion, and norm-referenced testing in several ways. The criterion behaviors are complex, rather than basic. The tasks require production rather than selection responding. Data for determining mastery are collected from a variety of sources, rather than solely on the basis of a test. Students and teachers have more influence over assessment content and evaluation criteria.

Performance-based assessments require students to demonstrate/produce criterion behaviors, which are rated by judges. A performance-based spelling task would require students to spell dictated words rather than select correctly spelled words when given multiple choices. Baker, O'Neil, and Linn (1993) describe several common features of performance assessments. The tasks are open-ended and focus on higher-order or complex skills. Context-sensitive strategies are employed, and group performance is emphasized over individual performance. Several types of performance and significant student time are required for task completion, and a significant amount of student choice is allowed. Performance-based assessments measure criterion skills directly, thus increasing their diagnostic and instructional utility.

Authentic assessments are similar to performance-based assessments in the type of behaviors assessed and method of data collection. The real-world context in which students perform criterion behaviors is the primary distinguishing feature. For example, authentic tasks often require students to collaborate with each other because collaboration skills often are used when solving real-world problems.

Portfolio assessment, as defined by Paulson, Paulson, and Meyer (1991), is a "purposeful collection of student work that exhibits the student's efforts, progress, and achievements in one or more areas. The collection must include student participation in selecting content, criteria for selection, criteria for judging merit, and evidence of student reflection" (p. 60). Portfolio assessments provide evidence (e.g., permanent products) that students have mastered instructional objectives. They also facilitate effective communication between parents and teachers at school conferences.

Performance, authentic, and portfolio assessments are rooted in current school restructuring efforts and are offered as alternatives to standardized, norm-referenced,* multiple-choice tests, which have historically dominated school testing programs. Standardized, norm-referenced, multiple-choice testing increased as a result of the basic skills movement. Restructuring efforts began, in part, when educators realized that these increases failed to improve educational outcomes for students. While the alternative assessments, arguably, are more content-valid and useful for instructional planning than the traditional assessments, they have several drawbacks. Perhaps most critical is their limited technical adequacy, which, as Linn, Baker, and Dunbar (1991) argue, should include evidence that intended, rather than unintended, consequences result when the assessments are used. The newer approaches are based on assumptions about their intended and unintended consequences. Proponents believe the assessments increase student and teacher motivation, guide instruction and intervention development, and improve educational outcomes for students. Proponents also believe the assessments do not limit instructional scope, a primary criticism and unintended outcome of traditional testing practices. In addition to limited technical adequacy, performance, authentic, and portfolio assessments are time-intensive to gather and score and lack definitional and procedural clarity, as well as an educational, decision-making framework. Collectively, these drawbacks seriously limit their utility. See Linn et al. (1991) for a discussion of advantages and disadvantages.

See also ALTERNATIVE SERVICE DELIVERY; ASSESSMENT (DIRECT AND INDIRECT).

REFERENCES

Baker, E. L., H. F. O'Neil, and R. L. Linn. (1993). Policy and validity prospects for performance-based assessment. *American Psychologist* 48, 1210–1218.
Linn, R. L., E. L. Baker, and J. B. Dunbar. (1991). Complex, performance-based assessment: Expectations and evaluation criteria. *Educational Researcher* 20 (8), 15–21.
Mizell, M. H. (1979). A citizen's introduction to minimal competency testing. In P. W. Airasian, G. F. Madaus, and J. J. Pedulas (Eds.), *Minimal competency testing* (pp. 5–22). Englewood Cliffs, NJ: Educational Technology Publications.
Paulson, F. L., P. R. Paulson, and C. A. Meyer. (1991). What makes a portfolio a portfolio? *Educational Leadership* 48, 60–64.

Vicki L. Collins

CURRICULUM-BASED ASSESSMENT/CURRICULUM-BASED MEASUREMENT. Curriculum-based assessment (CBA), broadly defined, represents strategies that use direct and repeated assessment of student academic performance in the curriculum to obtain information for educational decision making. CBA procedures emerged within the context of both professional and political change (Shinn, Rosenfield, and Knutson, 1989) as the need to better equip teachers with functional tools for measuring academic progress became increasingly apparent. Specific concerns included the lack of connection between assessment and material students were being taught, as well as the insensitivity of published norm-referenced tests to student growth.

CBA strategies have several commonalities, including (1) materials drawn from the curriculum; (2) tests of relatively short duration; (3) frequent and direct (i.e., production, rather than selection, responses) assessment of students' skills; and (4) direct linkage between data collected and intervention planning. Although not all models are useful or validated for all educational decisions, CBA strategies are not incompatible. Rather, they can be combined, with the selection of a particular strategy depending on the assessment question(s) being answered, logistics, and training (Shinn, Rosenfield, and Knutson, 1989).

Four common CBA models are curriculum-based assessment for instructional design (CBA-ID), criterion-referenced, curriculum-based assessment (CR-CBA), curriculum-based evaluation (CBE), and curriculum-based measurement (CBM). CBA-ID, CR-CBA, and CBE primarily were designed for making instructional planning decisions. CBM was designed primarily for making pupil progress decisions (Shinn, Rosenfield, and Knutson, 1989), although it may be used for a variety of educational decisions. CBM differs from the other models in three crucial ways: (1) it focuses on long-term, rather than short-term, monitoring; (2) it uses standardized assessment procedures; and (3) it has excellent technical adequacy data, especially in the area of reading. Because the three other models do not use standardized procedures and do not have sufficient technical adequacy data, they are limited in their utility for some educational decisions (e.g., eligibility).

Curriculum-based assessment for instructional design (CBA-ID) is defined by Gickling, Shane, and Croskery (as cited in Shinn, Rosenfield, and Knutson, 1989) as a system using a student's ongoing performance in current course content to determine instructional needs, as well as effective and efficient instructional delivery to meet those needs. Its focus is on remediating academic skill deficits for which the curriculum is responsible by ensuring appropriate placement level in curriculum materials. An assumption of this model is that if students are placed appropriately, they will make progress. Long-term progress is not assessed directly. While a drawback of CBA-ID is that it does not employ specific assessment procedures or decision rules, an appealing feature of this model is that a great deal of experience or background in test construction is not needed (Shinn, Rosenfield, and Knutson, 1989).

Criterion-referenced, curriculum-based assessment (CR-CBA) is defined by Blankenship (as cited in Shinn, Rosenfield, and Knutson, 1989) as the direct and frequent measurement of student skills on a series of sequential classroom curriculum objectives. The focus is on determining appropriate instructional content by assessing a variety of behaviors, using formats similar to teacher-made classroom tests (Shinn, Rosenfield, and Knutson, 1989). Although a drawback of CR-CBA is that its use may require more extensive test construction skills, it may be the best available means of assessing student performance in secondary-level curriculum content (Shinn, Rosenfield, and Knutson, 1989).

Curriculum-based evaluation (CBE), according to Howell and Morehead (as cited in Shinn, Rosenfield, and Knutson, 1989), involves testing students on essential components of instruction, analyzing errors, and identifying and incorporating into remediation plans the skills students are lacking. This "task-analytic" model of CBA emphasizes analyzing student errors and providing information in the basic skills areas (e.g., reading). CBE also has been used in the social skills and language areas. In contrast to other CBA models, CBE utilizes a variety of materials, including published norm-referenced tests, if they match the curriculum. If published measures are not used, this model requires extensive test construction skills (Shinn, Rosenfield, and Knutson, 1989).

Curriculum-based measurement (CBM) is a set of systematic procedures for assessing student performance in the basic skill areas of reading, mathematics, spelling, and writing (Deno, 1989). CBM was developed during the late 1970s and early 1980s at the University of Minnesota Institute for Research on Learning Disabilities (IRLD). According to Deno (1985), these measures were conceptualized as "vital signs" of student achievement. Characteristics of CBM measures include that they are technically adequate, simple and efficient to use (e.g., brief), easily understood, inexpensive, and sensitive to student growth over short periods of time (Deno, 1985). Also, both level and slope of progress can be obtained, and CBM data can be displayed graphically.

CBM is unique in that it provides a continuous database useful across a variety of educational decisions from problem identification to problem solution, and it can be tied to local norms (Shinn, Rosenfield, and Knutson, 1989). Importantly, CBM is useful for evaluating instructional plans and outcomes. The other models are more prescriptive for instruction. CBM "theoretically is based on the assumption that effective instruction can be determined only by evaluating the effects of teaching plans. CBM assumes that determining what will work with individual students cannot be determined in advance with any certainty, regardless of the amount or quality of the assessment data" (Shinn, Rosenfield, and Knutson, 1989, p. 302). When CBM is used to evaluate and alter instructional programs, student achievement increases.

See also ACADEMIC ASSESSMENT; ASSESSMENT (DIRECT AND INDIRECT); CRITERION-REFERENCED ASSESSMENT.

REFERENCES

Deno, S. L. (1985). Curriculum-based measurement: The emerging alternative. *Exceptional Children* 52, 219–232.
———. (1989). Curriculum-based measurement and special education services: A fundamental and direct relationship. In M. R. Shinn (Ed.), *Curriculum-based measurement: Assessing special children* (pp. 1–17). New York: Guilford Press.
Gickling, E. E., and S. Rosenfield. (1995). Best practices in curriculum-based assessment. In A. Thomas and J. Grimes (Eds.), *Best practices in school psychology—III* (pp. 587–595). Washington, DC: National Association of School Psychologists.
Shinn, M. R., S. Rosenfield, and N. Knutson. (1989). Curriculum-based assessment: A comparison of models. *School Psychology Review* 18, 299–316.

Kelly A. Powell-Smith

CUTTS, NORMA E. Norma Estelle Cutts was born in New Haven, Connecticut, on September 23, 1892, and died in Deerfield Beach, Florida, on September 3, 1988. After graduating from Mount Holyoke College in 1913, she worked with Henry Goddard* at the Vineland Training School and then with Arnold L. Gesell* in Connecticut. She received her master's degree in 1922 and her Ph.D. in 1933 at Yale University. She was a special-class teacher of mentally handicapped children (1914–1918), and supervisor, Department of Testing, Psychology, and Atypical Education in the New Haven public schools (1918–1947). She was among the earliest school psychologists in Connecticut and fostered the improvement of services, including the establishment in 1942 of certification* through the State Board of Education. She edited the proceedings of the

Thayer conference* on school psychology* published in 1955. Her last position was as principal of Florida's Hillsboro County Day School (1957–1963). In 1966, she was awarded the Florida Association of School Psychologists' first honorary membership.

REFERENCE

Fagan, T. K. (1989). Obituary: Norma Estelle Cutts. *American Psychologist* 44, 1236.

Thomas K. Fagan

D

DEFAMATION OF CHARACTER. Defamatory communications expose another person to ridicule, diminished esteem, or contempt in the estimation of the community. "Libel" refers to a publication that injures the reputation of another; "slander" refers to spoken words that harm the reputation of another. In defamation lawsuits, the courts consider issues such as whether the communication was false, whether it was made with malicious intent, whether the person's reputation was damaged, and whether the defamed person suffered other losses as a result of the communication. Courts generally recognize the special circumstances of communications made by psychologists in their professional role. Statements made by psychologists are "conditionally privileged." This means that when psychologists make reports about their clients, their communications will not be held libelous as long as their statements are professionally sound and in good faith and made only as required or permitted by their jobs.

See also CONFIDENTIALITY; DUTY TO WARN; PRIVILEGED COMMUNICATION.

REFERENCES

Eades, R. W. (1986). The school counselor or psychologist and problems of defamation. *Journal of School Law* 15, 117–120.
Iverson v. Frandsen, 237 F.2d 898 (10th Cir. 1956).

Susan Jacob-Timm

DEPARTMENT OF HEALTH AND HUMAN SERVICES. The U.S. Department of Health and Human Services (HHS) is a presidential, cabinet-level department and the U.S. government's principal agency for protecting health and providing essential human services to Americans. Administering some 250 separate programs, the department's budget of $641 billion (fiscal year [FY]

1994) is the largest budget among federal departments and higher than the total budgets of most governments. The largest single program within the department is Social Security and Medicare. HHS's National Institutes of Health (NIH) comprise the world's largest medical research center, and the Food and Drug Administration (FDA) regulates products that account for some twenty-five cents of every dollar spent by American consumers. The department's 127,000 employees work in every state and several other countries. HHS has four operating divisions: Public Health Service, Social Security Administration, Health Care Financing Administration, and Administration for Children and Families. The department provides services that protect and advance the quality of life for all Americans, with an emphasis on those least able to help themselves. HHS provides income support or direct services to more than one in every five Americans.

The Department of Health, Education and Welfare was established in 1953 by President Dwight Eisenhower. It was previously a part of the Federal Security Agency, formed in 1939. Earlier activities related to these services were developed as far back as 1789, when the first marine hospital was established. This national hospital was the forerunner of today's Public Health Service, which remains a military service under the command of the surgeon general. The present focus on children and families is attributed to President Theodore Roosevelt's first White House Conference on Children (1912). In 1979, the Department of Education became a separate cabinet-level department, and the present Department of Health and Human Services was established in 1990. Contact: Department of Health and Human Services, 200 Independence Avenue, SW, Washington, DC 20201.

See also OFFICE OF SPECIAL EDUCATION PROGRAMS.

Kevin P. Dwyer

DEVELOPMENTAL THERAPY. Developmental therapy is a comprehensive approach to treatment of emotionally disturbed, behaviorally disordered, and autistic children ages two through sixteen. Mary M. Wood produced a system that draws from theory and research in social learning, operant learning, developmental psychology, and psychodynamics. Her system, first reported in the early 1970s, focuses on five stages of development, beginning with rudimentary skills in the social, behavioral, communication, and (pre)academic areas and progressing to independent skill mastery allowing the student to function within the regular classroom.

The curriculum is designed to be used with four to eight students in a resource-room structure as well as in a full-day program. A lead teacher and a support teacher provide an individualized program for each student; however, the focus of the classroom environment is positive participation. The four areas of curriculum and the teaching techniques are dependent on formative and summative assessment utilizing the Referral Form Checklist, composed of fifty-four behaviorally stated problems, and the Developmental Therapy Objectives Rating

Form, composed of 171 objectives. Both are utilized as criterion-referenced as-sessment* instruments, referenced to the scope and sequence of the curricular areas.

Thirteen primary therapeutic teacher techniques are presented, stressing the suitability of each technique for each stage of development. For instance, to build trust and social belonging, body contact and touch are a major technique at stage one but either seldom or not used at stage five; the opposite is true for another technique, life-space intervention. Home programs and services for par-ents/guardians are included in the system.

REFERENCES

Wood, M. M. (1982). Developmental therapy: A model for therapeutic intervention in
    the schools. In C. R. Reynolds and T. B. Gutkin (Eds.), *The handbook of
    school psychology* (pp. 609–628). New York: Wiley.
————. (Ed.). (1975). *Developmental therapy.* Baltimore: University Park Press.
————. (1979). *The developmental therapy objectives: A self-instructional workbook*
    (3d ed.). Baltimore: University Park Press.

Paul G. Warden

DIAGNOSTIC TEACHING. The term "diagnostic teaching" was first used by Lightner Witmer* in 1925 to describe the process whereby a psychologist uses test instruments to examine "teachability on a minimum of instruction" (p. 4). A term synonymous to diagnostic teaching is "precision teaching."* In the early 1970s, the term "precision teaching" was used to describe the system-atic evaluation of instruction and curricula by a teacher (Lindsley, 1974). More recently, "diagnostic teaching" has been used to describe the relationship be-tween assessment and instruction (Lerner, 1981). The teacher or other school staff member carefully identifies the reasons a student is failing to learn targeted skills, through an analysis of the student's current level of functioning. A stu-dent's current level of functioning can be assessed through such procedures as curriculum-based assessment* or measurement, task analysis, or other objective assessments. Following the assessment, the teacher uses the information ob-tained to develop specific instructional activities and sequences in order to en-sure that the student makes gains.

See also DYNAMIC ASSESSMENT.

REFERENCES

Lerner, J. W. (1981). *Learning disabilities: Theories, diagnosis, and teaching
    strategies* (3d ed.). Boston: Houghton Mifflin.
Lindsley, O. R. (1974). Precision teaching in perspective. In S. Kirk and F. Lord
    (Eds.), *Exceptional children: Educational resources and perspectives* (pp. 477–
    482). Boston: Houghton Mifflin.
Shapiro, E. S. (1989). *Academic skills problems: Direct assessment and intervention.*
    New York: Guilford.

Karen T. Carey

DIFFERENTIAL DIAGNOSIS. Differential diagnosis involves distinguishing between the types of disorders included in the official nomenclature systems. In differential diagnosis, the goal is to differentiate and identify the etiological factors that distinguish two disorders by discovering the critical symptoms that are specific to one but not the other. Woody, LaVoie, and Epps (1992) indicated that for school psychology, the *Diagnostic and Statistical Manual of Mental Disorders IV* (American Psychiatric Association, 1994) and federal legislation (i.e., Public Law 94-142*) define the primary nosological categories used in the process of making a differential diagnosis. When properly used, differential diagnosis expedites the planning of appropriate treatment and research (Weiner, 1977). In addition, differential diagnosis based on the criteria defined in the nomenclature increases communication among professionals by creating consistency within the profession. Weiner (1977) also recommends the use of the following data when making a differential diagnosis: (1) presenting symptoms, (2) case history, (3) behavioral observations, and (4) psychological tests.

See also CLASSIFICATION: EDUCATIONAL; CLASSIFICATION: PSYCHIATRIC.

REFERENCES

American Psychiatric Association. (1994). Diagnostic and statistical manual of mental disorders (4th ed.). Washington, DC: Author.
Weiner, I. B. (1977). Differential diagnosis: Mental tests. In B. Wolman (Ed.), *International encyclopedia of psychiatry, psychology, psychoanalysis, and neurology* (pp. 104–108). New York: Aesculapius.
Woody, R. H., J. C. LaVoie, and S. Epps. (1992). *School psychology: A developmental and social systems approach.* Boston: Allyn and Bacon.

David E. McIntosh, Jr.

DIPLOMATE. Professionals who practice their specialties within a profession often are expected to hold special credentials that signify their advanced levels of abilities in prescribed and important areas. Special credentials may be awarded after one has obtained suitable academic and professional preparation, has been licensed at the state level, has been in both general and specialized practice for some years, and has successfully completed an examination process that focuses on the specialty. Following this process, professionals may use such terms as ''board-certified,'' ''board-certified specialist,'' or ''diplomate'' when referring to their specialized competencies.

The American Board of Examiners in Professional Psychology was established in 1947 and later evolved into the American Board of Professional Psychology (ABPP). The primary purpose of ABPP is to credential advanced levels in the practice of psychology. ABPP initially awarded diplomates in clinical, counseling, and industrial psychology. It began awarding the diplomate in school psychology* in 1968; the first recipient was Virginia Bennett. Mary Alice White, a member of the ABPP Board of Trustees, was instrumental in encouraging the board to provide a diplomate in school psychology. Others instrumental in this movement included Jack Bardon,* Julia Vane, and Jan Duker. By 1980, about 12 percent of all diplomates awarded by the board were in the specialty of school psychology. In 1992, the once-monolithic ABPP was divided into nine separately incorporated specialty boards, each responsible for credentialing one specialty; all specialty boards remain affiliated with ABPP. The American Board of School Psychology was charged with responsibilities for conducting the credential review process, developing and administering the diplomate examinations, and recommending the names of candidates for receipt of the diplomate in school psychology to ABPP, which continues to award the diplomates in all nine areas (Pryzwansky, 1993).

REFERENCE

Pryzwansky, W. B. (1993). The regulation of school psychology: A historical perspective on certification, licensure, and accreditation. *Journal of School Psychology* 13, 219–235.

Thomas Oakland

DIRECT SERVICE DELIVERY. Direct service delivery refers to the personal provision of services to clients, such as psychotherapy, counseling, or skills training. Within the practice of school psychology,* direct services include activities such as crisis counseling with a suicidal student, self-management or social skills training* of individuals or groups, or counseling of pregnant teens. Assessment* activities are sometimes considered ''direct services'' because the psychologist collects information directly from the client* (interviewing, testing), although it can also be argued that assessment per se is not a ''service'' but an activity that leads to client services.

Direct psychological services require a significant commitment of professional time and are often impractical in school settings due to the limited availability of psychologists. Schools and other agencies must balance the immediate impact of direct services on a small number of clients versus the potential and longer-term impact of indirect services* on a much larger pool of clients. Although generally less cost-effective, direct services have no intermediary steps; the treatment is not dependent on the training, motivation, or resources of a third party. A combination of direct and indirect services, balanced to best fit the needs of the student population, offers the most flexible model of comprehensive service delivery.

See also ASSESSMENT (DIRECT AND INDIRECT); INTERVENTION (DIRECT AND INDIRECT).

REFERENCE

Conoley, J., and T. Gutkin. (1986). School psychology: A reconceptualization of service delivery realities. In S. Elliott and J. Witt (Eds.), *The delivery of psychological services in schools: Concepts, processes, and issues* (pp. 393–424). Hillsdale, NJ: Erlbaum.

Thomas, A., and J. Grimes (Eds.). (1995). *Best practices in school psychology—III.* Washington, DC: National Association of School Psychologists.

Andrea Canter

DISCREPANCY IN ASSESSMENT OF LEARNING DISABILITIES. Federal rules and regulations specify (in part) that "a severe discrepancy between achievement and intellectual ability in one or more" of seven specified achievement areas must be noted in determining the existence of a specific learning disability (LD) (U.S. Department of Education, 1992, p. 44823). Over the past thirty years, several approaches to assessing severe discrepancies have been proposed. Early models examined prescribed deviations from grade level or used expectancy formulas. *Grade-level deviation* methods (i.e., one to two years below grade level or graduated deviations for older students) fail to consider intellectual differences and tend to overidentify students with below-average intelligence while underidentifying those with above-average intelligence. *Expectancy formula* methods attempt to estimate or predict expected achievement from mental and/or chronological ages and intelligence test (IQ) scores. These methods also tend to overidentify students with below-average IQs and underidentify students with above-average IQs. Statistical assumptions are violated in treating grade-equivalent values as interval data in performing mathematical operations.

The *standard score difference* method provides a simple comparison between the child's intellectual ability and academic achievement when both measures are expressed in the same units of measurement. This method, although popular and simple, fails to consider regression to the mean effects and thus overidentifies children with above-average IQs while underidentifying children with below-average IQs. Another method of discrepancy used in diagnosis of LD examines profiles or patterns in subtest performance on intelligence tests like the Wechsler Intelligence Scale for Children-Third Edition (WISC-III). Discrepancies between verbal and performance IQs as well as the ACID pattern (low Arithmetic, Coding, Information, and Digit Span) have been hypothesized to reflect LD. These methods should not be used to diagnose LD, as they have yet to be validated and fail to consider levels of academic achievement.

A federal work group on measurement issues in LD assessment recommended the use of a regression approach in quantifying the severe discrepancy between achievement and intellectual ability (Reynolds, 1984). The regression definition is based on comparing the difference between predicted achievement (based on the individual's intellectual ability) and actual achievement. This difference is then evaluated with regard to the standard error of estimate to determine if the difference is statistically significant based on a selected significance level.

See also ACADEMIC ASSESSMENT: TRADITIONAL; NORM-REFERENCED ASSESSMENT.

REFERENCES

Heath, C. P., and J. C. Kush. (1991). Use of discrepancy formulas in the assessment
    of learning disabilities. In J. E. Obrzut and G. W. Hynd (Eds.),
    *Neuropsychological foundations of learning disabilities: A handbook of issues,
    methods, and practice* (pp. 287–307). San Diego: Academic Press.
Kavale, K. A., S. R. Forness, and M. Bender. (1987). *Handbook of learning
    disabilities,* Vol. 1, *Dimensions and diagnosis.* Boston: Little, Brown.
Reynolds, C. R. (1984). Critical measurement issues in learning disabilities. *Journal of
    Special Education* 18, 1–26.
U.S. Department of Education. (1992). Assistance to states for the education of
    children with disabilities program and preschool grants for children with
    disabilities. *Federal Register* 57, 44794–44852.

Gary L. Canivez

DISSENTING OPINION. A dissenting (or minority) opinion occurs when the
school psychologist* is in disagreement with the conclusions and/or actions
taken by a decision-making team of which the psychologist is a part. Dissenting
opinions were considered important enough to be referenced in the first and
each revised edition of the National Association of School Psychologists*
(NASP) *Standards for the Provision of School Psychological Services.* "The
School Psychologist communicates a written minority position to all involved
when in disagreement with the multi-disciplinary team position" (NASP, 1992,
section 3.5.2.3).

While not specific to school psychology, the Rules and Regulations for the
Individuals with Disabilities Education Act (Public Law 101-476*) (57 FR
44823, September 29, 1992) require a written statement attached to the team
report when the report does not reflect a team member's conclusions.

Underscoring the importance of a dissenting opinion is the school psychologist's ethical responsibility as an advocate for clients' rights and welfare (NASP,
1992, section IV.A.1). A minority opinion may also be an essential document
if the ultimate team decision proves ineffective.

See also CODES OF ETHICS; PROFESSIONAL STANDARDS; SECOND
OPINION; TEAM APPROACH.

REFERENCE

NASP (1992). *Professional conduct manual.* Silver Spring, MD: Author.

Timothy S. Hartshorne

DIVISION OF SCHOOL PSYCHOLOGY. The Division of School Psychology of the American Psychological Association* (APA) was the first national
organization explicitly chartered to represent the interests of school psychologists in the United States. It came into existence as the sixteenth of the nineteen
charter divisions in the reorganized APA of 1945–1946. The restructuring of
APA at this time was stimulated by the merger of APA with several groups,

including the American Association of Applied Psychologists,* which had an educational, as well as clinical, section, to which many school psychologists belonged (Fagan, Hensley, and Delugach, 1986).

In 1948, the division had 90 members (1.8 percent of APA membership); by 1953, it had 298 (2.7 percent); by 1963, it had 856 (4.1 percent); and by 1973, it had 2,505 (7.1 percent). The largest membership reached was in 1976, with 2,629 members, which represented 6.3 percent of APA membership. By 1983, membership had dropped to 2,233 (4.0 percent), a figure that has remained fairly stable up to 1993, when membership was 2,104 (3.0 percent of APA membership).

The 1987 divisional bylaws state the objectives of the division:

a. To promote and maintain high standards of professional education and training within the specialty, and to expand appropriate scientific and scholarly knowledge and the pursuit of scientific affairs;
b. To increase effective and efficient conduct of professional affairs, including the practice of psychology within the schools, among other settings, and collaboration/cooperation with individuals, groups, and organizations in the shared realization of Division objectives;
c. To support the ethical and social responsibilities of the specialty, to encourage opportunities for ethnic minority participation in the specialty, and to provide opportunities for professional fellowship;
d. To encourage and effect publications, communications, and conferences regarding the activities, interests, and concerns within the specialty on a regional, national and international basis. (APA, 1991, p. 3)

The first presidents of the division were Warren Coxe* (1944–1945), Morris Krugman* (1945–1946), Harry J. Baker* (1946–1947), and Margaret A. Hall (1947–1948). Other early officers were Milton A. Saffir (1946–1949), first secretary-treasurer; and Fred Brown (1945), first representative to counsel. The position of treasurer, first held by James R. Hobson, was created in 1952 (Fagan, 1993). The division's name was changed in 1969 from Division of School Psychologists to Division of School Psychology.

In 1977, the division phased in four additional positions, termed monitors in place of the members-at-large offices. These positions were restructured in 1987 as vice president for education and training and scientific affairs, vice president for professional affairs, vice president for social and ethical responsibility and ethnic minority affairs, and vice president for publications, communications, and convention affairs.

Besides activities in publication, policy development, convention organization, and working with the boards and committees of APA, the division recognizes members through awards, including fellow status, Lightner Witmer* Award, Distinguished Service Award, Senior Scientist Award, and Dissertation Award.

See also AMERICAN PSYCHOLOGICAL ASSOCIATION ANNUAL CONVENTION; CODES OF ETHICS; PROFESSIONAL STANDARDS.

REFERENCES

American Psychological Association, Division of School Psychology. (1991). *Policy and procedures handbook.* Washington, DC: Author.
Fagan, T. K. (1993). Separate but equal: School psychology's search for organizational identity. *Journal of School Psychology* 31, 3–90.
Fagan, T. K., L. T. Hensley, and F. J. Delugach. (1986). The evolution of organizations for school psychologists in the United States. *School Psychology Review* 15, 127–135.

Jonathan Sandoval

DOCTORAL DEGREE. The doctoral degree is currently awarded by 80 of 208 school psychology* programs responding to a recent survey of training programs (Smith and Henning, in press). Of these programs, 25 offer a doctoral degree only, while the remaining 55 programs offer a doctoral degree as well as a master's* and/or specialist degree.* Consistent with previous studies (Brown, 1990; McMaster, Reschly, and Peters, 1989), the Ph.D. is the most common doctoral degree offered, followed by the Ed.D. and Psy.D. The number of programs offering the Ph.D. increased from 59 in 1988 (McMaster, Reschly, and Peters, 1989) to 71 in 1993 (Smith and Henning, in press), while the number of programs offering the Psy.D. increased from 6 to 7, and the number of programs offering the Ed.D. decreased from 16 to 10. Required credits for doctoral degrees range from 81 to 140 semester credits, with an average of 104 credits.

See also PROFESSIONAL TRAINING MODEL; SCIENTIST-PRACTITIONER MODEL; TRAINING MODELS.

REFERENCES

Brown, D. T. (1990). Professional regulation and training in school psychology. In T. B. Gutkin and C. R. Reynolds (Eds.), *The handbook of school psychology* (2d ed., pp. 991–1009). New York: Wiley.
McMaster, M. D., D. J. Reschly, and J. M. Peters. (1989). *Directory of school psychology graduate programs* (3d ed.). Washington, DC: National Association of School Psychologists.
Smith, D. K., and A. Henning. (in press). *Directory of school psychology graduate programs* (4th ed.). Washington, DC: National Association of School Psychologists.

Douglas K. Smith

DOCTORAL-NONDOCTORAL ISSUE. The doctoral-nondoctoral issue represents the historical debate over the minimum amount of training necessary for practice as a psychologist. This is commonly referred to as the *entry level.* This debate has perhaps been most strident in the areas of school psychology* and clinical psychology.* After World War II, the American Psychological Association* (APA) directed most of its resources toward representing academic and clinical psychology. This was a precipitating factor in the formation of the National Association of School Psychologists* (NASP) in 1969. In 1977, the APA adopted a new set of standards for providers of psychological services. These standards specified that the doctoral degree* was the minimum or entry-level degree for practice as a "psychologist." The adoption of this position further alienated APA from NASP. It was contrary to the NASP philosophical position of allowing a *continuum* of training to exist for psychologists, as had been advocated by NASP since the early 1970s (Patros, Gross, and Bjorn, 1972). The NASP position was also based on the lack of any significant research to support the doctoral degree as the entry level. At that time, over two-thirds of training programs for school psychologists in the country were at the nondoctoral level. In 1977, NASP began advocating the sixth-year or specialist degree* as the entry level for school psychology. Even this position met resistance from individual states and graduate training programs throughout the country, many of which were training at the master's* level.

From the standpoint of most school psychologists, APA appeared to have adopted the doctoral-level standard for political reasons. Central to this political process was the desire on the part of many clinical psychologists to achieve parity with the medical profession. As Bardon (1979) argued, other motivations existed for requiring the doctoral degree. APA was in the process of revising accreditation standards and attempting to standardize accreditation* and service provision standards for psychologists throughout the country. APA also was attempting to standardize the licensure and certification process. This effort was represented as an attempt to improve the minimum quality of services provided by psychologists nationally. It was viewed by many school psychologists as an attempt to restrain trade by requiring the doctoral level for comprehensive practice in or outside schools.

By 1979, the field of school psychology was experiencing rapid growth. The number of training programs for school psychologists had increased from 45 in 1962 to 203 (Brown and Lindstrom, 1978). An explosion in the number and diversity of school psychologists was emerging, and many initiatives had been undertaken by NASP in conjunction with Division 16 of APA to lay the foundation for the complete professionalization of school psychology. These included two important initiatives: the development of service provision standards for school psychologists and the development and implementation of accreditation standards for school psychology at the doctoral and nondoctoral levels. The training standards were, in part, implemented through the National Council for Accreditation of Teacher Education* (NCATE).

At about the same time, discussions began regarding the apparent jurisdictional conflict between APA and NCATE in accrediting doctoral-level school psychology programs. The NCATE was, and still is, the sole accrediting agency for nondoctoral school psychology programs. In 1978, the APA/NASP Task Force on Accreditation and Credentialing was formed to improve collaboration among NASP, APA, Division 16, and NCATE. The task force developed joint criteria for accreditation of training programs at the doctoral level in school psychology. As a result of these efforts, a permanent communication link was established among NASP, Division 16, APA, and NCATE. A closer alliance among Division 16, NASP, and APA eventually developed and led to greater advocacy for the needs of children. These groups continue to collaborate in the joint accreditation of the doctoral programs in school psychology. APA does not participate in the accreditation of nondoctoral programs but does, in essence, accept the specialist degree as entry level for school psychology as recognized by NASP.

See also CERTIFICATION; LICENSING; PROFESSIONAL STANDARDS; SPECIALTY TRAINING AND CREDENTIALING.

REFERENCES

Bardon, J. (1979). How best to establish the identity of professional school psychology. *School Psychology Digest* 8, 162–167.
Brown, D. T., and J. P. Lindstrom. (1978). The training of school psychologists in the United States: An overview. *Psychology in the Schools* 15, 37–45.
Fagan, T. K. (Ed.). (1994). Symposium: Will the real school psychologist please stand up?: Is the past a prologue for the future of school psychology. *School Psychology Review* 23, 560–603.
Patros, P. G., F. P. Gross, and N. Bjorn. (1972). *A survey of institutions offering graduate training in school psychology.* Washington, DC: National Association of School Psychologists.

Douglas T. Brown

DOLL, EDGAR A. Edgar Arnold Doll was born on May 2, 1889, in Cleveland, Ohio, and died on October 22, 1968, in Bellingham, Washington. Doll received the A.B. degree in education at Cornell (1912), the Pd.M. (master of paedology) in education at New York University (1916), and his Ph.D. at Princeton (1920). His career positions included an instructorship at the University of Wisconsin (1912–1913), assistant psychologist with H. H. Goddard* at the Vineland (New Jersey) Training School (1913–1917), director of the Division of Education for the New Jersey Department of Institutions and Agencies (1919–1923), assistant professor of clinical and abnormal psychology at Ohio State University (1923–1925), director of research at Vineland (1925–1949), coordinator of research at the Devereux Schools (Devon, Pennsylvania, 1949–1953), and consultant to the Bellingham, Washington, Public School District from 1953 until his death. His contributions to the history of school psychological services include his classification of the mentally retarded, especially their social and adaptive behavior, and the development of special educational programs. His accomplishments included the Vineland Social Maturity Scale (first published in 1935), his book *The Measurement of Social Competence* in 1953, and his Preschool Attainment Record in 1966. He also served in leadership positions and received several awards.

See also ADAPTIVE BEHAVIOR.

REFERENCES

Doll, E. E. (1969). Edgar Arnold Doll, 1889–1968. *American Journal of Mental Deficiency* 73, 561–682.
Doll, E. E. (1969). Edgar A. Doll: Research and application. Unpublished manuscript presented at the Annual Convention, American Psychological Association, San Francisco, 1991.

Thomas K. Fagan

DUAL DIAGNOSIS. Dual diagnosis is defined as the use of two diagnoses when a patient meets the diagnostic criteria of two different and/or related disorders. Dual diagnosis has also been referred to as comorbidity or the copresence of two disorders (First and Gladis, 1993). The application of a dual diagnosis by clinicians has become more common in recent years with the increased complexity of patients who present with multiple symptomatology. For example, the use of a dual diagnosis appears to be most common among older children and adults who present with a psychiatric disorder and a substance disorder or developmental disorder. Among children diagnosed with an oppositional defiant disorder, it is not uncommon for them also to be diagnosed with an attention-deficit disorder with hyperactivity or a developmental learning disability. Children diagnosed as having a learning disability are also often diagnosed with mild depression. The copresence of a disruptive behavior disorder with a diagnosis of mental retardation is also common. Typically, patients with a dual diagnosis are more difficult to treat and have a poorer prognosis. When making a dual diagnosis, most practitioners identify the primary diagnosis that results in the secondary diagnosis. In other situations, both disorders are considered primary, indicating that neither disorder is secondary to the other. Clinicians also identify the "principal" diagnosis that is the main focus of treatment as compared to "primary" diagnosis that identifies the disorder that occurred first (Moras and Barlow, 1992).

See also CLASSIFICATION: EDUCATIONAL; CLASSIFICATION: PSYCHIATRIC.

REFERENCES

First, M. B., and M. M. Gladis. (1993). Diagnosis and differential diagnosis of psychiatric and substance use disorders. In J. Solomon, S. Zimberg, and E. Shollar (Eds.), *Dual diagnosis: Evaluation, treatment, training, and program development* (pp. 23–37). New York: Plenum Medical Book.
Moras, K., and D. H. Barlow. (1992). Dimensional approaches to diagnosis and the problem of anxiety and depression. In A. Ehlers, W. Fiegenbaum, I. Florin, and J. Margraf (Eds.), *Perspectives and promises of clinical psychology* (pp. 23–37). New York: Plenum Press.

David E. McIntosh, Jr.

DUE PROCESS. The Fourteenth Amendment of the U.S. Constitution states, "No State shall make or enforce any law which shall abridge the privileges or immunities of citizens of the United States; nor shall any State deprive any person of life, liberty, or property, without due process of law." Courts have identified two aspects of due process: substantive and procedural. Substantive due process applies to the content of a law. A state may not pass a law that deprives citizens of life, liberty, or property if the law is not related to a legitimate governmental purpose; arbitrary and capricious laws that infringe on citizen rights will be declared unconstitutional. In the public schools, substantive due process has been interpreted to mean that school rules that restrict student rights must be reasonably related to the purpose of schooling (see *Tinker v. Des Moines Independent Community School District,* 1969).

Procedural due process means that a state may not take away life, a liberty interest, or a property right (often a right granted under statutory law) without some sort of procedural fairness to safeguard citizens from unfair or wrongful infringement of rights by the government. Notice (being told what action the state proposes to take and the reason for that action) and the opportunity to be heard (e.g., a hearing) are the minimum requirements of procedural due process. Access to a public school education is a property right created by state law and protected by the Fourteenth Amendment due process clause. In *Goss v. Lopez* (1975), the Supreme Court held that schools may not suspend pupils for more than ten days (and thereby deprive them of their property right) without some sort of fair, impartial due process procedures that include notice and the opportunity to be heard. Statutory law also grants pupils with disabilities the right to a free education appropriate to individual needs in the least restrictive setting. Special education law specifies a number of due process safeguards (e.g., impartial hearings) to ensure that schools do not deny eligible children their entitlement.

See also PROCEDURAL SAFEGUARDS; SUSPENSION AND EXPULSION.

REFERENCES

Bersoff, D. N., and P. T. Hofer. (1990). The legal regulation of school psychology. In T. B. Gutkin and C. R. Reynolds (Eds.), *The handbook of school psychology* (2d ed., (pp. 937–961). New York: Wiley.
Goss v. Lopez, 419 U.S. 565 (1975).
Tinker v. Des Moines Independent Community School District, 393 U.S. 503 (1969).

                                                                                    Susan Jacob-Timm

DUTY TO WARN (TARASOFF). In the mid-1970s, a young foreign student named Poddar, attending the University of California–Berkeley, fell in love with a young woman student from Brazil named Tatania Tarasoff. Poddar told a psychologist at the university's counseling center that unless Tatania responded positively to him when she started the fall semester, he intended to kill her. The psychologist took this threat seriously and notified campus security. He asked that Poddar be picked up and taken to the psychiatric unit at a local hospital as an emergency commitment. Two officers talked to Poddar, decided he was not serious, and released him. When Tatania returned in the fall, Poddar murdered her. Her family filed a lawsuit charging "wrongful death"; but common law said that in order for one to have responsibility for the safety of another, some "special relationship" (spouse, parent, child, and so on) had to exist between the two. The psychologist responded that he didn't even know Tatania, and the court dismissed the suit.

In a series of appeals, the case finally reached the California Supreme Court—at that time a highly respected court whose decisions often broke new legal ground. This court held that the Tarasoffs had a basis for their lawsuit and that the relationship between the psychologist and Poddar was enough to present a duty to act in Tatania's defense.

Since that time, a number of courts in other states have followed this precedent, defining further when a duty to warn exists: whenever a psychologist knows, or has reason to know, that his or her client intends to seriously harm someone in the immediate future. There must be a specific target for the client's hostility (not just, "He's going to hurt someone"), and even if that person is not named, if the therapist should be able to figure out who it is, he or she must act in some way that could reasonably prevent the client's intended act (e.g., call the police).

Recognizing that a therapist who acted thus might face a lawsuit for breach of confidence from a client who, in retrospect, was not serious, many states have now passed statutes (often called "Duty to Warn" or "Duty to Protect") that state that when a mental health professional warns of a client's intent to harm, he or she cannot be sued unless the client can prove the warning was prompted by malice.

See also CLIENT; CONFIDENTIALITY; *TARASOFF v. REGENTS OF CALIFORNIA*.

REFERENCE

Fulero, S. M. (1988). *Tarasoff*: Ten years later. *Professional Psychology: Research and Practice* 19, 184–190.

J. L. Bernard

DYNAMIC ASSESSMENT. This set of techniques seeks to assess a child's scholastic aptitude. In its methodologically soundest form, the child is pretested in a cognitive domain, then provided more and more specific prompts (in Reuven Feuerstein's Learning Potential Assessment Device procedures) or training in problem-solving strategies (in Milton Budoff's learning potential methods) and then posttested again with a device the same as, or similar to, the pretest. The gain score is seen as representing the child's "learning potential," which is distinguished as "dynamic" in contrast to the more static-, functioning-level description of intelligence tests. Dynamic assessment developed in a context in which limitations of intelligence tests in assessing culturally different children were evident and in which providing instructional direction and learning style information was very important. Problematic characteristics of gain scores, "learning potential" classification difficulties, and the relationship of such classifications to IQ scores have limited the acceptability of these techniques as measures of "learning potential."

See also COGNITIVE ASSESSMENT; PIAGETIAN ASSESSMENT.

REFERENCE

Glutting, J. J., and P. A. McDermott. (1990). Principles and problems in learning potential. In C. R. Reynolds and R. W. Kamphaus (Eds.), *Handbook of psychological and educational assessment of children: Intelligence and achievement* (pp. 296–347). New York: Guilford Press.

George C. Camp

E

ECOLOGICAL ASSESSMENT (NATURALISTIC ASSESSMENT). Ecological assessment includes a broad context for understanding adjustment and planning interventions by requiring multiple perspectives for each stage of problem solving (Bronfenbrenner, 1986; Cantrell and Cantrell, 1985). Environmental factors, behavior, and person variables all have potential importance in assessment decision making (Bandura, 1986). In addition, family and school environments are understood with respect to their impact on individual students and their potential for facilitating personal and social development.

Naturalistic assessment, a form of ecological assessment, focuses on the natural systems of families, classrooms, schools, and communities. Multiple perspectives of caregivers are assessed to determine the impact of the environment on the individual child. Naturalistic assessments are guided by the identification of a caregiver relationship characterized as warm, reciprocal, guiding, or supportive; the determination of an adaptive "educational" environment with the family or community where a wide range of learning experiences is provided; and the development of a continuum of support services for caregivers that stress essential skills and social adaptation as child-centered outcomes.

See also RECIPROCAL DETERMINISM; SYSTEMS ASSESSMENT.

REFERENCES

Bandura, A. (1986). *The social foundations of thought and action: A social cognitive theory.* Englewood Cliffs, NJ: Prentice-Hall.
Bronfenbrenner, U. (1986). Ecology of the family as a context for human development: Research perspectives. *Developmental Psychology* 22, 723–742.
Cantrell, M. L., and R. P. Cantrell. (1985). Assessment of the natural environment. *Education and Treatment of Children* 8, 275–295.

Karen T. Carey

ECOLOGICAL CONSULTATION. Ecological consultation is the result of the integration of two consulting models: behavioral consultation* (Bergan and Kratochwill, 1990) and problem-solving consultation.* Ecological consultation (Gutkin and Curtis, 1990) directs the consultant to maintain a focus on the many interactions between and among persons, environments, and behaviors relevant to the consultation. Central to the approach is a problem-solving process that consists of seven steps: (1) define and clarify the problem, (2) analyze the forces impinging on the problem, (3) brainstorm strategies, (4) evaluate and choose among strategies, (5) specify consultee and consultant responsibilities, (6) implement the selected strategy, and (7) assess the effectiveness of the strategy and recycle through the process if necessary. What is currently described by the term "ecological consultation" may be reconceptualized in the future as "ecobehavioral consultation," as strengths of ecological and behavioral perspectives come together to influence the overall practice of school-based consultation (Gutkin, 1993).

See also CONSULTATION; ECOLOGICAL ASSESSMENT.

REFERENCES

Bergan, J. R., and T. R. Kratochwill. (1990). *Behavioral consultation and therapy.* New York: Plenum Press.
Gutkin, T. B. (1993). Moving from behavioral to ecobehavioral consultation: What's in a name? *Journal of Educational and Psychological Consultation* 4, 95–99.
Gutkin, T. B., and M. J. Curtis. (1990). School-based consultation: Theory, techniques, and research. In T. B. Gutkin and C. R. Reynolds (Eds.), *The handbook of school psychology (2d ed.)*, (pp. 577–611). New York: Wiley.

William P. Erchul

EDUCATIONAL PROGRAMMER. The term "educational programmer" was used by Reger (1965) to describe the expanded role of school psychologists.* According to Reger, too much emphasis was being placed on testing and the pathologically oriented medical model.* School psychologists, he asserted, would soon move closer to an educational model that emphasized helping children grow rather than identifying their deficiencies. School psychologists would (or should) become educational programmers, using their advanced training to plan the most appropriate educational strategies for children with special needs. The emphasis of school psychology* should be on adapting the curriculum to the individual child rather than identifying the child's weaknesses and trying to force the child to adapt to the curriculum. By effecting these changes, Reger asserted that the school psychologist would be viewed as "a teacher, a programmer and a researcher" rather than "a technician who gives tests" (Reger, 1965, p. 9).

See also ROLE CHANGE AND DIVERSITY; ROLE RESTRICTION; ROLES AND FUNCTIONS.

REFERENCE

Reger, R. (1965). *School psychology*. Springfield, IL: Charles C. Thomas.

R. Scott Beebe

EDUCATIONAL PSYCHOLOGY. There is no single, agreed-upon definition of educational psychology. However, the American Psychological Association,* Division of Educational Psychology defined it as

the branch of psychology that is concerned with the development, evaluation, and application of a) theories and principles of human learning, teaching, and instruction and b) theory-derived educational materials, programs, strategies, and techniques that can enhance lifelong educational activities and processes. (see Wittrock and Farley, 1989, p. 196)

In addition to teaching, the field contributes to the knowledge bases for counseling, special education, school psychology, and evaluation and assessment.

In 1839, a normal school in Lexington, Massachusetts, offered the first educational psychology course in the United States, called Mental Philosophy. The first text, entitled *Educational Psychology,* was published by Louisa Hopkins in 1886. Around 1895, the first professorships of educational psychology were founded. The premier issue of the *Journal of Educational Psychology* was published in 1910.

The prominent shapers of the field include William James, G. Stanley Hall, Charles Judd, Raymond Cattell, R. J. Angell, John Dewey, and Edward L. Thorndike. Thorndike established educational psychology as a separate discipline and encouraged preservice teachers at Teachers College, Columbia University to choose instructional methods informed by science (Walberg and Haertel, 1992).

REFERENCES

Walberg, H. J., and G. D. Haertel. (1992). Educational psychology's first century. *Journal of Educational Psychology* 84, 6–19.
Wittrock, M. C., and F. L. Farley. (1989). Toward a blueprint for educational psychology. In M. C. Wittrock and F. L. Farley (Eds.), *The future of educational psychology* (pp. 193–199). Hillsdale, NJ: Erlbaum.

Judith S. Kaufman

EISERER, PAUL E. Paul E. Eiserer was born on July 5, 1912, in Hastings, Nebraska, and died on July 8, 1993, in Hendersonville, North Carolina, where he was in retirement. He received his Ph.B. in 1939 with a major in psychology and his M.A. in guidance and counseling in 1941 from Northwestern University. After serving as a personnel technician, rehabilitation counselor, and clinical psychologist for the military in World War II, he received his Ph.D. in psychology in 1948 from the University of Chicago. He held an assistant professorship of education and psychology (1948–1950) before accepting positions in clinical psychology,* special education,* and counseling psychology* with Teachers College, Columbia University for the remainder of his career. Among his contributions to school psychology* was his 1963 book, which was translated into a Spanish-language edition in 1971. He also helped to organize the Tri-State Conference on School Psychology* held at Teachers College in 1962.

REFERENCE

Eiserer, P. E. (1963). *The school psychologist.* Washington, DC: Center for Applied
    Research in Education.

Thomas K. Fagan

EMPLOYMENT TRENDS. Employment of school psychologists* in the United States has increased steadily since the mid-1940s. The most rapid growth occurred from about 1975 to 1985 as local schools and intermediate educational units hired additional personnel to staff the special education programs mandated by state and federal governments (Fagan, 1988).

The actual number of school psychologists in the United States working in public school positions was estimated at 19,527 by the Federal Office of Special Education Programs, based on a survey of state department of education divisions of special education (U.S. Department of Education, 1994). A slightly higher estimate of 21,251 was reported by Starkweather, Reschly, and Martin (1994) from a survey of the school psychology* leadership in each state. The first estimate may be low since only those school psychologists working primarily in special education programs likely were counted.

Significant numbers of school psychologists are employed as psychologists in nonschool settings such as mental health clinics, pediatric services, residential treatment centers, and private practice. Some persons with school psychology graduate training and experience work in administrative positions in school settings (e.g., director of special education) or teach in colleges or universities. The number of school psychologists working in these nontraditional settings is nearly impossible to enumerate. Most school psychologists employed in public school settings have completed specialist-level graduate training. School psychologists working in nonschool settings typically have completed doctoral-level graduate training in school psychology or a closely related area.

Schools continue to be the principal employer of school psychologists. The number employed depends on a number of factors, and trends vary significantly by state and region (Fagan, 1988; Starkweather, Reschly, and Martin, 1994). The best ratios of psychologists to students in the United States in the early 1990s were in the New England states (e.g., Connecticut, 1:600); the worst ratios were in the west-south-central states (e.g., Texas, 1:7,071). The current nationwide ratio is approximately 1 psychologist per 1,850 students.

The current job market in school psychology is excellent in nearly all U.S. locations, and some evidence suggests a future shortage due to a number of influences, including (1) decline in number of graduate students, (2) large numbers of persons retiring in the 1990 to 2005 period, and (3) gradual expansion of positions in public schools and other settings. The potential dangers of personnel shortages include (1) reversal of the long-standing trend toward improved psychologist-to-student ratios, (2) undermining progress in expanding roles to broader mental health services, and (3) erosion of standards for graduate training and certification/licensure. The favorable employment market makes school psychology an especially attractive career choice for persons seeking a human services career, with many opportunities in a variety of settings working with a diverse clientele.

See also COLLECTIVE BARGAINING; SALARY DETERMINATION.

REFERENCES

Fagan, T. K. (1988). The historical improvement of the school psychology service ratio: Implications for future employment. *School Psychology Review* 17, 447–458.

Starkweather, A. R., D. J. Reschly, and L. M. Martin. (1994). *School psychology personnel needs: A current look at a recent crisis.* Manuscript submitted for publication.

U.S. Department of Education (1994). *Sixteenth annual report to Congress on the implementation of the Education of the Individuals with Disabilities Education Act.* (1994). Washington, DC: Office of Special Education Programs, Author.

Daniel J. Reschly

EXAMINATION FOR PROFESSIONAL PRACTICE IN PSYCHOLOGY. A multiple-choice exam approximately 200 items in length, the Examination for Professional Practice in Psychology (EPPP) is standardized for use by psychology licensing* boards in order to obtain a license to practice psychology. The exam was developed and is administered semiannually (October and April) by the Association of State and Provincial Psychology Boards* (ASPPB). The exam measures knowledge of psychology relevant to basic practice, ethics, and professional activities.

The first form of the exam became available in 1961 and was followed by five revisions, which were declared obsolete in 1977. The Examination Committee of ASPPB since 1976 has been responsible for the item content of each exam, which is distributed by the Professional Examination Service (PES). Each licensing board using the exam contracts for the test with PES.

The content of the current examination was established by a job analysis of professional psychologists' work completed by 1,585 licensed psychologists, resulting in a delineation of fifty-nine responsibilities and sixty-one procedures, techniques, and resources. (Myers and Rosen, 1986). A twenty-five-member panel of psychologists combined the data from the job dimensions and the domains into five dimensions: (1) problem definition/diagnosis; (2) design, implementation, and assessment of intervention; (3) research and measurement; (4) professional/ethical/legal issues; and (5) applications to social systems.

Each state or provincial (Canadian) board has the authority to set its own passing score. However, ASPPB recommends a 70 percent pass score, which has been adopted by many states. An ASPPB brochure, *Information for Candidates,* is available from ASPPB or the state licensing board and explains how to apply and prepare for the exam.

See also CERTIFICATION TESTS.

REFERENCES

Myers, R. A., and G. A. Rosen. (1986). *Research digest: The examination of professional practice of psychology.* Montgomery, AL: Association of State and Provincial Psychology Boards.
Smith, I. L., R. K. Hambleton, and G. A. Rosen. (1988). Content validity investigations of the examination for professional practice in psychology. *Professional Practice of Psychology* 9(1), 43–80.

Robert N. Wendt

EXPERIMENTAL DESIGN. Experimental design is the logic and procedures that are used in research methods to allow an experimenter to make inferences regarding causal relationships between manipulated and outcome variables.

True experimental designs are characterized by a treatment(s) (independent variable[s]) that is manipulated, an outcome measure (dependent variable), subjects of study, a comparison (usually a control group), and random assignment of subjects to groups. The feature that most distinguishes true experiments from other types of experimental designs is the *random assignment* of subjects to groups. This feature, along with the use of control groups, allows investigators using true experiments maximum ability to rule out a variety of threats to internal validity.* True experimental designs include pretest-posttest control group designs, posttest-only control group designs, and the Solomon four-group design, as well as more complex designs such as factorial and mixed designs.

Quasi-experimental designs differ from true experiments in that quasi-experiments are *not* based on random assignment of subjects; otherwise, they retain all of the features of true experiments. Quasi-experiments tend to be more practical, feasible, and even ethical than true experiments in applied settings where random assignment to groups is not possible (Neale and Liebert, 1986). However, without random assignment, quasi-experiments tend to be weaker than true experiments in their ability to rule out threats to internal validity.

Two major categories of quasi-experimental designs are nonequivalent control group designs and interrupted time-series designs (within which single-case designs are subsumed). Nonequivalent control group designs include several variations but generally resemble true experiments except that membership in control and experimental groups is determined not randomly but often by a preexisting membership (e.g., members of a particular classroom, school, or organization).

In interrupted time-series designs, a particular experimental event (i.e., treatment) interrupts the periodic measurement of a group or individual, and the effects of this interruption on the time series are noted (Campbell and Stanley, 1966). The more familiar subset of time-series designs is single-case designs, commonly used in clinical and educational settings. Single-case designs employ continuous assessment procedures and baseline assessment (with some exceptions) and often include reversal or withdrawal of treatment phases (Kazdin, 1982). Commonly used single-case designs include ABAB designs,* multiple-baseline* designs, and changing criterion designs.* In an ABAB design, there is the alternation of a baseline (A) phase, during which there is no intervention, and an intervention phase (B). These two phases are then repeated.

Single-case design methodology (see, e.g., Kazdin, 1982) is rigorous in its design requirements necessary to rule out threats to internal validity.

Not to be confused with single-case design methodology, case-study research involves the descriptive, detailed account of the behavior of an individual with regard to life events, personality, course of therapy, and so on. Case studies or case histories tend to provide rich detail about an individual and, as such, may demonstrate important methods or procedures of therapy, provide accounts of rare phenomena, serve as a prototypical example of behavior, or serve as the basis for the generation of hypotheses (Neale and Liebert, 1986). However, because there is no manipulation of variables, and there is only the measurement or recording of events that exist/occur naturally, there is little or no power to draw causal inferences from case studies. Thus, although once prominent in psychology's history, case studies are found much less frequently in the psychological literature.

REFERENCES

Campbell, D. T., and J. C. Stanley. (1966). *Experimental and quasi-experimental designs for research.* Chicago: Rand-McNally.

Kazdin, A. E. (1982). *Single-case research designs: Methods for clinical and applied settings.* New York: Oxford University Press.

Neale, J. M., and R. M. Liebert. (1986). *Science and behavior: An introduction to methods of research* (3d ed.). Englewood Cliffs, NJ: Prentice-Hall.

Daniel H. Tingstrom

EXPERT POWER. Expert power is person A's ability to influence person B, given B's perception that A possesses knowledge or expertise in a designated area (French and Raven, 1959). Expert power and reward, coercive, legitimate, referent, and informational power constitute six well-established social power bases. A consultee may attribute expert power to a school psychologist*-consultant on the basis of the latter's specialized knowledge, perhaps indicated by the attainment of a graduate degree in psychology. Martin (1978) advocated that school psychologists should regard consultation* as an influence process and should develop their expert power and referent power* in order to consult most effectively. More recently, Erchul (1992) provided an analysis of expert power and the other five power bases in an examination of school psychologists' interactions with parents.

See also AUTHORITY; EXPERT WITNESS; POWER.

REFERENCES

Erchul, W. P. (1992). Social psychological perspectives on the school psychologist's involvement with parents. In F. J. Medway and T. P. Cafferty (Eds.), *School psychology: A social psychological perspective* (pp. 425–448). Hillsdale, NJ: Erlbaum.

French, J.R.P., and B. H. Raven. (1959). The bases of social power. In D. Cartwright (Ed.), *Studies in social power* (pp. 150–167). Ann Arbor, MI: Institute for Social Research.

Martin, R. (1978). Expert and referent power: A framework for understanding and maximizing consultation effectiveness. *Journal of School Psychology* 16, 49–55.

William P. Erchul

EXPERT WITNESS. The courts have long recognized that, in some instances, the layperson is simply not qualified to give testimony but that, instead, someone with expertise on the issue is needed. What this expert says is not binding on the jury but is intended to provide it with the information it needs to make its own judgment. Thus, anyone may be able to testify as to whether or not it was raining at a particular time or whether a car appeared to be speeding before an accident. But if the issue is the tensile strength of a failed steel beam that let a building collapse, a higher degree of expertise is needed. Interestingly, the courts have long held that the layperson is qualified to judge whether or not someone is mentally ill. However, expert testimony on this matter is obviously weighted more heavily by a jury.

If asked to be an expert witness, one would do well to know his or her limitations. The expert must be an expert and able to show this to the satisfaction of the court before being allowed to testify. Typically, education, experience, books written on the subject at hand, and so on are considered.

REFERENCES

Arcoren v. United States, 929 F2d 1235 (8th Cir. 1991).

Frye v. United States, 293 F2d 1013 (DC Cir. 1923).

Gorlow, L. (1975). The school psychologist as expert witness in due process hearings. *Journal of School Psychology* 13, 311–316.

Stumme, J. M. (1995). Best practices in serving as an expert witness. In A. Thomas and J. Grimes (Eds.), *Best practices in school psychology—III* (pp. 179–190). Washington, DC: National Association of School Psychologists.

J. L. Bernard

F

FACTOR ANALYSIS. Factor analytic methods were initially developed primarily by psychologists who were concerned about the organization and constructs of mental ability. The most prominent pioneers in the development of factor analytic techniques were Karl Pearson and Charles Spearman. Factor analysis refers to a variety of multivariate statistical techniques whose primary purpose is to reduce a larger set of observed variables into a smaller number of hypothetical constructs (Kim and Mueller, 1978). This reduction is accomplished by the analysis of the intercorrelations of variables and by determining which subsets of variables are more highly related compared to other subsets. On the basis of these observed interrelationships, factor analysis attempts to yield a smaller number of hypothetical constructs that convey essentially the same information as the original set of variables. Given the statistical complexity of factor analysis and the variety of methods and variations, factor analysis is done by computers. The majority of factor analytic studies conducted typically utilize one of two models: exploratory and confirmatory. Exploratory factor analysis models are usually employed when a researcher has little or no inclination as to the number and/or composition of the underlying constructs. In addition, exploratory applications are typically employed when a researcher is concerned with data reduction (Kim and Mueller, 1978). In confirmatory factor analysis, the researcher has hypotheses about the number and composition of the underlying dimensions and develops a theoretical model to test. The goal is to determine whether the sample data conform to the theoretical model generated by the researcher (Long, 1983). With confirmatory factor analysis, the researcher is able to incorporate meaningful constraints on the data (Joreskog, 1969) as compared to exploratory factor analysis, where the parameters of the model are difficult to ascertain. As a result, the utilization of confirmatory factor analysis has increased substantially in recent years. An alternative approach to factor analysis that gained popularity in the late 1970s and early 1980s was cluster analysis (Romesburg, 1984). In cluster analysis, the variables are mathematically grouped into similar sets and/or characteristics. The primary objective of researchers using cluster analysis is to make classifications (e.g., subtypes of children with learning disabilities). The advantage of utilizing cluster analysis is that it provides a mathematically and scientifically based procedure for classification. However, the major limitation of cluster analysis is the difficulty in making classification comparisons across studies. There appears to be little consistency in results across studies due to the large variety of mathematical applications, numbering in the hundreds, that are employed by researchers. Of the applications utilized, hierarchical cluster analysis outnumbers nonhierarchical cluster analysis ten to one (Romesburg, 1984). Methods that display similarities among subjects as a hierarchy are considered hierarchical cluster analysis, whereas applications that display similarities at a specified level are considered nonhierarchical cluster analysis.

See also MULTITRAIT-MULTIMETHOD MATRIX; VALIDITY.

REFERENCES

Joreskog, K. G. (1969). A general approach to confirmatory factor analysis. *Psychometrika* 34, 183–202.
Kim, J., and C. W. Mueller. (1978). *Introduction to factor analysis: What it is and how to do it.* Beverly Hills: Sage.
Long, J. S. (1983). *Confirmatory factor analysis.* Beverly Hills: Sage.
Romesburg, H. C. (1984). *Cluster analysis for researchers.* Belmont, CA: Lifetime Learning.

David E. McIntosh, Jr.
Nicole Nickens

FAMILY ASSESSMENT. The term "family assessment" covers a wide range of professional activities and fields, as well as describing the specific endeavor of developing and using instruments and assessment techniques to measure various aspects of the complex interactions within families and between families and their environments. Interactions of concern include those between family members—such as parent to parent, parent to sibling, and sibling to sibling— and extended-family interactions. Also of interest is measuring a wide range of individually held and family-wide attitudes. Many types of family assessment instruments exist. Typically, assessment instruments are of three types: questionnaires that use self-report techniques for acquiring information, instruments that acquire relevant information using observational techniques, and instruments that utilize a combination of self-report and observational methods. The future of family assessment appears to be congruent with other forms of psychological assessment in that a compilation of a variety of measures from a variety of sources appears to yield the most useful and valid information. *The Handbook of Family Measurement Techniques* (Touliatos, Perlmutter, and

Straus, 1990) provides a detailed listing of available family assessment devices as well as ordering information.

See also FAMILY ENABLEMENT/EMPOWERMENT; FAMILY THERAPY; MARRIAGE AND FAMILY THERAPY.

REFERENCE

Touliatos, J., B. F. Perlmutter, and M. A. Straus. (Eds.). (1990). *Handbook of family measurement techniques.* New York: Sage.

John S. C. Romans

FAMILY ENABLEMENT/EMPOWERMENT. Family enablement/empowerment is often considered a subtype or specialty of marriage and family therapy.* While both terms cover similar aspects of family counseling and therapy, general distinctions and broad differences can be discussed. While marriage and family therapy tends to focus on presenting problems of dysfunction within the family or couple, family enablement tends to deal more with working to increase currently adequate levels of functioning or enhance the growth and potential of a family or couple (L'Abate, 1981). Family enablement is more often conducted in a group setting, using psychoeducational techniques with a number of families present, while marriage and family therapy is more likely to be conducted in a more formal setting with a single family. Family enablement is also often used as an adjunct to family therapy during the course of therapy when the family is able to focus on growth and development issues. Family enablement is more likely to be time-limited and often centers around developing specific skills such as parent training.* The terms "enablement" and "empowerment" are often used interchangeably. Other related terms include skill training and family or marital enrichment.

See also FAMILY ASSESSMENT; FAMILY THERAPY.

REFERENCE

L'Abate, L. (1981). Skill training programs for couples and families. In A. S. Gurman and D. P. Kniskern (Eds.), *Handbook of family therapy* (pp. 631–661). New York: Brunner/Mazel.

John S. C. Romans

FAMILY THERAPY. The term "family therapy" has much in common with the term "marriage and family therapy."* Family therapy is often considered a subset of the larger field of marriage and family therapy, though much debate has occurred surrounding the issue of whether the two areas represent separate fields (Broderick and Schrader, 1981). The major difference between family therapy and marriage and family therapy is that the former has a primary focus on the family as the smallest unit for treatment while the latter at times may focus on the individual, the marital couple, or the family. The practice of family therapy typically involves conjoint therapy* sessions with all the members of the nuclear or, in some cases, extended family present for the therapy sessions. Other characteristics of the practice and profession of family therapy are shared with marriage and family therapy in general. The theoretical foundations of family therapy are similar to those of other mental health and helping professions, as many aspects of human development theory and psychological theory apply to family therapy work.

The beginnings of modern family therapy can be found in the decade of the 1950s. The most influential founders of family therapy include John Bell, Don Jackson, Nathan Ackerman, and Murray Bowen (Nichols and Schwartz, 1991). Major theoretical approaches to family therapy include systemic approaches, intergenerational approaches, communications family therapy, psychoanalytic and object relations approaches, group family therapy, extended family systems, experiential family therapy, strategic family therapy, structural family therapy, and behavioral approaches.

As with marriage and family therapy in general, there is no one, easily identified group of professionals solely associated with the practice of family therapy. In addition to those who identify themselves specifically as family therapists, a wide range of professionals, such as psychologists, counselors, social workers, and physicians, conduct family therapy as part of their general practice. The primary professional organization for family therapists is the American Association for Marriage and Family Therapy (AAMFT). In addition to the AAMFT, other professional organizations that are concerned with marriage and family therapy include the American Psychological Association* Division of Marriage and Family Therapy and the American Counseling Association.

See also FAMILY ASSESSMENT; FAMILY ENABLEMENT/EMPOWERMENT.

REFERENCES

Broderick, C. B., and S. S. Schrader. (1981). The history of professional marriage and family therapy. In A. S. Gurman and D. P. Kniskern (Eds.), *Handbook of family therapy* (pp. 5–35). New York: Brunner/Mazel.
Nichols, M. P., and R. C. Schwartz. (1991). *Family therapy concepts and methods.* Boston, MA: Allyn and Bacon.

John S. C. Romans

FEMINIZATION OF SCHOOL PSYCHOLOGY. School psychology* has become increasingly a profession of women. This phenomenon has caused substantial concern among some practitioners and academics who fear such outcomes as lowered prestige for the field, reduced salaries, and disruption in program development and research agendas. Others have seen the growing numbers of women in the profession as a hopeful sign for the emergence of new research and professional strategies more immediately responsive to social needs.

Rosa Hagin (1993) provided a thoughtful record of, and reflection on, the contributions of women to school psychology. The data she listed gave clearer perspective on the effects of the entry of women into the profession. In the larger context of American psychology, school psychology retains a comparative gender balance. Sixty percent of the people working in psychology as a whole are women, while there are nearly equal numbers of doctoral-level women and men (50.3 percent and 49.7 percent) who identify school psychology as their primary professional affiliation. These numbers are potentially misleading when compared with the membership of the National Association of School Psychologists* (NASP), currently 70 percent women. This apparent contradiction is clarified somewhat with the evidence that more women than men practice school psychology with master's* or specialist degrees* (61 percent), and the majority of NASP's membership is composed of practitioners at these degree levels.

The leadership of NASP and Division 16 of the American Psychological Association has not matched the trends in membership. Over the course of their respective histories, 46 percent of the presidents of Division 16 have been women, while only 30 percent of the presidents of NASP have been women (Hagin, 1993). This trend is reversing somewhat, with 40 percent of the presidents of Division 16 and 50 percent of the presidents of NASP being women in the past ten years.

Placed in historical context, the success of women in applied settings is illustrated by the movement of women into school psychology. In the first several decades of this century, women were essentially barred from gaining access to university positions (particularly if they were married). At the same time, applied psychology posts accounted for only about 20 percent of available positions (Russo and O'Connell, 1980). As applied positions increased, women psychologists were quick to earn them. By 1940, women held 51 percent of the positions in guidance centers, schools, educational systems, hospitals, and custodial centers, while constituting only 30 percent of all psychologists. By 1944, women held 60 percent of these positions, while the proportion of women in psychology as a whole remained unchanged (Conoley and Henning-Stout, 1990).

The discussion of the feminization of school psychology raises larger questions about the social context in which the profession exists and the biases to which school psychologists are subject. Within our current social structure, professions dominated by women are held in lower esteem, as illustrated by income levels and relative influence of professions on public policy. The term ''feminization'' is nowhere matched with similar concern about the ''masculinization,'' historically or contemporarily, of any professional discipline. Questions that might arise, given the stigmatization accruing to a profession that attracts women to its ranks, include, Are masculine professions (i.e., professions dominated by men) more valuable than professions in which women and men participate equally or in which women are more present? How is value determined? How does this assignment of value affect the profession of school psychology? In a system of higher education that prepares people to function in professions historically dominated by men, does the entry of women really connote feminization of the profession, or does the ''professionalizing'' of women masculinize them (i.e., training women to the system rather than adjusting the system to include women's ways of knowing)?

Questions of feminization are questions of the standards applied for determining what does and does not represent quality. The feminization of school psychology invites the profession and its members to consider the standards we apply for determining social worth and the biases those standards carry.

See also DIVISION OF SCHOOL PSYCHOLOGY; DOCTORAL DEGREE; GENDER ISSUES.

REFERENCES

Conoley, J. C., and M. Henning-Stout. (1990). Gender issues in school psychology. In T. R. Kratochwill (Ed.), *Advances in school psychology* Vol. 7 (pp. 7–31). Hillsdale, NJ: Erlbaum.

Hagin, R. A. (1993). Contributions of women in school psychology: The Thayer Report and thereafter. *Journal of School Psychology* 31, 123–141.

Russo, N. F., and A. N. O'Connell. (1980). Models from our past: Psychology's foremothers. *Psychology of Women Quarterly* 5, 11–54.

Mary Henning-Stout

FERNALD, GRACE M. Born in Clyde, Ohio, to James C. and Nettie Barker Fernald, Grace Maxwell Fernald (1879–1950) earned her A.B. (1903) and M.A. (1905) from Mount Holyoke College and her Ph.D. from the University of Chicago (1907). After short appointments at Bryn Mawr College and Lake Erie College, she became the first psychologist to work with William Healy at the Juvenile Psychopathic Institute in Chicago; the psychiatrist–psychologist–social worker team became a widely followed model.

Throughout her life, she worked effectively to improve schools, corrective institutions, and civic conditions with model practices, publications, and consultation with others. She helped establish many positions for school psychologists in California. Monographs on delinquency and mental tests were followed by her book on remediation and publications about bright underachievers. Her text on remedial techniques (Fernald, 1943) was reprinted often in the following twenty-five years.

Fernald advocated the use of kinesthetic and tactile stimulation as well as the visual and auditory modalities in teaching poor (or ''zero'') readers. Many case studies document the effectiveness of the visual, auditory, kinesthetic, tactile (VAKT) approach. This became known as the Fernald method of teaching reading, spelling, and writing, especially when combined with the use of words selected or stories dictated by learners.

Her sister Mabel* was another well-known psychologist.

REFERENCES

Fernald, G. M. (1943). *Remedial techniques in basic school subjects.* New York: McGraw-Hill.

Grace Maxwell Fernald. (1950). *Psychological Review* 57, 319–321.
Irvine, P. (1970) Pioneers in special education: Grace Fernald. *Journal of Special
   Education* 4, 258–259.

Joseph L. French

FERNALD, MABEL R. Born in Springfield, Ohio, Mabel Ruth Fernald (1883–
1952) followed her sister Grace Fernald to Mount Holyoke College for an A.B.
in 1906 and a Ph.D. at the University of Chicago in 1910. Mabel and Grace
and their four brothers, Charles, Henry, Dana, and James, made outstanding
records in various fields. Their father, James C. Fernald, was the author of many
well-received and much used books on English, including a dictionary and *English Grammar, Historic English,* and *Expressive English.*

Fernald held appointments at the Chicago Normal College, Laboratory for
Social Hygiene in Bedford Hills, New York, Office of the Surgeon General in
Washington, D.C., and the University of Minnesota, before becoming director
of the Division of Psychological Services in the Cincinnati public schools in
1921, a post she held until retirement in 1948.

She was one of the first psychologists certified by the American Psychological
Association* Committee on Certification of Consulting Psychologists (June 3,
1922).

REFERENCE

Fernald, M. R., M. Holmes, S. Hayes, and A. Dawley. (1920). *A study of women
   delinquents in New York state.* New York: Century.

Joseph L. French

FERNALD, WALTER E. The Walter E. Fernald State School, previously
known as the Massachusetts School for the Feebleminded, was named for its
first resident superintendent. Before his work in Massachusetts, Walter Elmore
Fernald (1859–1924), born of William A. and Margery C. F. Fernald in Kittery,
Maine, earned his M.D. at the Medical School of Maine at Bowdoin in 1881
and served as assistant physician at the State Hospital in Minnesota.

Well known for his humane treatment of the mentally retarded, he strongly
advocated diagnosing and classifying disabled people following assessment*
with a variety of tools, in addition to mental tests. By developing a twenty-four-
hour-a-day treatment plan for children under his care, the Massachusetts facility
became an international center for educating personnel concerned with the mentally retarded.

He was a correspondent with Lightner Witmer,* editor of *The Psychological
Clinic,* often making a case for "practical medical training and experience in
the diagnosis and care of the feebleminded" over "merely psychological measurements" such as the Binet (Farrell, 1914, pp. 30–31).

In 1922, he described the development of, and services delivered by, a statewide public school mental clinic in Massachusetts at the forty-sixth annual meet-

ing of the American Association for the Study of the Feebleminded in St. Louis. The clinic resulted from an act approved, with his urging, by the Massachusetts legislature in 1919 to establish special classes in each city in which there were ten or more children three or more years retarded.

REFERENCES

Farrell, E. E. (1914). A study of the school inquiry report on ungraded classes. *Psychological Clinic* 8, 29–47.
Fernald, W. E. (1922). The inauguration of a state-wide public-school mental clinic in Massachusetts. *Mental Hygiene* 6, 471–486.

Joseph L. French

FIELD EXPERIENCE. Field experience is used as a general term in school psychology* training to encompass practicum* (or extern) experiences as well as internships.* All such field experiences provide opportunities for students to apply their newly acquired knowledge and skills (e.g., assessment,* consultation,* and counseling) in applied settings. Some type of field experience in school psychology training has been around nearly as long as the profession itself. Lightner Witmer* provided demonstrations of practical skills to prospective school psychologists* in the early years of the twentieth century. Internships in school psychology have been traced back as early as 1908 (Morrow, 1946).

Currently, training programs and state departments of education* differ in the amount of time students are required to spend in field experiences. Smith and Henning (in press) reported that specialist*-level programs averaged 421 clock hours of required practicum experience and that doctoral* programs averaged 651 clock hours of practicum work. Regarding internships, specialist-level programs averaged 1,169 clock hours in a school setting, and doctoral programs averaged 1,559 clock hours of internship in a school setting.* Wide variations exist among programs in the number of practicum and internship hours required. In addition, some training programs require practicum work and/or internship in nonschool settings (e.g., on-campus psychoeducational clinics) in addition to the number of hours spent in schools.

Ideally, field experiences should match the training level of the student. As the student acquires skills, the requirements of the practicum should become increasingly demanding. New students may try out their testing skills with ''nonproblem'' cases, while advanced students may be required to complete case studies on students with difficulties. Internships provide a next step in the school psychology training process, offering a transition between schooling and full-time employment.

The National Association of School Psychologists* (NASP) and some state departments of education publish standards for, and information about, school psychology field experience requirements. Readers are advised to consult these sources for up-to-date information (NASP, 1994).

See also PROFESSIONAL STANDARDS; TRAINING MODELS; UNIVER-
SITY-BASED CLINICS.

REFERENCES

Morrow, W. R. (1946). The development of psychological internship training. *Journal
     of Consulting Psychology* 10, 165–183.
National Association of School Psychologists. (1994). *Standards for training and field
     placement programs in school psychology.* Washington, DC: Author.
Smith, D. K., and A. Henning. (in press). *Directory of school psychology training
     programs* (4th ed.). Washington, DC: National Association of School
     Psychologists.

Paula Sachs Wise

FIRST PSYCHOLOGICAL CLINIC. The founding of the first psychological
clinic and the practice of its founder, Lightner Witmer,* are considered points
of origin in the history of school and clinical psychology.* The clinic, founded
at the University of Pennsylvania (UPenn) in 1896, evolved from the psychological laboratory of James McKeen Cattell, who preceded Witmer at UPenn.
The clinic functioned in conjunction with Witmer's instruction in clinical psychology during the period 1896–1907 but expanded and diversified thereafter.
The clinic served as a training site for psychologists and special educators in
the early decades of the twentieth century and as a model for other clinics
emerging in that period.
     See also BUREAUS OF CHILD STUDY.

REFERENCES

Brotemarkle, R. A. (Ed.). (1931). *Clinical psychology: Studies in honor of Lightner
     Witmer to commemorate the thirty-fifth anniversary of the founding of the first
     psychological clinic.* Philadelphia: University of Pennsylvania Press.
Levine, M., and J. Wishner. (1977). The case records of the psychological clinic at the
     University of Pennsylvania. *Journal of the History of the Behavioral Sciences*
     13, 59–66.

Thomas K. Fagan

FLORIDA STATE UNIVERSITY INVITATIONAL CONFERENCE. Held
December 7 and 8, 1964, at the Holiday Inn in Tallahassee, Florida, the Florida
State University Invitational Conference on School Psychology was one of several historic conferences of the 1960s. The meeting was supported, in part, by
funds from the National Institute of Mental Health and intentionally engaged
dialogue among and between educational administrators, school psychologists,
trainers of school psychologists, and others. The overall theme was contributions
of the behavioral sciences to quality education and included addresses by Gordon Lippitt, Susan Gray,* and Eli M. Bower.*

REFERENCE

Nelson, W. H., and D. F. Driggs, (Eds.). (1964). *Contributions of the behavioral sciences to quality education: Proceedings of an invitational conference on school psychology.* Tallahassee: Florida State University.

Thomas K. Fagan

FOLLOW-UP SERVICES. The term "follow-up services" refers to the nature and amount of professional contact maintained or reinitiated between the psychologist and client following termination of primary services. Certain responsibilities of the school psychologist* necessitate greater emphasis on follow-up services than others. These services could include follow-up on the effectiveness of evaluation recommendations, evaluating the success of prescribed treatment, including counseling, and the effectiveness of teacher modifications. In all situations, ethically, it is appropriate for the school psychologist to make his or her future services available and to explain how contact can be made.

See also PROFESSIONAL STANDARDS; ROLES AND FUNCTIONS.

REFERENCES

Gutkin, T. B., and C. R. Reynolds (Eds.). (1990). *The handbook of school psychology.* New York: Wiley.

National Association of School Psychologists. (1992). *Standards for the provision of school psychological services.* Washington, DC: Author.

Reynolds, C. R., T. B. Gutkin, S. N. Elliot, and J. C. Witt. (1984). *School psychology: Essentials of theory and practice.* New York: Wiley.

Kathleen R. Ryter

FORMATIVE EVALUATION. The term "formative evaluation" is usually used by school psychologists* in two contexts: professional accountability* and program evaluation.* Formative evaluations are carried out during an ongoing program to provide a progress check. Formative evaluations use observations, curriculum-based measures,* questionnaires, and other feedback mechanisms to help improve the performance of an individual or fine-tune a program. Formative evaluations may be especially effective when planning instructional interventions* for children with disabilities since such evaluations provide multiple measures of students' progress rather than relying on the score from a single administration of a test of ability or achievement.

See also SUMMATIVE EVALUATION.

REFERENCES

Fagan, T. K., and P. S. Wise. (1994). *School psychology: Past, present, and future.* White Plains, NY: Longman.

Ysseldyke, J. E., and D. Marston. (1990). The use of assessment information to plan instructional interventions: A review of the research. In T. B. Gutkin and C.R.

Reynolds (Eds.), *The handbook of school psychology* (2d ed., pp. 661–682).
New York: Wiley.

Paula Sachs Wise

FORREST v. AMBACH. Murial Forrest was employed by the Edgemont School
District in New York from 1967 to 1979. The school board claimed it was
dissatisfied with her work during the 1976–1977 school year and terminated her
employment in 1979. Forrest alleged that the manner in which she was asked
to perform her duties violated state and federal laws and her professional ethics.
Specifically, she contended that the policies and practices of the district prevented proper identification of children with handicaps and failed to extend due
process rights to parents.

In 1980, Forrest appealed to the commissioner of education for the state of
New York, Gordon Ambach, who dismissed her appeal. Forrest appealed the
commissioner's decision in a lower supreme court in Albany County. Local and
national psychological associations joined in amicus support of Forrest. The case
was remanded back to the commissioner to investigate allegations made by
Forrest. In 1981, Commissioner Ambach replied that he found no support for
the allegation that the school neglected statutory duties to children with handicaps, nor was there support that her constitutional right of free speech had been
abridged. Forrest returned to the court, contending that the school board had
presented Commissioner Ambach with inadequate records and that a different
time frame was used to gather information about her performance.

In 1983, the Appellate Division of the New York Supreme Court affirmed
the decision of a lower court, upholding her dismissal on quality of work-related
evaluations, specifically, lack of cooperation.

This case, which brought a school psychologist in conflict with the school
system, though unsatisfactorily resolved for Murial Forrest, did yield a decision
from the lower court in the initial appeal (1980): "The ethical standards of any
professional employed by a school board cannot be cavalierly dismissed as ir-
relevant to the employer-employee relationship" (p. 122).

See also CODES OF ETHICS; PROFESSIONAL STANDARDS; TENURE.

REFERENCES

Forrest case appealed again. (1983). *Communique* 12(1), 6.
Forrest v. Ambach, Supp., 436 N. Y. S. 2nd 119 (1980).
Jacob-Timm, S., and T. Hartshorne. (1994). *Ethics & law for school psychologists.*
      Brandon, VT: Clinical Psychology.
Prasse, D.P. (1980). In the matter of *Forrest v. Ambach. Communique* 9(4), 3.
Ramage, J. C., and M. Johnston. (1982). Forrest case: Commissioner's rebuttal.
      Communique 10(5), 1.

Paul G. Warden

FREE APPROPRIATE PUBLIC EDUCATION. The term "free appropriate
public education" (FAPE) means, as defined by the Individuals with Disabilities

Education Act of 1990 (IDEA; Public Law 101-476*), that special education and related services* are provided at public expense, without charge, and that they meet the standards of the State Education Agency. The services are provided in conformity with an individualized education plan* (IEP) for each student with disabilities. Each child presents unique needs; therefore, appropriateness varies with each child. Most of the litigation under IDEA focuses on appropriateness as operationalized by provisions for related services and placement in the least restrictive environment.*

See also PUBLIC LAW 94-142; PUBLIC LAW 101-476.

REFERENCE

Tucker, B. P., and B. A. Goldstein. (1992). *The educational rights of children with disabilities: A guide to federal law.* Horsham, PA: LRP.

Paul G. Warden

G

GATEKEEPER ROLE. Historically, one of the primary and predominant reasons for employing school psychologists* was to have them assist educators in reliably sorting students into groups. Segregating the exceptional children facilitated the school system's goal to efficiently educate large numbers of students. The role of regulating the flow of students into special education classes or from one sector to another developed into the concept of school psychologists' being viewed as "gatekeepers." From this perspective, the school psychologist was an ancillary member of the system.

See also ROLE RESTRICTION; ROLES AND FUNCTIONS.

REFERENCES

Fagan, T. K., and P. S. Wise. (1994). *School psychology: Past, present, and future.* White Plains, NY: Longman.
Pfeiffer, S. I., and R. S. Dean. (1988). School psychology in evolution. *School Psychology Review* 17, 388–390.

Kelly J. Griffith

GAY AND LESBIAN STUDENT SERVICES. Gay and lesbian youth represent 30 percent of all teen suicides and 25 percent of all homeless youth and, as a group, nearly half repeatedly attempt suicide (Gibson, 1989). Despite these numbers, there is only a handful of services for gay, lesbian, and bisexual (hereafter, GLB) youth.

Project 10, in the Los Angeles Unified School District, provides services and support for GLB students in each of fifty-two high schools. This same district uses a prejudice-reduction curriculum, entitled "Homophobia: Discrimination Based on Sexual Orientation," developed by the Gay and Lesbian Alliance against Defamation in L.A. The Harvey Milk School is an alternative public school in New York City for (primarily, but not exclusively) GLB youth. Along

with a traditional curriculum, services are available to students through the He-
trick-Martin Institute, the umbrella organization for the school.

The Toronto Board of Education provides services for Canadian GLB students, parents, and teachers. Massachusetts became the first state to pass a law
prohibiting discrimination against gay and lesbian students in public schools.
Additionally, the Governor's Commission on Gay and Lesbian Youth (1993)
developed a school program, "Making Schools Safe for Gay and Lesbian
Youth."

Slater (1988) discusses the homophobia and institutional resistance that psychologists may face who wish to work with GLB youth. She provides background on developmental processes related to moving from an initial awareness
of sexual orientation toward an integrated gay and lesbian identity, and she also
discusses some of the major issues and problems faced by gays and lesbians.
Reynolds and Koski (1994) discuss the role of the school counselor in advocating for GLB youth and in building a positive school climate. They provide
a list of resources for both teens and counselors.

See also GENDER ISSUES.

REFERENCES

Gibson, P. (1989). Gay male and lesbian youth suicide. *Report of the Secretary's
    Task Force on Youth Suicide. Volume 3: Preventions and Interventions in
    Youth Suicide.* Washington, DC: U.S. Department of Health and Human
    Services.
Reynolds, A. L., and M. J. Koski. (1994). Lesbian, gay and bisexual teens and the
    school counselor: Building alliances. *High School Journal* 77, 88–94.
Slater, B. R. (1988). Essential issues in working with lesbian and gay male youths.
    Professional Psychology: Research and Practice 19, 226–235.

                                                                Judith S. Kaufman

GENDER ISSUES. Gender is the cultural construct attached to the fact of
biological sex. The construct of gender has come to carry significant meaning
especially with regard to the valuing of people or behaviors according to their
gender qualifications. In contrast to other areas of psychology where gender
issues have been a primary focus of research and theory for decades, school
psychology* has historically been unresponsive to gender as an area of practical
or scholarly concern. As recently as 1988, Alpert and Conoley (1988) noted that
school psychology had been essentially inactive relative to discussion and consideration of issues of gender.

In the years since 1988, noticeable increases have occurred in attention to
issues of gender in the profession. Writings in the area have included inquiry
into the links between psychological research findings related to gender and the
practice of school psychology (Henning-Stout and Conoley, 1991), investigation
of the experiences of women in the profession (Conoley and Henning-Stout,
1990), and exploration of gender as a cultural construction that influences re-

search in the profession (Henning-Stout, 1994). Early research can be found on topics such as leadership, gender climate in academic and practice settings, and teacher expectations for female and male consultants. In addition, there has been the establishment of an active Committee on Women in School Psychology within the Division of School Psychology* (16) of the American Psychological Association* (APA).

School psychologists* work to meet the needs of children who are struggling in schools. Research on the experiences of women and girls, men and boys indicates that there are deeply enculturated scripts for social behaviors and that these expectations are conveyed, in large measure, in schools. The study of gender influences is immediately relevant to the practice of school psychology.

See also ASSERTIVENESS TRAINING; FEMINIZATION OF SCHOOL PSYCHOLOGY; GAY AND LESBIAN STUDENT SERVICES.

REFERENCES

Alpert, J. L., and J. C. Conoley (Eds.). (1988). Miniseries: Women and school psychology: Issues in the professional life cycle. *Professional School Psychology* 3(1).

Conoley, J. C., and M. Henning-Stout. (1990). Gender issues in school psychology. In T. R. Kratochwill (Ed.), *Advances in school psychology,* Vol. 7 (pp. 7–31). Hillsdale, NJ: Erlbaum.

Henning-Stout, M. (1994). Consultation and connected knowing: What we know is determined by the questions we ask. *Journal of Educational and Psychological Consultation* 5, 5–21.

Henning-Stout, M., and J. C. Conoley. (1991). Gender: A subtle influence in the culture of the school. In F. J. Medway and T. P. Cafferty (Eds.), *School psychology: A social psychological perspective* (pp. 113–135). Hillsdale, NJ: Erlbaum.

Mary Henning-Stout

GENERIC TRAINING AND CREDENTIALING. Generic training and credentialing underlie the licensing* approach of most state boards of psychology.* They assume that there is a common knowledge base in psychology that should be mastered by all individuals seeking to practice professional psychology. This knowledge base includes training in professional areas of psychology, including ethics and standards, research design and methodology, statistics, biological bases of behavior, social bases of behavior, cognitive/affective bases of behavior, and individual behavior (Brown, 1990). An individual's knowledge is typically assessed through a multiple-choice exam that encompasses these major areas of psychology. Most states also require the completion of a doctoral degree in order to use the title ''psychologist.'' As Brown (1990) notes, generic licensing is the current position held by the American Psychological Association.* Many states require applicants for a license to indicate specific areas of competence based on their training and experiences. The recognition of specialty areas within psychology and by state psychology boards began in the middle to late 1970s

(Pryzwansky, 1993). Licensing in a specialty area, for example, school psychology, is often associated with a nondoctoral level of training. Brown (1990) points out that Virginia, California, Kentucky, and Wisconsin were among the first states to grant licensure for the title school psychologist.* In such cases, however, there are usually "substantial restrictions on the nature of the practice encompassed by this title as compared to licensure at the doctoral level" (Brown, 1990, p. 1005).

See also SPECIALTY TRAINING AND CREDENTIALING.

REFERENCES

Brown, D. T. (1990). Professional regulation and training in school psychology. In T. B. Gutkin and C. R. Reynolds (Eds.), *The handbook of school psychology* (2d ed., pp. 991–1009). New York: Wiley.
Pryzwansky, W. B. (1993). The regulation of school psychology: A historical perspective on certification, licensure, and accreditation. *Journal of School Psychology* 31, 219–235.

Douglas K. Smith

GESELL, ARNOLD L. Arnold Lucius Gesell was born on June 21, 1880, in Alma, Wisconsin, and died on May 29, 1961, in New Haven, Connecticut. He graduated from Alma High School (1896) and Stevens Point Normal School (1899), received the Ph.B. at the University of Wisconsin (1903), the Ph.D. at Clark University (1906), and the M.D. at Yale University (1915). Gesell was the first person in the United States to be employed with the title "school psychologist." In his position with the Connecticut State Board of Education (1915–1919), he made numerous contributions to the history of psychological services in the schools and to the field of special education. His most notable contributions were in the fields of developmental pediatric medicine and child psychology, which he pursued throughout the remainder of his career.

REFERENCES

Fagan, T. K. (1987). Gesell: The first school psychologist, Part I. The road to Connecticut. *School Psychology Review* 16, 103–107. Part II. Practice and significance. *School Psychology Review* 16, 399–409.
Gesell, A. (1952). Autobiography. In E. G. Boring, H. Werner, H. S. Langfeld, and R. M. Yerkes (Eds.), *A history of psychology in autobiography,* Vol. 4 (pp. 123–142). Worcester, MA: Clark University Press.
Miles, W. R. (1964). Arnold Lucius Gesell 1880–1961. A biographical memoir. In National Academy of Sciences, *Biographical memoirs,* Vol. 37 (pp. 55–96). New York: Columbia University Press.

Thomas K. Fagan

GESTALT THERAPY. "Gestalt" is a German word meaning whole or configuration. Gestalt therapy originated through the work of Frederick "Fritz" Perls, who fled Nazi Germany and later migrated to North America in 1947.

His therapeutic approach was heavily influenced by German Gestalt psychology, psychoanalysis, psychodrama, and the burgeoning human potential movement of the 1960s. The result was a highly existential and phenomenological therapy.

Theoretically, Gestalt therapy views people as continuously attempting to achieve homeostasis or balance in their lives. Humans are holistic in that body and mind are inseparable as is their interdependence with the environment. Aggression is essential to human growth and development because it facilitates contact with the environment. Individuals become maladjusted when they fall out of homeostasis. They are then said to have unfinished business or figures, which are submerged from conscious awareness in an unconscious background.

Gestalt therapy involves a here-and-now orientation that focuses on present psychological and physical awareness by linking affect to behavior. Becoming aware of specific figures and separating them from background are viewed as curative for the client.* Therapeutic techniques commonly involve active confrontation and frustration by the therapist of the client's attempts to remain emotionally unaware of unfinished business. Role play, psychodrama, guided imagery, and dream work are all common techniques used to enable the client to take action and experience new insights long after therapy is over.

REFERENCES

Perls, F. (1969). *Gestalt therapy verbatim.* New York: Bantam.
Polster, E., and M. Polster. (1973). *Gestalt therapy integrated.* New York: Brunner/ Mazel.
Wheeler, G. (1991). *Gestalt reconsidered: A new approach to contact and resistance.* New York: Gardner Press.

Richard K. James

GODDARD, HENRY H. Internationally acclaimed researcher, author, and speaker, Henry Herbert Goddard (1866–1957) was born in Vassalboro, Maine, of Quaker parents. Finishing an A.B. (1887) and an A.M. (1889) at Haverford, Goddard was a secondary school principal for six years before completing his Ph.D. at Clark University (1899). After six years as state college professor in West Chester, Pennsylvania, he became director of research at the Vineland (New Jersey) Training School for the Feebleminded, a leading research institution in the first quarter of the century. Here, Goddard developed the team (housemother, field-worker, "Binet tester," and psychologist) concept for diagnosis and treatment, published in *The Training School Bulletin* the first English translation (with the help of Elizabeth Kite) of the Binet-Simon scale (Goddard, 1908), and paved the way for inclusion of adaptive behavior in the diagnosis of mental retardation.

Using what is recognized today as the qualitative method, Goddard's research direction supported mental retardation as a Mendelian trait related to criminal behavior. He coined the word "moron" to characterize mildly retarded people and published extensively about the lineage of one family, feeble-mindedness, and criminal imbeciles (Goddard, 1912). As time went by, his evangelistic zeal and uncritical earnestness were recognized as too influential for a scientific scholar (Smith, 1985).

In 1918, he became director of the Ohio State Bureau of Juvenile Research, established to deal with juvenile delinquents, and published about delinquency and the psychology of normal and subnormal behavior. Later, as a professor of psychology at Ohio State, he broadened his interests to include multiple personalities and gifted children. Retiring in 1938, he continued to preach about the heritability of many human traits. A man with many interests, he was a skilled mountain climber and the first football coach at the University of Southern California in 1887.

REFERENCES

Goddard, H. H. (1908). The Binet and Simon tests of intellectual capacity. *Training School Bulletin* 5, 3–9.
———. (1910). A measuring scale for intelligence. *Training School Bulletin* 6, 146–155.
———. (1912). *The Kallikak family, a study in the heredity of feeblemindedness.* New York: Macmillan.
Smith, J. D. (1985). *Minds made feeble, the myth and legacy of the Kallikaks.* Rockville, MD: Aspen.

Joseph L. French

GRAY, SUSAN W. Susan W. Gray was born on December 5, 1913. She received the A.B. degree at Randolph-Macon Woman's College in 1935 and the M.A. degree in 1939 and the Ph.D. degree in 1941 at George Peabody College. She was a fourth grade teacher (1936–1938); assistant professor of psychology at Florida State University (1941–1945); associate professor (1945–1958), professor (1958–1978), and then professor emerita at George Peabody College, where she codirected its school psychology* program, founded in 1957. She served as the American Psychological Association* (APA) Division 16 president 1965–1966, was a recipient of an American Board of Examiners in Professional Psychology (ABEPP) diploma in school psychology, and was the 1983 recipient of the Division 16 Distinguished Service Award. She died in Nashville on December 30, 1992, at age seventy-nine. Her contributions were to both school psychological services and the education of disadvantaged children.

REFERENCES

Fagan, T. K. (1993). Centennial perspectives: Susan W. Gray: 1913–1992: A data-oriented problem solver. *The School Psychologist* (Division 16, APA Newsletter), 47(2), 2, 16.
Gray, S. W. (1963). *The psychologist in the schools.* New York: Holt, Rinehart and Winston.

Thomas K. Fagan

GROUP ASSESSMENT. Group assessment is a psychological technique allowing simultaneous assessment of more than one examinee, often large groups of examinees. It may sample a wide range of behaviors, including academic achievement, intelligence,* abilities, creativity, and interests, as well as occupational aptitudes and personality variables, and some are used for selection purposes, including college entrance and personnel screening. Typically, group assessments are in a paper-and-pencil format, although computer formats are becoming common. They most frequently use a multiple-choice response format and permit objective machine scoring. Thus, the techniques are valued for their efficiency in gathering large amounts of information from groups of examinees and scoring it with machines quickly and reliably. Many group assessment devices are well standardized with appropriate norming procedures. They are generally regarded as providing useful research and screening information and information useful at an individual client level when additional individual assessment data are available.

Group assessment commenced with the use of the Army Alpha and Beta tests in World War I (1917), which were developed by Robert Yerkes and other psychologists. Soon after, Arthur Otis (1918) published the first group intelligence test, and Monroe and Buckingham (1919) published the first group achievement test for use in schools.

See also SCREENING ASSESSMENT.

REFERENCES

Anastasi, A. (1988). *Psychological testing* (6th ed.). New York: Macmillan.
Salvia, J., and J. E. Ysseldyke. (1995). *Assessment.* Boston: Houghton-Mifflin.
George C. Camp

GROUP PRACTICE. In offering psychological services to the public, numerous business and professional configurations are possible. Group practice refers to several professionals' practicing in a common office setting, usually with an arrangement to share business expenses. Psychologists often form group practices in order to create financial and professional support for themselves. Sometimes the practice includes other psychologists with the same or different specialties or other health or mental health care providers, such as social workers, speech pathologists, educational consultants, occupational/physical therapists, or physicians.

Generally, group practice refers to a less formal arrangement than an incorporated business entity. Practitioners operate under their own license, with their own liability insurance,* and maintain their own business records. Each professional offers the subset of services for which he or she has the necessary training and expertise. Interoffice referrals are common, although separate records and confidentiality* are maintained. One advantage is that group liability insurance may be available at substantial savings over individual coverage.

See also INDEPENDENT PRACTICE; LICENSING; PRIVATE PRACTICE; THIRD-PARTY REIMBURSEMENTS.

REFERENCE

Kendall, P. C., and J. D. Norton-Ford. (1982). *Clinical psychology: Scientific and professional dimensions.* New York: Wiley.

Robbie N. Sharp

GROUP THERAPY. Group therapy involves the use of group interaction to assist an individual change thinking, feeling, or behavior to relieve severe emotional distress. Group therapy differs from group counseling, which involves the use of group interaction to assist an individual improve self-understanding and trigger behavior change. Both approaches draw upon the theory, research, and practice literature within counseling* and clinical psychology.*

In schools, group approaches to counseling are common, given that self-understanding and behavior change are priorities. Attention to more severe emotional distress can occur within school counseling services but is more likely in community or private mental health settings.

Application of counseling therapies to groups includes Adlerian,* Gestalt,* transactional analysis,* behavior therapy,* cognitive-behavioral, and reality therapy* approaches. Corey (1991) acknowledges that the average counselor develops an eclectic approach to therapy and is thus responsible for creating an integrative perspective.

Goals of therapy are as diverse as the perspectives of the counselor and the issues presented by clients.* Corey notes that counseling goals include "restructuring personality, uncovering the unconscious, creating social interest, finding meaning in life, curing an emotional disturbance, examining old decisions and making new ones, developing trust in oneself, attaining self-actualization, reducing anxiety, shedding maladaptive behavior and learning adaptive patterns, and gaining more effective control of one's life" (p. 431). Goals can range from the very specific, behaviorally defined to the global and long-term.

Therapists function to guide and modify the client's behavior. The extent to which their responsibility extends beyond the counseling context varies according to the theoretical orientation of the therapist. The responsibility for the implementation of change resides with the client.

Research on therapy and counseling has been extensive but has failed to provide clear understanding of the therapeutic process. One limitation to practice has been the hesitancy of therapists to engage in ongoing evaluation of effort and outcome. Ehly and Dustin (1989) support the evaluation of group therapy with clients and programs of therapy offered by organizations.

Practitioners have a wealth of materials from which to develop and apply group therapy interventions. With more than 200 theories, many of which overlap, to guide research and practice, therapists must rely on professional resources and colleagues to sort through available information and select strategies that match client needs and personal competencies.

See also COGNITIVE THERAPY; CONJOINT THERAPY; FAMILY THERAPY; MARRIAGE AND FAMILY THERAPY.

REFERENCES

Corey, G. (1991). *Theory and practice of counseling and psychotherapy* (4th ed.). Pacific Grove, CA: Brooks/Cole.
Ehly, S., and D. Dustin. (1989). *Individual and group counseling in schools.* New York: Guilford Press.
Garfield, S. L., and A. E. Bergin (Eds.). (1986). *Handbook of psychotherapy and behavior change* (3d ed). New York: Wiley.

Stewart W. Ehly

GUADALUPE v. TEMPE ELEMENTARY DISTRICT. Guadalupe was filed as a class-action suit seeking redress for misclassification of ethnic minority students under equal protection and due process clauses of the Fourteenth Amendment to the U.S. Constitution. The suit was filed on behalf of Yaqui Indian and Mexican-American students. The consent decree in 1972, as in *Diana v. California State Board of Education* (1970), required assessment in the child's primary language. *Guadalupe* went further than *Diana* and required that intelligence* shall not be the exclusive or primary basis for classifying students as mentally retarded. If the student's primary language is other than English, classification decisions are to be based on performance or nonverbal measures. Assessment of adaptive behavior* must be done, including an interview with the parents or guardian in the home.

Other required procedures, such as informed consent* for evaluation and placement and integration of special and regular education programs, were incorporated into Part B of the *Education of the Handicapped Act of 1975* (Public Law 94-142).*

See also NONBIASED ASSESSMENT; NONVERBAL ASSESSMENT.

REFERENCES

Diana v. California State Board of Education. (F. Supp. N.D. Cal. 1970).
Jacob-Timm, S., and T. Hartshorne. (1994). *Ethics & law for school psychologists.* Brandon, VT: Clinical Psychology.
Phye, G. D., and D. J. Reschly. (1979). *School psychology perspectives and issues.* New York: Academic Press.

Paul G. Warden

GULLION, MARY ELIZABETH. A pioneering school psychologist,* Liz was born on November 5, 1912, to Oscar Ray Gullion and Anna Elizabeth (Wright) Gullion. She attended Eugene, Oregon, public schools, including the University High School affiliated with the School of Education at the University of Oregon. Unknown to her family until much later, she took flying lessons and at age seventeen was the first woman south of Portland to solo (in a two-passenger biplane.) She obtained a bachelor of science degree from the University of Oregon in 1935.

Upon graduation, she took courses in several universities, supporting herself in a variety of jobs. She was the first female ski instructor at Oregon's Timberline Lodge and spent the war years teaching skiing in Banff, Canada. She returned to Eugene and obtained a master's degree in educational psychology.* In 1956, she joined the Eugene School District as a school psychologist, advocating for a sympathetic understanding of the unique gifts of each student. Following retirement, she continued to volunteer in the Eugene district.

With Gerald R. Patterson, she coauthored *Living with Children: New Methods for Parents and Teachers* (1968). Published by Research Press, this classic child management guide for parents has been translated into several languages. She was one of the founders of the Oregon School Psychologists' Association (OSPA), insisting that the association provide training activities for continuing professional development so that its members could keep up with the changes in the field.

Liz was a world traveler, spending many vacations touring the Orient. She was active in the International School Psychology Association* (ISPA) and read a paper at the 1980 ISPA colloquium in Jerusalem, Israel. When she retired, she shipped most of her textbooks and materials to a school psychologist in India whom she had befriended on one of her trips.

She was diagnosed with lung cancer shortly after her return from China in 1985. With medical treatments for a variety of ailments, she continued to be active in the National Association of School Psychologists* and the Oregon School Psychologists' Association, where she served as an emeritus member of the Executive Board. She died in February 1988.

Philip B. Bowser

H

HALL, G. STANLEY. Granville Stanley Hall was born in Ashfield, Massachusetts, on May 1, 1844, and died in Worcester, Massachusetts, on April 24, 1924. He graduated from Williams College (1867) and Union Theological Seminary (1871) and then became America's first Ph.D. recipient in psychology under William James at Harvard University (1878). Hall is considered the father of American child study and developmental psychology and a significant influence on the origins of school psychological services. He employed nomothetic methods of inquiry and cultivated the questionnaire method of research. A controversial figure in American psychology, Hall founded the American Psychological Association* in 1892 and several journals, including the *American Journal of Psychology* in 1887 and *Pedagogical Seminary* in 1891 (now *Journal of Genetic Psychology*).

See also IDIOGRAPHIC VERSUS NOMOTHETIC RESEARCH.

REFERENCES

Hall, G. S. (1923). *Life and confessions of a psychologist.* New York: D. Appleton.
Ross, D. (1972). *G. Stanley Hall: The psychologist as prophet.* Chicago: University of Chicago Press.
Sanford, E. C. (1924). Granville Stanley Hall 1846–1924. *American Journal of Psychology* 35, 313–321.

Thomas K. Fagan

HATCH AMENDMENT. The Hatch amendment was enacted in 1978 and is part of Public Law 95-561, which amended the Elementary and Secondary Act of 1965. The intent of the amendment is to protect students' and their family's privacy. The Hatch amendment and the Family Educational Rights and Privacy Act of 1974 (FERPA, Public Law 93-380)* provide statutory protection of privacy rights of students and their families.

The Hatch amendment regulations state that no student is required to submit to psychiatric or psychological examination, testing, or treatment without prior consent of parents if the primary purpose is to reveal information about political affiliations; mental or psychological problems embarrassing to the student or the family; sex behavior and attitudes; illegal, antisocial, self-incriminating, and demeaning behavior; critical appraisal of others in the family; legally recognized privileged relationships; and income other than that needed to determine program participation or financial assistance. Although the Hatch amendment applies only to federally funded experimental, demonstration, or testing programs, the provisions of the regulations are viewed, according to current legal opinion, as appropriate conduct in the schools.

The provisions of the amendment address the work of the school psychologist* in the areas of assessment,* counseling, and consultation.* Clearly, parental prior consent is required for assessment and counseling. Legal opinion is that consent is probably needed and desirable for consultation if the focus (client) of the consultation is a single child.

See also CONFIDENTIALITY; PRIVILEGED COMMUNICATION.

REFERENCE

Jacob-Timm, S., and T. Hartshorne. (1994). *Ethics and law for school psychologists.*
     Brandon, VT: Clinical Psychology.

                                                                Paul G. Warden

HEALTH PROMOTION. Health promotion is an encompassing term that refers to a variety of behavioral, educational, economic, spiritual, social, and/or environmental efforts designed to support the establishment, maintenance, and improvement of behaviors and lifestyles conducive to emotional and physical well-being (Elias et al., 1994; Millstein, Petersen, and Nightingale, 1993). The emphasis is on increasing skills and competencies, such as problem-solving and social decision-making skills, to encourage the development of positive, health-enhancing behaviors, while eliminating or reducing health-compromising actions. Comprehensive health promotion in schools, which results in creation of an array of integrated pupil support services, involves the collaborative efforts of disciplines such as health education, nursing, physical education, food services, counseling, and school psychology*; the modification of the overall school health environment; and the coordination of school and community resources and energies (Dryfos, 1994).

REFERENCES

Dryfos, J. G. (1994). *Full-service schools: A revolution in health and social services
     for children, youth, and adolescents.* San Francisco: Jossey-Bass.
Elias, M. J., R. P. Weissberg, D. P. Hawkins, C. L. Perry, J. E. Zins, K. A. Dodge, P.
     C. Kendall, D. C. Gottfredson, M. J. Rotheram-Borus, L. A. Jason, and R.
     Wilson-Brewer. (1994). The school-based promotion of social competence:

Theory, research, practice, and policy. In R. J. Haggerty, L. R. Sherrod, N. Garmezy, and M. Rutter (Eds.), *Risk, stress, and resilience in children and adolescence: Processes, mechanisms, and interaction* (pp. 268–316). Cambridge, England: Cambridge University Press.

Millstein, S. G., A. C. Petersen, and E. O. Nightingale (Eds.). (1993). *Promoting the health of adolescents: New directions for the twenty-first century.* New York: Oxford University Press.

Joseph E. Zins

HEARING (HEARING OFFICER). As guaranteed by the Individuals with Disabilities Education Act (Public Law 101-476)*, parents or guardians of a child with a disability have the right to bring complaint relating to any matter concerning the identification, evaluation, or placement of their child for special education* services to a due process hearing. Conversely, the representative educational agency has the corresponding right to present complaint over the same issues. The hearing is presided over by a hearing officer who is an appointee of the state education agency. The hearing officer neither is an employee of the agency nor has a personal or professional interest that would conflict with the objectivity of the hearing (Turnbull, 1993). Responsibilities of the hearing officer include establishing the hearing at a time and place convenient to the parents, hearing testimony and cross-examination from representatives of both parties, and judging in a neutral fashion an appropriate solution consistent with the law and student's need. Upon conclusion of the proceedings and determination of judgment, the hearing officer issues written findings of fact and conclusions of law (McCarthy, 1988). The decision of the hearing officer is final unless either party appeals after the initial hearing. If an appeal is instigated, an appellate hearing officer, different from the first hearing officer, examines the original proceeding and issues an independent decision.

See also DUE PROCESS; PROCEDURAL SAFEGUARDS; SECOND OPINION.

REFERENCES

McCarthy, G. (1988). *A handbook for hearing officers.* Columbia: South Carolina State Department of Education. (ERIC Document Reproduction Service No. ED 306 757)

Turnbull, H. (1993). *Free appropriate public education: The law and children with disabilities.* Denver, CO: Love.

Denise Cutbirth
Diane Montgomery

HILDRETH, GERTRUDE H. Gertrude Howell Hildreth was born in Terre Haute, Indiana, on October 11, 1898, and died in Bethesda, Maryland, on March 6, 1984. She received preparatory training at Garfield High School (Terre Haute), an A.B. degree from North Central College, an M.A. in education from the University of Illinois (1921), and the Ph.D. in educational psychology* at Teachers College, Columbia University (1925). After receiving her M.A., she was a school psychologist* in the Okmulgee, Oklahoma, schools until June 1923, perhaps the first such appointment in that state. Her career at Columbia University and wide range of contributions are documented in her papers in the Archives of the Educational Testing Service in Princeton, New Jersey. She authored or coauthored several tests, including the Metropolitan Achievement Tests and the Metropolitan Readiness Tests. In 1930, she published the first text on school psychology,* *Psychological Service for School Problems.*

REFERENCES

Fagan, T. K. (1988). Historical moments: The first school psychologist in Oklahoma. *Communique* 17(3), 19.
Hildreth, G. H. (1930). *Psychological service for school problems.* Yonkers-on-Hudson, NY: World Book.

Thomas K. Fagan

HOBBS, NICHOLAS. Nicholas Hobbs was born in Greenville, South Carolina, on March 13, 1915, and died in Nashville, Tennessee, on January 23, 1983. He received the A.B. degree in 1936 from The Citadel and the M.A. and Ph.D. in educational psychology* from Ohio State University in 1938 and 1946, respectively. His career ranged from secondary school teacher while working on his master's degree to provost at Vanderbilt University (1967–1975). In the interim, he served in several positions, including Project Re-ED (a demonstration program for the reeducation of emotionally disturbed children). He is known to school psychologists* for his works, *The Futures of Children* (1975) and *Issues in the Classification of Children, Volumes 1 & 2* (1975). He was president of the American Psychological Association* (APA) in 1966 and earlier chaired a committee that developed proposals for the original APA ethical principles. He was among the participants of the Thayer conference* on school psychology in 1954 and spoke at the 1976 National Association of School Psychologists* (NASP) convention. Two issues of the *Peabody Journal of Education* (1983, 60[3]; 1984, 61[3]) are devoted to the legacy of his contributions.

See also LABELING.

REFERENCE

Smith, M. B. (1985). Nicholas Hobbs (1915–1983). *American Psychologist* 40, 463–465.

Thomas K. Fagan

HOLLINGWORTH, LETA S. Leta Stetter Hollingworth was born on May 25, 1886, and died of abdominal cancer on November 27, 1939. Born and raised in Nebraska, she completed her undergraduate work at the University of Nebraska in 1906. She moved to New York City to marry Harry Hollingworth in 1908, where she completed her M.A. (1913) and Ph.D. (1916) at Columbia University. She worked as a psychological examiner and was the first psychologist hired under New York civil service. She was active in the American Association of Clinical Psychologists,* in which she served as secretary, and in the early years of the American Psychological Association* (APA) section on clinical psychology.* Her research spanned the areas of mental subnormality, giftedness, special talents and defects, nervous children, adolescents, and children with very high ability. Her early research studies helped to dispel myths about women and giftedness and have been cited in the history of both fields. She was an early contributor to both clinical and school psychology.*

REFERENCES

Fagan, T. K. (1990). Contributions of Leta Hollingworth to school psychology. *Roeper Review* 12(3), 157–161.
Hollingworth, H. L. (1943). *Leta Stetter Hollingworth: A biography.* Lincoln: University of Nebraska Press.

Thomas K. Fagan

HOME–SCHOOL–COMMUNITY COLLABORATION. The difficulties faced by children are diverse and complicated. Often these difficulties can be addressed only by cooperative efforts among the various systems in the child's life—the family, the school, and the community. Home-school-community collaboration can be viewed as a way of getting all of the systems in a child's life to work cooperatively in order to bring about positive changes for the child. Such cooperative intervention efforts may be complicated by the logistics of bringing everyone together and then getting everyone to agree on what needs to be done. In addition, the individual parties may resist cooperative efforts because each party blames one or more of the others for the problems the child is experiencing. Thus, teachers may blame the parents for not getting a child ''ready to learn,'' while the parents may blame the teachers for not providing an appropriate learning environment for the child. Community resources may present barriers to cooperative efforts because of complicated funding procedures, ''turf'' issues,* and lack of awareness of services offered by other agencies and individuals.

The school psychologist* is in an ideal position to assume a leadership role in establishing linkages among schools, homes, and community services, particularly with respect to students with disabilities (Apter, 1992). School psychologists are often accustomed to acting as case managers, completing paperwork, following up on recommendations, and resolving conflicts between teachers and parents. Working with community agencies is a natural extension of these tasks. In addition, school psychologists have the professional credentials and the training to interact effectively and confidently with mental health personnel, with physicians, and with other community resources and to act as a liaison among parents, schools, and community agencies.

See also COLLABORATION; COLLABORATIVE CONSULTATION.

REFERENCES

Apter, D. (1992). Utilization of community resources: An important variable for the
    home-school interface. In S. L. Christenson and J. C. Conoley (Eds.), *Home-
    school collaboration: Enhancing children's academic and social competence*
    (pp. 487–498). Silver Spring, MD: National Association of School
    Psychologists.
Carlson, C., and J. Hickman. (1992). Family consultation in schools in special
    services. *Special Services in the Schools* 6, 83–112.
Woody, R. H., J. C. LaVoie, and S. Epps. (1992). *School psychology: A developmental
    and social systems approach.* Boston: Allyn and Bacon.
                                                                                                          Paula Sachs Wise

HOSPITAL SETTINGS. Hospitals are institutions that provide medical, surgical, psychiatric, and rehabilitative services. In medical settings, the discipline
of school psychology* utilizes assessment,* diagnosis, intervention,* and research in order to promote intellectual, emotional, and social development for
individuals across the life span. Medical services are conceptualized from a
unique interdisciplinary perspective, with a focus on creating individual rehabilitation plans. Individual, group,* and family therapy* and parent education
are additional services that may be provided in a hospital setting.

The school psychologist's* understanding of the educational enterprise is a
major asset when working as a vital liaison among the home, school, hospital,
and community (Wodrich and Pfeiffer, 1989). A school psychologist may practice in a multiplicity of positions within a medically related facility, including
work in departments of neurology, family medicine, pediatrics, psychiatry, and
day treatment programs (Pfeiffer and Dean, 1988). Knowledge in the areas of
learning, development, consultation,* program evaluation,* and case management places the school psychologist in an ideal position to coordinate the resources necessary for helping any individual or family achieve optimal health.

See also HOME-SCHOOL-COMMUNITY COLLABORATION; MEDICAL
MODEL; PEDIATRIC SETTINGS.

REFERENCES

Pfeiffer, S. I., and R. S. Dean (Eds.). (1988). Psychologists in non-traditional settings.
    School Psychology Review 17(3), 388–446.
Wodrich, D. L., and S. I. Pfeiffer. (1989). School psychology in medical settings. In
    R. C. D'Amato and R. S. Dean (Eds.), *The school psychologist in
    nontraditional settings: Integrating clients, services, and settings* (pp. 87–105).
    Hillsdale, NJ: Erlbaum.
                                                                                                      Rik Carl D'Amato
                                                                                                Susan M. DiUglio-Johnson

HYBRID YEARS. The term "hybrid years" is used to describe the period in
school psychology* history from 1890 to 1969, characterized by the emergence
of school psychological services from a mixture of services provided by persons

holding credentials in psychology, regular and special education, guidance and counseling, or other psychology and education fields. The school psychologist's* dominant function was psychoeducational assessment for special class placement. Decade descriptors include origins of practice (1890–1909), expansion and acceptance (1910–1929), emerging regulation (1930–1939), organizational and professional identity (1940–1959), and training and practitioner growth (1960–1969). The period ended near the time of the founding of the National Association of School Psychologists* in 1969.

See also THOROUGHBRED YEARS.

REFERENCES

Fagan, T. K. (1990). Research on the history of school psychology: Recent developments, significance, resources, and future directions. In T. R. Kratochwill (Ed.), *Advances in school psychology,* Vol. 7 (pp. 151–182). Hillsdale, NJ: Erlbaum.

Fagan, T., and P. Wise. (1994). *School psychology: Past, present, and future.* White Plains, NY: Longman.

Thomas K. Fagan

HYPNOSIS. Trance has been used in healing throughout history, making hypnosis one of the oldest treatments in medicine and mental health. Mesmer (1766) introduced hypnosis as a discernible medical intervention. His animal magnetism theories fell into disfavor, and not until the early nineteenth century did James Braid introduce the term "hypnosis," noting the similarity of trance to sleep. Charcot later revived interest in hypnosis, and his work attracted Freud, who then rejected hypnosis as unreliable. Other analysts and psychotherapists continued to explore hypnosis in clinical and research settings. In World Wars I and II, hypnosis reappeared in medicine as treatment for "war neurosis" or combat stress. Hypnosis has since flourished as a psychological and medical intervention.

Hypnosis is most clearly defined by its phenomena. These are predominated by an altered state of consciousness, concentrated focus, suggestibility, and recall. Hypnotherapists use these to determine the presence and depth of hypnotic induction. Relaxation training,* guided imagery, and biofeedback* can trace their antecedents to hypnosis.

Medicine and surgery use hypnosis for control of pain and bleeding. Psychotherapeutically, it has been used to reduce, eliminate, or substitute for psychopathological symptoms; change attitudes; and change values. The school psychologist* can use hypnosis for direct psychotherapeutic intervention, reducing classroom stress, test anxiety, difficulty in concentration, and improvement in recall memory. School psychologists using hypnosis generally are trained in postgraduate workshops such as those offered by the American Society of Clinical Hypnosis.

See also INTERVENTION (DIRECT AND INDIRECT).

REFERENCES

Crasilneck, H. B., and J. A. Hall. (1975). *Clinical hypnosis: Principles and applications.* New York: Grune and Stratton.

Klauber, R. W. (1984). Hypnosis and education in school psychology. In W. C. Wester and A. H. Smith (Eds.), *Clinical hypnosis: A multi-disciplinary approach* (pp. 591–622). Philadelphia: Lippincott.

Spiegel, H., and D. Spiegel. (1978). *Trance and treatment.* New York: Basic Books.

Christopher R. Ovide

I

IDIOGRAPHIC VERSUS NOMOTHETIC RESEARCH. Research can be separated into two distinct categories: idiographic and nomothetic (Baltes, Reese, and Nesselroade, 1977). While nomothetic research has predominated the field of psychology in recent years, idiographic research is gaining renewed status. Idiographic research is conducted with individual people through the case study method. Data are interpreted and conclusions are drawn based on the particulars of an individual case (Barnett and Carey, 1992). Different interpretations of data are meaningful for different realities experienced by individuals (Lincoln and Guba, 1985).

Nomothetic research refers to lawful generalizations that pertain to classes or groups of people. Research constructed through a nomothetic approach generally meets the traditional criteria of the scientific method. Thus, results of nomothetic research are generalized to larger populations, and differences between individuals who participate in such research are not considered.

Idiographic research refers to the naturalistic analysis of a particular student, family, or classroom. Hypotheses are developed, tested, and evaluated in terms of a single case. Nomothetic research is conducted with large sample sizes, and hypotheses are developed based on how people, on average, will respond. Researchers employing either one of the two methods must attend to the threats of internal and external validity,* as well as issues of reliability.*

See also EXPERIMENTAL DESIGN; NATURALISTIC OBSERVATION; QUALITATIVE RESEARCH.

REFERENCES

Baltes, P. B., H. W. Reese, and J. R. Nesselroade. (1977). *Life-span developmental psychology: Introduction to research methods.* Monterey, CA: Brooks/Cole.
Barnett, D. W., and K. T. Carey. (1992). *Designing interventions for preschool learning and behavior problems.* San Francisco: Jossey-Bass.

Lincoln, Y. S., and L. G. Guba. (1985). *Naturalistic inquiry.* Newbury Park, CA:
    Sage.

Karen T. Carey

INCLUSION. Inclusion is a significant trend in special education* involving
the integration of students with disabilities into regular classrooms as an alternative to pull-out programs (Sailor, 1991). The goal is to educate each child to
the maximum extent appropriate in the general education environment. Special
education and support services are sent to the child, rather than taking the child
to the services (Rogers, 1993). Primary criticisms of inclusion have involved
the concept that children with disabilities require special instruction under some
circumstances, and special training is required for teachers to instruct students
with disabilities (Sailor, 1991).

Courts favor inclusion by encouraging schools to consider the full range of
supplemental aids and services that could be provided to maintain students in
regular classrooms (Data Research Inc., 1993). Sailor (1991) maintains that there
is poor support in the research literature for pull-out programs. He suggests that
all resources, school and community, should be coordinated and integrated for
successful inclusion.

See also LEAST RESTRICTIVE ENVIRONMENT; MAINSTREAMING;
SEGREGATED SERVICES.

REFERENCES

Data Research Inc. (1993). *Students with disabilities and special education* (10th ed.).
    Rosemount, MN: Author.
Rogers, J. (1993). *The inclusion revolution.* Bloomington, IN: Phi Delta Kappa.
Sailor, W. (1991). Special education in the restructured school. *Remedial and Special
    Education* 12(6), 8–22.

Laqueta D. Pardue-Vaughn
John C. Vaughn

INDEPENDENT PRACTICE. Independent practice within the field of psychology refers to the offering of one's services to the public at a fee. An independent practitioner is more likely to provide desired interventions rather than
required ones and optional plans of evaluation and treatment rather than only
mandated ones, which school-based psychologists are more likely to offer.
Within school psychology,* independent practice is seen as a means of incorporating a broader role definition for school psychologists.* Many find that the
private business setting offers enhanced professional status and financial rewards
unattainable to the school-based psychologist. Others state concerns over the
legal, professional, ethical, and business problems that may be associated with
offering psychological services as an independent practitioner.

Independence in practice is a legal status that recognizes psychology as a
profession independent of others, with its own knowledge base, ethical standards

and practices, and identity. It refers to the ability to present oneself as a professional, fully capable and competent to provide the stated psychological services under the licensing* laws of the state in which one practices. This includes the freedom to be included in health insurance plans for reimbursement of services and to be able to compete in the marketplace with other mental health care professionals. Independent practice is appropriate only with a license or with appropriate supervision and only for provision of services in which one has training and expertise. Licensing by an appropriate state agency for the provision of psychology services in that state is necessary. The licensure law for each state mandates the requirements for procuring and practicing with all the duties and privileges of that license. Adherence to state or professional ethical standards and practices is required. Malpractice liability insurance* is generally necessary.

Independent practice is usually undertaken with a business plan that addresses the entrepreneurial nature of the enterprise ahead. Many of the details and expenses that are provided by working in an agency, school district, university, or other setting will fall to the practitioner. Differing business arrangements are possible. One can engage in independent practice and still be a part of a corporation or agency. Many psychologists engage in contractual or consultative services with schools or other businesses.

See also CODES OF ETHICS; LIABILITY INSURANCE; NONSCHOOL SETTINGS; PRIVATE PRACTICE; PROFESSIONAL IDENTITY; PROFESSIONAL STANDARDS; SCHOOL SETTINGS; STATE BOARD OF EXAMINERS IN PSYCHOLOGY; THIRD-PARTY REIMBURSEMENTS.

REFERENCES

American Psychological Association, Division 42. (1977). *Psychologists in independent practice.* Washington, DC: Author.
Phares, E. J. (1992). *Clinical psychology: Concepts, methods, and profession.* Pacific Grove, CA: Brooks/Cole.
Rosenberg, S. I. (1995). Best practices in maintaining an independent practice. In A. Thomas and J. Grimes (Eds.), *Best practices in school psychology—III* (pp. 145–152). Washington, DC: National Association of School Psychologists.
Rosenberg, S. L. and D. M. Wonderly. (1990). Best practices in establishing an independent practice. In A. Thomas and J. Grimes (Eds.), *Best practices in school psychology—II.* Washington, DC: National Association of School Psychologists.

Robbie N. Sharp

INDIRECT SERVICE DELIVERY. Indirect service delivery refers to the provision of services to clients through a third party. In school psychology* practice, indirect services include consultation* with staff and parents regarding students; designing interventions,* which are actually carried out by others; in-service training; and research/program evaluation activities. In most situations, school psychologists* are primarily engaged in indirect services or in assessments* (direct, such as tests; indirect, such as parent ratings) that lead to indirect services. For example, a school psychologist might use results of a classroom rating scale to help a teacher design an intervention to improve attention to task. Indirect models of service delivery are most consistent with behavioral and ecological frameworks that consider environmental and systems variables as key components to intervention and treatment.

Indirect services are cost-effective compared to labor-intensive, direct services* such as therapy. Through consultation and training, new skills and concepts eventually will be applied in other situations, thus extending the impact of the initial service. Indirect services also address the needs of students and families in their natural environments (home, school, community), thus enhancing generalization.

School psychologists providing indirect services must determine which treatments or interventions can be most effectively carried out by others and how to best communicate skills and procedures to the direct providers.

See also ASSESSMENT (DIRECT AND INDIRECT); INTERVENTION (DIRECT AND INDIRECT).

REFERENCES

Conoley, J., and T. Gutkin. (1986). School psychology: A reconceptualization of service delivery realities. In S. Elliott and J. Witt (Eds.), *The delivery of psychological services in schools: Concepts, processes, and issues* (pp. 393–424). Hillsdale, NJ: Erlbaum.
Thomas, A., and J. Grimes (Eds.). (1995). *Best practices in school psychology—III.* Washington, DC: National Association of School Psychologists.

Andrea Canter

INDIVIDUAL ASSESSMENT. Individual assessments are one-on-one interactions between a client* and a psychologist that are designed to provide information related to some diagnostic question(s). They include intelligence,* achievement, projective and personality testing as well as structured observations, assessment in play therapy, and interviews. They are central to defining intervention issues for clients with special needs. They require the professional involved to be well trained. They contribute rich hypothesis generation/testing opportunities because of direct observation of client behavior in structured and standardized tasks. Examiners observe such things as activity level, mood, motor, problem-solving techniques, anxiety, frustration, attention, and persistence. Professionals can consider the extent to which the reliability* and validity* of findings have been affected by individual and situational variables. They can also adapt procedures to specific client characteristics.

Historically, early significant contributors in the development of these techniques include Francis Galton, Alfred Binet* and Theodore Simon, Lewis Terman,* and David Wechsler* in intelligence assessment and Emil Kraepelin,

Robert Woodworth, Hermann Rorschach, and Henry Murray in personality assessment.*

See also ACADEMIC ASSESSMENT; COGNITIVE ASSESSMENT; COMPREHENSIVE ASSESSMENT; NEUROPSYCHOLOGICAL ASSESSMENT; PERCEPTUAL-MOTOR ASSESSMENT; PERSONALITY ASSESSMENT; PERSONAL-SOCIAL ASSESSMENT.

REFERENCES

Lanyon, R. I., and L. D. Goodstein. (1982). *Personality assessment* (2d ed.). New York: Wiley.
Salvia, J., and J. E. Ysseldyke. (1995). *Assessment.* Boston: Houghton Mifflin.
Sattler, J. M. (1990). *Assessment of children.* San Diego: Author.

George C. Camp

INDIVIDUAL DIFFERENCES. "Individual differences" is a phrase used to convey the fact that people vary. English and English (1958) define the term as "any psychological character, quality, or trait, or difference in the amount of a character, by which an individual may be distinguished from others" (p. 152). The term has been applied in psychological and educational contexts to refer primarily to cognitive, affective, and motor variability. Galton's *Hereditary Genius,* published in 1869, represents the first effort to address individual differences as subject matter of psychology (Murphy and Kovach, 1972).

Individual difference comparisons are important for a variety of reasons (e.g., job or educational selection). Because experts disagree about the level of knowledge required to "master" a content domain, they often use individual difference measures (e.g., test scores) as indices of relative knowledge and as points of reference (Aiken, 1988).

See also IDIOGRAPHIC VERSUS NOMOTHETIC RESEARCH; NORM-REFERENCED ASSESSMENT.

REFERENCES

Aiken, L. R. (1988). *Psychological testing and assessment.* Newton, MA: Allyn and Bacon.
English, H. B., and A. C. English. (1958). *A comprehensive dictionary of psychological and psychoanalytical terms.* New York: David McKay.
Murphy, G., and J. K. Kovach. (1972). *Historical introduction to modern psychology.* New York: Harcourt Brace Jovanovich.

R. Steve McCallum

INDIVIDUALIZED EDUCATIONAL PLAN. Public Law 94-142* (Education for All the Handicapped Children Act of 1975) and the reauthorization known as IDEA (Individuals with Disabilities Education Act of 1990, Public Law 101-476*) guarantee all students with disabilities a free, appropriate education based on specific needs defined by a comprehensive multidisciplinary evaluation. An individualized educational plan (IEP) is a written statement designed to delineate the student's unique needs and describe how these needs will be met by special education in the least restrictive environment.* The contents of the IEP must include a statement of the student's present level of educational functioning, annual goals with accompanying short-term instructional objectives, a list of special education and related services,* and an indication of the percentage of the school day spent in regular education. Projected dates for initiation of services and anticipated duration of services must be specified. IEPs should list objective criteria and evaluation procedures with a schedule for determining whether short-term instructional objectives have been met. Legislation mandates that the student's IEP be reviewed and revised at least annually. Developed in a school-based committee meeting, the IEP must be implemented as defined in the document, but service providers are not held liable if goals are not met. Practically speaking, the IEP serves as a basis for communications between school and home.

See also INDIVIDUALIZED FAMILY SERVICE PLAN; INDIVIDUALIZED TRANSITION PLAN.

REFERENCES

Federal Register. (1977, August 23), 42 (163), 42474–42518. Washington, DC: U.S. Government Printing Office.
————. (1992, September 19), 57 (189), 44794–44852. Washington, DC: U.S. Government Printing Office.
Griffin, L. B., and M. Y. Carson. (1989). *How to write a what?? Handbook on writing an individualized educational program and Public Law 94-142.* Charlotte, NC: Sanddollar Tree.

Peggy A. Hicks

INDIVIDUALIZED FAMILY SERVICE PLAN. Whereas Public Law 94-142* emphasized parent involvement through implementation of educational services, Public Law 99-457* views parents of children from birth through age two as direct recipients of intervention* services. After age two, the child becomes the direct recipient of intervention services. Unique needs and appropriate services required to meet the needs of infants, toddlers, and their families are determined through a multidisciplinary assessment.* Physical development (including vision, hearing, and health status), cognitive development, language and speech development, psychosocial development, and mastery of self-help skills should be evaluated. A multidisciplinary team,* including the parent or guardian, other family members as requested by the parents, an advocate if requested, the case manager, evaluators, and service providers should meet to develop a written plan within a reasonable time after the assessment. The individualized family service plan (IFSP) should include a statement of present level of functioning, family strengths and needs, expected outcomes, specific early intervention services required to meet the needs, projected dates of initiation and anticipated duration of services, the name of the case manager, and an outline of transitioning procedures from preschool to public school. Semi-annual reviews for the family with annual reevaluations* and revisions are mandated.

See also INDIVIDUALIZED EDUCATIONAL PLAN; INDIVIDUALIZED TRANSITION PLAN.

REFERENCES

Federal Register. (1992, September 29), 57 (189), 44794–44852. Washington, DC: U.S. Government Printing Office.

North Carolina Interagency Coordinating Council. (1993). *Early intervention in North Carolina: Services to Children with disabilities birth to age five.* Raleigh, NC: State Printing Office.

Peggy A. Hicks

INDIVIDUALIZED TRANSITION PLAN. Public Law 101-476,* or Individuals with Disabilities Education Act (IDEA) of 1990, mandates that individual educational plans* (IEP) for students sixteen years or younger, if appropriate, must include statements of needed transition and related services.* Not only does IDEA mandate statements of needed services, but it also requires that agency responsibilities and/or linkages be specified. Needed modifications in instruction, opportunities for community experiences, appropriate training and employment options, and other adult living objectives must be addressed. Transition planning must take place in an IEP/career development team with membership drawn from regular, vocational and special education, vocational rehabilitation,* business, other appropriate agencies, the parents, and student. As an integral part of the IEP, timelines, confidentiality* requirements, rights to due process,* annual review, triennial reevaluation,* and review by the Administration Placement Committee are mandated. Statutory provision assigns the primary role for coordinating efforts and assuring follow-through to the public agency responsible for the student's education. Statutes stipulate that participating agencies are responsible for providing and/or paying for services that would be otherwise provided to students with disabilities who meet eligibility criteria of that agency. Interagency agreements designed to assure successful integration of services are recommended but not required.

See also INDIVIDUALIZED FAMILY SERVICE PLAN.

REFERENCES

Federal Register. (1992, September 29), 57 (189), 44794–44852. Washington, DC: U.S. Government Printing Office.

Levinson, E. M. (1995). Best practices in transition services. In A. Thomas and J. Grimes (Eds.), *Best practices in school psychology—III* (pp. 909–915). Washington, DC: National Association of School Psychologists.

O'Leary, E. (October 1993). Transition services and IDEA: Issues for state and local programs. *Newsletter: South Atlantic Regional Resource Center* 2, 1–11.

Peggy A. Hicks

INFORMED CONSENT. In ethics and law, the requirement for informed consent grew out of deep-rooted notions of the importance of individual privacy. "It is now universally agreed, though not always honored in practice, that human beings must give their informed consent prior to any significant intrusion of their person or privacy" (Bersoff, 1983, p. 150).

Ethical codes,* professional standards,* and law show agreement that informed consent should be obtained prior to the provision of school psychological services. The three elements of informed consent are that it must be knowing, competent, and voluntary. *Knowing* means that individuals giving consent must have a clear understanding of what it is they are consenting to. In seeking informed consent for the provision of psychological services, the practitioner is obligated to provide information about the nature and scope of services offered, assessment-treatment goals and procedures, the expected duration of services, any foreseeable risks or discomforts for the client,* the cost of services (if any), the benefits that can reasonably be expected, the possible consequences of not receiving services, and information about alternative services that may be beneficial. The information must be provided in language understandable to the person giving consent.

The individual giving consent must be *legally competent* to do so. The law presumes that all adults are competent to consent unless they have been judged incompetent following a formal hearing. Children, however, are generally presumed to be incompetent. Consequently, in the school setting, informed consent is sought from the parent or guardian of a minor child or from the student, if an adult.

The third element of informed consent is that it must be *voluntary,* that is, freely given and obtained in the absence of coercion, misrepresentation, or undue enticement. A school may request a hearing under special education law to override parent refusal to consent to psychological assessment if it is suspected that a child has a disability that adversely affects educational performance.

See also PARENT/GUARDIAN PERMISSION.

REFERENCES

Bersoff, D. N. (1983). Children as participants in psychoeducational assessment. In G. B. Melton, G. P. Koocher, and M. J. Saks (Eds.), *Children's competence to consent* (pp. 149–177). New York: Plenum Press.
Jacob-Timm, S., and T. S. Hartshorne. (1994). *Ethics and law for school psychologists* (2d ed.). Brandon, VT: Clinical Psychology.

Susan Jacob-Timm

INTEGRATED SERVICES. The term "integrated services" describes a comprehensive model of service delivery in which medical, mental health, social services, and educational services are provided to a community's individuals and families in a coordinated way. Key components of integrated service models include identification of a spectrum of child and family services delivered through multiple public and private agencies; coordinated referral and intake processes, permitting families to apply to all service agencies with a single application; case planning and management procedures that are coordinated across agencies to identify those services a child or family requires; and comprehensive case-monitoring systems to track service delivery and evaluate service impact. Many integrated service models also emphasize consensus building and collaboration as central to their models and utilize multiagency planning teams that include families and community leaders in decision making. Some, but not all, integrated service models designate a single site for service delivery that is easily accessible; when this site is in a community school, the services may be called school-linked services. Integrated service models have been proposed as a response to two primary criticisms of traditional agency-specific services: that the lack of coordination among traditional services wastes human service funds with unnecessary redundancies in services for some and gaps in services to others; and that the agencies' conflicting regulations and service procedures threaten service effectiveness and are unnecessarily confusing.

See also HOME-SCHOOL-COMMUNITY COLLABORATION; TRANSITION SERVICES.

REFERENCES

Dryfoos, J. G. (1993). Schools as places for health, mental health and social services. *Teachers College Record* 94, 540–567.

Nelson, C. M., and C. A. Pearson. (1991). *Integrating services for children and youth with emotional and behavioral disorders.* Reston, VA: Council for Exceptional Children.

Beth Doll

INTELLIGENCE. Nearly unanimous agreement by over 1,000 experts in psychology, education, genetics, and sociology is that abstract thinking or reasoning, the capacity to acquire knowledge, and problem-solving ability are important elements of intelligence. Seven other areas chosen by the majority of experts were adaptation to one's environment, creativity, general knowledge, linguistic competence, mathematical competence, memory, and mental speed (Sattler, 1988, pp. 45–46).

Modern concern with individual differences in intelligence had its beginning in the sixteenth century, but most notable attention was directed to cognitive functioning beginning with the nineteenth century. Early in the nineteenth century, focus was on mental retardation; later, Sir Francis Galton promulgated a hereditarian view of individual differences* based on his work with prominent persons. The early part of the twentieth century was a period of pragmatic efforts to differentiate children who would benefit from schooling from those who would not (e.g., the work of Binet and Simon). This approach found utility, particularly with the development of the intelligence quotient, the Stanford Binet Intelligence Scale in 1916 and the Wechsler scales in 1939, 1949, 1955, and

1963, and their revisions, which have dominated intellectual assessment to the present.

For the last ninety years, theoreticians have attempted to discern the nature and structure of intelligence. Using factor analysis,* two broad camps have emerged. First, following Spearman's two-factor theory, Vernon proposed a variation of a general intelligence factor, *g,* and multiple specific factors. Second, following the work of Thorndike, Thurstone and Guilford rejected *g* for various multifactor theories of intelligence. Currently, factor analytic approaches wed the two approaches in hierarchical theories of intelligence.

For decades, the measurement of intelligence has been driven by the need for determining special education* classifications or for diagnostic information regarding organic or functional pathology. With changes in beliefs about what constitutes good educational opportunities for learners with disabilities, the usefulness of intelligence tests has been questioned, with the emphasis shifting from product to process. Some school psychologists and educators want to know about the processes of cognitive functioning rather than the IQ of a child for special education placement. Others, however, are de-emphasizing cognitive process variables and preferring behavioral approaches to assessment.

These shifts in focus toward process variables make hierarchical theories of intelligence with developmental perspectives appealing. Equally intriguing are the information-processing theories of intelligence. During the 1960s, the electronic computer, work with the structure of language, and information theory coalesced into information-processing models. With much work having been done over preceding decades in areas such as attention, perception, and memory, whole pieces of the models had abundant research. Wider appeal for information-processing models developed when the domination of the early computer-analog models ended because they were deemed inadequate to account for the decision making or executive function operating in multiple contexts. Newer work supports general theories of intelligence incorporating a structural dimension and a control dimension. The structural components of capacity, durability, and efficiency are supposedly biologically or genetically based, while the control components are learned and guide problem solving. These control components can be taught. Piaget's work with schemata and adaptation is applicable to the control dimension. In this tradition, the work of Sternberg presents three dimensions: componential, experimental, and contextual. The latter two address cultural differences. The bridge between information processing and neuropsychology is best represented by the information-processing model of Das. Based on the work of the Russian neuropsychologist Luria, Das's ideas of simultaneous and successive processing have been incorporated into the development of the Kaufman Assessment Battery for Children and, more recently, the PASS model.

Currently, an interesting mix of information-processing theory, cognitive psychology, and neuropsychology is beginning to take form in the theoretical propositions presented earlier. Assessment instruments for segments of theories are appearing. The demands for treatment-linked assessment might allow for more comprehensive assessment instruments that provide cognitive processing information to supplant the traditional single index—the IQ.

See also BINET, ALFRED; COGNITIVE ASSESSMENT: NONTRADITIONAL; COGNITIVE ASSESSMENT: TRADITIONAL; PIAGETIAN ASSESSMENT.

REFERENCES

Glover, J. A., and A. J. Corkill. (1990). The implications of cognitive psychology for school psychology. In T. B. Gutkin and C. R. Reynolds (Eds.), *The handbook of school psychology* (2d ed., pp. 104–125). New York: Wiley.
Naglieri, J. A., and P. N. Prewett. (1990). Nonverbal intelligence measures: A selected review of instruments and their use. In C. R. Reynolds and R. W. Kamphaus (Eds.), *Handbook of psychological and educational assessment of children: Intelligence and achievement* (pp. 348–370). New York: Guilford Press.
Sattler, J. M. (1988). *Assessment of children* (3d ed.). San Diego: Author.
Vernon, P. E. (1979). *Intelligence: Heredity and environment.* San Francisco: W. H. Freeman.

Paul G. Warden

INTERDISCIPLINARY MODELS. The terms "interdisciplinary," "transdisciplinary," and "multidisciplinary" are used interchangeably by many educators, although they actually refer to three different staffing patterns or styles of professional interaction among members of school teams. When members of several disciplines are engaged in activities such as assessment,* planning and decision making, case management, intervention* design, and outcome evaluation, they often provide their services as members of a team. Such patterns of service delivery are especially useful in assisting students who have several areas of special need.

The multidisciplinary team,* which has its roots in the medical model* and which is one of the oldest forms of teaming, is characterized by having team members from several disciplines work with a child independently of one another and then report their findings to a single person (e.g., case manager, parent). In this model, there tends to be relatively little interaction among the disciplines, and team members usually take charge of those aspects of the program specific to their discipline (e.g., the school psychologist* assesses cognitive abilities or addresses behavioral problems, and the speech and language therapist provides instruction in communication skills). There is often a reliance on traditional models of service delivery (e.g., resource rooms* for special education instruction).

In an interdisciplinary model, professionals from different disciplines also work independently with a child, but, in addition, they participate as members of a team to jointly discuss and plan the child's program. However, each specialist usually retains responsibility for that part of the child's program related to his or her professional specialty and provides this assistance via traditional service delivery approaches. The interdisciplinary model was developed as a means of improving communication among team members.

With a transdisciplinary staffing pattern, professionals from various disciplines typically work jointly with the child and with one another, similar to the mental health collaboration process. Thus, team members must purposefully coordinate their efforts and share their information and skills. In addition, because they are knowledgeable about the roles of other team members, they are able to engage in role release, that is, to accept and share roles and responsibilities with one another (Linder, 1990). The role release aspect of the transdisciplinary approach challenges team members to reconsider their traditional roles and to respect the abilities of one another as they interchange professional roles. However, releasing roles does not indicate that expertise specific to each discipline is no longer required; rather, it is shared among team members across traditional disciplinary boundaries in support of children. A further implication is that parents and children are considered potential participants in the information exchange and role release process (Landerholm, 1990). As team members, parents are also expected to provide support related to their child's educational goals.

The transdisciplinary arrangement attempts to overcome some of the limitations or confines of each discipline, especially related to the fragmentation of services, by forming a team that crosses disciplinary boundaries, that learns and shares new information, and that provides services in a more unified fashion within the educational setting. The goal is to maximize communication, interaction, and cooperation among team members, to promote an integrated, interactive view of the child, and to increase the generalizability of skills. Professionals in early childhood education serving young children with disabilities have been the primary advocates of the transdisciplinary model.

Although distinctions among the three terms have been made, in practice it is common to find some combination of each being adopted. This fact may account for why these terms are often used interchangeably.

See also COLLABORATION; TEAM; TEAM APPROACH.

REFERENCES

Huebner, E. S., and B. M. Hahn. (1990). Best practices in coordinating multidisciplinary teams. In A. Thomas and J. Grimes (Eds.), *Best practices in school psychology—II* (pp. 235–246). Washington, DC: National Association of School Psychologists.
Landerholm, E. (winter, 1990). The transdisciplinary team approach. *Teaching Exceptional Children,* 66–70.
Linder, T. W. (1990). *Transdisciplinary play-based assessment: A functional approach to working with young children.* Baltimore: Paul A. Brookes.

Joseph E. Zins

INTERESTS. Interest assessment is one of the most important aspects of overall vocational assessment.* Essentially, interests are an individual's likes and dislikes as they relate to different career functions. Interest assessment is divided into three different approaches. *Expressed* interests are assessed by simply asking students what vocational areas they are attracted to and what areas they are not attracted to. *Measured* interests are determined by assessing students' knowledge about the various career areas, usually in the form of questionnaires. *Inventoried* interests are assessed through the use of standardized vocational interest inventories. The most popular of these are the Self-Directed Search and the Strong Interest Inventory. There are also picture-type interest inventories that do not require a student to have significant reading skills, such as the Wide Range Interest and Opinion Test. School psychologists are becoming increasingly involved in the interest assessment of adolescents with disabilities who may select vocational education programs at the secondary and postsecondary levels.

See also VOCATIONAL ASSESSMENT; VOCATIONAL SCHOOL PSYCHOLOGY.

REFERENCES

Anderson, W. T., T. H. Hohenshil, K. Herr, and E. Levinson. (1990). Vocational assessment procedures for students with disabilities: An update. In A. Thomas and J. Grimes (Eds.), *Best practices in school psychology—II* (pp. 787–798). Washington, DC: National Association of School Psychologists.
Cohen, R. J., M. E. Swerdlik, and D. K. Smith. (1992). *Psychological testing and assessement: An introduction to tests and measurement.* Mountain View, CA: Mayfield.

Thomas H. Hohenshil

INTERMEDIATE AGENCY. Regional education structures, also known as cooperatives or intermediate units, are defined as the uniting of local educational districts for the purpose of providing services in the most efficient and effective manner. These regional structures typically exist in an intermediate position between the local school district and the state educational agency.

Regional educational units provide a variety of services, including administrative services, planning and development, vocational-technical education programs, educational and instructional media services, purchasing, specialized instructional programs, and specialized pupil personnel services.* The range of services possible through regional cooperative agreements and the concept of regional structures in general is much broader than services to students with disabilities. However, the growing demand for these special education services and subsequent passage of Public Law 94-142* resulted in a proliferation of regional educational units in the 1970s.

Regional structures became especially important in rural districts as these districts were mandated to provide specialized teaching staff, program options to severely and low-incidence handicapped students, psychological services, and specialized medical services (e.g., psychiatrists, occupational therapists, physical therapists, audiologists), while facing issues of uneven local funding, the non-availability of sufficient numbers of qualified staff, and geographical and cultural barriers.

In the period of the 1970s through the mid-1980s, the most common regional service delivery model was the state-mandated special district or state-sanctioned agency. The purpose of these regional units was explicitly direct service delivery,* especially to students with disabilities. Common models included the Board of Cooperative Educational Services (BOCES) in New York, the Intermediate Units (IU) in Pennsylvania, and the Regional Education Service Agency (RESA) or Cooperative Education Service Agency (CESA), used widely throughout other portions of the nation. The BOCES, legislatively mandated in 1948, and IUs, begun in 1971, represent state-mandated intermediate, regional units that hold governing and/or funding responsibilities for the participating local school districts. Other regional programs formed voluntarily from the collaborative initiatives of the local educational agencies. Developmentally, as the immediate staffing service needs of the local districts were met, and these districts were able to employ qualified staff themselves, regional educational structures have become more of a locally initiated collaborative arrangement. Subsequently, in many regional units the role of the school psychologist* has changed from direct service to a large geographical area to direct service to students served by regional programs and indirect services to the local district staff (e.g., consultation,* supervision, continuing professional development* services).

Benefits of regional special education service models have been noted to include improved cost efficiency, access to program and service specialists, assessment and reallocation of resources, facilitation of staff retention, facilitation of compliance with federal and state mandates, and maintenance of a sense of local autonomy. Looking at school psychological services, the advantages include the possibility of having a wider sphere of influence, being able to employ multiple school psychologists with diversity in areas of interest/expertise, providing appropriate supervision, and having a support group of fellow professionals. In a regional model, the local school districts also have each other as a reference group, which is useful in facilitating system-level changes. Practical issues for the school psychologist in a regional position may include being perceived as an outsider by the local districts, the process of goal setting and dynamics of serving various expectations, and the travel and time involved.

See also RURAL SCHOOL PSYCHOLOGY.

REFERENCES

Benson, A. J. (1985). School psychology service configurations: A regional approach. *School Psychology Review* 14, 421–428.
Helge, D. (1984). *Problems and strategies regarding regionalizing service delivery.* Murray, KY: National Rural Research and Personnel Preparation Project. (ERIC Document Reproduction Service No. ED 242 449)

                                                                    A. Jerry Benson

INTERNATIONAL COLLOQUIUM ON SCHOOL PSYCHOLOGY. The International School Psychology Association* (ISPA) sponsors an annual colloquium to further the goals of the association. The primary purpose of this meeting is the promotion of professionalism of school psychology* at national and international levels. The five- to six-day event includes meetings of its executive officers and committees, invited addresses by scholars, practitioners, and policy planners, symposia, presentation of scientific and professional papers, and social and cultural activities. Escorted tours of important professional activities and other locations within the host country or nearby countries also are arranged.

The first colloquium was held in Munich, Germany, in 1975. Subsequent sites included Denmark, England, Jerusalem, Sweden, United States, Switzerland, Yugoslavia, Portugal, Turkey, and Brazil. Future colloquia are planned for Scotland and Hungary (Oakland, 1993). Colloquium themes often coincide and support those emphasized by the United Nations.

REFERENCE

Oakland, T. (1993). A brief history of international school psychology. *Journal of School Psychology* 31, 109–122.

Thomas Oakland

INTERNATIONAL SCHOOL PSYCHOLOGY ASSOCIATION. The International School Psychology Association (ISPA) is a professional association consisting of 300–400 members from more than forty countries. Its purposes are to promote the use of sound psychological principles within the context of education throughout the world, to promote communication between professionals committed to the improvement of children's mental health, to encourage the use of school psychologists* in countries where they are not currently being used, and to initiate and promote cooperation with other organizations working for purposes similar to those of ISPA. Its administrative structure includes elected officers: president-elect (who later assumes the office of president and immediate past president), secretary, and treasurer. They appoint an executive secretary. ISPA maintains an active committee structure, including membership, nominations, constitution and bylaws, child development and services, communications, historic preservation, research and evaluation, peace and conflict, professional development, international exchange, and financial aid. Its members meet at yearly colloquia held in different countries. In addition, communication between members occurs through its quarterly newsletter. ISPA also cosponsors a scholarly journal, *School Psychology International.*

ISPA was formed following years of growth within school psychology. Various forms of psychological services for children and youth, often school-based, emerged about the turn of the twentieth century in Europe and North America (Oakland, 1993). The first university-based child clinic was established by Witmer* in the United States in 1896, the first school-based department of child study began in Belgium before 1899, one of the first valid measures of mental abilities was developed by Binet* in France in 1911, and the first United Nations-sponsored international conference on school psychology was held in 1948.

The International School Psychology Committee (ISPC) was formed in 1972 under the direction of Calvin Catterall, Frances Mullen, and Anders Poulsen. The ISPC evolved into the ISPA in 1982 in an effort to promote directions for school psychology internationally as well as to provide assistance to school psychologists and to foster fellowship among them.

See also INTERNATIONAL COLLOQUIUM ON SCHOOL PSYCHOLOGY.

REFERENCE

Oakland, T. (1993). A brief history of international school psychology. *Journal of School Psychology* 31, 109–122.

Thomas Oakland

INTERNSHIP. The internship in school psychology* provides a transition between the classroom learning environment of a university and the "real world" of school psychology practice. Morrow (1946) wrote that interns were being trained at the Vineland Training School in New Jersey as early as 1908. A 1963 conference held at the George Peabody College for Teachers in Nashville, Tennessee, addressed the topic of doctoral-level school psychology internship experiences. Many of the topics discussed at the so-called Peabody conference* (e.g., the internship should provide a balance between service and training) are relevant to today's school psychology internships at all levels of training.

Currently, internships for sixth-year or specialist*-level students follow two years of classroom and practicum* experiences. In most cases, internships must be completed prior to the granting of state certification.* Doctoral*-level internships typically follow all classroom experiences, although the doctorate degree is not granted until the internship is successfully completed. Recent data indicate that interns in specialist-level programs complete an average of 1,169 clock hours in the schools while interns in doctoral-level programs complete an average of 1,559 clock hours in the schools (Smith and Henning, in press).

During the internship, the intern is usually employed by a school district or special education cooperative and works full-time for that district for one school year under close supervision from an experienced school psychologist. In some instances, the internship occurs over a two-year period, during which the intern is employed on a half-time basis. Universities maintain contact with interns through site visits by university personnel, return visits to campus by the interns, and letters and telephone contacts. It is generally the on-site supervisor, however, who provides the day-to-day supervision.

Internship experiences provide opportunities for interns to apply knowledge and skills acquired during training and to acquire additional knowledge and

skills. Ideally, interns should have the chance to observe the roles and functions*
of other professionals in the schools with whom school psychologists work
closely (e.g., school counselors, speech and language therapists) and to famil-
iarize themselves with the workings of the school system and the agencies and
resources available outside the schools. The internship is also the time to become
familiar with federal, state, and local rules and regulations that govern the practice of school psychology.

The National Association of School Psychologists* (NASP) and some state
departments of education publish standards for, and information about, school
psychology internships. Readers are advised to consult these sources for up-to-
date information (NASP, 1994).

See also INTERNSHIP SUPERVISION; INTERNSHIP SUPERVISOR;
PROFESSIONAL STANDARDS; SCHOOL SETTINGS; TRAINING MOD-
ELS; UNIVERSITY TRAINER.

REFERENCES

Morrow, W. R. (1946). The development of psychological internship training. *Journal
    of Consulting Psychology* 10, 165–183.
National Association of School Psychologists. (1994). *Standards for training and field
    placement programs in school psychology.* Washington, DC: Author.
Smith, D. K., and A. Henning. (in press). *Directory of school psychology training
    programs* (4th ed.). Washington, DC: National Association of School
    Psychologists.

Paula Sachs Wise

INTERNSHIP SUPERVISION. Receipt of intensive, individual supervision is
perhaps the single greatest distinction between an internship* and regular employment as a practicing school psychologist.* The nature and quality of internship supervision are so critical in the training of school psychologists that
at least four national professional organizations have guidelines applicable to
the supervision of school psychology interns, in addition to guidelines issued
by state credentialing agencies. All standards require that interns receive at least
two hours per week of direct supervision from a qualified supervisor (NASP,
1986).

Internship supervision focuses on both the development and formal evaluation
of the intern's competencies. Because internships are the capstone of preprofes-
sional training, occurring after practicums but before entry-level practice, internship supervision includes reinforcement of already-existing exemplary
practices, refinement of emergent competencies, and initial development of
whole new skills. Building the intern's confidence is also a critical element of
internship supervision.

Supervision of school-based internships is typically a joint effort between the
school site and the intern's university training program. While the school system
provides administrative supervision,* other aspects of internship supervision

may be provided by a site- or university-based supervisor(s) or by both. Interns also often receive group supervision, including case presentations, topical discussions, and lectures by persons with expertise in a particular area.

The evaluative component of internship supervision is critical. Detailed feedback to the intern provides a guide for professional development. Summative evaluations* resulting from internship supervision serve as the job applicant's single most important reference.

See also ADMINISTRATIVE SUPERVISION; CERTIFICATION; LICENSING; INTERNSHIP SUPERVISOR; PRACTICUM; PROFESSIONAL STANDARDS; PROFESSIONAL SUPERVISION; UNIVERSITY TRAINER.

REFERENCES

Alessi, G., K. J. Lascurettes-Alessi, and W. L. Leys. (1981). Internships in school psychology: Supervision issues. *School Psychology Review* 10, 461–469.
Conoley, J. C., and T. Bahns. (1995). Best practices in supervision of interns. In A. Thomas and J. Grimes (Eds.), *Best practices in school psychology—III* (pp. 111–122). Washington, DC: National Association of School Psychologists.
Knoff, H. M. (1986). Supervision in school psychology: The forgotten or future path to effective services? *School Psychology Review* 15, 529–545.
National Association of School Psychologists. (1986). *Standards for training and field placement programs in school psychology.* Silver Spring, MD: Author.

William Strein

INTERNSHIP SUPERVISOR. Internship supervisors take responsibility for the intern's work, as well as guiding the intern's training. Historically, in school psychology,* interns receive supervision from both a university-based and field-based supervisor. Multiple site-based supervisors are also common, but one individual (primary supervisor) must take the responsibility for organizing the training experience and monitoring the intern's work. According to National Association of School Psychologists* (NASP) and American Psychological Association* (APA) training standards, interns must receive at least two hours per week of individual, face-to-face supervision from their internship supervisor(s). At least one hour per week of this supervision must be provided by the primary supervisor. In addition to being appropriately credentialed and highly competent practitioners, internship supervisors must possess supervisory and teaching skills.

See also INTERNSHIP; INTERNSHIP SUPERVISION; PROFESSIONAL STANDARDS.

REFERENCES

Alessi, G., K. J. Lascurettes-Alessi, and W. L. Leys. (1981). Internships in school psychology: Supervision issues. *School Psychology Review* 10, 461–469.
Conoley, J. C., and T. Bahns (1995). Best practices in supervision of interns. In A.

Thomas and J. Grimes (Eds.), *Best practices in school psychology—III* (pp. 111–122). Washington, DC: National Association of School Psychologists.

William Strein

INTERPROFESSIONAL RESEARCH COMMISSION ON PUPIL PER-SONNEL SERVICES. Emerging from an invitational meeting in 1961, the Interprofessional Research Commission on Pupil Personnel Services (IRCOPPS) was founded in 1963 with funding from the National Institute of Mental Health. IRCOPPS was a congress of representatives of at least eighteen professional groups whose overall purpose was to foster improvement of pupil personnel services* and the contributions of IRCOPPS member groups to education (Liddle and Ferguson, 1968). Operating out of the University of Maryland with a director and associate director, the commission conducted research on pupil services programs across the country and was assisted by four regional research and demonstration centers (University of Texas, University of Michigan, Chico State College in California, and University of Maryland). The effort produced several research reports of local and national scope, including *Pupil Services for the 70's in Maryland, Special Education and Pupil Services in RESA 10* (Iowa), *Pupil Services in the Worcester Public Schools* (Massachusetts), and *Pupil Services Department: Functions, Organization, Staffing.* IRCOPPS appears to have been funded only from 1963 to about 1969.

REFERENCES

Liddle, G. P. (1968). IRCOPPS: A five year progress report. *Journal of the International Association of Pupil Personnel Workers* 12, 167–171.
Liddle, G. P., and D. G. Ferguson. (1968). *Pupil services department: Functions, organization, leadership.* Washington, DC: Administrative Leadership Service, Educational Service Bureau.

Thomas K. Fagan

INTERVENTION (DIRECT AND INDIRECT). Interventions can be defined as strategic reactions by psychologists and others to students' inappropriate behavior or unsuccessful learning (Reynolds et al., 1984). The ultimate goal of an intervention (prevention and/or treatment) should be the successful resolution of the learning or adjustment problem.

Interventions can be direct or indirect and specific or global (Reynolds et al., 1984). In direct interventions, the school psychologist* is working directly with the student. In indirect interventions, the school psychologist is working with a third party (e.g., consultation-based services with a teacher or parent) who will be responsible for implementing the intervention with a students(s). Specific interventions are designed to meet a specialized need of an individual child or a classroom. Global interventions are designed to meet the more general needs of a student or classroom.

Examples of direct, specific interventions include counseling, cognitive behavioral therapy, and direct instruction for an academic difficulty. Examples of direct, global intervention are the implementation of an effective education curriculum by the school psychologist in a classroom setting or a recommendation for placement in a special education class. An example of an indirect, specific intervention is a school psychologist who, through collaborative consultation,* facilitates the implementation of a behavioral program for a student by a teacher or parent. An example of an indirect, global intervention is an in-service training program conducted by a school psychologist on such issues as general intervention approaches with students with attention-deficit hyperactivity disorder (ADHD).

School psychology* has moved in the direction of indirect (specific and global) interventions that include both prevention and treatment services. Research has supported the efficacy of indirect (individual and group) service delivery interventions as equivalent to, or greater than, that of direct service delivery interventions (Prout and DeMartino, 1986). In addition, research has supported that behavioral and cognitive therapy* interventions are more effective than nonbehavioral (client-centered) interventions (Casey and Berman, 1985).

Indirect interventions are more common in school settings for a number of reasons. First, due to the number of students referred and encountered by school psychologists, it is virtually impossible to affect a significant number of students using direct interventions. Indirect service delivery is a more efficient use of time. Second, there is significant support in the literature for behavior change occurring more quickly and generalizing more fully when the intervention occurs in the natural environment. Teachers and parents are the most likely parties to implement interventions in the natural environment. Third, through the use of collaborative consultation, teachers and parents learn the intervention strategies themselves and can use them with other students (siblings) or use them in future applications. This increases the efficiency of the school psychologist's service.

See also BEHAVIOR THERAPY; ECOLOGICAL CONSULTATION; INDIRECT SERVICE DELIVERY; SYSTEMS INTERVENTION.

REFERENCES

Casey, R. J., and J. S. Berman. (1985). The outcome of psychotherapy with children. *Psychological Bulletin* 98, 388–400.
Prout, J. T., and R. A. DeMartino. (1986). A meta-analysis of school-based studies of psychotherapy. *Journal of School Psychology* 24, 285–292.
Reynolds, C. R., T. B. Gutkin, S. N. Elliott, and J. C. Witt. (1984). *School psychology: Essentials of theory and practice.* New York: Wiley.
Thomas, A., and J. Grimes (Eds.). (1995). *Best practices in school psychology—III.* Washington, DC: National Association of School Psychologists.

George M. Batsche

INTERVIEWING (DIAGNOSTIC INTERVIEW). The diagnostic interview, also referred to as the clinical, intake, or assessment interview, is often the single most valuable source of data for psychological evaluation. Its purpose, consistent with that of other assessment procedures, is to obtain valid, pertinent information for hypothesis testing, form a clinical picture of the client,* and determine appropriate intervention and treatment.

The interview has several advantages as an assessment procedure. It allows for rapport building, flexible questioning, motivating responses, clarifying or expanding ambiguous responses, obtaining a chronology of events, matching verbal and nonverbal behaviors, evaluating receptivity to intervention options, and addressing client expectations. Often it is the first and only direct means of obtaining data from clients and/or third-party referents. Several drawbacks to this method cannot, however, be overlooked. Reliability* and validity* of data are difficult to establish; inaccurate information may be provided; and interviewer subjectivity and bias can distort the clinical picture.

One consideration for interviewing is the degree of structure desired. Idiosyncratic and low-incidence data can be obtained only through an open-ended, flexible, person-centered approach that encourages rapport, self-exploration, and expanded expression. Structured interview formats have more psychometric precision, reliability, norm comparability, and objectivity in interpretation but give up the personal touch, depth, and sensitivity of the open-ended format. While behavioral clinicians prefer the structured format, psychodynamic and humanistic-oriented clinicians prefer the unstructured. Many interviewers lean toward a middle ground that depends on an outline of questions that can be elaborated upon when needed.

Interviewer style is strongly influenced by theoretical orientation and practical considerations. Psychodynamic, client-centered, and behavioral interviewers focus on the process from different perspectives and frame the data from different orientations. Thus, the same responses may not be elicited or, if elicited, may not be interpreted in the same way. Also, interview style is heavily influenced by the circumstances surrounding the client visit. Emergent situations call for a quick mental status and triage-type assessment, whereas insight-oriented outpatient interviewing may be extended to cover a broad range of topics.

The standard interview focuses on the following types of information: understanding the presenting problem; family history and dynamics; developmental history; physical and medical history; social history; educational history; vocational/career skills and interests*; behavioral patterns and habits; and prediction for intervention/treatment.

When interviewing children, Bierman (1990) suggests that care must be given to reducing the complexity and ambiguity of questions by providing concrete referents during the interview. Supplementing the interview with standardized self-report measures enables the interviewer to gather specific information about adjustment and allows for age-related comparisons. Standardized diagnostic interviews are also available for eliciting information about symptoms and behavioral patterns that aid in formally diagnosing disorders. Since they do not allow for the natural communication pattern typical of counselor-child relationships that becomes the foundation for further therapeutic interaction, the structured diagnostic and self-report formats should not supplant the open-ended child interview.

The interview and behavioral observation methods for data collection and analysis are basic tools of clinical practice and rely on trained skill development.

See also COMPREHENSIVE ASSESSMENT.

REFERENCES

Bierman, K. L. (1990). Using the clinical interview to assess children's interpersonal reasoning and emotional understanding. In C. R. Reynolds and R. W. Kamphaus (Eds.), *Handbook of psychological and educational assessment of children*. New York: Guilford Press.

Grath-Marnat, G. (1990). *Handbook of psychological assessment* (2d ed.). New York: Wiley.

Lentz, F. E., and B. A. Wehmann. (1995). Best practices in interviewing. In A. Thomas and J. Grimes (Eds.), *Best practices in school psychology—III* (pp. 637–649). Washington, DC: National Association of School Psychologists.

Sattler, J. M. (1992). *Assessment of children* (rev. 3d ed.). San Diego: Author.

Susan Kupisch

INVOLUNTARY HOSPITALIZATION/COMMITMENT. Most states have two types of involuntary commitment: emergency and judicial. Emergency commitment recognizes that, in some instances, the urgency of the need to commit (e.g., suicide attempts) may not allow for all the formal niceties of the law (a hearing, cross-examination of witnesses, and so on). Thus, an emergency commitment may be obtained by having qualified mental health practitioners agree that the individual is (1) an immediate danger to himself or herself or others and (2) in need of care and treatment. Such a commitment, since it skirts due process, is typically for a limited time only (e.g., five days), during which the person may be evaluated for possible judicial commitment.

Judicial commitment "touches all the bases" of the law. There must be a hearing, the person is entitled to legal representation, witnesses may be cross-examined, and the person may even demand a jury trial. Here again, professionals have to testify that the person is mentally ill, dangerous to self or others, and in need of care and treatment and that all less restrictive alternatives are unsuitable (*Lake v. Cameron,* 364 F2d 657, D.C. Cir., 1966; a state law example is TCA 33-6-101-et seq.).

See also DUTY TO WARN; PRIVATE PRACTICE.

J. L. Bernard

IOWA CHILD WELFARE RESEARCH STATION. Founded in 1917 at the University of Iowa in Iowa City, the Iowa Child Welfare Research Station was modeled after the Agricultural Experiment Station at Iowa State College in Ames. Assisted by Carl E. Seashore, dean of the Graduate College and professor of psychology at Iowa, Cora Bussey Hillis used her contacts with the state Women's Christian Temperance Union (WCTU) and the Iowa Federation of Women's Clubs to pressure the state legislature to establish the station and provide funding. In Hillis's view, the role of the station was to promote practical child-saving, but Seashore and the first director, Bird T. Baldwin, saw it as a vehicle for promoting psychological research on children at the university. A grant from the WCTU and increased funding from the state enabled the station to add a preschool nursery for research purposes—the first of its kind in the country—in 1922. Soon after, the station began receiving grant money from the Laura Spelman Rockefeller Memorial—at first, small amounts and then major funding during the 1920s as a part of the grand design by Lawrence K. Frank of the memorial to create a new science of child development and to disseminate its findings through a program of parent education. With George Stoddard as director in the 1930s, the station was at the center of a major controversy involving the issue of the constancy of IQ in young children. Iowa researchers Beth Wellman and Harold Skeels found evidence to suggest that the IQs of children could be improved, but key figures in child development research led by Lewis Terman disagreed and were able to maintain the view of the fixity of the IQ in young children. Recent research and the success of the Head Start program have led to renewed respect for the Iowa research in the 1930s.

See also PRESCHOOL INTERVENTIONS; PREVENTION.

REFERENCES

Cravens, H. (1985). Child saving in the age of professionalism. In J. M. Hawes and N. R. Hiner (Eds.), *American childhood: A research guide and historical handbook* (pp. 415–488). Westport, CT: Greenwood Press.

———. (1993). *Before Head Start: The Iowa Station and America's children.* Chapel Hill: University of North Carolina Press.

Joseph M. Hawes

J

JASTAK, JOSEPH F. Joseph Florian Jastak was born in Gostycsyn, Poland, on March 19, 1901, and died in Greenville, Delaware, on May 27, 1979. After attending the University at Poznan from 1920 to 1925, Jastak obtained a scholarship through the Kosciuszko Foundation in New York City to pursue his studies in the United States. He arrived in New York in 1926 and received his doctorate in clinical psychology* from Columbia University in 1934. He completed an internship at New York's Bellevue Hospital. Jastak moved to Delaware in 1936 to serve as chief psychologist at the Delaware State Hospital. In the 1950s, he entered full-time private practice.* In 1936, he first published the Wide Range Achievement Test (WRAT), perhaps his most noted accomplishment among publications that spanned the period 1934 to 1974. The highly successful test has been revised several times and is still widely used in school and nonschool settings. With his wife, Sarah, he organized Jastak Associates in Wilmington, Delaware. Jastak was a founder and president of the Delaware Psychological Association and was honored by several groups, including the National Rehabilitation Association, Delaware Association for Retarded Citizens, and the National Association of School Psychologists,* which granted him honorary life membership in 1977.

REFERENCE

Jastak, J. F. (1936). *Wide Range Achievement Test.* Wilmington, DE: C. L. Story.

Thomas K. Fagan

JOB SATISFACTION. Working as a school psychologist* has tremendous potential for satisfaction. Through their various roles and functions,* school psychologists have opportunities to help children, assist teachers and parents, and improve the overall school environment through systemwide change. Perhaps not surprisingly, more has been written about job stressors and burnout among school psychologists than about job satisfaction. This may be attributable to the fact that school psychology* is a problem-oriented or problem-solving profession. We may have a tendency to focus on how to change weaknesses rather than on how to enjoy strengths.

Research on job satisfaction and job stress suggests that job satisfaction occurs when the tasks required are at the proper level of difficulty (i.e., the individual feels neither overtrained nor undertrained to perform the job demands); when the workload is manageable; when there are sufficient opportunities for advancement; when the individual feels appropriately compensated for his or her skills and training; when the individual receives feedback of on-the-job successes; and when the job climate (coworkers, physical environment, gender issues, and so on) is pleasant (Fagan and Wise, 1994). Affiliation with professional associations also seems to be a factor (Levinson, Fetchkan, and Hohenshil, 1988). A recent study indicates that 41 percent of school psychologists intend to stay in the field until retirement (up from 31 percent in the mid-1980s) and that 77 percent would again choose school psychology* as a career (Reschly and Wilson, 1995).

See also EMPLOYMENT TRENDS.

REFERENCES

Fagan, T. K., and P. S. Wise. (1994). *School psychology: Past, present, and future.* New York: Longman.

Levinson, E. M., R. Fetchkan, and T. H. Hohenshil. (1988). Job satisfaction among practicing school psychologists revisited. *School Psychology Review* 17, 101–112.

Reschly, D. J., and M. S. Wilson. (1995). School psychology faculty and practitioners: 1986 to 1991 trends in demographic characteristics, roles, satisfaction, and system reform. *School Psychology Review* 24, 62–80.

Paula Sachs Wise

K

KELLY, GEORGE. George Kelly was born on April 28, 1905, in Kansas. He completed an M.A. in educational sociology from the University of Kansas, and in 1931 he completed a Ph.D. in psychology at Iowa State University. He spent the next ten years at Fort Hays State College (now, University) in Kansas and established a program of clinics that traveled throughout the western portion of the state providing psychological services to schools and children. During World War II, he served in the navy as an aviation psychologist. In 1946, George Kelly was appointed professor and director of clinical psychology at Ohio State University, where he remained for twenty years. During this time, he made his major contribution to the study of personality with the publication of *The Psychology of Personal Constructs* (1955). A primary application of Kelly's personal construct theory is repertory grid technique. He moved to Brandeis University in 1965 as the Riklis Chair of Behavioral Science. George Kelly died on March 6, 1966. He was an early personality theorist in the cognitive approach to psychotherapy and an advocate of providing clinical psychology* services in the schools.

REFERENCES

Jankowicz, A. D. (1987). Whatever became of George Kelly? Applications and implications. *American Psychologist* 42, 481–487.
Maher, B. (1969). *Clinical psychology and personality. The selected papers of George Kelly.* New York: Wiley.

Mark D. Shriver
Jack J. Kramer

KOPPITZ, ELIZABETH M. Elizabeth Munsterberg Koppitz was born in Germany on February 9, 1919, and died in New York on October 5, 1983. She earned her B.A. in sociology at George Peabody College for Teachers (1951) and her M.A. (1952) and Ph.D. (1955) in clinical psychology* at the Ohio State University. After employment in Columbus, Ohio, she became the first school psychologist* to be hired by the Endicott, New York, public schools. She worked for other New York school districts from 1961 to 1982. Koppitz was a significant contributor to psychoeducational assessment, with publications on the Bender Gestalt Test, children's human figure drawings, and the Visual Aural Digit Span Test. She lectured widely and contributed to the literature of school and clinical psychology. She also published a widely cited study on a five-year follow-up of children with learning disabilities (1968). She was active in professional organizations, receiving distinguished service awards from both the Westchester County Psychological Association and the National Association of School Psychologists* (NASP).

REFERENCE

Fagan, T. K. (1983). In memoriam: Elizabeth M. Koppitz, 1919–1983. *Communique* 12(4), 1,3.

Thomas K. Fagan

KRUGMAN, MORRIS. Morris Krugman was born July 1, 1898, in Bialystok, Russia, and moved to Brooklyn, New York, in childhood. He obtained his B.S. at Brooklyn Polytechnic Institute (1919) and his A.M. (1925) and Ph.D. (1928) in clinical psychology* from New York University. He lectured at several New York area colleges and universities and held leadership positions with the New York State Association of Applied Psychologists, the Rorschach Institute, and the New York Region of the American Orthopsychiatric Association. He served as the first elected president of the Division of School Psychologists* of the American Psychological Association* (1945–1946). He helped to develop psychological services in the New York City public schools and was chief psychologist for the Bureau of Child Guidance (1932–1947), assistant superintendent of schools for guidance and curriculum development (1947–1961), and associate superintendent for child welfare (1961–1964). He died in Tompkins Cove, New York, on February 23, 1993.

REFERENCES

Fagan, T. K. (1994). Morris and Judith Krugman: Division 16's only spousal presidents. *The School Psychologist* (Division 16, APA Newsletter), 48(3), 8, 14–15.
Krugman, M. (Ed.). (1958). *Orthopsychiatry and the school.* New York: American Orthopsychiatric Association.

Thomas K. Fagan

L

LABELING. Labeling or classification is the usual consequence of the assessment* process employed to identify children with mental, emotional, or physical conditions that create a need for the provision of specialized educational services. The process of identifying, labeling, and placement in a specialized educational setting is based on the assumption that it will accrue some benefit to the child (Hobbs, 1975). The impetus for the formalization of the practice of labeling children dates from the passage of Public Law 94-142,* the Education for All Handicapped Act, in 1975. The law, together with subsequent legislation (Public Law 99-457,* 1986; Public Law 101-476,* 1990), requires the identification and provision of services for all students with disabilities.

Generally, ten broad labels or conditions encompass approximately 11 percent of the population aged three to twenty-one: learning disabled; mentally disabled; emotionally disturbed; speech-impaired; hearing-impaired; visually impaired; orthopedically impaired; other health-impaired; multidisabled; and deaf-blind. Diagnostic characteristics, including incidence estimates, of the psychologically based conditions are further described in the *Diagnostic and Statistical Manual of Mental Disorders IV* (American Psychiatric Association, 1994).

There is considerable ambiguity regarding the definition of students with learning disabilities. This category of disability encompasses approximately 45 to 50 percent of all children served in special education. Whether or not a child is eventually labeled learning disabled depends, in part, on the particular assessment process employed and school district policies and guidelines.

Closely aligned with psychological assessment and the provision of special education services, labeling is controversial in that there exists the suspicion that the labels themselves promote biased expectations that may ultimately prove to be injurious to children. Undoubtedly, in accord with Reynolds and Kaiser (1990), labeling would occur informally even in the absence of any formally codified labels afforded by the elimination of normative testing or the employment of noncategorical funding. However, of concern throughout the history of labeling as a requirement for the provision of special services is the efficacy of the resulting services. The process of formal, codified labeling without demonstrable subsequent benefit does not provide much logical support for its continued use.

See also CLASSIFICATION: EDUCATIONAL; CLASSIFICATION: PSYCHIATRIC.

REFERENCES

American Psychiatric Association. (1994). *Diagnostic and statistical manual of mental disorders* (4th ed.). Washington, DC: Author.
Hobbs, N. (Ed.). (1975). *Issues in the classification of children,* Vols. 1, 2. San Francisco: Jossey-Bass.
Reynolds, C. R., and S. M. Kaiser. (1990). Test bias in psychological assessment. In T. B. Gutkin and C. R. Reynolds (Eds.), *The handbook of school psychology* (2d ed.). New York: Wiley.

Thomas J. Kehle

LANTZ, C. M. BEATRICE. Born in Chicago, C. M. Beatrice Lantz (1899–1957) moved west for her collegiate education, receiving an A.B. from the University of California at Berkeley in 1920 and an M.A. in 1922 and Ph.D. in 1940 from Stanford University. She practiced in several California communities until she became coordinator of research and guidance in the Los Angeles schools in 1941. She was a lecturer in psychology for the University of Southern California from 1945 to 1960.

As administrators of psychological services in a large city, Lantz, Frances Mullen from Chicago, and Bertha Luckey from Cleveland were key spokespersons across the country on issues related to psychological practice. With Mullen, T. Ernest Newland, and Harriet O'Shea, Lantz was a driving force in planning the Thayer conference. She was an early diplomate in clinical psychology* through the American Board of Examiners in Professional Psychology; a fellow in the American Psychological Association* and a member of its Council of Representatives from the Division of School Psychologists* (1951–1954); and a member of the American Educational Research Association,* Pi Lamba Theta, and Sigma Xi.

Joseph L. French

LARRY P. v. RILES. The *Larry P. v. Riles* case was a special education* placement litigation case brought in U.S. federal district court in California. *Larry P.* was a class-action suit filed on behalf of African-American students who had been placed in classes for the educable mentally retarded (EMR) in the San Francisco public school system. The impetus for the lawsuit was an allegation of overrepresentation of African-American students in EMR classes.

The central issues argued during the litigation were (1) the assessment techniques and procedures used to classify and place minority students in EMR classes and (2) the educational value of EMR classes. Specifically, the use of standardized intelligence* tests was challenged during the trial. The plaintiffs asserted that standardized, individually administered intelligence tests were culturally biased and at fault for the overrepresentation* of African-American students in the EMR classes. The plaintiffs further asserted that these EMR class placements were not educationally beneficial to students.

Judge Robert Peckham found for the plaintiffs and held that the California State Department of Education was in violation of the Civil Rights Act of 1964, Section 504 of the Rehabilitation Act* of 1973, and Public Law 94-142.* Judge Peckham's decision specifically addressed the use of the Wechsler and Stanford-Binet intelligence tests for classification and placement and found the tests to be racially and culturally biased, to have discriminatory impact against African-American children, and not to be validated for the purpose of placement of African-American children into EMR classes. Further, Judge Peckham found the EMR classes themselves to be stigmatizing, isolated, and essentially "dead-end" placements. The decision was upheld by the Ninth Circuit Court of Appeals.

As a result of this decision, the court ordered that IQ tests not be used as part of the EMR classification process for African-American students in California. In 1986, the plaintiffs won an expansion of the original injunction. The amended decision prohibited the use of individually administered intelligence tests with black students for *any* special education* placement decision. In 1988, a group of parents filed suit, alleging that the prohibition of IQ tests imposed by the court was unfair and discriminatory since it denied African-American children the opportunity to use these tests to assess their educational needs. This action resulted in a 1992 order from Judge Peckham allowing the use of IQ tests for African-American children, with parental permission,* in placement decisions for disabilities other than EMR.

In a ruling on the appeal of Judge Peckham's 1992 order, the appellate court upheld his decision and reaffirmed that the 1986 extended ban applied only to EMR classes. It also ruled that no evidence had been presented in the original 1979 trial or in the subsequent 1986 suit to justify an extension of the ban to students with disabilities other than EMR.

Further legal action regarding *Larry P.* is possible, but for now it represents a landmark case and legal opinion on both intelligence testing and classes for the mildly retarded. The decision of Judge Peckham has been widely analyzed and criticized on a number of grounds from a psychology/social science perspective.

See also NONBIASED ASSESSMENT.

REFERENCES

Bersoff, D. N., and P. T. Hofer. (1990). The legal regulation of school psychology. In T. B. Gutkin and C. R. Reynolds (Eds.), *The handbook of school psychology* (pp. 937–961). New York: Wiley.

Jacob-Timm, S., and T. Hartshorne. (1994). *Ethics and law for school psychologists.* Brandon, VT: Clinical Psychology.

Larry P. v. Riles, 343 F. Supp. 1306 (D.C. N.D. Cal., 1972), *aff'd.,* 502 F.2d 963 (9th Cir. 1974), *further proceedings,* 495 F. Supp. 926 (D.C. N.D. Cal., 1979), *aff'd.,* 502 F.2d 693 (9th Cir. 1984).

Reschly, D. J., R. Kicklighter, and P. McKee. (1988). Recent placement litigation Part II, minority EMR overrepresentation: Comparison of *Larry P.* (1979, 1984, 1986) with *Marshall* (1984, 1985) and *S-1* (1986). *School Psychology Review* 17, 22–38.

Todd C. Reiher

LEAST RESTRICTIVE ENVIRONMENT. Although the term ''least restrictive environment'' (LRE) does not appear in the Individuals with Disabilities Education Act of 1990 (IDEA, PUBLIC LAW 101-476*), the least restrictive environment principle is stated in the act:

To the maximum extent appropriate, children with disabilities, including children in public or private institutions or other care facilities, are educated with children who are not disabled, and that special classes, separate schooling, or other removal of children with disabilities from the regular educational environment occurs only when the nature or severity of the disability is such that education in regular classes with the use of supplementary aids and services cannot be achieved satisfactorily. (Tucker and Goldstein, 1992, p. H-21)

When integration into a regular classroom with supplementary aids and services can provide an appropriate education, integration is favored over segregation, but LRE is secondary to appropriateness. Current efforts by some advocates of full inclusion of all students with disabilities into the general education classrooms, along with recent court rulings, suggest a possible shift so that appropriateness may become secondary to LRE.

See also PUBLIC LAW 94-142; PUBLIC LAW 101-476.

REFERENCES

Osborne, A. G., Jr., and P. Dimattia. (1994). The IDEA's least restrictive environment mandate: Legal implications: *Exceptional Children* 61, 6–14.

Tucker, B. P., and B. A. Goldstein. (1992). *The educational rights of children with disabilities: A guide to federal law.* Horsham, PA: LRP.

Paul G. Warden

LEGAL-ETHICAL DILEMMA. A legal-ethical dilemma develops when legal statutes and professional standards* conflict. These situations occur when there are philosophical differences or ambiguities between, and in, the federal and state laws and the various standards that create for the professional a decision-making dilemma.

Psychologists who belong to professional organizations such as the American Psychological Association* or the National Association of School Psychologists* or a state association* agree to adhere to the standards of practice set by the respective association. Each association has its own set of ethical principles by which psychologists agree to conduct their professional practice.

Over the last twenty years, federal legislation, state legislation, and court decisions have increasingly regulated the practice of psychology. The legal system has become more influential than professional standards with the advent of state licensure laws and insurance ''freedom of choice'' laws at the state level relative to third-party reimbursement. Additionally, legislation pertaining to the education of handicapped children, access to records, the delivery of mental health services, and developmental disabilities has had an influence on the profession. Adding to legislative regulation are court decisions relative to testing and evaluation and malpractice that have directly influenced the practice of school psychology.*

Dilemmas develop because professional standards and regulations are often unclear relative to a specific situation or are in direct conflict with each other. For example, all states have laws requiring professionals to report child abuse, yet all professional standards uphold the concept of confidentiality* for the client,* and, in some instances, state statutes protect the client through privileged communication* status with psychologists and school psychologists.* The issue of client welfare versus professional welfare versus public interest creates for the professional situations where highly complex value judgments require rigorous critical analysis.

While, most often, legal considerations may dictate a course of action, it is still important to have knowledge of, and to fully understand, the complexities of both professional standards and the legal system. When confronted with such dilemmas, consultation with colleagues and legal experts is imperative prior to taking action.

See also CODES OF ETHICS; DUTY TO WARN.

REFERENCES

Bersoff, D. N., and P. Hofer. (1990). The legal regulation of school psychology. In C. Reynolds and T. Gutkin (Eds.), *The handbook of school psychology* (2d ed., pp. 937–961). New York: Wiley.

Fischer, F., and G. P. Sorenson. (1996). *School law for counselors, psychologists, and social workers* (3d ed.). New York: Longman.

Pryzwansky, W., and R. Wendt. (1987). *Psychology as a profession: Foundations of practice.* New York: Pergamon Press.

Robert N. Wendt

LIABILITY INSURANCE. Liability insurance is coverage purchased by professionals to protect themselves from such potential malpractice lawsuits as negligence, infliction of mental distress, and defamation due to the release of confidential materials. Professional liability insurance is available to members of the National Association of School Psychologists* and the American Psychological Association.* Successful litigation against professionals employed in school settings* is limited. However, mental health services provided via agency or private practice* settings increase the potential for liability suits. Most managed care facilities will not approve psychological services unless the provider can document liability insurance coverage. Although limits of liability are flexible, most insurance companies and referral agencies require a minimum $1 million for wrongful acts, with an additional $1 million as an aggregate.

See also CONFIDENTIALITY; PRIVILEGED COMMUNICATION.

REFERENCES

Appelbaum, P. S. (1993). Legal liability and managed care. *American Psychologist* 48, 251–257.
Fagan, T. K., and P. S. Wise. (1994). *School psychology: Past, present, and future.* White Plains, NY: Longman.

LeAdelle Phelps

LICENSING. Much of the professional regulation of school psychology* occurs through credentialing—a procedure for granting titles and functions to persons following their training. In school psychology, credentialing occurs through certification* and licensing. Though the terms are often used interchangeably, certification has referred to practice credentials granted by a state education agency for practice in settings under the authority of that agency (usually referred to as the school sector), and licensing has referred to practice credentials granted by a state board of examiners in psychology* for private, independent, and agency practice (usually referred to as the nonschool sector).

The earliest state-level credentials for school psychologists* were state education agency certification originating in the 1930s. Following World War II, psychologists began to be licensed for private practice by a separate state-level board of examiners in psychology whose jurisdiction was statewide, with broad practice exemptions for government agencies, including the public schools. In 1945, Connecticut became the first state to grant licensing for nonschool practice. There were fifteen states licensing by 1960, and Missouri, in 1977, completed the licensing of psychologists in all states.

The requirements for licensing vary, with titles and practice responsibilities aligned with degree and field experiences. However, almost all states require the doctoral degree* for licensing with the title ''psychologist,'' and only about a dozen permit licensure at the subdoctoral level, employing titles like ''psychological examiner'' or ''psychological assistant.'' Licensing requirements are often aligned with the American Psychological Association's* Model Licensure Act* and/or the guidelines of the Association of State and Provincial Psychology Boards* (ASPPB).

REFERENCES

Britt, S. H. (1941). Pending developments in the legal status of psychologists. *Journal of Consulting Psychology* 5, 52–56.

Fretz, B. R., and D. H. Mills. (1980). *Licensing and certification of psychologists and counselors.* San Francisco: Jossey-Bass.

Hollingworth, L. S. (1922). Existing laws which authorize psychologists to perform professional services. *Journal of Criminal Law and Criminology* 12, 70–73.

Prus, J., M. J. Curtis, A. Draper, and S. Hunley. (1995). A summary of credentialing requirements for school psychologists in public school settings. In A. Thomas and J. Grimes (Eds.), *Best practices in school psychology—III* (pp. 1237–1247). Washington, DC: National Association of School Psychologists.

Prus, J., and K. Mittelmeier. (1995). A summary of licensure requirements for independent practice in psychology and school psychology. In A. Thomas and J. Grimes (Eds.), *Best practices in school psychology—III* (pp. 1249–1256). Washington, DC: National Association of School Psychologists.

Pryzwansky, W. B. (1993). The regulation of school psychology: A historical perspective on certification, licensure, and accreditation. *Journal of School Psychology* 31, 219–235.

Thomas K. Fagan

LITERATURE IN SCHOOL PSYCHOLOGY. The literature of school psychology* evolved in three periods. The first period, from 1890 to about 1930, was characterized by the absence of journals or books specifically on the topic of school psychological services. In this era, the published information about, or related to, school psychology appeared in educational and psychological journals such as *Pedagogical Seminary, American Journal of Psychology, The Psychological Clinic,* and the *Journal of Educational Psychology.* There were no books specifically on the topic of school psychology, though several texts relevant to such practice were available.

The second period was initiated with the publication of Gertrude Hildreth's* *Psychological Service for School Problems* (1930) and extended to the early 1960s. During this period, the literature of the field continued to be scattered across several educational and psychological journals, but a more focused literature appeared by way of the publication of Hildreth's book, state education agency publications, a special issue of *The Consulting Psychologist* in 1942, the initiation of a newsletter by the Division of School Psychologists (APA),* and the division's 1955 publication of its Thayer conference* proceedings.

The third period began with the publishing of the *Journal of School Psychology (JSP)* in 1963 and extends to the present. The decade of the 1960s was especially productive, reflecting a rapidly growing identity of school psychology. In that decade, at least a dozen texts were published, and, in addition to *JSP, Psychology in the Schools* (appearing in 1964) added to the journal literature. School psychology literature continued to appear in related educational, special educational, and psychological journals, but to a decreasing extent. The National Association of School Psychologists* (NASP) first published its journal, *School Psychology Digest* (now *School Psychology Review*) (1972), and *School Psychology International* initiated publication in 1979, and another dozen texts directly or closely related to school psychology were published. In the 1980s, school psychology's fifth journal, *Professional School Psychology* (now *School Psychology Quarterly*), began publication (1986), another dozen or more texts were published, and the school psychology literature developed greater diversity than at any previous time.

In addition to commercially published books and journals, the publications of NASP, Division 16 (APA), and state associations added considerably to this diversity. By the early 1990s, there were almost fifty state associations for school psychologists producing newsletters, and the national newsletters of NASP (*Communique*) and Division 16 (*The School Psychologist*) had increased well beyond their earlier levels of production. After the late 1970s, association-sponsored products included texts (e.g., NASP's *Best Practices in School Psychology*), media products (e.g., Division 16's *Conversation Series* videotapes), proceedings, training program directories, certification and licensure handbooks, and numerous survey documents. Closely related journals such as *Journal of Psychoeducational Assessment, Professional Psychology: Research and Practice,* and *Special Services in the Schools* reflected the expansion of literature in related fields. State education agencies also added to the literature of school psychology, but such contributions were inconsistent; those of New York, Ohio, and Iowa were most noticeable. Since the initiation of field-specific journals, the journal literature of school psychology has been concentrated in outlets primarily for school psychologist audiences, in contrast to earlier eras, when its literature was in sources available to wider audiences of educators and psychologists. The three literary periods, with journals, books, and other media production, reflect the increasing professionalization and specialization of school psychology.

See also PUBLISHERS.

REFERENCES

Fagan, T. K. (1986). The evolving literature of school psychology. *School Psychology Review* 15, 430–440.

Fagan, T. K., F. J. Delugach, M. Mellon, and P. Schlitt. (1986). *A bibliographic guide to the literature of professional school psychology 1890–1985.* Washington, DC: National Association of School Psychologists.

French, J. L. (1986). Books in school psychology: The first forty years. *Professional School Psychology* 1, 267–277.

Whelan, T., and C. Carlson. (1986). Books in school psychology: 1970 to the present. *Professional School Psychology* 1, 279–289.

Thomas K. Fagan

LONGITUDINAL STUDIES. Longitudinal studies represent a class of techniques in which inferences are drawn regarding stability and change over time based on data collected over time. Longitudinal research designs include simultaneous cross-sectional studies, trend studies, time-series studies, intervention studies, and panel studies. A longitudinal design (time-series, in this example) would be appropriate to study any continuous process (e.g., human development) that could be meaningfully examined by a series of "snapshots" recorded at appropriate points in time. Longitudinal data are typically multivariate since the resources necessary to conduct and maintain contact with the sample are considerable. Consequently, data analytic techniques often involve the detection of hidden structures embedded in the database in order to simplify interpretation. Procedures such as factor analysis,* multidimensional scaling,* cluster analysis, and configural frequency analysis are useful for this purpose. Mortality (subjects who drop out of a group) represents the greatest threat to the validity* of a longitudinal study. Strategies for preventing the bias that results from considerable attrition of the sample over time—potentially invalidating the findings—are mandatory in longitudinal studies. Selected examples of major longitudinal studies include the Berkeley Growth Study, Fels Study, Harvard Growth Study, Kansas City Study of Adult Life, McFarland Guidance Study, Oakland Growth Study, and Stanford Studies of Gifted Children.

See also EXPERIMENTAL DESIGN.

REFERENCES

Keeves, J. P. (1988). Longitudinal research methods. In J. P. Keeves (Ed.), *Educational research, methodology, and measurement: An international handbook* (pp. 113–126). New York: Pergamon Press.
Wohlwill, J. F. (1970). Methodology and research strategy in the study of developmental change. In L. R. Goulet and P. B. Baltes (Eds.), *Life-span developmental psychology* (pp. 149–191). New York: Academic Press.

William T. Coombs

LOW-INCIDENCE ASSESSMENT. Low-incidence disabilities occur infrequently in the population (e.g., visual impairment, cerebral palsy, hearing impairment). Assessment should involve the integration of functional, behavioral, and traditional assessment approaches. Functional approaches focus on individuals' range of capabilities and limitations in functional domains—just what can they do? Skills are functional if they are (1) chronologically age-appropriate, (2) required in a variety of environments, and (3) used often. The interaction between development and disabilities is emphasized. This stresses the realization that disabilities do not involve distinct domains but are related to dysfunctions in other domains (Sattler, 1992; Zambone, 1988).

Behavioral assessments* are conducted to provide (1) clear, unambiguous definitions and (2) the conditions for guiding and maintaining behavior. Assessment* may be anecdotal recordings and direct observations in both contrived and natural environments (Wacker, Steege, and Berg, 1990; Zambone, 1988).

Traditional assessment involves intellectual, developmental, and adaptive behavior.* For students with severe skill deficiencies and multiple sensory and motor disabilities, it may be difficult to determine the students' level of intellectual functioning. There are several standardized tests of intelligence* and development that may be used (e.g., Battelle Developmental Inventory, Bayley Scales of Infant Development, Hiskey-Nebraska Test of Learning Aptitude, Test of Nonverbal Intelligence). If more than one assessment instrument is used, and these instruments provide similar information, then validity* may be increased (Wacker, Steege, and Berg, 1990; Sattler, 1992).

The assessment process must be individualized for each student. Evaluations should be made by a multidisciplinary team* using multiple procedures. Information should be gathered from a variety of sources, including intelligence and achievement/developmental tests, social-cultural background, health/physical information, and adaptive behavior*. Assessment procedures should have a direct relationship to the skills the student will need to develop. Assessment should be ongoing to provide for continuity of instruction and development (Wacker, Steege, and Berg, 1990).

See also CLASSIFICATION: EDUCATIONAL; CLASSIFICATION: PSYCHIATRIC.

REFERENCES

Berg, W. K., D. P. Wacker, and M. W. Steege. (1995). Best practices in assessment with persons who have severe or profound handicaps. In A. Thomas and J. Grimes (Eds.), *Best practices in school psychology—III* (pp. 805–816). Washington, DC: National Association of School Psychologists.

Sattler, J. M. (1992). *Assessment of children.* San Diego: Author.

Wacker, D. P., M. W. Steege, and W. K. Berg. (1990). Best practices in assessment and intervention with persons who have severe/profound handicaps. In A. Thomas and J. Grimes (Eds.), *Best practices in school psychology—II* (pp. 81–92). Washington, DC: National Association of School Psychologists.

Zambone, A. M. (1988). *Principles of assessment for children with severe multiple disabilities.* New York: American Foundation for the Blind.

Laqueta Pardue-Vaughn
John C. Vaughn

LUCKEY, BERTHA M. Bertha Musson Luckey (1890–1966) was born in Ontario, California, where her father was superintendent of schools. She entered public school at age nine in New York City, where her father was completing a doctorate, and she graduated in Lincoln, Nebraska, when she was sixteen. She received three collegiate degrees from the University of Nebraska, where her father was a professor: B.A. in 1910, M.A. in 1912, and Ph.D. in 1916—one of fewer than fifty Ph.D.'s in psychology granted to women by that date (Rossiter, 1982).

With a degree in chemistry and a certificate to teach, Bertha Luckey became a teacher of handicapped children and psychologist in Lincoln, Nebraska, in 1916 and then a teacher in Cleveland, Ohio, the following year. She organized a psychological clinic in the Cleveland public schools in 1917 (Luckey, 1920b), which she directed until her retirement in 1960. Initially, under the supervision of the Medical Department, the Psychology Department became a unit in the Bureau of Educational Research.

As director of psychological services, she became a leading spokesperson in Ohio and the nation. She was president of the American Psychological Association* (APA) Division of School Psychologists* in 1949–1950 and the Division of Consulting Psychologists in 1951–1952, the American Association for the Mentally Retarded in 1952–1953, and the Ohio Psychological Association in 1940–1941.

She was active in the governance of APA as well, the only woman on the six-person committee on training in clinical psychology* that produced the *Recommended Graduate Training Programs in Clinical Psychology,* a 1947 report providing the basis for accreditation of doctoral programs in psychology. Luckey made a number of visits to programs seeking accreditation (most visitors in the 1940s were male professors).

She published on atypical children, physical conditions of children referred to as problems in the schools, credentialing of psychologists, and racial differences in mental ability. She was among the first to question the implications of heredity espoused by Goddard.

REFERENCES

Luckey, B. M. (1920a). Correlation between psychological tests and educational
    progress in the schools. *Journal of Psycho-Asthenics* 25, 104–108.
———. (1920b). The psychological clinic in practice. *School and Society* 12, (288),
    6–12.
Rossiter, M. W. (1982). *Women scientists in America: Struggles and strategies to 1940*
    (p. 31). Baltimore: Johns Hopkins University Press.

Joseph L. French

LUKE S. AND HANS S. v. NIX ET AL. A class-action suit brought against the state of Louisiana on behalf of the class of children, suspected of being handicapped, who had not received a "timely" evaluation. The regulations governing evaluation services and special education in Louisiana required that the evaluation of children suspected of being exceptional should be completed in sixty operational days of the receipt of parental permission. Historically, thousands of children did not receive this timely evaluation. In 1978, the "backlog" of children still awaiting evaluation in Louisiana exceeded 27,000. The Louisiana State Department of Education and the Advocacy Center for the Elderly and Disabled (plaintiff) entered into a consent decree that had a profound effect on school psychology* services and other appraisal services. The decree immediately resulted in a special legislative allocation of $1,037,500 for contracted and overtime evaluation services, in order to eliminate the estimated 5,000-student "backlog" existing in January 1981. In addition, new ratios were established for the allocation of school psychologists,* school social workers, and educational assessment teachers. This new allocation resulted in approximately 200 new positions at a cost of more than $2.5 million for the remainder of the 1981–1982 school year and an ''annualization'' of these positions in future years. The *Luke S.* consent decree also established certain ''minimum'' compliance levels of evaluation services for each school district and sanctions for those that fall short. By June 30 of each year, each school system must have evaluated in timelines a certain percentage of all children referred for services or be placed on ''a plan of rapid compliance.'' By December 31, 1982, all school systems in Louisiana were to have achieved a compliance figure of 97 percent evaluations completed in timelines.

The value of the consent decree was that it implemented and mandated the use of Louisiana procedures for evaluating students (Bulletin 1508). This new bulletin required prereferral intervention,* curriculum-based assessment,* systematic behavior observation, and other informal assessment practices. With the assistance of a special court-ordered consultant, James Tucker, Louisiana was released from the consent decree in 1983.

See also PUBLIC LAW 94-142.

REFERENCES

Louisiana Department of Education. (1978). *Pupil appraisal handbook, bulletin 1508,* Baton Rouge: Louisiana State Department of Education.

Luke S., Hans S. v. J. Kelly Nix, United States District Court, Eastern District of Louisiana (C.A. NO. 81-3331.). 1981.

James Canfield

M

MCCANDLESS, BOYD R. A pragmatic scholar who contributed much to developmental and school psychology* through his research, teaching, writing, editing, and advising graduate students and colleagues, Boyd Rowden McCandless (1915–1975) began life in St. John, Kansas. Most of his life was spent in the Midwest, contributing to its reputation for "dust bowl empiricism." His first degree, under George Kelley, was from Ft. Hays State College (1936), and his M.A. (1938) and Ph.D. (1941) were under George Stoddard at the University of Iowa.

Holding eight different postdoctoral positions, he was most productive during his nine years as director of the Iowa Child Welfare Research Station* (1951–1960). Here, under his direction, experimental child psychology was christened, and he wrote the first of seven major texts on children and/or adolescents (McCandless, 1961). Later, he was director of the University School Clinic complex at the University of Indiana, where, with Walter Hodges and Howard Spicker, he developed the diagnostically based curriculum for psychosocially deprived children. In this period, McCandless became more actively involved with school psychology and special education.* He was elected by American Psychological Association's* Division of School Psychologists* to the Council of Representatives (1963–1966) and to president of the division (1967–1968) (McCandless, 1968–1969).

In 1966, he moved to Emory University. Here, he issued a series of papers with Norman Thompson on psychosexual development and became editor of *Developmental Psychology* for its first ten volumes.

REFERENCES

Hartup, W. W. (1976). Boyd R. McCandless 1915–1975. *Child Development* 47, 900–902.
In Memoriam: Boyd McCandless. (1976). *The School Psychologist* 30(3), 1.

McCandless, B. R. (1961). *Children and adolescents, behavior and development.* New
    York: Holt, Rinehart, and Winston.
————. (1968–1969). Points at issue between practical and academic school
    psychology. *Journal of School Psychology* 7, 13–17.

Joseph L. French

MAINSTREAMING. The placement of children with disabilities in the regular
classroom is known as mainstreaming. While mainstreaming and the least restrictive environment* (LRE) are used interchangeably, they are not synonymous. The term "least restrictive environment" is legally mandated. The
Individuals with Disabilities Education Act (Public Law 101-476*) requires that
children with disabilities should be educated in the least restrictive environment,
which means to the maximum extent appropriate with nondisabled children in
regular classes.

Mainstreaming is a term that originated during the application of the LRE
regulations when mildly disabled children were placed in the regular classroom
as the most feasible learning environment; mainstreaming is not a legal term
(Vergason and Anderegg, 1992). The right to placement in an integrated or
regular educational environment is not an absolute right but is secondary to the
primary purpose of education in the public schools, which is an appropriate
education. The appropriateness of an educational setting relies on the individualized education plan* (Turnbull, 1993).

See also INCLUSION; SEGREGATED SERVICES.

REFERENCES

Turnbull, H. R. (1993). *Free appropriate public education* (4th ed.). Denver: Love.
Vergason, G. A., and M. L. Anderegg. (1992). Preserving the least restrictive
    environment. In W. Stainback and S. Stainback (Eds.), *Controversial issues
    confronting special education* (pp. 45–54). Boston: Allyn and Bacon.

Laqueta Pardue-Vaughn
John C. Vaughn

MANAGED CARE. As the cost of health care in the United States increased
well out of proportion to the overall cost of living, insurance and business groups
implemented plans of cost containment known as managed care. The traditional
model where a patient acquires services from an individual provider has shifted
to a variety of group models, including health maintenance organizations
(HMOs) and preferred provider organizations (PPOs). In both, the growth of
health care costs is managed by arrangements where individual or groups of
providers agree to deliver specified services at set fees.

The concept of managed care via HMOs has been associated with the medical
profession since the 1920s but has been a prominent aspect of health care cost
reform since the early 1980s; PPOs have a very recent history (Frankel, 1990).
Both HMOs and PPOs have spread rapidly since the 1980s and have had a
profound impact on the medical profession and related health service providers,

including psychologists. Psychological services do not always fit conveniently into managed care arenas dominated by health insurance and medical groups. The changes have emphasized the importance of viewing service delivery from business as well as professional perspectives (Bennett et al., 1990; Rosenberg and Wonderly, 1990). A large portion of the population is provided services via managed care (Frankel, 1990). The impact on school-based psychological services has been minimal, but continued growth of managed care and/or a system of national health insurance that included school psychological services could change the situation dramatically.

See also GROUP PRACTICE; INDEPENDENT PRACTICE; PRIVATE PRACTICE.

REFERENCES

Bennett, B. E., B. K. Bryant, G. R. Vandenbos, and A. Greenwood. (1990). *Professional liability and risk management.* Washington, DC: American Psychological Association.
Frankel, A. S. (1990). Health care delivery by organized providers: HMOs and PPOs. In E. Margenau (Ed.), *The encyclopedic handbook of private practice* (pp. 442–449). New York: Gardner Press.
Rosenberg, S. L., and D. M. Wonderly. (1990). Best practices in establishing an independent practice. In A. Thomas and J. Grimes (Eds.), *Best practices in school psychology—II* (pp. 339–351). Washington, DC: National Association of School Psychologists.

Thomas K. Fagan

MANDATORY SERVICES. An important development in federal education policy is the emergence of the federal service mandate, a strategy for accomplishing equal educational opportunity for all citizens. Under a federal service mandate, the state educational agency or the local educational agency is required to satisfy federal standards in serving certain categories of children. Federal mandates require that children be served appropriately and specify qualifications of services to be provided. The federal service mandate is distinguished from antidiscrimination regulations (which require equal or equivalent treatment of all) and federal grants (which provide a fixed monetary disbursement). Mandatory services are intervention strategies, intensive and specialized, designed to overcome learning problems of certain populations.

Examples of mandatory services include accessibility (Section 504 of the Rehabilitation Act* of 1973); assessment and placement (Public Law 94-142*); development of individualized educational plans* (Public Law 94-142); related services* such as speech pathology, physical therapy, and transportation that are deemed necessary for educational integration (Public Law 94-142); early intervention programs (Public Law 99-457*); and transition* programs (Public Law 101-476)*.

REFERENCES

Barrow, Stephen. (1983). *Federal service mandates in education.* Washington, DC:
    SMB Economic Research.
Jacob-Timm, S., and T. Hartshorne. (1994). *Ethics and law for school psychologists.*
    Brandon, VT: Clinical Psychology.

Denise Cutbirth

MARRIAGE AND FAMILY THERAPY. The essential defining characteristic of marriage and family therapy as compared to other forms of therapy is a primary concern with the marital relationship and family relationships and functioning as opposed to concerns with the functioning of the individual. Marriage and family therapy typically involves conjoint therapy* sessions with both members of the marital relationship present or with all family members present for family therapy sessions. Other essential characteristics of the practice and profession of marriage and family therapy are shared with other forms of individual and group counseling and therapy,* such as a concern with issues of ethical practice. The basic theoretical foundations of marriage and family therapy are similar to those of other mental health and helping professions, as many aspects of human development theory and psychological theory apply to marriage and family work. A large body of theoretical literature, however, modifies and expands upon these shared bases as they apply to marriage and family therapy and also develops novel constructs and approaches that explicitly concern marriage and family therapy (Becvar and Becvar, 1993). Major theoretical approaches to marriage and family therapy include systemic approaches, intergenerational approaches, psychoanalytic and object relations approaches, and behavioral approaches.

The roots of the marriage and family therapy movement can be traced back to several early influences. The marriage counseling movement, family education movement, social work movement, and family therapy* movement all exerted influences upon the development and current state of marriage and family therapy (Broderick and Schrader, 1981).

Marriage and family therapy is conducted by a wide range of professionals, including not only those who define themselves specifically as marriage and family therapists but also psychologists, counselors, social workers, and physicians who conduct marriage and family therapy. Many areas of special interest exist within the field of marriage and family therapy, such as family therapy, sex therapy, and marital and relationship counseling. The primary professional organization for marriage and family therapists is the American Association for Marriage and Family Therapy (AAMFT), which was founded in 1945 as the American Association of Marriage Counselors. In addition to the AAMFT, other professional organizations that are concerned with marriage and family therapy include the American Psychological Association* Division of Marriage and Family Therapy and the American Counseling Association.

See also FAMILY ASSESSMENT; FAMILY ENABLEMENT/EMPOW-
ERMENT.

REFERENCES

Becvar, D. S., and R. J. Becvar. (1993). *Family therapy: A systemic integration.*
    Needham Heights, MA: Allyn and Bacon.
Broderick, C. B., and S. S. Schrader. (1981). The history of professional marriage and
    family therapy. In A. S. Gurman and D. P. Kniskern (Eds.), *Handbook of
    family therapy* (pp. 5–35). New York: Brunner/Mazel.

John S. C. Romans

MARSHALL v. GEORGIA. *Marshall v. Georgia* was a class-action suit filed
in 1981 in Georgia on behalf of African-American students. The suit alleged
that a disproportionately large number of African-American students were
placed in lower achievement groups in the regular education elementary programs of eight school districts in Georgia. Also, the suit alleged that a disproportionately large number of African-American students were placed in educable
mentally retarded classes and that a disproportionately small number of students
were placed in learning-disabled (LD) classes.

The U.S. District Court for the Southern District of Georgia found for the
defendants in 1984, as did the Eleventh Circuit Court of Appeals in 1985. The
decision allowing achievement grouping in regular education appears to contra-
dict the previous landmark decision in *Hobson v. Hansen,* which found tracking
of students by IQ tests unacceptable because such tests failed to assess innate
ability. *Marshall* established grouping to be acceptable because the criteria for
placement were related to achievement, and benefits in achievement due to
grouping were demonstrated by the defendants, the schools.

The *Marshall* decision regarding disproportionate representation in special
education classes also found for the defendants. The court decided to be guided
by American Association Mental Deficiency (AAMD) classification and later by
Public Law 94-142* and found the schools to be essentially in compliance;
consequently, disproportionate representation of a minority group did not constitute discrimination. This ruling is in contrast to *Larry P. v. Riles.**

REFERENCES

Reschly, D. J., R. Kicklighter, and P. McKee. (1988). Recent placement litigation, Part
    I, regular education grouping: Comparison of *Marshall* (1967, 1969) and
    Hobson (1967, 1969). *School Psychology Review* 17, 9–21.
———. (1988). Recent placement litigation, Part II, minority EMR overrepresentation:
    Comparison of *Larry P.* (1979, 1984, 1986) with *Marshall* (1984, 1985, and S-
    1, 1986). *School Psychology Review* 17, 22–38.

Paul G. Warden

MASTER'S DEGREE. The master's degree is the most commonly awarded
degree in school psychology* (Brown, 1990; Reschly and McMaster-Beyer,

1991). A recent survey of training programs indicated that a master's degree is awarded by 151 school psychology programs. Of these programs, 70 offer the master's degree only, while the remaining 81 offer the master's degree along with a specialist* or doctoral* degree (Smith and Henning, in press). Exact titles of the degrees include master of science (MS), master of science in education (MSEd), master of education (MEd), and master of arts (MA). Master's degree programs in school psychology range from thirty to ninety-nine semester credit hours, with an average of fifty-four semester credit hours. While a majority of programs require sixty to sixty-nine semester credit hours, a large number of programs require less than forty-five semester credit hours, resulting in the average of fifty-four semester credit hours.

See also CERTIFICATE OF ADVANCED STUDY; TRAINING MODELS.

REFERENCES

Brown, D. T. (1990). Professional regulation and training in school psychology. In T. B. Gutkin and C. R. Reynolds (Eds.), *The handbook of school psychology* (2d ed., pp. 991–1009). New York: Wiley.

Reschly, D. J., and M. McMaster-Beyer. (1991). Influences of degree level, institutional orientation, college affiliation, and accreditation status on school psychology graduate education. *Professional Psychology: Research and Practice* 22, 368–374.

Smith, D. K., and A. Henning. (in press). *Directory of school psychology graduate programs* (4th ed.). Washington, DC: National Association of School Psychologists.

Douglas K. Smith

MASTERY LEARNING. Mastery learning is an organizational process for learning that allows students with different learning history, abilities, and motivation sufficient time, based on their needs, to master the curriculum (Bloom, 1976). The underlying assumption of mastery learning is that, if given enough time, nearly all students can attain mastery (Carroll, 1963). The amount a student learns in school is a function of the time spent as a proportion of the amount of time needed. To improve student learning, provide more time or less content. Learners can master 95 percent of the material with concomitant increases in motivation because of higher success rates (Stallings and Stipek, 1986). The curriculum is divided into small units with pre- and postassessment. Students who do not master the content initially are remediated, using prescriptions based on posttest analyses. Curricular options for student prescriptions following nonmastery include additional lectures, small-group instruction, different textbooks, filmstrips, study guides, work-sheets, or computer-assisted instruction/computer-managed instruction programs. There is some question as to whether mastery learning is appropriate for high-ability students if all students must complete the unit before they go on. Waiting time will build up. Some experimental evidence shows that mastery learning has stronger effects on the weaker students in class. When mastery learning is done correctly, students begin the program normally

distributed across pretest scores and end the program with the distribution negatively skewed. Most perform at high levels, and there should be little variation
in student performance. This implies that the correlation between initial aptitude
and final performance should approach zero. There is still some argument from
meta-analytic studies as to the effects of mastery learning. Generally, students
seem to do better on locally prepared tests than on standardized tests.

See also CURRICULUM-BASED ASSESSMENT/CURRICULUM-BASED
MEASUREMENT.

REFERENCES

Bloom, B. S. (1976). *Human characteristics and school learning.* New York:
    McGraw-Hill.
Carroll, J. (1963). A model of school learning. *Teachers College Record* 64, 723–733.
Stallings, J. A., and D. Stipek. (1986). Research on early childhood and elementary
    school teaching programs. In M. C. Wittrock (Ed.), *Handbook of research on
    teaching* (3d ed., pp. 727–753). New York: Macmillan.

Kay Sather Bull

MEDICAL MODEL. The ''medical model'' was the diagnostic scheme birthed
by the psychoanalytic theory of psychopathology. Consequently, it has long
been, and still remains, the sine qua non of psychiatric and clinical psychology*
services. Emphasis is placed on assessing the patient's mental status and prescribing treatment accordingly. An array of assessment strategies is used, em-
bracing methods that are both standardized (e.g., psychometric tests) and
nonstandardized (e.g., interviews and observations). Often the information or
data are conceptualized as a ''mental status examination'' (dealing with appearance and behavior, form and content of thought, affect and mood, memory
and intellectual functioning, and insight and judgment) (Goodwin and Guze,
1989). After the collection of clinical information, the medical model necessitates a diagnosis, that is, ''the determination of the nature, origin, precipitation,
and maintenance of ineffective abnormal modes of behavior'' (Arbuckle, 1965,
p. 220). The diagnosis has three components (Woody and Robertson, 1988).
First, there is a clinical description of the patient's current psychological functioning (with consideration for physical concomitants as well). Second, the chronology of the pathology is traced, leading to a statement of etiology or causation.
Third, predictive or prognostic consideration is given to alternative therapeutic
interventions, and recommendations are posited. There is usually application of
a nosological system. Certain modern-day clinicians disapprove of the medical
model, alleging that it is overly simplistic and based on faulty or unproven
theories, relies too heavily on subjectivity, stigmatizes by labeling, ignores po-
tentials for positive functioning, and aggrandizes pathology. Nonetheless, it appears that the medical model still dominates assessment practices in clinical
settings. Moreover, there is reason to assert that the current health care reform
movement, with its emphasis on detailing the patient's clinical history, catego-

rizing the patient's mental status, establishing an individualized treatment plan, subjectively predicting the required course of treatment, and prescribing interventions directed at a targeted behavioral or emotional problem, may create a resurgence of interest in the medical model.

See also CLASSIFICATION: PSYCHIATRIC; INTERVIEWING.

REFERENCES

Arbuckle, D. S. (1965). *Counseling: Philosophy, theory, and practice.* Boston: Allyn and Bacon.

Goodwin, D. M., and S. B. Guze. (1989). *Psychiatric diagnosis* (4th ed.). New York: Oxford University Press.

Woody, R. H., and M. Robertson. (1988). *Becoming a clinical psychologist.* Madison, CT: International Universities Press.

Robert Henley Woody

MENTAL HEALTH CONSULTATION. The early beginnings of preventive psychiatry can be tracked to the study of bereavement reactions of survivors of the Coconut Grove nightclub fire in 1943. Erich Lindemann's 1944 work presented the fundamentals of crisis theory, which relied on clergy and other community caregivers, through psychiatric consultation, to help the bereaved to mourn adequately. As a colleague of Lindemann, Gerald Caplan certainly had formulated some key concepts of mental health consultation by 1949 and presented these concepts of the now famous four-type model of mental health consultation in his 1964 work about preventive psychiatry. His 1970 work on mental health consultation was expanded and recently revised (Caplan and Caplan, 1993).

Caplan delineates four types of mental health consultation: (1) client-centered case consultation, where the problems of the client encountered by the consultee are the focus, (2) consultee-centered case consultation, where the focus is on the consultee's difficulties in dealing with the client, (3) program-centered administrative consultation, where a consultee or group of consultees is having problems with any aspect of administering a program for prevention, treatment, or rehabilitation of mental disorder, and (4) consultee-centered administration consultation, which focuses on the interpersonal aspects and the consultee's problems as an administrator of a program.

Mental health consultation was initially presented as one dimension of preventive psychiatry; the others are social planning and community organization directed at primary prevention. In 1964, Caplan perceived that the methods of mental health consultation were more clearly developed than those of social planning and community organization.

Over the last twenty years, a number of modifications have been proposed that have modified Caplan's work as presented in his 1970 book. Contrary to Caplan's model, some authors suggest the inclusion of nonprofessionals in the category of consultees. Systems theory has been used to broaden the administrative consultation dimension of Caplan's model. In discussion of school settings, collaboration has been proposed as an alternative to consultation. Behavioral psychology has been injected into mental health consultation by placing more emphasis on ecology and events surrounding the client. The method of consultee-centered consultation has received a great deal of attention, both by Caplan and by his critics. Critics contend that defenses of the consultee can be confronted without damaging the professional relationship. The process of theme interference used to alleviate lack of objectivity has been criticized for the underlying psychodynamic assumptions, particularly that of displacement. Also, group consultation has emerged as a modification of the original model.

Gerald Caplan and his daughter Ruth Caplan authored *Mental Health Consultation and Collaboration* (1993) after encouragement from school psychologists* at the 1990 convention of the American Psychological Association.* At that time, Caplan was honored, and the twentieth-anniversary commemoration of his 1970 book was celebrated. Essentially, mental health consultation remains much the same as it was presented in 1970, except that group applications are discussed. A large portion of the book is devoted to mental health collaboration, which Caplan believes is more applicable to school psychologists and other professionals employed in the same organization as their consultees. Mental health consultation, as conceptualized currently by Caplan, is designed for professional caregivers. In fact, Caplan is critical of the popularization of mental health concepts when such use makes the general public overly dependent on support groups and professional caregivers.

See also BEHAVIORAL CONSULTATION; CASE CONSULTATION; COLLABORATIVE CONSULTATION; CONSULTATION; PROCESS CONSULTATION.

REFERENCES

Caplan, G., and R. B. Caplan. (1993). *Mental health consultation and collaboration.* San Francisco: Jossey-Bass.
Dougherty, A. M. (1990). *Consultation: Practice and perspectives.* Pacific Grove, CA: Brooks/Cole.

Paul G. Warden

MENTAL MEASUREMENTS YEARBOOK. The *Mental Measurements Yearbooks* (*MMY*) are a collection of volumes that review the psychometric qualities of psychological and educational tests and scales. The first *MMY,* published in 1935, was a brief bibliography of 250 tests developed between 1933 and 1934 (DuBois, 1970). The 1936 version comprised a bibliography of 503 tests; neither the 1935 nor 1936 volumes of the *MMY* contained actual reviews of any tests. The 1937 volume contained test reviews, but these reviews were reprinted from journals (Thorndike and Lohman, 1990). The first volume to publish commissioned test reviews was published in 1938. As a supplemental compendium to the *MMY,* the Buros Institute also publishes the reference book

Tests in Print (TIP). *TIP* provides a comprehensive list and description of commercially published tests and scales, without reviews. Intended as a guide for consumers, *TIP* describes the content or constructs purportedly assessed by various tests, as well as the test publishers, authors, and references related to each instrument.

Oscar K. Buros was the founder and editor of the *MMY* until his death in 1978. After Buros's death, the Mental Measurements Institute was moved from Rutgers University to the University of Nebraska under the directorship of James V. Mitchell. Mitchell also edited the ninth *MMY* in 1985. Jane Close Conoley and Jack J. Kramer edited the tenth *MMY* in 1989, and the most recent *MMY* in print is the eleventh, edited by Kramer and Conoley. The eleventh *MMY* includes reviews of over 700 tests organized into eighteen separate categories (e.g., achievement, sensory-motor, vocational) and a total of 4,382 references related to the development, psychometric quality, and use of tests.

REFERENCES

DuBois, P. H. (1970). *A history of psychological testing*. Needham Heights, MA: Allyn and Bacon.
Thorndike, R. M., and D. F. Lohman. (1990). *A century of ability testing*. Chicago: Riverside.

Bruce A. Bracken

METACOGNITIVE SKILLS. Metacognitive skills are part of the conscious executive control process in an information-processing system that controls cognitive processes leading to learner action and thought during learning and that influences motivation, acquisition, encoding, retention, retrieval, and transfer. It controls the processes used to recall, control, organize, sequence, and otherwise manipulate cognitive processes. It also involves thinking about one's own thinking—comprehension monitoring, where the student, knowing the objectives of instruction, assesses the degree to which these are being met and modifies the strategies, when necessary, to actualize them. When learning new content, this is done by linking new information to prior knowledge, selecting which thinking abilities to use directly, and looking at the amount of time to be invested. It also involves knowing what you don't know. Naturally occurring metacognition includes determining what the goal is and planning the steps needed to reach that goal. There must be questioning, self-interrogation, to determine consciously if goals are being met. By asking questions, students self-monitor, hypothesize and predict, assess self-understanding, and self-correct if necessary. Metacognitive skills may also be used in the affective domain, as in anxiety reduction, and in the psychomotor domain, as in mental practice for physical events in sport psychology. Metacognitive knowledge reflects on the self. The reflections begin with personal attributes, as modified by one's cognitive style, one's cognitive strategies, and finally one's knowledge schemes. Metacognition relates to knowledge in and of a particular area of content. Unless the learner is fairly skilled, he or she will not understand the processes sufficiently to be consciously aware of them and to be able to articulate what is being done. Without this knowledge base, metacognition, except in an imposed rote mechanical sense, is unlikely.

There are also developmental aspects to metacognition. Most children do not recognize their own cognitive processes until the age of ten, and some adults never become metacognitive. There is substantial developmental variability in the development and recognition of individuals' metacognitive skills. For young children and for those with learning difficulties, metacognitive skills need to be externally imposed by teachers if they are to be useful (Loper and Murphy, 1985). Creating externally imposed metacognitive skills involves developing a strategy or a checklist that is used when a certain class of problems is encountered. Strategies can be developed for a wide variety of purposes, including planning strategies (setting goals, skimming, generating questions), monitoring strategies (self-testing, focusing attention, monitoring comprehension, using test-taking strategies), and regulating strategies (adjusting reading rate, rereading, reviewing, using test-taking strategies). When a teacher imposes an atypical metacognitive process, it will look like this (illustrated by Meichenbaum and Asernow, 1978, pp. 13–14): (1) define the problem and the necessary self-interrogation skill ("What do I have to do?"), (2) focus attention and response guidance ("Now, carefully stop and repeat the instructions"), (3) apply self-reinforcement, which involves self-evaluation comparison to a set standard ("Good, I'm doing fine"), and (4) self-directions on how to deal with error correction ("That's OK . . . even if I make an error I can go slowly"). In the implementation of metacognitive skill training, both children and adults are unlikely to use time-demanding strategies if they believe they will fail with or without the strategies. Therefore, self-initiated strategy use without high self-esteem and effort attributions is unlikely either for initiation or for persistence.

See also INTELLIGENCE; SELF-MANAGEMENT.

REFERENCES

Loper, A. B., and D. M. Murphy. (1985). Cognitive self-regulatory training for underachieving children. In D. L. Forrest-Pressley, G. E. Mackinnon, and T. G. Waller (Eds.), *Metacognition, cognition and human performance* (pp. 223–265). New York: Academic Press.

Meichenbaum, D., and J. Asernow. (1978). Cognitive-behavior modification and metacognitive development: Implications for the classroom. In P. Kendall and S. Hollen (Eds.), *Cognitive-behavioral interventions: Theory, research, and procedures* (pp. 3–37). New York: Academic Press.

Kay Sather Bull

MINIMUM COMPETENCE. Minimum competence refers to the lowest level of knowledge or skills necessary for some task or credential (e.g., basic literacy, high school diploma, teaching certificate). Determination of minimum competence is often associated with formal testing, most often in the form of objective tests, although criterion-referenced* "performance assessments" are also used. There has been considerable debate (and legal challenges) concerning the use of minimum competency testing for high school graduation, admission to teacher education programs, and initial teacher certification, particularly with regard to disproportionate impact on minorities and persons with disabilities. The National Association of School Psychologists* (NASP) has provided leadership in determining minimum standards of competence in school psychology*; it developed a minimum competency statement early in its history and later published standards for credentialing and training programs. It also participated in the development of the National School Psychology Certification System,* which includes a competency examination in school psychology.

See also COMPETENCY-BASED CERTIFICATION.

REFERENCES

National Association of School Psychologists. (1984, 1994). *Standards for training and field placement programs in school psychology.* Washington, DC: Author.
————. (1985). *Standards for the credentialing of school psychologists.* Washington, DC: Author.
Valente, W. D. (1994). *Law in the schools (3d ed.).* New York: Macmillan.

Kathleen M. Minke

MODALITY ASSESSMENT. Modality assessment is a theoretical and controversial approach toward the evaluation and instruction of atypical and handicapped learners in which the sensory modality used to present information is viewed as highly influential in affecting initial learning, storage, retention, and recall of these materials. The contention began first with Munsterberg's findings in 1894 that information presented to two sense modalities simultaneously produced more efficient learning that required fewer trials-to-criterion and improved retention than when it was presented through only one sense modality. This perspective has been influential in the development of a number of educational curricula for atypical and handicapped learners, as well as the basis for many psychological and psychoeducational tests, such as the Illinois Tests of Psycholinguistic Abilities, the Visual-Aural Digit Span Test, the Learning Efficiency Test-II, and the Woodcock-Johnson Tests of Cognitive Ability.

Support for modality assessment is derived from at least six basic areas of research related to human learning and memory. These areas are cognitive developmental psychological research indicating that children undergo distinct shifts in their modality preferences during learning as they get older; research supporting Penney's "separate streams" hypothesis in which it has been shown that recall and recognition are significantly improved when bimodal presentations are used during learning as compared with single modality presentations; neuropsychological research highlighting the modality-specific effects of head trauma on learning, retention, and communication (as exists with the aphasias and apraxias) and also indicating the necessity of routinely examining modality-specific processing characteristics as part of the neuropsychological examination; direct studies of modality matching and its impact on educational achievement; a long history of empirical research showing that intact adults learn more effectively through the auditory modality than the visual modality; and the presence of relatively independent, modality-based codes during learning that differentially reflect the selective impact of verbal interference on retention.

Educational research examining the efficacy of modality assessment has been equivocal and confusing. Two general types of research designs have been used. In the first approach, the modality preferences of children are identified using available norm-referenced* or criterion-referenced* tests, which are followed by implementation of specific teaching strategies to determine the effect on learning rates and gains. The second type of research design examines the effectiveness of a specific modality-based instructional procedure with no adjustment made for the individual modality-based characteristics of the students. Many of the studies of the second type have presumed that the students are either visual or auditory learners and have attempted to determine whether visual or auditory short-term memory is more important during learning.

Difficulties in evaluating these research findings result from (1) the use of norm-referenced instruments to measure learning gains, because they are not sufficiently sensitive to make these types of measurements; (2) use of statistical procedures that obfuscate individual differences because of the pooling of participants; and (3) widely differing research designs that make cross-study comparisons difficult. Further, the time intervals used to implement the instructional interventions vary widely across studies, specific methods used are often vague in presentation, which makes replication difficult or impossible, and dependent variables often involve criterion-referenced procedures.

Many studies have found that special education* teachers accept modality assessment and instructional matching as appropriate and necessary components of an individualized educational program. Many teacher training programs also commonly offer specific training in these assessment strategies and instructional methods.

See also CLASSIFICATION: EDUCATIONAL; INTELLIGENCE; NEUROPSYCHOLOGICAL ASSESSMENT; PERCEPTUAL-MOTOR ASSESSMENT.

REFERENCES

Arter, J., and J. Jenkins. (1977). Examining the benefits and prevalence of modality considerations in special education. *Journal of Special Education* 11(3), 281–298.

Gillingham, A., and J. Stillman. (1965). *Remedial training for children with specific disability in reading, spelling, and penmanship.* Cambridge, MA: Educators.

Paivio, A. (1971). *Imagery and verbal processes.* New York: Holt, Rinehart, and Winston.

Webster, R. (1992). *The Learning Efficiency Test-II.* Novato, CA: Academic Therapy.
Raymond E. Webster

MODELING. Modeling is defined as the behavioral and cognitive change that occurs as a result of observing a model's behavior. The model can be live, filmed, or even imagined. Bandura's (1986) social-cognitive theory explains the relatively efficient learning that occurs as a result of observing and modeling other individuals' behaviors or vicariously experiencing their successes and failures. The effectiveness of modeling is related to the degree the observer identifies with the model, has an incentive to imitate the model, attends to the model, and has an opportunity to practice and match the model's behavior. Although children can learn through observing the model's behavior, the children's newly acquired knowledge may not necessarily be reflected in their performance.

Self-modeling is defined as the behavioral and cognitive change that results from observations of oneself on edited videotapes that depict only desired or exemplary behaviors. Self-modeling maximizes observer identification with the model in that the observer is also the model. Self-modeling has been employed as an intervention in school psychology* (Dowrick, 1991; Kehle, Owen and Cressy, 1990) for a variety of externalizing and internalizing problems.

See also BEHAVIOR THERAPY.

REFERENCES

Bandura, A. (1986). *Social foundations of thought and action: A social-cognitive theory.* Englewood Cliffs, NJ: Prentice-Hall.

Dowrick, P. W. (1991). *Using video: Psychological and social applications.* New York: Wiley.

Kehle, T. J., S. V. Owen, and E. T. Cressy. (1990). The use of self-modeling as an intervention in school psychology: A case study of an elective mute. *School Psychology Review* 19, 115–121.

Thomas J. Kehle

MODEL LICENSURE ACT. The Model Act serves as a prototype for state legislatures in drafting legislation relative to the professional practice of psychology. The American Psychological Association* (APA) developed in 1987 a model act in order to provide encouragement and language and to serve as a guide for states in the process of drafting legislation.

The process of drafting state laws and subsequent changes to the law inevitably reflect compromises peculiar to each state. As a result of these compromises, there has developed considerable variance among states relative to specific aspects and overall quality of the law. By providing a model, it is hoped that the state regulatory boards will then be able to develop more effective rules and regulations.

This is the fourth set of guidelines proposed by APA, with the first in 1955. The first revision, which was more comprehensive and detailed, came in 1967.

Another revision was developed in 1977 after all the states and the District of Columbia had enacted legislation, and it was felt that the 1967 guidelines were outdated. However, the APA Council of Representatives failed to adopt the new guidelines, leaving the 1967 guidelines as official APA policy until the 1987 model was passed after three years of study, compromises, and revisions.

See also LICENSING; REGISTRATION; STATE BOARD OF EXAMINERS IN PSYCHOLOGY.

REFERENCE

American Psychological Association. (1987). Model Act for state licensure of
    psychologists. *American Psychologist* 42, 696–703.

Robert N. Wendt

MOUNTAIN, VAN W. Van Mountain was born in Carbondale, Illinois, on August 2, 1917, and died of a heart attack on October 24, 1972. He received his B.S. and M.S. degrees from Southern Illinois University–Carbondale in 1953 and 1954, respectively. Mountain was a school psychologist* for the South Macoupin County area of the Madison Region III Cooperative located in Staunton, Illinois. A charter member of the National Association of School Psychologists* (NASP), he served as chair of the Nominations and Elections Committee during its first year of operation and as NASP's second treasurer (1970–1972). He was also active in the Illinois and Southern Illinois Psychological Associations.

REFERENCE

Treasurer: Van W. Mountain, Illinois. (1970, Summer). *NASP Newsletter* 2(2), 5.

Frederick Dornback
Thomas K. Fagan

MULLEN, FRANCES A. Frances Andrews Mullen was born in Chicago on November 27, 1902, and died in Sherman Oaks, California, on April 14, 1991. She earned her Ph.B., M.A., and Ph.D. (1939) in educational psychology* at the University of Chicago. In the Chicago public schools, she taught and then worked as a psychologist (1939–1947), elementary school principal (1947–1948), director of the Bureau of Mentally Handicapped Children (1949–1953), and assistant superintendent of schools for special education* (1953–1966). She was president of the Division of School Psychologists (APA)* 1953–1954 and edited *The Psychologist on the School Staff* (1958). She held leadership roles in international psychology and international school psychology and was an outdoors enthusiast.

See also INTERNATIONAL SCHOOL PSYCHOLOGY ASSOCIATION.

REFERENCES

Mullen, F. A. (1981). School psychology in the USA: Reminiscences of its origin. *Journal of School Psychology* 19, 103–119.
———. (1985). Origins of the International School Psychology Association: Reminiscences. In F. M. Culbertson (Ed.), *Voices in international school psychology* (pp. 5–18). Madison, WI: Editor.

Thomas K. Fagan

MULTICULTURAL COUNSELING. Multicultural counseling is a mental health service delivery model based on an understanding and consideration of cultural factors that affect the counseling process. This model is applicable in almost all psychotherapeutic and counseling situations, but it is particularly relevant in instances where the client is different from the counselor in terms of race, social class, or ethnicity. Historically, multicultural counseling had its formal origins in the 1970s in the field of counseling psychology* and is based on an understanding of the role of culture in the manifestation and expression of mental health problems and, more specifically, a concern with the unique counseling needs of culturally and linguistically diverse groups. Multicultural counseling has become increasingly relevant for school psychology,* given the increase in the number of immigrant and culturally diverse children in the schools. These children often experience stressors related to migration, poverty, the acculturation process, limited language proficiency, and differences in learning and behavioral styles. The underutilization by these children of traditional mental health services in clinical settings offers an opportunity for providing culturally appropriate counseling services and interventions in the school setting.

See also MULTICULTURAL TRAINING; MULTICULTURAL UNDERSTANDING.

REFERENCES

Costantino, G., R. G. Malgady, and L. H. Rogler. (1986). Cuento therapy: A culturally sensitive modality for Puerto Rican children. *Journal of Counseling and Clinical Psychology* 54, 639–645.
Esquivel, G. B., and M. Keitel. (1990). Counseling immigrant children in the schools. *Elementary School Guidance and Counseling* 24, 213–221.
Pedersen, P., and J. C. Carey. (1994). *Multicultural counseling in schools: A practical handbook.* Boston: Allyn and Bacon.

Giselle B. Esquivel

MULTICULTURAL TRAINING. Multicultural training entails the development of a set of multicultural perspectives, competencies, and standards for the profession. Two major approaches for developing multicultural competencies are the training of bilingual and/or culturally diverse school psychologists* and the training of monolingual school psychologists. These approaches are not mutually exclusive and, ideally, should occur simultaneously in any one program.

Rosenfield and Esquivel (1985) provided a model, based on a bilingual school psychology* program developed at Fordham University in 1981, for preparing bilingual school psychologists who are competent in the field of school psychology and have specialized competencies for working with children and families of culturally and linguistically diverse backgrounds. Since 1981, a number of recognized multicultural school psychology programs have been developed nationwide (e.g., San Diego State University, University of Massachusetts, Texas A. & M. University).

The training of monolingual school psychologists, initially proposed as part of in-service training, has been expanded by many of the programs providing formal multicultural training by integrating multicultural competencies as part of the regular curriculum. Multicultural training includes competencies in non-biased assessment,* psycholinguistic issues, multicultural clinical and consultative skills (e.g., Vasquez-Nuttall, De Leon, and Valle, 1990), and qualitative research methods (Ponterotto and Casas, 1991).

See also MULTICULTURAL COUNSELING; MULTICULTURAL UNDERSTANDING.

REFERENCES

Ponterotto, J. G., and J. M. Casas. (1991). *Handbook of racial/ethnic minority counseling research.* Springfield, IL: Charles C. Thomas.
Rosenfield, S., and G. B. Esquivel. (1985). Educating school psychologists to work with bilingual/bicultural populations. *Professional Psychology: Research and Practice* 16, 199–208.
Vasquez-Nuttall, E., B. De Leon, and M. Valle. (1990). Best practices in considering cultural factors. In A. Thomas and J. Grimes (Eds.), *Best practices in school psychology—II* (pp. 219–233). Washington, DC: National Association of School Psychologists.

Giselle B. Esquivel

MULTICULTURAL UNDERSTANDING. Multicultural understanding refers to a perspective on culture as a critical aspect of human behavior. Culture may be defined as diversity in religious belief, sex-role definition, language, ethnic identity, and other group characteristics and values that influence an individual's personal orientation and interactions (Pedersen, 1988). Although the concept of multicultural understanding originated in the counseling literature and has been primarily related to the counseling role, school psychologists* are increasingly concerned with issues of diversity and implications for the profession and for research, training, and practice (e.g., Gopaul-McNicol, 1992; Ingraham, 1992).

Multicultural awareness is the first stage in the development of multicultural understanding and forms the basis for the subsequent attainment of knowledge and expertise stages. Multicultural awareness involves a recognition of the importance of culture, an understanding of one's own culturally based dispositions, and the ability to accurately perceive the attitudes, opinions, and assumptions of the cultural group in question, without preconceived bias (Pedersen, 1988). Knowledge about a culture includes an understanding of factors such as group values, behavioral patterns, and within-group differences. Multicultural understanding culminates in the development of expertise or the integration of skills attained through a combination of clinical training and experience.

See also BILINGUAL ASSESSMENT; MULTICULTURAL COUNSELING; MULTICULTURAL TRAINING; NONBIASED ASSESSMENT.

REFERENCES

Gopaul-McNicol, S. A. (Ed.). (1992). Understanding and meeting the psychological and educational needs of African-American and Spanish-speaking students. *School Psychology Review* 21(4).
Ingraham, C. (1992). Attracting a diverse applicant pool to your school psychology program. *Trainers Forum* 11(2), 6–8.
Pedersen, P. (1988). *A handbook for developing multicultural awareness.* Alexandria, VA: American Association for Counseling and Development.

Giselle B. Esquivel

MULTIDIMENSIONAL SCALING. Multidimensional scaling refers to a variety of mathematical techniques that enable a researcher to detect the structure embedded in a database, often making the data much easier to understand. The procedures are applied to input measures of similarity among objects, resulting in a map as output. The more similar the objects, the closer their proximity on the map. Interpretations are based on geometric configurations such as the clustering of points for homogeneous groups and the meaningful placement of axes on the map. The optimal choice of scaling method depends on the type of embedded structure, accuracy of the spatial model specification, and the input measures of similarity. Multidimensional scaling methods are used for such diverse applications as (1) studying the structure of intelligence based on standardized student aptitude scores, (2) examining the ideological structure of a high school faculty based on teachers' attitudes, (3) comparing different minority groups based on their beliefs, (4) understanding the social structure of a classroom environment based on students' perceptions of their interaction patterns, and (5) analyzing perceived association of psychological traits based on subjects' sorting of trait terms (e.g., humorless, moody) into similar categories.

REFERENCES

Carroll, J. D., and P. Arabie. (1980). Multidimensional scaling. *Annual Review of Psychology* 31, 607–649.
Defays, D. (1988). Scaling of nominal data. In J. P. Keeves (Ed.), *Educational research, methodology, and measurement: An international handbook* (pp. 316–320). New York: Pergamon Press.
Kruskal, J. B., and M. Wish. (1978). *Multidimensional scaling.* Beverly Hills, CA: Sage.

William T. Coombs

MULTIDISCIPLINARY TEAM. Prior to 1975, school psychologists* were the primary, if not only, persons involved in the regulation of special education* diagnosis, placement, and review. With the advent of Public Law 94-142* and its state-level corollary mandates, the decision-making process for assessment and placement into special education programs became a team or group task. Consequently, multidisciplinary teams were formally incorporated as a part of special educational procedures. Section 121 a.532(e) of Public Law 94-142 states that "the evaluation is made by a multidisciplinary team or group of persons, including at least one teacher, or other specialist, with knowledge in the area of suspected disability." These multidisciplinary teams have been referred to as child-study teams, evaluation and placement committees, planning and placement committees, school-appraisal teams, assessment teams, dismissal committees, and evaluation and placement committees. The rationale for multidisciplinary teams is based on the belief that group decision making provides safeguards against individual errors in judgment and benefits students by providing broader input and greater accuracy in assessment, classification, and placement decisions. The educational decision-making team typically comprises parents, teachers, counselors, speech pathologists, nurses, social workers, school psychologists, administrators, medical doctors, and any other professional or individual who can provide information to assist in the best possible placement/ educational delivery system to a student.

See also PUPIL PERSONNEL SERVICES; RELATED SERVICES; TEAM; TEAM APPROACH.

REFERENCES

Fenton, K. S., R. K. Yoshida, J. P. Maxwell, and M. T. Kaufman. (1979). Recognition of team goals: An essential step toward rational decision-making. *Exceptional Children* 45, 638–644.
Kaiser, S. N., and R. W. Woodman. (1985). Multidisciplinary teams and group decision-making techniques: Possible solutions to decision-making problems. *School Psychology Review* 14, 457–470.
Ross, R. P. (1995). Best practices in implementing intervention assistance teams. In A. Thomas and J. Grimes (Eds.), *Best practices in school psychology—III* (pp. 227–237). Washington, DC: National Association of School Psychologists.
Yoshida, R. K. (1980). Multidisciplinary decision making in special education: A review of issues. *School Psychology Review* 9, 221–226.

Kelly J. Griffith

MULTIPLE BASELINE. Multiple baseline is one type of single-case research design. Consistent with all single-case designs, the objective is to demonstrate that the observed change in behavior is related to the implementation of the intervention procedure rather than extraneous events. This relationship, known as functional control, is shown by the repeated change of the target behavior only at the time when the intervention is put in place.

A multiple baseline design begins by determining the different dimensions across which the intervention will be implemented. This can be different subjects, settings, or behaviors within the same subjects. Baseline behavior rates are established across each dimension, and then the intervention is implemented sequentially in one baseline (dimension) at a time. Data are collected each day across all baselines. Because the behavior change occurs only when the intervention is started for each student, the intervention is viewed as having a functional (causal) relationship to the behavior change.

See also ABAB DESIGNS; MULTITRAIT-MULTIMETHOD MATRIX; QUALITATIVE RESEARCH; TREATMENT INTEGRITY.

REFERENCES

Kazdin, A. E. (1982). *Single-case research designs: Methods for clinical and applied settings.* New York: Oxford University Press.
Steege, M. W., and Wacker, D. P. (1995). Best practices in evaluating the effectiveness of applied interventions. In A. Thomas and J. Grimes (Eds.), *Best practices in school psychology—III* (pp. 625–636). Washington, DC: National Association of School Psychologists.

Edward S. Shapiro

MULTISTATE ASSOCIATION MEETINGS. Multistate association meetings describe professional gatherings of school psychologists* from more than one state in a geographic region. Due to distance and cost, many school psychologists are unable to attend national conferences. Also, associations with a smaller membership may find it difficult to conduct a diversified, high-quality state conference. By pooling financial resources, several associations have sponsored quality state conferences within driving distance of all members. Three such regional associations are presented as examples.

Kansas–Missouri–Oklahoma–Arkansas form the Central-State Conference, founded in 1982. Originally, Nebraska and Iowa also were part of the region. Meetings are held annually.

Oregon–Washington–Idaho, Tri-Sate Conference, originated in 1983 and meets every other year. Financial obligations are shared, and members from the three state associations present and assist with all organizational activities.

Alabama–Mississippi–Tennessee, Mid-South Conference, was established in 1988 as a result of a National Association of School Psychologists (NASP) regional meeting in which members expressed an interest in sponsoring a regional conference on an every-other-year basis.

See also STATE ASSOCIATION.

Gerald J. Spadafore

MULTITRAIT-MULTIMETHOD MATRIX. The multitrait-multimethod matrix is an experimental design* used to investigate the construct validity of measures by examining, simultaneously, convergent and discriminant validity. For tests to demonstrate construct validity, they must not only correlate highly with measures to which they should theoretically relate but also not correlate significantly with measures that are theoretically dissimilar. Convergent validity refers to the high correlations and strong relationships that should exist between different tests designed to measure the same (or similar) construct or trait. Discriminant validity refers to the low correlations and nonsignificant relationships that should exist between different tests designed to measure different constructs or traits. Campbell and Fiske (1959) indicated that tests may be deemed invalid if they correlate too highly with tests developed to measure a different construct.

Multitrait refers to examining two or more traits or hypothetical constructs, while multimethod means examining two or more methods used to measure those traits or constructs (Campbell and Fiske, 1959). Data generated through these correlational methods are summarized in a correlation matrix where reliability estimates of the separate measures are placed along the principal diagonal (see Anastasi, 1988; Campbell and Fiske, 1959; Cohen et al., 1988). Other correlation coefficients presented in the matrix include convergent validity coefficients, correlations between different traits using the same method, and correlations between different traits using different methods. The highest correlations in the matrix should be the reliability coefficients of the individual measures. Validity coefficients between different methods measuring the same trait (heteromethod-monotrait) should be higher than both the correlations between different methods measuring different traits (heteromethod-heterotrait) and correlations between different traits using the same method (heterotrait-monomethod) in order to demonstrate construct validity.

If convergent validation is not obtained due to nonsignificant correlations between two different methods measuring the same trait, then three possibilities need to be examined: (1) neither method adequately measures the trait, (2) one of the measures does not adequately measure the trait, or (3) responses provided on the test relate to different characteristics not associated with the proposed trait (Campbell and Fiske, 1959).

See also TREATMENT INTEGRITY; VALIDITY.

REFERENCES

Anastasi, A. (1988). *Psychological testing* (6th ed.). New York: Macmillan.
Campbell, D. T., and D. W. Fiske. (1959). Convergent and discriminant validation by the multitrait-multimethod matrix. *Psychological Bulletin* 56, 81–105.
Cohen, R. J., P. Montague, L. S. Nathanson, and M. E. Swerdlik. (1988). *Psychological testing: An introduction to tests and measurement.* Mountain View, CA: Mayfield.

Gary L. Canivez

MUNSON, GRACE E. Grace Esther Munson was born near Orleans, Nebraska, on October 17, 1883, and died in Morongo Valley, California, on August 8, 1980. She completed her B.A. at the University of Nebraska (1911), M.A. at Wellesley College (1912), and Ph.D. at the University of Nebraska (1916) in clinical psychology* and speech disorders. She was a teacher and principal in a Nebraska high school before completing her college degrees. Her career was most visible during the years she was employed in the Chicago public schools. There she worked as a school psychologist* (1918–1935), director of the Bureau of Child Study (1935–1946), and assistant superintendent in charge of special education* (1946–1949). Under her guidance, the bureau expanded in personnel and programs, including her development of the Chicago Adjustment Program, during the depression era. In retirement, she was a pioneer in the development of Morongo Valley, a remote desert community in California.

REFERENCES

Mullen, F. A. (1980). Grace Munson, Ph.D. October 17, 1883–August 8, 1980. *The School Psychologist* 35(1), 8.

———. (c. 1980). Grace Esther Munson, 1883–1980. Unpublished paper, 5 pp.

Thomas K. Fagan

MUSIC THERAPY. The development of the field of music therapy began in 1946 in response to the burgeoning populations in Veterans Administration (VA) hospitals at the conclusion of World War II. Music therapy was thought of as an activity therapy or adjunctive therapy to provide a vehicle for the patient's constructive use of time along with other activities, for example, occupational therapy.

Now, music therapy is grouped with drama, art, and dance as one of the creative arts therapies or expressive therapies. Music therapy has undergone a shift from a psychoanalytic basis to a behavioral basis because of the powerful nature of music as a stimulus and a reinforcer. Music can have either a stimulating or calming affect. By its introduction or withdrawal, music can function as a reinforcer.

During the first three decades as an organized profession, music therapists functioned primarily in institutional settings for the emotionally disturbed and the mentally retarded. Music therapists viewed the schools as a proper setting to work, with the passage of Public Law 94-142* and with music therapists' finding themselves operating more independently than during the early days of ancillary therapy employed under the direction of psychiatrists. Music could be used to teach academic, social, motor, and language skills. Used to evoke affect, as stimulus control or reinforcement, and as a vehicle to learn sequential material or behaviors, music can be applied effectively as a tool for learning with any type of disability, even deafness. Music provides a resource for integrating students with disabilities with peers who have no disabilities.

The profession is tightly regulated by the National Association for Music Therapy, which prescribes training, has developed a national certification examination, and certifies registered music therapists (RMT). Contact: National Association for Music Therapy, 8455 Colesville Road, Suite 993, Silver Spring, MD 20910.

REFERENCES

Alley, J. M. (1982). Music therapy. In C. R. Reynolds and T. B. Gutkin (Eds.), *The handbook of school psychology* (pp. 667–678). New York: Wiley.

Michael, D. E. (1985). *Music therapy: An introduction, including music in special education* (2d ed.). Springfield, IL: Charles C. Thomas.

Paul G. Warden

N

NATIONAL ASSOCIATION OF SCHOOL PSYCHOLOGISTS. The National Association of School Psychologists (NASP) was founded at its first convention, March 14–15, 1969, at the Sheraton-Jefferson Hotel in St. Louis, Missouri. Its first president was Pauline Alexander, a practitioner* from Ohio. Established as a grassroots organization to better represent practitioner issues, especially those of nondoctoral practitioners, NASP has been governed by an executive board of elected officers and regional directors and a separate delegate assembly, with each state having one elected delegate. The activities of the association are managed by a complex committee structure and a central office staff. The official NASP newsletter is the *Communique,* and its official journal is the *School Psychology Review.* NASP has other publications, including a code of ethics, standards relating to the provision of services and training, credentialing and training directories, and topical books. Its annual convention, usually held in March or April, is attended by more than 2,000 persons and is the largest national convention in the world exclusively for school psychologists.* A system of national certification* is also available through its National School Psychology Certification Board. NASP participates in national program accreditation* through the National Council for Accreditation of Teacher Education.* NASP members are primarily practicing school psychologists, university trainers,* and state department of education school psychologists, but associate membership is available for other interested persons. Archives of the association are maintained in the Special Collections Library of the University of Memphis Libraries, Memphis, Tennessee. Contact: NASP, 4340 East West Highway, Suite 402, Bethesda, MD 20814.

See also NATIONAL CERTIFICATION IN SCHOOL PSYCHOLOGY.

REFERENCES

Fagan, T. K. (Guest Editor). (1989). NASP at 20. *School Psychology Review* 18(2), 149–224.

———. (1993). Separate but equal: School psychology's search for organizational identity. *Journal of School Psychology* 31, 3–90.

Farling, W. H., and J. Agner. (1979). History of the National Association of School Psychologists: The first decade. *School Psychology Digest* 8, 140–152.

Thomas K. Fagan

NATIONAL ASSOCIATION OF SCHOOL PSYCHOLOGISTS ANNUAL CONVENTION. Beginning with the formation of the National Association of School Psychologists* (NASP) in March 1969, the annual convention has been an important, visible event in school psychology.* Conceived as both a gathering of school psychologists* and an opportunity to gain new information and skills, the convention also hosts the governing body of the association known as the Executive Board/Delegate Assembly. The location of the convention is typically in a major city in the United States, although one convention was held in Toronto, Canada. Sites of the NASP conventions are listed in historical editions of the *School Psychology Review* 8(2) and 18(2). The first convention, held in St. Louis, was attended by approximately 400 school psychologists. During the next twenty years, attendance increased significantly, making the convention a major source of revenue for the organization. In recent years, attendance has been more than 2,300 persons. The first NASP convention lasted two days, while recent conventions have lasted five days, including preconvention workshops and governing body meetings.

Planning for a convention begins with determining the location and the assets of the facilities to be used. The location of the convention was rotated among the five geographic regions of NASP governance until the late 1980s. Site selection has changed in recent years, with the location of sites determined with less regard for regional rotation, and sites are selected five or more years in advance. A convention committee determines the program content, while the NASP president has input on who will be the general session speakers. Presentations and workshop proposals are solicited in the summer of the year previous to when the convention will be held. A "call for papers" is published in the *Communique,* the NASP official newsletter. In recent years, more than 500 papers have been presented during the convention. The convention committee periodically conducts evaluations to determine both participant satisfaction and revenues generated.

See also AMERICAN PSYCHOLOGICAL ASSOCIATION ANNUAL CONVENTION; CONTINUING PROFESSIONAL DEVELOPMENT.

W. Alan Coulter

NATIONAL ASSOCIATION OF SCHOOL PSYCHOLOGISTS INTEREST GROUPS. The purpose of interest groups within the National Association of School Psychologists* (NASP) is to provide a forum, or network, for school psychologists* with particular specialty interests. Sharing information occurs during annual conferences, through newsletters, and through encouragement of ongoing communication links within the professional community.

The period of initial interest group development (the late 1970s to early 1980s) paralleled the increasing specialization of school psychology* training at various universities (Knoff, 1985). Though providing a core curriculum, some training programs were considered to "specialize" in a specific area, such as preschool or vocational applications of school psychology. From the onset, NASP interest groups have been informal networks, with NASP providing modest funding (for mail and phone communication), with major ongoing costs (newsletter printing and distribution) absorbed by members or member institutions. Due to the informal nature of the interest groups, the viability and eventual survival of these networks were dependent on the energy and commitment of those who volunteered to coordinate these activities.

Initial interest groups were entitled vocational, preschool, CTASP (Committee on Technological Applications in School Psychology), and rural. There have also been NASP interest groups for postsecondary services, urban, prevention, crisis management, international, families, neuropsychology, school psychologists for the deaf, systems/indirect services, and autism/developmental.

NASP continues to support interest groups, and, in 1995, there were thirteen groups listed.

See also INTERNATIONAL SCHOOL PSYCHOLOGY ASSOCIATION; LITERATURE IN SCHOOL PSYCHOLOGY; TRAINING MODELS; VOCATIONAL SCHOOL PSYCHOLOGY.

REFERENCE

Knoff, H. (1985). Interest group development in NASP: Current status and future trends. *Communique,* 14(4), 5–8.

Alex Thomas

NATIONAL ASSOCIATION OF STATE CONSULTANTS FOR SCHOOL PSYCHOLOGICAL SERVICES.

The National Association of State Consultants for School Psychological Services (NASCSPS) was officially incorporated on August 20, 1976. The association's founder and first president was James Eikeland. Although the organization dates only from 1976, school psychologists* have been employed by state education agencies since Arnold Gesell's* appointment in 1915 to the Connecticut State Board of Education (Fagan, 1987a,b).

NASCSPS was organized to establish a communication network among state department of education* (SDE) state consultants* of school psychology* to more cooperatively address issues and current events. The individual membership of the NASCSPS is composed of state education agency (SEA) employees who serve as consultants in school psychology. Typically, state consultants are employed for administrative purposes, including the improvement of services, interpretation of state policies and regulations, facilitation of employment for school psychologists, and coordinating internship* programs. One of the most significant contributions of the association was its impact on the original rules and regulations of Public Law 93-380* and Public Law 94-142* (Fagan, 1993). The group has worked with the National Association of School Psychologists* (NASP) and the American Psychological Association* (APA) to address important issues to the field of school psychology. The association works closest with committees engaged in issues of training and accreditation,* legislation, and children's services. The NASCSPS maintains contact through its current president.

See also STATE ASSOCIATION.

REFERENCES

Fagan, T. K. (1987a). Gesell: The first school psychologist, Part I. The road to Connecticut. *School Psychology Review* 16, 103–107.

———. (1987b). Gesell: The first school psychologist, Part II. Practice and significance. *School Psychology Review* 16, 399–409.

———. (1993). Separate but equal: School psychology's search for organizational identity. *Journal of School Psychology* 31, 3–90.

Jonathan Pedro

NATIONAL ASSOCIATION OF STATE DIRECTORS OF SPECIAL EDUCATION. The National Association of State Directors of Special Education (NASDSE) was founded in 1938 with a mission to assist state agencies to maximize their efforts to serve individuals with disabilities. The 2,100 NASDSE members are state directors of special education,* consultants, supervisors, administrators, and others who have statewide responsibilities for special education programs. The association seeks to improve educational opportunities of individuals with disabilities through a variety of activities such as legislative efforts and recognizing outstanding contributions of individuals by bestowing awards.

NASDSE also maintains a clearinghouse for professionals in special education. NASDSE has two publications: *Counterpoint,* which is a quarterly journal, and *National Association of State Directors Special Education Liaison Bulletin,* which is a periodic newsletter covering special education issues at a national level, including action in Congress, the executive branch, and federal agencies. NASDSE holds an annual convention each fall. Contact: NASDSE, 1800 Diagonal Road, Suite 320, Alexandria, VA. Phone: (703) 519-3800, FAX: (703) 519-3808, electronic mail via Special Net.

See also NATIONAL ASSOCIATION OF STATE DIRECTORS OF TEACHER EDUCATION AND CERTIFICATION.

REFERENCE

Daniels, P. K., and C. A. Swartz, (Eds.). (1994). *Encyclopedia of associations,* Vol. 1 (28th ed., p. 8354). Detroit: Gale Research.

James W. Batts

NATIONAL ASSOCIATION OF STATE DIRECTORS OF TEACHER EDUCATION AND CERTIFICATION. The National Association of State Directors of Teacher Education and Certification (NASDTEC) was founded in 1922 and currently has approximately 100 members. The association is divided into four regional groups. The members are the administrative representatives of states, District of Columbia, and the Commonwealth of Puerto Rico who have the primary responsibility for the preparation and certification* of professional school personnel and professional standards of practice. NASDTEC's mission is to improve the skills of members and interested persons and to improve teacher education programs and certification procedures. Workshops, training programs on a variety of topics, including performance/outcome-based certification, and a national clearinghouse of school personnel who have had their certification revoked are among the services offered. The association publishes annually the *Directory of State Certification Personnel* and periodically publishes *Standards for State Approval of Teacher Education* and *Manual on Certification and Preparation of Education Personnel in the United States.* NASDTEC's annual convention is in June and is rotated regionally. Contact: NASDTEC, 3600 Whitman Avenue N, Suite 105, Seattle, WA 98103; phone (203) 547-0437; FAX: (206) 548-0116.

See also NATIONAL ASSOCIATION OF STATE DIRECTORS OF SPECIAL EDUCATION.

REFERENCES

Daniels, P. K., and C. A. Swartz, (Eds.). (1994). *Encyclopedia of associations,* Vol. 1 (28th ed., p. 8354). Detroit: Gale Research.

James W. Batts

NATIONAL CERTIFICATION IN SCHOOL PSYCHOLOGY. National certification in school psychology* was initiated by the National Association of School Psychologists* (NASP) through the creation, in 1988, of the National School Psychology Certification Board. The board established the Nationally Certified School Psychologist (NCSP) certificate to recognize those school psychologists who met national standards for certification in school psychology* as set forth in the NASP *Standards for Training and Field Placement Programs in School Psychology* (1984).

The purposes of the national certification system are to (1) provide consumers of school psychological services with a consistent level of training and experience in service providers who are nationally certified; (2) encourage professional growth and development by school psychologists at a national level; (3) allow the profession of school psychology (through NASP) to set the standards for credentialing at a national level; and (4) facilitate the acceptance of national standards by individual states and hasten the recognition of the NCSP as equivalent to state certification. In this way, school psychologists who were nationally certified could move to other states without the barriers of recertification in each state. As well, consumers could have greater access to school psychologists from throughout the United States who might choose to relocate.

The initiation of the national certification system (NCS) was triggered by early efforts in the school reform movement to raise the standards of professional educators through the establishment of state-level certification examinations in all areas of professional educator certification, including school psychology. This effort was initiated by the Southern Regional Education Board. Each of these states was establishing its own criteria for the knowledge base of the examination. NASP became involved in order to provide a unified approach and a national, professional association perspective to the test development. In 1987, over twelve different titles were used in the United States to certify school psychologists, including "school psychologist," "school psychometrist," "associate school psychologist," "school psychological examiner," and "educational diagnostician." It was clear that a national effort was necessary both to define who a school psychologist was and to define the criteria for certification of an individual with that title.

The requirements for the NCSP certificate include (1) a sixth-year/specialist degree* in school psychology with a minimum of sixty graduate semester hours, consisting of course work, practicums, and internship* from an accredited institution of higher learning; (2) successful completion of a full-year (1,200 clock hours) internship, at least 600 hours of which must be in a school setting; and (3) successful completion of the national school psychology examination administered by Educational Testing Service. Graduates of a NASP-approved school psychology program automatically meet the first requirement and do not undergo transcript review. The certificate is valid for three years and must be renewed triennially.

Nationally certified school psychologists must complete seventy-five contact hours (or 7.5 continuing education units) of continuing professional development* (CPD) within each three-year renewal cycle. The criteria for types of acceptable CPD activities are set forth by NASP.

At the time of the implementation of the NCS, a "grandparent" clause was created for those individuals who were already credentialed as a school psychologist (or its equivalent) by a state credentialing agency. Individuals who desired grandparenting had to meet the following criteria: (1) hold a master's degree (or higher) from an accredited institution; (2) hold a credential to provide school psychological services as of December 31, 1988; (3) take the national school psychology examination by April 15, 1989; and (4) apply to NASP for the NCSP certificate by December 31, 1988. Individuals grandparented into the system had until December 31, 1991, to meet the NASP standards of forty-eight semester hours (or equivalent) of academic credit and a full-year internship (or two years' experience) in order to renew their certification.

Approximately 14,000 school psychologists hold the NCSP certificate. The NCSP is recognized for certification or licensure in twelve states.

REFERENCES

Batsche, G. M. (1987). National school psychology certification system proposed. *Communique* 16(3), 1–2.

———. (1988). Q and A on the national certification system. *Communique* 17(3), 1.

National Association of School Psychologists. (1988). *National school psychology certification board policy manual.* Silver Spring, MD: Author.

George M. Batsche

NATIONAL CONFERENCE ON LEVELS AND PATTERNS OF PRO-FESSIONAL TRAINING IN PSYCHOLOGY. Following the 1949 Boulder, Colorado, conference and the development of the scientist-practitioner training model, the American Psychological Association* has sponsored additional conferences to examine and make recommendations about training in psychology. The National Conference on Levels and Patterns of Professional Training in Psychology, held in Vail, Colorado, in 1973, is one example. While conferees did not abandon the Boulder model of training, the conference endorsed programs that defined themselves by a basic service orientation. The Psy.D. was determined to be an appropriate degree if the primary emphasis in training was on the direct delivery of professional services. The Ph.D. was considered appropriate for programs emphasizing the development of new knowledge in psychology. Other issues addressed at the Vail conference included multilevel training, delineating desirable characteristics of professional training, doctoral-level training, master's-level training, submaster's-level training, continuing professional development,* professional training and minority groups, professional training and women, and service delivery systems and the social context.

See also BOULDER CONFERENCE; PROFESSIONAL TRAINING MODEL.

REFERENCES

Korman, M. (1974). National conference on levels and patterns of professional training in psychology: The major themes. *American Psychologist* 29, 441–449.

——— (Ed.). (1976). *Levels and patterns of professional training in psychology.* Washington, DC: American Psychological Association.

Mark D. Shriver
Jack J. Kramer

NATIONAL CONGRESS OF PARENTS AND TEACHERS. Originally the National Congress of Mothers, the Parent-Teachers Association (PTA) was founded in Washington, D.C., by Alice McClellan Birney in 1897 as an outgrowth of the kindergarten movement in Chicago. In Chicago at a meeting called by the Chicago Kindergarten College, Birney called on the nation to "recognize the importance of the child." The first national meeting attracted 2,000 delegates and led to the creation of state associations that sponsored mothers' clubs across the country. By 1910, twenty-one states had mothers' clubs, with 50,000 members. By 1920, there were clubs in thirty-six states with a membership of

190,000. In 1924, the congress changed its name to the National Congress of Mothers and Parent-Teachers Association, although its membership remained overwhelmingly female. In 1976, the organization assumed its present name, the National Congress of Parents and Teachers.

The goal of the organization was to mobilize educated mothers on behalf of the nation's children; although the leadership was to be from the educated elites among women, others less fortunate were welcome to join. The hope was that, through organization, a broad program of social improvement would emerge. Specific parts of its program included granting mothers equal guardianship of children, the establishment of kindergartens, the use of foster homes in place of orphanages, widow's pensions, and the creation of juvenile courts. In addition, the founders lobbied for courses in domestic science or home economics for women college students. During the 1920s, the PTA strongly supported efforts for international peace in spite of conservative criticism. In 1994, the congress had 7 million members organized in 27,000 local groups. It claims to unite the forces of home, school, and community on behalf of children and youth, and it works for legislation on behalf of children and youth.

See also HOME-SCHOOL-COMMUNITY COLLABORATION.

REFERENCES

Cott, N. (1987). *The grounding of modern feminism.* New Haven, CT: Yale University Press.
Rothman, S. (1978). *Woman's proper place, A history of changing ideals and practices, 1870 to the present.* New York: Basic Books.

Joseph M. Hawes

NATIONAL COUNCIL FOR ACCREDITATION OF TEACHER EDU-CATION. The National Council for Accreditation of Teacher Education (NCATE), a nongovernmental, specialized accrediting organization, was established in 1954 through the efforts of five major organizations interested in teacher education: the American Association of Colleges for Teacher Education (AACTE), the National Association of State Directors of Teacher Education and Certification* (NASDTEC), the National Commission on Teacher Education and Professional Standards of the National Education Association (NEA), the National Council of Chief State School Officers (now CCSSO), and the National School Boards Association (NSBA). The NCATE replaced AACTE in the accreditation* process within teacher education. NCATE is the only agency recognized by the U.S. Department of Education for the purpose of accrediting college and university units engaged in the preparation of all professional school personnel who function at the elementary, middle, and secondary levels.

NCATE comprises representatives of more than two dozen professional organizations that have a significant interest in the preparation of professional education personnel, as well as student and public representatives. The professional organizations represent four general constituencies: (1) persons engaged in the preparation of professional educators (e.g., American Association of Colleges of Teacher Education), (2) practicing professionals (e.g., National Education Association, American Federation of Teachers), (3) state and local policymakers (e.g., Council of Chief State School Officers, National School Boards Association), and (4) professional specialty areas (e.g., International Reading Association, National Association of School Psychologists*).

NCATE accredits professional education "units," which are defined as the school, college, department, or other administrative body that is primarily responsible for the preparation of professional education personnel. Accreditation is based on compliance with standards and criteria in the general areas of curriculum (including foundation, design, and delivery), clinical and field experiences, students (including recruitment, quality, advisory services, and program completion), faculty (including qualifications, working conditions, development, and evaluation), governance, and resources.

In addition to generic unit standards, NCATE also reviews and approves guidelines developed by its specialty organization members for the review of professional preparation programs (e.g., specialist and doctoral programs in school psychology*). Programs are evaluated by the respective specialty organizations in terms of compliance with NCATE-approved guidelines. Those programs approved by specialty organizations are identified by NCATE as "nationally recognized" in its annually published list of accredited units.

See also TEACHER ORGANIZATIONS.

REFERENCES

National Council for Accreditation of Teacher Education. (1995). *Standards, procedures, and policies for the accreditation of professional education units.* Washington, DC: Author.
————. (annual). *Teacher preparation: A guide to colleges and universities.* Washington, DC: Author.

Michael J. Curtis

NATIONAL INVITATIONAL CONFERENCE OF SCHOOL PSYCHOLOGISTS.

This conference was organized and hosted by the Ohio School Psychologists Association in order to improve communication among school psychologists* nationwide and to consider establishing a national organization. The conference was held at the Christopher Inn in Columbus, Ohio, on March 21–22, 1968. According to the *Proceedings,* invitations were sent to persons and organizations expressing interest, and the meeting was attended by thirty-nine people representing eleven states, including practicing school psychologists, state education agency employees, and university trainers.* One outcome was the formation of committees whose work would assist in the founding of the National Association of School Psychologists* one year later. The keynote address, "An Overview of the National Scene in School Psychology," was presented by William Farling, chief psychologist for the Ohio Department of

Education. The *Proceedings* name the fifty-four original contributors to the General Planning Committee for the Establishment of NASP and the participants of the invitational conference.

REFERENCE

Proceedings of the National Invitational Conference of School Psychologists, March 21–22, 1968. Christopher Inn, Columbus, OH.

Thomas K. Fagan

NATIONAL MENTAL HEALTH ASSOCIATION. The National Mental Health Association (NMHA) was founded in 1909. It was originally called the National Committee for Mental Hygiene, and its founder was a former psychiatric patient named Clifford W. Beers. NMHA is a charitable organization with more than eighty years of success in addressing the mental health needs of our communities, states, and nation. It has 358 affiliate organizations in thirty-five states, each dependent on the efforts of volunteers to help change the way America thinks about mental health and mental illness.

NMHA volunteers all over the country work to meet the mental health needs of their communities through support groups, community outreach and education, information and referral programs, patient advocacy, and a wide array of other services. The national office has information materials on over 140 mental health topics, many of which are directed toward the mental health of children and families.

Nationally, NMHA works with the media to keep the public informed about mental health and mental illness, with the federal government to promote research and coordinated services for people with mental health problems. NMHA works collaboratively with other major organizations to ensure that the nation's mental health needs are understood and addressed. The National Association of School Psychologists* and the American Psychological Association* work in coalitions with NMHA, including the National Consortium for Child and Adolescent Mental Health Services and the Mental Health—Special Education Coalition. Contact: National Mental Health Association, 1021 Prince Street, Alexandria, VA 22314.

See also COALITIONS.

REFERENCE

National Mental Health Association. (1994). *Mission statement.* Alexandria, VA: Author.

Kevin P. Dwyer

NATIONAL REGISTER OF HEALTH SERVICE PROVIDERS IN PSYCHOLOGY. *The National Register of Health Service Providers in Psychology* was established in 1974. The *National Register* is a publication that lists psychologists who are licensed or certified by a state regulatory board and who have met the register's criteria as health service providers in psychology. The criteria include the holding of a doctoral degree* and at least two years of supervised experience in health services in psychology, of which at least one year is in an organized health service training program, and one year is post-doctoral.

As of 1994, there were approximately 16,000 psychologists in the nonprofit publication. In addition to basic identifying information, theoretical orientation and characteristics regarding general and specialized health services are provided.

The *Register* makes this list available to consumers of health services, health service organizations, governmental agencies such as the National Institute of Mental Health, and the general public. A number of public and private insurers have informally recognized the *Registry* for purposes of insurance reimbursement.

In addition to the application fees, there is an annual renewal fee. Guidelines also exist for removal of a psychologist from the listing for ethical or legal violations in professional practice. Contact: National Register of Health Service Providers in Psychology, 1120 G Street, NW, Suite 330, Washington, DC 20005.

See also CERTIFICATION; LICENSING.

REFERENCE

Wellner, A. M., and C. A. Zimet. (1983). The national register of health service providers in psychology. In B. Sales (Ed.), *The professional psychologists handbook* (pp. 185–200). New York: Plenum Press.

Robert N. Wendt

NATIONAL SCHOOL PSYCHOLOGY INSERVICE TRAINING NETWORK.

The National School Psychology Inservice Training Network (NSPITN) was established in 1978 with the assistance of funds from the Office of Special Education and Rehabilitative Services,* U.S. Department of Education. In existence until 1984, the goals of the network were to provide in-service training for school psychologists* in the wake of Public Law 94-142* and to provide a stimulus for reconsidering the roles and functions* of school psychologists and their future training needs. Housed at the University of Minnesota, the network helped to organize the Spring Hill Symposium on the Future of School Psychology,* published in-service training modules on the appraisal process, nonbiased assessment,* and nontest-based assessment, and published two culminating works to help define the future needs of school psychology (NSPITN, 1984; Ysseldyke, 1984).

REFERENCES

National School Psychology Inservice Training Network. (1984). *School psychology: A blueprint for training and practice.* Minneapolis: Author.

Ysseldyke, J. E. (Ed.). (1984). *School psychology: The state of the art.* Minneapolis: Author.

Thomas K. Fagan

NATIONAL TEACHER EXAMINATION. The National Teacher Examination (NTE) was developed by the Educational Testing Service (ETS) of Princeton, New Jersey, to provide data to colleges and school districts regarding the academic preparation of teachers and other educational personnel. Typically administered three times a year at the numerous ETS sites across the country, the exam consists of multiple-choice items that are responded to on optically scored "bubble" sheets.

The "common" examination was first developed in 1940. It tests knowledge in the areas of professional education, social studies, literature and the fine arts, science and mathematics, and English expression. In 1993 the NTE became the Core Battery for the Educational Testing Service's PRAXIS Series. Exams are also available for a wide variety of "specialty" teaching areas. NTE#40, the school psychologist examination,* is one of these specialty areas.

See also CERTIFICATION TESTS.

REFERENCES

Buros, O. K. (1978). *The eighth mental measurements yearbook.* Highland Park, NJ: Gryphon Press.

Lanier, J. E., and J. W. Little. (1986). Research on teacher education. In M. C. Wittrock (Ed.), *Handbook of research on teaching* (pp. 527–569). New York: Macmillan.

Philip B. Bowser

NATURALISTIC OBSERVATION. Naturalistic observation is a data-gathering approach employed when the researcher desires to make a "functional analysis of behavior in the setting and at the time the behavior occurs" (Gresham and Elliot, 1984, p. 297). By gathering data in the setting where the researcher's questions exist, the results of studies based on naturalistic observations are judged to have greater face validity, while maximizing ecological validity.

Numerous studies considering the social context of schooling have incorporated naturalistic observations. From Wright and Barker's (1950) work on psychological ecology to more contemporary works dealing with cooperative learning* in the classroom, observing subjects in their natural settings continues to provide invaluable data to the field of school psychology* (Evertson and Green, 1986).

For many years, field notes, checklists, and sociograms* were techniques of naturalistic observations. The recent rise of qualitative research* (i.e., ethnographic), however, has had an impact on the approaches taken as part of naturalistic observations. An evolving trend is to employ less structured observational techniques that enable the researcher to make more informed assessments of the meaning of the subjects' behavior within the mores of their culture.

See also IDIOGRAPHIC VERSUS NOMOTHETIC RESEARCH; VALIDITY.

REFERENCES

Evertson, C. M., and J. L. Green. (1986). Observation as inquiry and method. In M. C. Whittrock (Ed.), *Handbook of research on teaching* (3d ed., pp. 162–213). New York: Macmillan.

Gresham, F. M., and S. N. Elliot. (1984). Assessment and classification of children's social skills: A review of methods and issues. *School Psychology Review* 13, 292–301.

Hintze, J. M., and Shapiro, E. S. (1995). Best practices in the systematic observation of classroom behavior. In A. Thomas and J. Grimes (Eds.), *Best practices in school psychology—III* (pp. 651–660). Washington, DC: National Association of School Psychologists.

Wright, H. F., and R. G. Barker. (1950). *Methods in psychological ecology.* Lawrence: University of Kansas Press.

Tracy L. Cross

NEEDS ASSESSMENT. Needs assessment is the practice of gathering and evaluating information essential to the planning and implementation of modifications in educational programs. Needs refer to discrepancies between existing programs and standards established by school authorities. They include data regarding the psychoeducational status of students and parent and professional issues, as well as information regarding the sophisticated equipment essential to the successful achievement of educational objectives. With expanded services being provided for all students, those in regular education as well as those with special needs in mainstreamed classrooms, staff development is a primary focus in school districts nationwide. In addition to educational/training needs and appropriately qualified personnel, special students often require that attention be paid to potential crisis situations.

Effective assessments begin with a comprehensive analysis of current conditions in the target area(s) to be addressed. Issues to be considered relate to the current status of a district and a comprehensive plan for getting the district to "where it wants to be." An outline of the most important data sources available is employed to help target the design of the best data collection techniques. Methods utilized include interviews, questionnaires, nominal group process, and the "Delphi" technique. Needs assessment instruments should be attractive and interesting, so that resistance to change can be overcome, and a commitment to high-quality programming can be established. Consultants often use needs assessment devices to break particular topic areas into component parts (Goldstein, Krasner, and Garfield, 1992). For maximum effectiveness, teachers, as well as administrators and support staff, should be included. Burke, Heideman, and Heideman (1990) strongly urge districts to consider teachers as primary in-service presenters. Such peer group presentations have proven very effective.

School psychologists* must possess the knowledge and skill to act as consultants in all areas previously mentioned, as well as providing assistance in the implementation and evaluation processes. Outcome measures involve the administration and interpretation of standardized test scores and/or competency-based test results. Analyses of various school records and survey techniques, as well as classroom observations, are also of value. The gathering and analyzing of appropriate data should involve all participants. This should enhance their knowledge of target issues and improve the quality of the decisions that eventuate.

Crucial areas for consideration are the processes of goal setting, translating needs into objectives, understanding the change process, and designing evaluation techniques. Regardless of what methods are employed, staff development programs must be tailored to meet the needs of the target population.

See also ACCOUNTABILITY; PROGRAM EVALUATION.

REFERENCES

Burke, P., R. Heideman and C. Heideman (Eds.). (1990). *Programming for staff development: Fanning the flame.* New York: Falmer.
Goldstein, A., L. Krasner and S. Garfield (Eds.). (1992). *Psychology practitioner guidebooks: School consultation.* New York: Macmillan.

Barbara W. Wonderly

NETWORKING. The earliest derivation of the term ''networking'' can be traced to the mid- to late 1500s (Simpson and Weiner, 1989). Usage referred to a work in which threads, wires, or other materials were arranged in some order, much like a net. ''Network'' has evolved from referring to an arrangement of materials to an arrangement of linking transmitters, eventually to the linkages of computers, and currently referring to an interconnected group of people.

Professional networking within school psychology* generally refers to both structured and unstructured methods of facilitating communication within a discipline for a specific purpose. In a structured setting, networking is accomplished by instituting procedures to ensure communication among individuals primarily involved in some project or activity. Examples of structured networking include the requirement to have specific participants for planning individualized education programs* or to be members of a building assistance or multidisciplinary evaluation team.*

Unstructured networking refers to informal activities that develop social and professional interaction, presumably enhancing the accomplishment of participants' goals. Involvement in professional conferences or continuing education activities, attendance at social functions, and interactions during professional activities are likely to encourage informal communication that may establish useful relationships or increase the likelihood and benefits of future professional contact.

See also AMERICAN PSYCHOLOGICAL ASSOCIATION ANNUAL CONVENTION; COLLABORATION; NATIONAL ASSOCIATION OF SCHOOL PSYCHOLOGISTS ANNUAL CONVENTION; NATIONAL AS-SOCIATION OF SCHOOL PSYCHOLOGISTS INTEREST GROUPS; STATE ASSOCIATION; TEAM.

REFERENCE

Simpson, J. A., and E.S.C. Weiner (Eds.). (1989). *The Oxford English dictionary,* Vols. 1–2. (2d ed.). Oxford: Clarendon Press.

Alex Thomas

NEUROPSYCHOLOGICAL ASSESSMENT. Applied neuropsychology (i.e., the study of brain–behavior relationships) began in 1935, when Ward Halstead established the first full-time laboratory for investigating the psychological outcomes of cerebral lesions. Prior to that time, research was limited to identifying specificity of brain functions (e.g., Broca's examination of speech production, Lashley's investigations of the visual cortex). Primarily studying patients with frontal lobe damage, Halstead systematically developed a variety of psychometric tests that were sensitive to brain injury. The resulting Halstead Neuropsychological Battery was published in 1947.

One of Halstead's students, Ralph Reitan, continued the work of his mentor. In 1951, Reitan started a neuropsychology laboratory investigating brain–behavior relationships with both children and adults. Following Halstead's advice, Reitan completed blind evaluations on thousands of persons with known diversified cerebral damage, as well as normal control subjects. Only after drawing conclusions based *solely* on the neuropsychological findings would Reitan match his data with the neurological information provided by neurosurgeons or neuropathologists. This laborious technique was deemed essential in separating test results critical to aspects of brain pathology from those that were only spuriously related. Many techniques originally assumed sensitive to brain damage were eliminated by this rigorous research methodology (e.g., coin differentiation while blindfolded). Thus, Reitan greatly expanded previous research and was highly instrumental in the development of the Halstead-Reitan Neuropsychological Battery (HRNB) and the Halstead-Reitan Neuropsychological Battery for Older Children (HRNB-C), both published in 1969.

In a 1982 survey of neuropsychologists, Reitan was ranked as the *most* significant contributor to the field of neuropsychology since 1940. Likewise, portions of the Halstead-Reitan Battery (e.g., Category Test, Tactile Performance Test, Speech-Sounds Perception Test) were ranked the second most frequently used psychometric tools, surpassed only by the Wechsler (i.e., WISC-R, WAIS-R). The entire Halstead-Reitan Battery was reported to be the fourth most frequently used assessment tool. The overwhelming emphasis on psychometric assessment (as opposed to nuclear/radiographic techniques such as computerized axial tomography [CAT] or position-emission tomography [PET] scans, magnetic resonance imaging [MRIs]) is clearly a function of the contribution of Reitan.

The Luria-Nebraska Neuropsychological Battery (LNNB) is gaining acceptance as a valid and reliable assessment tool. Based on A. R. Luria's (1902–1977) functional systems theory of brain organization, Golden, Hemmeke, and Purisch published the LNNB in 1980 as a tool to utilize the acclaimed Russian's methodology. It has been reported that Luria was opposed to the standardization of his techniques, and he died before the LNNB was published. However, Golden has stated that only through publication of the LNNB would this valuable technique be accepted by neuropsychologists in Western society. The LNNB differs from the Halstead-Reitan approach by focusing on a theory-driven processing paradigm as compared to an injury/insult model. Items within the LNNB essentially represent A. L. Christensen's 1975 standardization of Luria's procedures. Golden and associates provided further standardization in administration/scoring as well as statistical norms for comparative purposes.

Many neuropsychologists utilize tests independent of the HRNB or LNNB. The Wisconsin Card Sorting Test and the Stroop Color and Word Test are two such examples.

See also MODALITY ASSESSMENT; NEUROPSYCHOLOGY LABORATORY; PERCEPTUAL-MOTOR ASSESSMENT.

REFERENCES

Puente, A. E., and R. J. McCaffrey. (1992). *Handbook of neuropsychological assessment: A biopsychosocial perspective.* New York: Plenum Press.
Reitan, R. M., and D. Wolfson. (1993). *The Halstead-Reitan Neuropsychological Test Battery: Theory and clinical interpretations.* Tucson, AZ: Reitan Laboratory.

LeAdelle Phelps

NEUROPSYCHOLOGY LABORATORY. Neuropsychology, the study of brain–behavior relationships, offers a dynamic approach to assessment and rehabilitation. Neuropsychological examinations, which incorporate sensory, perceptual, motor, cognitive, emotional, and educational data, are the most comprehensive evaluations presently available (D'Amato, 1990). Most exams are conducted in specialized clinics called neuropsychology laboratories. While neuropsychology can be traced back some 2,500 years, the first formal laboratory was developed by Halstead in 1935 (Whitten, D'Amato, and Chittooran, 1992). Neuropsychology looks both inward at the brain and outward at behavior to determine which psychotherapeutic interventions will be most beneficial. There is much common ground between school psychology* and neuropsychology, including intellectual and personality assessment,* intervention strategies, consultation,* and research. Neuropsychology has yielded reliable subtypes of disorders, preferential processing styles, and prognostic information concerning daily living. Neuropsychology laboratories have the potential to link medicine, education, and the psychological sciences to offer superior services to patients. See also NEUROPSYCHOLOGICAL ASSESSMENT.

REFERENCES

D'Amato, R. C. (1990). A neuropsychological approach to school psychology. *School Psychology Quarterly* 5, 141–160.
Whitten, J. C., R. C. D'Amato, and M. M. Chittooran. (1992). A neuropsychological approach to intervention. In R. C. D'Amato and B. A. Rothlisberg (Eds.), *Psychological perspectives on intervention: A case study approach to prescriptions for change* (pp. 112–136). New York: Longman.

Rik Carl D'Amato
Susan M. DiUglio-Johnson

NEW DIRECTIONS IN SCHOOL PSYCHOLOGY CONFERENCE. This conference was planned by the American Psychological Association* (APA) central office and the Division of School Psychologists,* sponsored by the National Institute for Mental Health (NIMH), and held June 22–24, 1964, in Bethesda, Maryland. Participants included NIMH-supported school psychology* program trainers, consumers of services, school administrators, and others. Doctoral-level training and desired roles by consumers were conference emphases. This was the first major national conference since the Thayer conference* in 1954.

REFERENCE

Bardon, J. I. (Ed.). (1964–1965). Problems and issues in school psychology—1964: Proceedings of a conference on New Directions in School Psychology. *Journal of School Psychology* 3(2), 1–44.

Thomas K. Fagan

NEWLAND, T. ERNEST. A Ph.D. recipient of Ohio State University (1931), T. Ernest Newland (1903–1992) served as chief of the Division of Special Education for the Pennsylvania State Department of Public Instruction (1938–1942), director of clinical training at the University of Tennessee (Knoxville) (1948–1951), and professor of educational psychology* at the University of Illinois (Urbana) (1951 until his retirement in 1971). At Illinois, Newland founded one of the earliest formal doctoral programs in school psychology,* which blended his interests in educational and clinical psychology* and special education. He published widely and developed the Blind Learning Aptitude Test. Newland was active in the American Psychological Association's* Division of School Psychologists,* helping to organize the Thayer conference* and chairing the committee that established the annual preconvention institute. He earned diplomas from the American Board of Examiners in Professional Psychology in clinical and school psychology.

REFERENCES

Fagan, T. K., G. McCoy, and S. McCoy. (1992). Obituary: T. E. Newland (1903–
    1992). *American Psychologist* 48, 988.
Newland, T. E. (1981). School psychology—observation and reminiscence. *Journal of
    School Psychology* 19, 4–20.

Thomas K. Fagan

NONBIASED ASSESSMENT. Nonbiased assessment refers to the valid, reliable, and appropriate assessment of children from diverse cultures, including those whose language is different from that of the majority culture. Nonbiased assessment is conducted for the purpose of improving the educational and social opportunities for minority children who have been referred for assessment* because of learning or social problems. School psychologists* conducting nonbiased assessment strive to develop a deep understanding, acceptance, and respect of cultural diversity; recognize their own stereotypes and erroneous beliefs about different minority groups; and take steps to assure that these stereotypes do not influence the assessment process, results, or interpretations of the results.

Nonbiased assessment is comprehensive and multidimensional and involves multiple methods, instruments, and procedures. The assessment is conducted in a language spoken by the child and the family (or in two languages if the child is bilingual). Interpretation of the assessment results takes into account the child's background, family, and educational experiences, as well as the child's interest and motivation in taking the test and other test-taking behaviors and attitudes (such as test anxiety and attitude toward the examiner).

Nonbiased assessment requires the utilization of assessment instruments that contain valid and reliable psychometric properties. Because criticisms of the use of psychological tests with individuals from minority groups have largely focused on the psychometric properties of the tests themselves, investigation of test bias has traditionally involved statistical examination of the predictive, content, or construct validity* of tests.

Bias in predictive validity exists when there is constant and systematic error in the predictive meaning of test scores for different groups. The most widely used statistical method for examining predictive bias in the use of tests has been regression analysis. This procedure compares the regression line (the line in a scatter diagram that forms best fit through the points marking individuals' scores on both the test and the criterion measure) of the majority and minority groups. It is assumed that no test bias in predictive validity exists if the regression lines for the majority and the minority groups are identical. If the regression line of the majority group has a different slope or a different intercept (the point of intercept of the regression line with the Y or criterion axis), there is a differential validity. The use of a common regression line in the prediction of the criterion score may then either underpredict or overpredict the performance on the criterion measure. Most studies have not found consistent differential predictive validity with tests of strong psychometric properties and breadth of content.

Bias in content validity exists when certain groups (typically, minority or economically disadvantaged children) systematically fail or receive a lower score on an item or subscale of a test due to different experiential or linguistic backgrounds. Extensive research examining test items' difficulty has not found consistent patterns of content bias in well-constructed standardized tests. Further, research utilizing professional and college student members of minority groups showed that minority judges do not consistently detect items that are more difficult for minority children than for nonminority children.

Bias in construct validity occurs when a test measures different theoretical constructs or traits for different groups, or when the test serves as a better measure of the construct or trait (e.g., *g* factor) for one group than for another. The most common approach to evaluate construct validity has been with the utilization of factor analysis,* a mathematical technique used to examine intercorrelation of test items or clusters of items that have been administered to a large number of individuals. Research has not found consistent bias in the construct validity of reliable psychological tests. Well-constructed cognitive and educational tests are therefore considered equally valid across groups in respect to measuring underlying constructs.

Because of the serious consequences of assessment bias, school psychologists continue to address issues of bias in both research and practice. In situations where bias exists, school psychologists make appropriate adjustments, discontinue the use of a test, or change the assessment procedures.

See also *LARRY P. v. RILES*; OVERREPRESENTATION; *PASE v. HANNON*.

REFERENCES

Reynolds, C. R., and S. M. Kaiser. (1990). Test bias in psychological assessment. In T. B. Gutkin and C. R. Reynolds (Eds.), *The handbook of school psychology* (pp. 487–525). New York: Wiley.
Sattler, J. M. (1992). *Assessment of children.* San Diego: Author.

Shani Beth-Halachmy

NONSCHOOL SETTINGS. Although much has happened throughout history to influence the profession of school psychology,* the fundamental goal has essentially remained unchanged since its inception—to educate and improve the psychological well-being of children, youth, families, and school personnel. Some have advocated that practitioners must work both in and out of the schools to achieve this important goal. School psychologists* working in schools are seen as serving in traditional settings, whereas those working outside the educational enterprise are seen as serving in nontraditional settings (D'Amato and Dean, 1989).

Training and accreditation* standards set forth by the American Psychological Association* (APA) and the National Association of School Psychologists* (NASP) mandate a broad array of courses and practicum* experiences to ensure that school psychologists are equipped to provide a full range of psychological services regardless of the setting. Training for the school psychologist involves the areas of psychological foundations, professional education, assessment,* consultation,* direct and indirect intervention,* statistics, and research design— all within the context of the biological, cognitive-affective, and social bases of behavior.

When school psychology is not limited to practice in a school building, the emphasis becomes a melding of client needs with appropriate services. This shift stresses that school psychology is an approach to problem solving, not a setting-specific profession. From this view comes a model of school psychology services that can be applied to medical facilities, residential treatment centers, businesses, private practices,* community agencies, universities, correctional facilities, and the like (e.g., Pfeiffer and Dean, 1988). Depending on the setting, school psychologists tend to emphasize different skills. In medical settings, psychologists often conduct diagnostic evaluations, develop rehabilitation plans, and provide individual and family therapy.* In business and industry, they may serve as program evaluators, consultants, researchers, and providers of vocational evaluations and counseling. Psychologists working in residential treatment may assess adaptive behaviors, design behavioral interventions, lead multidisciplinary teams, and intervene with family members. Correctional facilities often require professionals who can diagnose educational disabilities, provide vocational counseling, and teach a variety of social and daily living skills.

Bardon (1989) has argued that the title ''school psychologist'' may be too limiting for a professional trained to provide a full range of psychological services. He has suggested the term ''applied educational psychologist'' to more accurately reflect the multitude of services that a school psychologist may offer to individuals in diverse settings. The discipline of school psychology, by virtue of its training and focus, brings the technical insights of behavioral science to bear upon problems that may hinder the full development of individuals. If education is best conceptualized as a lifelong process spanning multiple environments, then school psychology practice must not be restricted to school settings.

See also CORRECTIONAL SCHOOL PSYCHOLOGY; GROUP PRACTICE; HOSPITAL SETTINGS; INDEPENDENT PRACTICE; PEDIATRIC SETTING; POSTSECONDARY SCHOOL SETTING; PRIVATE PRACTICE; RESIDENTIAL CENTER; VOCATIONAL SCHOOL PSYCHOLOGY.

REFERENCES

Bardon, J. I. (1989). The school psychologist as an applied educational psychologist. In R. C. D'Amato and R. S. Dean (Eds.), *The school psychologist in nontraditional settings: Integrating clients, services, and settings* (pp. 1–32). Hillsdale, NJ: Erlbaum.

D'Amato, R. C., and R. S. Dean. (1989). The past, present, and future of school psychology in nontraditional settings. In R. C. D'Amato and R. S. Dean (Eds.), *The school psychologist in nontraditional settings: Integrating clients, services, and settings* (pp. 185–209). Hillsdale, NJ: Erlbaum.

Pfeiffer, S. I., and R. S. Dean (Eds.). (1988). Psychologists in nontraditional settings. *School Psychology Review* 17 (3).

Rik Carl D'Amato
Susan M. DiUglio-Johnson

NONVERBAL ASSESSMENT. In the purest sense, nonverbal assessment refers to an assessment* technique that requires no spoken or written words to communicate task demands or to respond to those demands. Nonverbal assessment often requires use of a test designed specifically for administration to deaf, hard-of-hearing, or limited-English-proficient individuals. The most famous group-administered, nonverbal test of intelligence, the Army Beta, was developed during World War I as a cognitive screening test for illiterate recruits (Aiken, 1988). Several individually administered tests exist (Raven Progressive Matrices, Test of Nonverbal Intelligence-II, Leiter International Performance Scale), and another, the Universal Nonverbal Intelligence Test, is under development. Some verbal tests of intelligence offer modified directions for nonverbal administration (e.g., Kaufman Assessment Battery for Children). Some tests have been referred to as nonverbal if the response is nonverbal, even though they require comprehension of oral language. Anastasi (1982) discusses controversial assumptions that guide use of nonverbal tests (e.g., that nonverbal and verbal tests can measure the same functions, that nonverbal tests are culture-fair).

See also NONBIASED ASSESSMENT.

REFERENCES

Aiken, L. R. (1988). *Psychological testing and assessment.* Newton, MA: Allyn and Bacon.

Anastasi, A. (1982). *Psychological testing* (5th ed.). New York: Macmillan.

R. Steve McCallum

NORM-REFERENCED ASSESSMENT. Norm-referenced assessment is a means of comparing an individual's behavior with the behavior of a group of persons who are representative of the individual on key variables. Thus, "the emphasis is on relative standing of individuals, rather than on absolute mastery of content" (Salvia and Ysseldyke, 1991, p. 32). The comparison or norm group provides the standard for interpreting the individual's performance. Issues impacting norm group representativeness are that: (1) people in the norm sample must be the same as the population they are intended to represent (e.g., in ethnicity, age, grade) and (2) the norm group should be proportionally equal to those in the reference population (e.g., matching census data). The size of the normative sample also is important because it impacts the stability of the norms and increases the likelihood that unusual elements in the general population will be represented (Salvia and Ysseldyke, 1991). Thus, normative samples must be large enough to accomplish the goals of stability and representativeness.

Typically, screening and eligibility decisions for special education services are based on norm-referenced assessment data. Norm-referenced assessment methods utilize standardized administration and objective scoring procedures that minimize the influence of examiner bias in scoring. Although norm-referenced assessments are standardized, not all standardized tests are norm-referenced. For example, curriculum-based measurement* (CBM), while standardized, is norm-referenced only when norms are developed and used in decision making.

Reducing examiner scoring bias was the impetus for the beginning of norm-referenced assessment. These types of assessment devices were developed to overcome the limitations of observation and decision making based on subjective feelings about a student (Witt et al., 1994). Thus, a benefit of using this kind of assessment is that it may protect children from the negative consequences of arbitrary decision making. These issues are especially critical when making important educational decisions like screening and eligibility.

Although norm-referenced assessment data can be collected in a variety of ways, they are typically obtained via *norm-referenced tests*. For example, commercially prepared, published, norm-referenced ability and achievement tests likely are the most common tests of this kind used by school psychologists.* Norm-referenced tests are designed to answer such questions as, How does Sarah compare in reading comprehension to the rest of the class? Does Dustin have the math aptitude needed for a college engineering program? Are Julie's SAT [Scholastic Aptitude Test] scores high enough to qualify her for admission to the university of her choice?'' (Witt et al., 1994, p. 28). Because of their wide appeal and application, norm-referenced tests have received much attention and research investigating their technical adequacy.

Several considerations should be kept in mind when considering norm-referenced assessment. For example, extreme care should be taken when decisions based on results from norm-referenced tests are made for persons from populations who were not included in the standardization sample. Students with severe disabilities often are not included in standardization samples when tests are normed. Regarding the use of commercially prepared, norm-referenced tests, the information obtained may not be helpful to teachers in knowing how or what to teach or for developing direct classroom interventions (Witt et al., 1994). These concerns arise when the overlap of the test with what is being taught in any specific classroom is uncertain (Marston, 1989). Commercially prepared, norm-referenced tests also are not sensitive to individual students' growth over time because they are not designed for such purposes, the types of scores often reported (e.g., grade equivalents) are misleading (Marston, 1989), and they have limited item sampling. Also, because the primary purpose of norm-referenced assessment is to compare one person's behavior with the behavior of others, it may draw attention away from the idea that problems may be related to the curriculum, instruction, or setting and may cause one to attend more to a within-person explanation for performance (Witt et al., 1994).

Despite these concerns, norm-referenced assessment has its benefits. For example, the use of norm-referenced assessment methods may help protect children from arbitrary or biased decision making. Also, this type of assessment can provide information on relative standing comparisons at local, state, and national levels. Finally, it is important to remember that norm-referenced and criterion-referenced assessment* methods are complementary, not exclusive approaches to assessment.

See also ACADEMIC ASSESSMENT; ASSESSMENT (DIRECT AND INDIRECT); COGNITIVE ASSESSMENT; PUBLISHERS.

REFERENCES

Marston, D. B. (1989). A curriculum-based measurement approach to assessing academic performance: What is it and why do it? In M. R. Shinn (Ed.), *Curriculum-based measurement: Assessing special children* (pp. 18–78). New York: Guilford Press.
Salvia, J., and J. E. Ysseldyke. (1991). *Assessment* (5th ed.). Boston: Houghton Mifflin.
Witt, J. C., S. N. Elliott, J. J. Kramer, and F. M. Gresham. (1994). *Assessment of children: Fundamental methods and practices.* Madison, WI: Brown and Benchmark.

Kelly A. Powell-Smith

O

OFFICE OF CIVIL RIGHTS. The Office of Civil Rights (OCR) within the U.S. Department of Education (USDOE) enforces the federal civil rights statutes that prohibit discrimination based on race, color, national origin, sex, disability, or age in USDOE programs and activities. OCR also assists USDOE in carrying out the civil rights requirements of certain grant programs. The civil rights laws enforced by OCR extend to a wide range of federal fund recipients, including education and rehabilitation agencies and their subrecipients in all states and territories. This includes approximately 16,000 school districts, 3,600 postsecondary institutions, and 6,800 proprietary schools, libraries, museums, and other institutions that receive federal assistance. OCR is headed by an assistant secretary for civil rights, who is the principal civil rights adviser to the secretary of education. OCR headquarters in Washington, D.C., provides legal, policy, and management support, while its ten regional offices are responsible for investigating complaints and providing technical assistance. A complaint can be filed by anyone who believes that an educational institution (receiving federal funds) has discriminated. OCR assists in school desegregation, magnet school assistance programs, special education,* and bilingual and postsecondary education. OCR is responsible for monitoring many laws, including Section 504 of the Rehabilitation Act* of 1973 and the Individuals with Disabilities Education Act (IDEA, Public Law 101-476*). Contact: U.S. Department of Education, Office of Civil Rights, Mary E. Switzer Building, 330 C Street, SW, Washington, DC 20202.

See also DEPARTMENT OF HEALTH AND HUMAN SERVICES; MANDATORY SERVICES; OFFICE OF SPECIAL EDUCATION PROGRAMS.

REFERENCE

U.S. Department of Education. (1992). *ED Facts: Information about the Office for Civil Rights.* Washington, DC: Author.

Kevin P. Dwyer

OFFICE OF SPECIAL EDUCATION PROGRAMS. The Office of Special Education Programs (OSEP) provides federal leadership and fiscal resources for the initiation, expansion, and improvement of education and services for disabled persons. Its programs assist public education agencies to provide all handicapped children with a free and appropriate public education* that emphasizes special education* and related services* and assures that the rights of handicapped children and their parents or guardians are protected. OSEP accomplishes this mission by communicating and disseminating federal policy and information on the education of handicapped children and adults; administering formula grants and discretionary programs authorized by Congress; fostering and supporting research and the development of knowledge and innovations for the education of handicapped children and adults; promoting and supporting the training of educational, related services, and leadership personnel and parents and volunteers; evaluating, monitoring, and reporting on the implementation of federal policy and programs and the effectiveness of efforts to educate handicapped children and youth; and coordinating with other federal agencies, state agencies, and the private sector, including parent and professional organizations, private schools, and organizations of handicapped persons for the review of policy, program planning, and implementation issues.

OSEP is under the supervision of a director who reports directly to the assistant secretary for special education and rehabilitative services. The director of the Office of Special Education Programs provides overall direction, coordination, and leadership to five divisions: Assistance to States Division; Innovation and Development Division; Program Analysis and Planning Division; Personnel Preparation Division; and Educational Services Division. Contact: Office of Special Education Programs, U.S. Department of Education, Mary E. Switzer Building, 330 C Street, SW, Washington, DC 20202.

See also DEPARTMENT OF HEALTH AND HUMAN SERVICES; MANDATORY SERVICES; OFFICE OF CIVIL RIGHTS.

REFERENCE

U.S. Department of Education. (1992). Washington, DC: Author.

Kevin P. Dwyer

OLYMPIA CONFERENCE. From November 17 to 20, 1981, 322 invited participants convened in Oconomowoc, Wisconsin, for the Olympia Conference on the Future of School Psychology. Attendance at the conference was determined by a committee that attempted to balance both political considerations and the need to ensure representation of the various roles and needs of school psychologists.* This planning conference, jointly designed and sponsored by the National Association of School Psychologists,* Division 16 of the American Psychological Association,* and the National School Psychology Inservice Training Network* at the University of Minnesota, utilized a unique format composed of paper presentations by a futurist and the current presidents of the two sponsoring groups, analysis of survey results from school psychologists throughout the United States and Canada, and action-planning groups. Approximately seventy of the participants were recruited as staff to facilitate the conference's action-planning tasks. Called "linkers," these facilitators were trained during the first day of the conference. The second day's activities, following a welcoming of the major body of participants, focused on knowledge and awareness of both projected conceptions of society and the needs of school psychology* as a profession in the coming years. The third day, linkers, facilitating small groups, utilized the results of a preconference survey yielding high-impact, high-agreement issues to determine the actions to be taken by the profession in coming years. The conference concluded with presentations of the action plans that had been developed that were subsequently published in the *School Psychology Review.*

See also SPRING HILL SYMPOSIUM.

REFERENCE

Brown, D. T., B. W. Cardon, W. A. Coulter, and J. Meyers. (1982). The Olympia proceedings. *School Psychology Review* 11, 107–214.

W. Alan Coulter

OPERANT CONDITIONING. Operant conditioning refers to the process in which the frequency of a behavior is influenced by the consequences that follow that behavior. Thus, operant conditioning states that behavior is a function of its consequences. Although first described by Skinner (1938, 1953), operant conditioning represented a reformulation and reconceptualization of an earlier concept described by E. L. Thorndike in the early twentieth century as the law of effect (Thorndike, 1913).

Operant conditioning (sometimes called instrumental conditioning) focuses on the relationship between behavior and environment and is concerned with the objective, controlled, and scientific description of environmental events and their functional relationships to behavior. Explanations of why behavior occurs are restricted to a description of the conditions under which behavior occurs. The cause(s) of behavior is made clear when it can be demonstrated that systematic and controlled changes in the environment lead to systematic changes in behavior.

Operant conditioning rests upon a "three-term contingency" that specifies the relationships among antecedents, behavior, and consequences. Antecedents that occur immediately prior to, and set the occasion for, behavior are known as discriminative stimuli or Sds. Antecedent stimuli that do not set the occasion for, or cue, behavior are known as S-deltas. Some discriminative stimuli may be removed in time and place from the actual occurrence of behavior but may be functionally related to that behavior. These are more accurately termed setting events.

Most of the emphasis in operant conditioning has focused on the consequences of behavior. Consequent stimuli can be either reinforcing stimuli or reinforcers or punishing stimuli or punishers. Reinforcers always increase the probability of behavior that they follow, and punishers always decrease the probability of behavior that they follow. There are two types of reinforcers: positive and negative. Positive reinforcers are stimuli presented subsequent to behavior that increase that behavior's probability. Examples of positive reinforcement are food and money. Negative reinforcers are stimuli removed by a behavior that increase that behavior's probability. Negative reinforcement always involves either escape or avoidance learning. Examples of negative reinforcers are putting on a coat before going out in the cold or studying to avoid a failing grade.

Punishers also consist of two types: positive and negative (or Type I and Type II). A positive punisher is a consequent stimulus that, when presented, decreases the probability of behavior. Examples of positive punishers include spanking and verbal reprimands. A negative punisher is a consequent stimulus that, when removed, decreases the probability of behavior. Examples of negative punishers are taking away privileges or withholding allowance money for curfew violations.

The frequency with which behaviors are reinforced or punished determines their frequency. The plan for determining how often a behavior will be reinforced or punished is known as the schedule of reinforcement. Schedules of reinforcement or punishment can be continuous (after every response) or intermittent. Intermittent reinforcement/punishment can either be ratio (after a certain number of responses) or interval (after passage of a certain amount of time). Ratio and interval schedules can be fixed (after a certain number of responses or a certain amount of time) or variable (on average, after a certain number of responses or a certain amount of time). The more often a behavior is reinforced, the more often it will occur, and vice versa.

See also BEHAVIORAL ASSESSMENT; BEHAVIORAL CONSULTATION; BEHAVIOR MODIFICATION; BEHAVIOR THERAPY; CLASSICAL CONDITIONING.

REFERENCES

Hergenhahn, B. R., and M. H. Olson. (1993). *An introduction to theories of learning* (4th ed.). Englewood Cliffs, NJ: Prentice-Hall.
Skinner, B. F. (1938). *The behavior of organisms: An experimental analysis.* New York: Appleton-Century-Crofts.
———. (1953). *Science and human behavior.* New York: Free Press.
Thorndike, E. L. (1913). *Educational psychology: The psychology of learning.* New York: Teachers College.

Frank M. Gresham

ORGANIZATION DEVELOPMENT THEORY. Organization development involves ''coherent, systematically planned, sustained effort at system self-study and improvement, focusing explicitly on change in formal and informal procedures, processes, norms, or structures, and using concepts of behavioral science. The goal is to improve organizational functioning and performance'' (Fullan, Miles, and Taylor, 1980, p. 135). Organization development (OD) theory and strategies evolved from work in the areas of laboratory training (T-groups), survey research and feedback, and action research. Fullan and colleagues have applied OD interventions in schools.

A related definition defines organization development as a ''planned, systematic process in which applied behavior science principles and practices are introduced into an ongoing organization toward the goals of effecting organization improvement, greater organizational competence, and greater organizational effectiveness'' (French and Bell, 1990, p. 1). The emphasis on the importance of applied behavior science (with contributions from psychology, sociology, economics, and anthropology) extends throughout the OD literature.

While numerous theories have been proposed, practitioners have relied more on personal experience than theory to guide their actions. French and Bell argue that research on organization development interventions is not theory-guided and propose that ''there is essentially no comprehensive theory to explain the process of planned change in organizations'' (p. 273).

In the absence of a comprehensive theory, researchers and practitioners apply more limited theoretical explanations to organizational functioning and change processes (see PROCESS CONSULTATION for example of one attempt to integrate theoretical, research, and practice agendas).

At the level of practice, organization development has been very successful, attracting broad attention and implementation since the 1960s. OD, in practice, often operates from several important assumptions: (1) productivity in the work site is optimal when workers' needs are balanced with organizational requirements; (2) people are motivated to work. They work best when their efforts are recognized, and they can engage in satisfying interpersonal relationships; (3) workers can develop a sense of ownership of their work tasks if placed in a position of responsibility for their actions.

Organization development involves clients in the assessment, diagnosis, and transformation of their own organizations. With the assistance of external or internal change agents/consultants, clients examine past or current issues and participate in the formulation of goals and objectives to address limitations in system functioning. Many writers on OD interventions stress the importance of a long-term commitment by the organization to efforts at planned change. One frequent recommendation in the literature is that organizations develop an internal cadre of personnel responsible for monitoring and promoting long-term change efforts.

A broad variety of interventions has been promoted under the OD rubric. Activities that have proven popular include training and education of system personnel, process consultation, confrontation interventions, data feedback/diagnostic exercises, problem-solving training, planning and goal-setting training, and technostructural activities (alteration of an organization's work flow, structure, means of accomplishing tasks).

Ethical dilemmas have been cited in the literature. In common with other approaches to consultation,* OD change agents confront issues of power,* informed consent,* and confidentiality* during interventions. As research and theory on organizational intervention develop through the 1990s more attention is needed on resolving discrepancies in power and control between consumers, who are affected by OD interventions, and clients, who are able to purchase the expertise of consultants.

See also SYSTEMS AND ORGANIZATIONAL CONSULTATION; SYSTEMS ASSESSMENT; SYSTEMS INTERVENTION.

REFERENCES

French, W. L., and C. H. Bell, Jr. (1990). *Organization development. Behavioral science interventions for organization development* (4th ed.). Englewood Cliffs, NJ: Prentice-Hall.

Fullan, M., M. B. Miles, and G. Taylor. (1980). *OD in schools: The state of the art.* Cited by R. A. Schmuck and P. J. Runkel (1985), *The handbook of organization development in schools* (3d ed.). Palo Alto, CA: Mayfield.

Stewart W. Ehly

O'SHEA, HARRIET E. For seventy years, Harriet Easterbrooks O'Shea (1895–1986) was a major influence on the application of psychology in schools and preschools and to children and their families. Born in Madison, Wisconsin, Harriet was one of four children in a family steeped in education. Finishing a B.A. (1916) and an M.A. (1917), O'Shea accepted a variety of positions in the East—statistical analyst, survey researcher, teacher, principal, school psychologist,* and professor. After completing a Ph.D. at Columbia University (1931), she became an associate professor and later professor at Purdue University; she taught many different courses, organized and directed a nursery school, established a psychological clinic, where she conducted therapy with children and university students, and was the women's personnel director.

Active in professional organizations, she brought to many meetings concerns for the unique needs of children, importance of early identification, and prevention of mental problems. She was active in development of policy and in legislative arenas. A participant in the Boulder conference on clinical psychology,* she understood the need for a similar conference about school psychology.* She became a principal organizer, along with Beatrice Lantz,* Frances Mullen,* and T. Ernest Newland,* of the Thayer conference, where her views of the role of psychology in education were well received.

In the 1950s, she was the American Psychological Association* (APA) Division of School Psychologists* secretary (1955–1958) and twice its representative to the APA legislative body, the Council of Representatives (1950–1953,

1955–1958). After retirement from Purdue, she moved East and continued to be active as a psychologist and consultant for twenty years.

REFERENCES

Crissey, M. S. (1988). Harriet Easterbrooks O'Shea (1895–1986). *American Psychologist* 43, 71.
O'Shea, H. E. (1935). *Essentials of nursery education with special reference to nursery schools.* Boston: National Association for Nursery Education.
———. (1960). Friendship and the intellectually gifted child. *Exceptional Children* 26, 327–335.

Joseph L. French

OVERREPRESENTATION. In overrepresentation, minority children are placed into special education* programs, particularly, educable mentally retarded (EMR) programs, in which the proportion of minority students in the special program exceeds the proportion of minority students in the general school population. This disproportionality was used as evidence of differential treatment for minority students and, thus, de facto discrimination against African-American students in litigation that challenged the procedures used to classify and place minority students into EMR programs. In some instances, the court cases presented evidence that minority students were overrepresented in EMR programs by a factor of two to three times the number expected from their presence in the general population. Examples of court cases brought as a result of overrepresentation include *Larry P. v. Riles** (1972, 1979, 1984, 1986) and *PASE v. Hannon** (1980). For example, factual evidence in the *Larry P.* case indicated that while African Americans accounted for 28.5 percent of all students in the San Francisco school system, they constituted 66 percent of EMR students in San Francisco. Likewise, while African Americans constituted 9.1 percent of the California school population, they represented 27.5 percent of the EMR students statewide.

According to many scholars, overrepresentation of minority students in programs for the EMR has had a fundamental impact on state and federal special education legislation, assessment* and placement procedures, and school psychology* practice (Reschly, Kicklighter, and McKee, 1988). As a result of these legal actions, the courts have intensely scrutinized a range of special education and school psychology issues, including (1) the efficacy of special education programs, (2) potential bias contained in intelligence* tests, (3) the role of psychological testing with nonnative English speakers, and (4) the nature of the assessment techniques used to place students into special education classes (Bersoff and Hofer, 1990; Jacob-Timm and Hartshorne, 1994).

REFERENCES

Bersoff, D. (1982). *Larry P.* and *PASE:* Judicial report cards of the validity of individual intelligence tests. In T. Kratochwill (Ed.), *Advances in school psychology,* vol. 2 (pp. 61–95). Hillsdale, NJ: Erlbaum.

Bersoff, D. N., and P. T. Hofer. (1990). The legal regulation of school psychology. In T. B. Gutkin and C. R. Reynolds (Eds.), *The handbook of school psychology* (pp. 937–961). New York: Wiley.

Jacob-Timm, S., and T. Hartshorne. (1994). *Ethics and law for school psychologists.* Brandon, VT: Clinical Psychology.

Reschly, D. J., R. Kicklighter, and P. McKee. (1988). Recent placement litigation Part II, minority EMR overrepresentation: Comparison of *Larry P.* (1979, 1984, 1986) with *Marshall* (1984, 1985) and *S-1* (1986). *School Psychology Review* 17, 22–38.

Todd C. Reiher

P

PARADOXICAL STRATEGIES. Paradoxical strategies, often called double-bind strategies, are based on the idea that people are to change by remaining unchanged (Weeks and L'Abate, 1982). The most commonly used form of paradox is to prescribe the symptom. For instance, the client who cannot sleep is told to get up and watch television or read a book.

Alfred Adler was the first psychotherapist to utilize paradoxical strategies. Learning theorist Knight Dunlap proposed that clients with stuttering problems use "negative practice," a form of symptom prescription. Clark Hull, in a similar vein, used "massed practice" for the treatment of tics. Victor Frankl, who is often credited with coining the term "paradoxical intention," advocated for its use with a wide range of problems (Brehm and Smith, 1986).

Brehm and Smith (1976) offer theoretical explanations for the therapeutic efficacy of paradoxical strategies. They propose that some behaviors are maintained through a circular anxiety process. In these cases, they theorize that prescribing the symptom breaks the anxiety chain. For instance, insomnia is often maintained by the anxiety of trying to go to sleep. When staying awake is prescribed, this breaks the anxiety chain and produces the desired behavior, sleep. For symptoms that are not anxiety-based, psychological reactance theory offers an explanation for the efficacy of paradoxical strategies. For example, the compulsive masturbator is told to masturbate every hour. The desired reaction is for the client to resist the therapist by not masturbating.

Concerns have been raised about the risks associated with the use of paradoxical strategies. Clients may prematurely terminate therapy, or the therapeutic relationship may be harmed. Further, Brehm and Smith (1986) warn that even the successful use of paradoxical strategies may harm the client's sense of self-efficacy.

See also ADLERIAN THERAPY.

REFERENCES

Brehm, S. S., and T. W. Smith. (1986). Social psychological approaches to psychotherapy and behavior change. In S. Garfield and A. Bergin (Eds.), *Handbook of psychotherapy and behavior change* (pp. 69–115). New York: Wiley.
Weeks, G. R., and L. L'Abate (1982). *Paradoxical psychotherapy: Theory and practice with individuals, couples, and families.* New York: Bruner/Mazel.

Donald L. Boswell

PARAPROFESSIONAL. A paraprofessional is a person who provides specific, limited services under the supervision of a professional. Within educational and mental health contexts, paraprofessionals may include paid assistants or aides, parents, and students. Paraprofessional activities may include tutoring and counseling, group facilitation, behavior management,* data collection and analysis, and assessment.* The use of paraprofessionals in special education* appears to be growing, although concern has been expressed about selection, training, and efficacy (Jones and Bender, 1993). Use of paraprofessionals in school psychology* has been limited; however, at least one state (Kansas) issues paraprofessional certificates and outlines appropriate duties and responsibilities for school psychology paraprofessionals (ERIC Documents Number ED330985). McManus (1986) provides the most recent review of using paraprofessionals in school psychological services.

REFERENCES

Jones, K. H., and W. N. Bender. (1993). Utilization of paraprofessionals in special education: A review of the literature. *Remedial and Special Education* 14, 7–14.
McManus, J. L. (1986). Student paraprofessionals in school psychology: Practices and possibilities. *School Psychology Review* 15, 9–23.
Supplement for school psychology. (1990). ERIC Documents Reproduction Services, Document number: ED330985.

Kathleen M. Minke

PARENT–CHILD INTERACTION TRAINING. Parent–child interaction therapy (PCIT) was designed for the treatment of a broad range of psychological disturbances in preschool-age children. It is distinct in that it emphasizes more traditional play therapy techniques incorporated into the initial phase of treatment and emphasizes problem-solving skills training incorporated in the second phase of treatment. While it has been used clinically for the treatment of a wide variety of emotional and behavioral problems, its empirical support has shown it to be very successful in the treatment of externalizing disorders (oppositional defiant disorder and attention-deficit hyperactivity disorder). The PCIT is an integrated approach incorporating both behavioral modification* and relationship enhancement techniques. It is conducted within the context of natural play situations between a parent and child and consists of two basic phases, labeled child-directed interaction (CDI) and parent-directed interaction (PDI). Each phase consists of multiple components designed to influence both the parents' and the child's behavior. The goals of PCIT are to teach parents skills to build a warm and mutually rewarding relationship with their child and to teach their child desirable, prosocial behaviors as well as decreasing the child's inappropriate behaviors. The treatment model provides a detailed structure within which parents and children can learn a global set of positive interaction skills that can be readily applied to their own unique problems.

See also PARENT TRAINING; PLAY THERAPY; SOCIAL SKILLS TRAINING.

REFERENCES

Eyberg, S. (1982). Parent–child interaction training: Effects on family functioning. *Journal of Clinical Child Psychology* 11, 130–137.
McNeil, C. B., and S. Eyberg. (1991). Parent–child interaction therapy with behavior problem children: Generalization of treatment effects to the school setting. *Journal of Clinical Child Psychology* 20, 140–151.

Kelly J. Griffith

PARENT CONSULTATION. Parent consultation is a problem-solving process in which a professional and parent work together with the goal of improving a student's social, emotional, or academic adjustment. The consultant's role is to provide the parent with expert knowledge and guidance in problem-solving structures. The parent retains responsibility for implementing any planned interventions with the student and, consequently, retains direct control over the manner and schedule according to which intervention will proceed. Necessary components of parent consultation include identifying and clarifying the problem that the parent will work to address, providing an objective perspective of the problem for the parent, assisting the parent in developing a plan for intervention, and assisting the parent in monitoring the intervention's impact on the student.

Parent consultation necessarily occurs within a family system, and the family's historical patterns of interactions and themes present both special challenges and special opportunities to the consultant. A student's problems can be better addressed with an understanding of the social context within which they evolved, but the family's systemic resistance to change can impede the intervention. Parent consultants necessarily enter into the family system as a consequence of their consultation and must balance their obligation to be objective against the press to become enmeshed in the system.

Two alternative models of parent consultation are prominent. Behavioral consultants assist parents in applying the principles of behavior analysis to students' maladaptive behaviors with the goal of increasing effective behaviors or decreasing ineffective ones (Kratochwill and Bergan, 1990). Conjoint behavioral consultation is a special case of parent consultation in which the behavioral consultation* process is implemented with a student's parents and teachers as joint consultees (Sheridan, Kratochwill, and Elliott, 1990); this holds special advantages in fostering familiarity between a student's family and school, providing a comprehensive description of problems occurring across settings, and promoting the generalization of interventions across settings. Family systems consultation is an application of systems concepts to parent consultation with the goal of improving the quality and functioning of the family system (Fine, 1991); systems theory contributes to parent consultation by framing the intervention as a part of family roles and relationships.

See also CONSULTATION; FAMILY THERAPY; PARENT TRAINING; SYSTEMS INTERVENTIONS.

REFERENCES

Fine, M. R. (1991). A systems-ecological perspective on family-school intervention. In M. J. Fine and C. I. Carlson (Eds.), *Handbook of family-school intervention: A systems perspective* (pp. 1–17). Boston: Allyn and Bacon.
Kratochwill, T. R., and R. Bergan. (1990). *Behavioral consultation in applied settings.* New York: Plenum Press.
Sheridan, S., T. R. Kratochwill, and S. N. Elliott. (1990). Behavioral consultation with parents and teachers: Delivering treatment for socially withdrawn children at home and school. *School Psychology Review* 19, 33–52.

Beth Doll

PARENT/GUARDIAN PERMISSION. Procedural due process* was established as part of the law (Public Laws 94-142* and 101-476*) defining the education of children with disabilities. To enable parents to be active in decision making about their child, parents must be informed that their child's educational agency is contemplating a change (Reynolds et. al, 1984). Parental consent must be obtained before conducting a preplacement evaluation and before the initial placement of a disabled child in a program providing special education* and related services.* A legal guardian and a designated surrogate parent can also give consent. From a broader perspective, parent permission may be needed for other interventions typically offered by school psychologists,* such as counseling, behavior modification,* and traditional psychotherapy. Court decisions have given some guidance, but there is no clear-cut rule. According to Bersoff (1982) and Jacob-Timm and Hartshorne (1994), there is a general trend to allow the adolescent greater freedom to obtain psychological assistance without parental permission. There is little debate that the treatment of preadolescents should occur with parental consent.

REFERENCES

Bersoff, D. (1982). The legal regulation of school psychology. In C. R. Reynolds and T. B. Gutkin (Eds.), *The handbook of school psychology* (pp. 1043–1074). New York: Wiley.

Jacob-Timm, S., and T. Hartshorne. (1994). *Ethics and law for school psychologists* (2d ed.). Brandon, VT: Clinical Psychology.

Reynolds, C., T. Gutkin, S. Elliott, and J. Witt. (1984). *School psychology: Essentials of theory and practice.* New York: Wiley.

Dennis A. Tomlinson

PARENT TRAINING. Parent training is an instructional activity with the purpose of (1) enhancing parent knowledge about children and parenting; (2) altering parent beliefs or attitudes; and/or (3) teaching parents new behavioral skills. Some of the earliest parent training programs were Adlerian child study groups, promoted in this country during the 1920s and 1930s to instruct caretakers in theories of child development (Adler, 1956). Contemporary Adlerian parent training teaches parents about the goals of children's misbehavior, encourages parents to respond to misbehavior in ways that redirect these goals, and emphasizes the importance of preparing children to be responsible citizens of democratic societies (e.g., Systematic Training for Effective Parenting). Client-centered parent training emerged in the 1950s to train parents to use the therapeutic skills of empathy, authenticity, and unconditional positive regard with their children (Rogers, 1951). Contemporary client-centered parent training teaches parents quasi-therapeutic skills that promote the child's actualization and enhance parent–child communication (e.g., Parent Effectiveness Training). Behavioral parent training came into prominence in the 1960s and 1970s to teach parents the skills of applied behavioral analysis: identifying, controlling, and correcting maladaptive behaviors and developing effective behaviors using contingent consequences. Contemporary behavioral parent training programs also teach more complex behaviors, such as giving effective commands, conflict resolution, contracting, managing token economies, and fostering self-control (e.g., Teaching Child Management Skills). Because studies comparing these different models of parent training have serious methodological flaws, no definitive empirical evidence exists to support the implementation of any one parent training program over another (Dembo, Sweitzer, and Lauritzen, 1985).

Current problems addressed in the parent training research include acceptability of interventions, the nature and incidence of parent resistance to intervention, and the differential effectiveness of various training formats. For example, explaining the principles of child management through reading selections or other media appears to improve parental commitment to the training and confidence in their ability to apply the strategies successfully. Providing opportunities for guided practice of the skills with corrective feedback is critical for parent mastery skills. Training conducted in a classroom or clinic can generalize to the home when the training programs use many concrete examples, give homework assignments, give specific instructions on how to implement the skills in the home, and give parents feedback about how accurately they are applying the skills. Programs that incorporate group discussions appear to effect changes in parental attitudes.

Parent training programs addressing specific problems of children and youth include Kazdin's (1985) Parent Management Training for antisocial and conduct-disordered children and adolescents; Robin and Foster's (1989) Communication Training for families of adolescents; Barkley's (1990) Parent Training Program for children with attention-Deficit Hyperactivity Disorder; and Forehand and McMahon's (1981) training program for parents of noncompliant children.

See also FAMILY ASSESSMENT; FAMILY ENABLEMENT/EMPOWERMENT; PARENT-CHILD INTERACTION TRAINING.

REFERENCES

Adler, A. (1956). *The individual psychology of Alfred Adler: A systematic presentation in selections from his writings.* Edited by H. L. Ansbacher and R. R. Ansbacher. New York: Basic Books.
Christenson, S. L., and Conoley, J. C. (Eds.). (1992). *Home-school collaboration.* Washington, DC: National Association of School Psychologists.
Dembo, M. H., M. Sweitzer, and P. Lauritzen. (1985). An evaluation of group parent education: Behavioral, PET, and Adlerian programs. *Review of Educational Research* 55, 155–200.
Rogers, C. R. (1951). *Client-centered therapy.* Boston: Houghton Mifflin.

Beth Doll

PASE v. HANNON. The case *Parents in Action on Special Education (PASE) v. Joseph P. Hannon* was a class-action suit brought in U.S. federal district court in Illinois on behalf of African-American students in the Chicago public schools because of overrepresentation* of African-American students in special education* classes for the educable mentally retarded (EMR). The plaintiffs alleged bias on the part of intelligence* tests and, thus, improper classification* and placement of students as mentally retarded. *PASE* was very similar to the *Larry P. v. Riles* case, which preceded it in California, as the factual issues regarding overrepresentation and cultural bias in intelligence tests were nearly identical in the two cases (Reschly, Kicklighter, and McKee, 1988).

However, the decision of the court in *PASE* was remarkably different from that in *Larry P.* The court ruled that individually administered intelligence tests were not racially or culturally biased and, when used with other procedures, did not discriminate against African-American students. In this case, Judge John F. Grady personally undertook a detailed examination of test items and concluded that they were essentially free from bias. His decision supported the use of IQ tests with procedural safeguards,* properly trained personnel, and inclusion of supplementary information as valid classification and placement procedure. He also ruled that EMR classes provided educational benefit.

This case was most remarkable in light of its juxtaposition with *Larry P.* In both cases, similar evidence was reviewed, and some of the same expert witnesses* were heard, yet opposite decisions were rendered regarding the use of intelligence tests and the efficacy of EMR classes.

See also NONBIASED ASSESSMENT.

REFERENCES

Bersoff, D. N., and P. T. Hofer. (1990). The legal regulation of school psychology. In T. B. Gutkin and C. R. Reynolds (Eds.), *The handbook of school psychology* (pp. 937–961). New York: Wiley.
Jacob-Timm, S., and T. Hartshorne. (1994). *Ethics and law for school psychologists.* (2d ed.). Brandon, VT: Clinical Psychology.
PASE (Parents in Action on Special Education) v. Hannon, 506 F.Supp. 831 (N.D. Ill. 1980).
Reschly, D. J., R. Kicklighter, and P. McKee. (1988). Recent placement litigation Part II, minority EMR overrepresentation: Comparison of *Larry P.* (1979, 1984, 1986) with *Marshall* (1984, 1985) and *S-1* (1986). *School Psychology Review* 17, 22–38.

Todd C. Reiher

PATH ANALYSIS. Path analysis was developed as a method for studying the direct and indirect effects of variables hypothesized as causes of variables treated as effects. Path analysis is not intended as a method for discovering causes, but instead is a method applied to a causal model formulated by the researcher on the basis of knowledge and theoretical considerations.

Path analysis has been applied in school psychology* in the form of path-referenced assessment. Path-referenced assessment refers to the strategy of describing test performance by indicating examinee position in a structural model specifying relations among categories of behavior. Suppose, for example, a school psychologist* believes that performance on learning task p affects performance on learning task q and that learning task q, in turn, influences performance on learning task r. The hierarchical nature of this ordered learning sequence is depicted graphically in the following path diagram: $p \rightarrow q \rightarrow r$. A child would be considered to be placed at position q—in terms of the path diagram—if she or he has mastered tasks p and q but not task r. The child's placement shows not only the learning skills thus far mastered but also what learning is next needed to progress in the sequence. Path analysis would be applied to the hypothesized hierarchical model to determine the extent to which learning patterns predicted under the model accurately match empirically based (observed) learning performance.

See also EXPERIMENTAL DESIGN; QUALITATIVE RESEARCH.

REFERENCES

Bergan, J. R. (1981). Path-referenced assessment in school psychology. In T. R. Kratochwill, *Advances in school psychology,* Vol. 1 (pp. 255–281). Hillsdale, NJ: Erlbaum.

Keith, T. Z. (1988). Path analysis: An introduction for school psychologists. *School Psychology Review* 17, 343–362.

Pedhazur, E. J. (1982). *Multiple regression in behavioral research: Explanation and prediction* (2d ed.). Fort Worth, TX: Holt, Rinehart, and Winston.

William T. Coombs

PEABODY CONFERENCE. The only national conference focusing on the internship* in school psychology,* the Peabody conference was held March 21–22, 1963, at George Peabody College for Teachers in Nashville, Tennessee. The goal of the conference was to develop guidelines for the internship in doctoral programs. About two dozen persons attended the conference, representing several doctoral programs, state department of education personnel, students, and internship supervisors.* The guidelines developed at the conference reinforced the certification* guidelines published by the American Psychological Association* (APA) Division of School Psychologists* in 1962 and in 1978 influenced the internship guidelines developed by the National Association of School Psychologists* (NASP). The conference affirmed the internship as a planned experience and an integral part of the training program, which should precede the granting of the doctoral degree.* The conference proceedings include the results of a 1963 survey of state education agency certification requirements.

REFERENCE

Gray, S. W. (Ed.). (1963). *The internship in school psychology: Proceedings of the Peabody conference, March 21–22, 1963.* Nashville, TN: George Peabody College for Teachers.

Thomas K. Fagan

PEDIATRIC SETTING. Often children who are chronically ill or medically fragile are provided an education in a pediatric setting. This term refers to articulation and implementation of a specialized curriculum that accounts for the social, emotional, and cognitive needs of children who are chronically ill or, in some cases, severely emotionally disabled. Depending on the degree to which the health impairment affects the ability of the student to be involved in the educational mainstream, instruction may occur at home, in the hospital, or at school. Although the use of technology is continually improving homebound or hospital instruction, the goal for students with health impairments is to return to the regular classroom as soon as possible for as much time as the health condition allows.

Transdisciplinary team planning is the preferred method for the care and management of children educated in a pediatric setting. Health care professionals, psychologists, and teachers, along with parents and the child, when appropriate, work together to plan an appropriate environment for growth.

REFERENCES

Bigge, J. L. (1991). *Teaching individuals with physical and multiple disabilities* (3d ed.). Columbus, OH: Merrill.

Giangreco, M. F., J. York, and B. Rainforth. (1989). Providing related services to learners with severe handicaps in educational settings: Pursuing the least restrictive option. *Pediatric Physical Therapy* 1, 57.

Morrow, G. (1985). *Helping chronically ill children in school.* West Nyack, NY: Parker.

Diane Montgomery

PEER COUNSELING. Peer counseling involves a relationship between two peers, one of whom functions as a counselor to help the peer explore and understand problems and consider strategies for personal change. Peer counseling is part of the broad continuum of paraprofessional services available from students (Ender and Winston, 1984). Given proper training and supervision, peer counselors are believed to be effective in assisting fellow students.

D'Andrea and Salovey (1983) propose key skills for peer counselors: be nonjudgmental; be empathic; do not give personal advice; avoid questions that begin with "why"; do not take responsibility for the client's problems; paraphrase instead of interpreting comments; focus on the here and now; and deal with feelings first.

Effective peer counselors supplement existing professional counseling services. Students with interpersonal problems (e.g., dating concerns, drug involvement) may approach a peer before being willing to discuss concerns with school staff. School districts have adopted peer counseling approaches to encourage students to talk about thoughts and feelings in the hope that professional services can be introduced as appropriate.

REFERENCES

D'Andrea, V., and P. Salovey. (1983). *Peer counseling. Skills and perspectives.* Palo Alto, CA: Science and Behavior Books.

Ender, S. C., and R. B. Winston (Eds.). (1984). *Students as paraprofessional staff.* San Francisco: Jossey-Bass.

Stewart W. Ehly

PEER REVIEW. The conduct of a professional is best judged by his or her peers. The development of school psychology* as an independent profession has been reflected in standards for peer review. The term has two current usages, both related to accountability. The first is accountability to professional codes of ethics.* Both the American Psychological Association's* (APA) and the National Association of School Psychologists'* (NASP) codes call for peer monitoring of ethical behavior and the reporting of code violations to the appropriate organization. Reported violations are subsequently reviewed by an ethics committee made up of professional peers, thus serving as a related form of peer review (Keith-Spiegel and Koocher, 1985). The second usage refers to professional development and supervision. While the 1978 NASP *Standards for the Provision of School Psychological Services* discusses the importance of professional growth experiences (Section 4.2.3), reference to peer review as a means becomes a specific section with the 1984 *Standards* (Section 3.2.5). The 1981 APA *Specialty Guidelines* makes brief mention of peer review in its "Accountability"* section (Section 3.1) as a way to ameliorate "those factors that inhibit the provision of services to particular users."

See also PROFESSIONAL STANDARDS.

REFERENCES

APA (1981). Specialty guidelines for the delivery of services by school psychologists. *American Psychologist* 36, 670–681.

Keith-Spiegel, P., and G. P. Koocher. (1985). *Ethics in psychology.* New York: Random House.

NASP (1978, 1984, 1992). *Standards for the provision of school psychological services.* Washington, DC: Author.

Timothy S. Hartshorne

PEER TUTORING. Peer tutoring involves the provision of instructional assistance and guidance to another person. Tutoring assists the student to master academic requirements. In schools, peer tutoring involves children's helping other children to acquire specific knowledge or skills, whether in same-age or cross-age arrangements. Reports of peer tutoring span several centuries (Foot, Morgan, and Shute, 1990).

Peer tutoring builds upon the social and instructional resources of family, school, or community settings to address the academic and social needs of students. Peer tutoring provides an effective means of introducing students to concepts, skill-building or practice materials, and social skills content. Peer tutoring serves as an extension of teacher instruction.

Research underlines the importance of preparing tutors for their responsibilities. Gerber and Kauffman (1981) consider peer tutoring a rational choice for teachers "*if* the resulting educational outcomes are improved with the expenditure of the same amount of teacher time, or *if* the educational outcomes remain the same with an investment of less time" (p. 162).

See also COOPERATIVE LEARNING.

REFERENCES

Foot, H. C., M. J. Morgan, and R. H. Shute, (Eds.). (1990). *Children helping children.* Chichester, England: Wiley.

Gerber, M., and J. M. Kauffman. (1981). Peer tutoring in academic settings. In P. Strain (Ed.), *The utilization of peers as behavior change agents* (pp. 155–188). New York: Plenum Press.

Stewart W. Ehly

PENNSYLVANIA ASSOCIATION FOR RETARDED CITIZENS. The Pennsylvania Association for Retarded Citizens (PARC) represents important litigation in special education.* The state court case of *Pennsylvania Association for Retarded Citizens (PARC) v. Commonwealth of Pennsylvania* (1972) resulted in the landmark decision that all children with mental retardation have the right to a free and appropriate public education* in Pennsylvania. Parents of children with mental retardation initiated the class-action suit against the state. Although fourteen students were named in the case, the results applied to all children with mental retardation in Pennsylvania, leading the way for future decisions about the rights of students with disabilities and federal Public Law 94-142* passed a few years later.

At the time, Pennsylvania had public school classes for students classified as educable mentally retarded, but no provisions for students who were more severely disabled. Administrators were using a procedure in the Pennsylvania School Code to avoid the compulsory attendance policy for these students whose parents were sending them to expensive private schools.

The *PARC* case had three main propositions: (1) children with mental retardation can learn, given an appropriate education program, (2) early education is essential, and (3) activities involved in education of these students must be defined more broadly. Pennsylvania was given a detailed plan in order to adhere to these points, and two professionals not working for the state were assigned to oversee the process.

REFERENCE

Tucker, B. P., and B. A. Goldstein. (1992). *The educational rights of children with disabilities: A guide to federal law.* Horsham, PA: LRP.

Diane Montgomery

PERCEPTUAL-MOTOR ASSESSMENT. Assuming a basis of satisfactory sensory reception, perceptual-motor assessment is a means of evaluating the strengths and weaknesses of combined (integrated) sensory/perceptual skills and those of motor movement. Perceptual-motor assessment has emerged over more than a century from various forms of nonverbal assessment* and from research related to adults and children with mental retardation, brain injury, and learning disabilities (Salvia and Ysseldyke, 1991).

In the practice of school psychology,* perceptual-motor assessment has been closely associated with visual-motor assessment, most often employing normative tests and informal drawing tasks requiring the subject to perform motor responses based on perceptions from the visual stimuli presented. Some tests are simply copying tasks, such as in the highly popular Bender Visual-Motor Gestalt Test. Others involve a variety of gross- and fine-motor responses such as in the Purdue Perceptual-Motor Survey, Developmental Test of Visual-Motor Integration, or the Developmental Test of Visual Perception. These and other tests enjoyed a period of considerable popularity in the 1960s and 1970s, when the field of learning disabilities gained official recognition, and included a major subfield of perceptual-motor problems. The general theory held that children's academic achievement was related to, if not dependent on, satisfactory perceptual-motor skills. The theory enjoyed considerable popularity despite the lack of research support for academic achievement outcomes of perceptual-motor training (Salvia and Ysseldyke, 1991). Nevertheless, it is generally accepted that satisfactory visual perceptual and motor skills are requisite to school success (Hallahan, Kauffman, and Lloyd, 1985).

While perceptual-motor tests continue to be widely observed in the practice of school psychology, the diagnosis of visual-motor learning disability has become less common. Among the criticisms of perceptual-motor assessment have been issues of reliability, predictive validity, distinguishing between the perceptual and the motor contributions to test responses, the limited nature of skills assessed, and the overinterpretation of test results (Salvia and Ysseldyke, 1991; Sattler, 1988). Despite the availability of motor-free tests of perception, this area of testing has lost favor, perhaps as a result of waning interest in process assessment and the modality assessment-instruction paradigm and the rising interest in direct assessment* linked to academic interventions.* Salvia and Ysseldyke (1991) suggest that, instead of employing available perceptual-motor skill tests, the examiner "engage in direct systematic observation in the natural environment in which these skills actually occur" (p. 321).

See also BEHAVIORAL ASSESSMENT; COMPREHENSIVE ASSESSMENT; CURRICULUM-BASED ASSESSMENT.

REFERENCES

Hallahan, D. P., J. M. Kauffman, and J. W. Lloyd. (1985). *Introduction to learning disabilities.* Englewood Cliffs, NJ: Prentice-Hall.
Salvia, J., and J. E. Ysseldyke. (1991). *Assessment.* Boston: Houghton Mifflin.
Sattler, J. (1988). *Assessment of children.* San Diego: Author.

Thomas K. Fagan

PERKINS, KEITH. Keith J. "Perk" Perkins was born on July 2, 1907, and died on January 12, 1987. He completed his A.B. degree at DePauw University in 1929, his M.A. in education at the University of Michigan in 1933, and the Ph.D. in clinical psychology* at Purdue University in 1941. Perkins worked for the Akron, Ohio, Child Guidance Center and then served in the U.S. Naval Reserve and as director of child study for the Akron Board of Education. In 1948, he moved to Phoenix, Arizona, as a psychologist with the U.S. Public Health Service and the Phoenix Mental Health Center. In 1952, he established the Child Study and Consultation Service (CSCS), a school psychological service for fifteen school districts in the Phoenix area. The CSCS was the first school psychology* service in Arizona and an early example of contractual comprehensive mental health services to the schools. He retired from the CSCS in 1975. Throughout his career and retirement, he maintained consultantships with the

Arizona Department of Public Instruction and local mental health and hospital groups. As an active member of the American Psychological Association,* Perkins held a diplomate* in clinical psychology, fellow membership in the educational, clinical, and school divisions, and in 1962–1963 served as president of the Division of School Psychologists.* The Arizona Association of School Psychologists, of which he was a founding member in 1968, grants a Keith Perkins Award for Lifetime Contributions to School Psychology in the State of Arizona.

REFERENCES

Perkins, K. J. (1953). Consultation service to public schools by a mental health team. *Mental Hygiene* 37, 585–595.

———. (1963–1964). School psychology: From identification to identity. *Journal of School Psychology* 2, 7–16.

———. (1984). On becoming a school psychologist: A semiautobiographical account. *Journal of School Psychology* 22, 1–15.

Thomas K. Fagan

PERSONALITY ASSESSMENT: TRADITIONAL. The traditional approach to personality assessment adheres to the medical model*; that is, it includes an emphasis upon pathology; a diagnosis with descriptions of present psychological functioning, the chronology of the pathology, and etiology or causation of emotional and behavioral problems; and a prediction or prognosis relevant to treatment alternatives, along with distinct recommendations for interventions. Most commonly, traditional personality assessment is aligned with psychoanalytically or psychodynamically oriented personality theories, with recognition of psychic determinism or unconscious/subconscious emotional conflicts. Consequently, assessment strategies are directed at presumed structural components of personality, primary and secondary need systems, emotional conflicts, ego defense mechanisms, and pathological operations and functioning. There is allegiance to clinical or subjective judgment. Even data from relatively objective psychometric instruments are subjectively interpreted, with the reliability* and validity* thereby becoming vulnerable to flaws in clinical judgment and acumen. Clinical judgment underlying personality assessment is a product of society; while clinical judgments may be only slightly better than, say, common sense or pure chance solutions, society has authorized and elevated the importance of problem-solving thinking by clinically trained persons with special levels of training, experience, and competence. Further, clinical judgment involves inferential accuracy, that is, the diagnostician's "ability, given limited information about a target person (patient) to judge correctly other pertinent characteristics about the person and to identify behavioral exemplars as part of a pattern of behavioral consistencies" (Reed and Jackson, 1975, p. 475). By definition, the traditional approach to personality assessment applies a diverse set of processes and procedures directed primarily at idiographic problem solving, with secondary consideration given to emotional factors manifested in social relationships.

Typically, traditional personality assessment collects information or test data relevant to personal history, observed behavior, intelligence, academic achievement, perception, neuropsychology, personality, and physical concomitants. Halleck (1978) indicates that personality assessment data for functional and dysfunctional behavior allow linking "the current existence of a cluster of behaviors with predictable maladaptive behavior in the future" (p. 33), which accommodates "the formulation and testing of multiple hypotheses as to the processes which cause various types of dysfunctional behavior" (p. 39). The controversy over actuarial* versus clinical methods has led to the development and usage of objective personality instruments, such as the Minnesota Multiphasic Personality Inventory-Second (MMPI-2), with data-based interpretive guidelines for determining both diagnosis and treatment. Criterion-based and factor analytic research methods are used to validate objective personality tests. Projective tests (or methods) rely on the principle of projection, which holds that what a person perceives or believes to be reality is tempered by his or her personality, and the person's private world (including at the unconscious level) will be revealed in expressions, such as what is perceived in an inkblot or what story is triggered by looking at a picture. Projective methods have received extensive criticism, primarily questioning the lack of empirical research relevant to reliability and validity. Nevertheless, surveys continue to reveal heavy reliance by psychologists on projective personality assessment methods, notably the Rorschach inkblot method and the Thematic Apperception Test and the latter's progeny (Lubin, Larsen, and Matarazzo, 1984). Surprisingly, even psychologists espousing behaviorism endorse personality assessment, including projective methods. Computerized scoring and interpretation systems are available for numerous objective personality instruments and projective methods.

See also ACTUARIAL ASSESSMENT VERSUS CLINICAL JUDGMENT; PERSONAL-SOCIAL ASSESSMENT.

REFERENCES

Halleck, S. L. (1978). *The treatment of emotional disorders.* New York: Aronson.
Knoff, H. M. (Ed.). (1986). *The assessment of child and adolescent personality.* New York: Guilford.
Lubin, B., R. M. Larsen, and J. D. Matarazzo. (1984). Patterns of psychological test usage in the United States: 1935–1982. *American Psychologist* 39, 451–454.
Reed, P. L., and D. N. Jackson. (1975). Clinical judgment of psychopathology: A model for inferential accuracy. *Journal of Abnormal Psychology* 84, 475–482.

Robert Henley Woody

PERSONAL-SOCIAL ASSESSMENT. Personal-social assessment is the evaluation of an individual's affective, intrapersonal, and interpersonal processes. Barnett and Zucker (1990) prefer the term "personal-social assessment" to "personality assessment,"* which many psychologists identify with the more traditional theories of personality. The term "personality assessment" tends to focus clinicians on the traditional theories of personality, instruments, and/or interpretations, causing them to overlook contributions from related areas (Barnett and Zucker, 1990). In contrast, the term "personal-social assessment" encourages a broader perspective focused on the understanding of personal and social processes when assessing an individual's problem. With a more ecological focus on how individuals function, more appropriate interventions can be developed. In school psychology,* personal-social assessment considers both the internal and environmental influences as they affect the academic performance of children. Besides academic performance, school psychologists* are also concerned with social functioning within school and within the home environment.

Barnett and Zucker (1990) indicated that, historically, child personal-social assessment emerged from personality assessment that had its origins in the personality theories developed earlier in this century. The foundations of personality assessment began with the work of James McKeen Cattell, Alfred Binet,* and Sir Francis Galton, who studied individual differences. Cattell in 1888 established the Psychological Laboratory at the University of Pennsylvania and supported the development of personality tests. Binet developed not only tasks that would be included in his intelligence test but tasks that were antecedents to later developed projective tests (Lanyon and Goodstein, 1982). Galton, with his research on the faculties of character or temperament, focused on direct observation of human behavior. This research on individual differences,* conducted before 1915, set the stage for the development of personality assessment.

From 1920 through the 1940s, there was a growing interest in personality theories. As a result, there was a dramatic increase in the number of personality tests developed during this period. Almost from the start, two different approaches toward assessing personality were developed: projective techniques and objective methods. The work in psychoanalysis by pioneers such as Freud, Jung, and Adler formed the foundations for the development of projective techniques during the 1930s and 1940s. Probably the best-known projective measure developed during this period was the Rorschach inkblot technique (Rorschach, 1942). The popularity of the Rorschach and the development of similar procedures (e.g., Thematic Apperception Test, Word Association Methods) resulted in Frank's (1939) coining the term "projective techniques" to describe these approaches to personality assessment. Besides the growth of projective methods during this period, objective measures of personality were being further refined and developed (Lanyon and Goodstein, 1982). Compared to projective measures, objective measures of personality were being used in the form of paper-and-pencil group tests as early as World War I. However, the popularity of these paper-and-pencil tests began to wane as projective measures were introduced in the 1930s and early 1940s. Not until after World War II and the development of psychometrically based, structured personality tests did a resurgence in these techniques occur. Probably the most popular of the structured personality tests developed during this period was the Minnesota Multiphasic Personality Inventory. By the end of the 1940s, many of the theories of personality and personality assessment techniques still used today had been developed (Barnett and Zucker, 1990).

Projective personality assessment techniques, historically, have been criticized for their questionable validity* and reliability,* while objective personality measures have had less criticism regarding their psychometric properties. For objective measures, the primary criticism has been that they are too rigid to allow the clinician to fully understand the individual. Today, the most difficult decisions that many psychologists have to make are choosing from the hundreds of projective and objective measures available when conducting a personality assessment. The approach most used and recommended is one that incorporates both projective and objective measures of personality along with other information.

See also COMPREHENSIVE ASSESSMENT; ECOLOGICAL ASSESSMENT; PERSONALITY ASSESSMENT: TRADITIONAL.

REFERENCES

Barnett, D. W., and K. B. Zucker. (1990). *The personal and social assessment of children: An analysis of current status and professional practice issues.* Boston: Allyn and Bacon.
Frank, L. K. (1939). Projective methods for the study of personality. *Journal of Psychology* 8, 389–413.
Lanyon, R. I., and L. D. Goodstein. (1982). *Personality assessment* (3d ed.). New York: Wiley.
Rorschach, H. (1942). *Psychodiagnostics.* Bern: Huber

David E. McIntosh, Jr.
Mardis D. Dunham

PERSON-CENTERED THERAPY. Initially called nondirective during its origin in the 1940s, client-centered in the 1950s, and experiential in the 1960s, person-centered therapy was developed by Carl Rogers.* Philosophically, it falls within the humanistic existential-phenomenological family of therapies that purport that individuals have self-actualizing tendencies. Persons are constantly striving to reach their full potential. Theoretically, the person-centered approach is not so much concerned with the causes of personality disturbances as it is with the process of personality change. Individuals are equipped with an organismic valuing process (inherent wisdom) that allows them to determine what is and is not actualizing. In childhood, as awareness of being develops, a self and self-concept* are generated from experiences, relationships, and beliefs that are translated into behavior. Congruence occurs when there is no dissonance among acting, thinking, and feeling states and when experiences are fully integrated into the self-concept. Maladjustment occurs when the individual's perception of experience is distorted or denied and is not recognized as incongruent with one's self-concept. Maladaptive behavior occurs along a continuum and differs not in kind, but only in degree of incongruence between one's self and one's experience.

Therapeutic focus is on the client's experiencing feelings in the here and now of the therapy session. Key to experiencing these feelings is the therapist's ability to create the three major facilitative conditions of unconditional positive regard, genuineness, and empathy. Nondefensiveness, spontaneity, sharing of self, freedom from roles, attending deeply to client concerns and feelings, reciprocity in the relationship, and a nonevaluative attitude are examples of helping skills used to facilitate these conditions. As clients experience these therapeutic conditions, they are able to shed defenses, more openly experience themselves, self-actualize toward their full potential, and regard themselves in a more positive and unconditional manner.

REFERENCES

Rogers, C. R. (1951). *Client-centered therapy.* Boston: Houghton Mifflin.
————. (1961). *On becoming a person.* Boston: Houghton Mifflin.
————. (1980). *A way of being.* Boston: Houghton Mifflin.

Richard K. James

PHI DELTA KAPPA. Phi Delta Kappa is an international professional education fraternity founded when the first chapter was organized in 1906 at Indiana University. The fraternity is dedicated to the ideals of research, service, and leadership. The purpose of the organization is to promote quality education, especially publicly supported education, as essential to the development and maintenance of a democratic way of life. It provides conferences, publications, scholarships, and a variety of professional services. Its journal, *Phi Delta Kappan,* is a widely respected source of information on education. Among its publications is an annual *Gallup Poll of the Public's Attitudes toward the Public Schools.* Originally for males only, the fraternity admitted women into membership in 1974. In 1992–1993, there were 677 chapters, with a total of 134,153 good-standing members. New members are initiated annually by recommendation of a good-standing member. Membership is available to worthy educators, including school psychological personnel. Contact: Phi Delta Kappa, P.O. Box 789, 8th and Union, Bloomington, IN 47402-0789.

See also TEACHER ORGANIZATIONS.

Thomas K. Fagan

PIAGETIAN ASSESSMENT. Jean Piaget (1896–1980) was trained as a biologist and was greatly interested in epistemology. While working in the Binet Laboratory in Paris, his interest turned to cognitive development. Though never having had a course in psychology, his work has influenced immensely our understanding of learning and cognitive development. His theory of genetic epistemology explicates how cognitive structures develop and change. Certain mental abilities tend to develop at certain ages and have been identified as appearing in four stages: sensorimotor (birth to two years), preoperational thinking (two to seven), concrete operations (seven to eleven, twelve), and formal operations (eleven, twelve to fourteen, fifteen).

The qualitative assessment of cognitive development differs from psychometric assessment in that it is nonnormative and focuses on the structural, developmental process of reasoning. The child is presented with a number of problem-solving tasks. The focus is on the operations a child uses rather than the number of problems solved correctly. The identification of the stage at which a child is functioning is helpful in planning interventions that are developmentally sequenced.

A few formal instruments have been developed: Infant Psychological Development Scale, Albert Einstein Scales of Sensori Motor Intelligence, and the Conservation Concept Diagnostic Kit. A number of informal measures and techniques have been developed, and these have been described by Simeonsson (1986). The informal procedures to assess the nature of a child's qualitative cognitive functioning include clinical interviews, think-aloud procedures, observation of problem solving, strategy interviews, observation of play, and the test-teach-test technique, the best known of which is Feurstein's Learning Potential Assessment Device (LPAD).

Interesting applications of Piagetian techniques with persons with mental retardation appear in the literature. Anecdotal information has been shared indicating that a disproportionate number of institutionalized children and adolescents with personal/social/emotional diagnoses and incarcerated adults are functioning at the preoperational level. Research is needed to address these observations.

See also DYNAMIC ASSESSMENT; COGNITIVE ASSESSMENT: NON-TRADITIONAL.

REFERENCES

Reynolds, C. R., and R. W. Kamphaus, (Eds.). (1990). *Handbook of psychological and educational assessment of children: Intelligence and achievement.* New York: Guilford Press.
Sattler, J. M. (1990). *Assessment of children.* San Diego: Author.
Simeonsson, R. J. (1986). *Psychological and developmental assessment of special children.* Boston: Allyn and Bacon.

Paul G. Warden

PLAY ASSESSMENT. Play assessment can provide useful data that may be otherwise difficult to obtain in traditional assessment procedures. Significant emotional and cognitive behaviors may become evident only when children participate directly in play activities. Because play activities can be influenced by numerous factors, specific attention must be directed toward types of toys, number of students in the play group, space, and peer homogeneity.

A child must be free to select toys, have adequate space to play in, and have peers available when social play is being assessed (Bailey and Wolery, 1989). Certain toys and materials, such as crayons and puzzles, foster isolated play, while dress-up clothes and balls lead to social play. Further, realistic toys produce more pretend play than do toys that are abstract in nature. Materials such as paints are likely to produce constructive play. Also, use of fewer toys promotes more social interaction among children.

When play activities are conducted in a physically restrictive area with limited space and lots of children, the probability of children's exhibiting aggressive tendencies toward each other is increased, but in settings that provide sufficient space, more socially appropriate behavior is expected. If observers are seeking a means to assess how a child deals with social conflict, they may want to consider placing the child in an overcrowded play situation.

Johnson, Christie, and Yankey (1987) have suggested that a child's gender also influences both the type of play as well as toy selection. Children in a mixed-gender group engage in activities quite differently than in a single-gender group.

Play assessment should be regarded as a legitimate procedure for gathering information about a child's social development. Single observations, however, may not always portray an accurate or typical description of a child's true behavior. Therefore, repeated observations (generally three) in a variety of different circumstances are recommended. Play observation is one of several observational techniques applied to young children.

See also ASSESSMENT; NATURALISTIC OBSERVATION; SOCIAL SKILLS TRAINING.

REFERENCES

Bailey, D. B., and M. Wolery. (1989). *Assessing infants and preschoolers with handicaps.* Columbus, OH: Merrill.

Cohen, D. H., and V. Stern. (1970). *Observing and recording the behavior of young children.* New York: Columbia University, Teachers College Press.

Johnson, J. E., J. F. Christie, and T. D. Yankey. (1987). *Play and early childhood development.* Glenview, IL: Scott Foresman.

Gerald J. Spadafore

PLAY THERAPY. The term "play therapy" refers to a collection of methods that utilize various forms of play to assist a child with resolving emotional or behavioral problems. The concept dates back to the work of Sigmund Freud, but the technique was developed by Melanie Klein and refined by Anna Freud. Other influential theorists and practitioners include Erik Erikson, Virginia Axline, and Clark Moustakas. Schaefer (1979) identified six major approaches or schools of play therapy: psychoanalytic, release, relationship, group, limit-setting, and behavioral. Specific play therapy techniques include drawing or painting, playing board or card games, puppet play, costume play, mutual storytelling, role playing, and play or activity groups. Play or activity groups often focus on a particular need or deficit, such as improvement of self-concept* or the development of specific social skills.* Proponents of play therapy argue that children cannot be helped by words alone but can learn and grow through their experiences, particularly in the context of a relationship that offers them warmth, safety, and understanding. Early play therapy approaches emphasized interpretation and insight; more recent ones emphasize relationships and experiences.

See also ART THERAPY; MUSIC THERAPY; PLAY ASSESSMENT.

REFERENCES

Gondor, E. I. (1954). *Art and play therapy.* Garden City, NY: Doubleday.
Schaefer, C. (1979). *The therapeutic use of child's play.* New York: Aronson.

W. Val McClanahan

POSTDOCTORAL STUDY. Postdoctoral study ''is another means of gaining continuing education while furthering one's doctoral specialization'' (Fagan and Wise, 1994, p. 190). It offers the opportunity to refine one's skills and develop areas of specific expertise as well as to expand one's skills in related areas of psychology. This training is usually a formal period of advanced study beyond the initial doctoral* training and thus, differs from continuing education activities that are often required in order to renew an individual's licensure or certification* to practice psychology. Examples of postdoctoral study include the postdoctoral residency in professional psychology, for which the American Psychological Association* is developing standards for a psychologist to move from one area of psychology into another. School psychology,* for example, is a specialty area in which there are shortages, and psychologists trained in other fields of psychology, including clinical and experimental, are pursuing postdoctoral study through school psychology training programs.

See also CONTINUING PROFESSIONAL DEVELOPMENT.

REFERENCE

Fagan, T. K., and P. S. Wise. (1994). *School psychology: Past, present, and future.* White Plains, NY: Longman.

Douglas K. Smith

POSTSECONDARY SCHOOL SETTING. The practice of school psychology* in a postsecondary or university setting is still unique to the field. Since 1977, literature has suggested that school psychologists* could serve university personnel and adult student populations in ways similar to those utilized in elementary and secondary school settings (Sandoval, 1988). Postsecondary school psychology might include indirect services* such as providing professional development and consultation* to college faculty. Assisting exceptional students, counseling individuals, developing interventions, and conducting research are direct services* that could be provided. Vocational school psychologists,* who sometimes serve in postsecondary vocational school settings, usually focus on career development,* assessment strategies, and specific work-related programming.

Steil (1994) focuses on the need for postsecondary school psychologists to understand adult problems and to develop the skills needed to help adults acquire personal resources. By utilizing their consultation, intervention, and research skills, postsecondary school psychologists can assist both faculty and adult students. It is suggested that persons interested in this specialty area should receive training that emphasizes lifelong human development and learning, assessment of adult functioning, counseling methods, and program evaluation* (Steil, 1994).

See also NONSCHOOL SETTINGS; SCHOOL SETTINGS.

REFERENCES

Sandoval, J. (1988). The school psychologist in higher education. *School Psychology Review* 17, 391–396.
Steil, D. (1994). Post-secondary school psychology: Come on in, the water's fine. *Communique* 22(8), 28–30.

Leslie Hale

POWER. Power refers to the ability to influence the behavior of others. However, school psychologists,* though they may exert considerable power, lack the authority* to make critical decisions. School psychologists are concerned with both referent power*—the projection of an image of close identification with school personnel as well as with the families of the pupils who are served—and expert power,* which refers to the possession of skill and knowledge and which often develops over a relatively short period of time. Both types of power are essential to effective performance as a consultant (Martin, 1978). Factors that contribute to the perception of such power include advanced professional training, the acquisition of a license where available, and participation in professional organizations. Power is essential to effective school psychological service. However, it is sometimes misperceived as decision-making authority, which results in conflict between professionals. The concept of ''empowerment'' must be dealt with, as students express an interest in participating in the decision-making process. Such power is related to political access and is championed by those who feel that minority groups have been consistently slighted. The task of the school psychologist is to encourage dialogue, to support essential program modification, and to work toward minimizing conflict in this area.

See also CENTRALIZED VERSUS DECENTRALIZED SERVICES.

REFERENCE

Martin, R. (1978). Expert and referent power: A framework for understanding and maximizing consultation effectiveness. *Journal of School Psychology* 16, 49–55.

Donald M. Wonderly

POWERS, MARGARET HALL. Margaret Hall Powers was born on March 22, 1905, and died in Chicago on August 10, 1983. She completed her B.A. at the University of Wisconsin (1927), M.A. at the University of Chicago (1931), and Ph.D. from the University of Iowa (1938) in clinical psychology* and speech disorders. In the Chicago public schools, she worked as a psychologist in the Bureau of Child Study (1939–1948), director of the Division of Speech Correction (1948–1956), and director of the Bureau of Physically Handicapped Children (1956–1968). Prior to working for the Chicago schools, she worked as a psychologist for the Institute for Juvenile Research (1928–1930) and the Illinois Soldiers and Sailors Children's Schools (1931–1935). She was president of the Division of School Psychologists,* 1947–1948, a fellow of Divisions 12 and 16, and a diplomate* in clinical psychology. She traveled widely and was active in community affairs during her retirement.

REFERENCE

Mullen, F. A. (1983). In memoriam: Dr. Margaret Hall Powers. *School Psychologist* 38(1), 4.

Thomas K. Fagan

PRACTICUM. The idea of a practicum component in the training of school psychologists* dates back to the early years of the field of school psychology.* Unlike internships,* which are typically completed at the conclusion of training, practicum experiences (sometimes known as extern experiences) are typically offered concurrently with academic course work. Such experiences provide opportunities for students to apply their newly acquired skills in such areas as assessment,* consultation,* and counseling immediately in an applied setting.

Training programs and state departments of education* differ in the amount of time students are required to spend in practica. Smith and Henning (in press) report that specialist programs required an average of 421 clock hours (actual time spent), and doctoral programs required an average of 651 clock hours of practicum work. Wide variations exist among programs in the number of practicum hours required. In addition, some training programs require practicum work in nonschool settings (often on-campus psychoeducational clinics) in place of, or in addition to, the number of hours spent in the schools.

Ideally, practicum work should be developmentally organized. That is, the practicum should match the training level of the student. Thus, as the student acquires skills, the requirements of the practicum should reflect the skill acquisition by becoming increasingly demanding. New students may try out their testing skills with "nonproblem" cases, while advanced students may be required to complete case studies on students with difficulties and/or disabilities.

In the practicum, a university faculty member (or, in some cases, an advanced graduate student) typically arranges for the experiences, makes assignments, assigns grades, and generally has primary responsibility. Although local and area school psychologists or school administrators may be involved, to some extent, in the practicum, the university trainer* is ultimately responsible.

The National Association of School Psychologists* (NASP) and some state departments of education* publish standards for, and information about, school psychology field experiences.* Readers are advised to consult these sources for up-to-date information (NASP, 1994).

See also PROFESSIONAL STANDARDS; TRAINING MODELS; UNIVERSITY-BASED CLINICS.

REFERENCES

Fagan, T. K., and P. S. Wise. (1994). *School psychology: Past, present, and future.*
    White Plains, NY: Longman.
National Association of School Psychologists. (1994). *Standards for training and field*
    placement programs in school psychology. Washington, DC: Author.
Smith, D. K., and A. Henning. (in press). *Directory of school psychology training*
    programs (4th ed.). Washington, DC: National Association of School
    Psychologists.

Paula Sachs Wise

PRACTITIONER. In the context of school psychology,* the term "practitioner" refers to a professional who provides direct and indirect school psychological services. The term is used to distinguish between school psychologists* who are working in practice settings and those working in nonpractice settings (e.g., university trainers* or state consultants*).

A practitioner must hold appropriate credentials, which vary from state to state. With few exceptions, to practice in a state-regulated school setting,* one must be credentialed as a school psychologist by the state's education agency. This typically requires at least a master's* or specialist* training from a school psychology program that includes an internship.* To be a practitioner in settings outside the regulation of a state's education agency, one must obtain a practice credential from a state's board of examiners in psychology* or comparable agency. Typically, to be credentialed by this agency for practice as a school psychologist, one must hold the doctoral degree* with preparation in school psychology and an appropriate internship. Some state boards license at the subdoctoral level of training and employ practitioner titles such as psychological examiner or psychometrist. In most states, nondoctoral practitioners credentialed by a state board of examiners in psychology must be supervised for some or all of their functions by a doctoral-level credentialed psychologist.

See also CERTIFICATION; LICENSING; NONSCHOOL SETTINGS; PRIVATE SCHOOL SETTINGS; SCHOOL SETTINGS.

REFERENCE

Fagan, T. K., and P. S. Wise. (1994). *School psychology: Past, present, and future.*
    White Plains, NY: Longman.

R. Scott Beebe

PRACTITIONER-BASED RESEARCH. Practitioner-based research refers to scientific investigations by field-based (rather than university-based) professionals that are intended to produce new knowledge or to improve practice related to education. Although research is an essential component of the theory and practice of school psychology,* practitioners* traditionally have been limited to consuming, rather than conducting, research. However, a growing number of practitioners are expanding their roles in order to investigate key questions regarding student performance and professional practice.

Practitioner-based research tends to address questions of efficacy and decision making, often involving surveys, rating scales, and descriptive methods. How accurately do specific assessment procedures differentiate specific populations, predict performance, or identify needs? What factors influence teacher judgments or instructional approaches? What approach to social skills training has the greatest impact on student behavior?

With limited time allocated to research and, usually, limited (if any) funding for research activities in schools, practitioners seek efficient research designs and data analysis procedures. Case study, time-series, and other single-subject designs are useful alternatives to group studies.

A number of barriers must be overcome by practitioners seeking to develop research programs in the schools: (1) time allocations; (2) systemic hurdles, including administrative approval, parental consent, and school schedules; (3) preservice training that usually overlooks small-scale research designs; (4) lack of district technical resources to support staff research; and (5) limited control of variables affecting the quality of research in real-world settings. Additionally, practitioners typically find limited incentives for conducting school-based research, compared to the rewards (tenure or promotion) and expectations (funding) for their colleagues in university settings. Regardless of administrative and technical support, the practitioner conducting research usually is expected to respond to the everyday demands of mandated services* to students.

School psychology practitioners seeking research opportunities (1) develop grant proposals to local, state, and federal agencies; (2) identify technical resources within the community or nearby universities; (3) work with school administrators to develop a district (school) research agenda; (4) enhance their skills through consultation and additional training; (5) collaborate with other school personnel to promote empirically based practice; and (6) seek collaborative arrangements with university faculty or students interested in school-based samples, pilot sites, and other resources.

See also EXPERIMENTAL DESIGN; QUALITATIVE RESEARCH.

REFERENCES

Fry, M. (1986). The connections among educational and psychological research and the practice of school psychology. In S. Elliot and J. Witt, (Eds.), *The delivery of psychological services in schools: Concepts, processes, and issues* (pp. 305–327). Hillsdale, NJ: Erlbaum.

Keith, T. Z. (1988). Research methods in school psychology: An overview. *School Psychology Review* 17, 508–526.

———. (1990). Best practices in applied research. In A. Thomas and J. Grimes, (Eds.), *Best practices in school psychology—II* (pp. 207–218). Washington, DC: National Association of School Psychologists.

Andrea Canter

PRAGMATIC MODEL. The pragmatic model of training is one of three master models, the others being the scientist-practitioner model* and the professional model.* The model is termed pragmatic because its essential feature is to take a practical approach to program curriculum development consistent with prescriptive certification* requirements of state departments of education* and the specialist-level standards of the National Association of School Psychologists* (NASP). As a master model, it influences the specific program model developed by individual training programs for school psychologists.* That is, the preparation of school psychologists is directed toward the credentialing requirements of the state in which the school psychology* training program is located. Individual program models vary as a function of the state's expectations.

Whereas the scientist-practitioner and professional models are applicable to doctoral programs, the pragmatic model is most applicable to nondoctoral programs. The pragmatic model is atheoretical and is primarily a descriptive model, whereas the scientist-practitioner and professional models are based on much broader consensus about the nature of preparation in professional psychology. The pragmatic model is heavily influenced by nondoctoral program accreditation* standards promulgated by the National Council for Accreditation of Teacher Education* (NCATE), which are closely aligned with NASP training and credentialing standards and with state education agency credentialing standards. Because nondoctoral programs are restricted in credit-hour requirements, their prescriptive nature reduces their flexibility of orientation or elective course work.

Though restrictive, the pragmatic model is necessary for preparing entry-level school psychologists. As practice expectations expanded, the importance of broad generalist preparation for the entry level has been emphasized in training and accreditation standards. These standards have increased in the past twenty years from the master's* to the specialist degree* level. The doctoral degree* is considered by NASP as an advanced preparation beyond the entry level, in contrast to American Psychological Association* (APA) ideology, which views the doctorate as the entry level.

See also TRAINING MODELS.

REFERENCE

Fagan, T. K., and P. S. Wise. (1994). *School psychology: Past, present, and future.* White Plains, NY: Longman.

Thomas K. Fagan

PRECISION TEACHING. Precision teaching (PT) describes a process in which operant conditioning* principles are applied to the teaching and learning process. Although he denies it, Ogden Lindsley is credited with developing PT (Lindsley, 1990). Lindsley, a former student of B. F. Skinner, argues that frequency of behavior should be measured continuously and monitored daily, students should use self-recording, and standard charts should be used to display major changes in academic or social behaviors. Each student is able to progress at his or her own rate, and instruction is thus individualized. Behaviors are charted on a logarithmic scale that communicates rate of learning or "celeration" (Lindsley, 1990, p. 11) and allows for a wide range of behavioral frequencies.

Principles of PT state that student behavior is the best measure of instructional effectiveness, behaviors should be continuously and directly measured, rate of responding is the best measure of behavior, standard charts should display performance, behaviors should be operationally and functionally defined, environmental influences on behavior should be examined, and building appropriate and functional behaviors should be emphasized, rather than the reduction or elimination of undesirable behaviors. Analysis of learning graphs provides feedback to the teacher in adjusting instruction based on objective data.

See also BEHAVIOR MODIFICATION; CURRICULUM-BASED ASSESSMENT; DIAGNOSTIC TEACHING.

REFERENCES

Lindsley, O. R. (1972). From Skinner to precision teaching: The child knows best. In J. B. Jordan and L. S. Robbins (Eds.), *Let's try doing something else kind of thing: Behavioral principles and the exceptional child* (pp. 1–11). Arlington, VA: Council for Exceptional Children.

———. (1990). Precision teaching: By teachers for children. *Teaching Exceptional Children* 22, 10–15.

———. (1992). Precision teaching: Discoveries and effects. *Journal of Applied Behavior Analysis* 25, 51–57.

Gary L. Canivez

PREREFERRAL ASSESSMENT. Prereferral assessment deals with the process of identifying conditions in the individual and/or in the school that prevent successful learning. The notion of "prereferral," related to this activity, means that the assessment (and prereferral intervention*) occurs prior to formal referral to special education.* The conditions adversely affecting learning may be related to intraindividual factors (e.g., an educational disability, attention difficulties) or may be related to the learning environment (e.g., instructional and social dimensions of the classroom).

Prereferral assessment has been proposed as a solution to the dramatic increase in the number of referrals made to special education since the inception of Public Law 94-142* (Fuchs, 1991).

With its roots in school consultation theory and practice dating back to the late 1970s, prereferral assessment is a model based on the principles of prevention.* A major component of prereferral assessments is collaborative problem-solving activities between general and special educators for the purpose of improving educational outcomes (Graden, 1989). Prereferral assessment (and intervention planning) typically takes place in a team format (e.g., teacher assistance teams, intervention assistance teams, instructional support teams). By design, the assessment process used is indirect in nature, with intervention typically taking place within the current classroom setting by the student's classroom teacher.

Prereferral assessment naturally leads to interventions intended to alleviate the concern. The lack of success of prereferral intervention is the rationale for referral to the special education multidisciplinary team, as this increases the likelihood of the presence of an educational disability. The process is consistent with the least restrictive environment mandates of the Individuals with Disabilities Education Act (IDEA, Public Law 101-476*) by using a less restrictive means of gathering data about student performance.

Prereferral assessment is viewed as intervention-oriented and thus should be curriculum-based and sensitive to the ecology (Fuchs, 1991). Curriculum-based measurement* (CBM) is often preferred at this step in the process as it is designed to be directly linked to intervention. CBM provides for a continuous measurement system. That is, it provides for a systematized procedure that is present at the development stage, the implementation stage, and the evaluation stage of the intervention.

Prereferral assessment is not without critics. Pugach and Johnson (1989) argue that the referral process leads to premature solidification of the problem, a transfer of problem ownership from teachers to a team of other professionals, and an overdependence on specialists for problem clarification and solutions. Further evidence suggests that parents' involvement in the team process is marginal at best, despite research heralding the importance of parental involvement.

See also ASSESSMENT (DIRECT AND INDIRECT); TEAM; TEAM APPROACH.

REFERENCES

Fuchs, D. (1991). Mainstream assistance teams: A prereferral intervention system for difficult-to-teach students. In G. Stoner, M. R. Shinn, and H. M. Walker (Eds.), *Interventions for achievement and behavioral problems* (pp. 241–267). Silver Spring, MD: National Association of School Psychologists.

Graden, J. L. (1989). Redefining ''prereferral'' intervention as intervention assistance: Collaboration between general and special education. *Exceptional Children* 56, 227–231.

Pugach, M. C., and L. J. Johnson. (1989). Prereferral interventions: Progress, problems, and challenges. *Exceptional Children* 56, 217–226.

John E. Brandt

PREREFERRAL INTERVENTIONS. Prereferral intervention deals with the process of changing or modifying conditions in an attempt to ameliorate learning difficulties and increase the chance of success in school. The notion of "prereferral," related to this activity, means that the intervention occurs prior to formal referral to special education.* The conditions adversely affecting school success may be related to intraindividual factors (e.g., an educational disability, attention difficulties) or may be related to the learning environment (e.g., instructional and social dimensions of the classroom).

Organized as an indirect, consultation-oriented activity, prereferral interventions typically follow an assessment process organized by a team of general and special educators. These teams, known by a variety of names (e.g., teacher assistance teams, intervention assistance teams, instructional support teams), are designed to offer a collaborative, problem-solving activity that provides immediate assistance to the pupil and the teacher (Fuchs, 1991). Prereferral interventions are prevention-oriented and based on an ecological model of viewing the student's learning and behavior within the context of the classroom.

As already noted, prereferral interventions are typically consultation*-oriented. School consultation may take many forms, ranging from case-specific (i.e., client-centered) to systemic (i.e., program-centered). Prereferral interventions similarly take these various forms. The intervention may be related to the specific needs of a student, a group of students, a teacher, or a classroom/program.

Fuchs (1991) noted that, most frequently, teachers target off-task or inattentive behaviors as the primary concern when bringing students to the attention of the team. Other teachers target poor work quality, difficulty relating to adults and peers, and poor academics as the concern. Interventions that are "client-centered" may range from individual behavioral contracts for disruptive students to modifications in instruction or curriculum. Systemic interventions may involve modification of the classroom environment, such as reorganizing the seating plan or using a token economy system. Interventions may involve changes in the teacher's behaviors or skills as a means of improving the learning environment.

The lack of success of the prereferral intervention often indicates the presence of an educational disability and promotes referral to the special education multidisciplinary team. This process is consistent with the least restrictive environment mandates of the Individuals with Disabilities Education Act (IDEA, Public Law 101-476*) by using a less restrictive means of gathering data about student performance and a less restrictive form of intervention (Graden, Casey, and Christenson, 1985).

As with all intervention, it is imperative to assess the effectiveness of the activities by collecting data at various points during the process. Consultants engaging in prereferral intervention must assure that the individuals implementing the intervention are doing so consistently and comprehensively.

See also INTERVENTION (DIRECT AND INDIRECT); PREREFERRAL ASSESSMENT; TEAM; TEAM APPROACH.

REFERENCES

Fuchs, D. (1991). Mainstream assistance teams: A prereferral intervention system for difficult-to-teach students. In G. Stoner, M. Shinn, and H. Walker (Eds.), *Interventions for achievement and behavioral problems* (pp. 241–267). Silver Spring, MD: National Association of School Psychologists.
Graden, J. L., A. Casey, and S. L. Christenson. (1985). Implementing a prereferral intervention system: Part I. The model. *Exceptional Children* 51(5), 377–384.

John E. Brandt

PRESCHOOL ASSESSMENT. Assessment of preschool children's cognitive functioning is an activity that has both historical roots and current importance. Historically, psychologists believed that intelligence* was fixed (i.e., not subject to change) and inherited. These tenets were commonly accepted as recently as the mid-1930s. Wellman, a psychologist who worked for the Iowa Child Welfare Research Station,* commonly administered psychological assessments to preschool-aged children. Wellman noted that over a period of several years, many of the children she tested evidenced an increase in assessed intelligence. As a result, in 1932 Wellman questioned the concept of fixed intelligence and attributed the change in assessed intelligence to a modifiable construct. In 1928 Florence Goodenough, on the other hand, also had noted a change in children's assessed intelligence over time, but she had attributed the variability to error in measurement as opposed to actual changes in children's intelligence.

The differences in opinion surrounding the Wellman-Goodenough controversy set the stage for a dramatic increase in preschool assessment and assessment-related research. Subsequent research has investigated the degree to which young children's intelligence is fixed, inherited, and affected by environmental deprivation and stimulation. From the subsequent research, public laws have been passed to fund early childhood educational programs (e.g., Head Start) and mandate educational services to preschool children with exceptional needs (e.g., Public Law 99-457*). To determine eligibility for preschool educational services for large numbers of American preschool children, the number of preschool assessments has grown concomitantly.

Preschool assessments may take many forms, reflect many formats, and measure many different constructs. For example, preschool children referred for psychological or educational evaluations are often administered traditional norm-referenced test batteries on which the children's performance on the standardized set of tests is compared to the performance of a normative sample of same-aged peers. Infants and young children may be observed, interacted with, and rated according to normative developmental schedules (e.g., Denver Developmental Screening Test; Bayley Scales of Infant Development). Developmental scales assess the rate, form, and sequence of children's developing skills across common and core areas of functioning. Play-based assessment is a rapidly growing means of evaluating preschool children in a nonthreatening, naturalistic fashion.

Common constructs assessed in preschool evaluations include intelligence, adaptive behavior,* fine and gross motor abilities, speech and language functioning, creativity, perceptual processing, social-emotional adjustment, neuropsychological functioning, and school readiness. Assessments may take the form of a brief screening of a singular skill (e.g., basic language concepts), a diagnostic evaluation of a broader skill area (e.g., speech and language assessment), or a comprehensive psychoeducational evaluation that includes and integrates several constructs (e.g., language, intelligence, adaptive behavior). The principal determinant of whether a screening instrument or a comprehensive battery is administered is the nature of the referral and services sought. Narrowly focused referral questions typically result in a specific skill assessment and intervention plan; likewise, a more nebulous or chronic referral problem may result in a more encompassing evaluation and treatment plan.

See also COGNITIVE ASSESSMENT; COMPREHENSIVE ASSESSMENT; NEUROPSYCHOLOGICAL ASSESSMENT; NONVERBAL ASSESSMENT; PLAY ASSESSMENT; PERCEPTUAL-MOTOR ASSESSMENT; PERSONAL-SOCIAL ASSESSMENT; PIAGETIAN ASSESSMENT; READINESS; SCREENING ASSESSMENT; SOCIAL SKILLS ASSESSMENT.

REFERENCES

Bagnato, S. J., J. T. Neisworth, and S. M. Munson. (1989). *Linking developmental assessment and early intervention: Curriculum-based prescriptions.* Rockville, MD: Aspen.
Bracken, B. A. (Ed.). (1991). *The psychoeducational assessment of preschool children* (2d ed.). Needham Heights, MA: Allyn and Bacon.

Bruce A. Bracken

PRESCHOOL INTERVENTIONS. Preschool intervention programs were widely introduced in the 1960s to provide educational services to young children and their families, to identify potential developmental or learning problems when children were young, and to prevent or reduce later problems. Programs were typically designed for preschool children who were economically disadvantaged or at risk for developing learning or behavior problems or for preschool children with developmental delays or disabilities. Research indicates that preschool intervention programs can have short-term and long-term benefits for children, families, schools, and communities.

Texts, such as those by the Consortium for Longitudinal Studies (1983) and Guralnick and Bennett (1987), contain reports of many experimental intervention programs for young children, including the Carolina Abecedarian project, the Perry Preschool Project, Head Start, and the Harlem Study. One of the most consistently replicated, short-term results of these and other preschool interventions projects was the significant gain in IQs for the participants. However, longer-term evaluation of the participants indicated that they usually had declines in IQs in the first one or two years following the preschool program and that the gains were no longer apparent after four or five years.

Long-term results for the preschool programs were more compelling than the initial, short-term gains in IQs. Longitudinal research investigated the characteristics of the children and their families for many years following participation in the preschool program. Reports in Consortium for Longitudinal Studies (1983) and Guralnick and Bennett (1987) described the following long-term results for children who participated in preschool intervention programs, when compared to children who did not participate in the programs: lower probability of grade retention* and placement in special education* programs, higher reading and mathematics performance, higher self-esteem, higher probability of graduating from high school, better classroom behavior, and greater commitment to school. The research reports also identified long-term benefits for families of children who participated in the programs, including better parent–child relationships and higher parental aspirations for their children.

The reports of longitudinal studies of preschool intervention programs suggested that family interventions and home services are critical factors. Involvement of both parents and children, inclusion of parent training,* and provision of services such as health care and nutrition training to families were key components of effective preschool intervention programs.

The benefits of preschool intervention programs have not always been consistently supported by research. Haskins (1989) conducted a comprehensive review of research on early intervention programs and concluded that the benefits of the programs are related to quality of the program and that results of research may be affected by flaws in the research methodology. Haskins indicated that good investigations of model, high-quality programs provided strong evidence of long-term benefits such as reduced special education placement and grade retention. Poorer investigations of lower-quality programs provided mixed evidence of long-term benefits.

See also PRESCHOOL ASSESSMENT; PREVENTION.

REFERENCES

Consortium for Longitudinal Studies. (1983). *As the twig is bent . . . lasting effects of preschool programs.* Hillsdale, NJ: Erlbaum.

Gettinger, M., S. N. Elliott, and T. R. Kratochwill (Eds.). (1992). *Preschool and early childhood treatment directions.* Hillsdale, NJ: Erlbaum.

Guralnick, M. J., and F. C. Bennett, (Eds.) (1987). *The effectiveness of early intervention for at-risk and handicapped children.* Orlando, FL: Academic Press.

Haskins, R. (1989). Beyond metaphor: The efficacy of early childhood education. *American Psychologist* 44, 274–282.

Patti L. Harrison

PRESCRIPTION PRIVILEGES. Broadening the authority beyond physicians to treat via administration of controlled substances is a hotly debated topic that has evolved during the last twenty years. In the early 1970s, the American Psychological Association* (APA) Board of Directors appointed a committee to review the matter. The committee determined that prescription privileges should not be pursued, as the field was progressing well without such authority.

However, by the mid-1980s, the profession had moderated its position. Other nonphysician disciplines such as optometrists and nurse practitioners had made substantial gains in prescription authority despite vigorous protests by organized medicine. By 1989, the APA Board of Professional Affairs endorsed the study of psychopharmacology for psychologists, and in 1990 the Council of Representatives established a special task force on prescription privileges.

Individual states have the authority to determine what professional groups may prescribe medications and under what conditions. Hawaii was the first state that seriously pursued legislation to allow licensed psychologists to administer and prescribe medication. Legislative action was attempted in 1985 and again in 1989. The bills were consistently opposed by the psychiatric community. At the end of the 1989 legislative session, a compromise resolution was adopted that referred the matter to the Center for Alternative Dispute Resolution for roundtable discussion.

The federal government, not individual states, determines the scope of practice of federal mental health providers. Under such authority, the Department of Defense established a training project to instruct military psychologists in the prescription of psychotropic medications. Although the project was intended to begin in 1988, organized medicine's persistent objections prevented its implementation until the fall of 1990. Within this training program, military psychologists enroll in physician assistant courses for approximately four months. Course work includes human anatomy, chemistry, and pharmacology. Clinical practicums in inpatient psychiatric services follow and last approximately eight months. All work and medical orders are completed under the supervision of a licensed psychiatrist.

See also PSYCHOPHARMACOLOGY.

REFERENCE

DeLeon, P. H., R. E. Fox, and S. R. Graham. (1991). Prescription privileges: Psychology's next frontier? *American Psychologist* 46, 384–393.

LeAdelle Phelps

PRESIDENTIAL COMMISSIONS AND WHITE HOUSE CONFERENCES. Presidential commissions are as old as the presidency itself and cover or pertain to a wide variety of topics. White House conferences, by contrast, have always pertained to children and have been held about every ten years since the first, the Conference on the Care of Dependent Children, was called by President Theodore Roosevelt in 1909. Organized by prominent social settlement workers Jane Addams and Lillian Wald, the first White House conference represented a major departure on the part of the federal government in the United States, as it brought the welfare of all American children under its purview. One result of this first conference was the establishment of the Federal Children's Bureau, approved by Congress in 1912. The conference in 1919 continued the focus of the Children's Bureau on infant mortality and carefully avoided offending any perceived interests. In sharp contrast, the conference of 1930 sought to broaden its scope to include almost every aspect of childhood and adolescence: the family, education, labor, recreation, and so on. The first two conferences numbered about 200 participants; the 1930 meeting attracted around 3,000 people and was dominated by experts in the new fields of child development and family studies. The 1940 White House Conference on Children in a Democracy reflected ideological concerns of a nation about to enter World War II, while the Midcentury Conference on Children and Youth (1950) seemed unable to do much more than worry about the threat of nuclear warfare, although Benjamin Spock did call for a greater reliance on professional expertise in child rearing. The 1960 conference, with 7,600 participants, focused on adolescents and youth and the national problem of juvenile delinquency. In 1970, there was concern over the social role of women and the need for day care; for the first time a White House conference focused on ordinary children instead of those "at risk" (e.g., dependent, handicapped, or abused). Rarely have recommendations been enacted, and strong opposition to the role of the federal government has been a consistent theme since the first conference. No conference on children and youth was held in 1980; instead, there was a White House Conference on Families. No conference on either topic was held in 1990.

One of the longest lasting and most influential presidential commissions was the President's Panel on Mental Retardation, established by John F. Kennedy in 1961. The panel issued its first report in October 1962, which, in turn, prompted a presidential message to Congress and the passage of the Mental Retardation Facilities and Community Mental Health Centers Act of 1963. The panel (later, the President's Committee on Mental Retardation) continued through the Johnson, Nixon, and Ford years, with its major role coming in the passage of the Education for All Handicapped Children Act in 1975 (Public Law 94-142*). A presidential commission strongly supported the legislation, commenting that "our children must not be deprived of educational opportunities until federal district courts of the 50 states have each ruled that their education is a present constitutional right" (Kindred, 1976, p. 267).

See also CHILD ADVOCACY.

REFERENCES

Beck, R. (1973). The White House Conferences on Children: An historical perspective. *Harvard Educational Review* 43, 653–668.

Kindred, M. (Ed). (1976). *The mentally retarded citizen and the law.* Sponsored by the President's Committee on Mental Retardation. New York: Free Press.

Tyor, P. L., and L. V. Bell. (1984). *Caring for the retarded in America: A history.* Westport, CT: Greenwood Press.

White House Conference on Families. (1980). *Listening to America's families: Action for the 80s; The report to the President, Congress and families of the nation.* Washington, DC: Author.

Joseph M. Hawes

PREVENTION: PRIMARY. Primary prevention refers to programs designed to promote adaptive functioning of individuals in schools, with families, with peers, and in the community. Primary prevention is the first of three components (including secondary* and tertiary* prevention) in the preventive psychiatry model developed by Gerald Caplan (1964). Caplan argued that "a program of primary prevention would focus on identifying current harmful influences, the environmental forces which support individuals in resisting them, and those environmental forces which influence the resistance of the population to future pathogenic experiences" (p. 27).

Primary prevention provides an important conceptual framework for school psychological services. With a schoolwide focus, it undertakes, as its goal, the promotion of abilities in individuals such as general ego strength, problem-solving skills, interpersonal skills, academic skills, and others (Bower, 1981).

Primary prevention does not neglect the promotion of ability in those individuals who have already been identified as having problems but focuses also on all others in the school community. It would therefore not eliminate the need for assessments* and interventions,* but the need for these services would be reduced.

Primary prevention programs can be implemented at multiple levels in the school and can include, for example, developing programs to enhance social skills in children; setting up parent education programs on facilitating cognitive and emotional functioning in children; and consulting with teachers about students' learning styles.

See also POWER; PREVENTIVE EDUCATION.

REFERENCES

Bower, E. M. (1981). *Early identification of emotionally disturbed children in school* (3d ed.). Springfield, IL: Charles C. Thomas.

Caplan, G. (1964). *Principles of preventive psychiatry.* New York: Basic Books.

Shani Beth-Halachmy

PREVENTION: SECONDARY. Secondary prevention is the second of three components of the preventive psychiatry model developed by Gerald Caplan (1964). Caplan referred to secondary prevention programs as those designed to "reduce the disability rate due to a disorder by lowering the prevalence of the disorder in the community" (p. 89). Reduction of prevalence can occur in two ways: (1) by changing factors that lead to a disability or (2) by developing early identification and effective intervention* programs that would shorten the duration of the disability. Because the first way would fall under primary prevention,* secondary prevention includes primary prevention within its conceptual framework.

Secondary prevention requires the maximum use of resources so as to affect the largest number of individuals in the school community. Further, it highlights the importance of early identification and intervention (Bower, 1981). Working within a secondary prevention model, school psychologists* consult with teachers to help them differentiate students who are having adjustment problems from those who have developmental or learning disabilities; consult with teachers and administrators to help set up early identification, referral, and intervention programs; conduct class- or schoolwide screening* for a wide variety of problems; and develop programs designed to facilitate children's functioning in different domains.

See also POWER; PREVENTION: TERTIARY; PREVENTIVE EDUCATION.

REFERENCES

Bower, E. M. (1981). *Early identification of emotionally disturbed children in school* (3d ed.). Springfield, IL: Charles C. Thomas.
Caplan, G. (1964). *Principles of preventive psychiatry.* New York: Basic Books.
                                                                    Shani Beth-Halachmy

PREVENTION: TERTIARY. Tertiary prevention is the third of three components of the preventive psychiatry model developed by Gerald Caplan (1964). Caplan defined tertiary prevention as programs aimed to ''reduce the rate in a community of defective functioning due to mental disorder'' (p. 113). To achieve its goals, tertiary prevention programs in schools are designed so that individuals with disabilities are brought to function in the mainstream environment at their highest potential.

To be successful, tertiary prevention programs must be one component in a comprehensive prevention philosophy that includes the development and implementation of primary* and secondary prevention* as well. This includes programs targeted at the overall school population that are designed to facilitate the development of attributes and skills promoting adaptive functioning in all individuals and programs for the early identification of individuals at risk of developing disabilities. But the focus of tertiary prevention lies in the development of programs for individuals whose functioning has been impaired due to a disability—programs that would facilitate their successful functioning in the mainstream environment.

Tertiary prevention programs can include, for example, developing intervention programs designed for students challenged with affective or cognitive disabilities; consulting with teachers of students with disabilities; or developing inclusion programs designed to support students with disabilities in the regular classroom.

See also POWER; PREVENTIVE EDUCATION.

REFERENCES

Bower, E. M. (1981). *Early identification of emotionally disturbed children in school* (3d ed.). Springfield, IL: Charles C. Thomas.
Caplan, G. (1964). *Principles of preventive psychiatry.* New York: Basic Books.

Shani Beth-Halachmy

PREVENTIVE EDUCATION. The primary focus of public school education centers around instruction in academic areas in which accountability* is a major concern. With vast numbers of single- and dual-working-parent families, as well as the mainstreaming of children with special needs, the school has become the principal vehicle for the provision of knowledge, skills, and services in nonacademic areas. The pressure for health, driver, and physical education that arose during the 1950s has been supplemented by a greater demand for information related to the prevention of physical, sexual, and drug abuse and other problems.

To make preventive programs successful, it is necessary to gain the cooperation and commitment of school and community. The consultative role embraced by school psychologists* at the end of the twentieth century provides service to a broader population than that addressed in the assessment/counseling model, which targets a relatively limited number of students (Fagan and Wise, 1994).

Primary prevention,* according to Wonderly et al. (1979), represents an attempt to prevent maladjustment. Adjustments in program strategies affecting the learning of all children are an example. Secondary prevention* relates to interventions such as counseling, placement in a learning disabilities program, or providing remedial reading strategies. Tertiary interventions are considered for a child whose inability to function in a regular education program requires a specialized placement such as a class for autism or severe behavior disorders.

At the preschool level, programs such as Head Start and day-care centers funded to provide skills and training for underprivileged children have become widely available. Parenting programs are being offered by hospitals, mental health facilities, and many public schools. Such programs as the Active Parenting Program, developed by Michael Popkin of Atlanta, Georgia, which includes a video-based segment, are becoming increasingly popular.

School psychologists function as consultants in the planning, execution, and evaluation of primary prevention strategies. The practice of intellectual and achievement evaluation has, in many districts, been considerably expanded to include program development in cooperation with school counselors at both the elementary and secondary levels.

Many schools are now mandated to provide information pertaining to personal protection, ranging from ''stranger danger'' to recognizing and reporting sex abuse at an early age. A myriad of programs such as Children Are People

(CAPS, from American Guidance Services) are available. Local community agencies, such as the Young Women's Christian Association (YWCA), offer awareness programs that can be previewed and utilized.

In addition to these formalized instructional programs, psychologists are often involved in coordinating and/or running small group counseling sessions. Groups often center around such topics as adjusting to a new school, coping with bullies, divorce, stepfamilies, drug abuse in the home, making friends, and reducing negative behavior patterns.

The public often perceives drug education programs in terms of only secondary schools. Awareness and prevention programs may, however, begin as early as kindergarten. Some districts employ chemical awareness coordinators. Within each building, starting at the elementary level, a team approach to providing information and enhancing awareness is established. The school psychologist is, once again, an integral and invaluable member of the team. Working in concert with local school personnel and parents, mutual concerns are diagnosed, common goals are established, and intervention strategies are developed.

At the secondary and tertiary levels of prevention,* pathological behaviors that have already occurred (teen pregnancies, substance abuse, contracting of (acquired immunodeficiency syndrome [AIDS], suicide attempts) are dealt with through the employment of remediation and/or assistance techniques. School psychologists must have an extensive knowledge of human behavior patterns, which is crucial to the development of intervention strategies if they are to be successful.

Some districts subject prevention programs to the rigors of research. This, too, incorporates the skill of the psychologist. If a program is applauded by school and community, the most significant problem may lie in attempts to establish control groups. Few parents are willing to deny their children access to current, potentially valuable information. Every aspect of the research design should be developed and evaluated to provide the best information possible for the enhancement of the nonacademic areas of a school system.

REFERENCES

Fagan, T. K., and P. S. Wise. (1994). *School psychology past, present, and future.* White Plains, NY: Longman.
Wonderly, D., J. Kupfersmid, R. Monkman, J. Deak, and S. Rosenberg. (1979). Primary prevention in school psychology: Past, present, and proposed future. *Child Study Journal* 9, 163–179.

                                                              Barbara W. Wonderly

PRIMARY MENTAL HEALTH PROJECT. The Primary Mental Health Project (PMHP) is a school-based program for early detection and prevention of young children's school adjustment problems. With ongoing changes and refinements, it has been in continuous operation since 1957. PMHP serves socioculturally diverse populations of young children in need.

PMHP has four main emphases: (1) it focuses on primary grade children before problems develop and worsen; (2) it uses a screening process, including brief objective screening measures, to identify systematically children in need as soon as possible; (3) its primary direct-help agents are carefully selected, trained, closely supervised paraprofessionals* called child associates; and (4) the school-based mental health professional's role features a new set of activities that include selection, training, and supervision of child associates; conducting screening to detect children at risk; and acting in a consulting, coordinating capacity with teachers and other school personnel. This program brings needed help to children sooner and sharply expands the reach of effective services.

The screening process profiles primary grade children's school problems and competencies early and systematically. Most referrals begin when teachers or parents observe signs of ineffective functioning. An initial assignment conference evaluates the child's situation and establishes appropriate intervention* goals and strategies. Child associates then see children in a playroom setting. School-based mental health professionals (e.g., school psychologists,* school social workers, or counselors) provide not only basic on-the-job training for child associates but also more advanced training on special topics. Teachers, child associates, and mental health professionals exchange information and coordinate goals throughout the year. Periodic conferences review each child's progress and, if needed, realign goals and procedures. End-of-year conferences evaluate children's overall progress and formulate recommendations for the next year. PMHP consultants visit schools regularly to provide stimulation and consider challenging cases. By helping professionals provide training, consultation,* and resources to school staff and child associates, PMHP can attend to many more problems early, when they are still manageable, and prevent future difficulties.

More than fifty program evaluation studies, some internal and others external, support the following conclusions: (1) PMHP works effectively to strengthen young children's adjustment and academic achievement; (2) such short-term gains endure over time; (3) PMHP is effective with diverse populations reflecting major sociocultural differences and, thus, offers a vehicle for reaching heretofore underserved groups; and (4) the approach costs less than most other interventions for children experiencing problems (Cowen, et al., 1975; Cowen et al., in press).

Currently, more than 500 school districts around the world are implementing PMHP. These programs bring effective preventive services to tens of thousands of children. PMHP has influenced how school mental health services are conceptualized and delivered in many schools.

See also PREVENTION; PREVENTIVE EDUCATION.

REFERENCES

Cowen, E. L., M. A. Trost, R. P. Lorion, D. Dorr, L. D. Izzo, and R. V. Isaacson.

(1975). *New ways in school mental health: Early detection and prevention of school maladaption.* New York: Human Sciences Press.

Cowen, E. L., A. D. Hightower, W. C. Work, J. P. Pedro-Carroll, P. A. Wyman, and W. G. Haffey. (in press). *Primary Mental Health Project.* Washington, DC: American Psychological Association.

A. Dirk Hightower
Emory L. Cowen

PRIVATE PRACTICE. Private practice refers to the practice of providing psychological services to the public, not as the employee of another business or agency but working alone or with a group of colleagues. Psychologists in private practice both operate a business and provide professional services.

Private practice represents an increasing trend in psychology. There is concern by some in the profession that private practice may not be an economical, efficient response to the nation's mental health needs. It is seen as having contributed a great deal to psychology's statutory regulation in legislation, credentialing, and political activism at a cost to research, academic, and altruistic approaches that form the basis of the profession. On the other hand, psychologists are being recognized as "practitioners of the healing arts" and are thus offering their services alongside other such professionals.

Independent private practice is limited to those who can practice within the licensure laws of their states. In many states, the doctoral level of training is required for a license at the entry level for independent practice. For those with nondoctoral degrees, practice in the private sector may require supervision or that they be under the auspices of a licensed psychologist, within one's area of competency in experience and training, or under a separate certification* or licensure that regulates the services provided.

See also INDEPENDENT PRACTICE; LIABILITY INSURANCE; LICENSING; NONSCHOOL SETTINGS; STATE BOARD OF EXAMINERS IN PSYCHOLOGY; THIRD-PARTY REIMBURSEMENTS.

REFERENCES

Kendall, P. C., and J. D. Norton-Ford. (1982). *Clinical psychology: Scientific and professional dimensions.* New York: Wiley.

Phares, E. J. (1992). *Clinical psychology: Concepts, methods, and profession.* Pacific Grove, CA: Brooks/Cole.

Robbie N. Sharp

PRIVATE SCHOOL SETTINGS. A growing demand for "school choice" on the part of parents has led to an increase in the opportunity for school psychologists* to find employment in private settings. Such settings include independent and church-related schools, as well as cooperatives that serve both types of institution. Working in such schools is an aspect of private practice,* and psychologists must be aware of potential problems of discrimination and church/state separation. The notion that such a practice is "backdoor clinical psychology''* (Pryzwansky, 1989) has changed in recent years, because those who work in private settings are usually licensed or work under supervision, in what has become recognized as a legitimate specialty within the profession of school psychology.* In spite of this, there is a persistent claim that such practices jeopardize psychological practice in institutions (Oakland, 1986). Advantages associated with working in private schools usually include more professional freedom and greater focus on student needs. Disadvantages lie in generally lower salaries, fewer benefits, and less job security. Because of this, it is estimated that, as the twentieth century comes to an end, fewer than 5 percent of school psychologists work in private settings.

See also NONSCHOOL SETTINGS; SALARY DETERMINATION; SCHOOL SETTINGS; TENURE.

REFERENCES

Oakland, T. (1986). Professionalism within school psychology. *Professional School Psychology* 1, 9–27.
Pryzwansky, W. (1989). Private practice as an alternative setting for school psychologists. In R. D'Amato and R. Dean (Eds.), *The school psychologist in nontraditional settings* (pp. 67–85). Hillsdale NJ: Erlbaum.

Donald M. Wonderly

PRIVILEGED COMMUNICATION. English law recognized a duty for witnesses to testify in court over 400 years ago. The rule that witnesses can be compelled to testify is based on the principle that the determination of justice requires full access to relevant information. However, the need for information in the determination of justice at times conflicts with the need to safeguard the trust and privacy essential to special relationships, such as the relationship between attorney and client.

Privileged communication is a legal term that refers to "the right of a person in a 'special relationship' to prevent the disclosure in legal proceedings of information given in confidence in the special relationship" (Fischer and Sorenson, 1996, p. 12). Special relationships protected in common law include attorney–client and husband–wife. Many states have enacted legislation to extend privilege to protect other special relationships, such as physician–patient and psychologist–client.

Privileged communication laws establish the right of the client* to prevent disclosure of confidential information in a legal proceeding. The client (or parent of a minor child) may voluntarily waive privilege, and then the psychologist must provide the relevant testimony. The psychologist has no independent right to invoke privilege against client wishes.

Practitioners need to consult their state laws to determine whether their state extends privilege to school psychologists.* In the absence of state legislation specifically granting them privilege, school psychologists can be required to testify in a legal proceeding. Even in states that grant privilege to school psychologists, the court may not view all disclosures to the psychologist as privileged. Most states allow the judge to waive privilege during a court proceeding to ensure justice. Psychologist–client privilege is typically waived in legal proceedings involving child abuse, danger to the client or others, court-ordered psychological examination of a client, and malpractice suits filed by a client against the psychologist.

See also CONFIDENTIALITY; DUTY TO WARN.

REFERENCES

Fischer, L., and G. P. Sorenson. (1996). *School law for counselors, psychologists, and social workers* (3d ed.). White Plains, NY: Longman.
Hummel, D. L., L. C. Talbutt and M. D. Alexander. (1985). *Law and ethics in counseling.* New York: Van Nostrand Reinhold.

Susan Jacob-Timm

PROBLEM-SOLVING ASSESSMENT. All psychological assessment involves problem solving on some level. However, problem-solving assessment has two functions: scanning problem behaviors and circumstances and analyzing problem situations in depth (Peterson, 1968). Problem-solving assessment is based on consultation* and structured interviews with teachers and/or parents.

Effective communication, both verbal and nonverbal, is basic to problem-solving assessment. Important factors include genuineness, listening and encouraging consultee verbalizations, empathy, questioning skills, clarification, summarization, and, at times, confrontation (Gutkin and Curtis, 1982). The following steps are utilized in problem-solving assessment:

1. Explain the problem-solving process and its purpose.
2. Define the problem behavior.
3. Prioritize multiple problems.
4. Define the severity of the problem.
5. Define generality of the problem.
6. Explore determinants of the problem behavior, including:
   a. Conditions that intensify the problem;
   b. Conditions that alleviate the problem;
   c. Caregivers' perceptions of the origin of the problem;
   d. Antecedents, personal and social influences; and
   e. Consequences.
7. Determine modification attempts.
8. Identify expectancies for improved behavior.
9. Summarize caregivers' concerns.
10. Explore each caregiver's commitment and motivation to work on the problem.

11. Have caregiver summarize the problems, treatment goals, and plans.

12. Discuss and mutually arrive at plans for the next step.

Problem-solving assessment is a basic technique for uncovering and clarifying caregiver concerns, problem settings, and possible contributions of individuals to intervention plans (Barnett and Carey, 1992).

See also BEHAVIORAL CONSULTATION; COLLABORATION; COLLABORATIVE CONSULTATION.

REFERENCES

Barnett, D. W., and K. T. Carey. (1992). *Designing interventions for preschool learning and behavior problems.* San Francisco: Jossey-Bass.

Gutkin, T. B., and M. J. Curtis. (1982). School-based consultation: Theory and techniques. In C. R. Reynolds and T. B. Gutkin (Eds.), *Handbook of school psychology* (pp. 577–611). New York: Wiley.

Peterson, D. R. (1968). *The clinical study of social behavior.* New York: Appleton-Century-Crofts.

Karen T. Carey

PROBLEM-SOLVING CONSULTATION. Because problem solving is the essence of consultation,* it follows that most models of consultation depict consultation as a problem-solving process in which consultant and consultee join forces to solve an identified problem (Zins and Erchul, 1995). One such model is behavioral consultation* (Bergan and Kratochwill, 1990), which breaks the process down into problem identification, problem analysis, plan implementation, and problem evaluation stages. Zins and Erchul (1995) similarly have described the problem-solving stages of school consultation as (1) establishing a cooperative partnership, (2) clarifying the problem, (3) analyzing the problem, (4) brainstorming and exploring intervention options, (5) selecting an intervention, (6) clarifying implementation procedures and responsibilities, (7) implementing the strategy, and (8) evaluating intervention effectiveness and following up.

Apart from underlying most recognized approaches to psychological consultation, problem solving has been considered a model of consultation in its own right (Gutkin and Curtis, 1982). These authors noted that the central feature of problem-solving consultation is a similar process consisting of seven steps: (1) defining and clarifying the problem, (2) analyzing the forces impinging on the problem, (3) brainstorming strategies, (4) evaluating and choosing among strategies, (5) specifying consultee and consultant responsibilities, (6) implementing the selected strategy, and (7) assessing the effectiveness of the strategy and recycling through the process if necessary.

See also CONSULTATION.

REFERENCES

Bergan, J. R., and T. R. Kratochwill. (1990). *Behavioral consultation and therapy.* New York: Plenum Press.

Gutkin, T. B., and M. J. Curtis. (1982). School-based consultation: Theory and
    techniques. In C. R. Reynolds and T. B. Gutkin (Eds.), *The handbook of school
    psychology* (pp. 796–828). New York: Wiley.
Zins, J. E., and W. P. Erchul. (1995). Best practices in school consultation. In A.
    Thomas and J. Grimes (Eds.), *Best practices in school psychology—III* (pp.
    609–629). Silver Spring, MD: National Association of School Psychologists.

William P. Erchul

PROCEDURAL SAFEGUARDS. In order to protect student rights, public school law outlines procedures schools must follow in making certain decisions about students. These procedural safeguards have their roots in the due process* clause of the Fourteenth Amendment of the U.S. Constitution. Under the Fourteenth Amendment, a state may not take away life, a liberty interest, or a property right without some sort of procedural fairness to safeguard citizens from wrongful infringement of rights by the government. Property rights include entitlements granted by statutory law, such as the right to a public school education and special education* for children with disabilities. The minimum requirements of due process are notice of what the state (school) proposes to do and why and the opportunity to be heard.

Statutory law grants pupils with disabilities the right to a free education appropriate to individual needs in the least restrictive setting. Special education law includes a number of specific procedural safeguards to prevent misclassification of students and to ensure that schools do not deny eligible children their entitlement. Many of these procedural safeguards involve the basic due process guarantees of notice and the opportunity to be heard. For example, special education law requires schools to implement procedures to ensure the parent's right to consent to a preplacement evaluation; right to notice prior to subsequent reevaluations*; right to participate in decision making regarding identification, placement, or educational planning; right to consent to, or refuse, the initial placement in special education; and right to written prior notice before changes are made in identification, evaluation, placement, or special services.

Special education law also grants both the parents and the school a right to a due process hearing on any disagreement regarding the identification, evaluation, placement, or education program of a child. The hearing* must be conducted by an impartial person at a time and place convenient to both parties, and each party has a right to be represented by counsel, to present evidence, and to confront, cross-examine, and compel the attendance of witnesses. Either party may appeal the decision of the hearing officer to a higher state authority or file a civil action in court.

See also INFORMED CONSENT; PARENT/GUARDIAN PERMISSION.

REFERENCE

Jacob-Timm, S., and T. S. Hartshorne. (1994). *Ethics and law for school psychologists*
    (2d ed.). Brandon, VT: Clinical Psychology.

Susan Jacob-Timm

PROCESS CONSULTATION. Process consultation is closely identified with the work of Edgar Schein, who provides the following definition: "a set of activities on the part of the consultant that help the client* to perceive, understand, and act upon the process events that occur in the client's environment in order to improve the situation as defined by the client" (1988, p. 11). Attention to process events is recommended in several strategies within organization development.

Process consultation has conceptual roots in Kurt Lewin's studies of group dynamics. Other notable influences include group dynamics training methods (piloted by the National Training Lab [NTL] Institute) and techniques for studying group process, the study of group relations and organizational processes in business and industry, and the work of Sherif (and others) who identified regularities in relations between and within groups. Since being proposed, the process consultation model has been applied in a wide array of public and private institutional settings.

The process consultation model allows the client and consultant to consider how problems are perceived and resolved within an organization. Schein (1988) identifies key assumptions underlying the process consultation model: (1) clients often are not aware or do not understand what is wrong within an organization. Clients benefit from assistance in diagnosing the nature and extent of their system's difficulties; (2) clients need direction and assistance in determining which services will deliver critically needed interventions; (3) most clients need the assistance of a consultant in identifying what to improve within an organization and how to improve it; (4) all forms of organization need help in becoming more effective in their functioning. Consultants can assist organizations to learn to diagnose and manage strengths and weaknesses; (5) understanding the culture of an organization is important to the consultant, who often will work with insiders to understand and apply information about the system's culture; (6) the consultant guides the client through problem-solving and decision-making activities. The responsibility for the selection of intervention goals and activities resides with the client; (7) the successful consultant succeeds in assisting the client to respond to immediate concerns and in preparing the client to apply diagnostic and intervention skills to address future organizational concerns (pp. 10–11).

The effective process consultant offers skills in interpersonal processes, individual processes, group processes, and intergroup processes. Schein emphasizes the importance of applying the skills to establish and define relationships with the client, conduct diagnostic interventions, influence (interpersonal, group, or intergroup) processes through confrontation, confront through the use of feedback, and coach, counsel, or provide structural suggestions.

In schools that have used process consultation interventions, consultants have been concerned with promoting the skills of listening, questioning, clarifying, and confronting (Schmuck and Runkel, 1985). Systematic problem solving is used to help individuals and groups move toward establishing problem solving as a rational, conscious, and public process for all participants. Success of a process consultation intervention in a school can be measured in terms of how effectively school personnel work together after the initial stages of diagnosis and planning. School personnel can be trained to become more successful in defining their problems and goals, identifying and tapping resources that support movement toward goals, and monitoring and evaluating the process and products of individual and group activities.

See also ORGANIZATION DEVELOPMENT THEORY; PROBLEM-SOLVING CONSULTATION; SYSTEMS AND ORGANIZATIONAL CONSULTATION.

REFERENCES

Schein, E. H. (1988). *Process consultation.* Vol. 1: *Its role in organization development* (2d ed.). Reading, MA: Addison-Wesley.
———. (1987). *Process consultation.* Vol. 2: *Lessons for managers and consultants.* Reading, MA: Addison-Wesley.
Schmuck, R. A., and P. J. Runkel. (1985). *The handbook of organization development in schools* (3d ed.). Palo Alto, CA: Mayfield.

Stewart W. Ehly

PROFESSIONAL IDENTITY. Identity formation, for the individual, is generally considered a process. That is, the development of the individual includes creating a cognitive structure that incorporates ideation about self. The process involves multiple reorganizations of identity's contents throughout the life span. Identity can never be said to be a finished product. In addition to an individual's self-generated ideas about self and identity, an identity can be partially defined by the observer. The observer remarks upon the behavior and characteristics of the individual, and this information has the potential to influence identity. School psychology's* professional identity has a developmental progression as well. The professional identity of school psychology, as defined historically by the observer, involved a series of landmark events that traced the evolution of the profession (Fagan, 1990). Development of an identity for school psychology began vaguely in the 1890s, with a blend of educational and psychological practitioners focused principally on psychoeducational assessment. The study of individual differences* and the use of standardized tests to segment school populations became an activity around which professional identity was organized. Arnold Gesell,* the first practitioner with the title of ''school psychologist,'' was much involved in the area of diagnostics. School psychology continued to enrich its identity during the 1900s by creating specialized journals, specialized training programs, state certification programs, American Psychological Association* (APA) accreditation,* a national association, and a national certification.* During this process of defining the identity of school psychology, a number of activities have been added to the original role of testing. The National Association of School Psychologists* (NASP) *Standards for the Provision of*

School Psychological Services (1992) is evidence of the expansion of the professional identity of school psychology. The standards suggest a comprehensive services delivery model that can be said to currently define school psychology's professional identity in terms of professional activities. Provision of a range of services, including consultation,* psychological and psychoeducational assessment, interventions,* supervision, research, and program planning and evaluation,* is now considered standard practice. Many school psychologists* today would add the goal of child advocacy* as an ethical component of their professional identity.

See also CERTIFICATION; LICENSING; LITERATURE IN SCHOOL PSYCHOLOGY; PROFESSIONAL STANDARDS.

REFERENCES

Fagan, T. K. (1990). A brief history of school psychology in the United States. In A. Thomas and J. Grimes (Eds.), *Best practices in school psychology—II* (pp. 913–929). Washington, DC: National Association of School Psychologists.

National Association of School Psychologists. (1992). *Standards for the provision of school psychological services*. Washington, DC: Author.

Dennis A. Tomlinson

PROFESSIONAL STANDARDS. A cornerstone of professionalism is self-control, or self-regulation. Professionals have generally maintained that their actions are best judged by their peers. The strength of a profession can be seen in its insistence on membership adherence to common standards for behavior (Oakland, 1986). Professional standards in school psychology* address training and accreditation,* service delivery, credentialing, and ethics.

A primary means of recognizing a profession is by its training. This was a primary concern of the Thayer conference* (Cutts, 1955), and recommendations were made for levels and content of training. The American Psychological Association* (APA) has developed and revised generic training standards for applied psychology, which have been used for accrediting doctoral programs since 1947 and school psychology programs since 1971. The National Association of School Psychologists* (NASP) developed standards for training programs and internships* in 1978 (revised 1984 and 1993). By its association with the National Council for Accreditation of Teacher Education* (NCATE), NASP's standards have been used to designate approved programs since 1986.

Services appropriately provided by school psychologists* have long been debated. In 1974, APA adopted generic standards for service providers. These were followed in 1981 with specialty guidelines in the various applied psychology areas. This was an effort to better define the qualifications held and nature of services provided by a specialist within the practice of psychology. NASP published its own standards in 1978 (revised 1984, 1992), intended as a guide to service organization and delivery at federal, state, and local levels. Standards related to particular practices also exist; for example, the APA has standards related to educational and psychological testing (1985) and computers (1986).

In an effort to protect the public, providers of certain services are required to obtain a credential, such as a license or certificate. In order to protect their profession, members have sought to develop and promulgate their own standards. APA has focused on independent practice* licensure, developing a model licensure act* for states to consider. NASP adopted credentialing standards in 1978 (revised 1985), which were meant to address both licensure* and certification.* In 1988, NASP implemented a national certification program to recognize school psychologists meeting NASP training and credentialing standards. Since the late 1960s, the American Board of Professional Psychology (ABPP) has awarded diplomas to school psychologists meeting its standards. ABPP recently initiated a specialty board for school psychology.

Ethical codes may serve to reduce the call for external regulation and control. By adopting codes of ethics,* professionals are agreeing to put the public welfare above personal self-interest. APA first adopted a code of ethics in 1953 (current edition, 1992). NASP adopted a code of ethics in 1974 (revised 1984, 1992).

See also DIPLOMATE; SPECIALTY TRAINING AND CREDENTIALING.

REFERENCES

Cutts, N. E. (Ed.). (1955). *School psychologists at midcentury.* Washington, DC: American Psychological Association.

Gutkin, T. B., and C. R. Reynolds (Eds.). (1990). *Handbook of school psychology* (section VI). New York: Wiley.

Oakland, T. D. (1986). Professionalism within school psychology. *Professional School Psychology* 1, 9–27.

Timothy S. Hartshorne

PROFESSIONAL STRESS/BURNOUT. Working in helping professions, such as school psychology,* can be simultaneously rewarding and frustrating. In the process of helping children, school psychologists* may encounter seemingly insurmountable obstacles (e.g., bureaucratic "red tape," inflexible or incompetent administrators, parents who deny that their children have difficulties, too many cases in too little time), leading to professional stress. Burnout is a consequence of, or a reaction to, professional stress in some individuals. According to Maslach and Jackson (1986), burnout has three components: emotional exhaustion (i.e., feeling that one cannot possibly meet all of the demands of the job); depersonalization (i.e., negative feelings about the people being served); and reduced personal accomplishment (i.e., feelings of professional incompetence and reduced productivity). Persons experiencing burnout often begin their professional careers with great enthusiasm and zeal. When confronted by the realities of job demands, however, such individuals may experience the components of burnout just described.

An initial exploration of stressful events in the professional lives of school psychologists was conducted by Wise (1985). In that study, the School Psychologists and Stress Inventory (Wise, 1985), a list of stressful events frequently encountered by school psychologists was presented; school psychologists were asked to rate the relative stressfulness of each of thirty-five events. The five most stressful events for the school psychologists responding to the survey were notification of unsatisfactory job performance; not enough time to perform job adequately; potential suicide cases; working with uncooperative principals and other administrators; and feeling caught between child's needs and administrative constraints.

Using the School Psychologists and Stress Inventory (Wise, 1985), along with the Maslach Burnout Inventory (Maslach and Jackson, 1986), Huebner (1992) found that burnout is a serious problem for many school psychologists. More than one-third of his respondents qualified as emotionally exhausted, while more than a fourth fitted into the reduced personal accomplishment category. Among the stressors contributing to burnout were items related to lack of resources (e.g., incompetent or inflexible supervisors, unavailability of test materials), time management (e.g., backlog of referrals), high risk to self and others (e.g., potential suicide cases), and interpersonal conflicts (e.g., meeting with resistant parents and teachers).

Antidotes to professional stress and burnout include forming professional support groups, improved supervision of school psychologists, organizational change strategies, and "generic" stress reduction strategies (e.g., regular exercise, dietary changes, meditation). Providing training in coping with professional stress and burnout has also been recommended.

See also ADMINISTRATIVE SUPERVISION; PROFESSIONAL SUPERVISION; RELAXATION TRAINING; STRESS REDUCTION THERAPY.

REFERENCES

Huebner, E. S. (1992). Burnout among school psychologists: An exploratory investigation into its nature, extent, and correlates. *School Psychology Quarterly* 7, 129–136.
Maslach, C. M., and E. Jackson. (1986). *Maslach Burnout Inventory* (2d ed.). Palo Alto, CA: Consulting Psychologist Press.
Wise, P. S. (1985). School psychologists' ratings of stressful events. *Journal of School Psychology* 23, 31–41.

Paula Sachs Wise

PROFESSIONAL SUPERVISION. Professional supervision may be defined broadly as a process that facilitates the effective delivery of school psychological services and promotes the continuing professional development* of practicing school psychologists.* Supervision is most typically an interpersonal activity between a designated supervisor and one or more supervisees but may take the form of "peer supervision" in which the role of "supervisor" passes among coequals depending on the activity being supervised. Professional supervision focuses primarily on maintenance and enhancement of the practicing school psychologist's competencies.

Historically, supervision of professional psychologists arose mainly in hospitals and clinics because, prior to World War II, most university-based graduate programs focused on academic preparation. There was little formal relationship between academic and professional training. Consequently, within the clinic/hospital settings, an apprentice-type model of supervision, closely resembling a counseling relationship, predominated. Following the formalization of professional psychology training in the late 1940s, other supervision models arose that were either more didactic or a combination of the didactic and counseling emphases. Supervision in school psychology* has been less counseling-oriented than in other areas of professional psychology. This stems from school psychology's close connection to education, in which supervision historically has been didactic and top-down (Murphy, 1981).

Although both National Association of School Psychologists* (NASP) and American Psychological Association* (APA) standards require some form of supervision for at least those school psychologists with three or fewer years of experience, a national survey by Zins, Murphy, and Wess (1989) found that fewer than a third of novice school psychologists received either individual or group supervision, and few school psychologists received more than an hour of professional supervision per week.

See also ADMINISTRATIVE SUPERVISION; INTERNSHIP SUPERVISION; PROFESSIONAL STANDARDS; PROFESSIONAL TRAINING MODEL.

REFERENCES

Knoff, H. M. (1986). Supervision in school psychology: The forgotten or future path to effective services? *School Psychology Review* 15, 529–545.

Murphy, J. P. (1981). Roles, functions and competencies of supervisors of school psychologists. *School Psychology Review* 10, 417–424.

Zins, J. E., J. J. Murphy, and B. P. Wess. (1989). Supervision in school psychology: Current practices and congruence with professional standards. *School Psychology Review* 18, 56–63.

William Strein

PROFESSIONAL TRAINING MODEL. Several models of graduate education have been utilized in school psychology,* which vary as a function of the level of training (i.e., master's, specialist, or doctoral). In the 1950s and 1960s, the scientist-researcher model was prominent in the few doctoral programs that existed in school psychology. At the nondoctoral level, programs tended to be derivatives of the clinical psychology* model. The 1973 Vail conference explored alternative models of training for applied psychologists. This resulted in a reaffirmation of the scientist-practitioner model, which was developed at the Boulder conference* in 1949. This model assumes that all applied psychologists receive basic course work in the core areas of psychology, including quantitative methods, personality, history and systems of psychology, developmental psychology, learning, motivation, cognition, social psychology, and biological bases of behavior. Course work in the applied specialization (e.g., school, counseling, or clinical psychology) is appended to this scientific core. Under the scientist-practitioner model, specialty preparation tends to be idiosyncratic to a given graduate training program. Conversely, the core psychology content tends to be fairly consistent from program to program.

During the late 1970s, the applied professional psychologist model was developed. This model focused on applied course work offered in graduate training programs and de-emphasized the core psychology content. The applied professional psychologist model resulted in the development of doctor of psychology (Psy.D.) programs, primarily in clinical psychology, during the 1970s and 1980s. An increase in the number of Psy.D. programs also was experienced in school psychology. In 1985, the National Association of School Psychologists* (NASP) revised its program accreditation standards by requiring both core psychology content and specialty content. This, in effect, was a reaffirmation of the scientist-practitioner model* recommended by the Boulder and Vail conferences. The continued emphasis on application while maintaining the scientific underpinnings of the profession has resulted in a steady increase in course requirements for graduate training programs. Brown and Minke (1986) identified twenty-six distinct areas of training in school psychology within doctoral and nondoctoral programs. By 1994, over forty areas of course work were identified. Areas of increased emphasis during that time included child therapy, family therapy,* educational intervention, neuropsychological therapy and assessment, early childhood assessment, advanced consultation techniques, crisis intervention, multicultural issues and techniques, group therapy,* and substance abuse interventions.

Recent studies of practitioners' continuing professional development suggest an increased need for applied doctoral training (Brown, 1994). Most recent studies (Brown and Minke, 1986; McMaster, Reschly, and Peters, 1989) on graduate training suggest that the scientist-practitioner model continues to dominate training in school psychology, as reflected in the stability of distribution of Ph.D., Ed.D., and Psy.D. programs. This is in contrast to the area of clinical psychology, in which the number of Psy.D. programs has increased steadily. School psychology continues to be confronted with integrating scientific method with practice at a time when the information and skill repertoire is increasing rapidly.

See also NATIONAL CONFERENCE ON LEVELS AND PATTERNS OF PROFESSIONAL TRAINING IN PSYCHOLOGY.

REFERENCES

Brown, D. T. (1994). Will the real school psychologist please stand up: Is the past a prologue for the future of school psychology? *School Psychology Review* 23, 589–600.

Brown, D. T., and K. M. Minke. (1986). School psychology graduate training: A
    comprehensive analysis. *American Psychologist* 41, 1328–1338.
McMaster, M. D., D. J. Reschly, and J. M. Peters. (1989). *Directory of school
    psychology graduate programs.* Washington, DC: National Association of
    School Psychologists.

Douglas T. Brown

PROFILE ANALYSIS. The concept of profile analysis, also known as ipsative
test interpretation (Cattell, 1944), is the intrascale process of comparing an examinee's individual subtest scores with the examinee's average subtest score.
The process assumes that the variability among a collection of scores* or the
variation of individual scores from an average score has inherent value in the
diagnosis of children's cognitive strengths and weaknesses. It is also believed
that certain patterns of subtest scores might be held in common among groups
of children with similar conditions (e.g., learning disabilities).

Though Cattell coined the term "ipsative test interpretation," and Davis
(1959) is best known for developing the working formula for implementation,
Kaufman (1979) made ipsative profile analysis popular with the Wechsler scales.
The process of ipsative profile analysis has been seriously challenged on methodological grounds in recent years.

REFERENCES

Cattell, R. B. (1944). Psychological measurement: Normative, ipsative, and interactive.
    Psychological Bulletin 51, 91–97.
Davis, F. B. (1959). Interpretation of differences among averages and individual test
    scores. *Journal of Educational Psychology* 50, 162–170.
Kaufman, A. S. (1979). WISC-R research: Implications for interpretation. *School
    Psychology Digest* 8, 5–27.

Bruce A. Bracken

PROGRAM APPROVAL. Most state educational agencies or state departments of education have an approval process for graduate training programs in
school psychology.* The approval requirements are usually quite specific, including the length of the program, number of hours of field experience, content
of the curriculum, nature of supervision, and requirements of the internship.*
Standards adopted by the state educational agencies are generally influenced by
the accrediting standards of professional organizations such as the National Association of School Psychologists* (NASP) and the American Psychological
Association* (APA). While APA and NASP provide voluntary accreditation,*
the state education agencies have the legal authority to impose standards on the
training programs as a requirement for gaining certification as a school psychologist* in the state. In several states, national accreditation and state approval
reviews are conducted cooperatively and concurrently. For a list of states employing program approval contact the National Council for Accreditation of
Teacher Education* (NCATE).

See also ACCREDITATION; COUNCIL ON POSTSECONDARY AC-
CREDITATION.

REFERENCES

Brown, D. T. (1990). Professional regulation and training in school psychology. In T.
     B. Gutkin and C. R. Reynolds (Eds.), *Handbook of school psychology* (pp.
     993–1009). New York: Wiley.
Fagan, T. K., and P. S. Wise. (1994). *School psychology: Past, present, and future.*
     White Plains, NY: Longman.
Woody, R. H., J. C. LaVoie, and S. Epps. (1992). *School psychology: A developmental
     and social systems approach.* Boston: Allyn and Bacon.

James W. Batts

PROGRAM EVALUATION. Program evaluation refers to the systematic process of gathering information about various components and effects of a program
in order to make objective judgments and decisions about that program. School
psychologists* engage in program evaluation activities in two broad areas: (1)
self-evaluation (evaluation of the implementation, efficiency, and effectiveness
of psychological services) and (2) evaluation of specific educational programs
and practices. Although evaluation activities are typically limited in school psychology* practice (and in most school districts), school psychologists nevertheless are often the most appropriately trained professionals available to conduct
evaluation activities in a school district.

Regardless of the subject of evaluation, program evaluation activities serve a
number of purposes: (1) identifying and clarifying program strengths, needs, and
modifications; (2) monitoring progress toward program goals; (3) identifying
patterns in a significant variable such as student achievement or service delivery;
(4) determining efficient and effective deployment of personnel and other resources; and (5) determining the degree of implementation of a given program
or activity.

Within school systems, school psychologists may design and carry out evaluation of intervention and instructional programs for individual students or
groups of students (from classrooms, to schools, to districts); they may evaluate
the relative costs and benefits of specific curricula or school organizations; they
may conduct a needs assessment* to identify key resources, strategies, or organizational structures; they may assess the impact of a given program on student achievement or behavior or compare the effects of several programs; and
they may assess the degree to which a new program has been implemented as
planned.

School psychologists also use program evaluation techniques to examine patterns in the delivery of their services, to identify service needs at a building or
district level, to identify staff development needs, to examine the relative cost-
effectiveness of various approaches to structuring services, and to compare dif-

ferent approaches to assessment or intervention. Accountability* practices are often conducted using program evaluation techniques.

In conducting program evaluations, school psychologists use a variety of measurement approaches: (1) opinion surveys/scales regarding perceived outcomes, degree of implementation, service needs, and consumer preferences; (2) documentation review, which addresses compliance with program procedures, costs, and timelines; (3) "focus groups" and other structured interactive procedures to assess consumer or staff satisfaction or perceived needs; (4) direct testing, such as assessment of reading skills to obtain objective outcome data, including group comparisons or time-series analyses; (5) product review (such as reviews of psychological reports) to compare goals and objectives with actual outcomes, as specified by an outcome checklist or other standard set of criteria for success; (6) direct observation of activities reflecting program implementation and/or outcomes; and (7) direct interviews with staff and/or consumers as an alternative to surveys regarding perceived outcomes and program implementation.

See also EXPERIMENTAL DESIGN; QUALITATIVE RESEARCH; TREATMENT INTEGRITY.

REFERENCES

Bennett, R. E. (1988). Evaluating the effectiveness of alternative educational delivery systems. In J. L. Graden, J. E. Zins, and M. J. Curtis (Eds.), *Alternative educational delivery systems: Enhancing instructional options for all students* (pp. 513–524). Washington, DC: National Association of School Psychologists.
McConnell, S. R. (1990). Best practices in evaluating educational programs. In A. Thomas and J. Grimes (Eds.), *Best practices in school psychology—II* (pp. 353–370). Washington, DC: National Association of School Psychologists.
Maher, C. A., and R. E. Bennett. (1984). *Planning and evaluating special education services.* Englewood Cliffs, NJ: Prentice-Hall.

Andrea Canter

PSI CHI. Psi Chi, founded in 1929, is the National Honor Society for Psychology. Its mission is to foster excellence in psychology, through both academics and research. Psi Chi largely operates through its chapters at individual colleges and universities. The chapters focus on both the induction of new members, which is based on academic excellence, and chapter activities, which promote the active exploration of the different facets of psychology by chapter members. Psi Chi convenes annually at the regional and national American Psychological Association* (APA) conventions, at which time national issues are discussed, and the election of officers is held.

REFERENCES

Cousins, R. H., C. Tracy, and P. J. Giordano. (1992). Psi Chi and Psi Beta: The two national honor societies in psychology. In A. E. Puente, J. R. Matthews, and C.

L. Brewer (Eds.), *Teaching psychology in America: A history* (pp. 403–427). Washington, DC: American Psychological Association.

Hunt, T. (1979). *History of Psi Chi: The national honor society in psychology.* Arlington, VA: Psi Chi.

Psi Chi National Honor Society. (1993–1994). *Chapter handbook.* Chattanooga, TN: Author.

Marie A. Sell

PSYCHODYNAMIC THERAPY. Psychodynamic therapy may be divided into three major branches: Freudian, Adlerian, and Jungian. Freudian or psychoanalytic therapy was originated by Sigmund Freud. Philosophically, Freudian therapy is deterministic, dualistic, and instinctual. Victorian-era Freudian therapy has evolved through neo-Freudian theorists such as Anna Freud, Karen Horney, and Henry Sullivan to its current use in object relations, self, and ego psychology.

Freudian personality is an interrelated energy system composed of the id (the source of psychic energy), the superego (the conscience and ego ideal), and the ego (the intermediary between the id and superego and the contact with the external world). The Freudian concept of mind is composed of the unconscious, preconscious, and conscious. Instincts or drives function as the motivation forces and direct psychological processes of the personality. Personality is developed through oral, anal, phallic, latency, and genital psychosexual stages. Maladjustment occurs when there is an inability to satisfactorily move through developmental stages (fixation). Fixation may result in repressed feelings, thoughts, and behaviors that reemerge in later life in maladaptive ways. Inability to resolve the Oedipus/Electra complex—castration fears in the male, penis envy in the female, and sexual love of the opposite-sex parent—is a major cause of later maladjustment. Displacement, repression, projection, reaction formation, and regression are adaptive defense mechanisms used to reduce anxiety associated with threatening situations and feelings. Taken to the extreme, these defense mechanisms serve to increase maladjustment.

Therapy commences with a comprehensive collection of conscious and unconscious material. Second, transference, the feelings the client has toward significant others of the past that are now directed toward, and manifested in, the therapist, is elicited. The therapeutic techniques of free association, dreams, fantasies, and projections are used to gain access to repressed material and create the transference. Finally, resolution occurs when insight and catharsis of major conflicts of the past have been worked out, and the client's attachment to the therapist is resolved.

Adlerian* or individual therapy was originated by Alfred Adler. It took root in America through the work of Rudolf Dreikurs's development of group therapy* and child guidance centers. Currently, it is extensively used in parent training programs and child counseling. Philosophically, Adlerian therapy is humanistic, holistic, phenomenological, teleological, and socially oriented. Theoretically, social interest or "belonging" is the primary motivator in the individual's drive toward superiority and a style of life. The family plays a major role as a socializing agent and determines how a person will attempt to work on the five major life tasks of friendship, occupation, love, spiritualness, and self. Maladjustment occurs because of fictional goals that were generated in childhood to fit into the family constellation but that have become mistaken and unrealistic goals in adulthood. When fictional goals interfere with a successful lifestyle, an inferiority complex is created.

Adlerian therapy progresses through four stages: establishment of the relationship, investigation of the lifestyle, interpretation of the lifestyle, and reorientation. Assessment of the lifestyle includes detailed analysis of the family constellation, birth order placement, early childhood recollections, and dreams. Dynamic interpretation of these patterns of "fitting in" to the family of origin is used to determine current life tasks and priorities and help the client gain insight into maladaptive fictional goals. Reorientation is designed to stop clients from safeguarding maladaptive behavior and become motivated enough to take risks necessary to change. Adlerian therapy uses a broad range of techniques, which include restatement, reflection, encouragement, paradoxical intention, interpretation, and confrontation.

Jungian or analytic therapy was originated by Carl Gustav Jung. Currently, it is used extensively in pastoral counseling and as the format for the Myers-Brigg Type Indicator, a popular personality assessment tool. Philosophically, Jungian therapy is genetic, transcendental, transpersonal, and spiritual. The Jungian concept of mind is composed of a conscious, which provides consistency and direction; a personal unconscious, which contains repressed material retrievable to memory; and a collective unconscious, which stores the genetically transmitted heritage of the culture. The Jungian ego consists of thoughts, feelings, and active memories and is the reality base for interaction with the environment. Covering the ego is the persona, which projects the everyday image of the person. The self is the personal unconscious, which is the unifying and stabilizing agent of the personality. The shadow comes from both the personal and collective unconscious and contains the primitive elements within us that are unacceptable to society. Anima and animus come from the collective unconscious and represent the feminine characteristics found in men and the masculine characteristics found in women. The self, shadow, and anima/animus are all archetypal or primordial images, which are inherited personality traits that are culturally and generationally transmitted. Maladjustment is seen as an imbalance between conscious and unconscious and the anima and the animus.

Jungian therapy involves a methodical exploration of the symbolic elements of the unconscious. The interpretation of dreams and what they attempt to compensate is the primary therapeutic technique. Individuation is the ultimate goal of therapy and occurs when the ego and shadow-self are in harmonic balance.

REFERENCES

Auld, F., and M. Hyman. (1991). *Resolution of inner conflict: An introduction to psychoanalytic therapy.* Washington, DC: American Psychological Association.
Campbell, J. (Ed.). (1971). *The portable Jung.* Translated by R.F.C. Hull. New York: Penguin Books.
Dinkmeyer, D. C., D. C. Dinkmeyer, Jr., and L. Sperry. (1987). *Adlerian counseling and psychotherapy* (2d ed.). Columbus, OH: Merrill.
Fine, R. (1979). *A history of psychoanalysis.* New York: Columbia University Press.
Porter, A. (Ed.). (1958). *Alfred Adler: What life should mean to you.* New York: Putnam's Capricorn Books.

Richard K. James

PSYCHOEDUCATIONAL CLINICS. Psychoeducational clinics provide a wide range of services associated with the practice of school psychology,* as well as specialized educational services. These clinics may be components of existing governmental agencies or private health care facilities or operated privately by school psychologists* and other licensed mental health and educational service providers.

The first school-based clinic was the Department of Scientific Pedagogy and Child Study established in the Chicago public schools in 1899 (later known as the Chicago Bureau of Child Study). The first child guidance clinic was established in Chicago by William Healy as the Juvenile Psychopathic Institute of Chicago in 1909. The focus of child guidance clinics changed from the initial purpose of evaluating juvenile delinquents and retardates to the examination of parent–child relationships in the 1920s. The first clinic to carry the name "psychoeducational clinic" was established in 1912 by Wallin* at the School of Education, University of Pittsburgh (Wallin, 1914). By the early 1930s, there were nineteen school-based clinics reported, and by the mid-1930s, 650 communities (primarily urban) were known to be receiving services by child guidance clinics in thirty-four states. The primary activities of these clinics included the classification of schoolchildren, supervision of speech classes, educational guidance, and conducting surveys and statistical analyses.

See also BUREAUS OF CHILD STUDY.

REFERENCES

Fagan, T. K. (1985). Sources for the delivery of school psychological services during 1890–1930. *School Psychology Review* 14, 378–382.
Reisman, J. R. (1976). *A history of clinical psychology.* New York: Wiley.
Wallin, J. E. W. (1914). *The mental health of the school child.* New Haven, CT: Yale University Press.

A. Jerry Benson

PSYCHOLOGY OF SCHOOLING. The concept of a psychology of schooling in contrast to that of school psychology* was popularized in the 1980s by Jack

Bardon* (1982, 1983). Bardon's conceptualization was put forth in an attempt to resolve differences between doctoral and nondoctoral practitioners, between the American Psychological Association* (APA) and the National Association of School Psychologists* (NASP), and between the present status of practice and the needs of future school psychologists.* Among his more controversial points of resolution was his recommendation that the title "school psychologist" be ceded to NASP and that APA proceed to develop a broader, doctoral specialization along the lines of "applied educational psychology, educator psychology, or practitioner educator psychology" (Bardon, 1983, p. 194).

A psychology of schooling implies a closer alliance to the knowledge base of educational psychology,* a shift from a mental health to an educational viewpoint, the recognition of learning as a lifelong process, the expansion of psychological applications to educational settings beyond the traditional elementary and secondary schools, and at least doctoral level of preparation as a professional psychologist. Bardon's conceptualizations were analogous to the Stage III school psychology level of practice discussed in his earlier book with Virginia Bennett. His ideas were heavily influenced by the positions in the 1960s of Susan Gray* (e.g., the data-oriented problem solver) and of Mary Alice White, both of whom saw school psychology as a distinct specialty of psychology and the need for role and setting expansion beyond traditional spheres of influence. The psychology of schooling concept permeated the thinking of the National School Psychology Inservice Training Network's* 1984 publication, *School Psychology: A Blueprint for Training and Practice.*

REFERENCES

Bardon, J. I. (1982). School psychology's dilemma: A proposal for its resolution. *Professional Psychology* 13, 955–968.

———. (1983). Psychology applied to education: A specialty in search of an identity. *American Psychologist* 38, 185–196.

Gray, S. W. (1963). *The psychologist in the schools.* New York: Holt, Rinehart, and Winston.

Thomas K. Fagan

PSYCHOPHARMACOLOGY. Psychopharmacology is the use of psychoactive substances in the treatment of emotional and behavioral dysfunctions. Prior to the 1950s, mental disorders were treated through the surgical technique of lobotomy. Although such surgery is considered barbaric by today's standards, the procedure was the only known method for subduing highly agitated patients. The technique was so highly valued that its developer, Egas Moniz, won a Nobel Prize in 1949.

The development in the early 1950s of antipsychotic drugs inaugurated the beginning of modern psychopharmacology. The first major breakthrough came with chlorpromazine (e.g., Thorazine). Chlorpromazine began as an anesthetic.

A French physician named Laborit, noting that chlorpromazine abolished anxiety and excitement, recommended the medication be investigated in the treatment of psychoses. The results were impressive, and modern psychopharmacology was launched. The use of chlorpromazine quickly altered the care of mentally ill patients and began the noteworthy release of thousands of inpatients in state mental hospitals. Today, Thorazine and other antipsychotic medications, termed neuroleptics (e.g., Mellaril, Haldol), are used in the treatment of autism, schizophrenia, Tourette's disorder, and severe aggression in children.

Many attempts were made to discover a substance that would have dramatic results on depression. Clinical trials with cocaine, amphetamines, and caffeine were attempted with little success. Monoamine oxidase inhibitors (MAOI) were first synthesized by Roche Laboratories in 1952 for the treatment of tuberculosis. When the mood-elevating properties of the medications were noted, clinical trials were initiated. Today, MAOIs are frequently prescribed in the treatment of childhood depression.

R. Kuhn, a Swiss psychiatrist, can largely be credited for the introduction of tricyclics (TCAs). The discovery of the tricyclic drug imipramine owes much to the development of chlorpromazine, for the two are similar in nature. Although imipramine proved ineffective in treating schizophrenia, Kuhn continued to explore its use and reported in 1958 that the drug had remarkable results in patients with deep depression. Another TCA drug, amitriptyline (Elavil), was synthesized in 1960. Today, the TCAs are the major mainstays of drug therapy for childhood depression, anxiety, and enuresis. TCAs also have been used to treat attention-deficit hyperactivity disorder (ADHD) when stimulant medication has failed.

Lithium, the element known worldwide since the 1960s as the most effective treatment for mania, was discovered in 1817 and purified in 1855. The medication was first used in the treatment of gout and seizure disorders. Then, in the 1940s, it was used as a salt substitute for cardiac and hypertensive patients. Many of these patients developed the now well-known toxic side effects due to overdosage. The resulting negative reputation, coupled with the lack of financial incentive by drug companies (an element cannot be patented), resulted in very slow acceptance of the substance. In 1949, physician Cade propelled lithium into the limelight by publishing a paper that cited the miraculous recovery of ten chronic and severe manic patients with lithium treatment. Today, lithium is used to treat manic-depression, depression, and severe impulsive aggression in children.

Stimulant medications such as Ritalin, Dexedrine, and Cylert are the most frequently prescribed drugs in pediatric psychopharmacology. Their efficacy in managing ADHD is well chronicled. Recent data document their effectiveness in treating oppositional, defiant, and conduct disorders as well.

See also PRESCRIPTION PRIVILEGES.

REFERENCES

Ayd, F. J. (1991). The early history of modern psychopharmacology.
    Neuropsychopharmacology 5, 71–84.
Healy, D. (1993). 100 years of psychopharmacology. *Journal of Psychopharmacology*
    7, 207–214.

LeAdelle Phelps

PSYCHSIM. PSYCHSIM is a simulation technique developed at Ohio State University in which a variety of practical on-the-job situations are simulated in school psychology* training (preservice) or through workshops (in-service). Needs of the participants are assessed, and simulation techniques are drawn from a variety of multimedia options, including discussion with feedback. The simulations are designed around a fictitious Monroe City, which is one of the twenty largest school systems in the country.
   See also TRAINING MODELS.

REFERENCES

Engin, A. W., and I. R. Klein. (1975). The effectiveness of a simulation technique as
    an integral part of a school psychology training program. *Journal of School
    Psychology* 13, 171–184.
Engin, A. W., and J. N. Miller. (1974). *PSYCHSIM: School psychology simulator.*
    Columbus, OH: University Council of Educational Administration.
———. (1975). The training of school psychologists through simulation: PSYCHSIM.
    Psychology in the Schools 12, 40–42.

Thomas K. Fagan

PUBLIC LAW 93-380: FAMILY EDUCATIONAL RIGHTS AND PRIVACY ACT. The Family Educational Rights and Privacy Act (FERPA), enacted in 1974, was sponsored by Senator James Buckley and, thus, was called the "Buckley amendment" in the early years of its enactment. It was an amendment to the Elementary and Secondary Education Act of 1965. The Russell Sage Foundation Conference Guidelines* for the collection, maintenance, and dissemination of student records (1969) influenced the content of FERPA. FERPA's regulations define records, specify the right to inspect, review, and request amendment of records, and includes the right to confidentiality of records. Also, the conditions of records disclosure are delineated.

   "Education records" are defined as any records maintained by the schools, or a party acting for the schools, that are directly related to the student. The term does not include records that are in the sole possession of the maker and not revealed to any other person except a substitute (often discussed as "notes"). The regulations specify other exclusions. The act defines a category of record, "directory information," that includes such things as name and address and degrees and awards received. This information can be freely released.

   The right to review and inspect records is accorded to parents, guardians, or a person acting as a parent in absence of parents or guardians or to an "eligible student," a student who has reached age eighteen or is attending an institution of postsecondary education. Annual notice is provided to these persons of their rights to inspect, review, and request amendments to the student's education records. A request to inspect records must be granted in a reasonable time but within no longer than forty-five days. The school must respond to requests for interpretations and explanations of education records.

FERPA is designed to protect the privacy of students and their families. The schools cannot disclose personally identifiable information from education records without written consent of the parents or eligible student. Certain exceptions are specified, that is, court order. Prior consent for disclosure is not required if disclosure is to other school officials who have a legitimate educational interest, to certain governmental officials, or to financial aid officials. Additional conditions for disclosure are specified.

The right to request an amendment to education records applies to amend information that is incorrect or inaccurate or violates the privacy or other rights of the student. The parent or eligible student has a right to a hearing if the school does not comply with the request to amend. Persons may file complaints with the U.S. Office of Education.

Psychological and educational test protocols have been deemed part of the student's educational record by policy statements by the Office of Special Education Programs.* Test protocols cannot be considered private notes. The parent can examine test protocols under school supervision but should not be allowed to copy test questions. The school is required to provide copies of protocols if the parent cannot come to school over a forty-five-day period due to illness or extended travel or if a due process hearing will have test questions introduced by either party as evidence.

Each school district must have a policy regarding access to education records. The school psychologist* can provide valuable assistance to ensure that the district's policies and procedures are in compliance with FERPA and sections of the Individuals with Disabilities Education Act (IDEA, Public Law 101-476*) which, in part, address records issues. With the use of computers to keep records, there is concern about unauthorized access and confidentiality of records.

See also PUBLIC LAW 94-142; PUBLIC LAW 101-476.

REFERENCES

Appendix D: Rules and regulations for PL 93-380 implementing section 438 (The Family Educational Rights and Privacy Act) (1982). In C. R. Reynolds, and T. B. Gutkin (Eds.), *The handbook of school psychology* (pp. 1158–1168). New York: Wiley.

Goslin, D. A. (1969). *Guidelines for the collection, maintenance and dissemination of pupil records.* Troy, NY: Russell Sage Foundation.

Jacob-Timm, S., and T. Hartshorne. (1994). *Ethics and law for school psychologists* (2d ed.). Brandon, VT: Clinical Psychology.

Public Law (P.L.) 93-380. Family Educational Rights and Privacy Act of 1974. (20 U.S.C. and 34 C.F.R.).

Paul G. Warden

PUBLIC LAW 94-142: EDUCATION FOR ALL HANDICAPPED CHIL-DREN ACT. Public Law 94-142 is known as the Education for All Handi-capped Children Act (EAHCA) and was enacted in 1975. After the 1954 landmark Supreme Court ruling, *Brown v. Board of Education,* declaring, under the equal protection clause of the Fourteenth Amendment, that states must pro-vide equal education to children regardless of their race, two cases addressed equal education for children with disabilities. *Pennsylvania Association for Re-tarded Children v. Commonwealth of Pennsylvania* (PARC, 1971, 1972) and *Mills v. Board of Education* (1972) spurred Congress, in part, to extend equal education to children with disabilities in 1975.

Public Law 94-142 mandated services for children ages three to twenty-one who had been identified with the following disabilities: mental retardation; hear-ing impairment, including deafness; speech and language impairment; visual impairment, including blindness; serious emotional disturbance; other health im-pairment; specific learning disability; and multihandicapped (two or more dis-abilities). These children also must require special education* and related services.*

Public Law 94-142 required child-find activities and nondiscriminatory testing and evaluation procedures. Once identified, the child's services were determined by a multidisciplinary team, including parents or guardians, to determine the most appropriate services (free, appropriate public education*/FAPE) for the child. Also, to the maximum extent appropriate, the child is to be educated with children who are not disabled (least restrictive environment*/LRE). The indi-vidual education plan* (IEP) is developed, specifying the nature, duration, and evaluation of services. The law provides procedural safeguards on provisions for recourse through a due process* procedure.

Public Law 94-142 was amended in 1986 by Public Law 99-457* to cover persons from birth through age two. In 1990, Public Law 101-476 changed the name to Individuals with Disabilities Education Act (IDEA).

REFERENCES

Jacob-Timm, S., and T. Hartshorne. (1994). *Ethics and law for school psychologists.* (2d ed.). Brandon, VT: Clinical Psychology.
Public Law (P.L.) 94-142. Education for All Handicapped Children Act of 1975. (20 U.S.C. and 34 C.F.R.).

Paul G. Warden

PUBLIC LAW 99-457. Public Law 99-457, enacted in 1986, amended Public Law 94-142,* the Education of Handicapped Act (EHA) of 1975. Public Law

99-457 established an additional subchapter, Part H, of the EHA, which extended services to infants and toddlers, ages birth through two years.

To be served under this law, infants and toddlers must have developmental delays in cognitive development, physical development, communication development, social or emotional development, or adaptive development. Services are provided in the home and through community settings. Services are prescribed in an individualized family service plan* (IFSP). This document is developed after a multidisciplinary assessment of the infant's or toddler's needs and strengths, and a family-directed assessment of resources, priorities, and concerns of the family has been conducted. A case manager assists the child and the family in receiving services, rights, and procedural safeguards. The law provides for recourse through a due process* procedure.

EHA and its provisions for infants and toddlers were amended in 1990 by Public Law 101-476, which amended the name to Individuals with Disabilities Education Act (IDEA).

REFERENCES

Jacob-Timm, S., and T. Hartshorne. (1994). *Ethics and law for school psychologists* (2d ed.). Brandon, VT: Clinical Psychology.
Public Law (P.L.) 99-457. Education of the Handicapped Amendments of 1986. (20 U.S.C. 1470).

Paul G. Warden

PUBLIC LAW 101-476: INDIVIDUALS WITH DISABILITIES EDUCATION ACT. The Individuals with Disabilities Education Act (IDEA), Public Law 101-476 (1990), was formerly called the Education of Handicapped Act (EHA) or the Education for All Handicapped Children Act (EAHCA), Public Law 94-142,* which was enacted in 1975. IDEA amended the name of the act and made some substantive changes.

After the 1954 landmark Supreme Court ruling, *Brown v. Board of Education,* declaring, under the equal protection clause of the Fourteenth Amendment, that states must provide equal education to children regardless of their race, two cases addressed equal education for children with disabilities. *Pennsylvania Association for Retarded Children v. Commonwealth of Pennsylvania* (PARC, 1971,72) and *Mills v. Board of Education* (1972) spurred Congress, in part, to extend equal education to children with disabilities in 1975.

IDEA has eight subchapters (often referred to as Parts A-H). Part A describes definitions and general provisions of the act. Part B, or Subchapter II, is permanent and does not require preauthorization and is the heart of the act. Subchapters III–VII include discretionary programs that were not permanently authorized. In 1986, Public Law 99-457* established the new subchapter VIII (Part H), which extended services to infants and toddlers. In 1990, regulatory changes were made to implement the 1990 amendments of PL 101-476, most notable of which were the additional categories of autism and traumatic brain injury. Again in 1991, Public Law 102-119 further amended Parts B and H of IDEA, focusing on preschool children and infants and toddlers.

IDEA mandates services for children from age six to twenty-one who have been identified with the following disabilities: mental retardation; hearing impairment, including deafness; speech and language impairment; visual impairment, including blindness; autism; traumatic brain injury; serious emotional disturbance; other health impairment; specific learning disability; and multihandicapped (two or more disabilities). These children also must require special education* and related services.* For children birth through five, they must have developmental delays in cognitive development, physical development, communication development, social or emotional development, or adaptive development.

IDEA requires child-find activities and nondiscriminatory testing and evaluation procedures. Once identified, the child's services are determined by a multidisciplinary team, including parents or guardians, to determine the most appropriate services (free, appropriate public education*/FAPE) for the child. Also, to the maximum extent appropriate, the child is to be educated with children who are not disabled (referred to as the least restrictive environment*/LRE). A document called the individual education plan* (IEP) is developed, specifying the nature, duration, and evaluation of services. The law provides procedural safeguards and provisions for recourse through a due process* hearing procedure.

For infants and toddlers birth to two years of age, services are provided in the home and through community settings. Services are prescribed in an individualized family service plan* (IFSP). This document is developed after a multidisciplinary assessment of the infant's or toddler's needs and strengths, and a family-directed assessment of resources, priorities, and concerns of the family has been conducted. A case manager assists the child and the family in receiving services, rights, and procedural safeguards. The manager coordinates all services across agencies and functions as a single contact point for the family.

School psychology,* a related service, has been dramatically transformed by IDEA and its predecessor, Public Law 94-142. Shortly after full implementation in 1977, there was a demand for more school psychologists* to provide assessment of children with disabilities. The demands for assessment have been attributed as a primary factor in narrowing the scope of services provided by school psychologists.

Currently, school psychologists are faced with a shift in role and function, with the emphasis on inclusion of children with disabilities in general education programs. Newer classroom-based assessment technologies are becoming necessary for school psychologists to remain helpful in the collaborative or consultation processes, with general education teachers and special education teachers serving children with disabilities in general education classrooms.

The shift to inclusion* has become controversial. Previous analyses of IDEA and relevant case law have indicated that the appropriateness of services (FAPE) takes precedent over the least restrictive environment* (LRE); however, there has been advocacy for full inclusion where all children with disabilities will be served in general education. Analysis of some recent case law indicates that a shift from emphasis on appropriateness to social development might be taking place, supporting the goals of advocates for full inclusion (Osborne and Dimattia, 1994).

See also NONBIASED ASSESSMENT.

REFERENCES

Jacob-Timm, S., and T. Hartshorne. (1994). *Ethics and law for school psychologists.* (2d ed.). Brandon, VT: Clinical Psychology.

Osborne, A. G., Jr., and P. Dimattia. (1994). The IDEA's least restrictive environment mandate: Legal implications. *Exceptional Children* 61, 6–14.

Public Law (P.L.) 101-476. Individuals with Disabilities Education Act, 1990. (104 Stat. 1103).

Tucker, B. P., and B. A. Goldstein. (1992). *The educational rights of children with disabilities: A guide to federal law.* Horsham, PA: LRP.

Paul G. Warden

PUBLIC RELATIONS AND SELF-PROMOTION. Public relations activities are necessary for communication of information and promotion of understanding between professionals and their audiences. Kelly (1990), in her description of public relations in educational settings, indicated that an improved public image for schools was needed historically in order to promote improvements in education. Public relations activities by schools continue to be important, according to Kelly, because of waning public confidence in education and increased competition for funding.

Public relations activities can include advertisements, announcements, direct communications, newspaper and magazine articles, television and radio appearances, and public speeches (Kelly, 1990). Public relations activities by school psychologists* can serve several purposes. Public relations can be used for self-promotion, including self-promotion of services to be provided within a school district as well as self-promotion of services to be provided in private practice.* Public relations can be used for promotion of the profession, for example, when school psychologists engage in a statewide campaign to inform the public about their roles. Public relations activities may also be used to provide services and information to an audience, such as when a school psychologist appears on a television news program to describe research on an educational issue.

The National Association of School Psychologists* (1992) and American Psychological Association* (1992) have specific ethical standards for public relations activities of school psychologists. If school psychologists are engaging in public relations activities for self-promotion, they must accurately represent all information about themselves, including training, expertise, experience, and credentials. The 1992 American Psychological Association ethical standards indicate that psychologists may directly solicit business from clients but must avoid false or deceptive solicitations or advertisements. School psychologists must not compensate media employees for publicity about them in a news item. If school psychologists are engaging in public relations activities for promotion of the profession or to provide information to an audience, they must base all information on sound educational and psychological theory, research, and practice and must ensure that all public statements are consistent with ethical standards.

See also CODES OF ETHICS; PROFESSIONAL IDENTITY.

REFERENCES

American Psychological Association. (1992). Ethical principles of psychologists and code of conduct. *American Psychologist* 47, 1597–1611.
Kelly, C. (1990). Best practices in building-level public relations. In A. Thomas and J. Grimes (Eds.), *Best practices in school psychology—II* (pp. 171–181). Washington, DC: National Association of School Psychologists.
National Association of School Psychologists. (1992). *Professional conduct manual.* Silver Spring, MD: Author.

Patti L. Harrison

PUBLISHERS. The term ''publishers,'' as applied to school psychology,* describes the business entities that develop, print, and market textbooks and tests used by school psychologists* (as well as other applied and academic professionals). Most school psychologists become involved with representatives of publishers primarily because they buy products of publishers; these products are displayed in catalogs distributed by the publishers. To a lesser extent, school psychologists become involved with publishers because they write textbooks or develop tests in collaboration with publishers. Typically, publishers specialize; that is, publishers focus on certain segments of the market, and some specialize more in the publication of tests, and others in books. Because school psychologists have invested considerable portions of their work time conducting assessment activities, test publishers have been particularly salient.

Historically, two publishers well known to school psychologists are the Stoelting Company and Houghton-Mifflin, publisher of earlier editions of the Stanford-Binet Intelligence Scale. Early literature related to the practice of school psychology was published by university presses (e.g., Columbia, Ohio State, Pennsylvania, Yale), book companies (e.g., Little, Brown; Macmillan; World Book), a few state departments of education (e.g., Connecticut, New York), and the U.S. Government Printing Office. Other highly relevant publishers for school psychologists include Allyn and Bacon; American Guidance Service; Clinical Psychology Publishing Company; Consulting Psychologists Press; Educational Testing Service; Grune and Stratton; Guilford Press; Wiley; Longman Publishing Group; Merrill/Macmillan; Pro-Ed; Pergamon Press; Prentice Hall; the Psychological Corporation; Psychological Assessment Resources; Riverside Publishing Company; Scholastic Testing Service; and Western Psychological Services.

See also LITERATURE IN SCHOOL PSYCHOLOGY.

R. Steve McCallum

PUPIL PERSONNEL SERVICES. Pupil personnel services (PPS) emerged from the expansion of compulsory schooling* in the early twentieth century and from the work of Arch O. Heck in the 1930s. These services are supportive of general administrative and educational services in school systems and may be referred to as ancillary, pupil, special, or support services. Hummel and Bonham (1968) identify ten service areas: counseling and guidance, psychological, school social work, school health, speech and hearing therapy, attendance, child accounting, pupil appraisal, remedial instruction, and special education.* Ferguson (1963) included psychiatric services. Increased school system responsibility for children with disabilities now includes physical therapy and occupational therapy. Primary functions of PPS include supportive-consultative, special instruction, and research and data processing. PPS organizations include the National Association of Pupil Personnel Administrators (NAPPA), founded in 1966, and the National Alliance of Pupil Service Organizations (NAPSO), founded in 1978.

See also RELATED SERVICES; TEAM APPROACH.

REFERENCES

Ferguson, D. G. (1963). *Pupil personnel services.* New York: Center for Applied Research in Education.

Hummel, D. L., and S. J. Bonham. (1968). *Pupil personnel services in schools.* Chicago: Rand-McNally.

Thomas K. Fagan

Q

QUALITATIVE RESEARCH (ETHNOGRAPHY). The term "qualitative research" refers to a paradigm of inquiry that includes numerous research approaches. The paradigm distinguishes itself from traditional quantitative research at the philosophical level (Guba, 1990). Qualitative research is predicated upon the epistemological assumption that what is knowable has no absolute truths. Moreover, the ontological assumption that the relationship between the researcher and what is being studied is necessarily enmeshed also distinguishes qualitative research from traditional research. The methodologies employed by qualitative researchers, therefore, attempt to provide descriptions of the socially constructed truths and meanings of people within specific contexts (Erickson, 1986).

Another feature of qualitative research is that its approaches (e.g., ethnography, phenomenology, grounded theory, case study) originated in disciplines outside education or psychology. For example, ethnography originated and is a mainstay within the discipline of anthropology, while phenomenology emerged from philosophy. Ethnographic research is field-based, with the researcher coexisting with the subjects of interest, interacting with them in their natural environment. Cultural anthropologists actually move into the culture being studied. It is believed that to understand the meaning of behaviors, one must become intimate with the nuances that define the culture. Since ethnographers attempt to understand behaviors and cognition as meaningful within the context of the culture being studied, the studies often continue for years. These time constraints, along with the fact that school environments are familiar settings to educational ethnographers, led educational researchers to create a research approach called microethnography. In these studies, the researcher spends less time immersed in the culture. Often, rather than living among the subjects for years, researchers immerse themselves within a school setting for a semester or academic year. Unlike true enthographies, microethnographies allow the researcher to leave the culture being studied. For example, the time spent during the school day and important evening school events often represents the time the researcher spends in the culture. An example of an ethnographic study being conducted today considers the interfacing of teachers and students with the new technologies introduced into schools.

To conduct ethnographic research, daily field notes are taken, interviews are conducted, and observations are made. Field notes are logged, and new hypotheses are created and tested in the field. This recursive process continues until the ethnographer believes a thorough understanding of the culture and the meaning of behaviors in the culture exists. For example, underachievement, violence, and teen pregnancy all can be understood in a manner different from the perspective that traditional research provides when the meaning of these behaviors is interpreted within the school culture.

See also IDIOGRAPHIC VERSUS NOMOTHETIC RESEARCH; NATURALISTIC OBSERVATION.

REFERENCES

Erickson, F. (1986). Qualitative methods in research on teaching. In M. C. Wittrock (Ed.), *Handbook of research on teaching* (3d ed., pp. 119–161). New York: Macmillan.
Guba, E. (1990). *Paradigm dialogue.* Newbury Park, CA: Sage.

Tracy L. Cross

QUALITY CIRCLES. Quality circles (QCs) are small groups (three to twelve members) that meet on a regular or as-needed basis to discuss problems and solutions in the workplace. Participation usually is voluntary, but employees may be assigned by a supervisor to a QC in order to deal with a problem that is shared by the participants.

QCs are based on the belief that employee empowerment, manifested by their participation in these mutual problem-solving groups, will improve the quality of the workplace and often will result in a decision that is better than what management would have developed on its own. Further, studies have shown that decisions reached by the constituents of a problem (i.e., those most closely associated with its effects) are more likely to be implemented by those constituents.

Some research suggests that groups should be limited to about five participants; others believe the ideal number is whatever the leader can manage. The benefits of a QC should include a clearer definition of the problem, increased feeling of belonging to an organization, reduced stress, and a willingness to explore problems rather than hiding them.

Japanese business corporations are credited with starting the idea of QCs; American companies copied this idea throughout the 1970s and 1980s. In the late 1980s, it became clear that there was little research to support the value of the QC movement. However, it has continued to be popular, especially in Japan, and current research is attempting to determine the reasons for its successes and failures.

See also ORGANIZATIONAL DEVELOPMENT THEORY; SYSTEMS AND ORGANIZATIONAL CONSULTATION.

REFERENCES

Ledford, G. E., G. G. Lawler, and S. Mohrman. (1988). The quality circle and its variations. In J. P. Campbell and R. J. Campbell (Eds.), *Productivity in organizations* (pp. 255–294). San Francisco: Jossey-Bass.
Wood, R., F. Hull, and K. Azumi. (1983). Evaluating quality circles: The American application. *California Management Review* 26, 37–53.

Thomas J. Kampwirth

R

RATIONAL-EMOTIVE PSYCHOTHERAPY. Rational-emotive psychotherapy is a counseling method that emphasizes logical reasoning and cognitive processes to resolve emotional difficulties. Developed by Albert Ellis as rational-emotive therapy (RET), the approach has been used widely and proven very adaptable in a broad array of settings.

RET is based on several assumptions proposed by Ellis: (1) people condition themselves, through self-talk, to feeling disturbed, rather than being conditioned by external sources; (2) people, through cultural and biological tendencies, think irrationally and needlessly disturb themselves; (3) people invent disturbing thoughts and keep themselves disturbed about their disturbances; (4) people can change their thoughts, emotions, and behaviors. They can train themselves to remain minimally disturbed in their lives (Corey, 1991).

Psychotherapists during RET use teaching, suggestion, persuasion, and homework assignments to challenge clients to adopt more rational belief systems. Therapists urge clients to validate observations and to think scientifically. Relying on cognitive and behavioral techniques, therapists vary in their personal styles and strategies with clients.

See also COGNITIVE BEHAVIOR MODIFICATION; COGNITIVE THERAPY.

REFERENCES

Corey, G. (1991). *Theory and practice of counseling and psychotherapy* (4th ed.). Pacific Grove, CA: Brooks/Cole.
Ellis, A. (1962). *Reason and emotion in psychotherapy.* New York: Stuart.
————. (1989). Rational-emotive therapy. In R. J. Corsini and D. Wedding (Eds.), *Current psychotherapies* (4th ed., pp. 197–238). Itasca, IL: F. E. Peacock.

Stewart W. Ehly

READINESS. "Readiness" is a term in school psychology* that is frequently used to describe the extent to which a child is developmentally, socially, educationally, and emotionally "ready" to participate in, and benefit from, the rigors of formal education or to acquire a specific skill (e.g., reading). Readiness implies an entry-level knowledge of social rules (e.g., following the lead of an adult; adhering to established rules of order, conduct, and discipline), personal self-help skills (e.g., is toilet trained; can tie one's own shoes), foundational educational attainment (e.g., basic understanding of numbers, letters, colors, sizes, shapes), functional academic skills (e.g., paper-pencil skills; proper use of scissors), and emotional development (e.g., doesn't cry without reasonable cause). Given an entry-level ability in each of these areas, it is assumed that the child is sufficiently prepared to benefit from the activities and structure found in a regular kindergarten classroom or to begin acquiring a specific academic skill, such as reading.

REFERENCES

Bracken, B. A. (Ed.). (1991). *Psychoeducational assessment of preschool children* (2d ed.). Needham Heights, MA: Allyn and Bacon.
Garwood, S. G. (Ed.). (1983). *Educating young handicapped children: A developmental approach.* Rockville, MD: Aspen.

                                                                                        Bruce A. Bracken

REALITY THERAPY. Reality therapy is a cognitive-behavioral-based therapy that was formulated in the 1960s by William Glasser. It has been extensively employed in corrections and schools. Theoretically, every action the individual undertakes is an attempt to control basic perceived needs such as survival, belonging, power, and freedom. The individual's perception about what needs are required for personal control and the way the individual goes about gaining that control result in a personal identity. Identity relates more to one's search for acceptance as opposed to doing things. Thus, a success identity is a social force based on experiencing both love and worth from others. A failure identity is learned early in life because of a lack of love and/or the inability of the individual to do something worthwhile and is the major cause of later maladjustment.

    Reality therapy focuses on current acting and thinking and is concerned little with past behavior. Current needs and perceptions are explored in order to determine the client's values and priorities. The client evaluates current behavior and makes a judgment as to whether it is fulfilling needs. If it is not, the client then develops a simple, positive behavioral plan of action that has specific, realistic, and attainable goals and makes a commitment to carry out the behavioral plan.

    Reality therapy is a "no punishment" approach that believes that plans fail, but people do not. It is also a "no excuses" therapy that holds people responsible for their actions and actively confronts them when they attempt to disown or disavow their inappropriate behavior. Thus, if the plan fails, therapist and client* conjointly confront what the problem is, troubleshoot what needs to be changed, and start a new plan.

REFERENCES

Glasser, W. (1969). *Schools without failure.* New York: Harper and Row.
———. (1986). *Control theory in the classroom.* New York: Harper and Row.
Wubbolding, R. E. (1988). *Using reality therapy.* New York: Harper and Row.

Richard K. James

RECIPROCAL DETERMINISM. Albert Bandura (1986) proposed an answer to the question of why people behave as they do that went beyond the ideas of either the environmentalists or those who emphasize inherited dispositions and traits. His proposition of reciprocal determinism consists of a three-way interaction of the environment, the person's behavior, and the person. Each of the three aspects influences, and is influenced by, the other two.

This work, called social cognitive theory, is a revision of social learning theory. Critical to the practitioner is the understanding of how and what the person learns. Actions of the person are controlled by self-regulated behavior. The person learns performance standards directly or vicariously (observational learning); these standards become the basis of self-evaluation. Also, critical to self-regulation is perceived self-efficacy, which is learned through experience or observation. One's moral code is an internalized set of performance standards from which departure can bring self-contempt. Persons find themselves more or less free, that is, have more or fewer options. Constraints to personal freedom are either personal (i.e., incompetence, fear, or faulty cognitive processes) or social (i.e., prejudice).

The application of modeling* (observational learning) has been employed to inhibit, disinhibit, or facilitate behavior. The most common application is the reduction of fears. Cognitive behavior modification* (CBM) employs modeling and self-efficacy training.

See also COGNITIVE THERAPY.

REFERENCES

Bandura, A. (1986). *Social foundations of thought and action: A social cognitive theory.* Englewood Cliffs, NJ: Prentice-Hall.
Hergenhahn, B. R., and M. H. Olson. (1993). *An introduction to theories of learning* (4th ed.). Englewood Cliffs, NJ: Prentice-Hall.
Nietzel, M. T., D. A. Bernstein, and R. Milich. (1991). *Introduction to clinical psychology* (3d ed.). Englewood Cliffs, NJ: Prentice-Hall.

Paul G. Warden

REEVALUATIONS. Federal regulations require that the individual education plan* (IEP) of each student with a disability be reviewed annually and that an evaluation of the student be conducted every three years or more frequently, if conditions warrant or if the student's parent or teacher requests an evaluation. Numerous researchers have questioned whether "testing" necessarily needs to be part of the process. Ross-Reynolds (1990) advocates strongly that evaluation must be linked to effective intervention. Numerous authors have suggested that annual and triennial evaluation should be "curriculum-based."

Reevaluation should meet four objectives: (1) to determine whether the student's program is implemented as intended and needed, (2) to determine how much progress the student has made in the last three years, (3) to determine whether the student's classification and placement are appropriate, and (4) to determine what changes need to be recommended in the student's program.

See also ASSESSMENT (DIRECT AND INDIRECT); CURRICULUM-BASED ASSESSMENT.

REFERENCES

Brandt, J. E. (1993). Triennial reevaluation of special needs students: A review of best practices and other considerations. *The annual convention of the National Association of School Psychologists,* Washington, DC. (ERIC Document)

Ross-Reynolds, J. (1990). Best practices in conducting reevaluations. In A. Thomas and J. Grimes (Eds.), *Best practices in school psychology—II,* Vol. 2 (pp. 195–206). Washington, DC: National Association of School Psychologists.

John E. Brandt

REFERENT POWER. Referent power is Person A's ability to influence Person B based on B's perception of some desirable and/or similar personal quality in A (French and Raven, 1959). Referent power and reward, coercive, legitimate, expert, and informational power constitute six recognized social power bases. A teacher-consultee may attribute referent power to a school psychologist*-consultant when the teacher perceives the psychologist to serve in a highly desirable professional role. Martin (1978) proposed that school psychologists should regard consultation* as an influence process and that, as consultants, they should develop their referent and expert power* in order to increase effectiveness. In addition, Erchul (1992) discussed referent power and the other five power bases in an examination of school psychologists' interactions with parents.

See also AUTHORITY; POWER.

REFERENCES

Erchul, W. P. (1992). Social psychological perspectives on the school psychologist's involvement with parents. In F. J. Medway and T. P. Cafferty (Eds.), *School psychology: A social psychological perspective* (pp. 425–448). Hillsdale, NJ: Erlbaum.

French, J. R. P., and B. H. Raven. (1959). The bases of social power. In D. Cartwright (Ed.), *Studies in social power* (pp. 150–167). Ann Arbor, MI: Institute for Social Research.

Martin, R. (1978). Expert and referent power: A framework for understanding and
    maximizing consultation effectiveness. *Journal of School Psychology* 16, 49–55.

William P. Erchul

REFERRAL PROCESS. The method by which children and families come to
the attention of pupil personnel* workers for direct or indirect professional service delivery is referred to as a referral process. The process can be formal or
informal and involve an individual specialist or a team of specialists and may
result in consultation* services, assessment,* and placement in special education* programs.

The referral process (to pupil personnel workers) is very important, as inappropriate referrals have been shown to provide disproportionate utilization of
available resources and may lead to inappropriate placements for children, particularly of minority or low socioeconomic students in categorical programs.

The total proportion of children in the United States receiving special education services has remained around 10 percent, though the relative percentages
of children with various disabilities within this population have fluctuated with
time and fluctuate by state (Meyen, 1995). Considering that 3–5 percent of the
schoolage population are referred yearly, the integrity of the referral process is
important.

Referrals for services come from two main sources: persons within the school
system and parents or agency professionals outside the school system. Each
school system has established referral procedures, including screening, prereferral, and formal referral to identify children with suspected disabilities.

Concerns about children's learning and behavior within the school system
generally follow procedures allowing specialists within the system to attempt
interventions* or do informal assessments prior to a formal referral. The concern
that most students who were referred were eventually deemed to be disabled
has led to initiation of prereferral procedures designed to identify problems and
implement interventions to reduce the number of unnecessary, multifactored
assessments.

The prereferral process usually involves a building-level team* of professionals who gather information regarding the child and then recommend, initiate,
and evaluate interventions within the child's building. If such methods of intervention are unsuccessful, a referral for multidisciplinary evaluation may occur.

The Education for All Handicapped Children Act (Public Law 94-142*),
passed in 1975, and the updated Individuals with Disabilities Education Act
(IDEA, Public Law 101-476*) provide the framework for the referral process,
subsequent evaluation, and provision of services for children deemed to have
disabilities.

The formal referral process is initiated when parents provide written consent
indicating they are aware of the nature of the assessment and possible programmatic recommendations and understand they are to be full participants in the
process.

See also CLASSIFICATION: EDUCATIONAL; INFORMED CONSENT; MULTICULTURAL TRAINING; MULTIDISCIPLINARY TEAM; NONBIASED ASSESSMENT; PREREFERRAL ASSESSMENT; PREREFERRAL INTERVENTIONS; PUBLIC LAW 101-476.

REFERENCE

Meyen, E. L. (1995). Legislative and programmatic foundations of special education. In E. L. Meyen and T. M. Skrtic (Eds.), *Special education and student disability* (pp. 35–95). Denver: Love.

Alex Thomas

REGIONAL ACCREDITORS. Nine regional associations currently accredit educational institutions ranging from high schools to colleges and universities. These organizations are identified by names suggestive of geographical areas (e.g., the Southern Association of Colleges and Schools). However, some of the states actually included in some regions might not necessarily be associated with that region.

The regional associations award "institutional," as opposed to "specialized," accreditation, focusing on the institutions as a whole, rather than on professional preparation programs within institutions. Evaluation of the institution is conducted in accordance with the mission that the institution has undertaken. In other words, the institution is judged with regard to how well it accomplishes the goals that it has established. Criteria and standards tend to be generic in nature and are largely intended to ensure the overall quality and stability of the institution. Attention is given to conditions that should exist for all students, such as general education requirements, as opposed to curricular requirements reflective of specific majors or specialties. In addition, consideration is given to many institutional variables that are not directly related to academic programs. For example, standards for the accreditation* of high schools typically address issues relating to support services for students.

All of the regional accrediting associations are independent, nongovernmental organizations. Until the dissolution of the Council on Postsecondary Accreditation* (COPA) on December 31, 1993, all of these associations were members of that organization. Although the eventual status of the agencies that emerged following the dissolution of COPA remains unclear, the regional accreditors initially joined one or more of the new associations (e.g., the Commission on Recognition of Postsecondary Accreditation).

The decision of an institution to seek accreditation by a regional association is technically voluntary. However, many decisions are either based on accreditation by a regional or national accrediting agency (e.g., admission to most colleges is contingent on graduation from an accredited high school; specialty accreditation for a professional preparation program requires that the institution administering the program is accredited; eligibility for federal funding is contingent on accreditation of the institution) or are influenced by institutional accreditation (e.g., foundations providing external funding, prospective students). Consequently, institutions face strong pressure to seek accreditation through a recognized regional or national accrediting agency.

REFERENCE

The Council on Postsecondary Accreditation. (1989). *The COPA handbook.* Washington, DC: Author.

Michael J. Curtis

REGISTRATION. The practice of psychology has become regulated by state legislation through the enactment of licensure laws. Each state has a regulatory board that governs the title and practice of psychology in its jurisdiction.

Licensing* is the process by which the regulatory board controls and regulates the professional practice of psychology. The state laws, however, may require only certification,* in which only the title is protected. In these instances, individuals who are deemed appropriate through education and training must be certified by the state regulatory board in order to use the title "psychologist" or the term "psychological" in reference to their practice. This term is also used by many state boards of education that issue a school psychology* certificate for practice in the schools when such practice is exempt in the state licensing law. A practice act that is more restrictive regulates both title and function and, as such, makes it illegal for any person not licensed or exempted to engage in the practice of psychology as defined by the law.

These laws are designed to protect the consumer relative to title and practice, with noncompliance having legal consequences. Registration is a more voluntary type of licensure in that the practitioner files relevant information (e.g., education, experience, training, methods, fees) with the state board of registration or specialty board (e.g., National Register of Health Service Providers in Psychology,* American Board of Professional Psychology*), which becomes responsible for the maintenance of professional standards* and disciplinary enforcement. Because a state license is often generic, registration becomes a vehicle for the practitioner to present to the public a specialty that meets the standards of the particular board.

See also SPECIALTY TRAINING AND CREDENTIALING.

REFERENCES

Genshaft, J. L., and J. J. Wisniewski. (1988). Present credentialing and prospects for the future. *Professional School Psychology* 3, 187–194.
Hogan, D. B. (1979). *The regulation of psychotherapists,* Vols. 1–4. Cambridge, MA: Balinger.

Robert N. Wendt

REGULAR EDUCATION INITIATIVE. The regular education initiative (REI) is a term that was developed by the U.S. Department of Education (Office of Special Education and Rehabilitative Services). The document that provided the groundwork for this initiative, *Educating Students with Learning Problems: A Shared Responsibility* (1986), was written under the direction of Madeline Will, then assistant secretary of education for special education and rehabilitative services of the U.S. Department of Education. The REI was a national model for integrating general and special education* services within the general education setting. The REI provided a focus on how special education and general education could build a more effective partnership to help the increasing number of students at risk for academic failure (Will, 1989). Will identified a number of difficulties with the special education service delivery model, including fragmented service delivery that focused on categorical labels, a dual system of segregated (general versus special education) services, potential stigmatization of students labeled handicapped, potential misclassification of students, and limited general education options for students not eligible for special education services.

Will (1986) proposed changes in service delivery to students with disabilities that emphasized the strengths of both the general and special education systems. These changes included increasing support systems for teachers in general education, increasing instructional time, giving building principals more influence over programs and service delivery, increasing effective educational approaches in general education in order to reach students with a broader range of abilities and behavior profiles, and providing incentives to implement alternative approaches to service delivery. Clearly, these proposals set the stage for school psychologists* and other support personnel to begin to focus on prevention and intervention services, rather than to continue to focus primarily on the ''assess-staff-place'' model. The impact of Madeline Will's effort focused on school psychology through the publication of *The Role of School Psychology in Providing Services to All Children* (1989).

The Will (1989) document was a collaborative effort between Will and the National Association of School Psychologists* (NASP) and was disseminated under the U.S. Department of Education's letterhead. Specifically, the document emphasized the role that school psychologists could assume relative to implementing new instructional approaches and to increasing instructional time. Will stated that school psychologists could help teachers implement effective academic, behavioral, and social skills interventions using a collaborative consultation* model. This document focused exclusively on the role school psychologists could assume in implementing effective interventions using a collaborative consultation model and in effectively linking assessment to these interventions. The Will (1989) document supported the expansion of the role of the school psychologist beyond that of assessment and provided federal-level support for consultation-based service delivery in school psychology.*

See also FREE APPROPRIATE PUBLIC EDUCATION; INCLUSION; LABELING; LEAST RESTRICTIVE ENVIRONMENT.

REFERENCES

Graden, J. L., J. E. Zins, and M. J. Curtis. (1988). *Alternative educational delivery systems: Enhancing instructional options for all students.* Silver Spring, MD: National Association of School Psychologists.
Will, M. (1986). *Educating students with learning problems: A shared responsibility.* Washington, DC: U.S. Department of Education.
———. (1989). *The role of school psychology in providing services to all children.* Washington, DC: U.S. Department of Education.

George M. Batsche

REHABILITATION FACILITY. A rehabilitation facility encompasses both organizational (the administration and service providers) and architectural (the building that houses the service) entities dedicated to providing integrated, multidisciplinary habilitative or rehabilitation programs. Habilitative programs focus on children and/or adults who have never experienced a normal state of functioning because of congenital disabilities. Rehabilitation is the third phase in a continuum that includes acute management and convalescent care. When a permanent physical loss has occurred, and individuals have returned to optimum functioning through extensive personal adaptation of individuals or environmental alterations, rehabilitation has taken place. Programs are designed to minimize the handicapping effects of physical, mental, developmental, social, and/ or vocational impairments. Treatment teams may include, but are not limited to, physicians with a wide array of specializations, nurses, physical therapists, occupational therapists, speech/language pathologists, audiologists, rehabilitation psychologists, clinical psychologists, neuropsychologists, social workers, vocational rehabilitation counselors, special educators, dietitians, recreational and art therapists, prosthetists, orthotists, rehabilitation engineers, and job coaches. In addition to physical restoration, these facilities focus on developing independent living and vocational skills and work activities. The Commission on Accreditation of Rehabilitation Facilities (CARF) is responsible for quality assurance and certification of rehabilitation facilities (Harrington, 1982).

See also VOCATIONAL ASSESSMENT; VOCATIONAL REHABILITATION.

REFERENCE

Harrington, T. F. (1982). *Handbook of career planning for special needs students.* Rockville, MD: Aspen Systems.

Peggy A. Hicks

RELATED SERVICES. "Related services" became part of the terminology used by school personnel and school psychologists* with the passage in 1975 of the Education of All Handicapped Children Act, otherwise known as EHA or Public Law 94-142.* In 1990, EHA was reauthorized and renamed the Individuals with Disabilities Education Act, or IDEA (Public Law 101-476*). This law (IDEA) mandates that special education* and related services are to be made available to all children and youth with disabilities who require them. Federal funds are to be made available to help state and local governments establish and maintain special education programs and to provide the related services necessary in order for students with disabilities to benefit from special education. IDEA defines related services as "transportation, and such developmental, corrective, and other supportive services (including speech pathology and audiology, psychological services, physical and occupational therapy, recreation, including therapeutic recreation, social work services, medical and counseling services, including rehabilitation counseling, except that such medical services shall be for diagnostic and evaluation purposes only) as may be required to assist a child with a disability to benefit from special education." Some states have legislated their own related services requirements, which may include services beyond those specified in federal law. A school district may not charge the family of a student with disabilities for the cost of related services. IDEA has made related services a component of the free appropriate public education* (FAPE) that is to be provided. The need for related services is identified during the process of evaluating a student for special education. The individual education plan* written for the student details necessary related services. Under IDEA, the student must be enrolled in special education to be considered eligible for related services. However, another federal law, Section 504 of the Rehabilitation Act* of 1973 (Public Law 93-112), in many cases, broadens a student's eligibility for related services. The definition of disability is broader under Section 504 and may include children who are ineligible under IDEA and still a part of regular education. If, however, the student meets the Section 504 definition of "handicapped person," then the provision of FAPE, along with necessary related services, is guaranteed. IDEA and Section 504 differ in another way. The former is a federal grant program authorizing funding, while the latter is a civil rights statute with no federal financial assistance designated for related services.

See also LEAST RESTRICTIVE ENVIRONMENT.

REFERENCES

Education of All Handicapped Children Act, 20 U.S.C. Sections 1400–1485.
Individuals with Disabilities Education Act, 20 U.S.C. Chapter 33, Section 1417(b), p. 14.
Rehabilitation Act of 1973, 29 U.S.C. Sections 701-794.
Tucker, B. P., and B. A. Goldstein. (1992). *The educational rights of children with disabilities: A guide to federal law.* Horsham, PA: LRP.

Dennis A. Tomlinson

RELAXATION TRAINING. Relaxation training is a procedure in which a person is taught to relax voluntarily major muscle groups and become more aware of internal sensations that accompany the relaxation of these muscle groups. The two major relaxation techniques are progressive relaxation, developed by Jacobson (1938), and autogenic training, developed by Schultz and Luthe. Wolpe (1958) popularized Jacobson's procedure, using a variation in which persons were taught relaxation in six sessions with a focus on six major body regions (Wolpe, 1973). Relaxation training is presently widely used in the treatment of several different types of stress-related psychological and physical disorders, including anxiety, hypertension, asthma, insomnia, stuttering, and alcohol and drug abuse. It is often used in conjunction with biofeedback* or progressive relaxation training to treat these disorders. For persons with difficulty relaxing initially, psychotropic medications may be given about one hour before the actual training begins, or hypnosis is used to enhance the effects of the relaxation procedures.

Research has shown that relaxation training can lower blood pressure effectively without the use of medications. It has also been used effectively with emotionally disturbed children to teach socially appropriate behaviors and enhance self-control (Walton, 1979).

See also CLASSICAL CONDITIONING; CLASSIFICATION: PSYCHIATRIC; PSYCHOPHARMACOLOGY; STRESS REDUCTION THERAPY; SYSTEMATIC DESENSITIZATION.

REFERENCES

Walton, W. (1979). The use of a relaxation curriculum and biofeedback training in the classroom to reduce inappropriate behaviors of emotionally handicapped children. *Behavioral Disorders* 5, 10–18.

Wolpe, J. (1958). *Psychotherapy by reciprocal inhibition.* Stanford, CA: Stanford University Press.

———. (1973). *The practice of behavior therapy.* New York: Pergamon Press.

Raymond E. Webster

RELIABILITY. Reliability is the extent to which a test performs consistently across test items, across test forms, and across periods of time. Reliability represents the proportion of variability in a test score that is attributable to true variability, as opposed to variation associated with error. A reliability coefficient of .85, for example, indicates that 85 percent of the variability in examinees' test scores is attributable to true differences in the subjects' abilities, knowledge, or whatever characteristic is assessed by the instrument. The remaining .15 or 15 percent of the variability (1.0 − reliable variance) is due to measurement error. High standards of reliability are sought in psychological and educational measurement to ensure that important diagnostic and placement decisions are based on reliable judgment rather than error.

Three basic forms of reliability exist: internal consistency, alternate-form, and stability. Internal consistency is the extent to which items within a scale consistently measure a singular construct. Items can be grouped by splitting a test in half (split-half reliability) or by creating an average of combined split halves (e.g., Chronbach's Alpha, Kuder-Richardson-20).

Alternate-form reliability, useful when a test has more than one form (e.g., Forms A and B), is represented as a correlation between scores obtained on the two or more respective forms of the same test. In this case, of concern is the consistency with which the multiple forms of the test produce comparable scores and thus provide consistent measurement across forms.

Stability, or test-retest reliability, is associated with the consistency of test scores when an individual is tested on the same instrument repeatedly over a period of time. Test-retest reliability is generally determined over an interval of four to six weeks, a short enough time not to allow developmental changes to significantly influence examinees' test performance and long enough that the examinees do not clearly recall the test content from the previous administration. Some constructs are known to be stable over time (e.g., intelligence,* self-concept*), while others (e.g., state anxiety) are less stable and are influenced more by environmental conditions and recent life events.

See also VALIDITY.

REFERENCES

Anastasi, A. (1988). *Psychological testing.* New York: Macmillan.
Cohen, R. J., M. E. Swerdlik, and D. K. Smith. (1992). *Psychological testing and assessment: An introduction to tests and measurement* (2d ed.). Mountain View, CA: Mayfield.

Bruce A. Bracken

REMEDIAL INSTRUCTION. Remedial instruction is the teaching of basic skill or content areas to a child who has demonstrated difficulty in learning in the conventional manner in the general classroom. Remedial instruction may be directed at a specific skill deficiency, such as memory or a perceptual problem, or skill may be remediated by teaching prerequisites in a content area, such as math or reading. It is specifically different from compensatory instruction, material adaptation, or curricular modification in that remediation refers to "correcting" a defined problem. Remedial instruction has as its purpose the goal of bringing the learner up to standards perceived to be necessary, whereas compensatory instruction provides adaptations to the method or content to be learned by the student. Most special education* programs are some combination of both remedial and compensatory approaches.

Several math or reading programs are offered by federal funds for schools that have demonstrated low achievement scores. Teachers with specialized content skills are employed to work with students who present achievement problems in the general classroom. The most common type of remedial program is funded federally and often called "Chapter One" in American schools.

REFERENCES

Meyen, E. L., G. A. Vergason, and R. J. Whelan (Eds.). (1988). *Effective instructional strategies for exceptional children.* Denver: Love.

Strickland, B., and A. Turnbull. (1993). *Developing and implementing individualized educational plans* (3d ed.). New York: Macmillan.

Diane Montgomery

REPORT WRITING. Report writing is among the major responsibilities of school psychologists* and refers to the written description of assessment* and intervention* and related activities. The child study report is built around the referral question and describes a problem-solving process leading to recommendations for intervention. Reports are also used to describe less traditional activities, including consultation,* interventions, follow-up, research, and evaluation. The school psychologist's report and that of other members of the team approach* to services serve as an official record of assessment activities, diagnoses, and recommendations for cases presented.

Traditionally prepared by the school psychologist with the assistance of secretarial services, modern technology allows the report to be prepared through word-processing programs and computerized report-writing* programs, several of which are commercially marketed. Reports are most often associated with the traditional case study assessment of children referred for suspected handicapping conditions. Comprehensive assessment* reports include identifying information; reason for referral; background information, including developmental, educational, medical, and social histories; test behavior and relevant observations; selection of instruments and assessment procedures; interpretation of results; and a section for summary, conclusions, and recommendations (Georgia Department of Education, 1988). The team approach to services necessitates that team reports be compiled based on the contributions of team members and collective decisions regarding diagnosis and intervention.

The terminology and content of reports are provided at levels appropriate for the audiences served (e.g., parents, teachers, physicians). Preparing comprehensive psychological reports and their maintenance and dissemination are important aspects of psychologists' ethical codes* and professional standards.* Separate standards and ethical guidelines exist for computer-generated reports. Tallent (1988) provides a comprehensive overview of psychological reports and relevant legal-ethical standards. A survey of research specific to school psychological reports and a discussion of the expository process model are provided by Ownby and Wallbrown (1986). A concise resource is provided in Ross-Reynolds (1990).

See also ACCOUNTABILITY; COMPREHENSIVE ASSESSMENT; COMPUTERIZED REPORT WRITING.

REFERENCES

Georgia Department of Education. (1988). *Psychological reports: Recommended practice illustrated with actual case studies.* Atlanta, GA: Author.

Ownby, R. L., and F. Wallbrown. (1986). Improving report writing in school psychology. In T. R. Kratochwill (Ed.), *Advances in school psychology, Vol. 5* (pp. 7–49). Hillsdale, NJ: Erlbaum.

Ross-Reynolds, G. (1990). Best practices in report writing. In A. Thomas and J. Grimes (Eds.), *Best practices in school psychology—II* (pp. 621–633). Washington, DC: National Association of School Psychologists.

Tallent, N. (1988). *Psychological report writing.* Englewood Cliffs, NJ: Prentice-Hall.

Thomas K. Fagan

RESIDENTIAL CARE. Residential care refers to the support, education, and management provided to individuals with disabilities by a specially trained staff on a twenty-four-hour basis. Considered a highly restrictive placement option for students with disabilities, residential schools are segregated, with little or no time planned with age peers without disabilities.

Historically, the residential school was developed in the early 1800s in Europe by physicians, altruistic individuals, and families with the belief that people who were deaf, blind, or, later, individuals with mental retardation would benefit from an education. The United States followed the European example and established early residential programs, such as the American Asylum for the Deaf in Connecticut in 1817, the Perkins School for the Blind in Massachusetts in 1831, or modern mental hospitals (Zilboorg and Henry, 1941). In contrast to the European model, these programs were generally state funded and operated. The residential school rooted as an American practice, and, not so long ago, children born with severe disabilities were placed in residential care at birth, never to experience a more normal family life.

The principle of normalization articulated by Wolfensberger (1972) led to the deinstitutionalization movement of the 1970s for students with sensory impairments, severe emotional disabilities, or mental retardation. The current trend reflects a steady decrease in the number of individuals with disabilities served in residential settings in favor of home or community placements.

Contrary to the deinstitutionalization of programs for students with disabilities, another trend in special education* is the establishment of residential schools in the sciences or humanities for students who are highly gifted. North Carolina, Louisiana, Illinois, Indiana, Oklahoma, and other states offer juniors and seniors a full-time residential setting for accelerated study with content experts.

See also RESIDENTIAL CENTER.

REFERENCES

Smutny, J. F., and R. H. Blocksom. (1990). *Education of the gifted: Programs and perspectives.* Bloomington, IN: Phi Delta Kappa.

Wolfensberger, W. (1972). *The principle of normalization in human services.* Toronto: National Institute on Mental Retardation.

Zilboorg, G., and C. Henry. (1941). *A history of medical psychology.* New York: Norton.

Diane Montgomery

RESIDENTIAL CENTER. The Child Welfare League of America (1972) defined a residential center, or residential treatment center, as a twenty-four-hour facility for children who are removed from their families and who require psychiatric treatment in a hospital setting. Current practice, however, distinguishes between hospital inpatient treatment, designed for acute care of individuals exhibiting dangerous behavior, and residential treatment, designed for intermediate and long-term treatment of individuals who do not require twenty-four-hour care and supervision.

Residential treatment centers, or RTCs, trace their roots back to the orphanages, correctional schools, convalescent hospitals, homes for deprived and neglected children, and special schools for emotionally disturbed or mentally retarded children that were founded in the United States after the Civil War. The primary treatment in these institutions was educational. Emerging knowledge about the efficacy of psychological treatments in the 1920s led to the development of more specialized facilities, offering the services of psychiatrists, psychologists, and social workers, as well as educators.

Weber and Haberlein (1972) identified twelve characteristics that distinguish RTCs from other children's institutions, including a focus on behavioral or psychiatric disorders, an emphasis on treatment rather than care and custody, a diagnostic process that guides the treatment, application of a specific theory or technique of treatment, the interrelation or integration of all program elements, the employment of clinically trained personnel, individualization of the treatment program, an emphasis upon community experiences and reintegration into the community setting, and a requirement for parental participation in the treatment program.

RTCs emphasize the importance of the total physical and social environment in assisting the treatment. Primary treatment components include group living and milieu therapy, the facility's school program, recreational and occupational therapies, and treatment services provided by the clinical staff. The latter include individual, group, and behavioral therapies, provided or directed by the facility's psychiatrists, psychologists, and social workers.

Some 473,000 children were treated in RTCs in the U.S. in 1966. Continuing social changes increased these numbers in the 1970s and 1980s. By the 1990s, an emerging emphasis upon less expensive, community-based services (such as day treatment) led to decreased utilization of RTCs.

See also RESIDENTIAL CARE.

REFERENCES

Child Welfare League of America. (1972). *From chaos to order.* New York: Author.
Morris, R. J., and Y. P. Morris. (1989). School psychology in residential treatment facilities. In R. C. D'Amato and R. S. Dean (Eds.), *The school psychologist in nontraditional settings* (pp. 159–183). Hillsdale, NJ: Erlbaum.
Weber, G. H., and B. J. Haberlein. (1972). *Residential treatment of emotionally disturbed children.* New York: Behavioral.

W. Val McClanahan

RESOURCE ROOM. Resource room is a placement option within regular schools designed to meet special educational needs of students with disabilities. The concept may be applied differently throughout the United States; however, resource room generally refers to a separate special education* setting in which students are pulled out of their regular classrooms and taught by a specially trained teacher for a portion of the instructional day. The intention of the placement decision is to provide special education instruction while maintaining contact with peers without disabilities.

Students are commonly referred for resource room support by regular classroom teachers. The instruction provided within the resource room may be remedial* (reteaching skills), tutorial (help with specific content area), or special skill training (study skills,* specific academic skills, computer skills, or transition to life skills). Students may receive instruction individually or in small groups based on age, grade, skill, academic need, or disability. The length of time and frequency of sessions spent outside the general classroom are determined by the type and degree of disability or problem of the student. The special education teacher in the resource room may work closely with the regular education teacher on educational goals for the student. Given the flexibility and variability of the program option, the resource room is often chosen for secondary students.

See also INCLUSION; SELF-CONTAINED CLASS.

REFERENCE

Strickland, B. B., and A. P. Turnbull. (1990). *Developing and implementing individualized education programs* (3d ed.). Columbus, OH: Merrill.

Diane Montgomery

RETENTION/NONPROMOTION. Grade retention is the strategy of requiring a child to repeat a grade in school. The practice began in the United States with the industrialization and urbanization that led to graded schools in the mid-nineteenth century. Nonpromotion was common; between 1840 and 1930, it has been estimated that half the children in graded schools were retained at least once during the elementary school years (Medway and Rose, 1986). Few students were expected to pass into high school.

At the beginning of the century, Ayers (1909) suggested that having large numbers of overage children in a classroom was not good practice. The number of retained children began to drop steadily after World War I.

During the depression, two forces led to a change in practice: the need to keep children in school and out of the crowded labor market and concern for the impact of retention on emotional well-being. "Social promotion" was used to move failing children on so they could remain with peers as they were grouped for instruction with other low-achieving children. Subsequently, the nonpromotion rate dropped to around 5 percent by 1940 (Saunders, 1941). These rates and attitudes generally continued into the 1970s.

During the 1960s, retention in the early grades received a boost from the influential work of Ilg and Ames of the Gesell Institute, who argued that some children needed more time to achieve school readiness* than others and might be successfully retained in kindergarten and first grade. Large numbers of schools followed their lead in instituting "developmental placement" in grades.

In the mid-1970s, calls for increased educational accountability and the development of minimal competency* testing resulted in a return to retaining children who did not achieve in school or pass competency tests. At the same time, however, two influential meta-analytic reviews by Jackson and by Holmes and Matthews led scholars to oppose the practice on the grounds that it did not lead to positive outcomes for children.

In 1988, the National Association of School Psychologists* published a position paper condemning the practice in general, recommending that alternatives for children be sought, and arguing for the participation of school psychologists* in such decisions.

REFERENCES

Ayers, L. P. (1909). *Laggards in our schools.* New York: Russell Sage.

Medway, F. J., and J. S. Rose. (1986). Grade retention. In T. R. Kratochwill (Ed.), *Advances in school psychology,* Vol. 5 (pp. 141–175). Hillsdale, NJ: Erlbaum.

Rafoth, M. A., and K. Carey. (1995). Best practices in assisting with promotion and retention decisions. In A. Thomas and J. Grimes (Eds.), *Best practices in school psychology—III* (pp. 413–420). Washington, DC: National Association of School Psychologists.

Saunders, C. M. (1941). *Promotion or failure for the elementary school pupil?* New York: Teachers College Bureau of Publications.

Jonathan Sandoval

ROGERS, CARL R. Carl Ransom Rogers (1902–1987) was a man with many careers. He finished a B.A. at the University of Wisconsin (1924) and M.A. (1928) and Ph.D. (1931) at Columbia University. In 1927–1928, he was a fellow at the New York City Institute for Child Guidance in an innovative collaborative program where he worked with S. J. Beck. While working on his doctorate, he was a psychologist with the Society for Prevention of Cruelty to Children in Rochester, New York, and became its director for eight years in 1930.

About 1940, his interests shifted to adolescents and adults. He accepted a position at Ohio State University for five years as professor and executive secretary of the counseling center. From there he moved to the University of Chicago. His most influential book, *Client-Centered Therapy,* was published in 1951, and his most widely read book, *On Becoming a Person,* in 1961. From 1957 to 1963, he was back at the University of Wisconsin as a professor. In retirement, he moved to the Center for the Study of the Person in La Jolla, California, where he focused more on group interactions and less on individual therapy.

Rogers is acknowledged by many as creator of a third force in counseling. His humanistic/client-centered orientation provided therapists with a process quite different from psychoanalysis and behaviorism.

See also PERSON-CENTERED THERAPY.

REFERENCES

Gendlin, E. T. (1988). Carl Rogers (1902–1987). *American Psychologist* 43, 127–128.

Rogers, C. R. (1939). *The clinical treatment of the problem child.* Boston: Houghton Mifflin.

———. (1942). *Counseling and psychotherapy, newer concepts in practice.* Boston: Houghton Mifflin.

———. (1951). *Client-centered therapy, its current practice, implications and theory.* Boston: Houghton Mifflin.

Joseph L. French

ROLE CHANGE AND DIVERSITY. Role change and diversity refer to the scrutiny of the traditional activities of school psychologists* and efforts to change those activities toward greater involvement with nontesting activities. Role debates often revolve around conceptions of school psychologists as primarily diagnosticians of problems that are treated by other professionals or as professionals who intervene directly through counseling or therapy activities or indirectly through problem-solving consultation. The origins of the tension between diagnosis and intervention can be identified in the earliest roots of school psychology* in the clinic established at the University of Pennsylvania by Lighter Witmer* (Sandoval, 1993). Every major national conference on school psychology,* from the Thayer conference* to the Spring Hill* and Olympia* conferences in the early 1980s, addressed issues related to roles, with nearly universal agreement that school psychology roles should be broad and diverse (Reschly and Ysseldyke, 1995).

Consistent results have been published in recent survey research on school psychology roles. Self-report data on roles revealed that over two-thirds of school psychologists' time is devoted to various activities related to determining, maintaining, or reevaluating students' eligibility for special education.* The major activity of school psychologists in eligibility determination and assessment of current intellectual functioning and achievement using standardized tests constitutes slightly over half of the professional activities of school psychologists (Reschly and Wilson, 1995). Other roles, such as problem-solving consultation* and direct intervention,* involve about 30–35 percent of school psychologists' time, with systems/organizational consultation* and research/evaluation accounting for 5 percent or less of the time.

Survey research on school psychologists' role preferences has consistently indicated preferences for greater amounts of time in problem-solving consultation and direct interventions, with time devoted to assessment to determine eligibility reduced to 25–30 percent of the role. Despite the admonitions of many national leaders and university faculty, practicing school psychologists have never expressed much enthusiasm for roles such as in-service training of other professionals, organizational consultation, or research/evaluation.

Role change and diversity are most often discussed today in the context of system reform. Contemporary delivery system reform schemes typically place emphasis on noncategorical eligibility for services and funding based on needed supports and services rather than categories of disability such as mental retardation or specific learning disability. System reforms dealing with funding mechanisms and eligibility for services could produce conditions that would lead to dramatically lower demands for school psychological services devoted to testing for eligibility determination and to markedly higher demands for functional assessment and intervention design services (Reschly and Ysseldyke, 1995).

See also ROLE RESTRICTION; ROLES AND FUNCTIONS.

REFERENCES

Reschly, D. J., and M. S. Wilson. (1995). School psychology faculty and practitioners: 1986 to 1991 trends in demographic characteristics, roles, satisfaction, and system reform. *School Psychology Review* 24, 62–80.
Reschly, D. J., and J. E. Ysseldyke. (1995). School psychology paradigm shift. In A. Thomas and J. Grimes (Eds.), *Best practices in school psychology—III* (3d ed., pp. 17–34). Washington, DC: National Association of School Psychologists.
Sandoval, J. (1993). The history of interventions in school psychology. *Journal of School Psychology* 31, 195–217.

Daniel J. Reschly

ROLE RESTRICTION. Role restriction refers to limitations on the services provided by school psychologists.* The degree to which school psychologists' roles are restricted ultimately depends on a combination of systemic and individual factors (Grimes, 1981). Systemic limitations usually are imposed because of special education* funding mechanisms that generate monies to school districts on the basis of the number of students identified with disabilities and in need of special education. Salaries for psychologists and other related services providers and special education program costs may be paid through moneys generated by the number of students eligible for, and in need of, special education. In such circumstances, district administrators and supervisors of psychological services are likely to view psychoeducational assessment to determine eligibility as the most important, if not the only, role of school psychologists.

Another form of role restriction originates in narrow graduate training in which persons are prepared only in restricted areas, such as standardized testing. These persons may not have the necessary skills to engage in broader roles, such as problem-solving consultation* and social skills interventions.* A final form of role restriction arises from the unwillingness of individual practitioners to attempt to change from traditional services, with which they may be truly comfortable, to broader roles that often require more initiative, greater individual responsibility, and greater accountability.*

The recent reform efforts in special education and school psychology* often advocate funding the necessary supports and services needed by children with learning and behavior problems without the use of categorical labels such as specific learning disability or educable mental retardation (Graden, Zins, and Curtis, 1988; Reschly, 1988). These and other changes may reduce concerns about role restriction and permit greater emphasis on (1) assessment related to identifying intervention target behaviors, monitoring progress, and evaluating outcomes; (2) problem-solving consultation; (3) direct interventions, such as counseling individuals and leading social skills groups; and (4) preventive mental health services, such as parent training.*

See also ROLE CHANGE AND DIVERSITY.

REFERENCES

Graden, J. L., J. E. Zins, and M. J. Curtis (Eds.). (1988). *Alternative educational delivery systems: Enhancing instructional options for all students.* Washington, DC: National Association of School Psychologists.
Grimes, J. (1981). Shaping the future of school psychology. *School Psychology Review* 10, 206–231.
Reschly, D. J. (1988). Special education reform: School psychology revolution. *School Psychology Review* 17, 459–475.

                                                                            Daniel J. Reschly

ROLES AND FUNCTIONS. Much has been written about the roles and functions of school psychologists.* Briefly, "roles" can be defined as overarching theoretical approaches to the profession of school psychology,* while "functions" refer to the day-to-day activities carried out by practicing school psychologists. Thus, when Susan Gray* (1963) proposed two major roles for school psychologists—"data-oriented problem solver" and "the transmitter of psychological knowledge and skill"—she was suggesting general ways of viewing the school psychologist's role in the school, rather than specific functions in which the school psychologist might engage.

The earliest empirical study of roles and functions of individuals performing psychological services within school settings* was conducted by Wallin* (1914). Wallin examined the training and testing practices of practitioners and found that his respondents were not particularly well trained and were providing a rather restricted range of services. Most of Wallin's respondents were providing testing services in order to "sort" children into educational categories. By the 1920s, school psychologists were providing some intervention services—namely, remedial instruction and/or counseling—in addition to the "sorting."

Reports from the 1954 Thayer conference* suggested that, in the early 1950s, testing and other assessment-related activities still consumed more than two-thirds of the school psychologist's professional time. While the Thayer conference (and other professional gatherings since then) devoted considerable time and attention to the establishment of a consensus regarding the role and function of school psychologists, such a consensus has never been achieved. Still, such discussions of role and function have been thought-provoking and have undoubtedly caused individual practitioners and trainers to modify their previous beliefs and practices.

The roles and functions of any given school psychologist are influenced by a number of factors, including what the individual brings to the job (e.g., personal characteristics and background, professional training and interests); job-related factors (e.g., job-site characteristics, expectations, and needs; available resources); and "external" factors (e.g., legislative developments, social problems, world events). School psychologists working in rural areas, for example, tend to function as generalists. Such practitioners may work with all ages of youngsters providing assessment,* counseling, and often special education* administrative duties for one or more school districts. Urban and suburban practitioners may specialize in a particular age group (e.g., early childhood, middle school students) and may be more limited to assessment since other professionals handle counseling cases or special education administration.

The passage of Public Law 94-142* in 1975 provides a dramatic example of how an external development can have a significant impact on the role and function of school psychologists. While this law was viewed as generally positive to school psychologists in that it mandated a place for psychological services for every child with a disability, it has also served to restrict school psychologists' professional functioning to students with disabilities and has emphasized the psychoeducational assessment role over intervention,* consultation,* and research roles.

Most school psychologists practicing today have been trained, and are expected, to perform certain standard functions—namely, assessments, interventions, and teacher and parent consultations.* Many have also been trained in individual and/or group counseling, research and program evaluation.* Recent surveys reported in Fagan and Wise (1994) indicate that psychoeducational assessment-related duties (e.g., testing, classroom observations, teacher and parent interviews) consume slightly more than 50 percent of school psychologists' time. Interventions (including counseling) and consultation (including in-service education) each accounts for about another 20–25 percent. Research and evaluation account for only about 1 or 2 percent of practitioners' time.

See also NONSCHOOL SETTINGS; PUBLIC LAW 101-476; RURAL SCHOOL PSYCHOLOGY; SCHOOL SETTINGS; SPECIAL EDUCATION; SUBURBAN SCHOOL PSYCHOLOGY; URBAN SCHOOL PSYCHOLOGY.

REFERENCES

Fagan, T. K., and P. S. Wise. (1994). *School psychology: Past, present, and future.* White Plains, NY: Longman.

Gray, S. W. (1963). *The psychologist in the schools.* New York: Holt, Rinehart, and Winston.

Wallin, J.E.W. (1914). *The mental health of the school child.* New Haven, CT: Yale University Press.

Paula Sachs Wise

RURAL SCHOOL PSYCHOLOGY. School psychology* as a profession is identified by certain methods, skills, and knowledge equally relevant to all school settings. However, it is commonly recognized that school psychological services are optimally delivered when offered in a way that considers and matches aspects of the broader community context.

Serving children in rural and/or small school districts presents special challenges. Services in many rural areas were nonexistent until the passage of Public Law 94-142.* Services in rural areas more than doubled from 1975 to 1980. In 1981, it was reported that 67 percent of all schools in America were classified as rural, remote, or isolated. These schools served 32 percent of all schoolchildren and had the majority of unserved and underserved handicapped children. Nationally, 74 percent of all school districts are small (fewer than 2,500 students) or very small (fewer than 1,000 students). Over 51 percent of all school districts are both small and rural.

Small and rural communities are typically characterized by sparse populations; geographic and climatic barriers; traditional value systems; being poorer in terms of spendable income; closeness of family and community, as evidenced by a ''make-do'' attitude of self-sufficiency; and insufficient mental health services. However, rural communities also vary widely in distinctive characteristics that define their individual context. Many typologies have been offered to assist the human service provider in assessing the specific community context for service delivery planning, for example, the differences among the rural poor, middle America, and transitional rural communities.

Rural school districts generally are less bureaucratic, more personal power-based, and staffed by personnel who function as generalists. These districts are faced with issues of providing a comprehensive range of educational services, given the lack of qualified personnel and, at times, a critical mass of students; difficulty in recruiting and retaining staff; and the social and professional isolation that exists. In addition, rural school psychologists may be challenged by heavy caseloads; limited access to other school psychologists for supervision, consultation,* and peer support; the lack of administrative and consumer understanding of one's role; and difficult work conditions, such as extensive travel and work space problems. Yet, these same issues or barriers may offer opportunities, such as an expanded role for the school psychologist, input at higher administrative levels affording the potential for influencing system-level changes, and spanning the boundaries between school and community.

See also INTERMEDIATE AGENCY; ROLE CHANGE AND DIVERSITY; SUBURBAN SCHOOL PSYCHOLOGY; URBAN SCHOOL PSYCHOLOGY.

REFERENCES

Benson, A. J., and S. Z. Petty. (1990). Best practices in rural school psychology. In A. Thomas and J. Grimes (Eds.), *Best practices in school psychology—II* (pp. 635–647). Washington, DC: National Association of School Psychologists.

Hughes, J. N., and T. K. Fagan (Eds.). (1985). Mini-series on rural school psychology. *School Psychology Review* 14, 400–456.

Jacob-Timm, S. (1995). Best practices in facilitating services in rural settings. In A. Thomas and J. Grimes (Eds.), *Best practices in school psychology—III* (pp. 301–310). Washington, DC: National Association of School Psychologists.

Meacham, M. L., and V. Triane. (1967). The role of the school psychologist in the community school. In J. F. Magary (Ed.), *School psychological services in theory and practice: A handbook* (pp. 68–98). Englewood Cliffs, NJ: Prentice-Hall.

A. Jerry Benson

RUSSELL SAGE GUIDELINES. In 1969, the Russell Sage Foundation convened a conference on ''Ethical and Legal Aspects of School Record Keeping.'' At that time, most schools maintained extensive records on individual pupils, but few had policies to safeguard pupil and family privacy in the collection, maintenance, or release of pupil records. Furthermore, pupil records were typically closed to parents. Parents were unable to review or challenge the accuracy of school records used in educational decision making. In recognition of these problems, conference participants developed a set of guidelines for the management of school records (Russell Sage Foundation, 1970). The Russell Sage guidelines called for policies and procedures to ensure the privacy of pupil records and parent access to them. The guidelines were influential in the development of federal legislation addressing school record-keeping practices, such as the Family Educational Rights and Privacy Act of 1974 (Public Law 93-380*).

REFERENCE

Russell Sage Foundation. (1970). *Guidelines for the collection, maintenance, and dissemination of pupil records.* Hartford: Connecticut Printers.

Susan Jacob-Timm

S

SALARY DETERMINATION. Historically, teachers were not allowed to organize, and salaries of school employees were subject to secret negotiations, political patronage, and a host of idiosyncratic factors. Contemporary laws, especially "sunshine" laws, have forced schools to make their financial dealings a matter of public record. As a result of these factors, most public school districts have established guidelines or salary schedules that are organized by steps, each representing a fixed salary increase. Steps are determined by years of experience and credentials, and the number of steps varies by district. Such schedules usually have a salary ceiling regardless of training and experience (e.g., master's degree* plus thirty semester hours and twenty-five years' experience). Some district schedules do not include the doctoral degree.* As a guideline for districts, minimal salary schedules may be specified by the state department of education.*

There is very little research specific to school psychology* salaries, their determination, or variation. Salary growth during the twentieth century was gradual until the post–World War II period, when salaries consistently rose above $3,000. By the 1960s, the median salary was in the $7,000–$8,000 range (Fagan, 1995). Since the 1970s, there have been several studies revealing the range of salaries in the field, and the 1994 average for school psychologist* practitioners was $43,230 (Dawson, Mendez, and Hyman, 1994).

Even though school psychologists are noninstructional personnel, their salaries may be on schedules that are (1) a teacher salary schedule, (2) an administrative salary schedule, (3) separate but above those of teachers and below those for administrators, or (4) personally negotiated with the local school administration (Hyman and Kaplinski, 1994). Currently, most school psychologists, especially those in states with collective bargaining* laws, appear to be on teacher salary schedules (Hyman and Kaplinski, 1994). The range of salaries is apparently influenced by such factors as years of experience, level of academic preparation, specific assignment, and setting. There exists no definitive study of the relative influence of factors on salary, though a recent analysis has revealed the influence of experience and degrees (Thomas, 1995). Since most school psychologists work in public school settings, salary comparisons across settings have not been reported. Salary differentials on the basis of gender are illegal, and no conclusive evidence exists of such bias in school psychology (Dawson, Mendez, and Hyman, 1994; Fischer and Sorenson, 1996; Thomas, 1995).

In most regions of the country, salaries of school psychologists, especially at the entry level of certification,* are very competitive with those of other non-doctoral psychologists. The rationale for salaries above those of teachers is that the entry level into the profession of school psychology is more rigorous and requires at least three years of additional training as compared to teachers. Further, unlike educators, psychological practice is defined by commonly accepted professional standards* that render psychologists subject to litigation for malpractice.

See also COLLECTIVE BARGAINING; GENDER ISSUES; JOB SATISFACTION.

REFERENCES

Dawson, P., P. Mendez, and A. Hyman. (1994). Average school psychologist's salary tops $43,000. *Communique* 23(1), 1, 6–7.

Fagan, T. K. (1995). Trends in the history of school psychology in the United States. In A. Thomas and J. Grimes (Eds.), *Best practices in school psychology—III* (pp. 59–68). Washington, DC: National Association of School Psychologists.

Fischer, L., and G. P. Sorenson. (1996). *School law for counselors, psychologists, and social workers.* White Plains, NY: Longman.

Hyman, I., and K. Kaplinski. (1994). Will the real school psychologist please stand up: Does the past offer a prologue for the future of school psychology? *School Psychology Review* 23, 364–583.

Thomas, A. (1995). A study of gender differences among school psychologists. Oxford, OH: Miami University. Unpublished manuscript.

Irwin A. Hyman

SCHOOL PSYCHOLOGIST. According to Fagan and Wise (1994), ''A school psychologist is a professional psychological practitioner whose general purpose is to bring a psychological perspective to bear on the problems of educators and the clients educators serve'' (p. 3). The school psychologist is trained in educational and psychological foundations and has specialty training in school psychology* that facilitates the provision of comprehensive psychological services of a direct and indirect nature. A school psychologist is defined in legal terms related to credentialing by a state department of education* (SDE) or a state board of examiners in psychology.* These agencies grant certification* and licensing,* which protect titles and functions proffered to consumers. Irrespective of training, for employment purposes, the person must hold one or more of these credentials to legally use the title ''school psychologist.''

The title emerged early in the twentieth century from the practice of generic clinical psychology* in school settings, and the title "school psychologist" was first held by Arnold Gesell.* Regulatory recognition emerged in the 1930s, when New York and Pennsylvania established SDE certification in school psychology. By the 1990s, every state department of education offered some form of school psychological credentialing.

See also SPECIALTY TRAINING AND CREDENTIALING; TRAINING MODELS.

REFERENCE

Fagan, T. K., and P. S. Wise. (1994). *School psychology: Past, present, and future.* White Plains, NY: Longman.

Thomas K. Fagan

SCHOOL PSYCHOLOGIST EXAMINATION. The School Psychologist Examination was created by the Educational Testing Service of Princeton, New Jersey, as a "specialty area test" for the National Teacher Examination* (NTE) program. First administered on March 26, 1988, it measured knowledge of six basic domains of school psychology.* Like the other specialty area exams, NTE #40 used a multiple-choice format, optically scanned "bubble" answer sheets, and a scoring system that penalized guessing. The standardization exam was held on July 9, 1988.

The six content areas included assessment,* intervention,* evaluation, professional practice, psychological foundations, and educational foundations. The examinee score report listed subtests, number of questions in the category, number and percent answered correctly/incorrectly, the number omitted, and the number not attempted. A total score resulted from summing all 131 items.

The test was one of the requirements for obtaining national certification in school psychology as administered by the National Association of School Psychologists* (NASP). In creating the National School Psychology Certification Board, NASP hoped to create a standard of training that was independent of the state boards that were originally designed to license or certify teachers. By establishing a constant national standard, NASP promoted high standards for training, with the intent of increasing uniformity of service and creating a greater potential for reciprocity of certification*/licensure* across states. Many school psychology programs renewed their efforts to meet NASP training standards as a result of national certification, and several states agreed to allow reciprocal certification. However, the majority of states maintained unique, individual requirements for their school psychologists* that prevented true reciprocity.

REFERENCES

Batsche, G. M. (1987). NASP endorses National School Psychology Exam. *Communique* 16(2), 1–2.

Educational Testing Service. (1988). *The School Psychologist Examination.* Princeton, NJ: Author.

Philip B. Bowser

SCHOOL PSYCHOLOGIST OF THE YEAR. At the March 1990 annual convention of the National Association of School Psychologists* (NASP) in San Francisco, the Executive Board/Delegate Assembly approved a proposal from the Ethical and Professional Standards Committee to establish a School Psychologist of the Year Award. Initially suggested by NASP presidents Michael Curtis and Howard Knoff, the award was designed to honor a practitioner* who provided comprehensive school psychological services of high quality.

The original selection procedure required a candidate statement, letters of support from colleagues, and extensive interviewing both in person and via conference calls. The selection committee consisted of leaders from all five NASP regions, carefully selected so as to avoid a conflict of interest. The procedure was later simplified to reduce costs and the burden of time on committee members.

Award recipients included:

• 1991—Melvin Franklin

• 1992—Paula Laidig

• 1993—Fred Krug

• 1994—award not given due to financial constraints

• 1995—Mary H. Arredondo

State affiliates of NASP typically nominated their own "outstanding school psychologist," except in those years when the individual received the state-level award for a lifetime of service to the association (which disqualified him or her for the national award). The finalists and the award recipient were honored at a ceremony at the annual NASP convention, which was also recorded in the newsletter, the *Communique.*

REFERENCE

National Association of School Psychologists. (1991). *Operations handbook* (p. 90). Washington, DC: Author.

Philip B. Bowser

SCHOOL PSYCHOLOGY. The application of psychological knowledge and skills within educational settings to directly or indirectly enhance the development and learning of children is the province of school psychology. The dual relationship of education and psychology is reflected in the diversity of academic curricula offered by colleges and universities, in the requirements for state credentialing as a school psychologist,* and in the range of professional responsibilities and activities of school psychologists.

School psychology training programs are usually located within an institu-

tion's college of education (guidance and counseling, educational psychology,*
or special education* departments) or college of arts and sciences (psychology
department). Of the approximately 220 higher education institutions offering
graduate training leading to school psychologist credentialing, most are at the
specialist's degree* level or higher.

Most states designate specific criteria for certification* as a school psychologist, including a supervised internship* in addition to prescribed academic
course work. Academic programs are typically related to the state credentialing
guidelines, although there is considerable variation among states in the propor-
tionate balance of required psychology and education courses. Many school
psychologists have teaching certificates and have pursued graduate training after
one or more years of teaching experience. Most states permit individuals without
teacher certification to be credentialed in school psychology, usually requiring
additional course work to provide the student with knowledge about educational
curriculum and school organization and the opportunity to observe in public
school classrooms.

A 1994 survey of over 17,000 members of the National Association of School
Psychologists* (NASP) indicated that the typical NASP member is a white female in her forties with a sixty-credit master's degree,* works for a public school
system as a school psychology practitioner, and earns a salary of $43,230 (Daw-
son, Mendez, and Hyman, 1994). Most school psychologists work within public
educational settings, although some may be employed by community mental
health agencies or private schools or may be in private practice.* Some states
have established specific criteria for ''school psychology'' licensure, although
most states offer a generic ''psychology'' license for eligible school psychologists, usually those who possess a doctoral degree.*

Twenty-six states have consultants for school psychology within the state
department of education,* usually attached to the division of special education*
or the division of pupil personnel.* The state consultant maintains a liaison
between the department of education and the field school psychologist, provides
leadership in interpreting psychological interventions* and strategies, as well as
state standards within the educational bureaucracy, and provides opportunities
for in-service and continuing professional development.*

Professional responsibilities of the school psychologist vary among the states
as well as within each state. The differing academic and certification requirements parallel the diversity in role and function* expectations of the local school
systems. Most school psychologists are integrally involved with extensive psychoeducational consultation, assessment,* intervention planning, and educational
programming for students with suspected or identified learning, behavioral, or
emotional problems. A primary role of the school psychologist is to ferret out
the circumstances hindering optimum school performance for referred children
and to assist the school system in the provision of educational plans for these
children. The school psychologist relies on a knowledge of learning theories,
child development, consultation* techniques, intervention strategies, psycho-

educational assessment, and family systems plus a functional understanding of classroom analysis, school organization, and curriculum. Contemporary developments within the field of school psychology increasingly emphasize indirect service provision to teachers and other personnel.

Depending on the school system's priorities and the personality and competencies of the psychologist, additional services may be provided, including group appraisal of schoolchildren, coordination with community child-serving agencies, counseling and psychotherapy, coordination with other pupil personnel workers, preventive mental health consultation on programs for children, participation on curriculum committees, research, provision of in-service training, collection and calculation of local normative data, and numerous other areas. Since school psychologists generally have the most formal training within public education systems (particularly in child development, research, and individual assessment), consultation in these areas of expertise is often a major responsibility.

The blending of psychological applications within an educational setting directly or indirectly to promote optimum learning for students is the purpose of school psychology. School psychology is distinguished from other specialties within psychology with respect to the applied nature of the field and with respect to the primary client* being the child within educational settings. There are approximately 22,000 school psychologists throughout the United States (Fagan and Wise, 1994). Directly or indirectly, there is a school psychologist responsible or assigned to every public school in the United States.

See also CERTIFICATION; CLASSIFICATION: EDUCATIONAL; CLASSIFICATION: PSYCHIATRIC; FAMILY ASSESSMENT; LICENSING; PROFESSIONAL STANDARDS; SCHOOL SETTINGS; STATE CONSULTANT FOR SCHOOL PSYCHOLOGICAL SERVICES; TEACHER CERTIFICATION ISSUE; TRAINING MODELS.

REFERENCES

Dawson, P., P. Mendez, and A. Hyman. (1994). Average school psychologist's salary tops $43,000. *Communique*, 23(1), 1, 6–7.

Fagan, T., and P. Wise. (1994). *School psychology: Past, present, and future.* White Plains, NY: Longman.

Alex Thomas

SCHOOL PSYCHOLOGY SPECIALIZATIONS. Because school psychology* is the practice of psychology in educational settings, the profession has informal subspecializations that reflect the broader field of psychology and education. School psychology training programs, for example, claim to offer "subspecializations" in such core areas as applied cognitive psychology, developmental psychology, educational psychology,* experimental psychology, learning, measurement, organizational psychology, neuropsychology, personality, and research. In addition to offering subspecializations in these basic areas of psychology, other training programs offer subspecializations in more applied psychological skill areas, such as assessment,* behavior analysis, consultation,* counseling, family systems, therapeutic approaches, and vocational assessment* and guidance. Also, some school psychologists* subspecialize in areas of practice or client "type," such as working with children with sensory limitations (e.g., blindness or deafness); children who have educational exceptionalities (e.g., attention-deficit, gifted, learning disabilities, mental retardation); children of a given age (e.g., adolescence, preschool); or children from different cultural and/or language backgrounds. Specializations in school psychology are typically not credentialed, regulated, or licensed as separate entities; rather, they tend to be areas in which training programs or individual psychologists profess identification and special skill.

See also SPECIALTY TRAINING AND CREDENTIALING; VOCATIONAL SCHOOL PSYCHOLOGY.

REFERENCE

Fagan, T. K., and P. S. Wise. (1994). *School psychology: Past, present, and future.* White Plains, NY: Longman.

Bruce A. Bracken

SCHOOL SETTINGS. School settings are the public and nonpublic elementary and secondary schools, as well as residential schools, comprising both regular education and special education.* Psychological services in these settings are provided by school psychologists* who are primarily employees of a school district; however, some schools, often rural, are provided services by employees of intermediate agencies* such as special education cooperatives.

An early survey of school psychologists indicated 72 percent working in city schools, 18 percent working in county schools, 5 percent working in state schools, that is, for the blind or deaf, and 5 percent working in private schools ("Results of Questionnaire," 1960). In a recent study, 86 percent of school psychologists were primarily employed in school settings. The school psychologist most often serves one district at the elementary level, the secondary level, or both. Those who worked in largely urban settings totaled 28 percent, in suburban settings 33 percent, in rural settings 21 percent, and in combined settings 17 percent (Reschly and Wilson, 1995). The apparent shift of having fewer school psychologists working in public school settings (95 percent to 86 percent) over the last thirty years indicates an expansion of employment opportunities in other settings. School psychologists now work in hospitals,* mental health clinics, postsecondary settings,* pediatric settings,* and private practice.* One must note that the 1960 research questioned only members of Division 16 of the American Psychological Association,* who were then required to be employed in school settings for membership.

Organizational structure can influence the delivery of services in the schools. In city or county districts, school psychological services can be found as a part of either special education or pupil personnel services.* In larger urban areas, school psychological services might be under the direction of an assistant superintendent. The relationship of school psychological services to special education can dictate which problems receive emphasis in the district. These same relationships can exist at the state department of education* (SED) and influence local models for service delivery. With only about half the states having school psychology state consultants, clearly other professions continue to strongly influence the role and function of school psychology.

Where school psychologists are housed, in a central facility or at a school building, can influence teachers' perceptions of their availability and loyalties. Small city and county districts often have few or only one school psychologist, invariably serving several buildings.

Rural areas can avail themselves of a cooperative agreement district where several rural districts or even multiple counties receive services from intermediate agencies. These agencies can be administratively attached to one of the school districts or function as agency districts under the direction of the SDE.

Noneducational agencies, such as mental health centers, can provide school psychological services to several rural districts. Some psychologists who are self-employed provide contractual services* to several districts. In some states, these self-employed psychologists may not be trained as school psychologists. Also, contractual services may not be comprehensive in nature.

With the shift toward inclusion,* the future of school psychology is uncertain, but the organizational structure and location of services will shape that future. Only with a reasonable psychologist/student ratio and access to classrooms and teachers can school psychologists become players in serving integrated special education students and other students at risk.

See also RURAL SCHOOL PSYCHOLOGY; SUBURBAN SCHOOL PSYCHOLOGY; URBAN SCHOOL PSYCHOLOGY.

REFERENCES

Fagan, T. K., and P. S. Wise. (1994). *School psychology: Past, present, and future.* White Plains, NY: Longman.
Reschly, D. J., and M. S. Wilson. (1995). School psychology faculty and practitioners: 1986–1991 trends in demographic characteristics, roles, satisfaction, and system reform. *School Psychology Review* 24, 62–80.
Results of questionnaire on working conditions of school psychologists. (1960). *Division of School Psychologists Newsletter* 14(2), 4.

Paul G. Warden

SCIENTIST-PRACTITIONER MODEL. The term ''scientist-practitioner'' refers to a specific conceptual model for the professional practice of psychology. Although the term often is used to refer to a model for training, it actually refers to the model for practice for which a training program is preparing its graduates.

The scientist-practitioner model originated from the Boulder conference* in 1949, which was organized following the initial American Psychological Association* (APA) accreditation of professional training programs in clinical and, later, counseling psychology (Lambert, 1993). Conference participants wanted to promote the scientific base of traditional experimental psychology as the foundation for the professional practice of psychology. They contended that the professional psychologist should not only have a solid foundation in scientific methods but actually engage in the conduct of research as well (Fagan and Wise, 1994). Relatedly, they desired to promote the preparation of psychologists accordingly. However, aside from emphasizing the inclusion of scientific inquiry in the preparation of psychologists, the conference generated little insight into the ways in which science and professional practice might be integrated (Lambert, 1993).

There tends to be considerable variation in the way school psychology* training programs implement the scientist-practitioner model. Fagan and Wise (1994) suggest that the programs fall along a continuum, with those on the scientist side giving greater emphasis to statistics and research, while those on the practitioner side emphasize professional knowledge and skills. However, even those programs that tend to lean more toward the practitioner side of such a continuum should emphasize a scientific knowledge base as the foundation to professional practice if they espouse adherence to the scientist-practitioner model.

See also PROFESSIONAL TRAINING MODEL; TRAINING MODELS.

REFERENCES

Fagan, T. K., and P. S. Wise. (1994). *School psychology: Past, present, and future.* White Plains, NY: Longman.

Lambert, N. M. (1993). Historical perspective on school psychology as a scientist-practitioner specialization in school psychology. *Journal of School Psychology* 31, 163–193.

                                                                        Michael J. Curtis

SCOPE OF PRACTICE. The term ''scope of practice'' refers to the general areas of knowledge and expertise accompanying psychological specialties, more specifically, to the knowledge and expertise of individual practitioners. While generalist orientations were common in the evolution of professional psychology specialties (e.g., clinical,* counseling, and school psychology*), a number of distinct subspecialties that require extensive specialized training have emerged over the past few decades. The person who is well trained as a psychotherapist with adults may be incompetent at neurological assessment, marriage counseling, or child educational practices. The ethical practitioner recognizes his or her practice limitations and does not exceed them.

The *Ethical Principles of Psychologists and Code of Conduct* (American Psychological Association, 1992) addresses this matter thus:

Principle A: Competence

Psychologists . . . recognize the boundaries of their particular competencies and the limitations of their expertise. They provide only those services and use only those techniques for which they are qualified by education, training, or experience.

If ethical strictures are overlooked by a practitioner so that the service he or she provides a client proves inadequate, and the client files suit, the courts would, in all likelihood, take a violation of such an ethical principle as evidence of malpractice.

See also CODES OF ETHICS; PROFESSIONAL STANDARDS.

REFERENCE

American Psychological Association. (1992). Ethical principles of psychologists and code of conduct. *American Psychologist* 47, 1597–1611.

J. L. Bernard

SCORES. A raw score represents a numerical summary of an individual's performance on a test. An isolated raw score provides little interpretive value unless it can be compared with either a distribution of other individuals' raw scores (norm-referenced interpretation) or standards indicative of mastery (criterion-referenced interpretation). Methods have been developed that allow for meaningful interpretation based on a single summary statistic that falls on a scale that has well-defined characteristics such as constant measures of central tendency and variability. The most common of these derived scores are grade equivalents, percentiles, and standard scores. A grade equivalent score represents the school grade group in which a student's raw score is average. A percentile score represents the percentage of students in the norm group whose raw score is less than the student's raw score. A standard score (e.g., z-score, T-score, norm-curve equivalent score, deviation IQ score, scaled score, stanine score) represents the standardized distance by which a student's raw score is less (or greater) than the average raw score of students in the norm group.

See also CRITERION-REFERENCED ASSESSMENT; NORM-REFERENCED ASSESSMENT.

REFERENCES

Crocker, L., and J. Algina. (1986). *Introduction to classical and modern test theory.* New York: Holt, Rinehart, and Winston.
Gronlund, N. E., and R. L. Linn. (1990). *Measurement and evaluation in teaching* (6th ed.). New York: Macmillan.
Lyman, H. B. (1986). *Test scores and what they mean* (4th ed.). Englewood Cliffs, NJ: Prentice-Hall.

William T. Coombs

SCREENING ASSESSMENT. Screening assessment is the assessment of every student in a population to pick out those who should be receiving a targeted service. Among the most frequent purposes of screening assessment are the identification of students who may benefit from special education* or related services,* the identification of students requiring counseling or psychotherapy services, determining whether young children are ready to begin formal schooling, and the identification of students requiring enrichment activities or programs for the gifted and talented.

Typically, screening procedures are part of a two-step process. A brief and easy-to-administer screening measure is given to all students; results of this brief measure are then used to identify a group of students who are most likely to meet criteria for the target services. These identified students are then administered a more comprehensive assessment* to determine whether or not they should be provided services.

Criteria for screening assessment procedures differ in important respects from the criteria for traditional assessments. First, it is imperative that the screening procedure be brief to administer and easy to score; procedures that can be administered simultaneously to large groups and computer-scored are ideal for screening assessments. Frequently, screening assessments are conducted by paraprofessionals* to conserve more expensive professional time. Second, it is imperative that the screening identify virtually all students who are appropriate targets for services. Finally, more effective screening assessment procedures minimize the need for assessment by identifying relatively few false positives.

Examples of contemporary screening measures that meet these criteria include the Child Behavior Checklist, used to screen for psychiatric disorders in epidemiological studies supported by the National Institute of Mental Health; the Reynolds Adolescent Depression Survey, used in a procedure to screen secondary schools for all instances of clinical depression; First Steps, used to screen preschool populations for instances of cognitive, language, or emotional delays; and Systematic Screening for Behavior Disorders, used to screen school populations for instances of significant emotional disorders.

See also PREREFERRAL ASSESSMENT; PRESCHOOL ASSESSMENT; PREVENTION.

REFERENCES

McLoughlin, C. S., and E. Rausch. (1990). Best practices in kindergarten screening. In A. Thomas and J. Grimes (Eds.), *Best practices in school psychology—II* (pp. 455–467). Washington, DC: National Association of School Psychologists.

Reynolds, W. M. (1986). A model for screening and identification of depressed children and adolescents in school settings. *Professional School Psychology* 1, 117–129.

Beth Doll

SECOND OPINION. According to the Rules and Regulations for the Implementation of P.L. [Public Law] 94-142* (the Education for all Handicapped Children Act of 1975; now Public Law 101-476,* the Individuals with Disabilities Education Act of 1990), parents or guardians have the right to contest the procedures and conclusions of evaluations conducted by employees of a local educational setting (see e.g., Gutkin and Reynolds, 1990, Appendix C). One means by which such evaluations are contested is by obtaining a second opinion via an evaluation conducted by practitioners independent of the educational setting. Parents or guardians may seek independent second opinions at their own expense at any time and present the results to the educational setting for consideration. Through the use of a due process* hearing, the parents/guardians may present the findings of their independently obtained second opinion. The presiding hearing* officer may conclude that the evaluation and findings by the school district or those of the independent evaluation were the more appropriate. The hearing officer may also judge whether the independent evaluation is to be paid for at public expense.

Parents or guardians also have the right to obtain an independent psychoeducational evaluation at their own expense prior to, or in the absence of, any evaluation being conducted by the school. In this case, the school system is required to consider these results or challenge them by conducting its own evaluation.

See also PUBLIC LAW 99-457.

REFERENCES

Gutkin, T. B., and C. R. Reynolds. (1990). *The handbook of school psychology.* New York: Wiley.
McKee, P. W., and R. H. Barbe. (1994). Independent evaluation: Maybe, at the school's expense. *Communique* 23(2), 1, 6.

R. Scott Beebe

SECTION 504 OF THE REHABILITATION ACT. The Rehabilitation Act of 1973 is a comprehensive act providing protection against discrimination on the basis of an individual's handicapping condition. Although the initial impact of Section 504 was felt in the area of employment of individuals with disabilities and minorities, the scope of the law was not limited to employment practices. The act extended to program accessibility, preschool through postsecondary education, and health, welfare, and social services. Provisions of Section 504 prohibit discrimination against all persons with disabilities, including staff and students in school systems receiving federal financial assistance. All programs and activities in school systems receiving federal funds are affected regardless of whether the specific program or activity in question is the direct recipient of federal dollars. The U.S. Department of Education regulations for Section 504 also require that students with disabilities must be provided a free and appropriate public education* (FAPE), including identification, evaluation, provision of appropriate services, and procedural safeguards.*

All students considered disabled under IDEA (Individuals with Disabilities Education Act, Public Law 101-476*) are also considered handicapped and protected under Section 504. However, the reverse does not always hold true. That is, some students identified under Section 504 may not be disabled under IDEA. Eligibility under IDEA requires that students be identified as handicapped in specified categories. In contrast, Section 504 protects all students who have any physical or mental impairment that substantially limits one or more major life activities, including learning. Students identified as handicapped under Section 504, but not IDEA, receive services from regular education. Examples of students who may be protected under Section 504, but not IDEA, include students with juvenile arthritis, acquired immunodeficiency syndrome (AIDS), and attention deficit disorder (ADD) who do not qualify as emotionally disturbed, other health-impaired, or learning-disabled under IDEA.

Identification under Section 504 requires that parents or guardians be provided with notice of actions affecting identification, evaluation, or placement. Parents and guardians are also entitled to an impartial hearing if they disagree with school decisions. Although more limited than multidisciplinary evaluations required by IDEA, these evaluations must be sufficient to accurately and completely assess the nature and extent of the disability and make recommendations for programming. Decisions about eligibility are made by a group of professionals who are knowledgeable about the student. Documentation of placement decisions is required, with accompanying periodic reviews.

See also OFFICE OF CIVIL RIGHTS; TEAM APPROACH.

REFERENCES

Council of Administrators of Special Education, Inc. (1993). *Student access: A resource guide for educators: Section 504 of the rehabilitation act of 1973* (Abbreviated Version). Washington, DC: U.S. Government Printing Office.
Federal Register. (1992, September 29), 57(189), 44794–44852. Washington, DC: U.S. Government Printing Office.

Peggy A. Hicks

SEGREGATED SERVICES. Segregation refers to the process of setting apart, separating, or isolating one or more persons from a larger group, often for the purposes of preventing anticipated difficulties, restricting social interactions, providing needed and different services, or punishing inappropriate behaviors.

Education traditionally has been provided in segregated settings. Various demographic qualities (e.g., age, gender, social class, race), sensory acuity and other physical deficiencies, levels of achievement, intelligence,* and social and emotional development, together with geographic area of residence, often have contributed to the formation of segregated educational settings. Segregated services based on race and handicapping conditions have been most objectionable; those associated with ability grouping* also have been challenged frequently.

Education historically has been provided to a small number of students, namely, males from well-educated and wealthy families. Following the Industrial Revolution and the movement of large numbers of families from rural to urban areas, public schools were established to educate more students. Preference initially was shown to boys between ages six and twelve, although larger numbers of girls also were educated. Throughout the first half of the twentieth century, children and youth with severe disorders typically were either excluded from school or educated in residential institutions, special schools, or self-contained day programs. Educators and parents increasingly relied on self-contained settings to best meet the needs of students with handicapping conditions.

Segregated services have been most numerous in the education of African-American students. In many smaller southern cities, separate schools were created for African-American and white students. Segregated schools also could be found in many larger cities, including those in the North, because neighborhood schools often reflected segregated living conditions.

The legality of segregated schooling was challenged in the 1954 U.S. Supreme Court decision in *Brown v. Board of Education in Topeka,** which banned racial segregation in schools. Advocates for students with handicapping conditions used *Brown* as legal precedent for implementing desegregation and improved services for them.

Congress amended the Elementary and Secondary Education Act of 1965 (Public Law 89-750) to promote and expand programs and personnel for the handicapped. Congress became dissatisfied with the states' progress and passed stronger legislation in Section 504 of the Rehabilitation Act* of 1973 (Public Law 93-380*) and the Education of All Handicapped Children's Act in 1975 (Public Law 94-142*). Subsequent legislation has contributed to the creation of educational, living, and working environments that minimize physical and other barriers for persons with handicapping conditions (Oakland et al., 1991).

See also FREE APPROPRIATE PUBLIC EDUCATION; LEAST RESTRICTIVE ENVIRONMENT.

REFERENCE

Oakland, T., J. Cunningham, P. Meazzini, and A. Poulsen. (1991). An examination of policies governing the normalization of handicapped pupils in Denmark, Italy, and the United States. *International Journal of Special Education* 6, 386–402.

Thomas Oakland

SELF-CONCEPT. Self-concept is the perception a person has of himself or herself as an individual functioning within several important life contexts. Self-concept is a stable human characteristic and is relatively resistant to change because it is a learned behavioral response pattern. A child who is repeatedly told that he is smart and experiences considerable school success is likely to develop a very positive academic self-concept. Given a consistent history of positive feedback, the examinee is likely to develop a very persistent, positive self-image in the academic domain.

Self-concept is a multidimensional construct; that is, rather than having a single self-concept, people have as many self-concepts as the contexts in which they operate. Six important contexts that influence children's developing self-concepts include social, competence, affect, academic, family, and physical domains. It is quite possible, for example, to have a negative self-concept in one domain (e.g., physical) and a very positive self-concept in another domain (e.g., academic), with the remaining self-concept domains being rated in the average range.

Self-concepts are acquired through the feedback individuals receive from two primary perspectives (self-perceptions and others' perceptions) and four standards (absolute, comparative, ipsative, and ideal). While an absolute standard represents the objective evaluation of what an individual can or cannot do, a comparative standard is the comparison a person makes with his or her performance and the performances of other individuals. The ipsative standard allows individuals to emphasize or de-emphasize individual successes and failures by comparing their performance in one domain (e.g., physical) with other domains (e.g., social, family). The ideal standards are the goals we strive for but seldom achieve.

Two commonly used historical measures of self-concept for children and adolescents include the Piers-Harris Children's Self-Concept Scale (Piers, 1984) and the Coopersmith Self-Esteem Inventory (Coopersmith, 1984).

REFERENCES

Bracken, B. A. (1992). *Multidimensional Self-Concept Scale.* Austin, TX: PRO-ED.
————. (Ed.). (1994). *Handbook of self-concept.* New York: Wiley.
Coopersmith, S. (1984). *Coopersmith Self-Esteem Inventory.* Palo Alto, CA: Consulting Psychologists Press.
Piers, E. V. (1984). *Piers-Harris Children's Self-Concept Scale.* Los Angeles: Western Psychological Services.

Bruce A. Bracken

SELF-CONTAINED CLASS. Self-contained class refers to the educational placement setting for children with diverse abilities or needs where the same teacher or team of teachers provides the instruction for most of the daily instructional sessions. Although less restrictive than special schools, the self-contained class is more restrictive than educational support received in a resource room* or the general classroom.

Before Public Law 94-142,* early efforts to provide special education* to students with disabilities utilized the self-contained special class as the preferred placement option. This practice led to a dual educational system of special education and general education with limited positive social and academic interaction between students with disabilities and students without disabilities. More recently, greater inclusion* into the general classroom with appropriate curricular modification and support is preferred over the special class model, except in circumstances involving students with more severe disability or students who need an alternative education for most or all of the school day. Most used at the secondary level for students with mental retardation or severe emotional disabilities, the curriculum taught within a self-contained classroom is functional, including skill training for job acquisition and work, community and life management, and social interaction skills.

See also CLASSIFICATION: EDUCATIONAL; RESOURCE ROOM.

REFERENCE

Smith, D. D., and R. Luckasson. (1992). *Introduction to special education: Teaching in an age of challenge.* Boston: Allyn and Bacon.

Diane Montgomery

SELF-MANAGEMENT. Self-management describes a variety of therapy techniques and programs prescribed from many theoretical backgrounds. It is a participant model that emphasizes the importance of the client's* responsibility, and, instead of offering a protective treatment environment, it encourages clients to accept increasing responsibility for their own behavior (Kanfer and Gaelick-Buys, 1991). This means that clients direct their change efforts by modifying aspects of the environment or by using and dispensing consequences (Cormier and Cormier, 1985).

The occurrence of self-management is a relatively recent arrival in counseling and therapy, and reports of therapeutic application have burgeoned since 1970 (Corey, 1990). These applications are temporary devices that help the learning process but do not necessarily become a part of the person's everyday repertoire (Kanfer and Gaelick-Buys, 1991). However, they are available for the client when he or she faces difficulties.

Specific strategies include, but are not limited to, problem solving, self-monitoring, self-reward, self-contracting, and stimulus control. Self-management strategies have been applied to many populations and many issues. Examples include anxiety disorder, depression, pain, agoraphobia, anger, test anxiety, and assertiveness. Psychologists who share these strategies are primarily concerned with teaching people the skills they need to manage their own lives effectively (Corey, 1990).

See also COGNITIVE BEHAVIOR MODIFICATION; COGNITIVE THERAPY.

REFERENCES

Corey, G. (1990). *Theory and practice of counseling and psychotherapy.* Pacific Grove, CA: Brooks/Cole.
Cormier, W. H., and L. S. Cormier. (1985). *Interviewing strategies for helpers, fundamental skills and cognitive behavioral interventions* (2d ed.). Monterey, CA: Brooks/Cole.
Kanfer, F. H., and L. Gaelick-Buys. (1991). Self-management methods. In F. H. Kanfer and A. P. Goldstein (Eds.), *Helping people change, a textbook of methods* (pp. 305–360). New York: Pergamon Press.

Sandy R. Locke
Donald L. Boswell

SENSITIVITY TRAINING. Sensitivity training (ST), often referred to as T-groups (training groups), is a general term used to describe a variety of small-group interactive experiences designed to develop understanding of intergroup issues and dynamics. Group size is generally below fifteen; meeting frequency and length vary according to need and interest.

The main goal of ST is to assist coworkers or parties-at-interest to some issue in understanding each other's beliefs, needs, reasoning styles, and concerns so that the group can move forward to more effective problem solving. Members are encouraged to speak their minds about issues central to the group's progress and to give and receive feedback from each other. Through the dynamics of group interaction, it is hoped that barriers to group harmony will be removed and that individuals will come to group consensus and understanding of each other.

The movement was begun in the 1940s by social psychologists Kurt Lewin and Ronald Lippitt. Based on some action-research results that suggested the power of these techniques, the National Training Laboratories (NTL) were established. This group served as the central force behind the spread of these techniques to business and the social sciences. Current critics of ST believe the experience can be too threatening for some participants and that the effects are only short-lived.

See also GROUP THERAPY.

REFERENCES

Appley, D. G., and A. E. Windsor. (1973). *T-groups and therapy groups in a changing society.* San Francisco: Jossey-Bass.
Golembiewski, Robert. (1972). *Renewing organizations.* Itasca, IL: Peacock.
                                                            Thomas J. Kampwirth

SERVICE RATIOS. The service ratio refers to the number of school-age children served per school psychologist.* It is expressed as a ratio of school psychologists to children. Historically, the ratio has improved from 1:60,000 in 1934, to 1:2,100 in 1986, and in 1992 it was reported to be approximately 1:2,000. In the nation's largest school districts, the median ratio has improved from 1:18,500 in 1950 to 1:2,000 in 1991. As a quantitative representation of the level of services provided, the service ratio is only a crude measure of service quality.

REFERENCES

Fagan, T. K. (1988). The historical improvement of the school psychology service ratio: Implications for future employment. *School Psychology Review* 17, 447–458.
Fagan, T. K., and M. Schicke. (1994). The service ratio in large school districts: Historical and contemporary perspectives. *Journal of School Psychology* 32, 305–312.
                                                            Thomas K. Fagan

SIBLING GROUPS. ''Sibling groups'' is a term applied to a classification of therapeutic groups, the members of which share a need for supportive assistance involving a familial relationship. Often considered an extension of parent support groups, sibling groups provide additional services for families in times of stress. A primary purpose of the group is to furnish information related to the targeted concern as well as to share coping strategies. Sibling groups focus on the need for clarification and support rather than psychotherapy.

A popular example is a sibling group whose participants are members of families that include children with disabilities. Families of children with special needs may require intervention services in order to foster the child's special developmental requirements. Additionally, siblings of children with disabilities may feel the need for added support due to increased parental demands on them or, conversely, lack of attention from parents. Sibling groups provide peer support from members who are experiencing similar feelings and problems. With sibling groups of elementary-age children, role playing and storytelling techniques provide problem-solving opportunities for developing coping strategies. Other types of sibling groups include groups whose members have experienced death or the effects of addiction.

See also FAMILY ASSESSMENT; FAMILY ENABLEMENT/EMPOWERMENT; FAMILY THERAPY; GROUP THERAPY; SUPPORT GROUPS.

REFERENCES

Powell, T., and P. Ogle. (1985). *Brothers and sisters: A special part of exceptional families.* Baltimore: Brookes.
Summers, M., J. Bridge, and C. Summers. (1991). Sibling support groups. *Teaching Exceptional Children* 23(4), 20–25.

Denise Cutbirth
Diane Montgomery

SOCIAL SKILLS ASSESSMENT. Social skills may be defined as socially acceptable learned behaviors that enable a person to interact with others in ways that elicit positive responses and assist in avoiding negative responses (Gresham and Elliott, 1990). Many children with social skills difficulties are unaccepted by peers, have poor relationships with adults, and often are at risk academically.

In general, the purposes of social skills assessments are either identification/ classification or intervention/program planning. The critical characteristic that differentiates assessment methods is the extent to which a method allows for a functional analysis of behavior (i.e., the extent to which an assessment procedure provides data on the antecedent, sequential, and consequent conditions surrounding a molecular behavior). Methods for assessing social skills vary along three primary dimensions: source, specificity, and temporal proximity of report to behavior performance. Thus, methods can rely on different sources, such as parents, teachers, peers, trained observers, or the child. From these sources, information is provided that varies in specificity, ranging from global or molar descriptions to molecular behaviors. Finally, these methods of assessment may differ with respect to temporal proximity of report or observation of behavior performance. For example, direct observations occur concurrently with the target behavior, whereas the completion of a behavior rating scale or analog role-play can be quite removed in time and space from the actual occurrence of a target behavior. The combination of these dimensions, plus the content focus of the method, influences the utility or purpose of an assessment.

The process of social skills assessment can be characterized by a series of hypothesis-testing sequences. Hypotheses are generated in an attempt to answer questions regarding identification, intervention,* and evaluation of treatment effects. Hypotheses may be generated based on information that is available at any given point in the assessment process and then tested at subsequent points through the gathering of additional information. Comprehensive assessment* allows one to draw conclusions regarding problem severity, interfering behaviors, necessary intervention strategies, and the degree of treatment success.

A standard battery of tests or methods for assessing social skills does not exist. Rather, hypotheses generated dictate the direction of assessment, the questions to be answered, and the methods to be used. Ideally, practitioners should use assessment methods possessing the attributes of reliability,* validity,* and practicality. Unfortunately, few social skills assessment methods meet all of these criteria. Easily administered instruments that are useful for screening purposes (e.g., self-report scales) are of little help in designing interventions. Other methods requiring considerably more effort from assessors and clients* (e.g., naturalistic observations* and self-monitoring) often have equivocal or unknown psychometric properties. Moreover, there is a tendency for assessment data obtained from different sources to correlate moderately at best and, more often, to correlate quite low. As a safeguard, multiple sources of information are required when assessing social skills.

To increase the likelihood of accurate identification/classification decisions, direct observations of the target child and nontarget peers in multiple settings are recommended, as well as behavioral interviews with both the referral source and the target child; rating scale data, preferably norm-referenced,* on both a social skills scale and a problem behavior scale completed by the referral source and possibly the target child; and sociometric data from the target child's classmates. Regarding intervention decisions, data contributing to a functional analysis of important social behaviors are imperative. This type of data usually results from multiple direct observations across settings; behavioral role-plays with the target child; and teacher and parent ratings of socially valid molecular behaviors. If individuals other than a psychologist will be involved in delivering the treatment, behavioral interviews with the treatment agent(s) also will be important to assess the treatment setting, the acceptability of the final treatment plan,* and the integrity with which the plan is implemented.

Behavior rating scales* have become one of the most common methods used to assess children's social behavior. Several such scales have been developed that have good-to-excellent psychometric qualities. In a comprehensive review of rating scales, Demaray et al. (in press) identified six published rating scales designed to assess children's social skills. The authors concluded that the most comprehensive instrument was the Social Skills Rating System (SSRS) because of its multisource (i.e., teacher, parent, student) rating approach and intervention linkages. The School Social Behavior Scales (SSBS, Merrell, 1993) and the Walker-McConnell Scale of Social Competence and School Adjustment (WMS, Walker and McConnell, 1988) were also considered useful tools for more limited, teacher ratings only (grades K–6) assessment of social skills.

Social skills assessment will continue to be an active area of research that has significant implications for practice. For example, much attention is being given to the use and interpretation of multiple sources of social behavior data to design interventions and the use of interactive computer and video technology to create common problem-solving situations to assess children's social problem-solving skills.

In summary, the state of social skills assessment emphasizes the use of multiple assessment methods that focus on a range of prosocial (e.g., cooperation, assertion, self-control, responsibility, empathy) and potentially disturbing behaviors (e.g., physical and verbal aggression, anxiety, withdrawal). The most common assessment methods include naturalistic observations and teacher-completed rating scales, although parent scales and self-ratings also are frequently included in comprehensive assessments.

See also BEHAVIORAL ASSESSMENT; INTERVIEWING; NATURALISTIC OBSERVATION; SOCIAL SKILLS TRAINING.

REFERENCES

Demaray, M. K., S. L. Ruffalo, J. Carlson, A. E. Olson, S. McManus, A. Levanthal, and R. T. Busse. (in press). Social skills assessment: A comparative evaluation of published rating scales. *School Psychology Review*.

Gresham, F. M., and S. N. Elliott. (1990). *Social Skills Rating System*. Circle Pines, MN: American Guidance Service.

Merrell, K. W. (1993). *School Social Behavior Scales*. Brandon, VT: Clinical Psychology.

Walker, H. M. and S. R. McConnell. (1988). *The Walker-McConnell Scale of Social Competence and School Adjustment*. Austin, TX: Pro-Ed.

Stephen N. Elliott

SOCIAL SKILLS TRAINING. Social skills training covers a wide range of interventions* that emphasize the acquisition and performance of prosocial behaviors and typically utilize nonaversive methods to teach these prosocial behaviors. Some social skills interventions, however, often must concurrently focus on the reduction of interfering problem behaviors as well as the teaching of prosocial behaviors. Thus, social skills training has four primary objectives: (1) promoting social skills acquisition, (2) enhancing social skills performance, (3) reducing or removing interfering problem behaviors, and (4) facilitating the generalization and maintenance of social skills.

Common social skills training tactics can be characterized as therapist-directed, therapist- and peer-directed, or peer-directed. These procedures can be further categorized into three theoretical approaches (operant, social learning, and cognitive-behavioral) that differ according to the focus of treatment (e.g., children's thinking and problem-solving skills, children's behavior) and to their active treatment procedures (e.g., modeling,* reinforcement of appropriate behavior).

Regardless of theoretical approach, teaching social skills involves many of the same methods as teaching academic concepts. Effective teachers of both academic and social skills model correct or appropriate behavior, elicit an imitative response, provide corrective feedback, and arrange for opportunities to practice the new skill. A large number of intervention procedures have been identified for teaching social skills to children. These procedures are based on the assumption that children learn social skills through the processes of observational and instrumental learning.

Five fundamental assumptions are central to the ongoing assessment and treatment of social skills:

1. Social skills are primarily acquired through learning that involves observation, modeling, rehearsal, and feedback.

2. Social skills include specific, discrete verbal and nonverbal behaviors.

3. Social skills require specific behaviors that are effective in initiating, maintaining, and terminating interpersonal interactions and relationships.

4. Social skills are interactive by nature and entail effective and appropriate behavioral performances.

5. Social skills are situationally specific behaviors and are influenced by the characteristics, demands, and expectations operating in specific environments.

Collectively, these five assumptions stress the multidimensional (verbal-nonverbal and initiating-responding), interactive, situation-specific nature of social skills. As such, effective interventions need to address (1) target behaviors involving both verbal and nonverbal communications used to initiate or respond to others and (2) the ability to discriminate when to exhibit certain social skills, given changing social situations. Children will likely have some combination of acquisition and performance deficits, some of which may be accompanied by interfering behaviors, and others of which will not. Thus, any given child may require some combination of acquisition, performance, and behavior reduction strategies. All children also require procedures to facilitate the generalization and maintenance of social skills. Procedures designed to facilitate generalization and maintenance of social skills must be incorporated from the very beginning for any social skills training program to be effective.

Although a number of procedures, such as modeling, coaching, cognitive

problem solving, and discrimination training, have been developed to teach social skills, four fundamental processes underlie all social skill intervention techniques. Ladd and Mize (1983) termed these processes "training variables."
These training variables are (1) instruction, (2) rehearsal, (3) reinforcement or
feedback, and (4) reductive processes.

Both qualitative and quantitative (Elliott and Gresham, 1993; Schneider,
1992) reviews of the social skills training literature suggest that it is an effective
intervention for changing social behavior and, to a lesser extent, in promoting
generalization/maintenance and peer acceptance and reducing antisocial behavior. Practical suggestions from the research literature include the extensive use
of operant* methods to reinforce existing social skills. The basic operant methods include the manipulation of environmental conditions to create opportunities
for social interactions that prompt or cue socially desired behavior in a child
and the manipulation of consequences so that socially appropriate behavior is
reinforced, and socially inappropriate behavior, whenever possible, is ignored
rather than punished. Some of the reasons for social skills training not producing
larger, more generalized effects, in part, are due to three things: (1) failure of
researchers and practitioners to "match" social skills instructional strategies
with specific types of social skills deficits, (2) failure to adequately program for
generalization, and (3) using "weak" treatments in restricted settings to change
behavior.

See also BEHAVIOR MODIFICATION; BEHAVIOR THERAPY; SOCIAL
SKILLS ASSESSMENT.

REFERENCES

Elliott, S. N. and F. M. Gresham. (1993). Social skills interventions for children.
    Behavior Modification 17, 287–313.
Ladd, G., and J. Mize. (1983). A cognitive-social learning model of social skills
    training. *Psychological Review* 90, 127–157.
Schneider, B. (1992). Didactic methods for enhancing children's peer relations: A
    quantitative review. *Clinical Psychology Review* 12, 363–382.

Stephen N. Elliott

SOCIETY FOR THE PREVENTION OF CRUELTY TO CHILDREN.
Founded in New York City in 1875, the Society for the Prevention of Cruelty
to Children (SPCC) grew out of a famous case in which a social worker could
find no agency to accept an abused ten-year-old girl. The social worker turned
to the Society for the Prevention of Cruelty to Animals (SPCA), which found
a foster home for the girl. The president of the SPCA, Henry Bergh, and the
general counsel, Elbridge Gerry, created the new organization, which would
provide foster homes for abused and neglected children and also attempt to
lessen the extent of abuse in urban families. The SPCC employed agents who
had wide discretion in handling cases. If, in the agent's judgment, a complaint
was based on spite, or if the child in question "deserved" corporal correction,

the agent did nothing. In other cases, the agent might lecture the abusing adults or remove the child from the home. About 30 percent of the SPCC cases resulted in foster home placement. The agency was a pioneer in child advocacy, but it was controversial. Working-class families viewed it as an attack on the family wage system, while reformers opposed the agency's policy of placing some of the children under its control in institutions such as the New York House of Refuge, a reformatory for juvenile delinquents. By the end of the nineteenth century, most major American cities had similar organizations.

Societies for the prevention of cruelty to children or equivalent child protection agencies continue to function in American cities. They have tended to become advocacy agencies rather than service providers, as state and local agencies have assumed most of the service burdens.

See also CHILD ADVOCACY; CHILDREN'S RIGHTS; CORPORAL PUNISHMENT.

REFERENCES

Child Welfare League of America. (1980). *Directory of member agencies.* New York: Author.
Hawes, J. M. (1991). *The children's rights movement: A history of advocacy and protection.* Boston: Twayne.
Pleck, E. (1987). *Domestic tyranny: The making of American social policy against family violence.* New York: Oxford University Press.

Joseph M. Hawes

SOCIOGRAMS. A sociogram is a diagram designed to indicate patterns of human interaction within a social structure. These patterns often depict underlying attractions as well as status dimensions. Sociograms enable individuals within a group to operationally define how they feel toward each other. More specifically, valuable information is provided through understanding how an individual is viewed by others, as well as how they see themselves.

In a classic study, Jennings (1943) was one of the first to use a sociogram as a technique for assessing individuals' preferences in associates. On the basis of this information, she drew a sociogram—a visual depiction of who liked whom. During the postdepression and World War II era, sociometric measures similar to sociograms thrived. Researchers doggedly charted the sociometric choices of literally thousands of groups. Unfortunately, the sociometric measures had one flaw, which led to their decline: as the group under study gets larger and larger, a sociogram becomes more and more complicated.

The sociogram may be used in a variety of settings and utilized in different ways. It may be an effective warming-up experience when a new group comes together. It may also be used as a technique for assessing interaction structures among members of groups and network phenomena. Sociograms may simply be used as a measure of group cohesiveness (Doreian, 1986).

See also FAMILY ASSESSMENT; SOCIAL SKILLS ASSESSMENT.

REFERENCES

Doreian, P. (1986). Measuring relative standing in small group and bounded social networks. *Social Psychology Quarterly* 49, 247–259.
Jennings, H. H. (1943). Leadership and isolation. In B. Seidenberg and A. Snadowsky (Eds.), *Social psychology* (pp. 284–285). New York: Free Press.

Timothy J. Daheim
Donald L. Boswell

SOUTHERN REGIONAL EDUCATION BOARD CONFERENCES. In the late 1950s, three conferences on school psychology* were sponsored by the Southern Regional Education Board (SREB) and supported by funds from the National Institute of Mental Health. The general intent was to encourage the creation of doctoral-level school psychology training programs in the South. A statement on the role of the school psychologist* was developed by an SREB commission and validated with discussions of school administrators and psychologists. The first SREB conference sought to further clarify the role of the doctoral school psychologist via a meeting of school administrators, educators, and psychologists in Asheville, North Carolina, June 26–28, 1958. The development of training programs was facilitated through two additional conferences, Seminar on University Programs for the Training of School Psychologists, held in Atlanta, Georgia, October 27–28, 1958, and Seminar on Internships in School Psychology, held in Pine Mountain, Georgia, May 10–13, 1959. The proceedings include brief descriptions of five planned or operating doctoral programs.

See also PEABODY CONFERENCE.

REFERENCE

Southern Regional Education Board. (1959). *Psychologists for schools.* Atlanta, GA: Author.

Thomas K. Fagan

SPECIAL EDUCATION. Special education is a major subpart of school systems, serving approximately 10 percent of the student population identified with one or more categorical disabilities (e.g., mental retardation, visual impairment, learning disability, emotional disturbance). In the United States, special education originated in the late nineteenth century, when public school systems initiated separate classroom programs for children with identifiable school-related problems (e.g., feeblemindedness, mental deficiency, sensory and health impairment). The necessity for a range of special education programs resulted from child-saving reform efforts of the period and especially from the implementation of state compulsory attendance laws. The resulting diversity of the pupil population necessitated a wide range of special programs observable in most large school systems by 1910 (Van Sickle, Witmer, and Ayers, 1911).

Special education programs have changed categorically and grown in enrollment across the twentieth century. Due to improved public health and medical care, some forms of special education disappeared (e.g., open-air schools for respiratory disorders), while others emerged as a result of improved psychoeducational diagnostic and intervention approaches (e.g., learning disabilities). The introduction of the standardized and normed intelligence test provided a reliable means of segmenting the population according to intellectual ability and, thus, a means of classifying the mentally retarded into different levels. The total number of "exceptional" children served has grown from approximately 26,163 in 1922, to 356,903 in 1948, 837,291 in 1958, 2,857,551 in 1971–1972, and approximately 4.5 million in the 1990s (Dunn, 1973; Fagan and Wise, 1994; Ysseldyke and Algozzine, 1990).

The diversity of the school population also necessitated the employment of child study experts to assist in the diagnostic classification of children. These specialists included school psychologists,* school social workers, school counselors, nurses, and others who would later be collectively referred to as pupil personnel services.* School psychology,* in particular, has had a very close association with the development of special education.

For most of its history, special education has been characterized by varying degrees of segregation from regular educational programs in school systems. Originating in an era when medical treatments often included isolation for the protection of the general public, special education children were often segregated from regular schoolchildren as well. As technological advancements and societal attitudes improved, the concept of more inclusive treatments that attempted to retain the patient in the community setting emerged. The changes are observed in the recent prevalence of outpatient medical care, deinstitutionalization, and community mental health centers and the concepts of mainstreaming,* least restrictive environment,* and inclusion* in special education.

Special educational programs, traditionally defined by specific legislative acts and criteria (e.g., Individuals with Disabilities Education Act, Public Law 101-476*), are being broadened to include students considered to be at risk for future problems (e.g., teen pregnancy) and those experiencing difficulties but not eligible by traditional categorical criteria (e.g., Section 504* referrals).

See also CLASSIFICATION: EDUCATIONAL; CLASSIFICATION: PSYCHIATRIC.

REFERENCES

Dunn, L. M. (1973). An overview. In L. M. Dunn (Ed.), *Exceptional children in the schools: Special education in transition* (pp. 1–62). New York: Holt, Rinehart, and Winston.

Fagan, T. K., and P. S. Wise. (1994). *School psychology: Past, present, and future.* White Plains, NY: Longman.

Van Sickle, J. H., L. Witmer, and L. P. Ayers. (1911). *Provision for exceptional children in the public schools* (U.S. Bureau of Education Bulletin No. 14). Washington, DC: U.S. Government Printing Office.

Ysseldyke, J. E., and B. Algozzine. (1990). *Introduction to special education.* Boston: Houghton Mifflin.

Thomas K. Fagan

SPECIALIST DEGREE. Although specialist-level training (a minimum of sixty semester credits) is considered entry-level for national certification in school psychology* (Brown, 1990; Reschly and McMaster-Beyer, 1991), the specialist degree is currently awarded by 68 of 208 school psychology programs responding to a recent survey of training programs (Smith and Henning, in press). Of these programs, 26 offer the specialist degree only, while 34 programs offer the degree in conjunction with master's* and/or doctoral* degrees. The exact title of the specialist degree varies and includes such titles as specialist in psychology, specialist certificate, school psychology specialist certificate, and specialist degree in education (Ed.S.). Many school psychology programs offer specialist-level training but do not award a specialist degree. Credit requirements for specialist degree programs in school psychology range from fifty-four to ninety-nine semester credits, with an average of sixty-nine credits. Two-thirds of the programs require sixty-five to seventy semester credits for the specialist degree.

See also CERTIFICATE OF ADVANCED STUDY; NATIONAL CERTIFICATION IN SCHOOL PSYCHOLOGY; TRAINING MODELS.

REFERENCES

Brown, D. T. (1990). Professional regulation and training in school psychology. In T. B. Gutkin and C. R. Reynolds (Eds.), *The handbook of school psychology* (2d ed., pp. 991–1009). New York: Wiley.

Reschly, D. J., and M. McMaster-Beyer. (1991). Influences of degree level, institutional orientation, college affiliation, and accreditation status on school psychology graduate education. *Professional Psychology: Research and Practice* 22, 368–374.

Smith, D. K., and A. Henning. (in press). *Directory of school psychology graduate programs* (4th ed.). Washington, DC: National Association of School Psychologists.

Douglas K. Smith

SPECIALTY TRAINING AND CREDENTIALING. Early training in applied and professional psychology in the United States was generic in nature. By the middle-1930s, however, specific certification* standards for school psychologists* were in place in New York and Pennsylvania. These standards were promulgated by state departments of education* rather than state licensing boards.* Training requirements were rather general, with Pennsylvania requiring twenty-four semester credit hours of theory, twelve hours of laboratory and practice, and twelve hours of experience. Specific topics of study included educational* and school psychology,* exceptional children, tests and measurements, statistics, and the psychology of childhood and adolescence (French,

1990). Current training standards as espoused by the American Psychological Association* (APA) (1981) and the National Association of School Psychologists* (NASP) (1994) overlap in some areas and are different in others. APA recognizes the doctoral degree* as the entry-level degree and requires training in professional psychology (ethics and standards, research design and methodology, statistics and psychometric methods), biological bases of behavior, cognitive and affective bases of behavior, social bases of behavior, individual behavior, social and philosophical bases of education, curriculum theory and practice, exceptionalities, and organization theory and administrative practice. NASP standards require completion of a master's* or specialist degree* at a minimum, including sixty semester credits of course work and a one-year, 1,200-clock-hour nondoctoral internship or 1,500-clock-hour doctoral internship (NASP, 1994). Specific topics of study include psychological foundations (biological bases of behavior, human learning, social and cultural bases of behavior, child and adolescent development, individual differences*); educational foundations (instructional design, organization and operation of schools); interventions/problem-solving (assessment,* direct interventions,* indirect interventions*); statistics and research methodologies (research and evaluation methods, statistics, measurement); and professional school psychology (history and foundations of school psychology, legal and ethical issues, professional issues and standards, alternative models for the delivery of school psychological services, emergent technologies, roles and functions* of the school psychologist).

Development of school psychology as a separate specialty area in the broader field of psychology was facilitated by two national conferences. The Boulder conference* in Boulder, Colorado, in 1949 addressed graduate education in psychology and focused on the training needs of clinical psychologists working with adults. The Thayer conference,* held five years later in New York, emphasized the role of the school psychologist as an adviser to school personnel, enumerated five specific functions of school psychologists, and presented a curriculum for their training (French, 1990). Two levels of training (doctoral and nondoctoral) were advocated.

Currently, all fifty states provide certification* in school psychology, primarily through their respective state departments of education, with the "school psychologist" title most commonly used. Most states utilize course-based requirements and require training in psychological foundations of education, consultation* and intervention,* tests and measurements, and special education.*

See also ACCREDITATION; TRAINING MODELS.

REFERENCES

American Psychological Association. (1981). *Specialty guidelines for delivery of services by school psychologists.* Washington, DC: Author.

French, J. L. (1990). History of school psychology. In T. B. Gutkin and C. R. Reynolds (Eds.), *The handbook of school psychology* (2d ed., pp. 3–20). New York: Wiley.

National Association of School Psychologists. (1994). *Standards for training and field placement programs in school psychology.* Washington, DC: Author.
————. (1994). *Standards for the credentialing of school psychologists.* Washington, DC: Author.

Douglas K. Smith

SPRING HILL SYMPOSIUM. During June 4–8, 1980, school psychology* turned its attention to the future of the profession for the first time since the Thayer conference* (1954). Three groups, the National School Psychology In-service Training Network,* the National Association of School Psychologists,* and Division 16 of the American Psychological Association,* collaborated in planning the agenda and selecting participants. Sixty-nine participants were chosen from lists submitted by the three groups, with consideration for geography, race, sex, and other variables. Three position papers were solicited prior to the symposium from three distinguished psychologists (G. Trachtman, J. Grimes, and coauthors D. Baer and D. Bushell). Each paper was to address three topics: recent findings in psychoeducational research, trends and problems in the application of psychology to schools, and current issues and practices in general and special education.* Six other distinguished psychologists wrote and presented reactions to these papers. The conference began with a paper on the history of school psychology, followed by a keynote address by William Bevan. Bevan focused on the major forces in society shaping the future, their effects on children and schools, and the implications for psychology. The authors of the position papers and their reactants made presentations. Symposium participants were divided into three groups to discuss implications of what had been presented. Don Peterson provided a synthesis of the symposium's events as a closing activity. This symposium formed the philosophical and political basis for the larger Olympia conference,* which followed in 1981.

REFERENCE

Ysseldyke, J., and R. Weinberg. (1981). The future of psychology in the schools: Proceedings of the Spring Hill symposium. *School Psychology Review* 10, 116–318.

W. Alan Coulter

STAFF DEVELOPMENT. Staff development includes a number of activities designed to train skills and upgrade competencies of staff members. According to the National Association of School Psychologists* (NASP) (1992) *Standards for the Provision of School Psychological Services,* school psychologists* may provide in-service and other staff development activities to individuals who play major roles in the education of children, including parents, teachers, other school personnel, and professionals in community agencies. Staff development consists of continuing professional development* for teachers and other professional staff and initial training activities for teacher assistants, volunteers, and others in a school.

In-service training, a traditional staff development activity provided by school psychologists, has often been described as an ineffective way of promoting staff development (Spitzer, 1979). However, Robinson (1990) noted that in-services can be effective when planned properly and not simply designed to fill the time during an in-service day. Activities in addition to in-service training should be incorporated into a comprehensive staff development program. For example, initial in-service training can be integrated with peer support groups, mentoring, supervision, and other activities that promote application of new skills to daily job performance. Agencies with limited resources can utilize the expertise of other agencies through distance learning and staff exchange programs.

See also PROFESSIONAL STANDARDS.

REFERENCES

Green, S. K. (1995). Best practices in implementing a staff development program. In A. Thomas and J. Grimes (Eds.), *Best practices in school psychology—III* (pp. 123–133). Washington, DC: National Association of School Psychologists.
National Association of School Psychologists. (1992). *Standards for the provision of school psychological services.* Silver Spring, MD: Author.
Robinson, G. A. (1990). Best practices in preparing and presenting in-service training. In A. Thomas and J. Grimes (Eds.), *Best practices in school psychology—II* (pp. 575–589). Washington, DC: National Association of School Psychologists.
Spitzer, D. R. (1979, November). Continuing professional education: A critique of a new challenge for the educational technologist. *Educational Technology* 26–28.
                                                                                Patti L. Harrison

STATE ASSOCIATION. State school psychological associations have existed since 1943; however, school psychologists* did not always have a separate identity among psychologists (Fagan, 1993). This lack of identity forced school psychologists to join either educational and/or clinical psychological associations. During the period 1890 to 1945, most applied psychologists were considered clinical psychologists regardless of setting; however, school psychology* did emerge as a separate entity.

From 1945 to 1965, only twelve school psychology state associations were created; however, from 1967 to 1981, an additional twenty-three associations were formed. Presently, every state has a psychological association affiliated with the American Psychological Association* (APA), while forty-nine states have school psychological associations affiliated with the National Association of School Psychologists* (NASP). APA's Division 16* is precluded from formal affiliation with state school psychology* associations; therefore, state associations affiliated with APA are generic psychological organizations that do not always address the needs of school psychologists.

The formation of NASP in 1969 played a significant role in promoting the organization of state associations. NASP was created exclusively for school psychologists, but, unlike APA, NASP focused primarily on nondoctoral school psychologists. Approximately 25 percent of school psychologists hold a doctoral degree (Fagan, 1993).

State associations have matured and now play a vital role in advocating for school psychology. Typically, state associations publish newsletters, hold state conferences, present practice and leadership awards, are active in legislative concerns, and, in general, serve as a local voice for school psychology. State associations are also part of a national network. This network permits school psychologists to speak in a strong, uniform voice.

The contribution of state school psychological associations cannot be over-emphasized. While many issues are national in scope, critical decisions are frequently made at the state level. States differ in rules and regulations; therefore, state associations are needed to communicate with local legislators and state departments of education.

See also MULTISTATE ASSOCIATION MEETINGS.

REFERENCES

Fagan, T. K. (1993). Separate but equal: School psychology's search for organizational identity. *Journal of School Psychology* 31, 3–90.

Fagan, T. K., L. T. Hensley, and F. J. Delugach. (1986). The evolution of organizations for school psychologists in the United States. *School Psychology Review* 15, 127–135.

Gerald J. Spadafore

STATE BOARD OF EXAMINERS IN PSYCHOLOGY. In the 1940s, state examining boards were established to ensure professional competence and ad-judicate ethical violations. As individual states have the legislative authority to determine what constitutes the practice of psychology, a wide variety of standards was implemented. To provide national guidelines, the American Psychological Association* in 1955 delegated the Committee on State Legislation Model Guidelines to publish licensure recommendations. The American Association of State Psychology Boards (AASPB) was chartered in 1961 to provide further models for state legislation. By 1978, the Educational Standards and Accreditation Committee of the AASPB presented general national guidelines and criteria for evaluating licensure applicants. However, there still exist diverse regulations governing the licensure of practitioners in psychology. The lack of nationally accepted definitions of training leaves state boards of examiners, which are frequently underfunded and understaffed, to function as the gate-keepers to licensure.

See also CODES OF ETHICS; LICENSING; PROFESSIONAL STANDARDS.

REFERENCE

Pryzwansky, W. B. (1993). The regulation of school psychology. *Journal of School Psychology* 31, 219–235.

LeAdelle Phelps

STATE CONSULTANT FOR SCHOOL PSYCHOLOGICAL SERVICES.
The state consultant for school psychological services is an appointed position within each state's department of education* (SDE).* The position is usually within the SDE's subdivision for pupil services or special programs. Though often a full-time position dedicated exclusively to psychological services in the schools, the position may be part-time in which the staff member is dedicated to broader duties in the SDE (e.g., guidance counseling, special education*). The state consultant serves dual roles of representing the interests, policies, and positions of the field of school psychology* to the state department of education and interpreting the state department's policies and positions relevant to psychological services to local practitioners* and school settings.* A position statement prepared by Leonard Pennington, then state consultant for Wisconsin, includes the rationale for employing state consultants (Anderson, 1982). This rationale includes the areas of training, credentialing, role and function, and the regulations governing the identification and services for exceptional children.

State consultants, or designated persons to represent the psychological services area, have historically been members of the National Association of State Consultants for School Psychological Services.* The organization's reports suggest that about half the states have consultants who are trained as school psychologists* and that other SDEs employ persons trained in related fields to represent psychological services. State consultants for school psychological services date to the time of Arnold Gesell's* appointment to the Connecticut Department of Education (1915–1919). In earlier times, some of these employees provided direct services to school districts. Regional services were provided in some states, with supervision provided by state department of education psychologists. These models diminished after the 1960s. The role has shifted from service provision and supervision to consultation within the state education agency and to the state's practitioners.

REFERENCES

Anderson, M. W. (1982). *Role and function of the state consultant for school psychology: Survey report.* Washington, DC: National Association of School Psychologists, Assistance to States Committee.
Fagan, T. K. (1993). Separate but equal: School psychology's search for organizational identity. *Journal of School Psychology* 31, 3–90.

Thomas K. Fagan

STATE DEPARTMENT OF EDUCATION. A state department of education (SDE) is the legislatively established agency in each state (or province) authorized to implement laws and regulations pertaining to education. Every state has an SDE, which serves as the central agency for education policy. The SDE is responsible for implementing and articulating both state and federal laws and rules and regulations for schooling. The agency has broad authority* and responsibility over the school districts and settings within its jurisdiction. Its authority usually extends to all preschool, elementary, and secondary settings, public or private. It may also include correctional education programs, vocational-technical schools, or higher education.

Administered by a chief state school officer (often called the state superintendent or commissioner of education), the agency has several subdivisions. Among the more relevant for school psychologists* are the subdivisions dealing with pupil personnel services,* special education* programs, licensure* and certification,* and preparation program approval.* The subdivisions facilitate the SDE's overall mission to implement education legislation and policies approved by the state's board of education. In many states, a state consultant for school psychological services* is employed in one of the subdivisions. In some states, the SDE is articulated with local districts via regional offices of the SDE.

Required by federal law to provide a plan for implementing federal education law and regulations in order to receive federal funds, the SDE is a major force in articulating federal legislation and policy at the local district level. These include policies related to training, credentialing, and role and function* of school psychologists and the regulations governing the identification and services for exceptional children. Implementation and enforcement of policies are related to the availability of state-level funding for education. For example, by monitoring practices of the local districts, the SDE may control the flow of state funds to local schools.

See also STATE DEPARTMENT OF EDUCATION MONITORING.

REFERENCES

Fagan, T. K., and P. S. Wise. (1994). *School psychology: Past, present, and future.* White Plains, NY: Longman.
Spring, J. (1989). *American education: An introduction to social and political aspects.* New York: Longman.

Thomas K. Fagan

STATE DEPARTMENT OF EDUCATION MONITORING. The state department of education* (SDE) is the governmental agency responsible for monitoring educational programs by encouraging innovative techniques, enforcing incurred program obligations, providing technical assistance in development, and overseeing corrections of deficiencies. The commission is programmatic, administrative, and fiscal. The SDE, as part of its monitoring activities, is mandated to guarantee that each child with a disability receives, to the maximum extent appropriate, an education with children who are nondisabled. Any removal from the regular education environment may occur only when the nature of the disability prevents successful integration in the regular classroom, even with the use of supplemental services.

Monitoring activities include a review of the local education agency's (LEA) justification for placements that are inconsistent with the mandated responsibility of the SDE; technical assistance in preparation for compliance reviews; and planning of any necessary corrective actions. Information for compliance reviews is collected from on-site examinations. An exit evaluation report containing findings and appropriate corrective actions is sent to the LEA for review and reply. If necessary, the LEA may either request a hearing or submit a corrective plan that delineates the elimination of noncompliance issues as well as documenting any preventive measures required. Sanctions for failure to correct a deficiency are decided on an individual basis and may include withholding of funds or suspension of accreditation.

See also INCLUSION; LEAST RESTRICTIVE ENVIRONMENT; MANDATORY SERVICES.

REFERENCE

Farrow, F. (1983). *Effective state monitoring policies.* Washington, DC: Center for
　　Study of Social Policy.

Denise Cutbirth

STATE TEACHER CERTIFICATION/LICENSING BOARD. A state teacher certification*/licensing* board is the regulatory and public policy arm of state government for licensing teachers and other educational personnel. The board sets standards and procedures for issuance of initial licensure and renewal of licenses.

The need for adequately trained teachers was formally recognized when Horace Mann established the first legislatively authorized normal school in Lexington, Massachusetts, in 1839 (Butts and Cremin, 1953). Slowly, other states began to create normal schools, but providing for well-trained personnel was only part of the problem. The local orientation and control of public schools resulted in local certification through examination and little or no statewide coordination for quality control or continuity. As public education grew, the solution to the quality question was the establishment of a well-organized state system of examinations managed at the local level by professional educators, superintendents, and professional teachers (Butts and Cremin, 1953). However, the nature of public schools as governmental agencies prevented the implementation of such certification practices based on lay examinations. Gradually, states began to pass laws for the certification of teachers, which led to the creation of regulatory agencies. State teacher certification boards evolved to implement the statutes and set policies relating to the qualifications and certification of teachers. Eventually, a quasi-professional system was adopted whereby teacher education colleges would prepare teachers and recommend certification of teachers to a state education board, which, in turn, would issue a teaching certificate or license (Alexander and Alexander, 1992). Today, there is a movement toward professional standards and practices boards (PSPBs) for school personnel licensure, and four states—California, Minnesota, Oregon, and Nevada—have autonomous PSPBs accountable only to the legislature of the state; forty-four other states have PSPBs with advisory prerogatives relative to setting licensure/certification standards and/or policing the conduct of teachers (Scannell, Anderson, and Hendrik, 1989).

See also CERTIFICATION; LICENSING; TEACHER CERTIFICATION ISSUE.

REFERENCES

Alexander, K., and M. D. Alexander. (1992). *American public school law* (3d ed.). St. Paul, MN: West.

Butts, R. F., and L. A. Cremin. (1953). *A history of education in American culture.* New York: Holt.

Scannell, D., D. G. Anderson, and D. G. Hendrik. (1989). Who sets the standards? The need for state professional standards and practices boards, occasional paper series. Association of Colleges and Schools of Education in State Universities and Land Grant Colleges and Affiliated Private Universities. (ERIC Document Reproduction Service No. ED 315 873)

George W. Etheridge

STERN, WILLIAM. William Stern was born in Berlin, Germany, on April 29, 1871, and died on March 27, 1938, while a professor at Duke University. He is known in school psychology* history for his contributions to the concept of the IQ, his research on child development, his early text, *The Psychological Methods of Testing Intelligence,* and the earliest known usage of the term ''school psychologist''* in the German language literature. With other exiled German scholars, Stern migrated from Europe to America in the mid-1930s and accepted a position at Duke University.

See also TERMAN, LEWIS M.

REFERENCES

Allport, G. W. (1938). William Stern: 1871–1938. *American Journal of Psychology* 51, 770–773.

Fagan, T. K., and F. J. Delugach. (1984). Literary origins of the term, ''school psychologist.'' *School Psychology Review* 13, 216–220.

Stern, W. (1930). Autobiography. In C. Murchison (Ed.), *A history of psychology in autobiography,* Vol. 1 (pp. 335–388). Worcester, MA: Clark University Press.

Thomas K. Fagan

STRESS REDUCTION THERAPY. Stress reduction therapy refers to interventions designed to combat the emotional and physical correlates of stress. Such intervention techniques may be useful to school psychologists* in addressing stressors in their own lives or in the lives of the students, teachers, and parents with whom they work. Many stress reduction techniques are founded on principles of cognitive behavior modification* as described in Meichenbaum (1977) and Hughes and Hall (1989). Stress reduction includes techniques such as deep muscle relaxation, stress inoculation training (Meichenbaum, 1977), aerobic exercise programs, breathing exercises, nutritional changes, biofeedback,* and enhancement of an individual's support systems. Forman (1993) reports the results of one successful approach that used a collaborative behavioral consultation (CBC) treatment with a group of teachers. The CBC system was unique in that it addressed reducing not only the teachers' stress levels but also one source of the stress (in this case, the school's organizational difficulties). Recent research on stress and children suggests that teaching coping skills (behaviors that help children respond in constructive ways to threatening situations) can lower stress levels while improving self-esteem and feelings of competence (Forman, 1993).

See also PROFESSIONAL STRESS/BURNOUT; RELAXATION TRAINING.

REFERENCES

Forman, S. G. (1993). *Coping skills interventions for children and adolescents.* San Francisco: Jossey-Bass.
Hughes, J. N., and R. J. Hall, (Eds.). (1989). *Cognitive behavioral psychology in the schools: A comprehensive handbook.* New York: Guilford Press.
Meichenbaum, D. (1977). *Cognitive-behavior modification: An integrative approach.* New York: Plenum Press.

Paula Sachs Wise

STUDY SKILLS. Study skills are processes that are naturally learned or taught to students to provide increased efficiency in attention, acquisition, storage, retrieval, and transfer of new information (Nisbet and Shucksmith, 1986). There are many types of study skills, but basically they can be divided into those that are done by rote and those that promote understanding or meaning. Rote skills include rehearsal strategies (mnemonics, the loci method, peg-word and keyword methods, and repeating a list) and elaboration strategies (rhyming imagery, e.g., ''one-a-bun, two-a-shoe''). Strategies that promote understanding include note taking, underlining, listing main ideas, self-testing, summarizing, or paraphrasing. There are also strategies for comprehension monitoring (e.g., self-questioning) and affective and motivational strategies (e.g., being alert and relaxed). A list of cognitive learning strategies includes dealing first with fundamentals, being actively involved in learning, spacing practice and overlearning, breaking information down into small chunks, tying new information to the old, learning sequentially, applying what you learn, and monitoring your learning strategies to see that they are effective (Pressley, Borkowski, and O'Sullivan, 1985). This last strategy is metacognitive. In addition to generic study skills, there are specific study skills in almost all disciplines. For example, in reading comprehension, students should be taught the processes of the restatement, backtracking, or problem formulation. In academic content reading, McWhorter (1992) suggests circling unknown words, marking definitions, marking examples, numbering lists, starring important passages, putting question marks next to confusing passages, making notes to yourself, creating possible test items, drawing arrows to show relationships, noting similarities/differences, and making summary statements. These and other strategies must be taught in each content area. This is particularly true at the secondary level; teachers must teach the skills they want students to exhibit.

See also METACOGNITIVE SKILLS; PEER TUTORING.

REFERENCES

McWhorter, K. T. (1992). *Study and thinking skills in college* (2d ed.). New York: HarperCollins.

Nisbet, J., and J. Shucksmith. (1986). *Learning strategies.* London: Routledge and Kegan Paul.

Pressley, M., J. G. Borkowski, and J. O'Sullivan. (1985). Children's metamemory and the teaching of memory strategies. In D. L. Forest-Pressley, G. E. Mackinian, and T. G. Waller (Eds.), *Metacognition, cognition, & human performance,* Vol. 1 (pp. 111–154). New York: Academic Press.

Kay Sather Bull

SUBURBAN SCHOOL PSYCHOLOGY. Professional literature in school psychology* has presented research and opinions on the similarities and differences between practice in rural and urban school districts. Typically, comparisons using this dichotomy have been the sole focus of such discussions, leaving out any reference to the suburban context. The most commonly held position at this time is that the practice of school psychology* involves certain methods, skills, and knowledge equally relevant to all school settings. However, these services are optimally presented when offered in a way that considers and matches aspects of the broader community.

In general, suburban school districts are seen as having the best characteristics of rural and urban districts without many of the inherent problems. For example, the per pupil expenditures are higher, community resources are more plentiful, traditional values and a family–community orientation still pervade, attracting qualified staff is easier, there is a lower turnover rate, and there are critical masses of students with similar educational needs within close proximity so that services to lower-incidence disabilities may be offered efficiently. These advantages supposedly come without the disadvantages noted elsewhere in this volume. In reality, while many of the advantages ascribed to suburban districts exist, many of the issues facing education, children, and families in general also pervade suburban systems.

Based on self-reports of school psychologists,* approximately 33 percent of practitioners work in a suburban setting, as compared to 28 percent in urban settings, 21 percent in rural settings, and 17 percent in a mixture of these settings. Recent reviews of employment trends indicate that the turnover rate for suburban settings is much lower than for the urban and rural settings (reported vacancies of 16 percent in suburban settings as compared to 27 percent in urban and 57 percent in rural settings).

See also RURAL SCHOOL PSYCHOLOGY; URBAN SCHOOL PSY-CHOLOGY.

REFERENCE

Reschly, D. J., and L. M. Connolly. (1990). Comparisons of school psychologists in the city and country: Is there a "rural" school psychology? *School Psychology Review* 19, 534–549.

A. Jerry Benson

SUMMATIVE EVALUATION. The term "summative evaluation" is usually used by school psychologists* in two contexts: professional accountability* and program evaluation.* Summative evaluations are carried out at the conclusion of a service or program. Such evaluations provide a measure of the overall quality of the service or program. While summative evaluations do not allow for ongoing program modifications, they can be helpful as overall summaries to be included in yearly reports. Summative evaluations can also help the professional reflect over past accomplishments and plan strategies for future self- or program improvement.

See also FORMATIVE EVALUATION.

REFERENCE

Fagan, T. K., and P. S. Wise. (1994). *School psychology: Past, present, and future.* White Plains, NY: Longman.

Paula Sachs Wise

SUPPORT GROUPS. Support groups are a therapeutic mechanism used to respond to the needs of people dealing with stress caused by life transitions, crises, or chronic conditions. The proliferation of support groups in recent years reflects the increasing need for formal and informal sources of assistance in a climate of rapid social change and geographical dispersion of families and friends (Schopler and Galinsky, 1993). Members of support groups dealing with common sources of stress find a social network that may potentially provide emotional support and guidance. Schools are recognizing the need to sponsor such groups for parents of students at risk for school difficulties.

Participation in support groups generally involves sharing of personal experiences in order to create a cohesive supportive system. With fewer therapeutic goals determined by the designated leader than a conventional psychotherapy group and greater structure than self-help groups, support groups are responsive to individual and group common needs. Normally considered member-centered, the leader shares authority with participants but is responsible for facilitation of discussion and promotion of a supportive environment. In addition to sharing experiences, members provide information, give advice concerning coping strategies, and discuss problem-solving techniques. Membership is normally on a volunteer basis. The range of concerns for support groups is extensive and includes addictions, aggressive behavior, disability, loss of children or spouse, weight control, and sexual orientation.

See also GROUP THERAPY; SIBLING GROUPS.

REFERENCE

Schopler, J., and M. Galinsky. (1993). Support groups as open systems: A model for practice and research. *Health and Social Work* 18, 195–207.

Denise Cutbirth
Diane Montgomery

SUSPENSION AND EXPULSION. Children who break school rules regarding behavior, particularly by engaging in aggressive acts, find themselves suspended from school by principals or expelled by school boards. Suspension for a set time, usually less than a month, results from less serious acts than does expulsion, which can lead to a child's being prohibited from ever returning to a school. These consequences of inappropriate behavior have undoubtedly been applied since the organization of the first classroom. Data on the prevalence of this practice of exclusion from school, particularly with children with disabilities, are hard to obtain. How many children dropped out and how many were "pushed out" are unclear.

Until the 1960s, the schools were considered to be acting in loco parentis, and suspension and expulsion decisions were less frequently challenged. The school has a duty to protect children and school property through exclusion of rule-violating children. Schools have long been able to exclude children for fighting, assaulting a teacher, persistent disobedience and insubordination, truancy, and, interestingly, membership in prohibited secret societies (Phay, 1977). Currently, gangs might be considered secret societies, and the banning of "colors" has a long history. From time to time, various reasons for school exclusion have been protested. An individual's marital status as a reason for exclusion was challenged in the courts in 1929 and found not to be a valid reason, and parental status (e.g., unwed mothers) was found not to be valid in the 1970s.

The schools began to face increased scrutiny over exclusion as students' First Amendment rights and Fourteenth Amendment due process* rights began to be recognized in the 1960s and 1970s. Free speech and the freedom of assembly prevented schools, in some cases, from excluding students who demonstrated or wrote controversial articles in school newspapers. However, because of concern for safety, exclusion can result from bringing weapons, narcotics, or unsafe dress to campus.

The landmark case on student suspension is *Goss v. Lopez* 419 U.S. 565 (1975), brought by nine Ohio students who had been suspended for ten days. The Supreme Court ruled that a hearing was required for short-term suspensions of up to ten days, that is, that children have due process rights. Among these rights are the notice of exclusion, the existence of clearly specified rules, the right to an impartial hearing, the right to counsel, and the right to inspect evidence.

Until the 1970s, children with special needs had no special status with respect to suspension or expulsion. Many children, particularly those with emotional disturbances, were routinely excluded from school. For children in special education,* the issue has become whether or not a suspension or expulsion is a change in a child's educational plan as required by Public Law 94-142,* the Education for All Handicapped Children Act. Courts have ruled that a suspension is not a change in the educational plan if the procedures required by *Goss* are followed. Various courts have ruled that children cannot be expelled for behavior related to their disability. However, appropriately placed children with disabilities can be expelled in the same way as other children if their offense is determined not to be related to their disability. Expulsion or a long-term suspension is a change in the plan, and an individualized educational plan* (IEP) meeting must be held first. Nevertheless, even though expulsion may be appropriate, it is not allowable to terminate all educational services for a child with disabilities (Leone, 1985).

See also RETENTION/NONPROMOTION.

REFERENCES

Leone, P. E. (1985). Suspension and expulsion of handicapped pupils. *Journal of Special Education* 19, 111–121.
Phay, R. E. (1977). *Student suspensions and expulsions*. Topeka, KS: National Organization on Legal Problems of Education.

                                                                              Jonathan Sandoval

SYMONDS, PERCIVAL. Percival M. Symonds was born in Newtonville, Massachusetts, on April 18, 1893, and died in Salem, Massachusetts, on August 6, 1960. He received the B.A. degree from Harvard University (1915) and then the A.M. (1920) and Ph.D. (1923) from Columbia University. Symonds was a member of the Teachers College, Columbia University faculty from 1924 until his retirement in 1958. He authored texts and tests that contributed to the fields of educational,* clinical,* and school psychology.* These included the Foreign Language Prognosis Test (1930), Symonds Picture-Story Test (1948), and The Personality Survey (1948). He did considerable work with the Thematic Apperception Test, developing his own work on the projective hypothesis summarized in Symonds (1949). Active in the development of professional organizations, he served as first chairman of the Educational Section of the American Association of Applied Psychologists* and as president of the American Psychological Association's* Division of Educational Psychology (1947–1948) and president of the American Educational Research Association* (1956–1967). His editing of a special issue of the *Journal of Consulting Psychology* provided a broad picture of the field in the early 1940s (Symonds, 1942). His wife, Johnnie P. Symonds, was the first editor of the *Journal of Consulting Psychology.*

See also LITERATURE IN SCHOOL PSYCHOLOGY.

REFERENCES

Symonds, P. M. (1933). Every school should have a psychologist. *School and Society* 38(976), 321–329.
———. (1949). *Adolescent fantasy: An investigation of the picture-story method of personality study.* New York: Columbia University Press.
———. (Ed.). (1942). The school psychologist—1942. *Journal of Consulting Psychology* 6(4), 173–228.

Thomas K. Fagan

SYSTEMATIC DESENSITIZATION. Systematic desensitization is an extinction-based therapeutic procedure developed by Wolpe (1958) in which an incompatible response is paired with an undesirable behavior to eliminate the targeted behavior. The two primary techniques used to desensitize persons involve relaxation training and counterconditioning. The procedure is used primarily for the treatment of phobias and anxiety disorders.

The initial process begins with completion of an intake history to determine the nature and extent of the anxiety and its impact on daily functioning. An anxiety hierarchy is then developed in which eight to twelve situations associated with the anxiety are identified and rank-ordered according to intensity. These situations are used to generate visual images during the relaxation training. The final step in treatment combines visual imagery and relaxation exercises with the anxiety hierarchy, beginning with the situation that evokes the lowest level of anxiety for the person. As tension occurs, the person is instructed to visualize the situation and then concentrate on relaxing.

The efficacy of systematic desensitization has been shown for treatment of anxiety disorders including public-speaking anxiety (Paul, 1966) and fear resulting from military combat (Kipper, 1977).

See also BIOFEEDBACK; CLASSICAL CONDITIONING; CLASSIFICATION: PSYCHIATRIC; RELAXATION TRAINING; STRESS REDUCTION THERAPY.

REFERENCES

Cohen, J. J., and M. C. Fish. (1993). *Handbook of school-based interventions.* San Francisco, CA: Jossey-Bass.
Kipper, D. (1977). Behavior therapy for fears brought on by war experiences. *Journal of Consulting and Clinical Psychology* 45, 216–221.
Paul, G. (1966). Physiological effects of relaxation training and hypnotic suggestion. *Journal of Abnormal Psychology* 74, 425.
Wolpe, J. (1958). *Psychotherapy by reciprocal inhibition.* Stanford, CA: Stanford University Press.

Raymond E. Webster

SYSTEM OF MULTICULTURAL PLURALISTIC ASSESSMENT. In the early 1970s, Jane Mercer, a sociologist, conducted a large-scale epidemiological research study of school-age children in California. Using the norming prepublication version of the Wechsler Intelligence Scale for Children—Revised and a variety of social and health measures, Mercer's staff evaluated a stratified random sample of whites, African Americans, and Hispanic Americans in California. Analysis of the results of this sample of more than 2,000 children encouraged her to combine the best of the measures into an assessment battery, the System of Multicultural Pluralistic Assessment (SOMPA).

The measures of SOMPA were organized into three models: medical, social, and pluralistic. Medical model measures were developed from commonly used, but largely informal, health screenings providing a basis for physician referral when indicated. Social measures included the Wechsler Intelligence Scale for Children—Revised (WISC—R) and a measure of adaptive behavior, the Adaptive Behavior Inventory for Children. The adaptive behavior* measure was unique in that parents were interviewed, rather than teachers, to determine levels of functioning. This was the first adaptive behavior measure available with norms for typical children and was thought by many to be the reason for SOMPA's initial popularity. Pluralistic measures included a sociocultural interview with the parent and a recalculation of intelligence* test scores based on a regression method for each ethnic group. This recalculation was termed the estimated learning potential of the child.

SOMPA introduced several innovations. A series of diverse measures was normed on the same sample of children. The tests' author carefully described the assumptions underlying each model and the purposes of the measures. For example, the traditional use of the IQ test was assumed to be a measure of functioning in the school environment. Mercer considered the intelligence test an achievement measure. Training to use SOMPA was explicitly designed by the author and provided to more than 5,000 assessment professionals throughout the United States. Trainers were personally trained by Mercer and had to adhere to high standards. Participants had to pass knowledge and scoring proficiency tests before receiving certification of training. During training, practitioners were encouraged to examine their own assumptions in using SOMPA.

SOMPA became immediately popular following its introduction by the Psychological Corporation in 1978. The requirement for nondiscriminatory assessment in federal regulations regarding public school assessment and the need for an appropriate adaptive behavior measure as part of the identification of mental retardation made SOMPA an important part of typical school assessments. At least one state (Louisiana) mandated the use of SOMPA whenever nondiscriminatory assessment was a consideration.

Two controversial aspects of SOMPA led to professional debate. For the first time, means and standard deviations for each of the three major ethnic groups for an intelligence test were published in a widely available form. Professionals learned of significant average score differences between ethnic groups, which were discussed during SOMPA training sessions. Questions about the suitability of the intelligence test as a nonbiased measure were raised, as was the feasibility of recalculating scores using regression equations. Determining whether the estimated learning potential scores should be used in the identification of gifted children expanded the controversial aspects of SOMPA beyond discussions of who had a mental disability.

The second controversy surrounded the use of parents, rather than teachers, as informants in the adaptive behavior interview. Mercer conceived adaptive behavior to be a measure of out-of-school functioning, where others (principally, Reschly, 1982) decried this nonschool measure for use in determination of a disability. Mercer contended that misidentification of minority ethnic children as mentally retarded occurred because only measures of school functioning were used. Others contended that the identification of mental retardation was for benevolent school purposes and therefore particularly benign. Further, the Adaptive Behavior Inventory for Children (ABIC) correlated poorly with the intelligence measure. Mercer considered this validation that a significant aspect of a child's functioning was being included with more traditional measures. This low correlation was interpreted by others as a rationale for using some other measure of adaptive behavior, presumably better correlated with achievement or intelligence, in the determination of mental retardation.

When the revision of the Weschler Intelligence Scale for Children (version III) was published in 1991, no revision of SOMPA was introduced, and no separate norms for ethnic groups were provided in the test's manual. Given the age of the norms of the measures within SOMPA, its reliance on the outdated WISC-R, and the failure to revise the system, its use faded rapidly in the late 1980s.

See also NONBIASED ASSESSMENT.

REFERENCES

Mercer, J. R. (1979). *System of Multicultural Pluralistic Assessment: Technical manual.* New York: Psychological Corporation.

Reschly, D. (Ed.). (1979). SOMPA: A symposium. *School Psychology Digest* 8, 5–115.

———. (1982). Assessing mild mental retardation: The influence of adaptive behavior, sociocultural status, and prospects for nonbiased assessment. In C. R. Reynolds and T. B. Gutkin (Eds.), *The handbook of school psychology* (pp. 209–242). New York: Wiley.

W. Alan Coulter

SYSTEMS AND ORGANIZATIONAL CONSULTATION. The practice of consultation* varies in scope from one-to-one meetings that last only a few minutes to processes that involve hundreds of people, extend over years, and culminate in major shifts in an organization's philosophy, methods of operation, efficiency, and effectiveness. Organizational consultation deals with large-scope issues that affect many or all of a system's subparts, such as management, production, or distribution of its products or services.

Daugherty (1990) lists seven organizational theories and a set of questions that are the central concerns of each. For example, in human relations theory, questions such as, What is the organization's psychological climate? are considered important, while in bureaucratic theory, an appropriate question might be, What are the strengths and weaknesses of this organization's structure? Analysis of these various models and theories suggests more overlap than differentiation among them. They all maintain a focus on at least these central questions: How is an organization structured? Is the organization working as effectively and efficiently as it can? How might it be improved in order to better achieve its goals?

Generally, an organization uses an external organizational consultant only when it appears that its own staff is unable (or unwilling) to deal with a problem pertaining to the way a product is being developed or a service is being delivered. Whether the consultant is internal or external, he or she is concerned with at least the following questions: What is the problem? How does it affect the mission of the organization? Who are the constituents (parties-at-interest; stakeholders)? What are the forces (i.e., barriers; possible solutions) that are important to understand? To whom does the consultant report? Within what time frame will the consultation take place? How will entry, both physical and psychological, take place? What is the financial remuneration? The external consultant usually works under a formal contract wherein details about lines of authority, time frames, and report expectations are spelled out.

Methods of conducting consultations within organizations vary as a function of the problem, the type of management currently operating, and the style of the consultant. Generally, however, consultants follow procedures analogous with the scientific method: a problem is identified and analyzed, hypotheses are formed, ideas are generated, some are tried, and effects are measured. Kurpius, Burello, and Rozecki (1990) present a model for organizational consultation that has the following seven stages: (1) sharing beliefs and creating the vision (Why are we here? What do we believe is important?); (2) mission, goals, and objectives (How can we operationalize our vision?); (3) internal and external analysis (What are the effects of social, political, economic, demographic, and technical factors that influence our system?); (4) essential policies (How do we currently attempt to implement our mission?); (5) strategies (What do we do specifically to achieve our objectives?); (6) action plans (How should we specify what we want to do, who is to do it, and so on?); and (7) recycling (What steps shall we take to keep the process of renewal alive?).

There are a number of opportunities for organizational consultation in schools. Sarason (1982) discusses the realities of school systems and points out that the "culture" of a school or district should be the central focus for change. Educators need to identify their most important purposes, generate a case for financial support of their mission, and evaluate results to demonstrate their successes.

Organizational consultation is a tool for systematically addressing these issues and is therefore a worthy activity for psychologists in the schools.

See also ORGANIZATIONAL DEVELOPMENT THEORY; SYSTEMS ASSESSMENT; SYSTEMS INTERVENTIONS.

REFERENCES

Daugherty, A. (1990). *Consultation: Practice and perspective.* Pacific Grove, CA: Brooks/Cole.
Kurpius, D., L. Burello, and T. Rozecki. (1990). Strategic planning in human service organizations. *Counseling and Human Development* 22, 1–9.
Sarason, S. G. (1982). *The culture of the school and the problem of change* (2d ed.). Boston: Allyn and Bacon.

Thomas J. Kampwirth

SYSTEMS ASSESSMENT. Systems assessment is founded in general systems theory. The term "system" refers to the combination of interactive parts that are organized to achieve a specific purpose. The term could be used to describe a wide range of such arrangements, including machines and electrical systems. A living system is "the orderly combination of two or more individuals whose interaction is intended to produce a desired outcome" (Curtis and Stollar, 1995) and could refer to as few as only two people working together or to very large, organized groups of people, such as community agencies or professional associations.

A school is an example of a living system. It is composed of component parts (e.g., students, teachers, support services personnel, cafeteria workers, principal) who interact in some organized way for the purpose of educating students. However, individual classrooms, grade-level teams, and intervention assistance teams are examples of systems that exist within the school. School districts and educational cooperatives are systems within which schools exist. Consequently, because systems exist at many different levels, it is important to define the specific system being targeted.

The concept of "reciprocal influence" is critical in understanding systems. Essentially, this concept refers to the tendency for each of the component parts of a system to influence each of the other parts, as well as the system as a whole. A change in one part of the system causes change in other parts of the system. Similarly, change in the environment in which the system exists influences both the system and the components within it. Understanding a system is dependent on knowledge of how the various parts of the system, the system itself, and the environment in which the system exists influence each other.

System assessment (also called system analysis) refers to the process through which an understanding is developed of a system (including its component parts and the larger environment in which it exists), the ways in which the system functions (i.e., the influence of the various parts on one another), and the extent to which the system succeeds in attaining its goals. The techniques utilized to develop that understanding depend on the system being analyzed. The following discussion may help to clarify this point.

In order to understand the problems being experienced by a particular student, a school psychologist* operating from a systems or ecological framework would view that student as one component in a larger interactive system (Bandura, 1977). Personal characteristics and behaviors, as well as various forces from the environment, all would have to be considered in terms of their interrelationships and their influences on one another. Consequently, in addition to techniques used to gain knowledge of the student and the student's behavior, procedures would be needed that would contribute to understanding other forces in the student's environment (e.g., the teacher, other students, parents, siblings) and how all of these forces influence the problem situation.

If a school building was the system for which analysis was to be completed, different assessment procedures would be utilized based on the problem(s) being addressed. However, the framework for assessment* would remain the same (i.e., understanding the subsystems within the school—[analogous to the characteristics of the student], how the school functions relative to the problem situation [analogous to behaviors of the student], forces within the larger environment that may be influencing the school, such as district policies, parents, state regulations, and how forces at these different levels are related and contribute to the problem situation). Discussion of techniques potentially helpful in assessing systems at the group or organizational level is typically found in the organization development literature (Schmuck and Runkel, 1985).

See also ECOLOGICAL ASSESSMENT; SYSTEMS AND ORGANIZATIONAL CONSULTATION; SYSTEMS INTERVENTION.

REFERENCES

Bandura, A. (1977). *Social learning theory.* Englewood Cliffs, NJ: Prentice-Hall.
Curtis, M. J., and S. A. Stollar. (1995). System-level consultation and organizational
    change. In A. Thomas and J. Grimes (Eds.), *Best practices in school
    psychology—III* (pp. 51-58). Silver Spring, MD: National Association of School
    Psychologists.
Schmuck, R. A., and P. J. Runkel. (1985). *The handbook of organization development
    in schools.* Palo Alto, CA: Mayfield.

Michael J. Curtis

SYSTEMS INTERVENTION. Systems intervention is founded in general systems theory. Systems intervention is typically associated with organization development principles and procedures.

The general purpose of systems intervention is to enhance the effectiveness with which a system achieves its objectives. Consistent with this overall purpose, systems intervention has two specific goals. The immediate goal is to help solve a specific problem that either is impeding the ability of the system to achieve its objectives or is causing significant stress within the system. However, the primary goal is to enhance the capacity of the system to effectively solve any problems that confront it. In other words, the system becomes more effective in analyzing forces that are influencing its functioning (or even anticipating them before they actually occur) and in making adjustments in its behavior in order to limit the negative impact (problems) or to maximize the positive impact (opportunities) of those forces. The more effective the system becomes as a problem solver, the less there is need for outside assistance to address specific issues.

As an example of these two goals, a school psychologist* is asked by a school for assistance in addressing a number of issues (e.g., school–parent relationships, behavior problems, a disjointed curriculum). Through the use of different techniques over a considerable span of time, including leading the school staff through a structured problem-solving process, the school psychologist helps the school develop strategies to address specific problems. In addition, the staff becomes skilled in the use of problem-solving procedures that they can use to address other issues confronting them, as well as issues that may confront them in the future.

Systems intervention itself is based on, and represents, one component in the implementation of a problem-solving process. Although different models may vary in terms of details, most problem-solving models incorporate four major stages: (1) problem analysis, (2) goal identification, (3) strategy development and implementation, and (4) evaluation. Systems assessment represents the first, and probably most critical, stage in problem solving. Systems intervention, as described here, incorporates the final three stages. The goals, strategies developed and implemented, and the framework for evaluating the effectiveness of those strategies are all based on the systems assessment carried out in stage one. Intervention strategies vary widely and address a broad range of issues, such as communication skills, conflict resolution, goal setting, and, of course, problem solving. Schmuck and Runkel (1985) provide a discussion of systems concepts, as well as a rather comprehensive review of many practical strategies and procedures relating to organization development and systems interventions in schools. Curtis and Metz (1986) and Snapp, Hickman, and Conoley (1990) have published case studies that illustrate key principles, as well as effective strategies in utilizing effective systems interventions.

See also PROBLEM-SOLVING CONSULTATION; SYSTEMS AND ORGANIZATIONAL CONSULTATION; SYSTEMS ASSESSMENT.

REFERENCES

Curtis, M. J., and L. W. Metz. (1986). System level intervention in a school for handicapped children. *School Psychology Review* 15, 510–518.

Schmuck, R. A., and P. J. Runkel. (1985). *The handbook of organization development in schools.* Palo Alto, CA: Mayfield.

Snapp, M., J. A. Hickman, and J. C. Conoley. (1990). Systems interventions in school settings: Case studies. In T. B. Gutkin and C. R. Reynolds (Eds.), *The handbook of school psychology* (2d ed., pp. 920–934). New York: Wiley.

Michael J. Curtis

T

TARASOFF v. REGENTS OF CALIFORNIA. In the mid-1970s, a young foreign student named Poddar at the University of California–Berkeley was enamored of a young Brazilian student named Tatiana Tarasoff. His feelings were not reciprocated. Tatiana had gone home for the summer, but Poddar was still on campus and seeing a psychologist at the counseling center. He told this man that if Tatiana continued to spurn him after her return in the fall, he intended to kill her. His therapist took this threat seriously and contacted campus security, asking that Poddar be picked up and taken to a local hospital for emergency commitment; but, after talking to Poddar they decided he was not serious and let him go free. When Tatiana returned in the fall semester, Poddar killed her.

The Tarasoff family filed a wrongful death suit. The case was dismissed based on a common-law precedent that since the psychologist didn't even know Tatiana, he had no responsibility to warn her of her danger. On appeal to the California Supreme Court, it was held that the defendants were responsible and that there had been clear duty to warn.* This ruling has since been followed by many other courts.

See also CLIENT; CONFIDENTIALITY.

REFERENCES

Jacob-Timm, S., and T. Hartshorne. (1994). *Ethics and law for school psychologists.* Brandon, VT: Clinical Psychology.
Merchant's National Bank and Trust Co. of Fargo v. United States, 272 F. Supp. 409. (1967).
Tarasoff v. Regents of the University of California, 551 P2d 533 (1976).

J. L. Bernard

TEACHER CERTIFICATION ISSUE. The issue of having been a teacher or trained as a teacher as a necessary or desirable requirement for functioning as a school psychologist* has been debated since at least the Thayer Conference* in 1954. Concretely, the issue is one of having classroom teacher certification and teaching experience. At present, available research and state department of education* certification* requirements indicate neither teacher certification nor teaching experience is necessary. Only three states have such requirements, a change from twelve of twenty states that had certification for school psychologists in 1954.

Four research studies employing teachers', supervisors', and principals' ratings have indicated no significant differences in patterns of critical functions between teacher-certified school psychologists and nonteacher-certified school psychologists. Two of the studies indicated that satisfaction with certain aspects of the psychologists' role, such as educational understanding and consultation skills, decreased with increased experience in teaching.

Two additional concerns are related to teacher certification. First, in a teacher walkout or strike, would a teacher-certified school psychologist be pressed into service as a teacher? Second, many states would preclude a nonteacher-certified school psychologist from obtaining other educational certifications such as that of an administrator.

See also COLLECTIVE BARGAINING; SALARY DETERMINATION; TENURE.

REFERENCES

Fagan, T. K., and P. S. Wise. (1994). *School psychology: Past, present, and future.* White Plains, NY: Longman.

Gerner, M. (1981). The necessity of a teacher background for school psychologists. *Professional Psychology* 12, 216–223.

Prus, J. S., G. W. White, and A. Pendleton. (1987). *Handbook of certification and licensure requirements for school psychologists.* Washington, DC: National Association of School Psychologists.

Paul G. Warden

TEACHER ORGANIZATIONS. The National Education Association (NEA) and the American Federation of Teachers (AFT) are the two professional and union organizations representing teachers, administrators, counselors, college and university professors, and others concerned with education. Both groups work with teachers and other educational employees in advocacy, legislation, organizing, collective bargaining,* research, information dissemination, educational issues, and public relations. Likewise, both groups provide members with a variety of services, such as professional liability insurance,* information hot line, public relations, a reference library, consultants, a national conference, and group rates on many things (e.g., health and life insurance, vacations).

The NEA is the oldest and largest (2,000,800 members) of the teacher organizations, with fifty-three state and 12,000 local affiliate groups. It was organized as the National Teachers Association (NTA) in 1857 in Philadelphia, with the purpose of elevating the character and advancing the interest of the profession of teaching and promoting the cause of education in the United States. In 1870, the NTA was incorporated under the laws of the District of Columbia and changed to the National Education Association. A special act of Congress in 1906 chartered the NEA under a new name, the National Education Association of the United States. The new charter was accepted, and bylaws were adopted at the Fiftieth Anniversary Convention in 1907. Today, NEA publications include *ESP [Educational Support Personnel] Annual, ESP Progress Handbook, Issues, NEA Today, Almanac of Higher Education, NEA Higher Education Advocate,* and *Thought and Action.* Contact: National Education Association, 1201 16th Street, NW, Washington, DC 20036; phone (202) 833-4000.

The AFT was founded in 1916 and has 790,000 members and 2,200 local groups. It is affiliated with the American Federation of Labor—Congress of Industrial Organizations (AFL-CIO). AFT publications include *AFT Action: A Newsletter for AFT Leaders, American Educator, American Teacher, On Campus,* and *Public Service Reporter.* Contact: American Federation of Teachers, 555 New Jersey Avenue, NW, Washington, DC 20001; phone (202) 879-4400.

Numerous organizations exist representing the special interest of some educators along lines of content areas, professional settings, and children served. Five main organizations serve professionals who work with individuals with handicapping conditions. The Council for Exceptional Children (CEC), founded in 1922, is the largest and serves teachers, school administrators, teacher educators, and others with direct or indirect concern for the education of the handicapped and gifted. CEC provides information concerning the education of exceptional children; sponsors workshops, academies, and symposia; holds an annual conference; provides technical assistance to legislators, state departments of education, and other agencies; disseminates information and conducts special projects; and operates the ERIC Clearinghouse on Handicapped and Gifted Children. Publications include *Exceptional Child Education Resources, Exceptional Children,* and *Teaching Exceptional Children.* Contact: Council for Exceptional Children, 1920 Association Drive, Reston, VA 22091-1589; phone (703) 620-3660.

The Learning Disabilities Association of America (LDA) was founded in 1964 to serve both parents of children with learning disabilities and interested professionals. LDA disseminates information to the public; provides assistance to state and local groups; facilitates local groups with direct services to parents and children—schools, camps, recreation programs, parent education, information services, and publications; and provides an information and referral service. Publications include *LDA Newsbriefs* and *Learning Disabilities.* Contact: Learning Disabilities Association of America, 4156 Library Road, Pittsburgh, PA 15234; phone (412) 341-1515.

The National Center for Learning Disabilities (NCLD) was founded in 1977 as a national voluntary organization to promote public awareness of learning disabilities. NCLD makes available resources and provides referrals to parents and professionals working with the learning disabled; develops and replicates programs; and conducts seminars. Publications include *Newsletter* and *Their World.* Contact: National Center for Learning Disabilities, 99 Park Avenue, 6th Floor, New York, NY 10016; phone (212) 687-7211.

The Council for Learning Disabilities (CLD) was founded in 1967 to serve professionals interested in the study of learning disabilities. CLD works to promote the education and general welfare of individuals having specific learning disabilities by improving teacher preparation programs and local special education* programs, resolving research issues, and sponsoring special meetings and an annual conference. Publications are the *LD Forum* and *Learning Disabilities Quarterly.* Contact: Council for Learning Disabilities, P.O. Box 40303, Overland Park, KS 66204; phone (913) 492-8755.

The American Council on Rural Special Education (ACRES) was founded in 1981 to enhance direct services to rural individuals and agencies serving exceptional students and to increase educational opportunities for rural handicapped and gifted students, to develop models for serving at-risk rural students, to forecast future needs, and to plan creative service delivery alternatives. ACRES serves as an advocate for rural special education, provides professional development opportunities, disseminates information, and offers a rural job placement service. Publications include *ACRES Membership Newsletter, Rural Special Education Quarterly,* and *RuraLink.* Contact: American Council on Rural Special Education, New Mexico State University, Department 3SPE, Las Cruces, NM 88003-0001; phone (505) 646-6812.

An example of a content education organization is the National Council of Teachers of Mathematics (NCTM). NCTM was founded in 1920 to serve teachers of mathematics in grades K–12, two-year colleges, and teacher education personnel on college campuses. Publications include the *Arithmetic Teacher,* featuring articles on innovative and practical methods of teaching arithmetic and information on metrics and problem solving; *Journal of Research in Mathematics Education,* reporting on research, philosophical and historical studies, and theoretical analysis; *Mathematics Teacher,* providing information for secondary and two-year college teachers of algebra and calculus plus new concepts; *National Council of Teachers of Mathematics—Yearbook,* presenting scholarly papers on selected mathematics related topics; and *NCTM News Bulletin,* reporting association activities, legislation affecting education, new teaching techniques and knowledge about learning, and new programs. Regional meetings and an annual convention are held. Contact: National Council of Teachers of Mathematics, 1906 Association Drive, Reston, VA 22091-1593; phone (703) 620-9840.

See also AMERICAN PSYCHOLOGICAL ASSOCIATION; NATIONAL ASSOCIATION OF SCHOOL PSYCHOLOGISTS.

George W. Etheridge

TEACHER RATINGS. Teacher ratings have been used to assess a wide variety of student behaviors, including adaptive, emotional, social, and academic behaviors and learning readiness skills. Historically, teacher rating scales can be traced back to 1928, when Wickman had both teachers and mental hygienists rate children on fifty behavioral traits. Assessment of emotional, social, and school adjustment continues to be the primary use of teacher rating scales. Consistent, broad-band patterns of problem behavior assessed by teacher rating scales include acting out, aggressive, externalized behaviors; shy, anxious, withdrawal, internalized functions; and learning difficulties, poor concentration, immature or attention deficit behaviors (Quay and Werry, 1986). Areas of strengths or competencies are rated less frequently by teacher rating scales and include such dimensions as the ability to tolerate frustration, assertive social skills, and peer social skills. Some teachers are highly accurate raters; others are less able judges. More observable dimensions typically have greater interrater reliability. More consistent and valid results occur when teachers are trained in observation skills and the use of rating instruments. Without training, rating biases related to children's socioeconomic status, age, sex, and race may appear (Spivack and Swift, 1973). Overall, teacher ratings have high indices of reliability* and validity* (Achenbach, McConaughy, and Howell, 1987), but standardization data are frequently limited.

See also BEHAVIORAL ASSESSMENT; COMPREHENSIVE ASSESSMENT; NATURALISTIC OBSERVATION.

REFERENCES

Achenbach, T. M., S. M. McConaughy, and C. T. Howell. (1987). Child/adolescent behavioral and emotional problems: Implications of cross-informant correlations for situational specificity. *Psychological Bulletin* 101, 213–232.

Quay, H. C., and J. S. Werry. (1986). *Psychological disorders of childhood* (3d ed.). New York: Wiley.

Salvia, J., and J. E. Ysseldyke. (1995). *Assessment.* Boston, MA: Houghton Mifflin.

Spivack, G., and M. Swift. (1973). The classroom behavior of children: A critical review of teacher-administered rating scales. *Journal of Special Education* 7, 55–89.

A. Dirk Hightower

TEAM. A team is a group of two or more autonomous individuals who engage in coordinated efforts to achieve a common goal. Direct lines of communication must be maintained among and between group members. Each participant must be actively involved in problem-solving and/or decision-making processes, implementation of recommendations, evaluation of effectiveness of solutions, and revisions. Role relationships, group and individual norms, and goals for the team are cooperatively established by the membership (Abelson and Woodman, 1983). Depending on the focus, teams may be identified as child study or prereferral teams. A child study team is a multidisciplinary team* of professionals that may include the child's teacher, a principal, a special education* teacher, a school psychologist,* and selected related service* providers. It is formed specifically to address the unique educational concerns of an individual child, and its sole purpose is to study the child and his or her presenting problems. In some states, prereferral and/or placement committees for special education are also called child study teams (West and Idol, 1990). Members of the prereferral team are selected based on expertise in a particular area of teaching or behavioral management consistent with the teacher's identified focus of concern and is established on an as-needed basis. Prereferral screening* may require documented evidence of at least two unsuccessful, systematic attempts to meet the child's needs in the regular education setting. These interventions must occur prior to formal referral for evaluation. Intervention* results are instrumental in determining if a referral for evaluation is appropriate.

See also TEAM APPROACH.

REFERENCES

Abelson, M. A., and R. W. Woodman. (1983). Review of research on team
    effectiveness: Implications for teams in the schools. *School Psychology Review*
    2, 125–136.
West, J. F., and L. Idol. (1990). Collaborative consultation in the education of mildly
    handicapped and at-risk students. *Remedial and Special Education* 11, 22–31.

Peggy A. Hicks

TEAM APPROACH. A team* is a group of interdependent persons working in a coordinated effort to achieve a common goal. A team consists of relatively few members who all share a recognition of each person's membership and the contributions each person is best prepared to provide.

With the educational reform movement of the 1980s, following the publication of numerous educational reform reports, teams were believed to be the best structures to make changes in education. Teams were formed for site-based management, professional development, and planning.

Two case-centered team structures have focused on students who have been identified as needing special or different provisions for their educational experiences. Even prior to Public Law 94-142,* case-centered teams were composed to attend to the learning and mental health needs of students. Public Law 94-142 required that multidisciplinary teams* implement evaluation, eligibility, and placement procedures for students with exceptionalities. The federal law did not specify the exact nature of team composition; subsequently, each state has developed regulations that have led to a variety of names for teams and differing team compositions.

The second notable case-centered team approach is the building-level, problem solving team. These teams, often called prereferral teams, were instituted to help teachers address, in the classrooms, problems they are having with students' learning and/or behaviors. In some instances, the focus on the term ''prereferral'' has led to the teams' efforts being considered perfunctory prior to referral for special education* placement and also to avoid formal referrals.

Teams at their best are envisioned as collaborative efforts of persons with differing skills and knowledge who share these for the ultimate benefit of the student. Shortcomings have been noted particularly in unsystematic data collection and analysis, loose decision-making procedures, lack of interdisciplinary trust, minimal parent and regular educator participation, and lack of participant experience in working together. A number of efforts have been initiated to investigate and remedy these shortcomings. Teams best function when goals are clear and shared, team members' interpersonal needs and professions' goals are met, and group process roles are shared (i.e., shared leadership).

See also PREREFERRAL ASSESSMENT; PREREFERRAL INTERVENTIONS.

REFERENCES

Dettmer, P., L. P. Thurston, and N. Dyck. (1993). *Consultation, collaboration, and teamwork for students with special needs.* Boston: Allyn and Bacon.
Friend, M., and L. Cook. (1992). *Interactions: Collaboration skills for school professionals.* New York: Longman.
Maher, C. A., and S. I. Pfeiffer (Eds.). (1983). Multidisciplinary teams in the schools: Perspectives, practices, possibilities. *School Psychology Review* 12, 123–189.

Paul G. Warden

TEMPERAMENT. Temperament refers to individual differences* in behavioral tendencies that are present early in life and are relatively stable across time and a variety of situations. Temperament is considered to be grounded in the biology of the organism, with some theorists giving particular emphasis to genetic determinants.

Factor analytic studies of temperament (Martin, Huttunen, and Wisenbaker, 1994) have consistently yielded five factors, with two other factors appearing less consistently across different measures and ages. The major factors are labeled *inhibition* (the initial tendency to withdraw versus approach a novel situation), *negative emotionality* (the tendency to intensely and persistently express negative emotions such as anger, sadness, or rage), *adaptability* (the speed and ease of adjustment to altered social circumstances), *activity level* (the tendency to engage in vigorous and fast motor movements), and *task persistence* (the tendency to remain engaged in difficult learning or performance tasks for a relatively long period of time). The two factors about which there is some theoretical disagreement and less consistent empirical support are *threshold* (the level of auditory, tactile, visual, and olfactory stimulation that is necessary to produce a response) and *biological rhythmicity* (the extent to which the biological functions of elimination, eating, and sleep occur at regular times during the day–night cycle).

Significant relationships have been found between temperamental dimensions and intelligence,* teacher estimates of intelligence, classroom behavior, behavior problems in the classroom, teacher ratings of ''teachability,'' teachers' classroom decisions, teachers' attitudes toward specific students, and achievement. Much of this research has demonstrated contemporaneous relations, although some has been predictive (e.g., Martin, 1992).

The only commercially available measure of temperament in childhood is the Temperament Assessment Battery for Children (Martin, 1988). The 1995 revision measures the five major temperamental factors listed earlier and is available in parent and teacher forms.

See also PERSONAL-SOCIAL ASSESSMENT.

REFERENCES

Martin, R. P. (1988). *Temperament Assessment Battery for Children—Manual.* Brandon, VT: Clinical Psychology.
———. (1992). Child temperament effects on special education: Process and outcome. *Exceptionality* 3, 99–115.
Martin, R. P., M. O. Huttunen, and J. Wisenbaker. (1994). The factor structure of instruments based on the Chess-Thomas model of temperament: Implications for the big-five. In C. F. Halverson, G. Kohnstamm, and R. P. Martin (Eds.), *The developing structure of temperament and personality: Infancy to adulthood* (pp. 157–172). Hillsdale, NJ: Erlbaum.

Roy P. Martin

TENURE. Tenure is a legal entity requiring that certain educational employees be granted employment security after a probationary period of employment. The practice of tenure appeared first in institutions of higher education, emerging in the early twentieth century and later spreading to elementary and secondary education (Spring, 1989). School psychologists* have tenure in most states that grant tenure to teachers. Tenure is not irremovable, and tenured school personnel can be terminated for documented "incompetence, immorality, and financial exigency" (Fischer and Sorenson, 1996). Termination procedures follow formal steps to protect the due process* rights of school employees.

Tenure for educators is considered important by many in order to assure that school personnel are guaranteed First Amendment rights. They should not be subjected to firing, for example, because of (1) problems involving political patronage, (2) political or religious beliefs expressed outside the school, (3) reprisals by unhappy parents over grades, (4) or refusal to comply with unreasonable demands by school administrators.

Tenured school psychologists and their positions have been terminated in some districts in order to save money or to eliminate psychologists who refuse to follow administrative suggestions or directives that the psychologists view as unethical. The reactions of courts to these attempts to undermine tenure of school psychologists have been mixed. In general, the courts have supported school psychologists if there was a clear demonstration that the schools were using abolishment of the position to merely eliminate an unpopular but competent employee. However, despite court orders, some districts have found other ways to terminate school psychologists. Practical advice for school psychologists is to have an active membership in an employee union that will help defend against loss of tenure by any of its members.

See also COLLECTIVE BARGAINING; *FORREST v. AMBACH;* LEGAL-ETHICAL DILEMMA.

REFERENCES

Fischer, L., and G. P. Sorenson. (1996). *School law for counselors, psychologists, and social workers.* White Plains, NY: Longman.

Spring, J. (1989). *American education: An introduction to social and political aspects.* White Plains, NY: Longman.

Irwin A. Hyman

TERMAN, LEWIS M. Lewis Madison Terman was born in Johnson County, Indiana, on January 15, 1877, and died on December 21, 1956. He received the B.S. and B.Pd. (bachelor of pedology) in 1897 from Central Normal College in Danville, Indiana; an A.B. and A.M. from Indiana University in 1902 and 1903, respectively; and his Ph.D. from Clark University in 1905, where he studied under G. Stanley Hall* and first met Arnold Gesell.* He had been a school-teacher and principal early in his career before pursuing graduate studies. Terman is best known in the history of school psychological services for his popularization of the IQ, his longitudinal studies of gifted children, and his development of tests, including the Stanford Achievement Tests and the Stanford Revision of the Binet-Simon Intelligence Tests, first published in 1916 (revised in 1937, 1960, 1972, and 1986), later known as the Stanford-Binet. His academic career was identified with educational psychology* in the College of Education at Stanford University and then the Stanford psychology department, where he served as chair from 1922 to 1942, when he retired. He was elected president of the American Psychological Association* in 1923. Though his career was identified with educational psychology, his contributions had an enormous impact on the practice and growth of school psychology.*

See also COGNITIVE ASSESSMENT; STERN, WILLIAM.

REFERENCES

Hilgard, E. R. (1957). Lewis Madison Terman (1877–1956). *American Journal of Psychology* 70, 472–479.

Minton, H. L. (1987). Lewis M. Terman and mental testing: In search of the democratic ideal. In M. M. Sokal (Ed.), *Psychological testing and American society 1890–1930* (pp. 95–112). New Brunswick, NJ: Rutgers University Press.

Terman, L. M. (1932). Autobiography. In C. Murchison (Ed.), *A history of psychology in autobiography,* Vol. 2 (pp. 297–331). Worcester, MA: Clark University Press.

Thomas K. Fagan

TEST SECURITY/ACCESS. Public disclosure of the content of psychological tests can invalidate the instrument for future examinees. The 1963 ethical code of the American Psychological Association* included a mandate to maintain test security by limiting test access to persons with professional interests who will safeguard their contents. Subsequent code revisions, however, recognized the need to balance the obligation to safeguard test security with the growing emphasis on the legal right of examinees to review test information used in making important decisions about them. Ethical codes now require psychologists to protect test security within the limits of legal mandates. In the public schools, the Family Educational Rights and Privacy Act of 1974 (Public Law 93–380*) has been interpreted as granting parents the right to examine their child's psychological test protocols under appropriate school supervision. Schools are not required to make copies of test protocols unless failure to do so would prevent parents from exercising their right to inspect records.

See also CODE OF ETHICS; PROFESSIONAL STANDARDS.

REFERENCE

Jacob-Timm, S., and T. S. Hartshorne. (1994). *Ethics and law for school psychologists* (2d ed.). Brandon, VT: Clinical Psychology.

Susan Jacob-Timm

THAYER CONFERENCE. The historic Thayer Conference was organized by the Division of School Psychologists* (Division 16 of the American Psychological Association* [APA]) with the support and assistance of the APA Education and Training Board and a grant from the Public Health Service of the U.S. Department of Health, Education, and Welfare. The name was derived from the conference site—Hotel Thayer in West Point, New York (the hotel was named after Sylvanus Thayer, superintendent of West Point from 1817 to 1833). Held August 22–31, 1954, this conference is the only national conference in the history of school psychology* to deal directly with issues of training for school psychologists,* and it is the longest national school psychology conference on any topic. The conference was attended by forty-eight persons representing a variety of psychological specialties, training backgrounds, and employment positions. It helped establish an agenda for the future of school psychology in terms of levels of training, certification,* and practice. The earlier Boulder conference* regarding training issues in clinical psychology* served as a stimulus for the planning of the Thayer Conference. Recommendations of the conference are still relevant to the training and practice of school psychologists.

See also CUTTS, NORMA E.

REFERENCE

Cutts, N. E. (Ed.). (1955). *School psychologists at mid-century* (A report of the Thayer

Conference on the functions, qualifications, and training of school psychologists). Washington, DC: American Psychological Association.

Thomas K. Fagan

THIRD-PARTY REIMBURSEMENTS. Third-party insurance reimbursements for services provided by psychologists became an issue in the 1970s. By the 1980s, professional psychologists (usually licensed, doctoral-trained psychologists by the state board of examiners of psychologists*) were eligible to be reimbursed for medical services from private insurance companies, federal and state employee insurance programs, Medicaid, and Medicare. A number of states have designated certain qualified licensed psychologists as health service providers. These psychologists must meet certain training criteria similar to those required by the Council of the National Register of Health Service Providers in Psychology.* These state and national health service provider designations are beginning to be required for reimbursement from insurance providers.

Most school psychologists* have not been concerned about third-party reimbursements because they have not pursued the doctoral degree and other requirements to become licensed and eligible for health service provider status. School psychology* was brought into the issue because of the American Psychological Association's (APA) proclamation in the late 1970s that, to use the title of ''professional psychologist,'' one had to have a doctoral degree; however, subsequent APA specialty guidelines and the model licensing act exempted school psychology, allowing the term ''certified school psychologist'' to be used while performing duties within the jurisdiction of the state department of education.* More recently, some states have developed separate licensing laws allowing school psychologists and licensed professional counselors to perform private practice,* albeit without the privilege of third-party reimbursements.

In 1990, the Medicaid law was amended to allow Medicaid money to be channeled into the public schools to cover the costs of needed services, including psychological services, to low-income, Medicaid-eligible students who were in special education.* By 1994, twenty-six states were using Medicaid money for school psychological services. Each state established its own rules regarding eligible services and eligible providers; consequently, each state has had to address the issue of eligibility of certified school psychologists. Dwyer (1994), speaking for the National Association of School Psychologists* (NASP), contends school psychologists should support efforts to acquire Medicaid reimbursement to school districts because eligible students will receive improved related services,* and the comprehensive services provided by school psychologists employed by the public schools will be more effective than contracted services. The latter has been a position of NASP for some time.

Earlier, Canter (1990) sounded an alarm regarding Medicaid reimbursements. Her concerns focused on use of DSM III (now IV) categories and the manipulation of services so that Medicaid reimbursement would be assured. Canter raised the question about what dependency on Medicaid would do to the recent professional shift away from emphasis on traditional diagnostic roles to more classroom-centered service delivery. Vigilant monitoring of school psychology's entrance into the world of third-party reimbursements will be needed to ensure the best available services to the students served.

REFERENCES

Canter, A. (1990). Issues related to third-party reimbursement. *Communique* 19(3), 14.

Dwyer, K. P. (1994). Medicaid used in 26 states for school psychological services. *Communique* 23(1), 7.

Fagan, T. K., and P. S. Wise. (1994). *School psychology: Past, present, and future.* White Plains, NY: Longman.

Paul G. Warden

THOROUGHBRED YEARS. The term "thoroughbred years" is used to describe the period in school psychology* history from 1970 to the present, characterized by growth in the number of training programs, practitioners, and state and national associations and the expansion of literature and regulations, contributing to a more stable professional identity. The period's name derives from the purification of training, practice, and regulation associated with this era. Employment was more consistently in positions titled "school psychologist,"* in states offering school psychology credentials, for persons who had completed training programs staffed by school psychologists and accredited in school psychology. Diversification of roles and functions* and practice settings has been a recognizable theme of the period.

See also HYBRID YEARS.

REFERENCES

Fagan, T. K. (1990). Research on the history of school psychology: Recent developments, significance, resources, and future directions. In T. R. Kratochwill (Ed.), *Advances in school psychology,* Vol. 7 (pp. 151–182). Hillsdale, NJ: Erlbaum.

Fagan, T. K., and P. S. Wise. (1994). *School psychology: Past, present, and future.* White Plains, NY: Longman.

Thomas K. Fagan

TIME ANALYSIS. Time analysis is one of several data-gathering methods used for purposes of professional accountability.* The school psychologist* keeps a personal journal or daily log of time spent in various professional activities (e.g., classroom observations, teacher consultations, report writing*). On a weekly, monthly, and yearly basis, the time spent in each activity is tabulated. In this manner, the relative time in which the school psychologist was engaged in each activity can be analyzed and subsequently reported as part of an overall accountability plan. Time analysis is considered an enumerative method of data collection in that the time spent in various activities is noted and counted but not analyzed in terms of one's professional skill level or the outcome or consequences of the time spent. Benefits of maintaining daily logs and conducting yearly time analyses include providing an accounting of professional activities for an individual school psychologist or an entire staff and demonstrating the school psychologist's involvement in a wide range of professional activities. Ultimately, such data collection may lead to the improvement of service delivery by school psychologists (Zins, 1990). A study by Zins and Fairchild (1986) found that approximately 25 percent of school psychologists responding to their survey collected time analysis data as a measure of accountability.

See also ACCOUNTABILITY: ENUMERATIVE DATA.

REFERENCES

Fairchild, T. N. (1975). Accountability: Practical suggestions for school psychologists. *Journal of School Psychology* 13, 149–159.

Zins, J. E. (1990). Best practices in developing accountability procedures. In A. Thomas and J. Grimes (Eds.), *Best practices in school psychology—II* (pp. 323–337) Washington, DC: National Association of School Psychologists.

Zins, J. E., and T. N. Fairchild. (1986). An investigation of the accountability practices of school psychologists. *Professional School Psychology* 1, 193–204.

Paula Sachs Wise

TINDALL, RALPH H. Ralph Harold Tindall (1914–1988), born in Cedarville, Ohio, graduated from Cedarville College in 1935 and from Ohio State with an M.A. in 1946 and a Ph.D. in 1952. During the 1930s and 1940s, he was a teacher in several Ohio schools. He became the resident psychologist in the Ohio Soldiers' and Sailors' Orphans Home in 1946. In 1953, he became the director of psychological services in the Milwaukee public schools, a post he held for ten years. From 1963 to 1979, he was a professor at the University of South Carolina (USC), where he developed a substantial graduate program for school psychologists.* To help integrate education and training, Tindall was also the director of special services for the Richland County schools for ten years, beginning with his appointment at USC.

REFERENCES

Nagle, R. J. (1988, May). In memoriam: Ralph H. Tindall 1914–1988. *School Scene* (newsletter of the South Carolina Association of School Psychologists) 20(5), 1.

Tindall, R. H. (1964). Trends in development of psychological services in the school. *Journal of School Psychology* 3, 1–12.

———. (1983). I didn't aspire to be a school psychologist: Reflections. *Journal of School Psychology* 21, 79–89.

Joseph L. French

TOTAL QUALITY MANAGEMENT. Total quality management (TQM) is a popular management theory growing out of W. Edwards Deming's work in organizational development* and Joseph Juran's work in statistical quality control. It is possibly the most profound variation in management theory that has influenced business in years and is considered a key to our economic survival. Although Deming's work helped transform the post–World War II Japanese industrial base, it was shunned by U.S. companies until the 1980s. Recently, the movement has grown and evolved as agencies, factories, businesses, and educational institutions shape it for their respective use.

Deming outlined fourteen points to achieve quality and maximum effectiveness, which are interdependent and systemic. These form the foundation for implementing TQM and emphasize the need to create a common vision and train employees to work effectively. Leadership, initiative, and teamwork are stated organizational values, minimizing the need for top-down management by objectives, inspection, quotas, and other traditional management control strategies.

Several principles characterize the quality movement:

1. A focus on the customer in which products and services address customer needs.

2. A prevention approach that supports proactive intervention and "do it right the first time" mentality.

3. Management based on factual information and data.

4. Respect for employees at all levels, who are empowered to analyze customer requirements, identify opportunities for improvement, implement change, and track the impact of the changes.

5. Cross-functional problem solving that cuts horizontally across organizational lines and functions, allowing people with different perspectives to work together to improve service delivery.

6. Constancy of leadership commitment that becomes a way of life and is built into the fabric of the organization.

A critical concept of TQM is continuous improvement, a process that undergirds the management approach and helps it meet its objectives. It symbolically forms the foundation of any TQM program and brings together the other principles and activities. It guides both leadership and methodology, which ultimately guide improvement efforts. To achieve improvement methodologically, the approach focuses on several tools or processes: customer identification; work process documentation; systematic problem-solving processes; competitive benchmarking; and employee surveys and focus groups.

TQM assumes that most people want to do a good job and that organizations need to build conditions supporting that effort. If problems arise, they are system-related, not people-driven. This is consistent with other basic organizational development theories of human systems and philosophically consistent with educational and psychological interpretations of organizational behavior. It is a person-friendly approach to management, incorporating the concepts of employee improvement, quality of action and product, and continued improvement through systematic problem solving and monitoring. It incorporates well-researched statistical tools and concepts and has demonstrated good applicability to various types of organizations worldwide.

Seymour (1992) and Covey (1991) have outlined basic principles of strategic quality management that cut across the various authors in the field. They elucidate the fundamental concepts inherent in the theory as articulated by its proponents: meeting and exceeding customer needs; constancy, consistency, and predictability; continuous improvement and progression; human resource development; teamwork and team ownership; recognition and reward; systematic problem solving; feedback from measurement and research; and virtue of truth in human relations.

TQM builds upon principles based on organizational development research and is currently being applied in many agencies and institutions. The spirit of the movement is to promote a learning organization built upon partnership, collaboration,* and continued improvement.

See also SYSTEMS AND ORGANIZATIONAL CONSULTATION.

REFERENCES

Covey, S. R. (1991). *Principled-centered leadership*. New York: Simon and Schuster.
Deming, W. E. (1986). *Out of crisis*. Boston: Massachusetts Institute of Technology.
Seymour, D. T. (1992). *On Q: Causing quality in higher education*. New York: American Council on Education, Macmillan.

Susan Kupisch

TRAINERS OF SCHOOL PSYCHOLOGISTS. Trainers of School Psychologists (TSP) was formed in 1972 to advance the standards of training in school psychology* programs; to inform member institutions of current trends in the graduate education of school psychologists*; to furnish opportunities for the professional growth of school psychology faculty; to encourage innovation in the development of more effective graduate training; to support the continuing education of practitioners of school psychology; and to support legislative efforts that promote satisfactory standards of training. TSP is a nonprofit, nonpartisan, and nonsectarian organization. Membership is primarily by institution and open to any university or college training program in school psychology, with one membership per degree-granting institution. Individual membership is open to any faculty person from institutions that do not have an institutional membership or to nonfaculty persons whose applications are approved by the Executive Committee. TSP is governed by a six-member Executive Committee, which has two members rotating on or off the committee each year after serving three-year terms. The Executive Committee elects its own president and secretary-treasurer. General membership meetings are held at least twice each year, usually at the conventions of the National Association of School Psychologists* and the American Psychological Association.* The *TSP Newsletter* is published quarterly.

REFERENCE

Phillips, B. N. (1993). Trainers of School Psychologists and Council of Directors of

School Psychology Programs: A new chapter in the history of school psychology. *Journal of School Psychology* 31, 91–108.

C. Sue McCullough

TRAINING MODELS. "Models of training" is a phrase used to characterize the philosophy, principles, and general guidelines adopted by graduate programs in psychology to guide training of their students. A parsimonious definition of "models of training" is offered by Fagan and Wise (1994), who use the phrase to "represent the salient characteristics of a particular program of preparation." Models of training are typically defined for applied specialties in psychology, specifically, school, clinical, and counseling psychology. The first and most widely endorsed model in psychology, the scientist-practitioner model,* was developed primarily to train clinical psychologists but has been adopted and/or adapted by other specialty programs. This model grew out of a training conference held in Boulder, Colorado, in 1949 and combines clinically oriented training with training in basic research. According to this model, a psychologist is a scientist and a competent researcher; a psychologist is also a practitioner who applies knowledge and techniques obtained from the research literature to solve problems of clients. Officially endorsed by the American Psychological Association,* the scientist-practitioner model has been the object of much controversy. Critics have called it a philosophy of training rather than a particular training model, and some have criticized it as too strongly research-oriented and too long; others claim that it allows some service areas to be neglected. Several alternative training models have been advanced. One alternative, the professional model,* was formalized during the Vail conference in 1973. The professional model emphasizes more practical training than the scientist-practitioner model, leads to the Psy.D. degree (doctor of psychology), and is often associated with free-standing schools of professional psychology rather than universities.

Fagan and Wise (1994) have referred to the scientist-practitioner model and the professional model as "master models," primarily because they have been so influential in guiding thinking about school psychology* training. One additional model is also referred to as a master model—the pragmatic model.* This model is used to describe the training in most nondoctoral programs and gets its name from the fact that many such programs are guided primarily by the entry-level credentialing requirements of states in which the programs exist. These three models overlap; they have provided the basic core characteristics used by proponents of other "hybrid" training models.

Two alternative models have been proposed that have unique applicability for school psychology training programs. The first is called the data-based problem solver model and is actually a variant of the scientist-practitioner model; the second is the behavior consultation model. The data-based problem solver model relies on use of scientific methodology, as does the scientist-practitioner model. Unlike the scientist-practitioner model, the data-based problem solver model provides considerable specificity, including a number of problem-solving steps

(Edwards, 1987). The utilization of this model encourages students to appreciate data as a basis for decision making and to approach all problems in a scientific manner, regardless of whether the problem is theoretical or practical. The behavioral consultation model emphasizes behavioral psychology and encourages the psychologist to use behavioral techniques. It requires the student to acquire a variety of consultation and direct service competencies during training (Kratochwill and Bergan, 1978) and describes a series of problem-solving steps.

Other training models include the psychologist-psychotherapist model, the research-clinician model, and the professional-psychologist model. Although these models have some unique characteristics, much of their substance comes from the early models (e.g., scientist-practitioner model).

See also BOULDER CONFERENCE; SPECIALTY TRAINING AND CREDENTIALING.

REFERENCES

Edwards, R. P. (1987). Implementing the scientist-practitioner model: The school psychologist as a data-based problem solver. *Professional School Psychology* 15, 417–435.

Fagan, T. K., and P. S. Wise. (1994). *School psychology: Past, present, and future.* White Plains, NY: Longman.

Kratochwill, T. R., and J. R. Bergan. (1978). Training school psychologists: Some perspectives on a competency-based behavioral consultation model. *Professional Psychology* 9, 71–79.

R. Steve McCallum

TRANSACTIONAL ANALYSIS. Transactional analysis (TA) was formulated by Eric Berne in the 1950s. TA was *the* self-help therapy of the 1960s and 1970s. TA has its own vocabulary, with very specific meanings for such words as "games," "rackets," "stamps," "discounts," "losers," and "drivers." Theoretically, it is psychodynamic and emphasizes ego states, life positions, parental injunctions from childhood, and interpersonal games people play. Whereas Freudian constructs exist in the unconscious, the parent, adult, and child ego states of TA are behavioral realities that are used to communicate or transact with the ego states of other individuals in attempts to gain strokes or attention. How strokes are given and received determines the four basic life positions: (1) I'm OK—You're OK; (2) I'm OK—You're not OK; (3) I'm not OK—You're OK; (4) I'm not OK—You're not OK. Maladjustment is the result of inappropriate childhood decisions made to parental injunctions and driver statements such as "don't grow up" or "be perfect." These injunctions and drivers form maladaptive behavioral scripts that are repeated endlessly through destructive interpersonal games.

Therapeutic change is accomplished by four kinds of rational analysis: structural (personality makeup), transactional (what people say to one another), game (how people act toward one another), and script (the overall life plans people follow). Therapy occurs in the following stages: clients must (1) be motivated to change, (2) become aware of what they want to change, (3) accept responsibility and deconfuse themselves by expressing unmet needs and feelings, (4) use redecision to change scripts, and (5) start relearning by engaging in new behaviors to stop old, maladaptive behavioral scripts.

See also PSYCHODYNAMIC THERAPY.

REFERENCES

Berne, E. (1964). *Games people play: The psychology of human relationships.* New York: Grove Press.
Harris, T. A. (1969). *I'm OK—You're OK.* New York: Harper and Row.
Woolams, S., and M. Brown. (1979). *TA: The total handbook of transactional analysis.* Englewood Cliffs, NJ: Prentice-Hall.

Richard K. James

TRANSITION SERVICES. Transition services are defined in Public Law 101-476* (the Individuals with Disabilities Education Act of 1990 [IDEA]) as "a coordinated set of activities for a student, designed within an outcome-oriented process, which promotes movement from school to post-school activities." These activities may include "post-secondary education, vocational training, integrated employment (including supported employment), continuing and adult education, adult services, independent living, or community participation." IDEA requires that a statement of transition services be included in the individual educational plan* (IEP) of all students with disabilities age sixteen and older (or younger, as appropriate). Best practice suggests that transition planning should begin as early as possible, preferably four years before the student will leave school.

Research in the field reveals that success in transition planning is increased when the student is offered vocational evaluation and vocational skills training, when the student's parents and family are involved, when the student has a paid work experience during high school, and when adult services agencies cooperate and collaborate in the IEP process.

See also CAREER ASSESSMENT; VOCATIONAL ASSESSMENT.

REFERENCES

Levinson, E. M., and L. M. McKee. (1990). Best practices in transitional services. In A. Thomas and J. Grimes (Eds.), *Best practices in school psychology—II* (pp. 743–755). Washington, DC: National Association of School Psychologists.
Wehman, P. (1992). *Life beyond the classroom: Transition strategies for young people with disabilities.* Baltimore: Brookes.
West, L. L., S. Corbey, A. Boyer-Stephens, B. Jones, R. J. Miller, and M. Sarkees-Wicenski. (1992). *Integrating transition planning into the IEP process.* Reston, VA: Council for Exceptional Children.

John E. Brandt

TREATMENT ACCEPTABILITY. Treatment acceptability refers to the degree to which consumers like or dislike psychological treatments (Witt and Elliott, 1985). It is a judgment by laypersons, clients,* and/or others whether treatment procedures are appropriate, fair, and reasonable for a client and problem behavior. Kazdin (1981) suggests that many potentially effective treatments for behavior problems are underutilized because they are unacceptable to treatment consumers. Reasons for the unacceptability of treatments range from the restriction of individual rights, equity, and the use of jargon in describing treatments (Witt and Elliott, 1985).

The concept of treatment acceptability can be traced to Wolf's (1978) conceptualization of social validity, which occurs on three levels: (1) the social significance of the goals of an intervention (i.e., Is this behavior worth changing?), (2) the social appropriateness of treatment procedures (Do the ends justify the means?), and (3) the social importance of the effects (Did the intervention make a difference in the client's functioning?). The social appropriateness of treatment procedures is more commonly referred to as treatment acceptability.

Witt and Elliott (1985) proposed a working model of acceptability that depicted the relationships among four elements: treatment acceptability, treatment use, treatment integrity,* and treatment effectiveness. This model was described by Elliott (1988) as sequential and reciprocal in which the acceptability of treatment predicts whether or not they will be used. A key element linking the use and effectiveness of treatments is treatment integrity. When integrity is high, the likelihood that the treatment will be effective is greater than if integrity is low.

The following factors are related to the acceptability of treatments:

- The jargon a psychologist uses to describe treatment. Teachers prefer treatments described in either humanistic or pragmatic terms rather than behavioral terms.
- The amount of time it takes (i.e., longer treatments are less acceptable than shorter treatments).
- The severity of target behavior. As severity of behavior increases, all treatments become more acceptable.
- Treatments based on positive reinforcement are more acceptable than treatments based on punishment.
- Perceived effectiveness of treatments is related to the acceptability of those treatments.

See also CODES OF ETHICS; LEGAL-ETHICAL DILEMMA; PROFESSIONAL STANDARDS.

REFERENCES

Kazdin, A. (1981). Acceptability of child-treatment techniques: The influence of treatment efficacy and adverse side effects. *Behavior Therapy* 12, 493–506.
Witt, J. C., and S. N. Elliott. (1985). Acceptability of classroom management strategies. In T. Kratochwill (Ed.), *Advances in school psychology,* Vol. 4 (pp. 251–288). Hillsdale, NJ: Erlbaum.

Wolf, M. M. (1978). Social validity: The case for subjective measurement or how applied behavior analysis is finding its heart. *Journal of Applied Behavior Analysis* 11, 203–214.

Frank M. Gresham

TREATMENT INTEGRITY. Treatment integrity refers to the degree to which an intervention or treatment to change behavior is implemented as planned (Gresham, 1989; Peterson, Homer, and Wonderlich, 1982). The most fundamental principle of intervention, particularly, behaviorally based interventions, is the demonstration that changes in behavior are functionally related to changes in the environment. That is, one must demonstrate that changes in a dependent variable are functionally related to systematic and controlled changes in an independent variable. Treatment integrity captures the essence of this relationship between independent variables (i.e., treatments) and dependent variables (i.e., behaviors).

If significant behavior change occurs, and if there are no data concerning the implementation of a treatment, then the internal validity of an experiment or intervention may be compromised. Similarly, if significant behavior change does not occur, and if the integrity of the treatment is not monitored, then one has difficulty in distinguishing between an ineffective treatment and an effective treatment implemented with poor integrity.

Practically speaking, one expects that treatment agents will implement an intervention as planned. When significant behavior changes occur, one assumes that these changes were due to the intervention. However, it may well be the case that the treatment agent (e.g., teacher or parent) changed the intervention in ways unknown to the school psychologist* and that these changes were responsible for behavior change. In contrast, if significant behavior changes do not occur, then the school psychologist may assume falsely that the lack of change was due to an ineffective or inappropriate intervention. In the latter, potentially effective treatments that would change behavior substantially if they were implemented properly may be eliminated in future considerations for similar problems. However, the cause of weak treatment effects in many cases may be poor integrity of potentially effective treatments.

In a review of 181 experimental studies conducted in school settings published between 1980 and 1990, Gresham et al. (1993) found that only 35 percent (64 studies) provided an operational definition of the treatment, and only 14.9 percent (27 studies) systematically measured and reported levels of treatment integrity for the independent variable. Correlational analyses showed a moderate correlation between level of treatment integrity and treatment outcome ($r = .58$), indicating that higher treatment integrity was associated with stronger treatment effects.

See also EXPERIMENTAL DESIGN; TREATMENT ACCEPTABILITY; VALIDITY.

REFERENCES

Gresham, F. M. (1989). Assessment of treatment integrity in school consultation and prereferral intervention. *School Psychology Review* 18, 37–50.

Gresham, F. M., K. Gansle, G. Noell, S. Cohen, and S. Rosenblum. (1993). Treatment integrity of school-based behavioral intervention studies: 1980–1990. *School Psychology Review* 22, 254–272.

Peterson, L., A. Homer, and S. Wonderlich. (1982). The integrity of independent variables in behavior analysis. *Journal of Applied Behavior Analysis* 15, 477–492.

Frank M. Gresham

TREATMENT PLAN. A treatment plan consists of a detailed, step-by-step method to achieve a determined goal (Dougherty, 1990). A treatment plan should address the following questions. What is the problem? What changes are required? How do we get there? Will the plan be developed by a team or an individual? Will it deal with long-term or short-term goals? Will the plan be implemented directly or indirectly? Further questions, such as who? what? when? and where? also need to be addressed.

A treatment plan may be designed to implement individualized educational plan (IEP) goals. However, IEP goals usually are long-term and written annually, whereas a treatment plan can be created to deal with a specific situation that requires immediate action.

After goals have been correctly framed and agreed upon, the next step is to sort out the existing alternatives. When appropriate alternatives do not exist, school psychologists* should attempt to either alter existing alternatives or devise new ones.

Because a direct link exists between assessment* and treatment, school psychologists should incorporate test findings when formulating treatment outcomes. The finalization of treatment goals should be based on diagnostic test data, observations, and teacher–parent input. Selecting appropriate goals ensures the relevance of the plan and also increases the likelihood of implementation.

Teachers and parents want to see results; therefore, a plan must not be overly complicated or difficult to implement. Plans that yield immediate results seem to enhance the credibility of the school psychologist. Unrealistic strategies that require tedious adherence to rigid timelines or procedures are doomed to fail.

A significant percent of treatment plans are expected to be unsuccessful; therefore, each plan should be evaluated after it is implemented. If a plan fails, it should not be abandoned; it should, however, be revised. Because many school psychologists are itinerant, they should strive to produce a tangible product such as a treatment plan. A treatment plan permits school psychologists to maintain a therapeutic influence on students at school, at home, or in other social settings.

See also INDIVIDUALIZED FAMILY SERVICE PLAN; INDIVIDUALIZED TRANSITION PLAN.

REFERENCES

Dougherty, A. M. (1990). *Consultation practice and perspectives.* Pacific Grove, CA: Brooks/Cole.

Spricks, R., M. Spricks, and M. Garrison. (1993). *Interventions.* Longmont, CO: Sopris West.

Gerald J. Spadafore

TRI-STATE SCHOOL PSYCHOLOGY CONFERENCE. Engaging school psychologist trainers,* representatives of state associations, and others from New York, New Jersey, and Connecticut, the Tri-State Conference addressed issues of identity, role and function,* and training. The conference was held at Teachers College, Columbia University in March 1962. It was among several lesser-known but historically important conferences on school psychology* held in the 1960s.

See also EISERER, PAUL E.

REFERENCE

Eiserer, P. E., S. Lieberfreund, and M. A. White, (Eds.). (1962, March). *Tri-State School Psychology Conference: Continuing professional development for school psychologists, proceedings.* New York: Teachers College, Columbia University.

Thomas K. Fagan

TURF ISSUES. Turf issues refer to disputes over the professional roles of different human services providers such as school psychologists,* clinical psychologists,* counseling psychologists,* social workers, and school counselors. Although these are separate and independent professions with unique state licensing* or certification* requirements, different state and national professional associations, and independent graduate programs at universities, there are common elements shared by each of the professions. Questions of ''turf'' often involve who has the authority to provide services in the areas of common training and practice (Fagan and Wise, 1994).

Several areas of common training and practice can be identified in the major human services professions. Virtually all involve training and practice in (1) counseling individual clients*; (2) interviewing* key individuals such as parents; (3) standardized methods of collecting information using tests or inventories; and (4) consultation* as a means to intervene with learning and behavior problems. There are, typically, differences as well in how these common skills are acquired in graduate programs and in how they are practiced in schools and other human services delivery systems. School psychologists are, for example, more likely to provide counseling services to children with disabilities, while school counselors are more likely to work with at-risk students who are not identified as educationally disabled.

Turf issues often have as much to do with funding or fears about loss of funding as with any genuine differences in professional competencies. Categorical or special program funding sometimes requires the involvement of a specific professional in order for the agency to receive the funds, and, parenthetically, the positions of certain professionals may be dependent on that categorical or special program funding. Some school psychologists are entirely dependent on special education* funding. Continued involvement in the diagnosis and programming services to students with disabilities, because of the funding mechanisms, often is crucial turf for school psychologists to defend because, without that role (turf), their jobs might be reduced or eliminated (Reschly and Wilson, 1995).

Turf battles in most situations are shortsighted and, in the long run, ineffective ways to preserve professional services and jobs. The need for mental health and educational interventions* far exceeds the supply of professionals in any human services agency. Ultimately, current turf issues may be resolved by which profession(s) can document positive outcomes as a result of the services provided (Ysseldyke, Thurlow, and Bruininks, 1992). The challenge, then, is not to protect turf but to capitalize on the strengths of different professionals and ensure that a comprehensive range of effective mental health and educational services is provided to children, youth, teachers, and families.

See also PUPIL PERSONNEL SERVICES; ROLE RESTRICTION; SALARY DETERMINATION.

REFERENCES

Fagan, T. K., and P. S. Wise. (1994). *School psychology: Past, present, and future.* White Plains, NY: Longman.

Reschly, D. J., and M. S. Wilson. (1995). School psychology faculty and practitioners: 1986 to 1991 trends in demographic characteristics, roles, satisfaction, and system reform. *School Psychology Review* 24, 62–80.

Ysseldyke, J. E., M. L. Thurlow, and R. H. Bruininks. (1992). Expected educational outcomes for students with disabilities. *Remedial and Special Education* 13(6), 19–30.

Daniel J. Reschly

U

UNIVERSITY-BASED CLINICS. The first psychological clinic* was established in 1896 by Lightner Witmer* at the University of Pennsylvania for the study and treatment of atypical children. University clinics were the primary facilities delivering broadly defined clinical and educational services to children and their families from the early 1900s until the 1940s. By 1914, there were twenty-six clinics at universities, colleges, and medical schools. With the growth of clinical psychology* training programs and the initiation of school psychology* programs in the early to mid-1930s, the primary focus of university clinics became training rather than service.

Until the early 1960s, psychoeducational services for children with learning or adjustment problems and counseling services for college students were the primary services provided by university clinics. Today, university clinics offer a wide variety of services and utilize various service delivery models. This variety reflects differences in program and university resources, administrative structures, program training goals, community resources, faculty interests and competencies, and the availability of alternative field placements for trainees. The program training needs receive primary attention over the service needs of the community in determining services offered by university-based clinics.

See also PSYCHOEDUCATIONAL CLINICS.

REFERENCE

Hughes, J. N., and A. J. Benson. (1986). University clinics as field placements in school psychology training. *Professional School Psychology* 1, 131–142.

A. Jerry Benson

UNIVERSITY TRAINER. A doctoral-level school psychologist* working in a university setting can function as a trainer of school psychologists. The trainer might be teaching undergraduate courses as well as graduate courses. The school psychology* program may be housed in a department of psychology, usually in a college of arts and sciences, or in a department in a college of education. In addition to teaching classes, a university trainer is involved in his or her own research, supervises student research, and is a member of departmental, college, and/or university committees. Student advisement, course development, program planning, and program direction also take place on campus. Off-campus activities involve school and agency consultation, attendance at meetings and professional development workshops, and, in some instances, supervision of practicum students and interns and involvement in a part-time private practice.*

Well beyond the establishment of the first training program at New York University in 1928, trainers came from the ranks of allied professions such as counseling and guidance, clinical psychology,* and educational psychology.* Only in the last decade has the number of doctoral programs grown (to approximately eighty) so that universities have preferred employing new trainers who have been graduated from doctoral-level school psychology programs. Currently, doctoral-level programs that have accreditation* from the American Psychological Association* (APA) or aspire to attain accreditation are seeking trainer candidates from APA-accredited programs.

University trainers often are members of the National Association of School Psychologists* (NASP) and APA, Division 16, Division of School Psychology.* An organization that has remained unaffiliated with either NASP or APA but meets concurrently at both associations' annual conventions is the Trainers of School Psychologists* (TSP). Another association, affiliated with APA, grants institutional membership to universities with doctoral-level school psychology training programs—the Council of Directors of School Psychology Programs.* Both of these associations focus on training issues as opposed to professional advocacy; consequently, they have remained peripheral to issues with which the field-based school psychologists are most familiar.

REFERENCES

Fagan, T. K. (1990). Best practices in the training of school psychologists: Considerations for trainers, prospective entry-level and advanced students. In A. Thomas and J. Grimes (Eds.), *Best practices in school psychology—II* (pp. 723–741). Washington, DC: National Association of School Psychologists.
Fagan, T. K., and P. S. Wise. (1994). *School psychology: Past, present, and future.* White Plains, NY: Longman.

Paul G. Warden

URBAN SCHOOL PSYCHOLOGY. Although the literature indicates varied opinions and findings as to differences among urban, suburban,* and rural* school psychologists,* there is agreement that the immediate context of the setting shapes and directs the specific nature of the practice of school psychology.* Jackson (1990) has noted that the context of the practice of urban school psychology includes the unique values and problems of students from many cultural and ethnic backgrounds, many of whom are poor.

The context of urban education is long-standing. In the latter nineteenth and early twentieth centuries, factors such as massive immigration from Central and Southern Europe to urban areas, significant migration within the United States from rural agrarian centers to urban industrial centers, compulsory school attendance, and child labor laws led to a doubling of the urban school populations, with increased cultural diversity of the student body and conditions of an economically impoverished urban life. Given these most pressing needs for adjustment of students to school, naturally, the growth of psychological services and special educational* services in the early 1900s was generally confined to urban or city schools.

The literature regarding urban education indicates that much the same situation exists today. While all schools are faced with distressing statistics on dropouts, students living in poverty, substance abuse, and an increasing rate of child suicide, these problems are more pressing for children in urban schools. The urban school is becoming more complex as the various types of minorities increase, and the minorities, in fact, become the majority. Urban settings present unique issues of socialized delinquency, social distance, and rejection inherent in racism; large numbers of at-risk students, with a shortage of relevant services; discontinuities between home and school that foster a cycle of failure; communities characterized by a sense of powerlessness and hopelessness; and, yet, communities with a greater availability of psychological services (e.g., agencies, clinics,* and hospitals). Given this unique definition of the nature of urban education, the prevailing education literature calls for preparing educators (teachers, school psychologists, administrators, and so on) specifically to serve in urban schools.

Urban school psychology, then, is defined as not only the application of the content, instruments, methods, and procedures of psychology in the urban setting but also a set of attitudes, sensitivities, and appreciations of the learners, staff, and parents that comprise the urban setting (Jackson, 1990).

REFERENCES

Jackson, J. H. (1986). Conceptual and logistical hurdles: Service delivery to urban schools. In S. N. Elliott and J. C. Witt (Eds.), *The delivery of psychological services in schools: Concepts, process, and issues* (pp. 171–202). Hillsdale, NJ: Erlbaum.

————. (1990). Best practices in urban school psychology. In A. Thomas and J. Grimes (Eds.), *Best practices in school psychology—II* (pp. 757–771). Washington, DC: National Association of School Psychologists.

Mullen, F. A. (1967). The role of the school psychologist in the urban school system. In J. F. Magary (Ed.), *School psychological services in theory and practice: A handbook* (pp. 30–67). Englewood Cliffs, NJ: Prentice-Hall.

Perry, D. D. (1995). Best practices in facilitating services in urban settings. In A. Thomas and J. Grimes (Eds.), *Best practices in school psychology—III* (pp. 289–299). Washington, DC: National Association of School Psychologists.

A. Jerry Benson

V

VALIDITY. Validity refers to the extent to which a test measures what it purports to measure, that is, whether the test accurately assesses the ability or construct it claims to assess. There are three basic forms of validity—content, criterion-related, and construct—though other types of validation are mentioned in the literature (e.g., face validity, social validity, commercial validity, treatment validity).

Content validity is the consideration of whether a test representatively samples a known universe of content. An arithmetic test should assess such basic topics as numerical concepts, rote counting, place value, numerical sets, equivalency, seriation, the four basic arithmetic functions, and so on to be a representative measure of elementary mathematical functioning.

Criterion-related validity is the extent to which a test either predicts or concurrently agrees with some objective criterion. For example, intelligence tests are among the very best predictors of future academic achievement, thus demonstrating predictive validity. Newly developed intelligence tests might demonstrate concurrent validity through a comparison with existing intelligence tests whose validity has been accepted. Test validity is never proven; rather, it is supported incrementally through ongoing and continuous validation studies.

Construct validity is the extent to which the theoretical underpinnings of a test are supportable. Tests constructed on the basis of a theoretical model should be shown empirically to reflect that underlying theoretical orientation. Construct validity is usually demonstrated through factor analysis* or multitrait-multimethod* research designs.

The various other sorts of ''validity'' are not widely accepted indications of a test's validity; rather, generally they are judgments about use or marketability sometimes imposed onto tests by others who want a given test to do more than it was originally intended to do. Treatment validity, for instance, holds a test accountable for leading to successful interventions. Commercial validity reflects the belief that tests that have high commercial value must, in fact, be good instruments; otherwise, knowledgeable professionals would not purchase and use them. Face validity is a reflection of whether a test "looks as if" it measures an important construct. Like face validity, social validity poses the question of whether a test assesses a construct that is important to society. Each of these various alternative types of validity is subjective in nature and does not lend itself well to empirical verification.

See also MULTITRAIT-MULTIMETHOD MATRIX; RELIABILITY; TREATMENT INTEGRITY.

REFERENCES

Anastasi, A. (1988). *Psychological testing*. New York: Macmillan.
Cohen, R. J., M. E. Swerdlik, and D. K. Smith. (1992). *Psychological testing and assessment: An introduction to tests and measurement* (2d ed.). Mountain View, CA: Mayfield.

Bruce A. Bracken

VOCATIONAL ASSESSMENT. Vocational assessment is a process through which information is gathered to assist students in their career decision making. It includes the generation of such information as a student's vocational aptitudes, vocational interests, vocational values, aspirations, social skills, and acquired academic skills. Federal legislation requires vocational assessment as part of comprehensive evaluations for students with disabilities who wish to enter vocational education programs. The information is also essential in the development of individual education plans* and for transition plans, especially at the middle and high school levels.

There is a wide variety of vocational assessment techniques, including group psychometric measures (paper-and-pencil tests), performance tests, vocationally oriented interviews, behavioral observation, computerized assessment systems, work sampling systems, simulated work experience, and work experience. Although group psychometric techniques are the most widely used vocational assessment techniques for students in general, youngsters with disabilities frequently require more applied measures that identify specific aptitudes relating to finger and manual dexterity, vocationally relevant social skills, and vocationally oriented adaptive behavior.* Here, the most important techniques are work sampling procedures, interviewing* and behavioral observation, and simulated work experience. These techniques tap individual attributes that paper-and-pencil tests may fail to identify.

In work sampling, certain job functions from an occupation or related occupations are performed by the student under the observation of a trained evaluator. The technique provides information about manual aptitudes, interests,* decision-making processes, and social skills. Simulated work experience also has similar, but less structured procedures and is especially helpful in the collection of information about vocationally relevant social and adaptive behavior skills. Performance tests, such as the General Aptitude Test Battery, and even the performance sections of the Wechsler intelligence scales can also provide vocationally relevant information; there have been attempts to develop vocational aptitude profiles from the Wechsler scales for use in career counseling. Interviewing and behavioral observation can be incorporated into some of the previous procedures and provide useful information about social skills and adaptive behavior. Assessment of basic academic skills is also an important part of a comprehensive vocational assessment program. Various training programs require different skill levels in reading, math, and writing, and it is important to determine student academic skills before a vocational training program is chosen.

In most states, vocational assessment programs for students with disabilities exist at two levels, depending on the degree of disability. Level I vocational assessments include all of the information included in a traditional psychological evaluation, with the addition of a vocationally oriented interview and vocational interest assessment. Level II is designed for students with more severe disabilities for whom vocational decisions cannot be made without more comprehensive vocational assessment. Level II assessments include all of the procedures included in Level I and additionally include expanded medical evaluations and require work sampling procedures.

Although school psychologists* may not actually administer many of these techniques, it is necessary to be able to interpret much of the resulting information in order to be an effective member of child study and transition teams. Also, in some states and local districts, school psychologists are expected to complete Level I evaluations for students evaluated at the middle and high school levels.

See also APTITUDES; CAREER DEVELOPMENT; COMPREHENSIVE ASSESSMENT; INDIVIDUALIZED TRANSITION PLAN; SOCIAL SKILLS ASSESSMENT.

REFERENCES

Anderson, W. T., T. H. Hohenshil, K. Herr, and E. Levinson. (1990). Vocational assessment procedures for students with disabilities: An update. In A. Thomas and J. Grimes (Eds.), *Best practices in school psychology—II* (pp. 787–798). Washington, DC: National Association of School Psychologists.

Hohenshil, T. H. (1984). Vocational aspects of psychological assessment: Part I. *Communique*, 13(3), 6–7. See also, W. E. Heinlein, M. D. Nelson, and T. H. Honeshil. (1984). Part II. 13(4), 7; and C. F. Capps, E. M. Levinson, and T. H. Hohenshil. (1985). Part III. 13(5), 5–6.

Levinson, E. (1993). *Transdisciplinary vocational assessment: Issues in school based programs.* Brandon, VT: Clinical Psychology.

Thomas H. Hohenshil

VOCATIONAL REHABILITATION. Vocational rehabilitation began in the United States with the passage of federal legislation in 1920 (Lassiter, Lassiter, and Gandy, 1987). This legislation demonstrated the federal government's concern for the welfare of a large number of individuals who were in need of retraining following World War I and who had injuries related to dangerous working conditions in many industrial settings (Goldenson, Dunham, and Dunham, 1978).

The overall goal of vocational rehabilitation programs is to assist persons with disabilities in achieving maximum economic and personal independence (*Disability Handbook,* 1994). Funding for vocational rehabilitation programs is provided through the federal government. Vocational rehabilitation counselors assume case management responsibilities to access services for individuals who possess a medically or psychologically diagnosed disability that results in a substantial impediment to employment. In addition, there needs to be a favorable prognosis that services will lead to employment. Services are available for individuals of high school age and above. These services may include medical, educational, vocational, and mental health assessment and intervention.

Rehabilitation professionals receive training in specialized university training programs and belong to an organization such as the National Rehabilitation Association.

See also REHABILITATION FACILITY; VOCATIONAL ASSESSMENT; VOCATIONAL SCHOOL PSYCHOLOGY.

REFERENCES

Disability handbook. (1994). Fayetteville: Department of Rehabilitation Education and Research, University of Arkansas.
Goldenson, R. M., J. R. Dunham, and C. S. Dunham (Eds.). (1978). *Disability and rehabilitation handbook.* New York: McGraw-Hill.
Lassiter, R. A., M. H. Lassiter, and G. L. Gandy. (1987). Historical antecedents of the rehabilitation movement. In G. L. Gandy, E. D., Martin, R. E. Hardy, and J. G. Cull (Eds.), *Rehabilitation counseling and services: Profession and process* (pp. 3–23). Springfield, IL: Charles C. Thomas.

C. Frederick Capps

VOCATIONAL SCHOOL PSYCHOLOGY. Vocational school psychology was first proposed as a field of research and study by Thomas H. Hohenshil in 1974. Hohenshil had an unusual background, which included training and experience in both school psychology* and vocational counseling. During the next twenty years, considerable support was generated to expand roles for school psychology in career development* programs. Federal legislation in special and vocational education mandated that children with disabilities have the same rights to career development services as other students and that all students with disabilities receiving vocational services must have a thorough vocational assessment* before receiving special vocational services. The National Association of School Psychologists* (NASP) strongly supported the development of vocational school psychology by devoting issues of its journal to the topic (Hohenshil, 1974, 1978). In 1979, NASP (with the strong leadership of Paul Warden) officially adopted vocational school psychology as its first officially recognized specialty. A special interest group in vocational school psychology was also developed and continues to provide support for the practice of vocational assessment, vocational counseling, and consultation* in school psychology.

REFERENCES

Hohenshil, T. H. (1984). The vocational aspects of school psychology: 1974–1984. *School Psychology Review* 13, 503–509.

——— (Ed.). (1974). School psychology in career education programs. *School Psychology Digest,* 3(3), complete issue.

———. (1978). School psychology in vocational education programs. *School Psychology Digest* 7(1), complete issue.

Thomas H. Hohenshil

VOCATIONAL SCHOOL PSYCHOLOGY CONFERENCES. In 1981 and 1982, Virginia Polytechnic Institute and State University in cooperation with the National Association of School Psychologists* and the Virginia Department of Education conducted two national conferences on the practice of vocational school psychology.* They were funded through grants from the Virginia Department of Education, Division of Vocational Education. The conferences drew more than 350 participants from throughout the United States and involved such nationally recognized speakers as Tom Fagan, Doug Brown, Tom Hohenshil, and Catherine Batsche. Major presentations and small work groups were devoted to such topics as vocational assessment* procedures for students with various types of disabilities, development of vocational individualized educational plans* (IEPs), roles of school psychology in career development* programs, university training programs in vocational school psychology, vocational counseling approaches for school psychologists,* and vocationally oriented consultation procedures. Proceedings for both conferences were developed and disseminated through the ERIC system and distributed to school psychology training programs throughout the United States.

REFERENCES

Hohenshil, T. H., and W. T. Anderson (Eds.). (1981). *School psychological services in secondary vocational education.* Richmond: Virginia Department of Education. (ERIC # ED 212929).

Hohenshil, T. H., W. T. Anderson, and J. Salwan (Eds.). (1982). *Secondary school psychological services.* Richmond: Virginia Department of Education. (ERIC # ED 229704).

Thomas H. Hohenshil

W

WALLIN, J.E.W. John Edward Wallace Wallin was among the most prolific authors and contributors to the development of school psychological* and special education* services in the first half of the twentieth century. Born in Page County, Iowa, on January 21, 1876, Wallin earned his A.B. degree from Augustana College (1897) and his A.M. and Ph.D. degrees at Yale in 1899 and 1901, respectively. He held numerous positions related to clinical psychology* and exceptional children's services, the more important being the establishment of psychoeducational clinics* and special education departments in the New Jersey State Village for Epileptics (1910), the University of Pittsburgh (1912), the St. Louis public schools (1914), Miami University of Ohio (1921), the Baltimore public schools (1929), and the Wilmington public schools and the Delaware Department of Public Instruction (1932). His Miami University position included a demonstration clinic from which examinations were conducted throughout the state, and special education teachers were trained under a state legislature grant. Photos of this clinic provide a glimpse of psychoeducational training and practice of the period (available from Akron University's Archives of the History of American Psychology). His book, *Mental Health of the School Child* (1914), includes the earliest survey data on the providers of school psychological services in the United States. Wallin developed several tests, including the Wallin Peg Boards. He died on August 5, 1969.

See also CLINIC; FIRST PSYCHOLOGICAL CLINIC.

REFERENCES

Irvine, Paul. (1969). John Edward Wallace Wallin (1876–1969): A biographical sketch. *Journal of Special Education* 3, 229–230.
Wallin, J.E.W. (1914). *The mental health of the school child.* New Haven, CT: Yale University Press.

———. (1955). *The odyssey of a psychologist: Pioneering experiences in special education, clinical psychology, and mental hygiene.* Wilmington, DE: Author.

Thomas K. Fagan

WECHSLER, DAVID. David Wechsler was born in Romania on January 12, 1896, and died on May 2, 1981. He emigrated to New York City with his family in 1902. After attending the New York City public schools, Wechsler completed his A.B. degree at City College of New York in 1916 and his M.A. and Ph.D. degrees at Columbia University in 1917 and 1925, respectively. He is known in school psychology* history for his contributions to the concept of the deviation IQ and his development of the Wechsler scales, including the Wechsler Intelligence Scale for Children (1949, revised in 1974, 1991), the Wechsler Adult Intelligence Scale (1955, revised in 1981), and the Wechsler Preschool and Primary Scale of Intelligence (1967). These scales evolved from his earlier Wechsler-Bellevue Scales (1939 and 1942). His contributions to the conceptualization and measurement of intelligence* led to many awards, including the American Psychological Association's* (APA) Award for Distinguished Professional Contributions. He was also honored by APA's Division of School Psychology* in 1973 and granted the first honorary life membership in the National Association of School Psychologists* in 1972.

See also COGNITIVE ASSESSMENT.

REFERENCES

Austin, J. A. (1981). David Wechsler 1896–1981. *Communique* 10(1), 2, 6.
Matarazzo, J. D. (1981). David Wechsler (1896–1981). *American Psychologist* 36, 1542–1543.
Wechsler, D. (1974). *Selected papers of David Wechsler.* New York: Academic Press.

Thomas K. Fagan

WITMER, LIGHTNER. Lightner Witmer (1867–1956) was born and spent most of his life and professional career in Philadelphia. He obtained the B.A. at the University of Pennsylvania in 1888 and the Ph.D. in psychology under Wilhelm Wundt at the University of Leipzig (Germany) in 1893. Witmer was on the faculty of the University of Pennsylvania until his retirement in 1937. Considered the father of both clinical* and school psychology,* he is acclaimed for founding the first psychological clinic* at the University of Pennsylvania in 1896, founding the first clinical psychology journal, *The Psychological Clinic,* in 1907, and coining the term "clinical psychology." He developed the Witmer Form Board and the Witmer Cylinders from adaptations of earlier tests. He was a charter member of the American Psychological Association* and president of the Pennsylvania Association of Clinical Psychologists.

REFERENCES

Fagan, T. K. (in press). Lightner Witmer. In *American National Biography.* Cary, NC: Oxford University Press.

McReynolds, P. J. (1987). Lightner Witmer: Little-known founder of clinical
    psychology. *American Psychologist* 42(9), 849–858.

Thomas K. Fagan

WOOLLEY, HELEN BRADFORD THOMPSON. Helen Bradford Thompson Woolley (1874–1947), born in Chicago, traveled only a few blocks to earn
a Ph.B. in 1897 and a Ph.D. (summa cum laude) in 1900 from the University
of Chicago. She then traveled to Berlin and Paris as an American Association
of University Women ''fellow'' and worked as an instructor at Mount Holyoke
College. In Yokohama, Japan, in 1905, she married Paul Gerhart Woolley, director of Serum Laboratory in Manila and, later, Bangkok. In 1909, she became
a lecturer in philosophy at the University of Cincinnati. In 1911, following
enactment of child labor laws, she joined the Cincinnati public schools to form
a vocational bureau that included a psychology clinic to investigate the vocational abilities of youth, to prevent school dropouts, and to combat inappropriate
child labor. This was one of the first seven clinics in public schools and the first
in Ohio. While in Cincinnati, Woolley and Charlotte Fischer (1914) were the
first persons to use percentiles in reporting about the cognitive ability of adolescents.

Woolley moved to the Merrill-Palmer School in Detroit in 1921 as a psychologist and assistant director when her husband affiliated with the Detroit
College of Medicine. There, her work centered on personality and mental development in young children. In 1926, she went to Teachers College, Columbia
University, to direct the newly funded Institute for Child Welfare Research. In
these posts, she studied and published about affective processes, theory of judgment, perceptions of infants, psychology of preschool children, nursery school
education, and parental education. Her very productive career faded in the late
1920s, when the separation from her husband became permanent, and she dealt
with the impersonal atmosphere of a large university in Manhattan.

REFERENCES

Rosenberg, R. (1982). *Beyond separate spheres: Intellectual roots of modern feminism.*
    New Haven, CT: Yale University Press.
Woolley, H. T., and C. R. Fischer. (1914). Mental and physical measurements of
    working children. *Psychological Monographs* 28, No. 1.
Zapoleon, M. W., and L. M. Stolz. (1971). Woolley, Helen Bradford Thompson. In
    James, E. T. (Ed.), *Notable American women 1607–1950,* Vol. 3 (pp. 657–
    660). Cambridge, MA: Belknap Press of Harvard University.

Joseph L. French

Y

YESHIVA UNIVERSITY INVITATIONAL CONFERENCE. Titled "The School Psychologist in the Midst of Urban Crisis," the invitational conference held at Yeshiva University on January 27, 1969, was among the lesser-known but historically important conferences of the 1960s. The conference was sponsored, in part, by funding from the National Institute of Mental Health and included individual presentations and group discussions on the role and training of school psychologists.* Among the speakers were Mary Alice White, Rachel Lauer, Gilbert Trachtman, and Lillian Zach.

See also TRI-STATE SCHOOL PSYCHOLOGY CONFERENCE.

REFERENCE

Zach, L. (Ed.). (1969). *The school psychologist in the midst of urban crisis: Proceedings of the invitational workshop.* New York: Ferkauf Graduate School of Humanities and Social Sciences, Yeshiva University.

Thomas K. Fagan

Z

ZERO REJECT. "Zero reject" means that no child with a disability may be excluded from school. Law provides for safeguards to ensure that programs are provided to meet the needs of children with disabilities. This policy is implemented through the requirement for a free appropriate public education* (FAPE), available to all children with disabilities from birth through twenty-one years of age (Turnbull, 1993).

Courts have emphasized the right of every child to an equal opportunity for education, and lack of funds was not an excuse for lack of educational opportunity. In *Timothy W. v. Rochester School District* (1st Cir. 1989), the school district argued that Timothy W. was incapable of benefiting from an education; therefore, it need not provide such education. The court rejected the benefit/eligibility test and ruled that all handicapped children, regardless of the severity of their handicap, were entitled to a public education. Children with disabilities cannot be unilaterally excluded from a public education on the grounds that they are unable to benefit from an education (Data Research, Inc., 1993).

See also INCLUSION; MAINSTREAMING; PUBLIC LAW 94-142; SEGREGATED SERVICES.

REFERENCES

Data Research, Inc. (1993). *Students with disabilities and special education* (10th ed.). Rosemount, MN: Author.
Turnbull, H. R. (1993). *Free appropriate public education* (4th ed.). Denver: Love.

Laqueta Pardue-Vaughn
John C. Vaughn

Appendix: Sources for Further Study

The study of school psychology can be approached from several directions. Research on the gathering and storage of information in the field suggests that multiple research techniques and sources are necessary (Fagan, 1990; Fagan and Schicke, 1994). In order to facilitate further investigation into the field of school psychology, the following sources are recommended.

ORGANIZATIONS AND ARCHIVES SERVING SCHOOL PSYCHOLOGISTS

American Psychological Association (APA), 750 First Street, NE, Washington, DC 20002. The APA maintains archival materials in both the Library of Congress and the APA headquarters facilities. For information about APA archival holdings, contact the Manuscript Division of the Library of Congress (James Madison Memorial Building, Washington, DC 20540) and/or the APA. For information regarding archives relevant to the Division of School Psychology, contact the current division president. The Library of Congress also contains the papers of Arnold Gesell, the first school psychologist by title.

Archives of the History of American Psychology (AHAP) is the largest archival facility on American psychology. Located at the University of Akron in Akron, Ohio 44325, AHAP has information on more than 80,000 entries of individuals and organizations. The facility is a major source of information on all aspects of American psychology. Its holdings relevant to school psychological services are incorporated in the papers of particular individuals. Like the collections in the Library of Congress, AHAP is a most useful resource for information about services early in the century.

Center for the History of School Psychology. The center is an informally organized collection of materials on the history of school psychology gathered by Thomas Fagan and maintained in his offices in the Department of Psychology, University of Memphis, Memphis, TN 38152. The collection includes a complete set of school psychology books and journals published in the United States and newsletter collections for the National

Association of School Psychologists (NASP) and the APA Division of School Psychology. Files are maintained on the lives of several significant school psychologists and on the proceedings of national conferences.

International School Psychology Association (ISPA), Hans Knudsen Plads 1A, 1. 2100 Copenhagen, Denmark. The ISPA archives are maintained at the School and Educational Counseling Centre in Biel, Switzerland. The collection includes some presidential papers, programs of the annual international colloquium, newsletters, and miscellaneous correspondence.

National Association of School Psychologists (NASP), 4340 East West Highway, Suite 402, Bethesda, MD 20814. NASP maintains current databases of its membership, fiscal, convention, and management affairs. Archival records are maintained in the Special Collections Library of the University of Memphis Library, Memphis, TN 38152. The archives are limited to presidential papers and a small number of additional items related to the history of NASP. For information about the NASP Archives, contact Dr. Thomas Fagan, Department of Psychology, University of Memphis, Memphis, TN 38152.

STATE ASSOCIATIONS

State associations can also be valuable sources of historical information, and many maintain an archive. Each state has an association for school psychologists. A list may be obtained from the National Association of School Psychologists. Every state also has a state psychological association that serves the interests of professional psychologists, though, to a lesser extent, the interests of school psychologists in school settings. A list of these associations may be obtained from the American Psychological Association.

JOURNALS IN THE FIELD OF SCHOOL PSYCHOLOGY

Prior to the founding of the *Journal of School Psychology,* the field of school psychology relied on a variety of journals in education and psychology as publication outlets. Since the 1960s, the following journals specific to school psychology have been established:

Journal of School Psychology (1963)

Psychology in the Schools (1964)

School Psychology Digest, now *School Psychology Review* (1972)

School Psychology International (1979)

Canadian Journal of School Psychology (1985)

Professional School Psychology, now *School Psychology Quarterly* (1986)

MAJOR BOOKS ON SCHOOL PSYCHOLOGY

Many books have been written on the field of school psychology. The following are considered major works that are related to the historical study of the field. They provide essential information and references for further study.

Cutts, N. E. (Ed.). (1955). *School psychologists at midcentury.* Washington, DC: American Psychological Association.

Fagan, T. K., F. J. Delugach, M. Mellon, and P. Schlitt. (1986). *A bibliographic guide to the literature of professional school psychology 1890–1985.* Washington, DC: National Association of School Psychologists.

Fagan, T. K., and P. S. Wise. (1994). *School psychology: Past, present, and future.* White Plains, NY: Longman.

Gutkin, T. B., and C. R. Reynolds (Eds.). (1990). *The handbook of school psychology* (2d ed.). New York: Wiley.

Hildreth, G. H. (1930). *Psychological service for school problems.* Yonkers-on-Hudson, NY: World Book. (Perhaps the earliest book on school psychology that employs the term "school psychologist.")

Jacob-Timm, S., and T. Hartshorne. (1994). *Ethics and law for school psychologists.* Brandon, VT: Clinical Psychology.

Magary, J. F. (Ed.). (1967). *School psychological services in theory and practice, a handbook.* Englewood Cliffs, NJ: Prentice-Hall.

Reynolds, C. R., and T. B. Gutkin (Eds.). (1982). *The handbook of school psychology.* New York: Wiley.

United Nations Educational, Scientific and Cultural Organisation. (1948). *School psychologists.* Geneva, Switzerland: Author. (International Bureau of Education Publication No. 105)

Wall, W. D. (Ed.). (1956). *Psychological services for schools.* New York: New York University Press (for UNESCO Institute for Education).

Wallin, J.E.W. (1914). *The mental health of the school child (The psycho-educational clinic in relation to child welfare, Contributions to a new science of orthophrenics and orthosomatics).* New Haven, CT: Yale University Press.

PRESIDENTS OF THE DIVISION OF SCHOOL PSYCHOLOGY (AMERICAN PSYCHOLOGICAL ASSOCIATION) AND OF THE NATIONAL ASSOCIATION OF SCHOOL PSYCHOLOGISTS

The writings and/or personal papers of school psychology leadership provide a unique source of historical information. The following is a complete list of the presidents of both the Division of School Psychology of the American Psychological Association and the National Association of School Psychologists. The following is the first published list of the national presidents of both organizations.

Presidents of the Division of School Psychology

Warren W. Coxe (1944–1945) (Temporary Chairman)

Morris Krugman (1945–1946)

Harry J. Baker (1946–1947)

Margaret E. Hall (1947–1948)

Ethel L. Cornell (1948–1949)

Bertha M. Luckey (1949–1950)

Wilda M. Rosebrook (1950–1951)

George Meyer (1951–1952)

Frances A. Mullen (1952–1953)

Milton A. Saffir (1953–1954)

Judith I. Krugman (1954–1955)

James R. Hobson (1955–1956)

Gertrude P. Driscoll (1956–1957)

May V. Seagoe (1957–1958)

Frederick B. Davis (1958–1959)

Thelma G. Voorhis (1959–1960)

Katherine E. D'Evelyn (1960–1961)

Albert J. Harris (1961–1962)

Keith J. Perkins (1962–1963)

Ralph H. Tindall (1963–1964)

Winifred S. Scott (1964–1965)

Susan W. Gray (1965–1966)

William Itkin (1966–1967)

Boyd R. McCandless (1967–1968)

Edward L. French (1968–1969)

Jack I. Bardon (1969–1970)

Mary Alice White (1970–1971)

Rosa A. Hagin (1971–1972)

James F. Magary (1972–1973)

Julia R. Vane (1973–1974)

Virginia Bennett (1974–1975)

Mary Jo MacGregor (1975–1976)

Joseph L. French (1976–1977)

Irwin A. Hyman (1977–1978)

Bartell W. Cardon (1978–1979)

Merle L. Meacham (1979–1980)

Calvin O. Dyer (1980–1981)

Marcia B. Shaffer (1981–1982)

Judith L. Alpert (1982–1983)

Thomas D. Oakland (1983–1984)

Joel Meyers (1984–1985)

Beeman N. Phillips (1985–1986)

Walter B. Pryzwansky (1986–1987)

Barbara R. Slater (1987–1988)

Jane Close Conoley (1988–1989)

Sylvia Rosenfield (1989–1990)

Roy P. Martin (1990–1991)

Jonathon Sandoval (1991–1992)

Stephen T. DeMers (1992–1993)

Cindy Carlson (1993–1994)

Randy Kamphaus (1994–1995)

Jan N. Hughes (1995–1996)

Presidents of the National Association of School Psychologists

Pauline Alexander (1969–1970)

Jerald Green (1970–1971)

John Austin (1971–1972)

Calvin Catterall (1972–1973)

Fred Dornback (1973–1974)

Jean Ramage (1974–1975)

Michael Chrin (1975–1976)

John Brantley (1976–1977)

Thomas Ciha (1977–1978)

Ann Engin (1978–1979)

Douglas T. Brown (1979–1980)

Thomas K. Fagan (1980–1981)

John Guidubaldi (1981–1982)

Stuart Hart (1982–1983)

W. Alan Coulter (1983–1984)

Daniel J. Reschly (1984–1985)

Carolyn Cobb (1985–1986)

Alex Thomas (1986–1987)

Thomas K. Fagan (1987–1988)

Michael J. Curtis (1988–1989)

Howard Knoff (1989–1990)

Margaret Dawson (1990–1991)

George Batsche (1991–1992)

Kathy Durbin (1992–1993)

Carol Kelly (1993–1994)

Susan Safranski (1994–1995)

Susan Vess (1995–1996)

HISTORICAL OVERVIEWS OF SCHOOL PSYCHOLOGY

The following publications provide specific information on the history of school psychology in the United States. They are valuable sources of additional information about the field.

Cutts, N. E. (Ed.). (1955). *School psychologists at midcentury.* Washington, DC: American Psychological Association.

Fagan, T. K. (1990). A brief history of school psychology. In A. Thomas and J. Grimes (Eds.), *Best practices in school psychology—II* (pp. 913–929). Washington, DC: National Association of School Psychologists.

———. (1990). Research on the history of school psychology: Recent developments, significance, resources, and future directions. In T. R. Kratochwill (Ed.), *Advances in school psychology,* Vol. 7 (pp. 151–182). Hillsdale, NJ: Erlbaum.

———. (1992). Compulsory schooling, child study, clinical psychology, and special education: Origins of school psychology. *American Psychologist* 47, 236–243.

———. (1993). Separate but equal: School psychology's search for organizational identity. *Journal of School Psychology* 31, 3–90.

———. (1995). Trends in the history of school psychology in the United States. In A. Thomas and J. Grimes (Eds.), *Best practices in school psychology—III* (pp. 59–67). Washington, DC: National Association of School Psychologists.

Fagan, T. K., F. J. Delugach, M. Mellon, and P. Schlitt. (1985). *A bibliographic guide to the literature of professional school psychology 1890–1985.* Washington, DC: National Association of School Psychologists.

French, J. L. (1984). On the conception, birth, and early development of school psychology: With special reference to Pennsylvania. *American Psychologist* 39, 976–987.

———. (1988). Grandmothers I wish I knew: Contributions of women to the history of school psychology. *Professional School Psychology* 3, 51–68.

———. (1990). History of school psychology. In T. B. Gutkin and C. R. Reynolds (Eds.), *Handbook of school psychology* (pp. 3–20). New York: Wiley.

Hildreth, G. H. (1930). *Psychological service for school problems.* Yonkers-on-Hudson, NY: World Book.

Symonds, P. M. (Ed.). (1942). *Journal of Consulting Psychology,* 6(4). (This issue is devoted almost entirely to school psychology.)

Wallin, J.E.W., and D. G. Ferguson. (1967). The development of school psychological services. In J. F. Magary (Ed.), *School psychological services in theory and practice, a handbook* (pp. 1–29). Englewood Cliffs, NJ: Prentice-Hall.

REFERENCES

Fagan, T. K. (1990). Research on the history of school psychology: Recent developments, significance, resources, and future directions. In T. R. Kratochwill (Ed.), *Advances in school psychology,* Vol. 7 (pp. 151–182). Hillsdale, NJ: Erlbaum.

Fagan, T. K., and M. C. Schicke. (1994). Historical preservation in school psychology: Who's minding the lore? *School Psychology Review* 23, 99–105.

Index

Page numbers in **boldface** indicate the location of main entries.

Contributors

GEORGE M. BATSCHE, University of South Florida, Tampa, FL

JAMES W. BATTS, Eastern Kentucky University, Richmond, KY

R. SCOTT BEEBE, University of Memphis, Memphis, TN

A. JERRY BENSON, James Madison University, Harrisonburg, VA

J. L. BERNARD, University of Memphis, Memphis, TN

SHANI BETH-HALACHMY, National-Louis University, Evanston, IL

DONALD L. BOSWELL, Oklahoma State University, Stillwater, OK

PHILIP B. BOWSER, Roseburg Public Schools, Roseburg, OR

BRUCE A. BRACKEN, University of Memphis, Memphis, TN

JOHN E. BRANDT, Maine Department of Education, Augusta, ME

DOUGLAS T. BROWN, James Madison University, Harrisonburg, VA

KAY SATHER BULL, Oklahoma State University, Stillwater, OK

GEORGE C. CAMP, University of Montana, Missoula, MT

JAMES CANFIELD, State of Louisiana Department of Education, Baton Rouge, LA

GARY L. CANIVEZ, Tempe School District #3, Tempe, AZ, and Northern Arizona University, Flagstaff, AZ

ANDREA CANTER, Minneapolis Public Schools, Minneapolis, MN

C. FREDERICK CAPPS, Woodrow Wilson Rehabilitation Center, Fishersville, VA

KAREN T. CAREY, California State University, Fresno, CA

VICKI L. COLLINS, University of Oregon, Eugene, OR

WILLIAM T. COOMBS, Oklahoma State University, Stillwater, OK

YVETTE J. CORNETT, Illinois State University, Normal, IL

W. ALAN COULTER, Louisiana State University Medical Center, New Orleans, LA

EMORY L. COWEN, Primary Mental Health Project/University of Rochester, Rochester, NY

TRACY L. CROSS, Ball State University, Muncie, IN

MICHAEL J. CURTIS, University of South Florida, Tampa, FL

DENISE CUTBIRTH, Oklahoma State University, Stillwater, OK

TIMOTHY J. DAHEIM, Oklahoma State University, Stillwater, OK

RIK CARL D'AMATO, University of Northern Colorado, Greeley, CO

SUSAN M. DIUGLIO-JOHNSON, University of Northern Colorado, Greeley, CO

BETH DOLL, University of Colorado-Denver, Denver, CO

FREDERICK DORNBACK, Elburn, IL

MARDIS D. DUNHAM, University of Missouri, Columbia, MO

KEVIN P. DWYER, National Association of School Psychologists, Bethesda, MD

STEWART W. EHLY, University of Iowa, Iowa City, IA

STEPHEN N. ELLIOTT, University of Wisconsin, Madison, WI

WILLIAM P. ERCHUL, North Carolina State University, Raleigh, NC

GISELLE B. ESQUIVEL, Fordham University, New York, NY

GEORGE W. ETHERIDGE, University of Memphis, Memphis, TN

THOMAS K. FAGAN, University of Memphis, Memphis, TN

THOMAS N. FAIRCHILD, University of Idaho, Moscow, ID

JOSEPH L. FRENCH, Pennsylvania State University, University Park, PA

EDWARD GAUGHAN, Alfred University, Alfred, NY

FRANK M. GRESHAM, University of California, Riverside, CA

KELLY J. GRIFFITH, Payne County Guidance Center, Stillwater, OK

LESLIE HALE, Tulsa Technology Center, Tulsa, OK

PATTI L. HARRISON, University of Alabama, Tuscaloosa, AL

STUART N. HART, Indiana University-Purdue University at Indianapolis, Indianapolis, IN

TIMOTHY S. HARTSHORNE, Central Michigan University, Mt. Pleasant, MI

JOSEPH M. HAWES, University of Memphis, Memphis, TN

MARY HENNING-STOUT, Lewis and Clark College, Portland, OR

PEGGY A. HICKS, Cumberland Hospital, New Kent, VA

A. DIRK HIGHTOWER, Primary Mental Health Project/University of Rochester, Rochester, NY

THOMAS H. HOHENSHIL, Virginia Tech, Blacksburg, VA

IRWIN A. HYMAN, Temple University, Philadelphia, PA

SUSAN JACOB-TIMM, Central Michigan University, Mt. Pleasant, MI

RICHARD K. JAMES, University of Memphis, Memphis, TN

WILLIAM B. JENNINGS, Memphis City Schools, Memphis, TN

THOMAS J. KAMPWIRTH, California State University, Long Beach, CA

JUDITH S. KAUFMAN, Oklahoma State University, Stillwater, OK

THOMAS J. KEHLE, University of Connecticut, Storrs, CT

JACK J. KRAMER, Learning Alternatives, Lincoln, NE

SUSAN KUPISCH, Mississippi University for Women, Columbus, MS

SANDY R. LOCKE, Oklahoma State University, Stillwater, OK

ROY P. MARTIN, University of Georgia, Athens, GA

R. STEVE MCCALLUM, University of Tennessee, Knoxville, TN

W. VAL MCCLANAHAN, Norman Counseling Clinic, Norman, OK

C. SUE MCCULLOUGH, Texas Woman's University, Denton, TX

DAVID E. MCINTOSH, JR., University of Missouri, Columbia, MO

JOEL MEYERS, University at Albany-State University of New York, Albany, NY

KATHLEEN M. MINKE, University of Delaware, Newark, DE

DIANE MONTGOMERY, Oklahoma State University, Stillwater, OK

JACK A. NAGLIERI, Ohio State University and the Nisonger Center, Columbus, OH

NICOLE NICKENS, University of Missouri, Columbia, MO

THOMAS OAKLAND, University of Florida, Gainesville, FL

CHRISTOPHER R. OVIDE, Medical College of Wisconsin, Milwaukee, WI

LAQUETA D. PARDUE-VAUGHN, Oklahoma State University, Stillwater, OK

JONATHAN PEDRO, University of Memphis, Memphis, TN

LEADELLE PHELPS, State University of New York at Buffalo, Buffalo, NY

KELLY A. POWELL-SMITH, University of South Florida, Tampa, FL

TODD C. REIHER, Wartburg College, Waverly, IA

DANIEL J. RESCHLY, Iowa State University, Ames, IA

JOHN S. C. ROMANS, Oklahoma State University, Stillwater, OK

KATHLEEN R. RYTER, Oklahoma State University, Stillwater, OK

JONATHAN SANDOVAL, University of California, Davis, CA

MARIE A. SELL, University of Memphis, Memphis, TN

EDWARD S. SHAPIRO, Lehigh University, Bethlehem, PA

ROBBIE N. SHARP, Baylor College of Medicine, Houston, TX

MARK D. SHRIVER, Rehabilitation Institute/University of Nebraska Medical Center, Omaha, NE

DOUGLAS K. SMITH, University of Wisconsin-River Falls, River Falls, WI

GERALD J. SPADAFORE, Idaho State University, Pocatello, ID

WILLIAM STREIN, University of Maryland, College Park, MD

MARK E. SWERDLIK, Illinois State University, Normal, IL

ALEX THOMAS, Miami University, Oxford, OH

DANIEL H. TINGSTROM, University of Southern Mississippi, Hattiesburg, MS

DENNIS A. TOMLINSON, Ponca City Schools, Ponca City, OK

TERRIE ANNE VARGA, Oklahoma State University, Stillwater, OK

JOHN C. VAUGHN, East Central University, Ada, OK

PAUL G. WARDEN, Oklahoma State University, Stillwater, OK

RAYMOND E. WEBSTER, East Carolina University, Greenville, NC

ROBERT N. WENDT, University of Toledo, Toledo, OH

PAULA SACHS WISE, Western Illinois University, Macomb, IL

BARBARA W. WONDERLY, Ponte Vedra, FL

DONALD M. WONDERLY, Ponte Vedra, FL

ROBERT HENLEY WOODY, University of Nebraska-Omaha, Omaha, NE

JOSEPH E. ZINS, University of Cincinnati, Cincinnati, OH

ISBN 0-313-29015-6

90000>

EAN

9 780313 290152

HARDCOVER BAR CODE

DATE DUE
